Inventors in the Colorado Territory and their U.S. Patents

1861-1876

An Annotated Index

Compiled by Dina C. Carson

Inventors in the Colorado Territory and their U.S. Patents, 1861-1876:

An Annotated Index

Compiled by Dina C. Carson

Published by:
Iron Gate Publishing
P.O. Box 999
Niwot, CO 80544
www.irongate.com

All rights reserved. No part of this book may be reproduced or transmitted in any form or by any means, electronic or mechanical, including photocopying, recording or any information storage and retrieval system without written permission from the author, except for the inclusion of brief quotations in a review.

The Publisher of this directory makes no representation that it is absolutely accurate or complete. Errors and omissions, whether typographical, clerical or otherwise do sometimes occur and may occur anywhere within the body of this publication. The Publisher does not assume and hereby disclaims any liability to any party for loss or damage by errors or omissions in this publication, whether such errors or omissions result from negligence, accident or any other cause.

Iron Gate Publishing has used its best efforts in collecting and preparing material for inclusion in *Inventors in the Colorado Territory and their U.S. Patents, 1861-1876: An Annotated Index,* but does not warrant that the information herein is complete or accurate, and does not assume, and hereby disclaims, any liability to any person for any loss or damage caused by errors or omissions in *Inventors in the Colorado Territory and their U.S. Patents, 1861-1876: An Annotated Index,* whether such errors or omissions result from negligence, accident or any other cause.

Copyright © 2016 by Dina C. Carson, Iron Gate Publishing

Printed in the United States of America

ISBN   1-68224-022-3   ISBN 13 978-1-68224-022-9

Introduction

The *Inventors in the Colorado Territory and their U.S. Patents, 1861-1876: An Annotated Index* contains the names of inventors from the Colorado Territory who were issued patents between 1861 and 1876. A copy of their patent filing is included, along with an index of the names of the patent holders, the witnesses to the patent filing, and the lawyers who filed the application.

Understandably, many of the inventions pertained to advances in mining techniques, but not all. There were changes to medical equipment, a machine to make cutting gloves easier, military gear, agricultural machinery—even a new horse shoe.

To learn more about the process of obtaining a patent, consult the U.S. Patent and Trademark Office online, or in one of the regional offices located in Silicon Valley, CA, Denver, CO, Dallas, TX, Detroit, MI, Alexandria, VA or at Cornell University in New York City.

Patent Directory

Patent No.	Date	Patent	Page	Name	Role
34,238	1862 Jan 28	Ore Amalgamator	1	Burrell [Burnett], James	inventor
				Munn (John Munn & Co)	attorney
				Livingston, M M	witness
				Van Deren, A J	witness
				Potter, W R	witness
				Coombs, J W	witness
37,479	1863 Jan 20	Axle Box	4	Weibling, Harmon G	inventor
				Dibble, Almon	witness
				Lathrup, Sperry L	witness
				Sorah, S I	witness
34,480	1863 Jan 20	Carriage & Wagon Axle	6	Weibling, H G	inventor
				Dibble, Almon	witness
				Lathrop, Henry S	witness
40,006	1863 Sept 22	Double-Acting Pump	9	Alexander, Calvin C	inventor
				Lynch, J A	witness
				Baldauff, Ph P	witness
				Feeser, Louis	witness
40,501	1863 Nov 3	Ore Amalgamator	11	Randall, John G	inventor
				Coombs, J W	witness
				Ruch, G W	witness
				Wilson, D P	witness
				Rudd, Anson	witness
42,372	1864 Apr 19	Ore Separator	13	Hicks, Charles D	inventor
				Merns, Henry	witness
				Coombs, J W	witness
				Jno Munn & Co	attorney
				Munn (John Munn & Co)	attorney
				Edson, O E	witness
				Witter, H	witness
42,568	1864 May 3	Machine for Amalgamating	15	Dodge, M B	inventor
				Livingston, M M	witness
				Morn, Henry	witness
43,589	1864 July 19	Amalgamator	17	Kenyon, Joseph	inventor
				Harold, Thos Geo	witness
				Smith, Chas H	witness
43,782	1864 Aug 9	Corn Seed-Planter	20	Loos, Fredrich	inventor
				Foster, C E	witness
				Delany, W R	witness
				Howery, Henry	attorney
				Bartels, Louis T	witness
				Menger, B O	witness

Inventors in the Colorado Territory and their U.S. Patents, 1861-1876

Patent No.	Date	Patent	Page	Name	Role
44,122	1864 Sept 6	Quartz Crusher	22	Stanton, J W	inventor
				Topleff, C L	witness
				Clovis, Henry	witness
				Munn & Co	attorney
				Dodge, M B	inventor
				Hale, J P	witness
				Livingston, M M	witness
44,767	1864 Oct 18	Dry Amalgamator	24	Crosby, Augustine B	inventor
				Thompson, Robert L	inventor
				Thompson, S V	witness
				Hedrick, B S	witness
45,062	1864 Nov 15	Elevator	28	McIntyre & Reeves	inventor
				McIntyre, Douglass	inventor
				Reeves, George C	inventor
				Munn & Co	attorney
				Young, John	witness
				Young, Nathaniel	witness
46,492	1865 Feb 21	Amalgamator	30	Peck, C C	inventor
				Dodge, W C	witness
				Drury, E N	witness
47,384	1865 Apr 25	Ore Amalgamator	32	Behr & Ward	inventor
				Ward (Behr & Ward)	inventor
				Havemeyer, H C	witness
				Keith, N Shepard	witness
				Behr, Adolph	inventor
				Ward, William James	inventor
47,557	1865 May 2	Gold Separator	35	Long, William H	inventor
				Maus, W E	witness
				Brown, F H	witness
49,258	1865 Aug 8	Composition for Exterminating Grasshoppers	38	Green, Samuel	inventor
				Nathan, S	witness
				Chase, I Q	witness
51,079	1865 Nov 21	Amalgamator	39	Peck, C E	inventor
				Crosby, W B	attorney
				Gould, F	witness
				Gleason, W B	witness
53,590	1866 Apr 3	Ore Amalgamator	42	Du Bois, F N	inventor
				Nesmith, J W	witness
				Armor, William	witness

Patent Directory

Patent No.	Date	Patent	Page	Name	Role
54,726	1866 May 15	Machinery for Separating Metals from Ores	45	Hitchings, J A	inventor
				Munn & Co	attorney
				Gallemore, Jas R	witness
				Chiniquy, Charles L	witness
56,480	1866 July 17	Ore Dumping Car	50	Williams, George	inventor
				Pettit, Charles A	witness
				Klaucke, Alexander A C	witness
56,481	1866 July 17	Ore Elevator	52	Williams, George	inventor
				Smith, C D	witness
				Hall, W F	witness
				Munn & Co	attorney
				Klaucke, Alexander A C	witness
56,842	1866 July 31	Furnace for Desulphirizing Ores	56	Worrall, Thomas D	inventor
				Coombs, J J	witness
				Coon, John	witness
57,430	1866 Aug 21	Apparatus for Desulphurizing Quartz	59	Worrall, Thomas D	inventor
				Coombs, Jos L	witness
				Brown, Edm F	witness
58,100	1866 Sept 18	Desulphirizing Ore	63	Hitchings, John A	inventor
				Wiedersheim, John	witness
				Hall, W F	witness
				Munn & Co	attorney
				Hobbs, B	witness
				Gallemore, J M	witness
58,709	1866 Oct 9	Speculum	65	Worrall, Thomas D	inventor
				Stanton, J O	witness
				Hill, Geo D	witness
69,025	1867 Sept 17	Smelting Furnace	68	Richardson, Alfred H	inventor
				Treurn, Wm	witness
				Fraser, John	witness
				Munn & Co	attorney
				Wagoner, H O	witness
				Ford, B L	witness
71,448	1867 Nov 26	Furnaces for Roasting Ores	70	Bruckner, William	inventor
				Martin, Charles A	witness
				Kurtz, Julius	witness
				Grannis, Henry	witness
				Parmelee, Ed C	witness

Inventors in the Colorado Territory and their U.S. Patents, 1861-1876

Patent No.	Date	Patent	Page	Name	Role
72,197	1867 Dec 17	Glove Cutter	73	Harlan, Jesse H	inventor
				Pomeroy, Thos	inventor
				Boyd & Co	attorney
				Boyd, Sam'l E	witness
				Dickson, Joseph	witness
				Harlan, William H	inventor
				Davidson, Alexander	witness
				Atkins, Alex W	witness
73,366	1868 Jan 14	Stamp Mill	75	Mitchell, George R	inventor
				Munn & Co	attorney
				Fusche, Theo	witness
				Irwin, Wm	witness
				Atkins, Horace H	witness
				Stillings, Edw'd B	witness
77,813	1868 May 12	Chart Roller	77	Hagar, E L	inventor
				Munn & Co	attorney
				Fusche, Theo	witness
				Adervice, J	witness
				Munson, Geo C	witness
				Ball, David J	witness
78,928	1868 June 16	Ore-Roasting Furnace	79	Collier, Cushman & Farrell	inventor
				Ashkettle, W C	witness
				Fusche, Theo	witness
				Collier, David C	inventor
				Cushman, Samuel	inventor
				Farrell, Newell E	inventor
				Munn & Co	attorney
				Wilder, Eugene	witness
				Hall, Frank	witness
82,528	1868 Sept 29	Horeshoe	84	Johnson & Froggott	inventor
				Morgan, Wm A	witness
				Cotton, G C	witness
				Johnson, P C	inventor
				Froggott, Edwin	inventor
				Munn & Co	attorney
				Kendall, S P	witness
				Sears, W F	witness
85,962	1869 Jan 19	Quartz Crusher	87	Reeves, George C	inventor
				Burridge, J H	witness
				Waite, E E	witness

Patent Directory

Patent No.	Date	Patent	Page	Name	Role
88,621	1869 Apr 6	Combination Tool	90	Froggatt, Edwin	inventor
				Munn & Co	attorney
				Raettig, C	witness
				Brooks, John F	witness
				Burrell, Harvey M	witness
				Schoenfeld, F	witness
89,476	1868 Apr 27	Machine for Concentrating and Separating Ores and Minerals	92	George, Robert	inventor
				Martin, Wm	witness
				Cammack, Wm	witness
90,565	1869 May 25	Process of Separating Iron and Other Metals from Potters Clay	98	Lynd, Wm J	inventor
				McCabe, Wm H	witness
				Harris, Arthur C	witness
92,009	1869 June 29	Process of Roasting Auriperous Sulphurets	99	Bruckner, William	inventor
				Dennis, J Jr	witness
				Dennis, Wm	witness
92,323	1869 July 6	Machine for Washing Dishes, Knives and Forks, etc.	100	Leland, Charles M	inventor
				D E Jones & Co	attorney
				Jones (D E Jones & Co)	attorney
				Eils, P Edw J	witness
				Herron, Charles	witness
				Johnson, P C	witness
				Wilcoxen, J N	witness
92,981	1869 July 27	Method of Extracting Iron and Other Oxides from Clay, Porcelain-Earth &c	102	Lynd, Wm J	inventor
				Armor, William	witness
				Harris, Richard H	witness
93,217	1869 Aug 3	Flooring Clamp	103	Nevin, David	inventor
				Munn & Co	attorney
				Henchman, O	witness
				Brooks, John F	witness
				Berkley, G	witness
				Wright, Alpheus	witness
93,447	1869 Aug 10	Horse Shoe	105	Johnson, P C	inventor
				Munn & Co	attorney
				Nida, Chas	witness
				Morgan, Wm A	witness

Inventors in the Colorado Territory and their U.S. Patents, 1861-1876

Patent No.	Date	Patent	Page	Name	Role
				Hall, Amos W	witness
				Cumings, J W	witness
93,629	1869 Aug 10	Preparing Coke from Coals	107	Lynd, William J	inventor
				Armor, Wm	witness
				Harris, Arthur C	witness
94,333	1869 Aug 31	Machine for Punching Metal Screens	108	Nesmith, J Wellington	inventor
				Vorlander, M	witness
				Mabee, Geo W	witness
				Munn & Co	attorney
				Backus, G B	witness
				Overhood, H M	witness
94,842	1869 Sept 14	Velocipede	110	Rood, M L	inventor
				Brooks, John F	witness
				Clark, Wm T	witness
				Munn & Co	attorney
				Roby, John D	witness
				Davids, Wm B	witness
94,879	1869 Sept 14	Land Roller	112	Evans, Elihu	inventor
				Munn & Co	attorney
				Pettit, C A	witness
				Revnon, T C	witness
				Boyd, H L	witness
				Cross, J M	witness
95,045	1869 Sept 21	Guides for Stamp Mill	114	Rice & Van Deren	inventor
				Rice, C A H	inventor
				Van Deren, A J	inventor
				Munn & Co	attorney
				Clark, Wm T	witness
				Brooks, John F	witness
				Seller, Willard	witness
				Kennedy, William R	witness
97,409	1869 Nov 30	Clothes Line	116	Johnson, P C	inventor
				Munn & Co	attorney
				Brennendorf, A	witness
				Roberts, Alex F	witness
				Johnson, Mary	inventor
				Kendall, S P	witness
				Chase, L W	witness
98,606	1870 Jan 4	Process of Preparing Coal for Smelting Ores	118	Lynd, Wm J	inventor
				Armor, William	witness

Patent Directory

Patent No.	Date	Patent	Page	Name	Role
				Harris, Richard H	witness
98,607	1870 Jan 4	Improvement in Using Colorado and Similar Coal for Metallurgical Operations	119	Lynd, William J	inventor
				Armor, William	witness
				Harris, Richard H	witness
98,669	1870 Jan 11	Time Register for Hiring Purposes	121	Courvoisier, Auguste	inventor
				Munn & Co	attorney
				Clark, W T	witness
				Roberts, Alex F	witness
				Hussey, Hyatt	witness
				Perrenoud, J G	witness
100,252	1870 Mar 1	Rock Drills	123	Blatchley, A	inventor
				Munn & Co	attorney
				Brooks, John F	witness
				Mabee, Geo W	witness
				Hart, A W	witness
				Haymanie, W	witness
				Kennedy, William R	witness
				Tappan, Henry S	witness
101,065	1870 Mar 22	Sheet Metal Seaming Machine	128	Veasey, John M	inventor
				Munn & Co	attorney
				Pettit, Charles A	witness
				Hagmann, Victor	witness
				Kemon, Solon C	witness
101,328	1870 Mar 29	Caster for Sewing Machines	130	Veasey, John M	inventor
				Munn & Co	attorney
				Hagmann, Victor	witness
				Pettit, Chas A	witness
				Kemon, Solon C	witness
102,504	1870 May 3	Horseshoe	132	Copeland, George C	inventor
				Munn & Co	attorney
				Veasey, John M	witness
				Taylor, James G	witness
103,006	1870 May 17		134	Arey, John P	inventor
				Mason, Fenwick & Lawrence	
				Haskins, K	witness
				Clarke, R W	witness

Inventors in the Colorado Territory and their U.S. Patents, 1861-1876

Patent No.	Date	Patent	Page	Name	Role
103,574	1870 May 31	Ore Separators	137	Copeland, George C	inventor
				Munn & Co	attorney
				Veasey, John M	witness
				Taylor, James S	witness
104,130	1870 June 14	Metallic Separator	140	Eysler, Christian S	inventor
				Holloway, D P & Co	attorney
				Grinnell, James S	witness
				Ruppert, A	witness
				Clausen, C F	witness
				Pool, S M	witness
105,010	1870 July 5	Electrolytic Sluice Tub for Saving Mercury from the Washings of Gold and Silver Ores	143	Spicer, Wells	inventor
				Watson, C H	witness
				Barnay, Henry	witness
				Wm Van Slarter & Co	attorney
				Modill, H J	witness
				Kirby, J P	witness
105,480	1870 July 19	Ore Separator	146	Nevin, David	inventor
				Munn & Co	attorney
				Becker, John	witness
				Maber, S S	witness
				Morgan, C H	witness
				Gunn, James	witness
106,047	1870 Aug 2	Machine for Separating Mineral and Fossil Substances	148	George, Robert	inventor
				Martin, Wm	witness
				Johnson, H C	witness
				Weber, E P	witness
				Schulze, Louis	witness
106,048	1870 Aug 2	Machine for Separating and Concentrating Ores and Other Materials of Different Specific Gravities	155	George, Robert	inventor
				Martin, Wm	witness
				Johnson, H C	witness
				Weber, E P	witness
				Schulze, Louis	witness
106,049	1870 Aug 2	Apparatus for Separating and Concentrating Ores	160	George, Robert	inventor
				Martin, Wm	witness
				Johnson, H C	witness

Patent Directory

Patent No.	Date	Patent	Page	Name	Role
				Weber, E P	witness
				Schulze, Louis	witness
106,553	1870 Aug 23	Roasting Furnace for Ores	166	Collom, John	inventor
				Munn & Co	attorney
				Henchman, O	witness
				Brooks, John F	witness
				Yenley, J H	witness
				Light, William	witness
108,214	1870 Oct 11	Gang Plow	171	Treadway, James Wilson	inventor
				Munn & Co	attorney
				Worland, M	witness
				Dietrich, Gustave	witness
				Brown, George	witness
				Gunnison, W C	witness
108,556	1870 Oct 25	Shoe Flasks for Casting Stamp-Shoes for Crushing Mills	174	Bolthoff, Henry	inventor
				Given, John W	witness
				Folelis, L C	witness
				Critchel, Wesley	witness
				Kennedy, Joseph W	witness
108,617	1870 Oct 25	Ore Mill	176	Moses, Frederick C	inventor
				Munn & Co	attorney
				Dietrich, Gustave	witness
				Mabee, S S	witness
				Hall, Assyria	witness
				Foster, J R	witness
110,301	1870 Dec 20	Grain Scourer	178	Smith, Austin	inventor
				Munn & Co	attorney
				Almquist, A W	witness
				Mabee, S S	witness
				Thomas, Jerome	witness
				Hartley, Jesse	witness
111,560	1871 Feb 7	Floor Clamp	180	Nevin, David	inventor
				Munn & Co	attorney
				Mabee, L S	witness
				Sieterich, P C	witness
				Yates, Lemuel F	witness
				Pollard, Chas W	witness
111,603	1871 Feb 7	Motor for Locomotives	182	Arnett, William D	inventor
				Campbell, R T	witness
				Campbell, J N	witness

Inventors in the Colorado Territory and their U.S. Patents, 1861-1876

Patent No.	Date	Patent	Page	Name	Role
				Mason, Fenwick & Lawrence	attorney
				Raymond, Wm	witness
				Horr, M L	witness
111,669	1871 Feb 7	Feeding Quicksilver to Stamps and Amalgamators	185	Munson, George C	inventor
				Thornton, John S	witness
				Ventz, Wm	witness
112,804	1871 Mar 21	Ore Mill	188	Griswold	inventor
				Munn & Co	attorney
				Becker, John	witness
				Mabee, S S	witness
				Cramer, Frederick	witness
				Hastings, John I	witness
113,872	1871 Apr 18	Fence Post	190	Gill, Andrew J	inventor
				Sarner, Phil F	witness
				Jackson, T A	witness
				Wood, Wm C	attorney
				Cass, J B	witness
				Woodworth, J B	witness
115,559	1871 June 6	Furnaces for Roasting Ores	192	Arey, John P	inventor
				Campbell, R T	witness
				Campbell, J N	witness
				Mason, Fenwick & Lawrence	attorney
115,659	1871 June 6	Repeating Ordnance	195	Townsend, Alfred H	inventor
				Almquist, A W	witness
				Smith, Wm H C	witness
				Munn & Co	attorney
				Drips, James W	witness
				Spruance, Wm	witness
117,031	1871 July 18	Improvement in Locomotives	199	Arnett, William D	inventor
				Mason, Fenwick & Lawrence	attorney
				Campbell, R T	witness
				Campbell, J N	witness
				Leas, George W	witness
				Webster, John W	witness
117,718	1871 Aug 8	Feeder for Roasting Furnaces	201	Arey, John P	inventor
				Campbell, R T	witness
				Campbell, J N	witness

Patent Directory

Patent No.	Date	Patent	Page	Name	Role
				Mason, Fenwick & Lawrence	attorney
119,400	1871 Sept 26	Improvement in Military Equipment for Soldiers	204	Penrose, William H	inventor
				Hill & Ellsworth	attorney
				Harkness, C A	witness
				Ellsworth, H K	witness
				Woodhull, Alfred A	witness
				Hatch, Saml F	witness
119,737	1871 Oct 10	Stencil Cutter	207	Bolthoff, Henry	inventor
				Raettig, C	witness
				Smith, Wm H C	witness
				Munn & Co	attorney
				Updegraff, Joseph S	witness
				Wilcox, Lewis V	witness
120,180	1871 Oct 24	Improvements in Locomotive Engines	209	Arnett, William D	inventor
				Campbell, R T	witness
				Campbell, J N	witness
				Mason, Fenwick & Lawrence	attorney
				Markham, Vincent D	witness
				Webster, John W	witness
120,530	1871 Oct 31	Improvements in Field Cots and Tents	211	Penrose, William H	inventor
				Ellsworth, N K	witness
				Rawlings, A C	witness
				Hill & Ellsworth	attorney
				Ellsworth (Hill & Ellsworth)	attorney
				Hatch, Samuel F	witness
				Adams, Charles B	witness
121,985	1871 Dec 19	Stamp Guides	215	Bolthoff, Henry	inventor
				Raettig, C	witness
				Smith, Wm H C	witness
				Munn & Co	attorney
				Lake, D D	witness
				Stokes, T T	witness
123,500	1872 Feb 6	Improvement in Governor Cut Offs	217	Meyer, Herman H	inventor
				Ludlow, W J	witness
				Peyton, W J	witness
				Van Santvoord & Hauff	attorney

Inventors in the Colorado Territory and their U.S. Patents, 1861-1876

Patent No.	Date	Patent	Page	Name	Role
				Webster, John W	witness
				Jensen, F	witness
124,349	1872 Mar 5	Improvement in Hooks for Wire Fences	222	Gill, Andrew J	inventor
				Sarner, Phil P	witness
				Jackson, F A	witness
				Wood, Wm C	attorney
				Clark, F A	inventor
				Matthews, E G	witness
				Resor, Edward A	witness
125,729	1872 Apr 16	Improvement in Ships' Berths	224	Evans, John	inventor
				Becker, John	witness
				Roberts, Alex F	witness
				Munn & Co	attorney
				Mosher, T B	witness
				Mabee, Geo W	witness
126,034	1872 Apr 23	Improvement in Ore Crushers	226	Cumings, James W	inventor
				Miller, Henry N	witness
				Evert, C L	witness
				Alexander & Mason	attorney
				Gribble, Edwin	witness
				Williams, C D	witness
126,523	1872 May 7	Improvement in Machines for Washing Grain	229	Copeland, George	inventor
				Van Santvoord & Hauff	attorney
				Bilhuber, Ernst	witness
				Wahlers, C	witness
				Smith, Percy B	witness
				Stanley, Gilbert	witness
128,161	1872 June 18	Improvement in Slide Valves	232	Meyer, Herman H	inventor
				Kastenhuber, E G	witness
				Bilhuber, E	witness
				Van Santvoord & Hauff	attorney
				Jensen, F	witness
				Webster, John W	witness
128,841	1872 July 9	Improvement in Spark Arresters for Locomotives	234	Arnett, William D	inventor
				Mason, Fenwick & Lawrence	attorney
				Campbell, R T	witness
				Campbell, J N	witness

Patent Directory

Patent No.	Date	Patent	Page	Name	Role
				Sarrell, Wm M B	witness
				Berthoud, Edward L	witness
129,015	1872 July 16	Improvement in Fluid Pressure Regulators	236	Fay, William J	inventor
				Cairns, Thomas A	inventor
				Bennerkendorf, A	witness
				Graham, W A	witness
				Munn & Co	attorney
				McCormic, T B	witness
				Levy, M W	witness
129,629	1872 July 16	Improvement in Sewing Machine Casters	238	Veasey, John M	inventor
				Lawton, Herm	witness
				Bendy, A	witness
				Brown, Geo E	attorney
				Kirby, John F	witness
				Hine, Henry B	witness
131,064	1872 Sept 3	Improvement in Ore Separators	240	Nevin, David	inventor
				Bennerkendorf, A	witness
				Graham, W A	witness
				Munn & Co	attorney
				Harrington, Henry C	witness
				Hutchinson, Wm N	witness
132,480	1872 Oct 22	Improvement in Slide Valves	242	Meyer, Herman H	inventor
				Wahlers, C	witness
				Bilhuber, Ernst	witness
				Van Santvoord & Hauff	attorney
				Reichard, Adolph L	witness
				Jensen, F	witness
133,314	1872 Nov 26	Skate Fastenings	244	Hunter, John	inventor
				Chenowith, Joel T	inventor
				Barth, Mortz	witness
				Barth, William	witness
134,609	1873 Jan 7	Washing Machines	246	Olds, Amandrin M	inventor
				Post, Wm H	witness
				Brush, Fred M	witness
137,473	1873 Apr 1	Wash Tub Holders	248	Olds, Amandrin M	inventor
				Post, Wm H	witness
				Bates, A C	witness
139,411	1873 May 27	Drawing Boards	250	Meyer, Herman H	inventor
				Haynes, Fred	witness

Inventors in the Colorado Territory and their U.S. Patents, 1861-1876

Patent No.	Date	Patent	Page	Name	Role
				Fusch, Fred	witness
				Wales, Brown & Allen	attorney
				Collins, S G	witness
				McNeil, J L	witness
140,425	1873 July 1	Stamps for Crushing Ores	252	McFarland, James Maxey	inventor
				Bennerkendorf, A	witness
				Sedgwick, C	witness
				Munn & Co	attorney
				Smith, L J	witness
				Coe, Edward D	witness
141,909	1873 Aug 19	Reversible Rotary Steam-Engines	255	Adams, Orwin	inventor
				Wolff, E	witness
				Sedgwick, C	witness
				Munn & Co	attorney
				Sayr, Hal	witness
				Nichols, J N	witness
142,491	1873 Sept 2	Governor Cut-off Gears	259	Meyer, Herman H	inventor
				Becker, John	witness
				Haynes, Fred	witness
				Brown & Allen	attorney
				Jensen, F	witness
				Webster, John W	witness
143,176	1873 Sept 23	Machines for Clearing Streets of Snow	261	Musgrove, William E	inventor
				Pearce, W H	witness
				Allen, Walter	witness
				Knight & Bros	attorney
				Knight, Saml	witness
				Burns, Robert	witness
143,524	1873 Oct 7	Car-Couplings	263	Merrill, Jay A	inventor
				Kempton, David W	inventor
				Brown, C F	witness
				Ellsworth, Nathan K	witness
				Hill & Ellsworth	attorney
				Church, Melville	witness
146,166	1874 Jan 6	Ore-Washers or Buddles	266	Collom, John	inventor
				Nida, Chas	witness
				Sedgwick, C	witness
				Munn & Co	attorney
				Dean, Thos J	witness
				Ross, W A	witness

Patent Directory

Patent No.	Date	Patent	Page	Name	Role
146,167	1874 Jan 6	Machines for Sampling Ores and other Materials	269	Collom, John	inventor
				Almquist, A W	witness
				Sedgwick, C	witness
				Munn & Co	attorney
				Dean, Thos J	witness
				Ross, W A	witness
146,168	1874 Jan 6	Ore Separators	271	Collom, John	inventor
				Wolff, E	witness
				Sedgwick, C	witness
				Munn & Co	attorney
				Dean, Thos J	witness
				Ross, W A	witness
146,193	1874 Jan 6	Sectional Cams	273	Mallinckrodt, John F	inventor
				Boone, John L	witness
				Richardson, C M	witness
				Dewey & Co	attorney
				Bonnell, C E	witness
				Hook, Charles H	witness
146,403	1874 Jan 13	Mitering Machines	275	Rowland, John Henry	inventor
				Wolff, E	witness
				Sedgwick, C	witness
				Munn & Co	attorney
				Stanley, Gilbert	witness
				Staples, James	witness
148,096	1874 Mar 3	Reverberatory Furnaces for Roasting Ores Etc	277	Stewart, James O	inventor
				Martin, James Jr	witness
				Hedrick, B S	witness
				Mason, Fenwick & Lawrence	attorney
				August, Anthony J	witness
				Mahany, Jerry G	witness
148,574	1874 Mar 17	Door Securers	282	Mowbray, Roscoe C	inventor
				Martin, James Jr	witness
				Campbell, J N	witness
				Mason, Fenwick & Lawrence	attorney
				Stebbins, G I	witness
				Arnold, A	witness
149,681	1874 Apr 14	Steam Mining Pumps	284	Rogers, Andrews N	inventor
				Bennerkendorf, A	witness

Inventors in the Colorado Territory and their U.S. Patents, 1861-1876

Patent No.	Date	Patent	Page	Name	Role
				Sedgwick, C	witness
				Munn & Co	attorney
				Thayer, A P	witness
				Mosher, T B	witness
150,567	1874 May 5	Circular Saw Mills	288	Hall, John N	inventor
				Mathys, G	witness
				Hart, A W	witness
				Munn & Co	attorney
				Benton, Edward V	witness
150,872	1874 May 12	Coking Fossil Coals or Lignites	294	Lynd, William John	inventor
				Dick, Ewell	witness
				Chaffee, Wm E	witness
				Holloky	attorney
				Elliott, Henry R	witness
150,873	1874 May 12	Coking Fossil Coals or Lignites	298	Lynd, William John	inventor
				Dick, Ewell	witness
				Smith, T C	witness
				Holloky	attorney
				Elliott, Henry R	witness
151,297	1874 May 26	Miners' Candle Holders	302	Larsen, Neils	inventor
				Wolff, E	witness
				Sedgwick, C	witness
				Munn & Co	attorney
				Ostrander, Othello R	witness
				Churchill, Caleb W	witness
151,763	1874 Feb 23	Improvement in Extracting Silver, Gold and other Metals from Their Ores	304	Stewart, James Oscar	inventor
				Douglas, James Jr	inventor
				Hunt, Thomas Sterry	inventor
				Mitchell, D H	witness
				Mahany, Jerry G	witness
152,532	1874 June 30	Apparatus for Conveying and Cooling Roasted Ores	306	Teats, Robert	inventor
				Gross, Edgar J	witness
				Hunter, R M	witness
				Millward, Frank	attorney
152,833	1874 July 7	Improvement in Medical Compounds or Salves	308	Dyer, John P	inventor
				Ward, R H	witness
				Lynch, Chas H	witness

Patent Directory

Patent No.	Date	Patent	Page	Name	Role
153,397	1874 July 21	Drying Ores	309	Teats, Robert	inventor
				Hunter, R M	witness
				Gross, Edgar J	witness
				Millward, Frank	attorney
				Wartmann, J L	witness
153,432	1874 July 28	Breech Loading Fire Arms	312	Freund, Frank W	inventor
				Martin, James Jr	witness
				Campbell, J N	witness
				Mason, Fenwick & Lawrence	attorney
				Hale, H M	witness
				Charles, L C	witness
154,412	1874 Aug 25	Smoke Stacks and Spark Arresters	314	Nesmith, J Wellington	inventor
				Bennerkendorf, A	witness
				Sedgwick, C	witness
				Munn & Co	attorney
				Manahan, Jas M	witness
				Armor, W C	witness
155,035	1874 Sept 15	Current Wheels	316	McCarty, Michael	inventor
				Wolff, E	witness
				Terry, A F	witness
				Munn & Co	attorney
				Miller, John D	witness
				Buckland, Wm J	witness
155,123	1874 Sept 15	Revolving Ore Roasters	318	Teats, Robert	inventor
				Gross, Edgar J	witness
				Hunter, H M	witness
				Millward, Frank	attorney
				Breed, Abel D	inventor
156,091	1874 Oct 20	Circular Saw Guides	324	Husted, Calvin R	inventor
				McPherson, Charles Henry	inventor
				Munn & Co	attorney
				Neveux, C	witness
				Platt, H H	witness
				Schuyler, Fred	witness
				Sedgwick, C	witness
156,270	1874 Oct 27	Slide Valves for Steam Engines	326	Bolthoff, Henry	inventor
				Nida, Chas	witness
				Terry, A F	witness
				Munn & Co	attorney

Inventors in the Colorado Territory and their U.S. Patents, 1861-1876

Patent No.	Date	Patent	Page	Name	Role
				Clark, James	inventor
				Sellers, Henry M	witness
				Welch, C C	witness
156,470	1874 Nov 3	Improvements in Baking Pans	328	Warner, Emma E O	inventor
				Ruppert, A	witness
				Perley, F L	witness
				Mungen, Theo	attorney
				Sayer, Daniel	witness
				Warner, J P	witness
				Lionberger, D C	witness
157,019	1874 Nov 17	Refrigerators	330	Mills, Joseph K	inventor
				Ryan, Michael	witness
				Haynes, Fred	witness
				Brown & Allen	attorney
				Greatorex, T A	witness
				Todd, Wm D	witness
158,703	1875 Jan 12	Saw Mills	332	Hall, Herman D	inventor
				Miller, Henry N	witness
				Evert, C L	witness
				Alexander & Mason	attorney
				Bramhall, Wm L	witness
159,105	1875 Jan 26	Whip Tip Ferrule	335	Light, Edward B	inventor
				McArdle, Francis	witness
				Terry, A F	witness
				Munn & Co	attorney
				Hanna, Jno R	witness
				Grosvenor, C G	witness
159,207	1875 Jan 26	Wind Mill	337	Parson, Warren D	inventor
				Dieterich, P C	witness
				Scott, H C	witness
				C H Watson & Co	attorney
				Church, Frank	witness
				Bishop, Edward F	witness
159,347	1875 Feb 2	Ore Separator	340	Nevin, David	inventor
				Martin, James Jr	witness
				Campbell, J N	witness
				Mason, Fenwick & Lawrence	attorney
				Nevin, Robert	inventor
				Stewart, J Oscar	inventor

Patent Directory

Patent No.	Date	Patent	Page	Name	Role
				Dolloff, L W	witness
				Campbell, Thos J	witness
159,973	1875 Feb 16	Improvement in Wireways	344	Smith, Andrew A	inventor
				Martin, James Jr	witness
				Campbell, J N	witness
				Mason, Fenwick & Lawrence	attorney
				Struance, Wm	witness
				Hough, Wm B	witness
160,145	1875 Feb 23	Improvements in Sash Balances	348	Berndt, John	inventor
				Hollingsworth, W W	witness
				Kernon, John C	witness
				Munn & Co	attorney
				Tenwinkle, Wm	witness
				Thomas, H H	witness
160,762	1875 Mar 16	Breech Loading Firearm	350	Freund, Frank W	inventor
				Martin, James Jr	witness
				Campbell, J N	witness
				Mason, Fenwick & Lawrence	attorney
				Elsner, John	witness
				Schleier, George C	witness
160,763	1875 Mar 16	Metallic Cartridge	357	Freund, Frank W	inventor
				Martin, James Jr	witness
				Campbell, J N	witness
				Mason, Fenwick & Lawrence	attorney
				Johnson, L K	witness
				Charles, L C	witness
160,819	1875 Mar 16	Sights for Fire Arms	360	Freund, Frank W	inventor
				Martin, James Jr	witness
				Campbell, J N	witness
				Mason, Fenwick & Lawrence	attorney
				Danielson, F M	witness
				Howe, Geo M	witness
162,217	1875 Apr 20	Door Check	363	Burt, George	inventor
				Willoughby, Edmund A	witness
				Watson, James F	witness
				Whitall, Jas C	witness
				Landon, Sam S	witness

Inventors in the Colorado Territory and their U.S. Patents, 1861-1876

Patent No.	Date	Patent	Page	Name	Role
162,224	1875 Apr 20	Breech Loading Fire Arm	365	Freund, Frank W	inventor
				Martin, James Jr	witness
				Campbell, J N	witness
				Mason, Fenwick & Lawrence	attorney
				Johnson, J W Hamilton	witness
162,373	1875 Apr 20	Pistol Grip Attachment for the Stocks of Fire Arms	372	Freund, Frank W	inventor
				Martin, James Jr	witness
				Campbell, J N	witness
				Mason, Fenwick & Lawrence	attorney
				Johnson, J W Hamilton	witness
162,374	1875 Apr 20	Guard Lever and Means for Operating the Breech Block of Breech Loading Fire Arms	375	Freund, Frank W	inventor
				Martin, James Jr	witness
				Campbell, J N	witness
				Mason, Fenwick & Lawrence	attorney
				Johnson, J W Hamilton	witness
163,104	1875 May 11	Ore Concentrator	379	Pomeroy, James V	inventor
				Nida, Chas	witness
				Terry, A F	witness
				Munn & Co	attorney
				Leonard, P A	witness
				Corning, Geo C	witness
163,754	1875 May 25	Water Wheel Gate		Dunn, George W	inventor
			382	Ourand, Chas H	witness
				Evert, C L	witness
				Alexander & Mason	attorney
				Hubbell, L D	witness
				Riland, Jas M	witness
164,424	1875 June 15	Rotary Measure	384	Chambers, Adam	inventor
				Smith, Chas H	witness
				Surrell, George	witness
				Terrell, Lemuel W	attorney
				Seward, H J	witness
				Pyle, John W	witness
164,639	1875 June 22	Combined Cradle and Bedstead	388	Chamberlain, Carrie Wells	inventor
				Godwin, Thomas J	witness
				Perley, F L	witness

Patent Directory

Patent No.	Date	Patent	Page	Name	Role
				Mungen, Theo	attorney
				Gallup, Francis	witness
				Horner, John W	witness
164,794	1875 June 22	Transom for Doors	391	Berndt, John	inventor
				Pettit, Chas A	witness
				Kennon, Solom C	witness
				Munn & Co	attorney
				Penwinkle, Wm	witness
				Goodridge, Henry	witness
165,484	1875 July 13	Car Coupling	393	Dinsmore, John	inventor
				Jacobs, C W J	witness
				George, Thomas	witness
				Gunnell, Hunter	witness
165,495	1875 July 13	Boring and Mortising Machine	395	Neamann, Henry	inventor
				Wolff, E	witness
				Terry, A F	witness
				Munn & Co	attorney
				Morse, Harley B	witness
				Wilcoxen, I N	witness
166,499	1875 Aug 10	Boot Trees	398	Cass, Henry Clay	inventor
				Rankin, George Read	inventor
				Wood, Geo H	witness
				Smith, G A C	witness
				Perkins, J M C	attorney
				Edgar, C E	witness
				Dexter, James V	witness
166,743	1875 Aug 17	Wet and Dry Ore Crushers	400	Bolthoff, Henry	inventor
				Neveux, C	witness
				Terry, A F	witness
				Munn & Co	attorney
				Hendrie, Charles F	inventor
				Withrow, Chase	witness
				Burrell, James	witness
167,191	1875 Aug 31	Ore Sizing Machine	403	Nevin, David	inventor
				Martin, James Jr	witness
				Lang, J F Theodore	witness
				Mason, Fenwick & Lawrence	attorney
				Stewart, James Oscar	inventor
				Nevin, Robert A	inventor
				Harrington, Henry C	witness

Inventors in the Colorado Territory and their U.S. Patents, 1861-1876

Patent No.	Date	Patent	Page	Name	Role
				Clark, Edward A	witness
167,674	1875 Sept 14	Key Fastener	405	Knight, James	inventor
				Lewis, W A	witness
				Brown, H A	witness
				Burt, George	witness
				Merrill, Jay A	witness
167,677	1875 Sept 14	Sash Balance	407	Lewis, William J	inventor
				Pole, B C	witness
				Parris, Albion K	witness
				Whitman, Charles S	attorney
				Anderson, H Y	witness
				Merrill, Jay A	witness
167,915	1875 Sept 21	Stove Leg	409	Lovejoy, Ira A	inventor
				Blood, James M	witness
				Blood, Eliza R	witness
				Munn & Co	attorney
168,089	1875 Sept 28	Baking Pan Improvements	411	Fristoe, Lydia A	inventor
				Nichols, W H J	witness
				Fristoe, C H	witness
				Newman, W S	witness
				Cutshaw, L	attorney
168,288	1875 Sept 28	Kitchen Table	413	Ricketts, John C	inventor
				Dyer, Geo W	witness
				Howard, Geo H	witness
				Whitman, Charles S	attorney
				Merrill, Jay A	witness
				Lewis, W A	witness
168,556	1875 Oct 11	Door Securer	415	Burt, George	inventor
				Willoughby, Edmund A	witness
				French, S Willis	witness
				Patterson, J O	witness
169,405	1875 Nov 2	Door Spring	417	Blood, James M	inventor
				Wolff, E	witness
				Terry, A F	witness
				Munn & Co	attorney
				Lovejoy, Ira A	witness
				Ryan, Jno A	witness
169,529	1875 Nov 2	Galvanic Battery	419	Duhem, Constant	inventor
				Gardner, A	witness
				Dunn, Edw W	witness
				Whitman, Charles S	attorney

Patent Directory

Patent No.	Date	Patent	Page	Name	Role
				Merrill, Jay A	witness
				Hefley, Bart C	witness
169,831	1875 Nov 9	Spark Arrester	421	Nesmith, J Wellington	inventor
				Hoffman, Benjamin W	witness
				Haynes, Fred	witness
				Brown & Allen	attorney
				Rollins, E W	witness
				Armor, W C	witness
170,073	1875 Nov 16	Bottle	424	Ernst, Joseph	inventor
				Snow, C A	witness
				Halleck, M F	witness
				Baggen, Louis	attorney
				Kempf, Joseph	inventor
				Morse, Harley B	witness
				Goetze, Henry	witness
170,636	1875 Nov 30	Portable Hay Press	426	McCarty, Michael	inventor
				McArdle, Francis	witness
				Roberts, Alex F	witness
				Munn & Co	attorney
				Bradford, M G	witness
				Sayles, Thomas W	witness
170,642	1875 Nov 30	Ore Concentrator	428	Pomeroy, James V	inventor
				Nida, Chas	witness
				Terry, A F	witness
				Munn & Co	attorney
				Graham, T J	witness
				Hubbard, E L	witness
171,238	1875 Dec 21	Sleeping Car	431	Mitchell, James L	inventor
				Danforth, Keyes	witness
				Pinckney, Henry K	witness
171,239	1875 Dec 21	Sleeping Car	436	Mitchell, James L	inventor
				Neveux, C	witness
				Roberts, Alex F	witness
				Munn & Co	attorney
				Thayer, A P	witness
171,597	1875 Dec 28	Gold Washer	439	Calvert, John S	inventor
				Lewis, W A	witness
				Brown, H A	witness
				Merrill, Jay A	agent
172,387	1876 Jan 18	Nut Lock	441	Cazin, Francis M F	inventor
				Townsend, F B	witness

Inventors in the Colorado Territory and their U.S. Patents, 1861-1876

Patent No.	Date	Patent	Page	Name	Role
				Evans, R K	witness
				A H Evans & Co	attorney
				LeFevre, Owen E	witness
				Fischer, C F Adolph	witness
174,187	1876 Feb 29	Car Coupling	443	Briggs, C H	inventor
				Neveux, C	witness
				Goethals, John	witness
				Munn & Co	attorney
				Mouster, Adrian	witness
				Beach, E C	witness
175,082	1876 Mar 21	Pen Extractor	445	Hard, Josiah A	inventor
				Proctor, Alexander	witness
				Cook, Jno Jr	witness
175,401	1876 Mar 28	Friction Clutch	447	Williams, Edwin F	inventor
				Wolff, E	witness
				Goethals, John	witness
				Munn & Co	attorney
				Andrews, DeForest H	witness
				McClure, Samuel	witness
175,799	1876 Apr 4	Wagon Brake	449	Welch, Lester B	inventor
				Burt, George	witness
				Lewis, W A	witness
				Merrill, Jay A	agent
				Duhem, Constant	witness
176,217	1876 Apr 18	Cake Cutter	451	Collins, James	inventor
				Nida, Chas	witness
				Goethals, John	witness
				Munn & Co	attorney
				Manville, J S D	witness
				Seymour, Ben E	witness
176,598	1876 Apr 25	Door Check	453	Collins, James	inventor
				Nida, Chas	witness
				Goethals, John	witness
				Munn & Co	attorney
				Manville, J S D	witness
				Seymour, Ben E	witness
176,994	1876 May 2	Reverberatory Furnace	455	Pearce, Richard	inventor
				Strong, Geo H	witness
				Bome, Jno L	witness
				Dewey & Co	attorney
				Cowenhoven, Henry P	witness

Patent Directory

Patent No.	Date	Patent	Page	Name	Role
				Williams, Henry	witness
177,361	1876 May 16	Sheet Metal Pipe Joint	457	Stanton, J Clark	inventor
				Grow, J W	witness
				Smith, J J	witness
				Hall, Cassius G	inventor
179,040	1876 June 20	Tag Holder for Mail Pouches	459	Metz, Julius	inventor
				Hinman, Egbert	inventor
				Howard, F W	witness
				James, Edwin	witness
				Holmead, J E F	attorney
				Anthony, W D	witness
				French, S W	witness
179,737	1876 July 11	Gearing	461	Smith, Anselmo B	inventor
				Smith, A M	witness
				Gardner, A	witness
				Walker, Joseph E	witness
179,740	1876 July 11	Billiard Table Leveler	463	Stanton, J Clark	inventor
				Storms, Thos G	witness
				DeBorneirre, Rufus	witness
				Hall, Fransana	inventor
				Kendrick, W F	witness
				Hall, Cassius G	witness
181,369	1876 Aug 22	Chucks for Metal Lathes	465	Smith, Anselmo B	inventor
				Smith, A M	witness
				Gardner, A	witness
				Cowl, D P	witness
182,214	1876 Sept 12	Spark Arrester	468	McMahon, Terrence J	inventor
				Everett, Robert	witness
				Alphonse, George E	witness
				Gilmore, Smith & Co	attorney
				Johnson, J M Jr	witness
				DeFrance, A H	witness
182,426	1876 Sept 19	Process of Preserving Animal and Vegetable Substances During Transportation	471	Everett, Charles J	inventor
				Becker, John	witness
				Haynes, Fred	witness
				Brown & Allen	attorney
				Lockwood, Radcliffe B	inventor
				Brown, Henry T	witness

Inventors in the Colorado Territory and their U.S. Patents, 1861-1876

Patent No.	Date	Patent	Page	Name	Role
182,839	1876 Oct 3	Combined Step and Hub Band	475	McDonald, Robert	inventor
				Rydquist, H	witness
				Goethals, John	witness
				Munn & Co	attorney
				Beighley, H B	witness
				Cautton, Thos S	witness
183,615	1876 Oct 24	Door Lock	477	Winter, Gustav	inventor
				Nida, Chas	witness
				Goethals, John	witness
				Munn & Co	attorney
				Merseburg, Chas	witness
				Holst, Herrman	witness
183,648	1876 Oct 24	Quartz Crusher	479	Davis, Francis Marion	inventor
				Bates, E H	witness
				Upshaw, George E	witness
				Gilmore, Smith & Co	attorney
				Ensminger, H C	witness
				Bemis, H M	witness
184,122	1876 Nov 7	Pulverized Fuel Feeder for Smelting Furnaces	482	West, William	inventor
				Rydquist, H	witness
				Goethals, John	witness
				Munn & Co	attorney
				Elkins, Ira S	inventor
				Bertensham, Silas	witness
				Stebbin, H H	witness
185,727	1876 Dec 26	Envelope	484	Collins, James	inventor
				Barrett, Franklin	witness
				Gerner, Richard	witness
				Gerner, Henry	attorney
				Sears, Nathan A	inventor
				Hendricks, Wm C	inventor
				Cameron, Robert	witness
				Nicholson, James	witness
188,098	1877 Mar 6	Shaft Furnaces for Treating Ore	486	Brett, Mathew D	inventor
				Zurns, Robert	witness
				Burdett, LeBlond	witness
				Knight & Bros	attorney
				Burns, Robert	witness
				Brown, C W H	witness

Patent Directory

Patent No.	Date	Patent	Page	Name	Role
reissue 1768	1864 Sept 13	Axle	490	Weibling, Harmon B	inventor
				Pomeroy, Julius R	witness
				Boughton, W H	witness
reissue 4380	1871 May 16	Improvement in Grinding and Amalgamating Ores	493	Bates, Thomas	inventor
				Bode, J	witness
				Merrell, Herman	witness
				Wood & Boyd	attorney
				Withrow, Chase	witness
				McLaughlin, M	witness
reissue 5412	1873 May 20	Lamps	495	Ambrose, Joshua E	inventor
				Shumway, J H	witness
				Tibbits, A J	witness
				Earle, John E	attorney
				Ambrose, Sarah T	inventor
				Miller, Edward	inventor
reissue 5944	1874 June 30	Ore Separators	498	Copeland, George	inventor
				Brown, C F	witness
				Church, M	witness
				Hill & Ellsworth	attorney
				Whitmore, Charles E	inventor
				Whitmore, H R	witness
				Church, Jno B	witness
reissue 6844	1876 Jan 11	Lamp	502	Ambrose, Joshua E	inventor
				Shumway, J H	witness
				Broughton, Clara	witness
				Earle, John E	attorney
				Miller, Edward	inventor
				Dearborn, N B	witness
				Ambrose, W H	witness

J. BURRELL.
Ore Amalgamator.

No. 34,238. Patented Jan. 28, 1862.

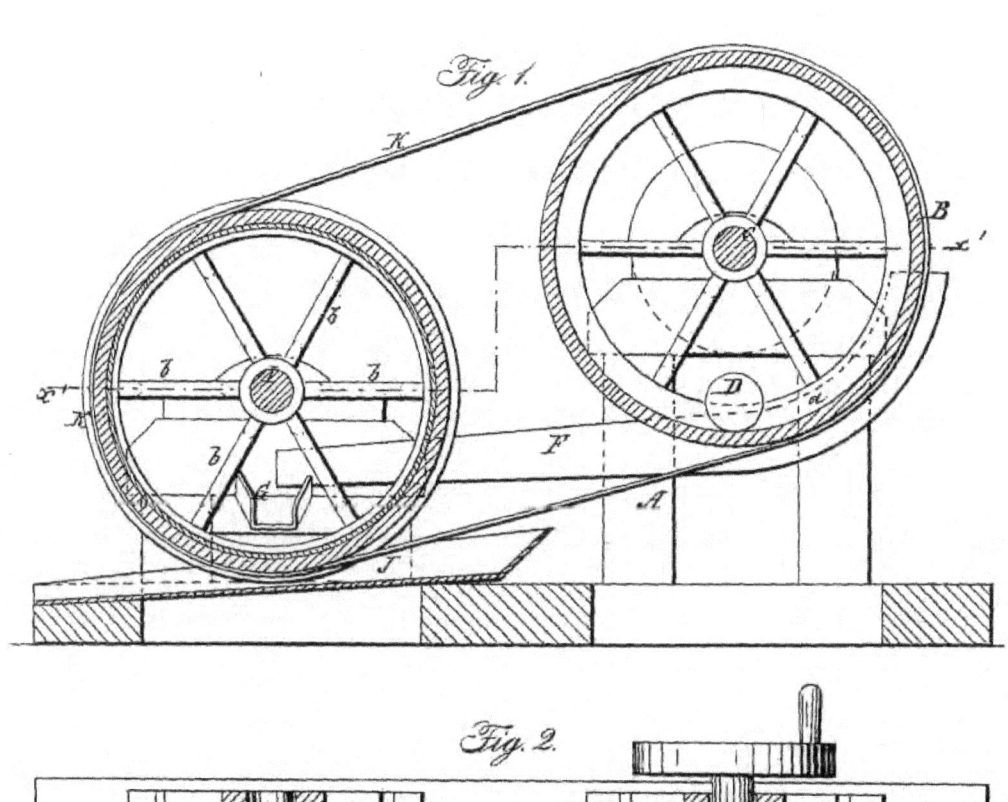

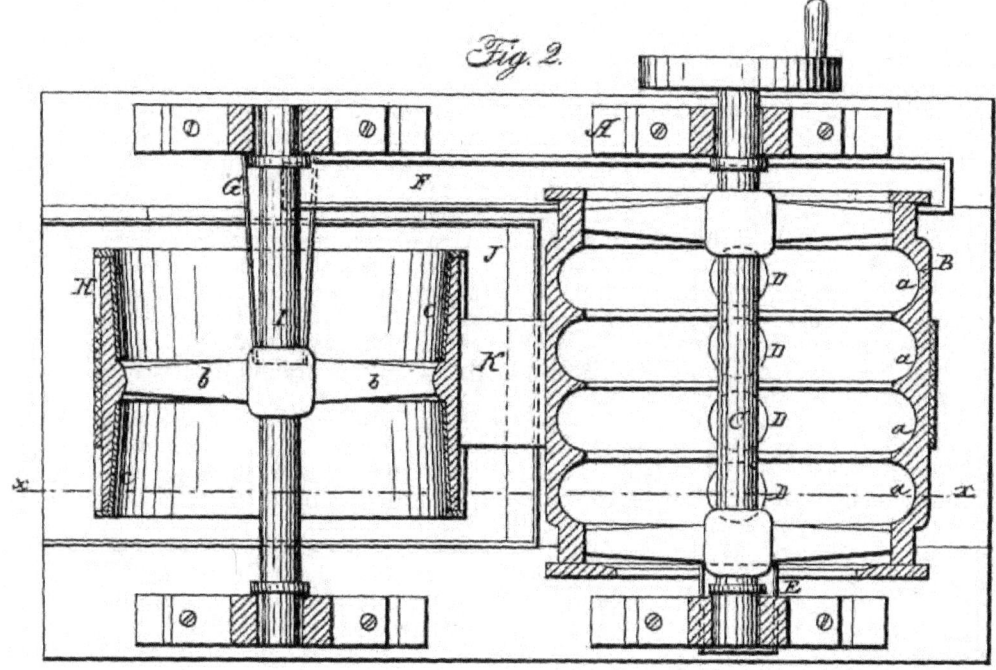

UNITED STATES PATENT OFFICE.

JAMES BURRELL, OF CENTRAL CITY, COLORADO TERRITORY.

IMPROVED AMALGAMATOR AND ORE-CRUSHER.

Specification forming part of Letters Patent No. **34,238**, dated January 28, 1862.

To all whom it may concern:

Be it known that I, JAMES BURRELL, of Central City, in the Territory of Colorado, have invented a new and Improved Pulverizer and Amalgamator for Separating Precious Metals from Ores; and I do hereby declare that the following is a full, clear, and exact description of the same, reference being had to the annexed drawings, making a part of this specification, in which—

Figure 1 is a side sectional view of my invention, taken in the line $x\,x$, Fig. 2; Fig. 2, a horizontal section of the same, taken in the line $x'\,x'$, Fig. 1.

Similar letters of reference indicate corresponding parts in the two figures.

The object of this invention is to obtain a machine which will complete the process of pulverizing the ore as it comes from the stamping-mills, and during the process of amalgamating the same, so that a more perfect separation may be obtained of the metal from the ore than by the ordinary amalgamating-machines.

The invention is chiefly designed for separating gold from quartz, and to receive the pulp as it is discharged from the ordinary stamp-batteries or stamping-mills.

The invention consists in the employment or use of a rotary or reciprocating pulverizer and amalgamator formed of a cylinder or semi-cylinder, provided with grooves which contain balls or spherical crushers, and using in connection therewith a rotary hollow cylinder or drum having an amalgamated inner surface, and so arranged as to receive the contents of the pulverizer and amalgamator, and separate any particles of gold that might have escaped amalgamation in passing through the pulverizer and amalgamator.

To enable those skilled in the art to fully understand and construct my invention, I will proceed to describe it.

A represents a framing, which may be constructed in any proper way to support the working parts of the machine, and B is a hollow cylinder, the shaft C of which is fitted in proper bearings on the framing A. This cylinder may be formed of cast-iron, and it is provided at its inner surface with a series of circumferential grooves, a, placed side by side and of semicircular form in their transverse section. Each groove a contains a metal ball, D, the diameter of which corresponds with the width of its groove. The cylinder B is slightly inclined in the direction of its axis, and into the elevated end of the cylinder a trough, E, passes, said trough being secured to the framing A.

F is a trough or spout, which is inclined and is fitted longitudinally in the framing A, the upper end of the trough being curved, so that it may fit under the lower or discharge end of the cylinder B and receive its contents. The lower end of the trough F projects over the upper or elevated end of a small inclined trough, G, which is placed at right angles to F, and conducts the contents of the latter into a hollow cylinder, H, the shaft I of which is placed on the framing parallel to the shaft C of cylinder B. The cylinder H is provided with one set of arms b, and these are at the center of the cylinder. The inner surface of cylinder H is of copper or other metal having an amalgamated outer surface. The inner end of trough G projects over the center of cylinder H, the latter having a slightly flaring inner surface from its center outward in both directions, as shown at c in Fig. 2. Underneath the cylinder H there is placed a trough, J, which is wider than the cylinder, so as to receive its contents from both ends.

K is a belt which passes around the two cylinders B H.

The operation of the machine is as follows: The cylinder B is rotated by any convenient power, and the pulp from the stamping-mill passes into cylinder B through trough E, which is supplied with a requisite quantity of quicksilver. The pulp is acted upon in the grooves a by the balls D, and further reduced or comminuted, so as to admit of the particles of gold amalgamating with the quicksilver. The pulp passes through the cylinder B from groove to groove, and is discharged into the trough F, which conducts it to the trough G, the latter discharging it in the center of the cylinder H, from which it flows toward both ends of the cylinder, and is discharged into the trough J. Any particles of gold that might chance to escape amalgamation in cylinder B will be caught in cylinder H, and hence all will be separated from the pulp and saved. Motion, it will be seen, is communicated to the cylinder H from the cylinder B by the belt K.

I would remark that the cylinder B, having a rotary movement, would be decidedly preferable to other motions. A reciprocating motion, however, might be given it, and a semi-cylinder, instead of a whole or entire cylinder, used.

Having thus described my invention, what I claim as new, and desire to secure by Letters Patent, is not, broadly, a rotating or reciprocating vessel provided with balls, irrespective of the construction and arrangement herein shown and described; but

1. A rotating or reciprocating pulverizer and amalgamator, B, when constructed with a series of circumferential grooves, a, each of which is provided with a ball, D, arrranged as described.

2. In connection with the pulverizer and amalgamator B, constructed as described, the cylinder H, provided with an amalgamated inner surface, and arranged to operate conjointly with B, substantially as and for the purpose set forth.

JAMES BURRELL.

Witnesses:
A. J. VAN DEREN,
W. T. POTTER.

H. G. WEIBLING.
Axle Box.

No. 37,479.

2 Sheets—Sheet 1.

Patented Jan'y 20, 1863.

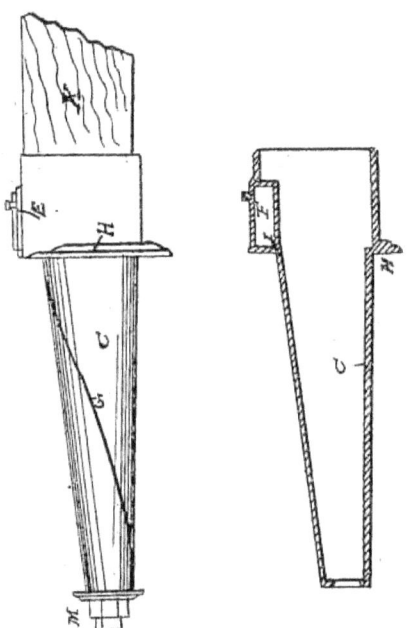

Witnesses
Almon Dibble
Henry S. Lathrop

Inventor
Harman G. Weibling

H. G. WEIBLING.
Axle Box.

No. 37,479.

2 Sheets—Sheet 2.

Patented Jan'y 20, 1863.

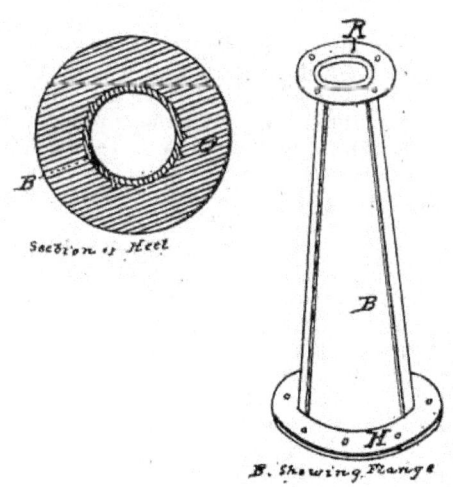

Section of Heel

B. Showing Flange

Witnesses
Almon Dibble
Henry S. Lathrop

Inventor
Hamm G. Weibling

UNITED STATES PATENT OFFICE.

HARMON G. WEIBLING, OF DENVER CITY, COLORADO TERRITORY.

IMPROVEMENT IN AXLES.

Specification forming part of Letters Patent No. **37,479**, dated January 20, 1863.

To all whom it may concern:

Be it known that I, HARMON G. WEIBLING, of Denver city, Colorado, have invented an Improvement in Method of Lubricating Carriage-Axles, of which the following is a specification.

The improvement: The peculiar construction of the boxes or thimbles and their attachments to the axles, having a lubricator at the shoulder connected with spiral grooves running the entire length of the spindle and friction-rollers inserted in its under side.

The improvements consist in having at the shoulder of the axle an oil-chamber or fountain, f, from which oil or other lubricating matter will flow through the aperture l into the spiral groove g, thus distributing the lubricator over the whole length of the axle from the shoulder to the point, and obviating the necessity of taking off the wheel to oil the spindle or axle.

The friction-rollers $e\ e$, placed in two grooves cut in the lower side of the spindle c and resting on the pipe or box b, also the friction-rollers $e'\ e'$ in the shoulder h and in the burr or nut m, the rollers in each case resting upon Babbitt metal, which will do away with much of the friction of the ordinary thimble-skein, these rollers to be so arranged as to act independently of each other, thereby making each to perform its own rotary motion in its own particular position.

The fastening of the box or thimble o to the hub o, and the spindle c to the axle k, with the gutta-percha packing a, the gutta-percha to be dissolved to the consistency of thick tar and then spread upon the surface of the axle k and the inner surface of the thimble or skein c. The thimble c is then to be forced upon the axle to its proper place, aided by an iron bar inserted in a groove in the lower side of the axle and extending from one end of the axle to the other. The box b is secured in the hub by the same process, with the addition of the flange r, which, after the box is forced to its place, is fitted onto the lower end of the box, and screwed to the hub by means of countersunk screws. By this means it will be impossible for the lubrication used upon the axle to penetrate or saturate the hub o or the axle k, and will thereby add durability to the wood of the axle or hub.

The flanges h and r, on the box b, by which strength is added to the axle and the oil is kept from the end of the hub o, also the friction between the flange h and the shoulder i, will keep the lubricating substance in a condition to flow through the groove l.

The peculiar shape of the spindle c and the box b, as shown in the drawing, giving it a greater amount of strength.

The spindle c is fastened to the axle k by means of the strap of iron d, running back the under side of the axle k to the bolt j, or through the entire length of the axle, the spindle c being drawn to its place and secured by means of the nut or burr n, the bar d to be secured to the axle by means of bolts running through the axle and bar, or by clasps passing over the two, and secured by screws and nuts.

I am aware that thimbles or journal-boxes covering the entire axle have been known and used, and that spiral grooves or axles are not new; therefore I do not claim them, broadly; but

What I do claim as my invention, and for which I desire to procure Letters Patent, is—

The peculiar construction of my axle-boxes or thimbles, with the flanges $h\ r$, oil-chamber f, and aperture l, when connected with a spiral groove terminating in a canal in which is placed friction-rollers e, the whole combined and operating as described.

HARMON G. WEIBLING.

Witnesses:
S. I. SORAH,
H. S. LATHROP.

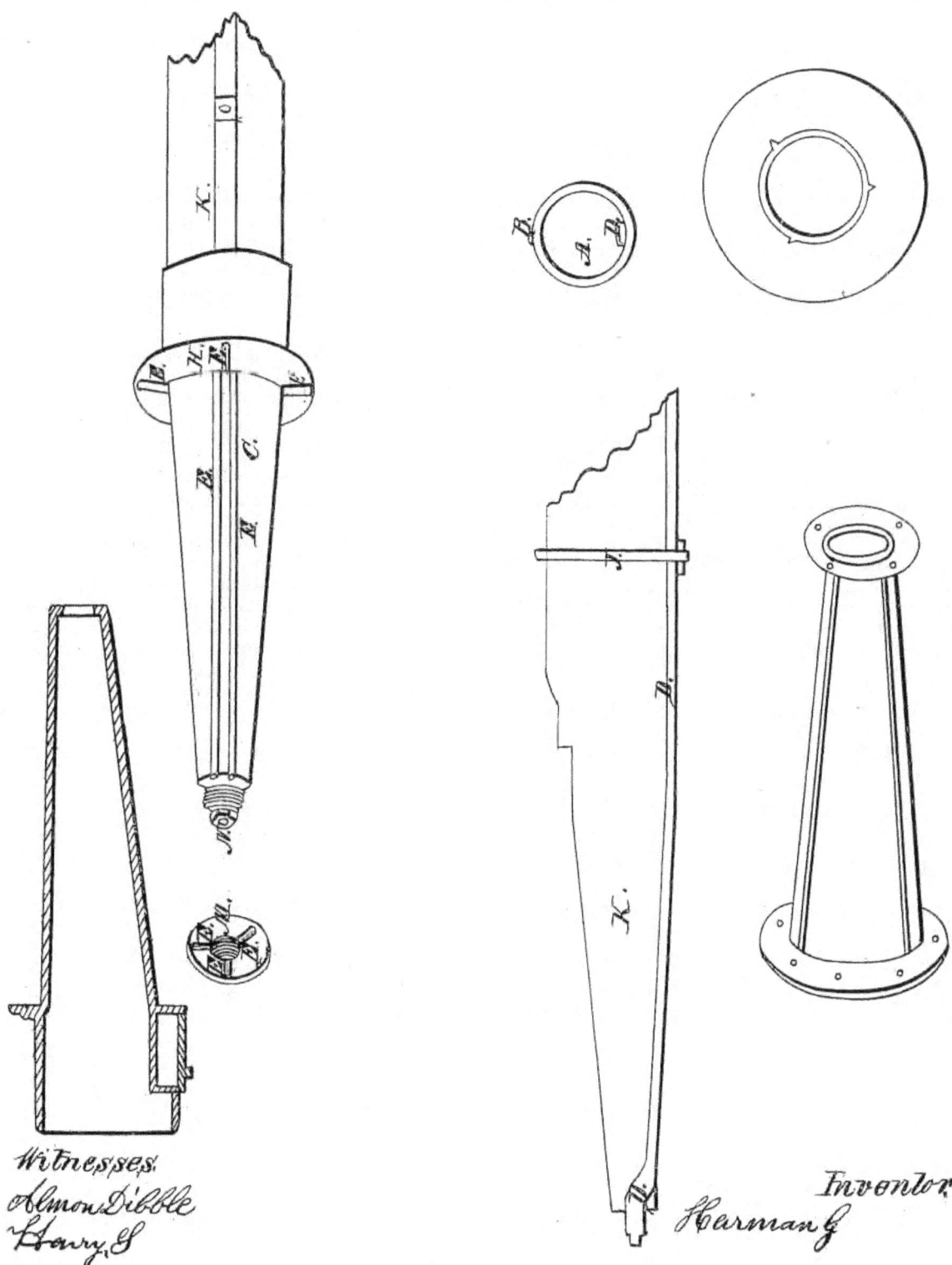

UNITED STATES PATENT OFFICE.

HARMON G. WEIBLING, OF DENVER CITY, COLORADO TERRITORY.

IMPROVEMENT IN CARRIAGE-WHEELS.

Specification forming part of Letters Patent No. **37,480**, dated January 20, 1863.

To all whom it may concern:

Be it known that I, HARMON G. WEIBLING, of Denver City, Colorado, have invented an Improvement in Carriage-Wheels, of which the following is a specification.

The description and general principles of the invention consist in having the friction-rollers E E placed in a groove cut in the lower side of the spindle c, and resting on the pipe or box b; also the friction-rollers E E in the shoulder H and in the burr or nut m, the rollers in each case to rest on "Babbitt metal," which will do away with much of the friction of the ordinary thimble-skein, these rollers to be so arranged as to act independently of each other, thereby making each perform its own rotary motion in its own particular position. The spindle c is fastened to the axle K with the gutta-percha packing A, the gutta-percha to be dissolved to the consistency of thick tar and then spread on the surface of the axle K, and the inner surface of the spindle c, which is then forced upon the axle to its proper place and secured by means of the iron strap or bar D, inserted in a groove in the lower side of the axle, and extending from one end to the other of the axle. The spindle c is fastened to the axle K by means of the strap of iron D, running back on the under side of the axle K to the bolt J, or through the entire length of the axle, the spindle c being drawn to its place and secured by means of the nut N, the bar D to be secured to the axle by means of bolts running through the axle and bar, or by clasps passing over the two and secured by nuts and screws.

What I claim as my invention, and desire to secure by Letters Patent, is—

My peculiar method of constructing the axle boxes or thimbles and attaching them to the axles, by means of the gutta-percha packing A and screws, where the boxes or thimbles are made to taper, as described, having a canal lined with Babbitt metal, in which rollers E are placed, the whole used in construction with the strap D on the under side of the axle, and the bolt J, the friction-rollers, spiral groove, and lubricator, all as described and set forth.

HARMON G. WEIBLING.

Witnesses:
ALMON DIBBLE,
HENRY S. LATHROP

C. C. Alexander,
Double-Acting Pump.
Nº 40,006.
Patented Sep. 22, 1863.

Witnesses

Inventor

UNITED STATES PATENT OFFICE.

CALVIN C. ALEXANDER, OF DENVER, COLORADO TERRITORY.

IMPROVEMENT IN PUMPS.

Specification forming part of Letters Patent No. 40,006, dated September 22, 1863.

To all whom it may concern:

Be it known that I, CALVIN C. ALEXANDER, of Denver, in the county of Arapahoe, Territory of Colorado, have invented a new and useful pump for the use of steam fire-engines, and engines of all kinds, mines, stone-quarries, cisterns, oil-wells, &c., requiring less motive power than any now in use; and I do hereby declare that the following is a full and exact description thereof, reference being had to the accompanying drawing, and to the letters of reference marked thereon.

I claim that the nature of my invention consists in the combination of four cylinders, (more or less,) A A A A, attached to a reservoir, B, by means of four pipes, (more or less,) C C C C, moving from cylinder-heads K K K K, to check-valve seats E E E E, the valves D and F on the inside cylinder-head, G, which allows the piston-head H to pass the whole length of cylinder A, the piston-rods M M M M, connected to cranks J J J J, working in rotation at right angles on shaft J, by pitmans N N N N. The water is drawn through pipes L and valve D into cylinder A and discharged at the same end through valve F and pipe C, check-valve E, into reservoir B, and through pipe O.

The arrangement is so ordered as that the valves and the inside cylinder-head allow the piston-head to pass the whole length of the cylinder, the piston-rod being connected to the crank, on a shaft, by a pitman, which works in rotation at right angles, thus driving a uniform, continuous, and unbroken stream of water into the reservoir, from which it is expelled without the pulsations or pauses incident to other pumps, the volume of water thus expelled being larger in diameter and capable of being lifted and thrown at a greater distance, with less motive power, than any other pump extant.

What I claim as original and new is—

The peculiar arrangement of the cylinder to a reservoir by means of the pipes fastened to a cylinder-head and to a check-valve seat, substantially as hereinbefore described.

CALVIN C. ALEXANDER.

In presence of—
PH. P. BALDAUFF,
LOUIS FEESER.

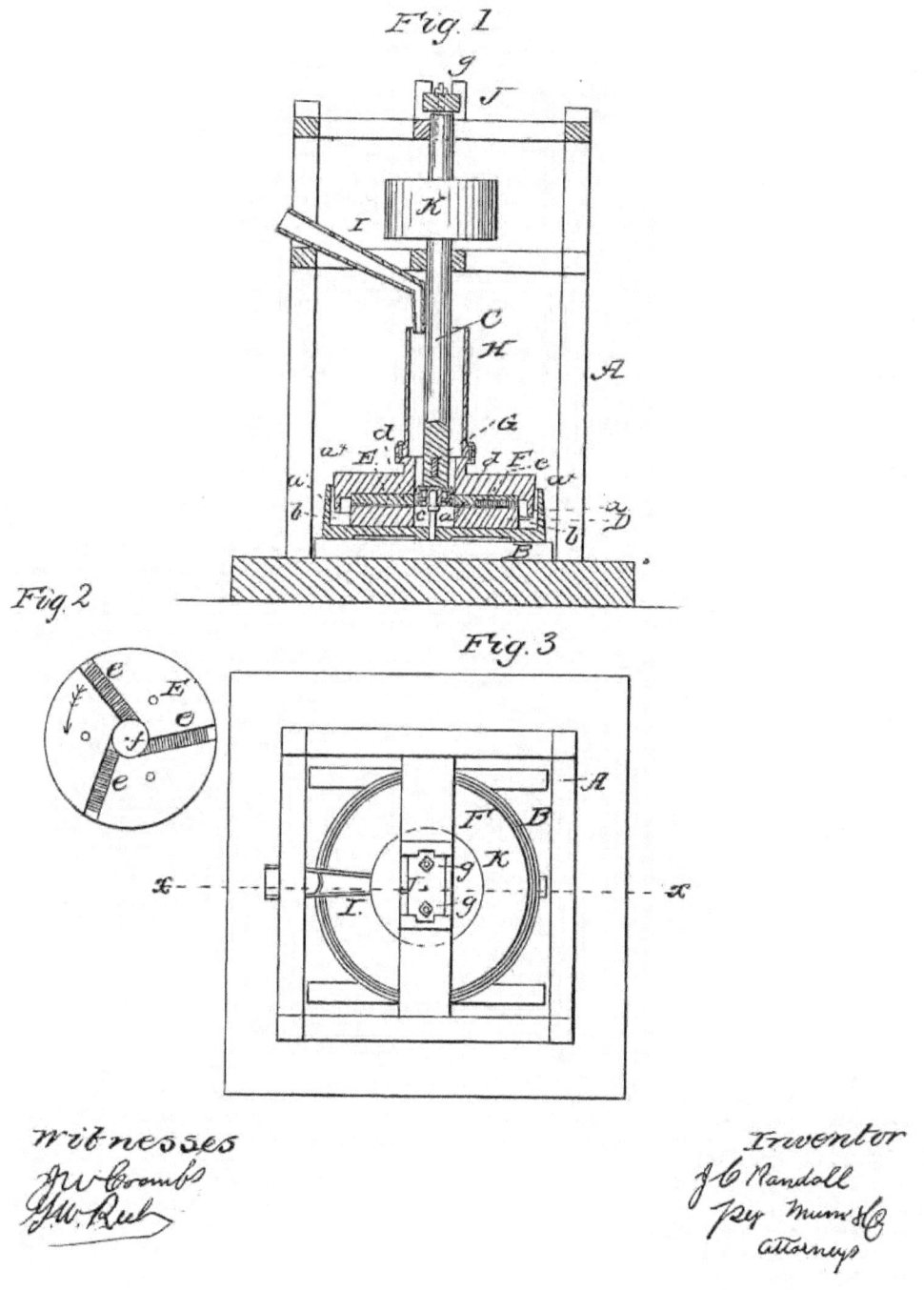

UNITED STATES PATENT OFFICE.

JOHN G. RANDALL, OF CAÑON CITY, COLORADO.

IMPROVED MACHINE FOR GRINDING ORES AND AMALGAMATING PRECIOUS METALS.

Specification forming part of Letters Patent No. **40,501**, dated November 3, 1863.

To all whom it may concern:

Be it known that I, JOHN G. RANDALL, of Cañon City, in the county of Fremont and Territory of Colorado, have invented a new and improved device for pulverizing ores and amalgamating the metals contained therein; and I do hereby declare that the following is a full, clear, and exact description of the same, reference being had to the accompanying drawings, making a part of this specification, in which—

Figure 1 is a vertical central section of my invention, taken in the line $x\,x$, Fig. 3; Fig. 2, a detached face view of the revolving muller-plate; Fig. 3, a plan or top view of Fig. 1.

Similar letters of reference indicate corresponding parts in the several figures.

The object of this invention is to obtain a device by which gold and silver ore, and particularly quartz, pulp, or tailings from a stamp-mill, may be pulverized and the metal it contains thoroughly amalgamated.

To enable those skilled in the art to fully understand and construct my invention, I will proceed to describe it.

A represents a rectangular frame, which supports the working parts of the machine; and B is a pan, at the center of which there is a vertical pin, a, on which a vertical shaft, C, is fitted and allowed to rotate freely. On the bottom of the pan B there is fitted a circular die, D, which may be of iron or other suitable material. This die does not reach the side of the pan B, a space, b, being allowed all around it, as shown clearly in Fig. 1. The die D has a circular opening, c, at its center, forming an eye, and the upper edge of said opening, c, is notched, as shown at d. The face or upper side of the die D is perfectly smooth, with the exception of the notches above referred to.

E is a circular die, which is attached to the under side of a circular pan, F, the rim a' of which extends down into the space b between the die D and the rim of the pan B. The face side of the die E is provided with three furrows or grooves, $e\,e\,e$, which are tangential with a circular opening, f, at the center of the die. (See Fig. 2.) The furrows or grooves e are corrugated transversely.

The pan F is connected with the shaft C by means of a driver, G, which passes transversely through the shaft, and has its ends fitting in recesses or notches in the circular opening at the center of the pan. To the top of the pan F there is attached a vertical tube, H, said tube encompassing the shaft and extending up a considerable distance.

I is a trough or spout, which leads into the upper end of the tube H.

On the upper end of the shaft C a block, J, rests or bears, and has screw-bolts g passing through it, by adjusting which the upper die, E, may be made to press upon the lower one, D, in a greater or less degree, as may be required.

K is a driving-pulley placed on the shaft C.

The operation is as follows: The shaft C is rotated by any convenient power, and the pulp is conducted into the tube H through the trough or spout I, and passes down and into the furrows $e\,e\,e$, but it cannot pass out at the ends of said furrows, owing to the position of the same, which gives them a tendency to throw the pulp to the center of the die as the latter rotates. The pulp is forced by static pressure between the faces of the two dies D E from the sides of the furrows e, and it is pulverized between said dies and the metal particles burnished, the pulp passing out and being forced through quicksilver placed in the space b, and the metal particles combining or amalgamating therewith. The refuse passes out at $a^\times$.

The whole device is simple and efficient, and may be constructed at a small cost.

The dies D E, when worn, may be removed and replaced by new ones, as it is designed to have them made detached and fitted to the pans in such a manner that they may be readily removed.

Having thus described my invention, what I claim as new, and desire to secure by Letters Patent, is—

The stationary die D, secured within a stationary pan, B, in combination with the revolving die E, provided with furrows e, and secured within the pan F, having the tube H attached to it, the pan B being arranged, as shown, to admit of a quicksilver-receptacle, b, into which the rim a' of the pan F projects, substantially as and for the purpose herein set forth.

JOHN G. RANDALL.

Witnesses:
D. P. WILSON,
ANSON RUDD.

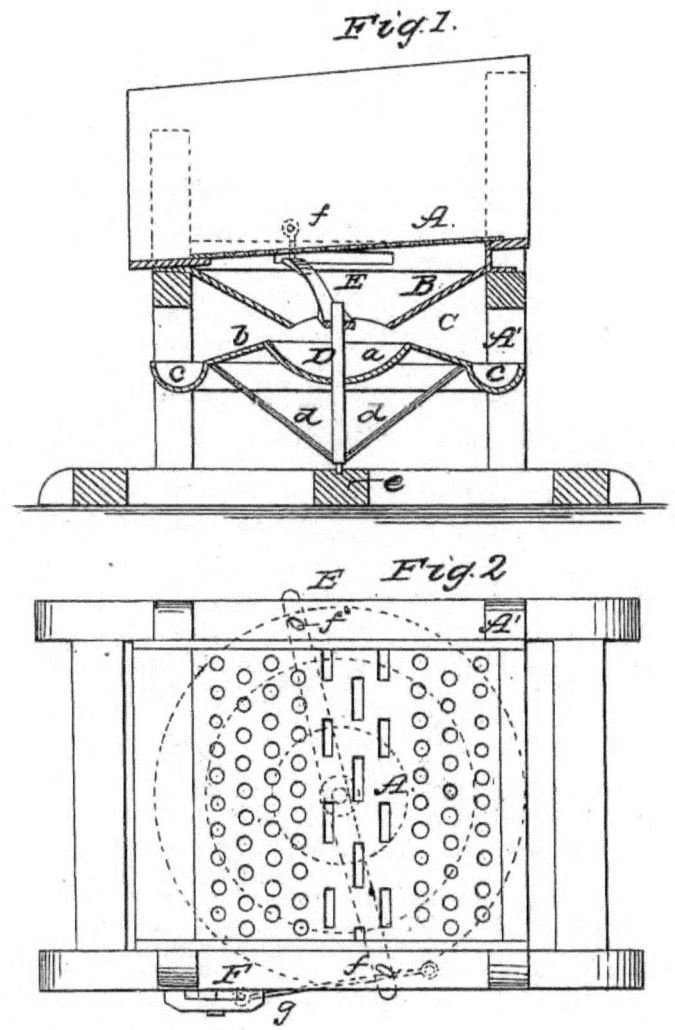

UNITED STATES PATENT OFFICE.

CHARLES D. HICKS, OF DENVER, COLORADO TERRITORY.

IMPROVED ORE-SEPARATOR.

Specification forming part of Letters Patent No. **42,372**, dated April 19, 1864.

To all whom it may concern:

Be it known that I, CHARLES D. HICKS, of Denver, in the county of Arapahoe and Territory of Colorado, have invented a new and Improved Ore-Separator; and I do hereby declare that the following is a full, clear, and exact description of the same, reference being had to the accompanying drawings, forming part of this specification, in which—

Figure 1 represents a longitudinal vertical section of my invention. Fig. 2 is a plan or top view of the same.

Similar letters of reference in both views indicate corresponding parts.

This invention consists in the employment of an oscillating separator, provided with a hemispherical central cavity, sloped sides, and an annular semicircular trough, in combination with an adjustable shaft, pyramidal chute, and common sluice, in such a manner that the small particles of quartz and gold passing through the perforated bottom of the sluice are conducted to the central cavity of the separator, and by the oscilliating motion imparted to said separator and by the action of its sloped sides, the gold contained in the quartz settles down to the bottom of the central cavity and annular trough, and the light particles are carried off by the water.

To enable those skilled in the art to make and use my invention, I will proceed to describe it.

A represents a section of a common sluice set upon a suitable frame-work, A', and provided with a perforated bottom through which the water and small particles of quartz with the gold pass, while the coarse stones run down the sluice.

The matter passing through the perforated bottom of the sluice is conducted by the pyramidal chute B to the center of the separator-wheel C. The chute is made of sheet metal, or any other suitable material, and it is secured to the frame-work A' under the bottom of the sluice, as clearly shown in Fig. 1 of the drawings.

The separator-wheel is made of sheet metal or other suitable material, and of any convenient size. Its center is depressed, forming a hemispherical cavity, *a*, and sloped sides *b*, and from said cavity to the annular semicircular trough *c* said separator is secured to a vertical arbor, D, and it is steadied by means of braces *d*, or in any other convenient manner.

The arbor D is stepped into a suitable socket, *e*, at the bottom of the frame-work A', and its upper bearing is in a bar, E, which is secured to the frame A' by means of pins *f* in such a manner that its position can be easily changed, and that it can be readily adjusted to bring the arbor in a vertical position. By these means the separator wheel can always be brought in a horizontal position independent of the formation of the ground on which the machine is placed.

A hand-lever, F, which connects by means of a rod, *g*, with a loop secured to the periphery of the separator-wheel, serves to impart to the same an oscillating motion, or instead of the hand lever any other suitable mechanism may be applied to produce the desired motion.

By the oscillating motion imparted to the separator-wheel the particles of quartz and gold passing down from the sluice arrange themselves in the central cavity and in the trough according to their specific gravity, the gold settling down to the bottom and the light particles being swept off by the current of water.

The separation is facilitated by the sloped sides of the separator-wheel, which spread the particles of quartz in thin layers and cause them to roll down slowly into the trough, so that the heavy particles have time to settle down in the annular trough.

By these means ore of any desired description can be readily separated according to the specific gravity of its component parts.

What I claim as my invention, and desire to secure by Letters Patent, is—

The separator-wheel C, provided with a central cavity, *a*, sloped sides *b*, and an annular trough, *c*, and secured to an oscillating adjustable arbor, D, in combination with the pyramidal chute B and sluice A, all constructed and operating in the manner and for the purpose substantially as shown and described.

C. D. HICKS.

Witnesses:
O. E. EDSON,
H. WITTER.

M. B. DODGE.
MACHINE FOR AMALGAMATING.

No. 42,568. Patented May 3, 1864.

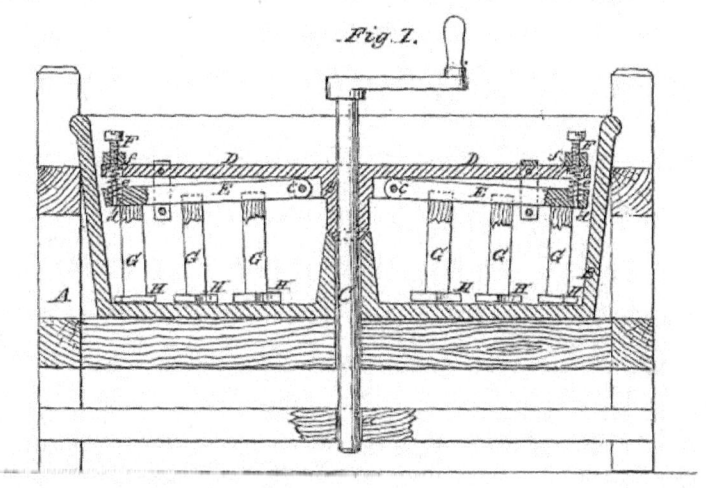

Fig. 1.

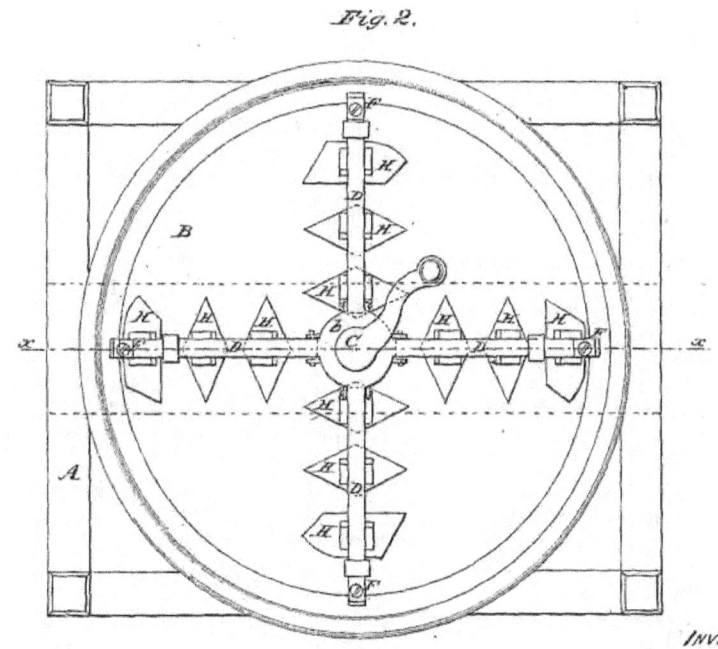

Fig. 2.

WITNESSES:

INVENTOR:
M B Dodge

UNITED STATES PATENT OFFICE.

M. B. DODGE, OF BLACK HAWK POINT, COLORADO.

IMPROVEMENT IN MACHINES FOR AMALGAMATING.

Specification forming part of Letters Patent No. 42,568, dated May 3, 1864.

To all whom it may concern:

Be it known that I, M. B. DODGE, of Black Hawk Point, in the county of Gilpin and Territory of Colorado, have invented a new and useful Improvement in Machines for Amalgamating the Precious Metals and Separating them from the Ore; and I do hereby declare that the following is a full, clear, and exact description of the same, reference being had to the accompanying drawings, making a part of this specification, in which—

Figure 1 is a vertical central section of an amalgamating device having my improvement applied to it; Fig. 2, a plan or top view of the same.

Similar letters of reference indicate corresponding parts in the two figures.

This invention relates to a novel arrangement of the rotary shoes of the machine, whereby the outer ones, which are subjected to the most wear, in consequence of having the greatest speed, may always be adjusted so as to run in contact with the bottom of the pan, and the wear thereby compensated for. In the ordinary amalgamating-machines the outer shoes, in consequence of being subjected to more wear than the inner ones, soon become comparatively useless, and thereby render the machine much less efficient than it otherwise would be.

To enable those skilled in the art to fully understand and construct my invention, I will proceed to describe it.

A represents a framing, which may be of rectangular or other suitable form; and B is a pan, which is fitted permanently in the framing A. C is a shaft which passes vertically and centrally through the pan B, and is stepped in the lower part of the framing A, as shown at a. On this shaft C there are placed horizontal radial arms D, four, more or less, said arms all projecting from a hub, b, keyed firmly on the shaft. The arms D extend nearly to the side of the pan B, and underneath each arm D there is a bar, E, the inner ends of which are connected by joints c to the hub b. The outer ends of the bars E have each a vertical pin, d, fitted in them, around which spiral springs e are placed. These springs e extend upward into recesses f in the under sides of the arms D, and have screws F bearing upon them, as shown clearly in Fig. 1. To the bars E there are secured a series of uprights, G, each one of which has a shoe, H, attached to its lower end. These shoes are designed to run in contact with the bottom of the pan B as the shaft C is rotated, and serve to bring the particles of quicksilver in contact with the particles of gold contained in the ore, the latter with a proper amount of quicksilver being placed in the pan B.

In the ordinary amalgamating-machines the uprights G are attached directly to the arms D, and it will be seen that the shoes H at the outer part of the arms, in consequence of having a more rapid motion than those at their inner parts, will be subjected to more wear, and, as they become worn, will become inefficient, in consequence of not being capable of being pressed or adjusted downward to compensate for the wear.

By my improvement it will be seen that this end is attained, for by turning the screws F the springs e may be compressed, so as to press or force down the outer ends of the arms D, and said springs will constantly keep the outermost shoes down to their work.

Having thus described my invention, what I claim as new, and desire to secure by Letters Patents, is—

The employment or use, in an amalgamating-machine, of adjustable shoes attached to or connected with supplemental bars or arms, which are arranged with springs and with the main or principal rotating arms, to operate in the manner substantially as and for the purpose herein set forth.

M. B. DODGE.

Witnesses:
  M. M. LIVINGSTON,
  HENRY MORN.

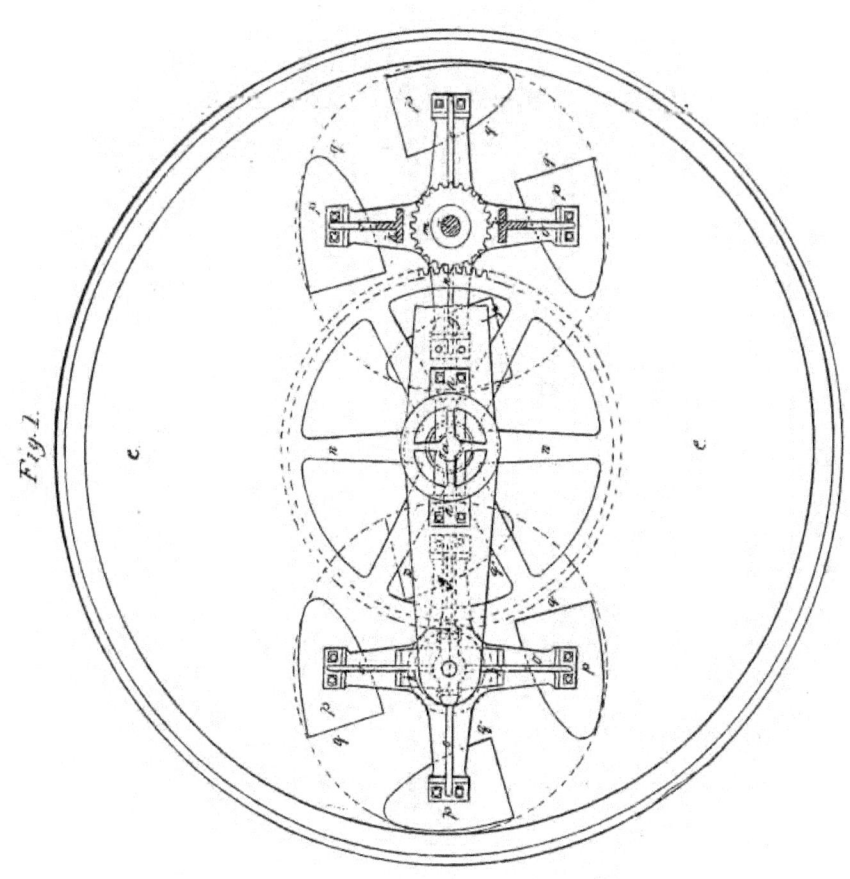

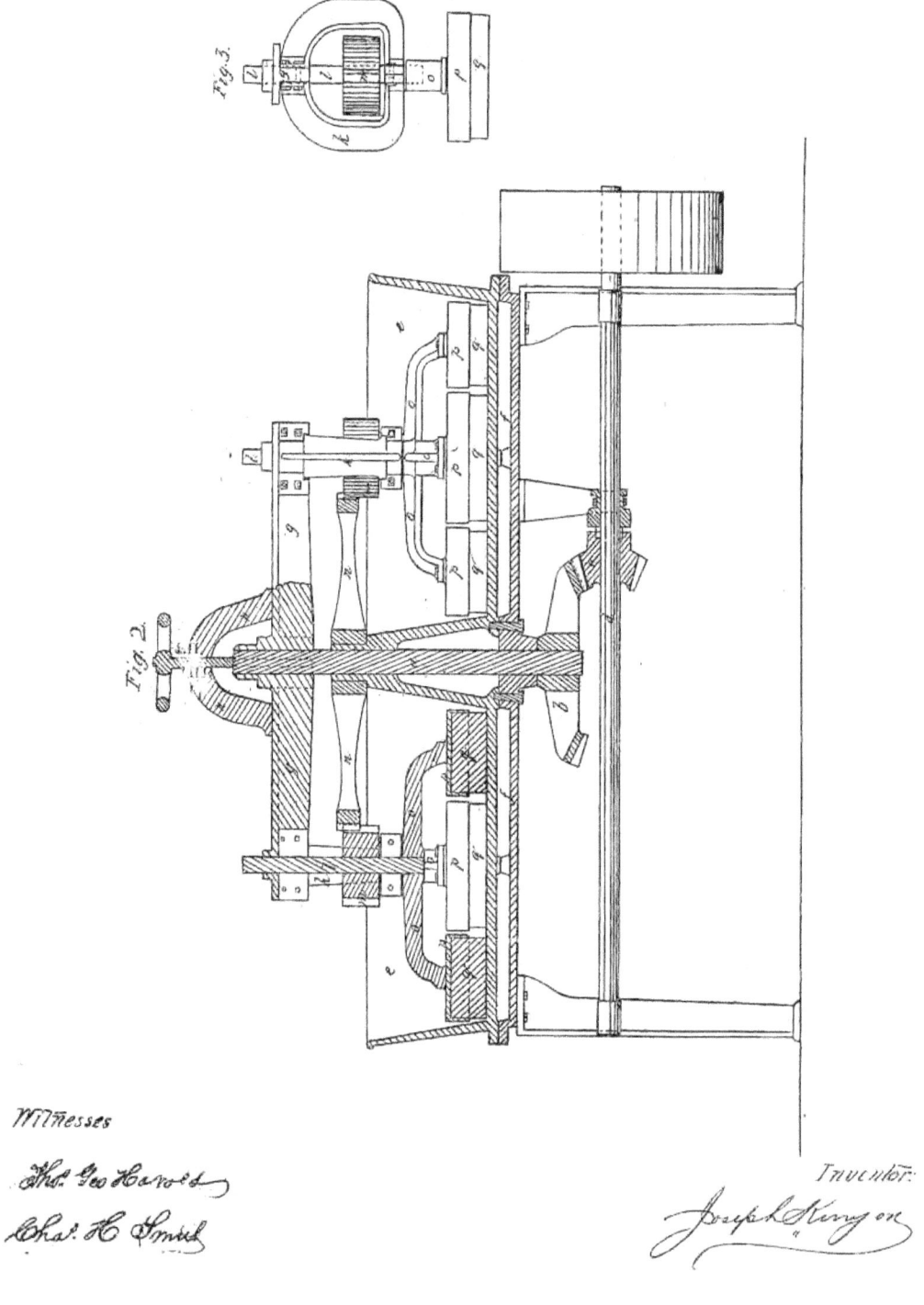

UNITED STATES PATENT OFFICE.

JOSEPH KENYON, OF BLACK HAWK, COLORADO.

IMPROVEMENT IN AMALGAMATORS.

Specification forming part of Letters Patent No. **43,589**, dated July 19, 1864.

To all whom it may concern:

Be it known that I, JOSEPH KENYON, of Black Hawk, in the Territory of Colorado, have invented, made, and applied to use a certain new and useful Improvement in Amalgamators; and I do hereby declare the following to be a full, clear, and exact description of the same, reference being had to the annexed drawings, making part of this specification, wherein—

Figure 1 is a plan of said amalgamator with part of the upper cross-bar removed. Fig. 2 is a vertical section of said apparatus with the mullers on one side in elevation, and Fig. 3 is a detached elevation of said mullers.

Similar marks of reference denote the same parts.

In amalgamators heretofore employed a circular basin has been used in which mullers are fitted to revolve and rub and grind the ores after they have been comminuted in order that the mercury contained in such vessel may amalgamate with the gold in the ore. In this class of amalgamators the ores sometimes accumulate and are pushed along in front of the mullers, and do not all come equally in contact with the quicksilver, and the water in the pan, that carries off the earthy matters, receives a whirling and centrifugal motion that is apt to throw the particles of amalgam off with the tailings.

The nature of my said invention consists in a series of mullers revolving upon a shaft that is itself revolved around the pan, so that each muller travels as a cycloidal curve around in the pan, and a much greater rubbing and amalgamating action is obtained, and the centrifugal action of the water is entirely prevented, so that the same remains nearly level and the banking up of the earthy matter in front of the mullers is prevented.

I also fit my mullers in such a manner that they can be gradually raised from the bottom of the pan while revolving, so as to maintain the agitation on the water for washing the earthy matters out of the amalgam while said amalgam gradually subsides in the pan, thereby there will be no loss of amalgam when the water and earthy matters are drawn off.

In the drawings, a is a vertical shaft propelled by the gearing b and c and shaft d to competent power. The shaft a is in the center of the circular or ring-formed pan e, which may be formed with a double bottom, f, so that steam may be introduced in cold weather to maintain a proper temperature of the contents of the pan.

g is a cross-head set on a feather upon the upper end of the shaft a, which cross-head is fitted with a yoke, h, through which the screw i passes and rests upon the end of the shaft a, so that the cross-head g can be either raised or lowered by turning the screw i, even while the apparatus is in motion.

At the ends of the cross-head g pendent frames or bows k k are firmly attached, carrying the vertical shafts l l, upon which are pinions m m, gearing into the stationary wheel n, and said pinions are wider than the wheel n, so as to remain in gear when the cross-head is raised by the yoke-screw i.

At the lower end of each shaft l are arms o o, which may be two or more in number. I have shown four such arms to each shaft l, and upon their ends are irons p p, receiving the mullers q q.

It will now be seen that as the shafts l l are themselves carried around with the cross-head g the said shafts l have a rotation imparted to them, which moves the mullers and causes them to travel in a cycloidal line around the pan, both thoroughly mixing the pulverized ore and water, and rubbing the same with the amalgam upon the bottom of the pan, thereby at the same time preventing any banking up of the earthy matter in front of the mullers and avoiding any centrifugal action on the water, so that the water remains nearly level.

What I claim, and desire to secure by Letters Patent, is—

1. A series of mullers connected by arms or supports with a shaft that revolves in its own bearings and also moves around the pan, so that each muller receives a cycloidal movement, for the purposes and substantially as specified.

2. The arrangement of the cross-head g, bows k, shafts l, wheel n, and pinions m m, for giving motion to the mullers, as set forth.

3. The yoke h and screw i, in combination with the cross-head g and cycloidal revolving mullers carried by the shafts l, as and for the purposes specified.

In witness whereof I have hereunto set my signature this 21st May, 1864.

JOSEPH KENYON.

Witnesses:
THOS. GEO. HAROLD,
CHAS. H. SMITH.

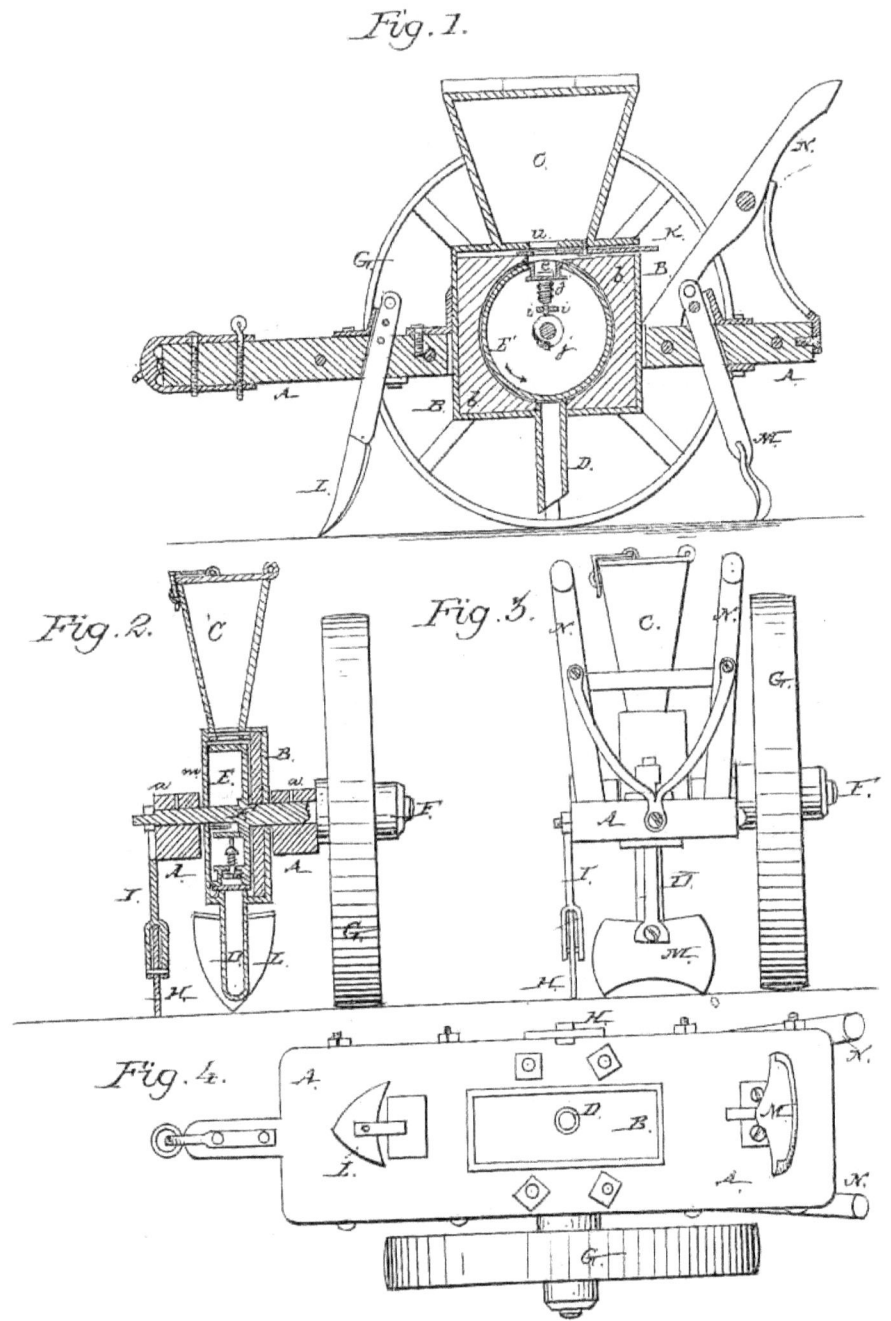

UNITED STATES PATENT OFFICE.

FREDRICH LOOS, OF DENVER, COLORADO TERRITORY.

CORN-PLANTER.

Specification forming part of Letters Patent No. **43,782**, dated August 9, 1864.

To all whom it may concern:

Be it known that I, FREDRICH LOOS, of Denver, Colorado Territory, have invented an Improved Corn-Planter; and I do hereby declare the following to be a full, clear, and exact description of the same, reference being had to the accompanying drawings, and to the letters of reference marked thereon.

My invention consists of certain mechanism, fully described hereinafter, for depositing kernels of corn in furrows at uniform intervals and in given quantities.

In order to enable others skilled in the art to make and use my invention, I will now proceed to describe its construction and operation.

On reference to the accompanying drawings, which form a part of this specification, Figure 1 is a vertical section of my improved corn-planter. Fig. 2 is a transverse vertical section; Fig. 3, a rear view of the planter; and Fig. 4, an inverted plan view.

Similar letters refer to similar parts throughout the several views.

A represents the frame-work of the planter, the front end of this frame being provided with suitable appliances, by means of which the machine is drawn over the ground. A box or casing, B, is secured to the frame, and this box is surmounted with a hopper, C, for receiving the corn, and is provided below with a tube, D, through which the kernels of corn are discharged into the furrows. The interior of the box B contains a packing, b, in which is a circular chamber for the reception of the hollow cylinder E, the latter being secured to the axle F, which passes through the box, and which turns in suitable bearings, $a\ a$, secured to the frame-work of the machine. A driving-wheel, G, secured to one end of the axle, serves to support one side of the frame, while the other side is supported by a wheel, H, turning in a hanger, I. A recess or pocket, e, is formed in the cylinder E, and in this recess fits a piston, f, attached to a spindle, h, which is guided by a projection, i, in the cylinder, the spindle being surrounded with a spring which tends to maintain the piston at the end of the recess. A projection, j, is secured to the cap m of the box B, this projection being inclined, as seen in Fig. 1, for a purpose described hereinafter.

In the bottom of the hopper C is an opening, n, and beneath the latter, and within the box B, is a slide, K, having a corresponding opening. In front of the box B, and to the frame, is secured the plow-pointed instrument L, which serves to open the furrows, and at the rear of the box another instrument, M, is secured to the frame, this instrument being of such a form that it will close the furrows as the machine passes over the ground. To the rear of the frame are also secured the two handles N, by means of which the machine is guided.

As the machine is drawn over the ground the cylinder E will turn in the direction of the arrow, and when the recess e coincides with the hole in the hopper, and thus in the slide K, it will receive the quantity of corn decided upon by the adjustment of the said slide. As the cylinder continues to revolve the corn will retain its place in the recess e, owing to the presence of the packing b, until the recess coincides with the tube D. As the recess approaches this point the end of the spindle h comes in contact with the inclined projection j, which forces the piston outward and causes the corn to be projected into the tube D, through which it falls into the furrow. After passing the projection j the spindle, owing to the spring with which it is surrounded, will recover its former position. As the machine is moved over the ground therefore a quantity of corn is received into the recess e and discharged from the same at intervals, the distance apart of the points where the corn is thus discharged into the furrows depending upon the circumference of the driving-wheel G.

I claim as my invention and desire to secure by Letters Patent—

The cylinder E, its recess e, piston f, spindle h, and the projection j, the whole being arranged within the packed box B, in respect to the hopper C and tube D, substantially as and for the purpose herein set forth.

In testimony whereof I have signed my name to this specification in the presence of two subscribing witnesses.

FREDRICH LOOS.

Witnesses:
LOUIS T. BARTELS,
B. O. MENGER.

J. W. STANTON.
Quartz Crusher.

No. 44,122. Patented Sept. 6, 1864.

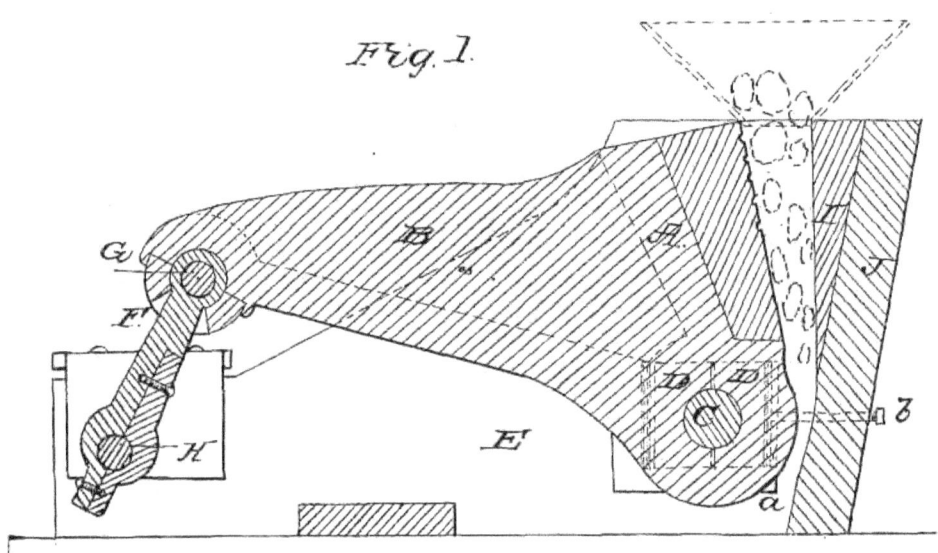

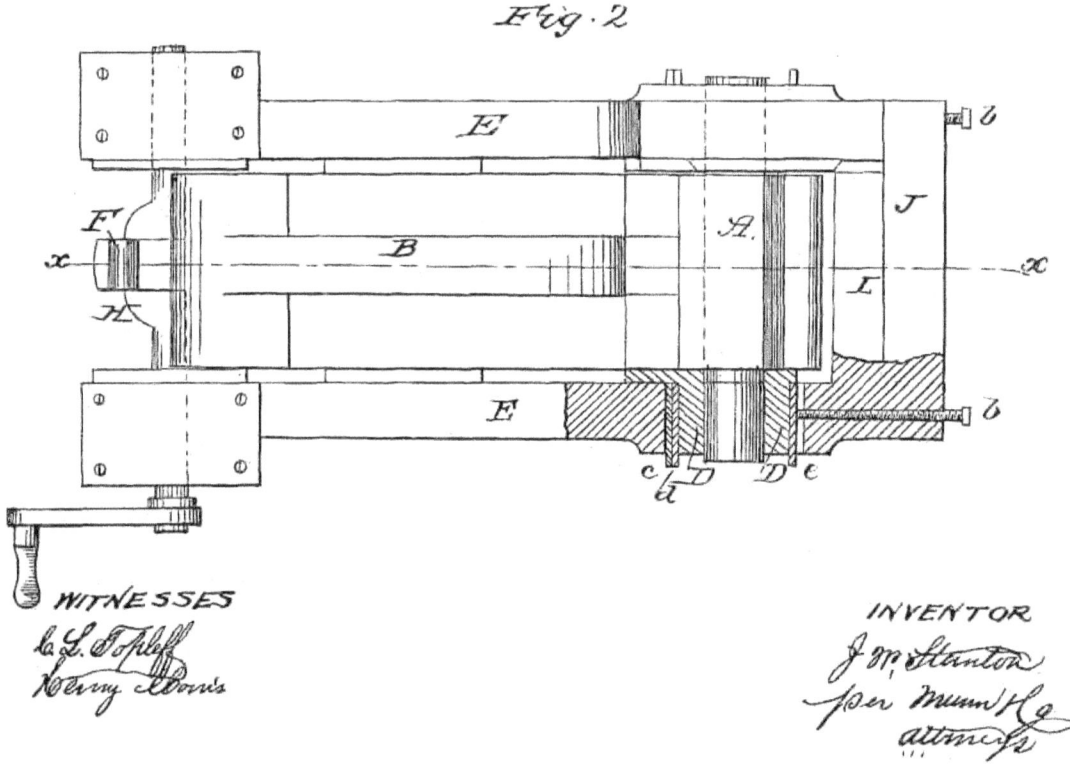

United States Patent Office.

J. W. STANTON, OF BLACK HAWK POINT, COLORADO, ASSIGNOR TO HIMSELF AND M. B. DODGE.

IMPROVEMENT IN QUARTZ-CRUSHERS.

Specification forming part of Letters Patent No. 44,122, dated September 6, 1864.

To all whom it may concern:

Be it known that I, JOHN W. STANTON, of Black Hawk Point, in the county of Gilpin and Territory of Colorado, have invented a new and useful Improvement in Quartz or Stone Breakers; and I do hereby declare that the following is a full, clear, and exact description thereof, which will enable others skilled in the art to make and use the same, reference being had to the accompanying drawings, making a part of this specification, in which—

Figure 1 is a side sectional elevation of my improvement; Fig. 2, a plan view of the same.

Similar letters of reference indicate like parts.

This invention pertains to that class of devices in which the quartz is broken during its passage between two crushing-jaws, one of which is movable, the other stationary.

Referring to the drawings, A is the movable jaw, attached to the front face of a strong movable lever, B, having its axis of motion C arranged in adjustable journal boxes D, between strong side frames, E E, as shown. The rear end of lever B is connected by means of a link, F, and lateral pin G with a driving crank-shaft, H, which is journaled between the rear ends of the frames E E, as shown. The crank-shaft H is to be driven by means of steam, water, or other suitable power. When motion is imparted to the crank-shaft H, the lever B oscillates on its axis C, causing the jaw A to move to and from the stationary crushing-jaw I, which is attached to the inner face of a front frame-piece, J, which connects the front ends of the side frames, E E, as shown. The position of the two jaws in reference to each other is somewhat like that of the sides of an inclined hopper, the upper ends of the jaws A I being separated, while the lower ends gradually approach each other.

The quartz to be crushed is introduced through a hopper at the upper ends of the jaws, as shown in Fig. 1, and is crushed by the approach of the jaws toward each other. The axis C of the movable jaw A is arranged in front of the fixed jaw I, so that when the jaw A oscillates toward the jaw I the jaw A will have a downward or drawing movement across the face of the fixed jaw I in direction of the arrow, by which drawing motion the quartz is most effectually crushed and forced downward and prevented from flying upward. Below the jaw A there is an open space, a, into which the crushed quartz falls.

In ordinary machines of this kind it is usual to arrange the axis of the movable jaw under the fixed jaw, which precludes the possibility of the drawing motion before described with its attendant advantages. The axis C is made laterally adjustable by means of screws b, which pass through the end frame-pieces, J, and side frames, E E, as shown, and bear against one of the filling-plates, c d e, which are placed at the sides of the journal-boxes D. By turning the screws b and shifting the plates c d e of the journal-boxes, it is obvious that the axis C may be adjusted laterally, so as to increase or diminish the space between the crushing-faces of the jaws A I at will, and thus regulate the crushing action of the jaws.

The jaws A I are to be so attached to their respective supports that they can be readily removed when they wear, and replaced by new jaws, or changed end for end in position, so as to bring new crushing-surfaces into use.

This improvement is intended to be used in the breaking of gold bearing quartz and other minerals or substances.

Having thus described my invention, I claim as new and desire to secure by Letters Patent—

In a machine for crushing ore, adjusting the axis of the movable jaw relatively to the stationary jaw by means of plates or blocks placed before or behind the journal-box.

JOHN W. STANTON.

Witnesses:
J. P. HALE,
M. M. LIVINGSTON.

CROSBY & THOMPSON.
Dry Amalgamator.

No. 44,767

Patented Oct. 18, 1864.

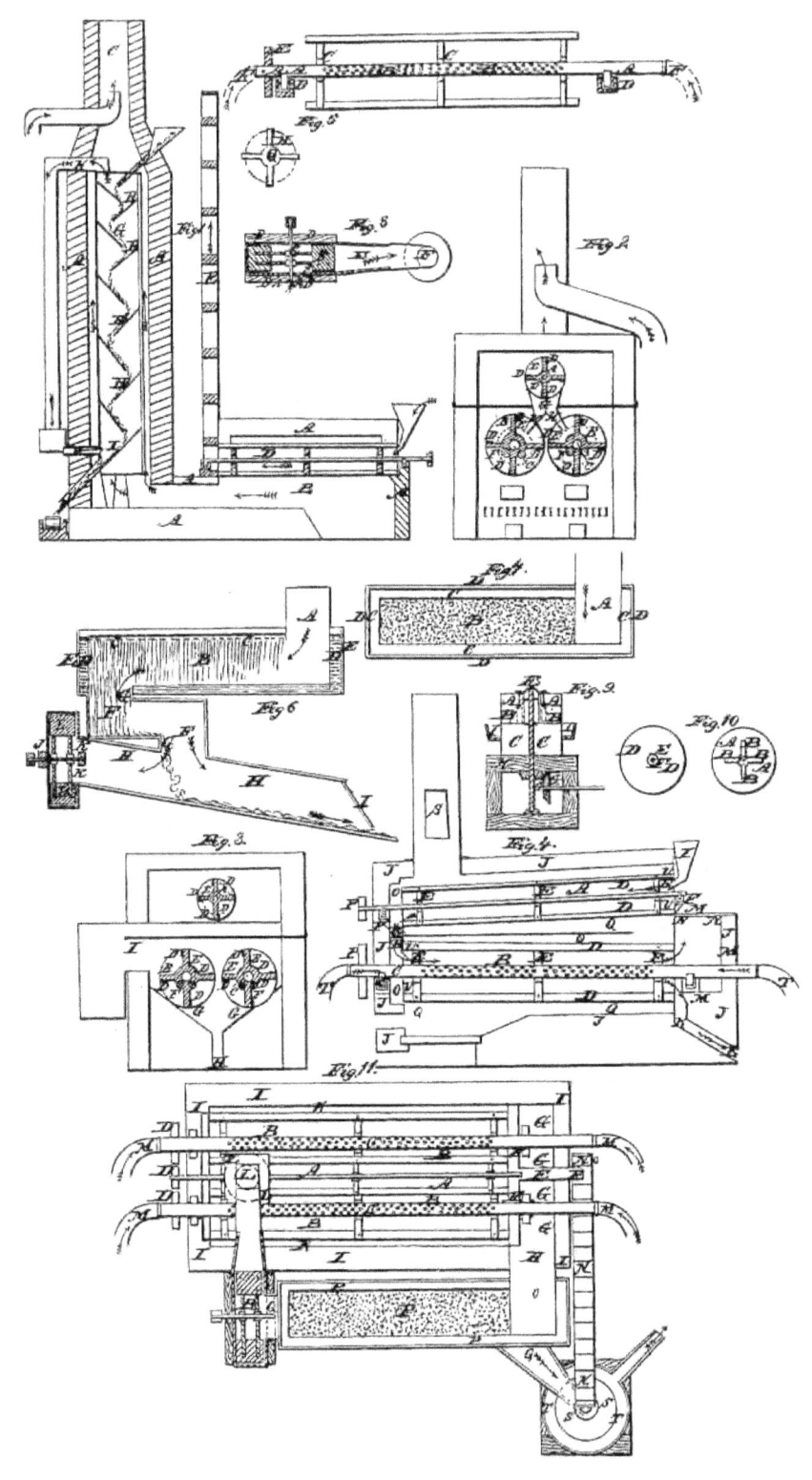

UNITED STATES PATENT OFFICE.

AUGUSTINE B. CROSBY AND ROBT. L. THOMPSON, OF GILPIN COUNTY, COLORADO TERRITORY.

IMPROVEMENT IN APPARATUS FOR ROASTING AND TREATING ORES OF GOLD AND SILVER.

Specification forming part of Letters Patent No. **44,767**, dated October 18, 1864.

To all whom it may concern:

Be it known that we, AUGUSTINE B. CROSBY and ROBERT L. THOMPSON, of Gilpin county, Colorado Territory, have invented a new and useful improvement or improvements on the modes and machinery now used for the separation of gold from its associated ores, its separation and condensation from its volatile combinations, and preparing it for amalgamation, called "Crosby and Thompson's Excelsior Gold-Saving Process," of which the following is a full and exact description.

The process consists in the oxidation of the gold-bearing sulphurets or other ores after they are finely pulverized by stamps or other machinery, and wet with a solution of salt, (common,) thereby completely destroying, or nearly so, the chemical combination of the mineralizing agents and the metals involved. The oxidation is effected by means of heat and a plentiful supply of air, in the manner hereinafter described. The effect of this burning is to produce oxides of metals, sulphurous and other acids, sulphates, metallic gold, and gold vapor. All these vaporous products are conveyed from the place of burning through a condenser, in the manner hereinafter described, using the gold-charged water from the stamps or other crushers for the purpose of condensation, and the absorption of sulphurous or other acid to aid amalgamation. The solids are allowed to fall from the place of burning onto an inclined sole, in the manner and for the purpose hereinafter described; also, that they may cool in thin layers in contact with air, so as to absorb their full amount of oxygen in cooling, and become peroxides. The products of condensation and the burned solids are conveyed to a grinding apparatus, in a manner hereinafter described, for the purpose of reducing the solids to a very fine pulp, and to remove by attrition any coating on the gold that might prevent amalgamation. When copper ores are treated, the burned solids must be leached by the condenser-water, and the copper precipitated before amalgamation. The burning is effected by means of one or more vertical cylinders (hollow) surrounded by fire in a furnace of suitable shape, the cylinders to have inclined planes or benches attached to their inside surfaces for the pulverized ore to fall upon and glide off again, so as to retard the progress of the ore through them sufficiently to secure its complete combustion, the supply of air to be taken in at the bottom of the cylinders and passed through them by means of a blower connected with a condenser, and conveyed to the grinders substantially in the same manner as when revolving cylinders are used. The ore is fed in at the top through an adjustable trap, after having been elevated from a drying-cylinder. At the bottom of the cylinders there is an incline plane, with a trap to receive and discharge the solid products of burning, substantially in the same manner as when revolving cylinders are used. When the burning is effected in revolving cylinders, one or more, the air is supplied through hollow axles or shafts perforated in such manner as to supply the air to all parts of the cylinders, to make the area of the perforations a little more than twice the hollow of the shaft, and not to materially weaken the shaft. The cylinders are from two to three feet in diameter and from ten to twenty feet in length, or of any suitable dimension, with four (more or less) lifts from one to four inches wide, so placed on their internal circumference that their rotation shall elevate and drop the pulverized ore through the air, and flanged in such manner at their receiving or feed ends as to prevent the escape of ore, their discharge ends hooded, sleeved, or arranged in any way to secure the ore from waste. The cylinders are placed in furnaces of suitable form and capacity, the fire passing around them. At their discharge end is placed a hood or chamber, at the bottom of which is an inclined plane for the burned solids to fall upon, and be discharged through a trap onto an endless belt or table that carries them to the grinders. At the top or side of the chamber an opening is made to connect with the condenser, through which all the metallic vapors must pass and be cooled to a condensing-point. The condenser is made of iron, copper, or any good conductor of heat, oblong or square in its cross-section, surrounded on all sides but the top by a tank filled with water constantly flowing through it. The top is perforated, so as to admit water from the stamps or other crushers for the purpose of condensation and forming a dilute acid. It connects and discharges itself into the supply-pipe of the blower in a manner substantially as hereinafter described. The supply-pipe of the blower is placed at an inclination, so that the water with the precipitated metal or ore (condensed) may be discharged by its specific gravity through a trap into a spout or trough extending to the top or feed-spout of the grinders or to the trough surrounding them. It is connected with the blower at and covering the center of one side. The blower receives its supply from the supply-pipe, is closed at all other points save the discharge-spout, it is of usual form, and the discharge-spout extends to the smoke-stack of the furnace and terminates at its center in a nozzle or spout pointing directly up. It is arranged in this manner to make an internal draft of air through the perforated shaft to supply the cylinder to carry the vapors and gases through the condenser and to make a draft to the furnace. The grinders are of the ordinary form of millstones, geared in a similar manner, and made of some soft wood, the lower one made with a smooth surface for ginding, the runner or upper one slotted from the center outward sufficiently to feed the capacity of the grinding-surfaces, and a trough round the lower one to convey the ground material to the amalgamator.

Figure No. 1 of the drawings exhibits by a vertical section the construction of the vertical burner above described; A, wall of furnace; B, fire-room; C, chimney or stack; D, drying-cylinder; E, elevator; F, trap through which the ore passes to G, the cylinder; H, inclined planes to impede the passage of the ore; I, inclined plane; J, trap to discharge the burned ores; K, flue to convey gases and vapors from the cylinder to the condenser.

Fig. No. 2 exhibits by a front view the construction of the burner when three cylinders (revolving) are used; A, the drying-cylinder and discharge end; B B, the two burning-cylinders and receiving ends; C C, the hollow and perforated axles; D D, the lifts; E E, the spider-centers connecting the axles with the cylinders; F F, friction-bearings; G, an adjustable partition to divide the ore falling from the drying-cylinder equally between the burning-cylinders; H H, inclined spouts to convey the ore from the drying to each burning cylinder.

Fig. No. 3 exhibits an end view at the discharge ends of the burners; A, feed end of the drying-cylinder; B B, the discharge ends of the burning-cylinders; C C, the hollow and perforated axles; D D, the lifts; E E, the spider-centers connecting the axles with the cylinders; F F, friction-bearings; G G, inclined planes or soles to receive the burned solids; H, trap through which the burned ore passes to an endless belt or carrier; I, opening for the gases to escape to the condenser, also the metallic vapors.

Fig. No. 4 exhibits a vertical section through the drying-cylinder and one of the burning-cylinders; A, drying-cylinder; B, burning-cylinder; C, the axle extending through the gas-chamber; D D, the lifts; E E, the spider-centers; F F, friction-bearings; G, the adjustable partition; H, the spout from the drying to the burning cylinder; I, the feed-spout to the drying-cylinder; J J J, &c., the walls of the furnace; K, the inclined plane or sole; L, trap at foot of the sole; M M, wall of gas-chamber at the end of the burning-cylinders; N N, top of gas-chambers; O O, hood to the front end of the cylinders; P P, pulleys to drive the cylinders; Q Q, fire-room and passages to the smoke-stack; R, the smoke-stack; S, the discharge-nozzle of the blower; T T, the supply-pipes of an auxiliary blower; U U, the flanges of the receiving ends of the cylinders; arrows, (→,) the direction of the ores and gases.

Fig. No. 5 exhibits a longitudinal section of the perforated hollow axle with its connected parts, and a cross-section of the same; A, the axle; B B, the perforations; C C, spider-centers; D D, bearings; E, pulley; F, pipe to the auxiliary blower, cross-section; G, axle; H, spider-center; dotted line, outline of the pulley.

Fig. No. 6 exhibits a vertical section of the condenser, the supply-pipe of the blower, and their connection, and a cross-section of the blower; A, flue connecting the gas-chamber with the condenser; B, the condenser; C, perforated top surrounded by low sides to receive water from the stamps or elsewhere; D D, water surrounding the condenser; E E, tank; F, opening from the condenser to the supply-pipe of the blower; G G, cascades and openings to the supply-pipe of the blower; H H, the inclined supply-pipe to the blower; I, trap through which the condensed matter and water passes to the grinders; J, cross-section of the blower; K, opening to the supply to the supply-pipe; L L, fans.

Fig. No. 7 exhibits a top view of the condenser; A, opening connecting with the gas-chamber flue; B, the perforated top of the condenser; C C, water around the condenser; D D, the tank.

Fig. No. 8 exhibits a longitudinal section of the blower with its connection with the smoke-stack; A, the opening from the supply; B B, fans; C, axles; D, the shell; E, discharge-flue leading to the smoke-stack; F, the nozzle or end of the discharge-flue terminating in the stack.

Fig. No. 9 exhibits a vertical section of the grinders; A, upper grinder or runner; B B, feed-slots; C, lower grinder; D, packing of spindle; E E, driver and bail of any usual device; F, spindle; G G, any usual driving-gear; H H, frame of any suitable form; I, trough running round the lower grinder and leading to an amalgamator.

Fig. No. 10 exhibits a view of the grinding-surfaces of both upper and lower grinders: A, smooth grinding-surface of the runner; B B, feed slots or channels; C, center hole for feeding; D D, the smooth grinding-surface of the lower grinder; E, spindle-hole; F, stuffing-box for the spindle.

Fig. No. 11 exhibits a top view of a horizontal section of all the parts combined when using a combination of three cylinders for burning; A, the drying-cylinder; B B, burning-cylinders with their several connections or parts; C C, the perforated hollow axles and their connections; D D D, pulleys; E E, inclined planes or soles; F, trap at the foot of the soles; G G, the gas-chamber; H, opening from the gas-chamber to the condenser; I I I, walls of the furnace; K K, fire-passages; L, cross-section of the smoke-stack and nozzle of the blower; M, the auxiliary blower; N, the endless belt or table for carrying the burned solids to the grinders; O, flue from the gas-chamber to the condenser; P P P, condenser and tank around it; Q, supply-pipe of the blower with the trap for the discharge of the water and condensed matter; R, the main blower with its connection with the smoke-stack; S, the grinders; T, trough around the lower grinder.

We do not claim the burning of ores in cylinders stationary or vertical, the use of lifts to scatter the ore, the use of chloride of sodium as an assistant to oxidation, nor the use of air as the source of oxygen to be of our invention, as we are aware of their previous use.

We do not claim the use of spray or water tanks for condensing purposes, the use of a blower for creating a draft, nor the grinding of burned ores to prepare them for amalgamation to be of our invention, as we are aware of their previous use.

We claim to be of our invention—

1. The application of the perforated hollow axle, substantially as above described, for the purpose of furnishing a sufficient supply of air at all points in the length of the burning-cylinder.

2. The application of the gas-chamber with the inclined plane or sole and trap, substantially as above described, for the purpose of separating the burned solids from the gaseous and vaporous products without admitting external air, so as to vitiate the draft.

3. The application of a condenser, substantially in the manner and of the form above described, for the purpose of condensing the metallic vapors and obtaining a hot dilute solution of acid to aid amalgamation.

4. The combination of a blower, substantially as above described, for the purpose of making an inward draft, with the cylinder, gas-chamber, and condenser, so that no metallic vapors may escape before condensation.

5. The application of grinders made of some soft wood or any kind of wood, or of any soft material suitable, substantially as above described, for the purpose of grinding burned ores and removing any coatings that may be on the gold particles.

6. The application of the general combination of the foregoing claims with the previously-known arrangements involved, substantially as above described, for the purpose of making a compact, practical, continuous, economical, and thorough mode and means of working gold ores.

In witness whereof we have hereunto subscribed our names the 2d day of August, 1864.

AUGUSTINE B. CROSBY. [L. S.]
ROBERT L. THOMPSON. [L. S.]

In presence of—
S. V. THOMPSON,
B. S. HEDRICK.

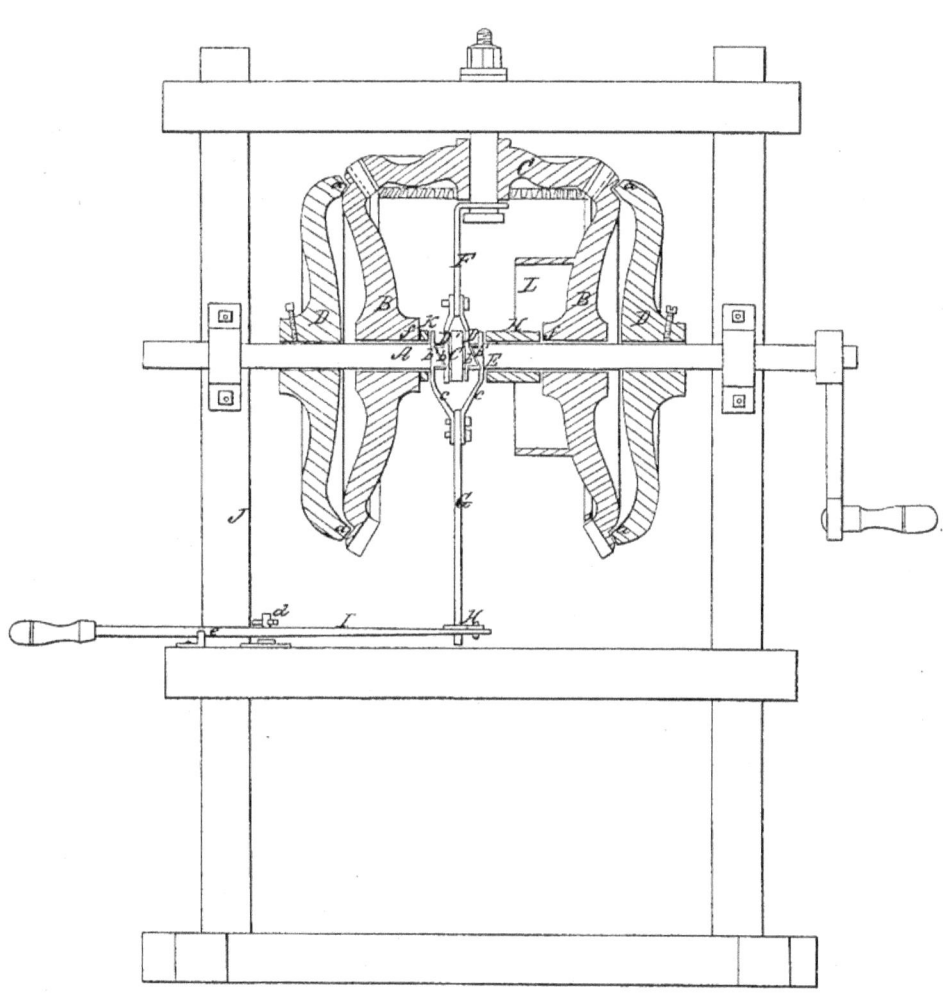

UNITED STATES PATENT OFFICE.

DOUGLASS McINTYRE AND GEORGE C. REEVES, OF CENTRAL CITY, COLO.

IMPROVEMENT IN HOISTING-MACHINES.

Specification forming part of Letters Patent No. **45,062**, dated November 15, 1864.

To all whom it may concern:

Be it known that we, DOUGLASS MCINTYRE and GEORGE C. REEVES, of Central City, in the Territory of Colorado, have invented a new and Improved Hoisting-Machine; and we do hereby declare that the following is a full, clear, and exact description thereof, which will enable those skilled in the art to make and use the same, reference being had to the accompanying drawing, forming part of this specification, said drawing representing a vertical central section of the invention.

This invention relates to a new and improved hoisting apparatus, designed more especially for elevating or drawing water, but applicable to other purposes.

The invention consists in a novel and improved arrangement of a friction-clutch and gearing, as hereinafter fully shown and described, whereby the motion of the gearing may be reversed at the will of the attendant and any number of devices operated from one and the same shaft.

A represents a shaft, on which two bevel-toothed wheels, B B, are placed loosely, and into which a horizontal bevel-wheel, C, gears.

D D are friction-pulleys, which are keyed or otherwise secured on the shaft A, one being at the outer side of each bevel-wheel B, and curved at their inner edges to form a rim, a, to bear against the rear of the wheels B when pressed in contact with them.

On the shaft A, between the wheels B B, there is a fixed collar or hub, C, and on the shaft A at each side of this fixed collar there is a ring, D', having two or more beveled projections, b, extending laterally from it, and which bear against similar projections, b', on rings E. The rings D' E are placed loosely on the shaft A, the rings D' being attached to a pendant, F, which is connected to the axis of the horizontal wheel C, and the rings E are attached by arms c to a rod, G, which extends downward, and is connected by a link, H, with a lever, I, the latter having its fulcrum at d, and projecting over a plate, e, secured to the framing J, which supports the shaft A and the axis of the wheel C. The outer surfaces of the rings E E are perfectly smooth, and bear against collars K, placed loosely on shaft A, between the rings E E and the hubs ff of the wheels B B, as clearly shown in the drawing. The projections $b\ b'$ of the two pairs of rings D' E are placed in reverse positions, and hence it will be seen that by actuating the lever I and turning the rings E E one of the collars K will be pressed against its wheel B and the latter pressed against its friction-pulley D, which, in consequence of being connected to the shaft A, will communicate motion to the wheel pressed in contact with it, said wheel turning with the shaft A, while the other wheel will turn loosely on the shaft in a reverse direction. By moving the lever I in a reverse direction the other wheel, B, which was previously loose on the shaft, will in the same way become connected to it, the one previously connected being freed from the shaft. Thus it will be seen that if a drum, L, be connected to each wheel B with a rope and bucket attached, said buckets may be alternately raised and lowered at the will of the operator or attendant and irrespective of any other number of similar devices which may be on the same shaft A, as each device will operate independently of the other.

We claim as new and desire to secure by Letters Patent—

The two bevel-toothed wheels B B, placed loosely on the shaft A, with the horizontal toothed wheel C, gearing into them, in combination with the friction-pulleys D D, keyed or otherwise secured on the shaft A, the stationary rings D', and the movable rings E, provided with the beveled projections $b\ b'$, and also placed on the shaft A, all arranged to operate in the manner substantially as and for the purpose herein set forth.

DOUGLASS McINTYRE.
GEO. C. REEVES.

Witnesses:
JOHN YOUNG,
NATHANIEL YOUNG.

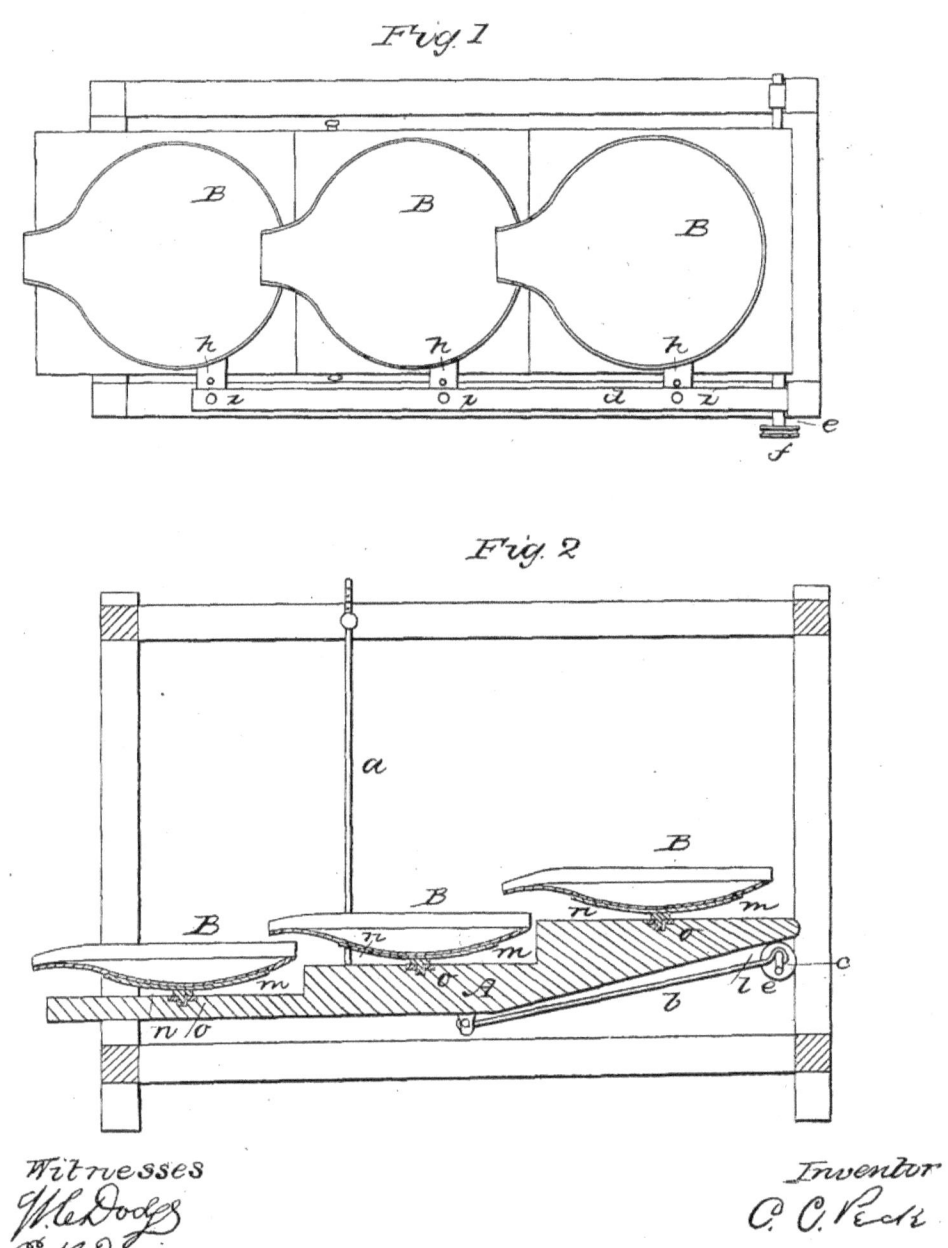

UNITED STATES PATENT OFFICE.

C. C. PECK, OF BLACK HAWK, COLORADO TERRITORY.

IMPROVED AMALGAMATOR.

Specification forming part of Letters Patent No. **46,492**, dated February 21, 1865.

To all whom it may concern:

Be it known that I, C. C. PECK, of Black Hawk, in the county of Gilpin and Territory of Colorado, have invented a new and Improved Apparatus for Amalgamating Ores; and I do hereby declare that the following is a full, clear, and exact description thereof, reference being had to the accompanying drawings, making part of this specification, and to the letters of reference marked thereon, in which—

Figure 1 is a top plan view, and Fig. 2 is a longitudinal vertical section.

A represents a platform or frame, so constructed that the pans B, when placed thereon, shall form an inclined series, as shown in Fig. 2. This platform is suspended by the rods a, which are attached to it—one on each side—in such a position that nearly its entire weight shall be brought to bear upon the rods. A shaft, e, is placed transversely under the upper end of the platform A, and on this shaft is secured an eccentric or cam, c, upon which the upper end of the platform rests, as shown in Fig. 2. The shaft e is also provided with a crank, l, to which is connected one end of the rod or pitman b, the opposite end being pivoted to the platform A, as shown in Fig. 2. A pulley, f, mounted on the shaft e, serves to communicate motion to the apparatus.

A spider or frame, m, of suitable shape, is constructed to receive and support the pans B. A hub or bearing, n, is secured to the spiders m, centrally underneath, and this bearing n has a journal projecting downward therefrom and fitting loosely into a socket in the metal plate o, secured upon the platform A. Each of the spiders m has an arm, h, projecting laterally therefrom, which arms are pivoted to one side of the frame or to the rod d, rigidly attached thereto, as shown in Fig. 1 at i.

Each of the pans B is constructed of copper, preferably, though other material may be used, and is provided with a spout, as shown. These pans are so located that the spout of each shall project over the pan next below it in the series.

The operation is as follows: The machine being suitably located to receive the crushed ore, together with a suitable supply of water, and a proper quantity of quicksilver being placed in the pans, motion is imparted to the apparatus in any suitable manner.

It will be observed that by the peculiar arrangement of the parts three motions are imparted to the pans B at one and the same time. While the eccentric e gives to the platform an up-and-down movement, the crank l, through the medium of rod b, gives to it a longitudinal movement back and forth. At the same time the pans, being attached by the arms h on one side, as described, have imparted to them by the longitudinal movement of platform A a to-and-fro rotary motion, these motions thus combined very nearly resembling the peculiar movements given to a pan when used by a skillful operator in the well-known hand process. By this means the particles of fine gold which are intermixed with the crushed quartz or other refuse matter is most thoroughly brought in contact with the quicksilver, with which it chemically unites, and is thereby extracted from the quartz and retained in the pan, while the refuse matter passes off with the water. By using a series of pans, as described, the gold which may by chance or otherwise pass out with the water and other material from the first or upper pan will be caught and retained in the second pan, where it is subjected to a repetition of the process already described, and thus all or a much larger proportion than usual of the gold is saved. Any number of pans may be used, but in practice I find three sufficient, little or no gold ever being found in the lower pan.

The apparatus is extremely simple, cheap, and efficient, and can be operated with a small expenditure of power.

Having thus described my invention, what I claim as new, and desire to secure by Letters Patent, is—

1. The pan B, constructed in the form and style shown and described.

2. A series of pans, arranged to operate in the manner and for the purpose set forth.

3. The spider m, provided with the bearing n and arm h, substantially as shown and described.

4. The suspended platform A, arranged to vibrate vertically and longitudinally, as and for the purpose set forth.

5. So arranging an amalgamator-pan as to give to it the three-fold motion, substantially as and for the purpose set forth.

                                  C. C. PECK.

Witnesses:
  W. C. DODGE,
  E. N. DRURY.

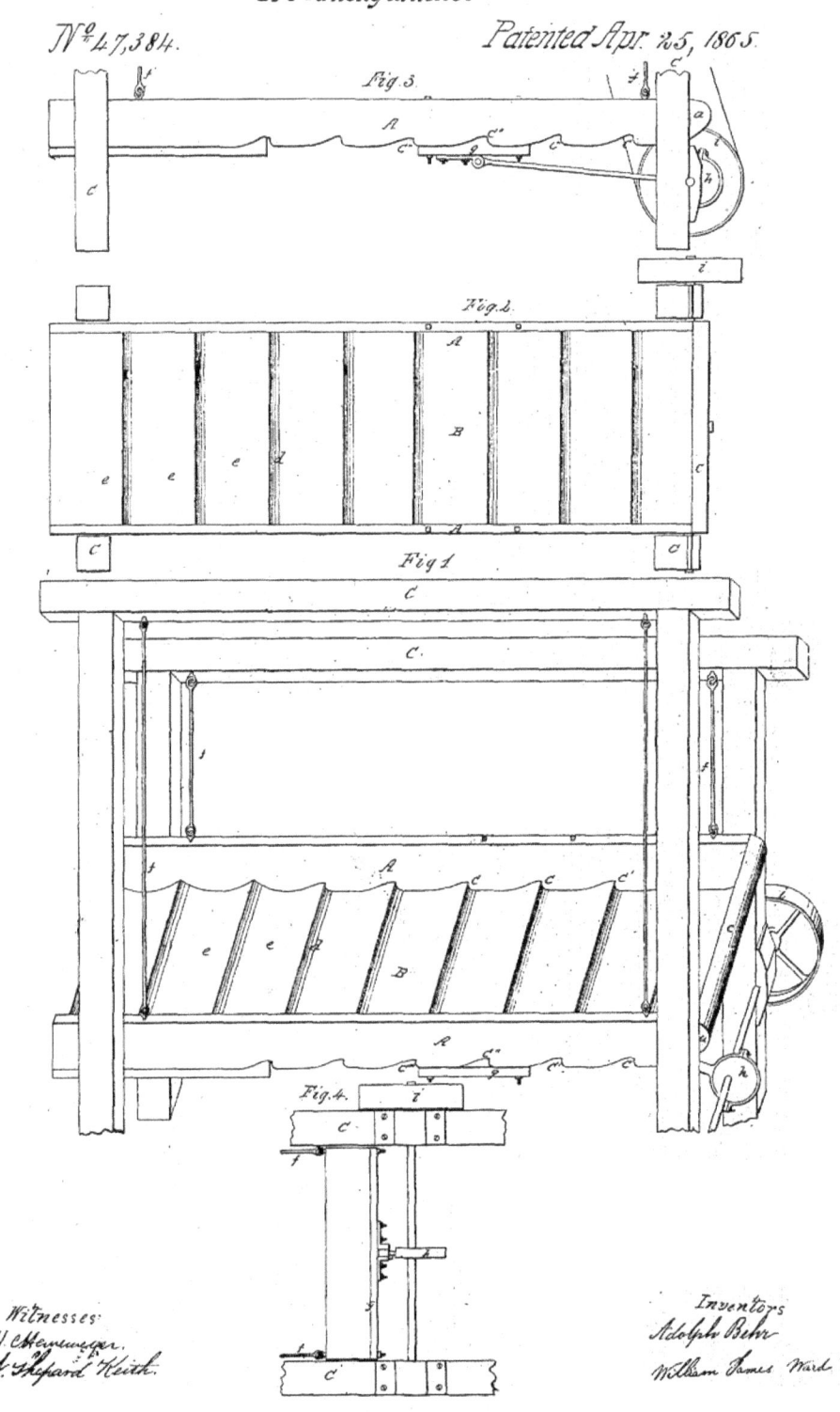

UNITED STATES PATENT OFFICE.

ADOLPH BEHR AND WILLIAM JAMES WARD, OF BLACK HAWK, COLORADO.

IMPROVED SHAKING AND ROCKING TABLE FOR AMALGAMATING GOLD, &c.

Specification forming part of Letters Patent No. 47,384, dated April 25, 1865.

To all whom it may concern:

Be it known that we, ADOLPH BEHR and WILLIAM JAMES WARD, of Black Hawk, in the county of Gilpin, and the Territory of Colorado, have invented a new and improved shaking or rocking table for the amalgamation and extraction of gold and silver from ores, minerals, and substances containing those metals; and we do hereby declare that the following is a full and exact description of the same.

The nature of our invention consists in an amalgamated sheet of copper or brass, bent in such a manner as to form furrows with projecting ribs, and screwed on tight to wooden sides, which are carved out in the desired shape. The end of the copper or brass opposite the ribs is bent over to form half of a circle, while the other end is secured to a series of wooden grooves or gutters. The table thus formed is suspended by iron rods on a level, and set in motion by means of an eccentric, to which the table is connected.

To enable others skilled in the art to make and use our invention, we will proceed to describe its construction and operation, reference being had to the annexed drawings, making a part of this specification, in which—

Figure 1 is a perspective view; Fig. 2, a top view; Fig. 3, a side view, and Fig. 4 an end view.

Two planks, A, Fig. 1, of pine or other wood, fourteen to fifteen feet long, eight or nine inches wide, and two inches thick, are rounded off on one of their ends to half of a circle, *a*, and curved out on one of their edges in the shape as shown by C, Figs. 1 and 3, the deepest cuts being twelve inches apart, and placed on a sheet of copper or brass, B, five feet wide and twelve feet long, the end *c* of which is bent over and screwed tight to the round *d* ends *a*, while the edges are fitted and screwed closely to the curved edges of the planks. The shape of the curves is thus communicated to the sheet, and is made to extend across its whole width, thus forming grooves or riffles with projecting ribs, which have a height of one and one half inch. The other end, *d*, of the copper or brass is connected with three or more wooden grooves or gutters, *e*, which are one foot in width, hollowed out in the center to the depth of one and one-half of an inch, and fitted in tight between the two planks A. These wooden grooves are added to collect any quicksilver which may be forced over by too heavy a feed of ore, &c. The table thus formed is suspended by the iron rods *f*, which are swinging in eyebolts fastened to the frame-work C.

g is a plank bolted to the sides A of the table, and connected with the eccentric *h*, Fig. 4, which has about a three-inch throw, and is set in motion by the pulley *i*, making one hundred and twenty revolutions in a minute. The upper side of the copper or brass is washed with a solution of concentrated lye to remove all grease, and by means of a solution of cyanide of potassium or ammonium zinc chloride quicksilver is evenly rubbed out on it till the copper or brass presents a bright quicksilver surface. The first copper or brass riffles or grooves are charged with liquid quicksilver—from ten to twenty pounds are sufficient—the table set in motion, and the powdered substances containing gold or silver are sluiced into the first copper or brass riffle by a moderate stream of water, five-eighths of an inch being sufficient. From this first riffle it passes into the second, third, and so on. The gold and silver coming in contact with the amalgamated copper or brass will adhere to it or be taken up by the liquid quicksilver, while the inert substances are carried away by the water. When sufficient amalgam is collected, it is, in connection with the liquid quicksilver, taken off the riffles and cleaned, separated as usual,

The advantages of our invention are as follows: First, a large quantity of substances containing gold or silver can be thus treated, as the apparatus can be worked continously at the same time requiring but very little motive power; second, by the peculiar shape of the copper or brass riffles the gold-bearing substances suspended in the water not only are subjected to a sifting motion, but are also, by the splash produced by the projecting ribs, thrown and forced in contact with the amalgamated copper or brass or liquid quicksilver, which constantly renews the surface by being in motion; third, no quicksilver, and consequently no amalgam, can be lost, as, if quicksilver should be forced over by any cause, the wooden grooves will collect it and save it—they having the greatest depth in the center, where the least motion is, the quicksilver, by its higher specific gravity, goes to the center and stays there; fourth, it offers a large amalgamating-surface, more so as every particle introduced therein is thrown to and fro again and again before it can leave the table; fifth, it is cheap in its construction and durable.

What we claim as our invention, and desire to secure by Letters Patent, is—

A shaking or rocking table with amalgamated copper or brass riffles or grooves, which may be charged with more or less additional quicksilver, alone or in connection with one or more wooden riffles or grooves, in the shape and manner above described, or constructed in any manner substantially the same, which will impart to substances suspended in water both the sifting and splashing motion, which throws and forces the particles in contact with the amalgamated surface of the copper or brass riffles or grooves.

ADOLPH BEHR.
WILLIAM JAMES WARD.

Witnesses:
H. C. HAVEMEYER,
N. SHEPARD KEFTH.

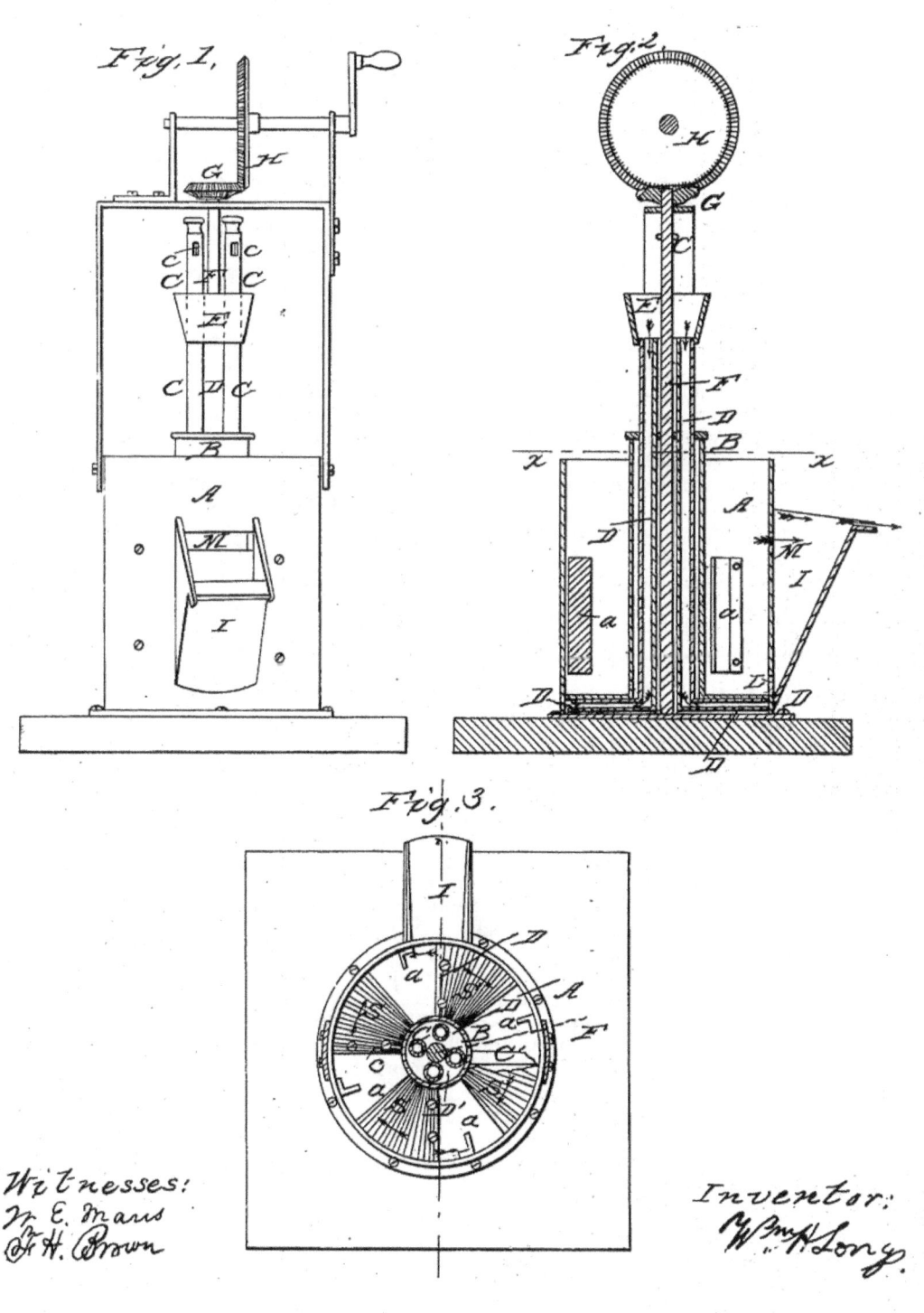

UNITED STATES PATENT OFFICE.

WILLIAM H. LONG, OF MOUNTAIN CITY, COLORADO TERRITORY.

IMPROVED GOLD-SEPARATOR.

Specification forming part of Letters Patent No. **47,557**, dated May 2, 1865.

To all whom it may concern:

Be it known that I, WILLIAM H. LONG, of Mountain City, in the county of Gilpin and Territory of Colorado, have invented a new and useful Improvement in Gold-Separators; and I do hereby declare that the following is a full, clear, and exact description of the same, reference being had to the accompanying drawings, and the letters and figures marked thereon, which form part of this specification.

My invention relates to that class of apparatus for separating gold from crushed quartz and other gold-bearing rocks and earths by means of quicksilver or mercury; and it consists in a novel arrangement whereby the entire mass of crushed rock and earths as it is washed from the battery or crushing apparatus is forced down through the mercury and discharged beneath it, the gold from its greater specific gravity, and also from its chemical affinity for the mercury, amalgamating with and remaining in the mercury, while all foreign ores and substances, from their less specific gravity, rise through the mercury and flow off.

To enable those skilled in the art to understand how to construct and use my invention, I will proceed to describe the same with particularity, reference being made, in so doing, to the aforesaid drawings, in which—

Figure 1 represents a side elevation of my invention; Fig. 2, a vertical central section of the same, and Fig. 3 a plan or top view thereof in section at the line x in Fig. 2.

Similar letters of reference in the different figures indicate the same parts of my invention.

A represents a cylindrical tub or vessel, of any required dimensions, in the bottom of which at the center, in a suitable box or support, the revolving vertical shaft (marked F) rests, to which motion is imparted by means of the gear-wheels G H, or by any other suitable appliances.

E represents a funnel-shaped pan or vessel, fixed rigidly upon the said vertical shaft, which passes through the center of the bottom thereof.

C C D D represent four vertical pipes or tubes arranged closely about said shaft, as shown, the tubes D D extending from the bottom of said funnel-shaped vessel E to the bottom of the separating-tub A, where they are bent out horizontally and extend radially toward the circumference of the vessel A, the tubes C C being bent in the same way and manner at the bottom of said vessel A, but extending up through the bottom of E and above said vessel, as shown. The upper ends of said tubes C C are closed by a movable cap with vertical sides extending down a short distance in said tubes, through the walls of which and the vertical sides of the aforesaid adjustable caps are cut openings for the admission of air into the tubes, as hereinafter mentioned. By turning the said movable caps slightly the apertures aforesaid may be wholly or partially closed, thereby wholly excluding the air or diminishing the quantity admitted into the tubes, as desired. The ends of the horizontal parts of the said tubes C C D D, which are marked C' C' D' D', are cut off diagonally with respect to their axes, as shown in Fig. 3. The said vertical tubes and shaft are inclosed within the cylinder B, so as to prevent the agitation of the contents of the vessel A by the rapid rotation of said tubes, as hereinafter mentioned.

Over and upon each of the radially-arranged tubes C' C' D' D' there is attached a shield or apron, (marked S,) extending outward from the inclosing-cylinder B to the wall of the tub A, one edge of the said apron lying upon said tubes and the other edge extending forward and downward gradually until it lies just at the bottom, so as to revolve freely above it.

$a\ a$ represent a series of vertical slots fixed radially upon the interior wall of the tub A, extending inward far enough to prevent the contents of the vessel A from revolving around by reason of the revolution of the tubes and shaft, as hereinafter mentioned.

M represents an opening or slot in the vertical wall of the vessel A, through which the refuse substances flow off out from the apparatus, I being an inclosure outside connected with the vessel A at the bottom through the slot L, in order that any particles of gold that might by any possibility flow through the opening M may return into the vessel A and be amalgamated with the mercury and saved.

Having described the construction of my invention, I will now proceed to describe its operation.

In the first place, the bottom of the vessel

A is covered with mercury rising high enough at least to completely cover the radially-arranged tubes C′ C′ D′ D′ and the aprons S S, which are arranged upon them. A rapid motion is then imparted to the shaft F, which communicates a rapid rotating motion to the aforesaid tubes C C′ D D′, the upper ends of the tubes C C being arranged so as to admit air into said tubes. The products of the battery or crushing-mill are then washed, by a current of water through any suitable conveyer, into the aforesaid funnel-shaped vessel E upon the shaft F, whence the crushed rock and earth issuing from the battery pass into and down the pipes D D, and are discharged at the extremities of the radially-arranged pipes D′ D′ beneath the mercury. By the rapid rotation of the apparatus in the direction indicated by the black arrows in Fig. 3, the front edges of the aprons S, moving close upon the bottom of the vessel A, throw the mercury up and back over the tubes and over the ends of the same, and thus a vacuum is created at the end of each of said tubes, and thus the crushed rock and earths from the crushing-mill are forced beneath and into the mass of mercury through the tubes D D, while the air is in like manner forced through the tubes C C into the mercury. The particles of gold, being of greater specific gravity than mercury, remain in and amalgamate with it, while all foreign substances, being of less specific gravity than the mercury, rise though it and pass out of the separator through the opening M, as indicated by the red arrows.

Should any gold by any possibility rise through the mercury and pass out through the opening M, there being an eddy in the compartment I, the gold would be carried down to the bottom of said compartment by its own weight, and enter the separator through the slot L into the mercury, where it remains, and is thus saved.

The object of introducing the currents of air into the mercury is to create a constant agitation by its upward passage and thus prevent the rock and baser minerals from settling upon the surface of the mercury and forming a crust or shell, which would prevent the foreign matter from escaping from the mercury, and retain it with the gold.

The number of tubes for conveying the product of the crushing-mill into and beneath the mercury is immaterial, as also the number of tubes for admitting the air; and, furthermore, the tubes for admitting the air may be omitted entirely, as the apparatus will operate without them, though not so satisfactorily and effectually.

Having described the construction and operation of my invention, I will now specify what I claim and desire to secure by Letters Patent—

1. Conveying the product of the battery through the mercury and discharging it beneath the same, by creating a vacuum at the end of the conveying-tubes D D′, substantially as and for the purposes herein specified and shown.

2. The employment of one or more tubes, D D′, arranged and operating substantially as and for the purposes set forth and described.

3. The combination of one or more air-tubes, C C′, with the tubes D D′, arranged and operating as and for the purposes shown and set forth.

4. The combination and arrangement of the aprons S with the tubes C′ D′, as and for the purposes described.

5. The combination of the shaft F, the funnel E, tubes C C′ D D′, and aprons S, arranged and operating as and for the purposes described.

WM. H. LONG.

Witnesses:
W. E. MAUS,
F. H. BROWN.

UNITED STATES PATENT OFFICE.

SAMUEL GREEN, OF DENVER, COLORADO TERRITORY.

IMPROVED COMPOSITION FOR EXTERMINATING GRASSHOPPERS.

Specification forming part of Letters Patent No. **49,258**, dated August 8, 1865.

To all whom it may concern:

Be it known that I, SAMUEL GREEN, of the city of Denver, in the county of Arapahoe and Territory of Colorado, have invented and discovered a new and Improved Method of Exterminating and Destroying Grasshoppers by Means of a Certain Composition of Matter; and I do hereby declare that the following is a full and exact description of the same.

The nature of my invention and discovery consists in the mixture and combination of certain articles, which when sprinkled over the field of the farmer, or locality infested by grasshoppers, will kill and destroy them, and thus prevent them from destroying any growing crop.

To enable others skilled in the art to make and use my invention and discovery, I will proceed to describe its construction and component parts and its operation.

I take three gallons of lime-water containing the entire strength or essence of one bushel of unslaked lime, five gallons strong lye made from ashes, one and one-fourth gallon of tobacco-juice containing the entire strength of ten pounds of tobacco-stems, four ounces phosphorus, four ounces of arsenic, one-half gallon of petroleum or coal oil, four ounces opodeldoc, four ounces spirits of camphor, four ounces spirits of turpentine, four pounds beef-gall, four ounces of flour of sulphur, and one-half pound cayenne pepper. These ingredients are compounded either in a liquid or solid substance, one pound of which compound dissolved in a barrel of water and sprinkled over the locality infested by grasshoppers is sufficient to destroy them on one acre of ground.

What I claim as my invention and discovery, and desire to secure by Letters Patent, is—

The combination and mixture and preparation of the above-enumerated ingredients in the aforesaid manner for the purposes above set forth, and the exclusive right to prepare the same for use and sale in those sections of the United States where grasshoppers are so numerous as to completely destroy growing crops.

SAMUEL GREEN.

Witnesses:
S. NATHAN,
I. Q. CHASE.

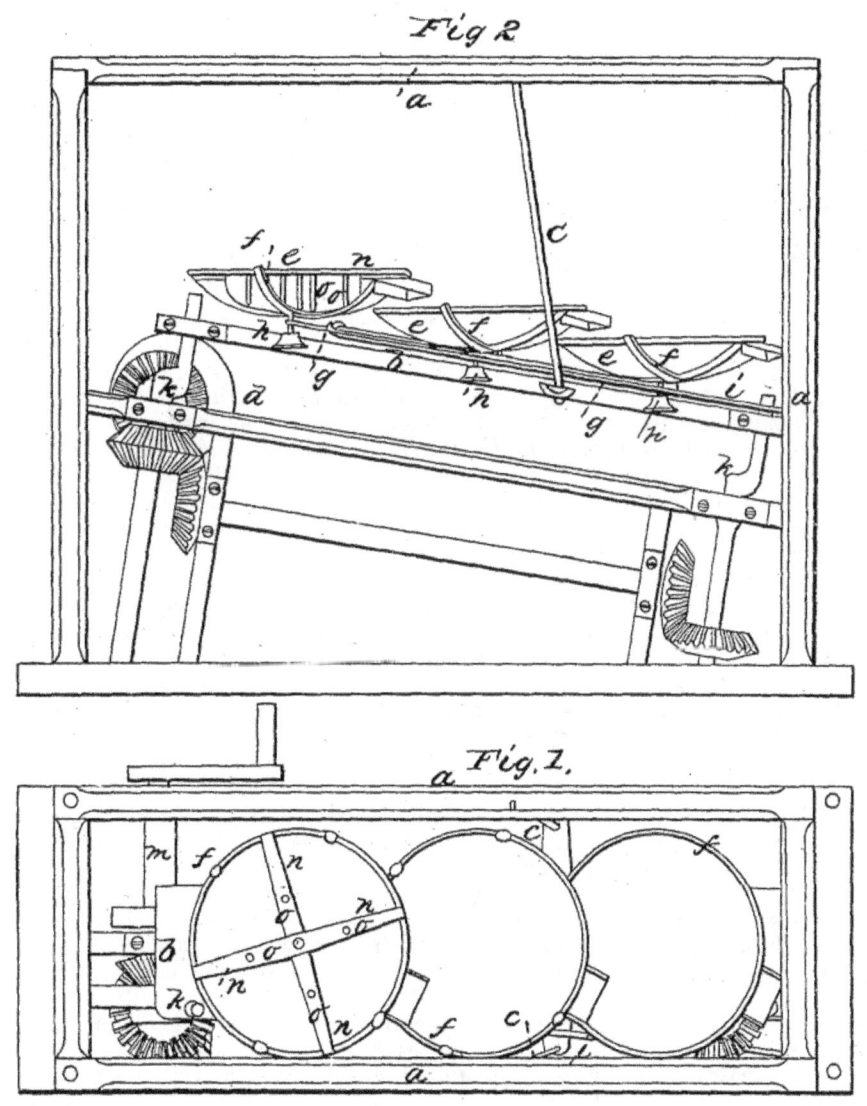

UNITED STATES PATENT OFFICE.

C. C. PECK, OF BLACKHAWK, COLORADO.

IMPROVED AMALGAMATOR.

Specification forming part of Letters Patent No. **51,079**, dated November 21, 1865.

To all whom it may concern:

Be it known that I, C. C. PECK, of Blackhawk, in the county of Gilpin and Territory of Colorado, have invented an Improved Amalgamator; and I do hereby declare that the following, taken in connection with the drawings which accompany and form part of this specification, is a description of my invention sufficient to enable those skilled in the art to practice it.

Letters Patent of the United States numbered 46,492, were granted to me on the 21st day of February, A. D. 1865, for an improved amalgamator. In said amalgamator a series of pans are arranged upon a frame or platform in such manner that the spout of each (excepting the lower one) shall project over the pan next below it, this platform being so hung in the main frame and arranged with reference to actuating mechanism that in operating the machine an up-and-down movement, a forward and back movement, and a vibrating movement are simultaneously communicated to the pans for the purpose of agitating the crushed gold containing quartz in the pans, to bring all particles of it intimately into contact with the quicksilver, as the current of water flows through the series of pans. It is to such or a similar organization that my present invention relates.

This invention consists in so organizing the mechanism that in addition to these motions imparted to the pans they shall also have a direct and simultaneous lateral movement imparted to them, which has the effect to more thoroughly agitate and bring into contact the quartz and quicksilver.

The improvement further consists in the manner of mounting one or more of the pans so as to be readily removable, and in the combination, with one or more of them, of stirrers which operate in the movement of the pans, to divide and break into separate currents the agitated masses of quartz and the stream of water running through the series of pans.

The drawings represent a series of pans embodying my present improvement, Figure 1 showing a plan, and Fig. 2 a side elevation, of the same.

a denotes the frame-work, in which the platform *b* is suspended by means of rods *c*, one end of the platform resting on the periphery of an eccentric or cam wheel, *d*. This platform supports the series of pans *e* by means of spiders, *f*, upon which each pan rests, and a journal-pin projecting therefrom into a bearing-plate upon the platform. The pans are connected together on one side by a rod, *g*, and a pin, *h*, fastened to the spider of each pan, and this rod *g* is connected to the stationary frame *a* by a rod, *i*, so that if the platform is moved to and fro endwise each pan will rock horizontally on its journal. Such a reciprocating endwise movement is imparted to the platform by means of cranks *k k*, the shafts of which are rotated by any suitable system of gearing, and the driving-shaft *m*, which bears the eccentric or cam wheel *d*. Thus it will be obvious that by rotation of the shaft the platform of pans receives a reciprocating vertical motion by means of the wheel *d* (the weight of the upper end of the platform keeping it in contact with this wheel) and a reciprocating longitudinal or endwise movement through the cranks *k*, while the endwise movement of the platform causes each pan to rock horizontally by means of the rods *g i*, these movements being imparted simultaneously, and being substantially the same as are given in the construction shown in my patent before referred to. In that construction, however, the longitudinal movement was imparted by a rod or link jointed at one end to the platform and at the other end to the cam or eccentric, while by my present improvement I impart this movement by means of the cranks *k*, which in their rotation carry the platform laterally as well as longitudinally, giving a reciprocating lateral movement to each pan. The result of this combined lateral and longitudinal movement is to give each pan a circular or nearly circular motion, which, taken in connection with the vibrating and vertical movement, proves very effective in producing the agitation of the contents of the pans, the contact of the mercury with all the crushed quartz, and the consequent separation of all or a large maximum of the particles of gold. Other means may be employed for imparting the lateral movement; but I consider the mechanism shown to be the simplest and most effectual.

One or more of the pans I support on its spider or arms in such manner as to permit of easy removal. This is done by extending each of the arms of the spider upon which the pan rests up to and over the top edge of the pan, which is then allowed to rest loosely in position, held down by the spider, and is removed by slightly turning up the ends of the spider-arms or by slipping the pan from under them, as will be readily understood. I also extend across the top of one or more of the pans cross-bars n, from the under surface of each of which a pin, o, projects down into the body of the pan, as seen in Fig. 2, where one of the pans is represented as broken at the side to show these pins. In the agitating movements of the pan these pins act as stirrers, to divide the contents of the pan and promote the intermixture of mercury and quartz.

I claim—

1. The arrangement of an amalgamating-pan or a series of pans and a mechanism for agitating the same, so that, in connection with a combined longitudinal and vertical or longitudinal and vibrating movement, said pan or pans shall have a reciprocating lateral movement, substantially as set forth.

2. Extending the spider-arms over the edge of the pan, thereby holding the pan in position and permitting its easy removal, substantially as set forth.

3. The pins or projections o, extending down into one or more of the pans, substantially in the manner and for the purpose specified.

In witness whereof I have hereunto set my hand this 12th day of June, A. D. 1865.

C. C. PECK.

Witnesses:
F. GOULD,
W. B. GLEASON.

F. N. DU BOIS.
Ore Amalgamator.

No. 53,590. Patented Apr. 3, 1866.

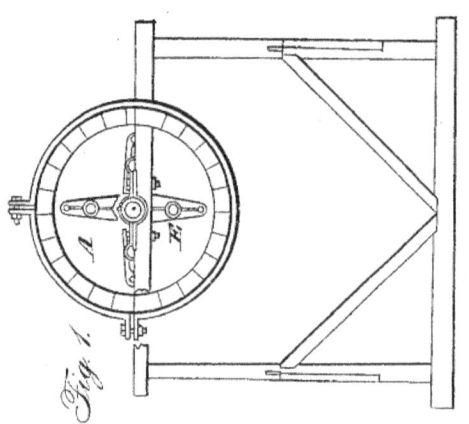

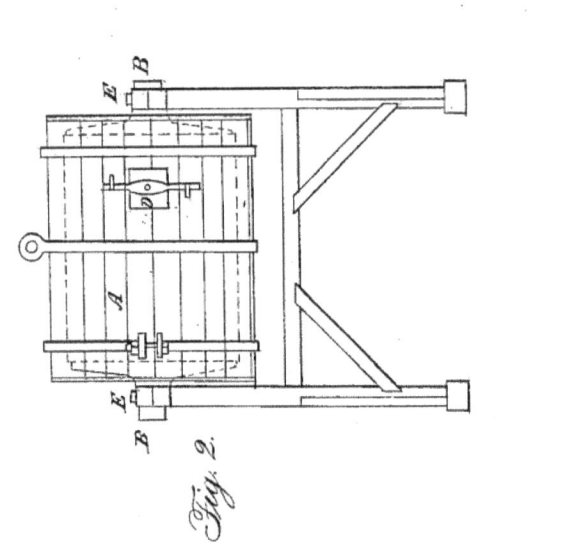

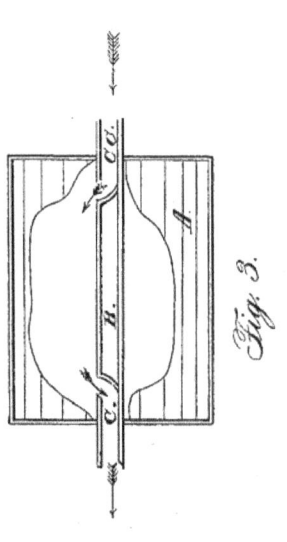

Witnesses:

Inventor:

UNITED STATES PATENT OFFICE.

F. N. DU BOIS, OF BLACK HAWK, COLORADO.

IMPROVED PROCESS FOR AMALGAMATING GOLD, &c.

Specification forming part of Letters Patent No. **53,590**, dated April 3, 1866.

To all whom it may concern:

Be it known that I, F. N. DU BOIS, of Black Hawk, in the county of Gilpin, in the Territory of Colorado, have invented a new and useful Improvement in a Method for Amalgamating Gold; and I do hereby declare that the following is a full and exact description thereof, reference being had to the accompanying drawings, and to the letters of reference marked thereon.

Figure 1 represents a side elevation. Fig. 2 represents an end elevation. Fig. 3 represents a cross-section view of the interior shaft.

Similar letters of reference in each of the several figures indicate corresponding parts.

The nature of my invention consists, first, in the use of the amalgamating-cylinder A; and, second, in the hollow wooden shaft or axle B, through which water is flowed for the purpose of discharging the ore after the gold has been amalgamated from it.

To enable others skilled in the art to make and use my invention, I proceed to describe its construction and operation.

The cylinder A, being of any convenient size, is to be constructed of wood with iron hoops. The shaft B, also of wood, is firmly fixed in the cylinder through the direction of its axis and revolves with the cylinder, resting on the journals E, the necessary power for revolving it being communicated by any convenient means.

The cylinder is to be filled to about two-fifths of its capacity with a charge consisting of the following materials and proportions, substantially: One-half ton of finely-ground desulphurized ore, about one hundred and fifty pounds of broken fragments of any kind of hard rock, not to exceed in size one and a half inch in diameter; also about two hundred and fifty ounces of an amalgam, consisting of mercury and the gold ordinarily obtained from the ore, which amalgam must at all times be maintained in such proportion of mercury and gold as to have a consistency about midway between a fluid and solid condition.

The above charge is introduced in the cylinder A through the opening D, together with a quantity of water sufficient to reduce the ore to the condition of a semi-fluid pulp. The opening D being then closed, the cylinder is revolved at a speed sufficient to produce the greatest amount of grinding effect from the fragments of rock and admixture of the material contained in the cylinder. The effect then produced is that the attrition of the fragments of rock grinds the ore and scours and brightens the particles of gold preparatory to their being picked up and held by the amalgam; and the nature of the amalgam is such that it does not divide into infinitely small particles, as liquid mercury does, and float away with the water beyond any possibility of being collected, but the amalgam retains its identity and consistency under any amount of agitation, being only divided into lumps and pieces, which diffuse themselves among the mass of ore and collect and hold the gold, which usually exists in the form of minute metallic particles.

There is also another point to be noticed. The nature of liquid mercury is such that it is entirely devoid of capillary attraction. It assumes the globular form, and is rather disposed to repel than to come in contact with particles of gold; but the presence of gold with the mercury in a state of amalgam not only destroys this tendency of the mercury to repel, but greatly facilitates its ability to adhere to and amalgamate the particles of gold.

The cylinder having been revolved for a time varying from six to twenty-four hours, according as the gold in the different ores requires more or less scouring, and the amalgamation being completed, a stream of water is introduced into the shaft B, Fig. 3, by applying a pipe with a water-tight joint to the opening C C in the end, causing the water to flow in the direction of the arrows until it enters the cylinder, where it mixes with the pulpy ore and dilutes it, so that it flows off with the water through the opening C in the opposite end of the shaft. During the operation the cylinder continues to revolve, and the ore is all flowed out with the water, while the fragments of rock and amalgam, being very heavy, remain in the cylinder. The cylinder is now stopped, and, the water being drained off a new charge of ore is introduced and the operation proceeded with as at first, except that thereafter ore and water only are introduced, and more fragments of rock are added as those already in are worn away, and as the amalgam becomes too stiff by its collecting gold it is softened to the proper consistency by the addition of more mercury, and as the amount of amalgam accumulates the surplus is from time to time removed from the cylinder, the whole forming a new and useful improvement in method for saving gold.

I do not claim as my invention either the cylinder or the hollow shaft through it, or the use of them in combination; but

What I do claim as my invention, and desire to secure by Letters Patent, is simply—

The use of an amalgam of gold and mercury substantially of such consistency as to render it adaptable for the purpose set forth.

The above specification of my improvement in method for amalgamating gold signed by me this 12th day of September, in the year 1865.

F. N. DU BOIS.

Witnesses:
J. W. NESMITH,
WILLIAM ARMOR.

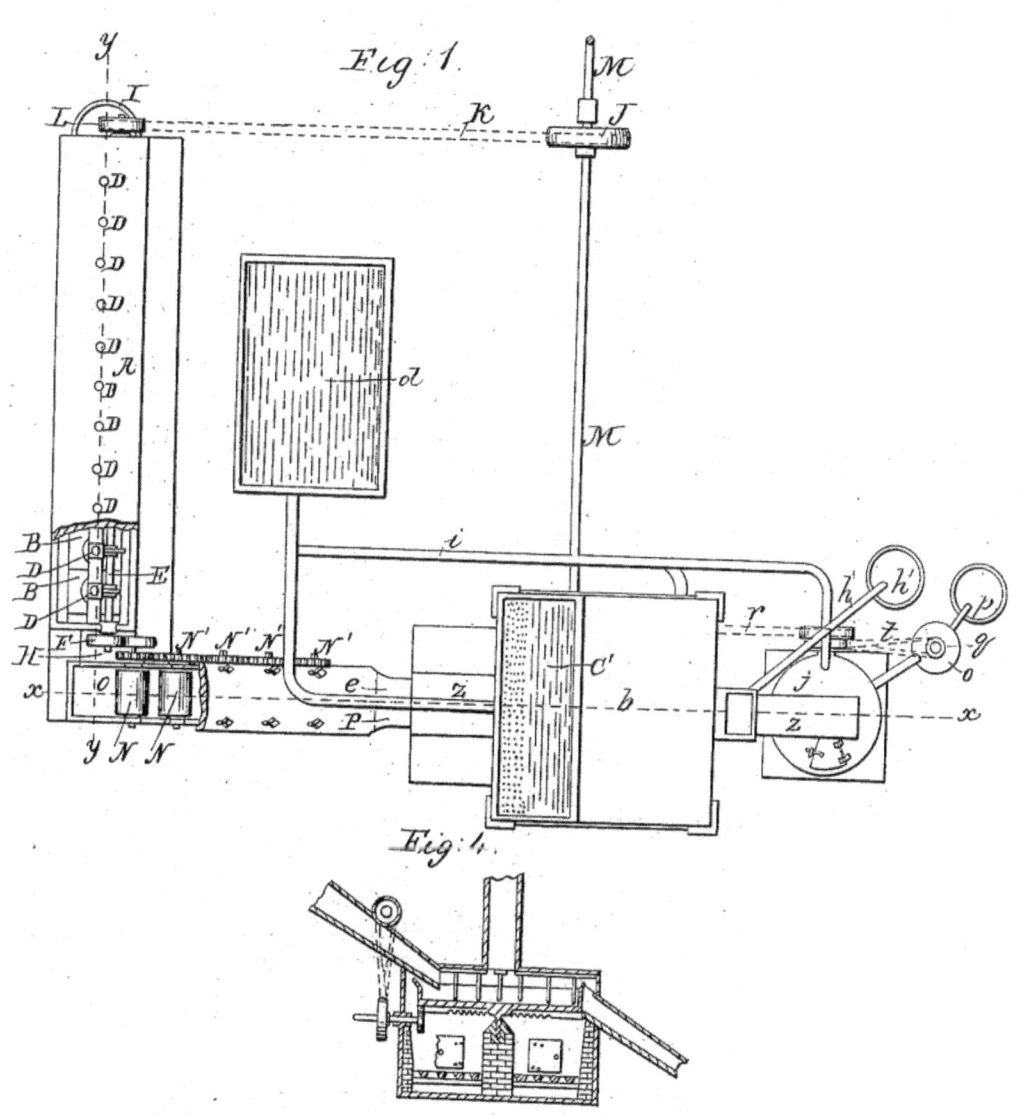

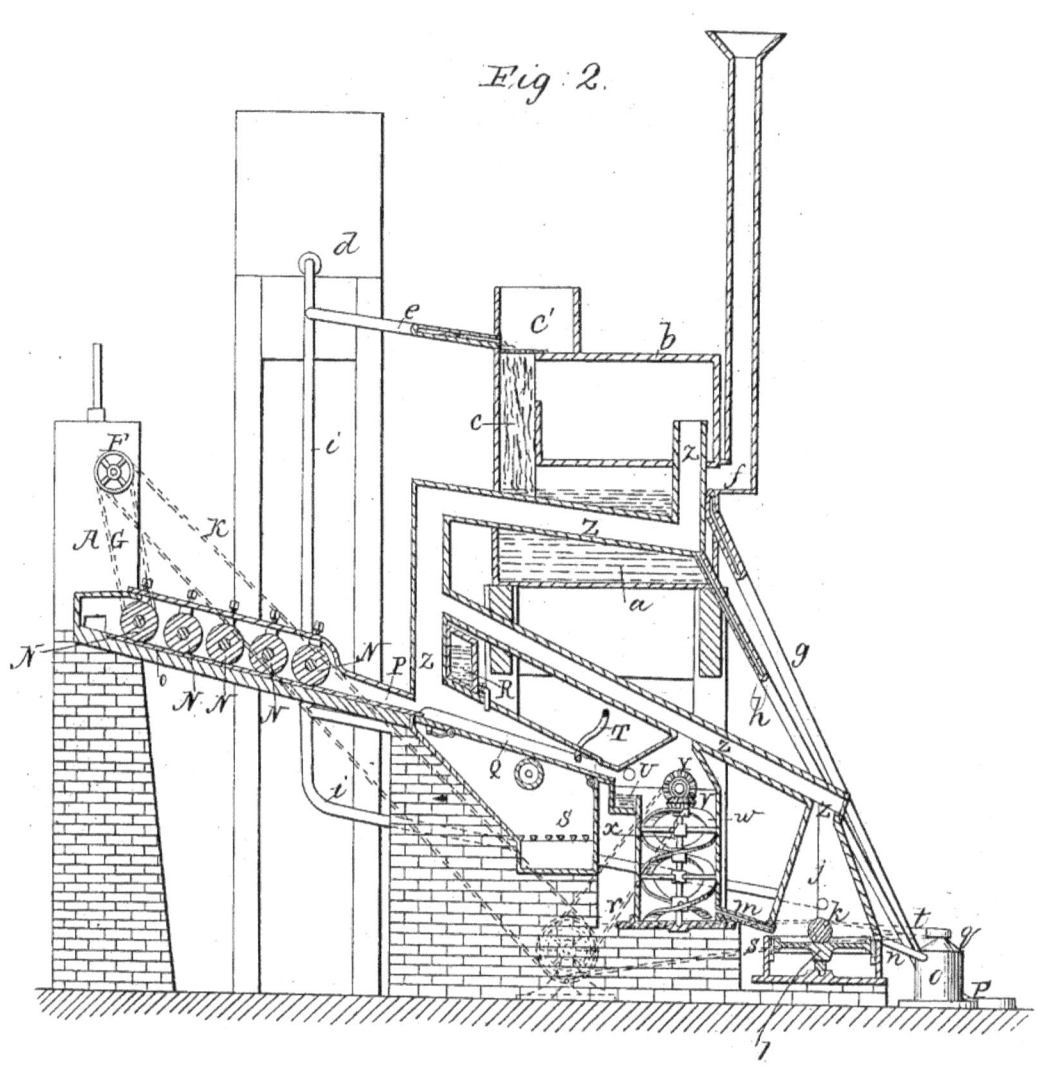

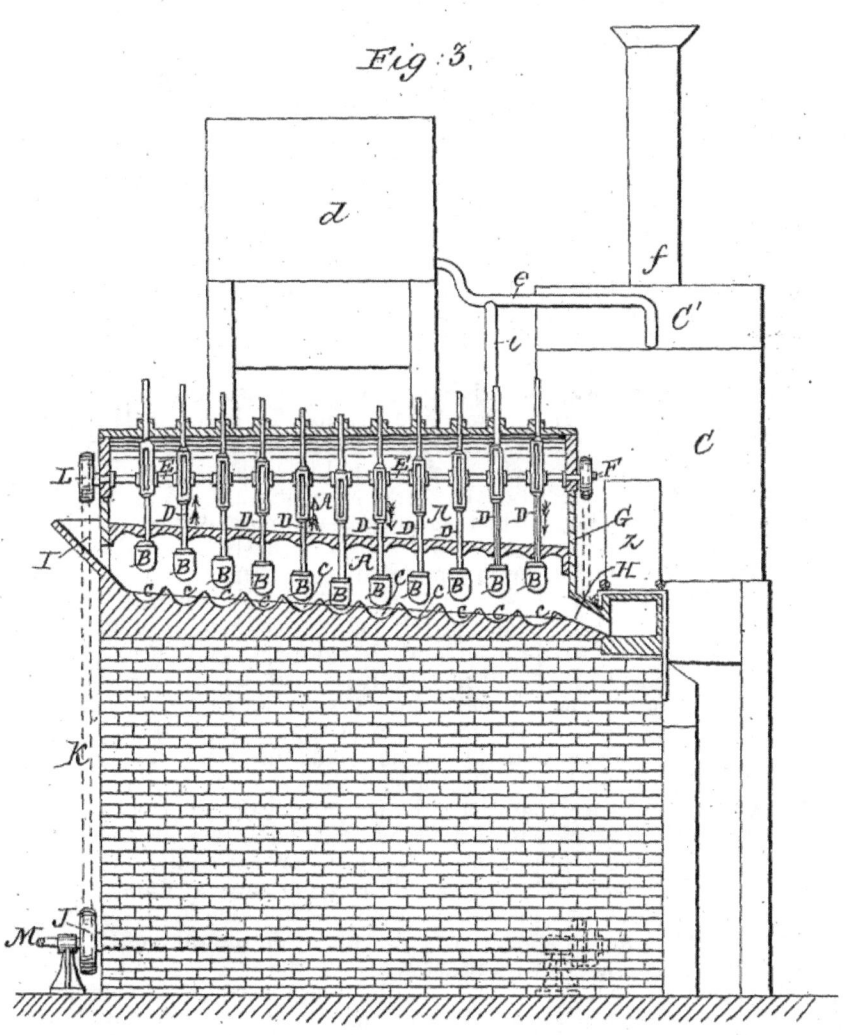

UNITED STATES PATENT OFFICE.

JOHN A. HITCHINGS, OF DENVER CITY, COLORADO.

IMPROVEMENT IN MACHINERY FOR SEPARATING METALS FROM ORES.

Specification forming part of Letters Patent No. **54,726**, dated May 15, 1866.

To all whom it may concern:

Be it known that I, JOHN A. HITCHINGS, of Denver City, in the county of Arapahoe and Territory of Colorado, have made new and useful Improvements in Machinery for Separating Metals from Ores; and I do hereby declare the following to be a full, clear, and exact description of the nature, construction, and operation of the same, sufficient to enable one skilled in the art to which appertains to construct and use the same, reference being had to the accompanying drawings, which are made part of this specification, and in which—

Figure 1 is a plan or top view. Fig. 2 is a vertical section on the line $x\,x$, Fig. 1. Fig. 3 is a vertical section on the line $y\,y$, Fig. 1. Fig. 4 is a detached view of the furnace-pan.

My invention consists of a number of portions through which the ores are consecutively passed, and which are, first, a stamping-mill; second, a series of crushing-rollers; third, a furnace; fourth, a cold-water tank; fifth, an amalgamator; sixth, an arrastra; seventh, a second amalgamator.

The ore descends in all these successive operations, so as not to require to be mechanically raised or lifted as it is passed from one to the other. The fumes are carried from the various portions where heat is applied, so as not to interfere with health, and the valuable vapors are condensed and returned to the apparatus at a point beyond the influence of the furnace.

The ore is fed into the machine at the hopper I, whence it passes to the chamber A, where it is exposed to the stampers B B, which are moved vertically by the shaft E and allowed to drop into the mortars C, which are in an inclined series, and which connect by slots which extend half of their depth, and by which the comminuted ore passes from one to another through the series until it is discharged at the spout H.

The motion of the stamps is produced by means of cams or cogs on the shaft E, which latter is rotated by the band K, which connects the pulley L on the shaft E with the pulley J on the main shaft M.

The pounded ore from the spout H passes along the inclined floor O under the crushing-rollers N N, which are rotated in the same direction by the cog-wheels N' N', which are rotated by a band, G, from the pulley F on the shaft E.

The ore, being further reduced by the action of the rollers N N, passes by the way of the spout P into a pan, Q, in the furnace S, where the ore is heated and a stream of mercurial vapor brought into contact with it by means of the pipe T. Water from the tank R, as may be required, (hot preferred,) is poured occasionally upon the heated pan Q to prevent the aggregation of the ore to the pan. The motion of the pan and its inclined position cause the comminuted and heated ore to be discharged into the chamber U, where the mineral oil which may not have been removed by the destructive distillation floats to the top and is carried off by a discharge-pipe.

From the chamber U the ore falls into the amalgamating-chamber V, which is charged with mercury, and in which is a revolving vertical shaft, X, on which are spiral wings W, which agitate the contents as the shaft is revolved by the bevel-wheels Y and the band r from a pulley on the shaft M.

The union of the quicksilver with the precious metals having been mainly completed in the chamber V, the amalgam is discharged by the pipe m into the arrastra j, where the roller K on the muller k on the revolving bed l has the effect of bringing the particles of mercury and precious metal into still closer contact. A stream of water from the pipe i is introduced into the arrastra and the amalgam-pulp is carried by the pipe n into the final amalgamator o, whose vertical shaft, with beater charged with mercury, revolves under the influence of the pulley q, which is rotated by the belt t from the pulley on the shaft of the arrastra-roller k.

The volatile fumes from the amalgamator V and the arrastra $k\,l$ are carried by the flue Z Z, together with those from the furnace, to the chamber b, having previously, in the chamber a, been exposed to the refrigerating action of cool water by the passage of the flue Z in a downwardly-inclined direction through the water-chamber a. Whatever fume or vapor becomes condensed in this angle of the pipe is returned by the pipe h to a chamber or pan, h', where it is utilized or collected.

The vapor escaping at the end of the flue Z into the chamber b is exposed to a shower-bath, c, to cleanse it of mercurial and sulphurous vapor, and is then allowed to escape by the chimney f.

The water for the supply of the various portions is derived from the tank d, which supplies the shower-bath chamber c' by means of the pipe e, and the arrastra by means of the pipe i. The condensed vapor of the chamber b is discharged, along with that from the lower descending angle of Z, into the pan h'.

The character of the furnace-pan which receives the comminuted ore from the rollers is designed to be as in Fig. 4, which consists of a cast-iron disk, u, four to six feet in diameter, placed over the furnace and supported by a pivot-pin on which it slowly revolves by means of the application of power to the pinion-shaft w coming through the wall of the furnace and gearing with a rack on the under side of the plate. A few inches above this plate is a rod, T, to which scrapers X are attached, which, by the revolution of the disk beneath, gradually remove the ore toward the periphery of the plate, where it falls into a spout which conducts it in its heated condition to the amalgamator. The flame of the furnace is admitted to pass around the edge of the disk and reverberates above it. The upper surface of the plate is covered with fire-clay, soapstone, or some fire-proof material thicker toward the center, and air is admitted by the discharge-sluice, furnace-doors, or through holes in the covering.

A small hollow cylinder is placed over the feed-sluice P, and is charged with soda, lime, or any other reagent, which is discharged into the passing ore and is fed with it to the roaster.

Set-screws above the rollers N N serve to gage their pressure upon the partially powdered ore which passes beneath them.

The arrastra has a circular concave cast-iron bed of four to six feet diameter, mounted on a stout table, Z, and revolving on a central pivot-ball and casters set in the frame under the periphery or rim of the bed. The bed is strengthened by flanges beneath, has a rim of several inches elevation, and has fixed across it an iron cylinder, K, of about sixteen inches diameter in the center and eight or ten at the ends, which is driven by a belt and connected to the bed by cog-and-pinion gear, thus producing a rubbing and sliding as well as grinding motion. Set-screws over the beams of the cylinder admit of an intimate and perfect pulverization and amalgamation. An opening in the rim through a fine screen with a circular catch-lift, carries the floating refuse to a copper amalgamator, o, shaped like a circular tea-caddy, which is provided with a revolving stirrer, and an opening near the bottom with slide-door to clean out its contents at. The pulp passes in at the side and out at the top. The inside is coated with quicksilver, and also charged with a few pounds of it. The copper amalgamator o, being coated with mercury, serves to arrest any floating particles of unamalgamized gold, and may be profitably used at the tail end of the quartz-mill to catch flour-gold in muddy water.

The cooler and first amalgamator and the arrastra are covered with dome-casings, and have pipes leading to the smoke-stack of the furnace to carry off the poisonous vapors liberated. The smoke-stack is bent down horizontally a few feet above the furnace and carried with a depressing angle of its own diameter below a horizontal line some eight feet into a sheet-iron vessel, and then turned up perpendicularly three feet and cut off in a dry chamber of several feet square. The vapors not settling in this chamber pass over a partition-wall at the end opposite their entrance, where a shower-bath of cold water from a reservoir above washes them down to the cistern below, the condensed vapors sinking therein to be drawn off by a pipe beneath, while the floating refuse passes out at a small opening to a waste-sluice with the surplus water. The smoke and other uncondensed vapors go out at a large opening near the turn-up elbow to an outside chimney, and thence to the open air.

These improvements are especially designed for pyritous ores, in which the presence of a mineral oil prevents the perfect amalgamation. The object, after reducing it to powder, is to heat it in contact with alkali and quicksilver fumes and then plunge it into cold water, when the mineral oil not previously dissipated will float and may be conveyed away, while the sediment being ground with mercury will be very perfectly amalgamated and the precious metals afterward separated.

Having described my invention, what I claim therein as new, and desire to secure by Letters Patent, is—

1. The arrangement of the mortars, rounded stamps, and slotted connecting-openings, substantially as and for the purpose set forth.

2. The arrangement, as a sequence to the subject-matter of the first claim, of the rollers N in the trough, for the further comminution of the ore received from the stamps.

3. A basin-shaped revolving roasting-plate, Fig. 4, provided with scrapers, as described, and with a vessel containing salts of soda, alum, or potash, which are intermingled with the ground ore.

4. The arrangement, with the revolving roaster, of the cold-water tank which receives the heated ore therefrom, as described.

5. The arrangement of the roasting-plate, cold-water bath, amalgamator, and arrastra, as described.

6. The quicksilver-coated copper amalgamator, acting as a final means of arresting non-mercurialized metals, arranged and operated as described.

7. The condenser, arranged as described, consisting of the flue Z, passing through the water-chamber, the discharge-pipes h, and the chamber b, the shower-bath c, and exit-flue f.

JOHN A. HITCHINGS.

Witnesses:
JAS. R. GALLEMORE,
CHARLES L. CHINIQUY.

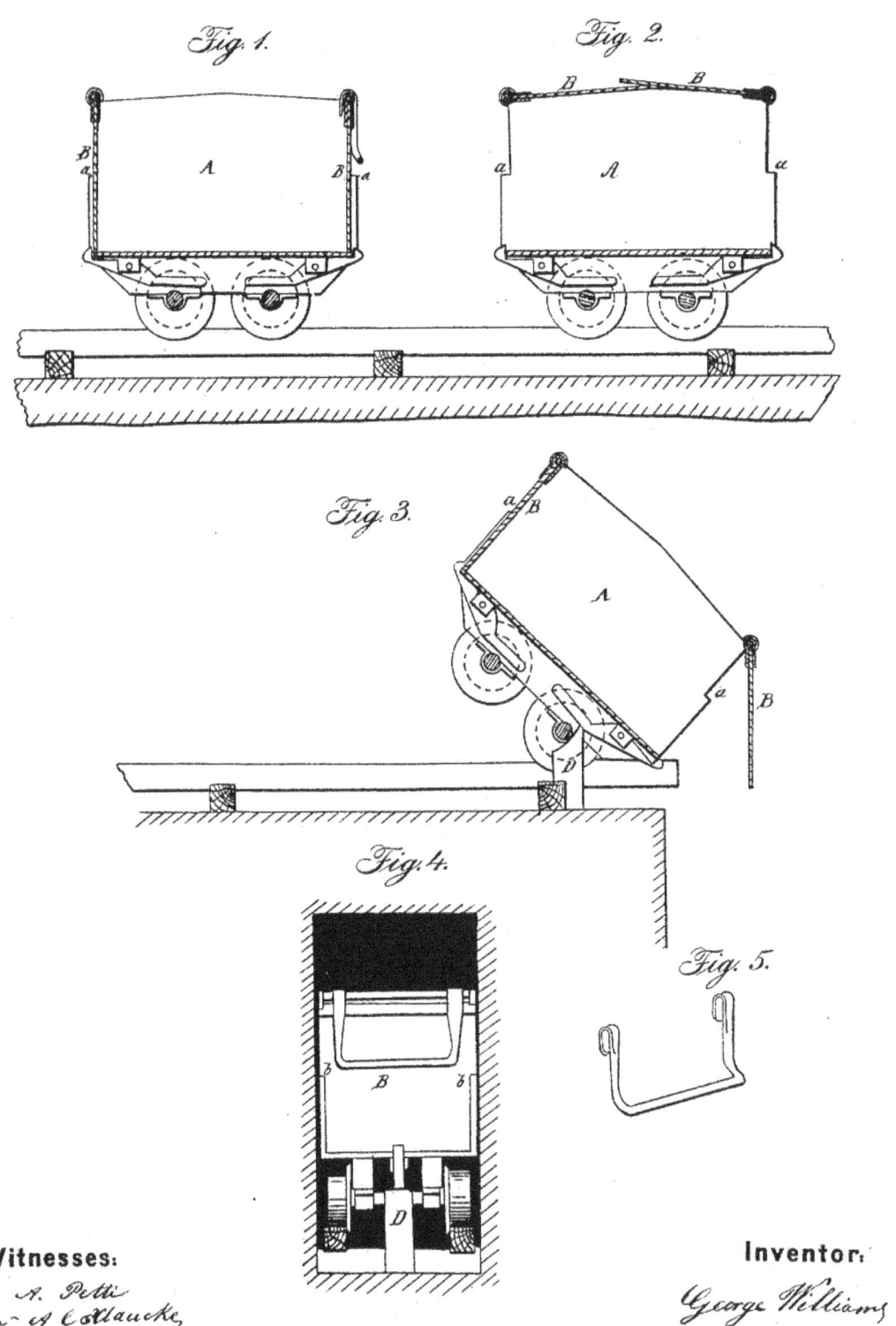

UNITED STATES PATENT OFFICE.

GEORGE WILLIAMS, OF STERLING, COLORADO TERRITORY.

IMPROVED ORE AND TIMBER CAR FOR MINES.

Specification forming part of Letters Patent No. **56,480**, dated July 17, 1866.

To all whom it may concern:

Be it known that I, GEORGE WILLIAMS, of Sterling, in the county of Park and Territory of Colorado, have made a new and useful Improvement in Combined Ore and Timber Car for Mines; and I do hereby declare the following to be a full, clear, and exact description of the nature, construction, and operation of the same, sufficient to enable one skilled in the art to which it appertains to construct and use the same, reference being had to the accompanying drawings, which are made part of this specification, and in which—

Figure 1 is a vertical longitudinal section, showing the ends of the car down in order to travel as an ore-car. Fig. 2 is a vertical longitudinal section of car arranged for carrying timber. Fig. 3 is a vertical longitudinal section, showing the car in the act of dumping. Fig. 4 is an end elevation, showing the car in the crevice. Fig. 5 is a perspective view of the detachable handle by which the hand-car is moved.

The improvement in the construction of the car, which is to be drawn or driven by manual power in the crevice of the mine, consists in so constructing the ends that they shall be self-supporting, either against the ends or upper edges of the sides of the car; in the arrangement whereby the car is adapted for containing ore or long timbers; in the arrangement for tripping the door-fastening, and in the detachable handle for manipulating the car.

In the drawings, A A are the sides of the car, which are notched at a, so that the door B may shut partially against and partially within the sides, as shown in Figs. 1 and 5, the under portion, b, of the door shutting against the end in the notch a. This arrangement secures the door from displacement in any direction save the one in which it is secured by the latch C, which is pivoted underneath the car in such a manner as to be actuated by the post D, which is placed in the track so as to trip the trigger at the desired point.

A blow or pressure against the forward end or beneath the outer end of the trigger will not open it, but it requires the contact of the post D with the inner end, which is attained when the car arrives at the discharging-point. (See Fig. 3.)

In the condition shown in Fig. 1 the car is prepared to carry ore, rock, or the detritus of the mine to the point of discharge, and in the condition shown in Fig. 2 it is prepared for carrying timbers into the mine for the support of the roof and sides, for laying track, or other uses familiar to mining experts.

The conversion from the condition Fig. 1 to that shown in Fig. 2 is made by raising the doors and folding them over, so as to form a temporary roof, the wide portions $b\ b$ resting upon the upper edge of the sides as they before rested against the ends.

The swinging handle, Fig. 5, is provided as a matter of convenience and security to the hands, which are thereby less exposed than when grasping the exposed upper edge of the door.

The car is designed to be used in crevices which have been opened by the removal of pay-rock, and the arrangement of duplicate doors permits the use of it without turning from either direction toward a common downcast shaft when used by two sets of miners whose tracks approach a common point of discharge from two different directions, and who use the car alternately.

The arrangement for change in the condition of the car permits it to carry loads each way with but little trouble in conversion, instead of compelling one car to be removed before the other can be put in position.

The form of the doors enables them to be supported by the sides without braces, cleats, or bars, and gives no occasion for the accumulation of trash therein or difficulty of discharge therefrom.

What I claim as new is—

1. The construction of the doors with a wider portion, b, to adapt them to be supported by the sides of the car, substantially as described.

2. A car constructed with end doors adapted to be folded over the top, for the purpose of converting it into a timber-car.

3. In combination with the above, a trigger, C, provided with an inward projection adapted to be tripped by the post D.

GEORGE WILLIAMS.

Witnesses:
CHARLES A. PETTIT,
ALEXR. A. C. KLAUCKE.

Sheet 1-2 Sheets.

G. Williams,

Elevator,

No. 56,481 Patented July 17, 1866.

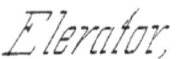

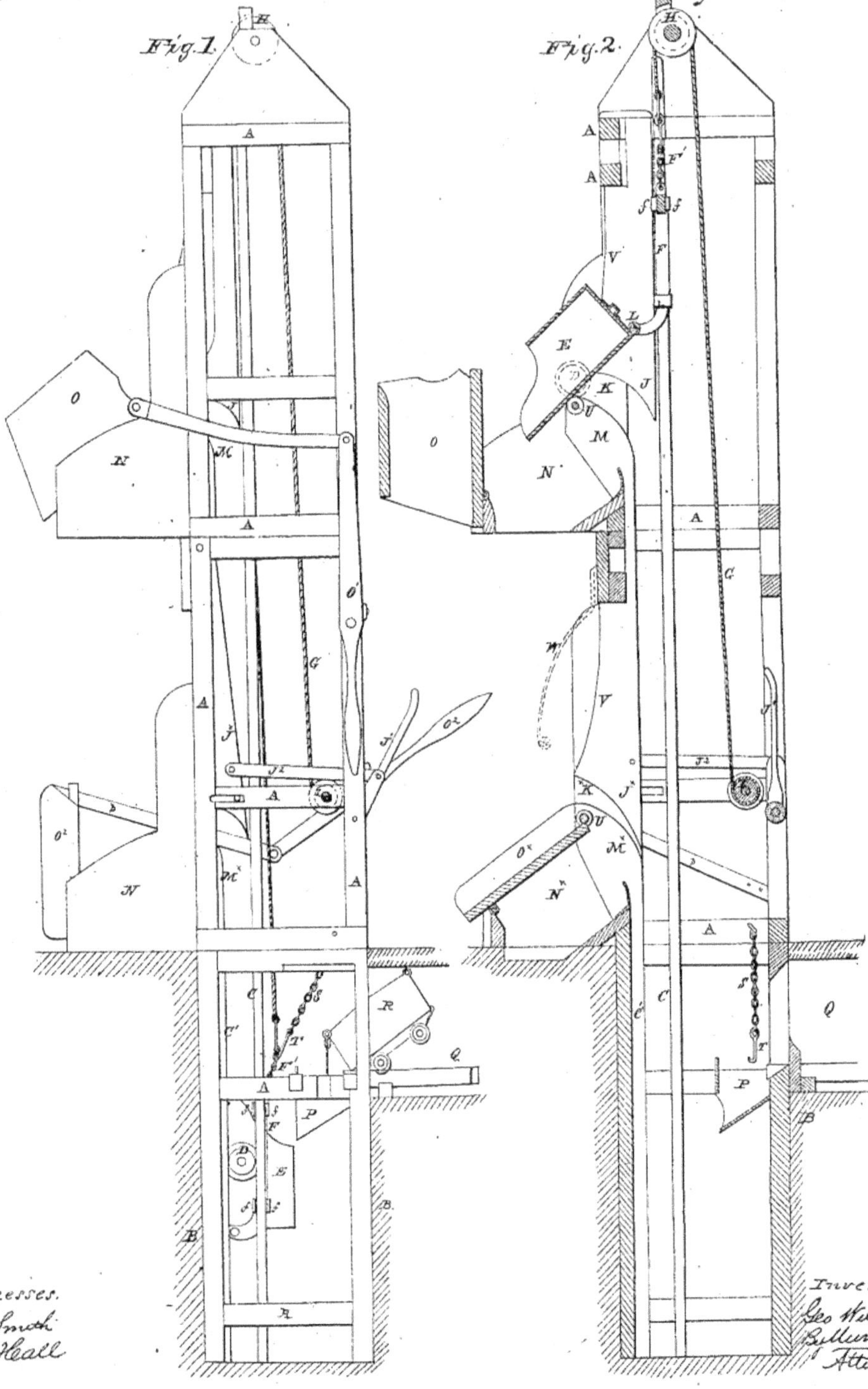

Witnesses.
O. D. Smith
W. F. Hall

Inventor
Geo. Williams
By Munn & Co.
Attorneys

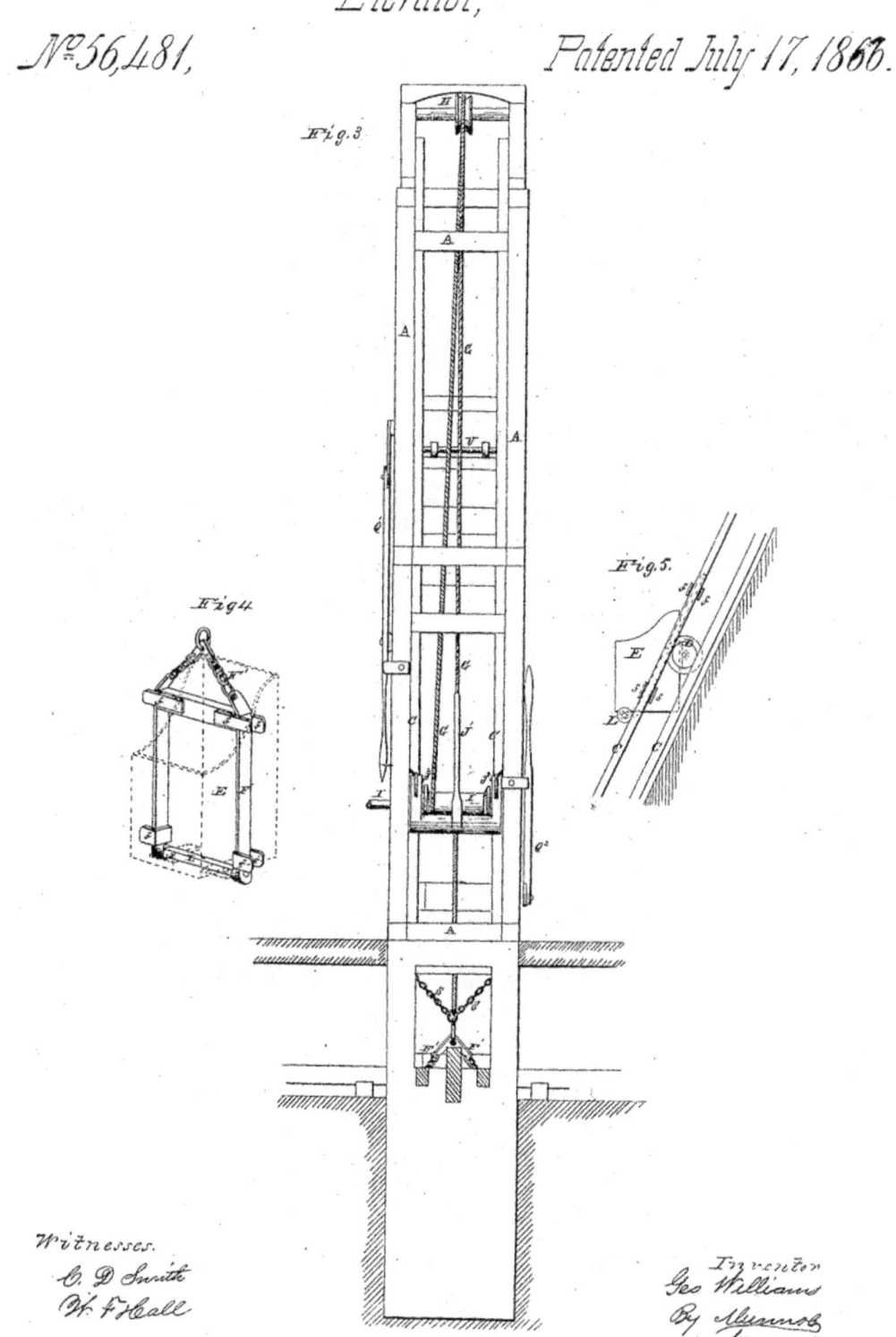

UNITED STATES PATENT OFFICE.

GEO. WILLIAMS, OF STERLING, COLORADO TERRITORY.

IMPROVEMENT IN ELEVATORS.

Specification forming part of Letters Patent No. **56,481**, dated July 17, 1866.

To all whom it may concern:

Be it known that I, GEORGE WILLIAMS, of Sterling, in the county of Park and Territory of Colorado, have made a new and useful Improvement in Elevators for Mines; and I do hereby declare the following to be a full, clear, and exact description of the nature, construction, and operation of the same, sufficient to enable one skilled in the art to which it appertains to construct and use the same, reference being had to the accompanying drawings, which are made part of this specification, and in which—

Figure 1 is a side elevation. Fig. 2 is a vertical section. Fig. 3 is also a vertical section, the plane of which is at right angle to the plane of Fig. 2. Fig. 4 is a detached view of the elevating-bucket and the bail upon which it is suspended and by which it is attached to the elevating-rope. Fig. 5 is a detached view, showing the mode of applying the bail to the bucket when the latter is working in an inclined shaft.

Similar letters of reference indicate corresponding parts in the several figures.

The improvement consists of an arrangement of an ascending and descending bucket operated by cord and windlass, and so supported as to be readily discharged by the deflection of the guide-wheels from their normal line of travel onto inclined ways, the axis of the guide-wheels forming a transverse line of support upon which the bucket is vibrated or tipped as it is raised by the bail attached to its lower end. By this means there is no additional power required to empty the bucket, as in ordinary cases, in which the bucket is suspended at a point between its upper and its lower end and upset by an obstacle which arrests its motion at one point—as, for instance, tipping it over by grasping and detaining the rim of the mouth.

Any obstacle placed in the way to tip the bucket increases the resistance at that point, and should be avoided, as the power must necessarily be equal to overcome the greatest resistance which under ordinary circumstances immediately precedes the emptying and causes great disturbance in the engine.

The arrangements permit the bucket to be loaded or discharged at various points in the shaft, so as to answer in turn for a number of drifts at different depths, and also to discharge water into an adit or ditch for carrying it off, to discharge ore at the surface, or to receive timber for transportation into the mine.

In the drawings, A A are the timbers of the frame, and B the wall-rock of the shaft. C C' are guide-timbers, between which the wheels D of the bucket E traverse. The bucket is lifted by the discharging-levers F F, to which the rope G is attached. The latter runs over the pulley H, and is wound upon the drum I of the hand-winch I'.

Power being applied to the winch I', the bucket rises until the wheels D of the bucket E meet an oblique deflecting-guide, which causes it to depart from its normal course, which is still maintained by the discharging-levers F F. This departure causes the bucket to vibrate on its axis L, where it is attached to the bail. It tips forward, the wheels D resting upon the curved track M, and as the discharging-levers still ascend in a direct line under the guidance of the timber C, the bucket is eventually tipped up, as in Fig. 2, sufficiently to discharge its contents into the chute N, or the trough O, if the latter be placed in the required position.

The curved deflector J in the upper section, Fig. 2, is a fixture, as it is the highest in the series; but in the case of those at a lower level, such as J^x, it is necessary to adjust it to the occasion which requires it. This is done by means of a lever, J', connecting-rods J^2, or equivalent devices, which vibrate the piece J^x on its upper pivot, so as to cause it to approach the guide C, and thus deflect the wheels D into the track K^x, the bucket then resting upon the curve M^x and discharging into the chute O^x or trough N^x, as occasion may require.

For each point of discharge a similar arrangement is required, and for each point where the bucket is to be loaded with ore a trough, P, is provided with a hook, T, and chain S, which detains the bucket in the required position for loading by being hooked to the chain F', which is applied to the top of the discharging-levers F F.

Q may represent a drift or gallery in the mine, and R the car traveling therein, which is rolled to the side of the shaft and discharged into the trough P, the bucket E being in position, Fig. 1, to receive the ore as it falls through the open bottom of the trough.

Each of the chutes O O˟ is pivoted within its corresponding adit, and the position of each is varied to permit the bucket to discharge into the chute or through the adit by means of a lever, O′ or O², and suitable connecting-rods.

When the bucket descends the hook T is applied by hand to the chain F′ of the discharging-levers F F; but when the bucket begins to ascend the central angular link of the chain F′ readily disengages itself from the hook T, and the latter swings over toward the side of the shaft, so as to be entirely out of the way.

As before stated, the discharging-levers F F always maintain an unvarying straight line of travel, and this is effected by the arms ff embracing the guide C; but as soon as the wheels D enter either of the ways K K˟ the bucket E begins to vibrate upon its lower point of support L, and this vibration continues until the bucket assumes the tilted position shown in Fig. 2. Now, it is manifest that when the wheels D enter the curved guideway a portion of the weight is immediately transferred to the curved point M or M˟, and the weight of the bucket devolves more and more upon this point as the bottom of the bucket continues to rise. Hence as the bucket approaches a horizontal position the strain upon the elevating-rope G diminishes to such an extent that the operation of tilting the bucket, instead of requiring additional power, as heretofore, is effected with greater facility or less power than the elevation of the bucket from the mine.

This is not the case under the old mode of operation, for in the latter the point on which the bucket is suspended is located between the top and bottom of the bucket, so that when the tilting commences, be the deflecting device of any character whatsoever, the weight of the bucket not only has to be lifted bodily by the elevating-rope, but the resistance of the deflecting device has also to be overcome. Hence it will be seen that an essential feature of my invention consists in having the point of suspension of the bucket located at the bottom of the latter and the deflecting-rollers somewhere between its ends, a central position for said deflecting-rollers being preferable.

By transferring the point of support L of the bucket E from the center of the bottom toward the edge, as shown in Fig. 5, the bucket may be tilted to a greater extent than before, because the pivoted heel of the bucket is made to rise higher relatively to the deflecting-rollers D than in the previous instance.

The point of support of the bucket is also transferred toward the edge of the bottom, for the purpose of adapting the bucket to be held in an upright position in an inclined shaft, as represented in Fig. 5. The detail in Fig. 4 shows the point of support applied to the center of the bottom of the bucket.

When the deflecting-rollers D of the bucket reach the upper extremity of the curved guides M or M˟ the mouth of the bucket, together with the rollers D, would be free to move inward and downward under the continued ascent of the pivoted heel of the bucket, and therefore I employ a fixed roller, U, upon which the bucket rests when the rollers D reach the upper extremity of the deflecting-guides, in order to prevent said rollers D from running back or downward in the ways K K˟. If the rollers were thus allowed to run back in the grooves they would become wedged or jammed within the same, and this sudden arresting of the parts would produce injury to the machinery and interfere with the operation of the engine. The roller U supports the bucket till the rollers run upon the guides V, and the rollers D may traverse upward upon those guides until the engine can be conveniently reversed. Then the rollers D, of course, move freely downward, traveling in the same guides as those in which they ascended.

The arm W (shown in Fig. 2) is fixed to the frame A, and by catching the lowest side of the rim at the top of the bucket may be made to answer the purpose of the roller U.

Having thus described my invention, the following is what I claim as new and desire to secure by Letters Patent:

1. The elevating-bucket E, with the discharging-levers F F applied to the bottom of the bucket, substantially as described.

2. In combination with the above, the deflecting-rollers D and curved guideways K K˟, arranged and operating substantially as described.

3. The adjustable sections J˟, employed to enable the bucket to be discharged at different heights, substantially as described.

4. The hinged chute O˟, in combination with the levers O² and p, operating substantially in the manner and for the purpose described.

5. The bucket E, in combination with the hook W, or its equivalent, the roller U, substantially as described.

GEORGE WILLIAMS.

Witnesses:
ALEXR. A. C. KLAUCKE,
W. F. HALL.

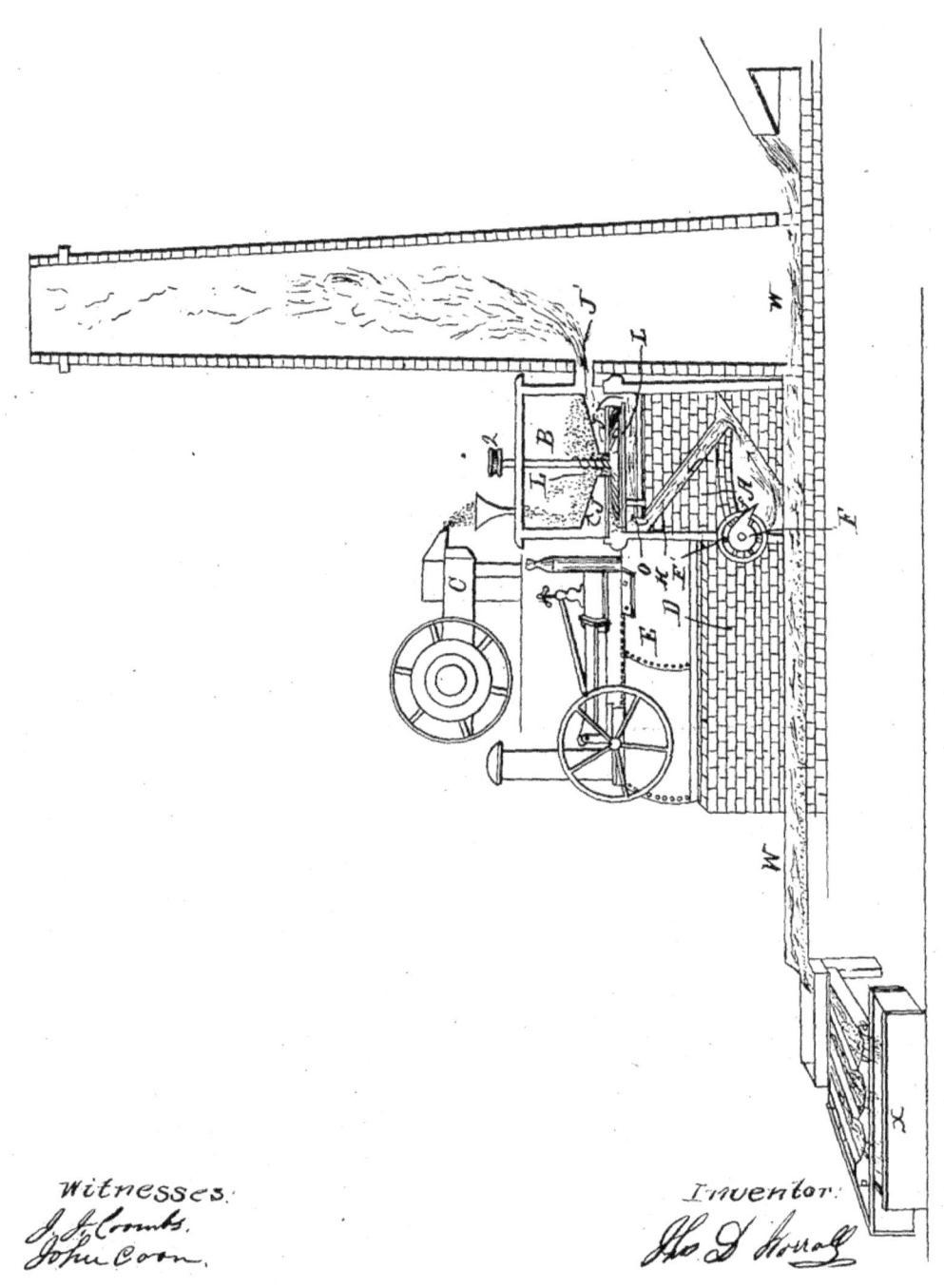

UNITED STATES PATENT OFFICE.

THOMAS D. WORRALL, OF CENTRAL CITY, COLORADO.

IMPROVED FURNACE FOR DESULPHURIZING ORES.

Specification forming part of Letters Patent No. **56,842**, dated July 31, 1866.

To all whom it may concern:

Be it known that I, THOMAS D. WORRALL, of Central City, in the county of Gilpin and Territory of Colorado, have invented certain new and useful Improvements in Furnaces for Desulphurizing Quartz-Rock, Pyrites, and other Metal-Bearing Substances; and I do hereby declare that the following is a full, clear, and exact description thereof, reference being had to the accompanying drawings, and to the letters of reference marked thereon.

My entire invention relates to a desulphurizing-furnace, in connection with which a steam-engine is used to operate a blower, and a quartz-pulverizing machine, if desired; but some of my improvements are equally applicable to a furnace used in connection with any other power.

In the accompanying drawings, A is a vertical section of the desulphurizing-furnace built in a square form. B is a cylindrical hopper above the furnace A, (also shown in section,) into which the pulverized quartz falls from any suitable quartz-pulverizing machine, as shown at C. D is the furnace under the boiler E, for generating steam to run the engine, as well as to supply heat to the desulphurizing-furnace. F is a drum in which a rotating fan is operated by means of a pulley, F', on the end of the fan-shaft, and f is a blow-pipe, or one of a series of blow-pipes, through which the air is forced onto a hearth in the desulphurizing-furnace. Said drum or cylinder F extends clear across the throat of the furnace D, through which all the flame and other products of combustion generated in said furnace D must escape into the desulpurizing-furnace, and said drum is so located that the flame, in passing from the furnace D into the desulphurizing-furnace, must pass under said drum.

I do not, however, limit myself to this particular form of blower. Any other bellows or device for forcing air through the blow pipe or pipes may be substituted.

G is an inclined hearth, of metal, soap-stone, fire-brick, asbestus, or any other suitable fire-proof material.

H is an inclined flame-flue, through which the flame ascends from the hearth G. The flue H may be made of fire-brick and covered with slabs of soap-stone, metallic plates, or any suitable fire-proof material.

I is a horizontal flue, constructed and covered in the same way, and J J is a circular flue below the bottom of the hopper B.

J' is the exit-flue, through which the flame and heated air and gasses pass into the chimney K.

L is a revolving stirrer or scraper in the space between the flues I and J, and operating on the plate or slab covering the flue I.

L' is a worm-screw on the shaft which carries the scraper for feeding the pulverized quartz from the hopper to the space or chamber in which the scraper revolves. This shaft is revolved by means of a pulley, l, on its upper end, geared by a proper band or strap with some other part of the machinery.

O is an aperture through the upper and lower plates of flue I, through which the pulverized quartz falls onto the covering-plate of flue H.

A fire being built in the furnace D, the flame passes under the blow pipe or pipes f, and by the current of air blown through said pipe or pipes is condensed on the hearth G; thence the flame passes through the flues H, I, and J, and through J', into the chimney K, in the course shown by the arrows.

The pulverized quartz falling from the quartz-crusher at C into the hopper B is fed down into the chamber in which the stirrer L revolves by means of the worm-screw L', and by the revolving stirrer is moved round on the heated plate which forms the bottom of said chamber, so that every particle will be likely to come in contact with the heated surfaces which surround said chamber, and finally falls, through the aperture O, onto the heated plate covering the flue H, runs down said plate to the aperture i, through which it falls onto the hearth G, and running down the same, passes through the flame condensed upon said hearth by the blow pipe or pipes f.

In the hopper B the pulverized quartz is dried and partially heated, and in being revolved upon the heated plate covering flue I by the stirrer it becomes still further heated and partially desulphurized. In passing down over the heated plate covering the flue H, down the hearth G, and through the flame condensed upon said hearth by the blow pipe or pipes f, the sulphur, arsenic, and other agents which prevent the yield of gold or silver by amalgamation are completely removed, and said pulverized quartz is prepared for amalgamation, smelting, or chlorinization.

W W is a sluice or water-way running under the furnace to carry the pulverized quartz, as it falls from the hearth G, to a buddle, arrastra, or shaking-table at X.

Having thus described my invention and the mode of carrying it into effect, what I claim as new, and desire to secure by Letters Patent, is—

1. In a desulphurizing-furnace used in combination with a steam-engine to operate a blower or quartz-pulverizer, or both, so combining and arranging the steam-generating furnace with the desulphurizing-furnace that the flame and other products of combustion escaping from the steam-generating furnace shall pass into and through the desulphurizing-furnace and supply the flame and heat necessary for effecting desulphurization therein, substantially as described.

2. Condensing flame, by means of a blow pipe or pipes, upon a hearth over which pulverized quartz is passed for the purpose of desulphurizing the same, substantially as described.

3. In combination with a hearth upon which flame is condensed by means of a blow pipe or pipes, for the purpose herein described, a fan-blower, air-pump, or other suitable air-generator, for the purpose of forcing air through said blow pipe or pipes to condense the flame upon the hearth, substantially as described.

4. An inclined or zigzag flue, with top of soap-stone, metal, or other suitable substance, for the purpose of securing a heated surface, over which pulverized quartz is passed, for the purpose set forth.

5. The horizontal flue I, with top plate of soap-stone, metal, or other suitable substance, in combination with the stirrer or scraper L, for the purpose described.

6. The hopper B, in combination with the worm-screw L' and the stirrer or scraper L, substantially as and for the purpose described.

7. The hopper B, in combination with the flue J J, under the same, for the purpose of drying and heating the pulverized quartz before leaving the hopper.

8. In combination with the stirrer or scraper L, and the horizontal flue I, the aperture O, (one or more,) through both the top and bottom plates of said flue, for the purpose of delivering the pulverized quartz down upon the heated plate covering the inclined flue H, substantially as and for the purpose set forth.

9. In combination with the hearth G, the sluice or water-course W W, for the purpose of conveying the pulverized quartz from said hearth to a buddle, arrastra, or shaking-table, as described.

THOS. D. WORRALL.

Witnesses:
J. J. COOMBS,
JOHN COON.

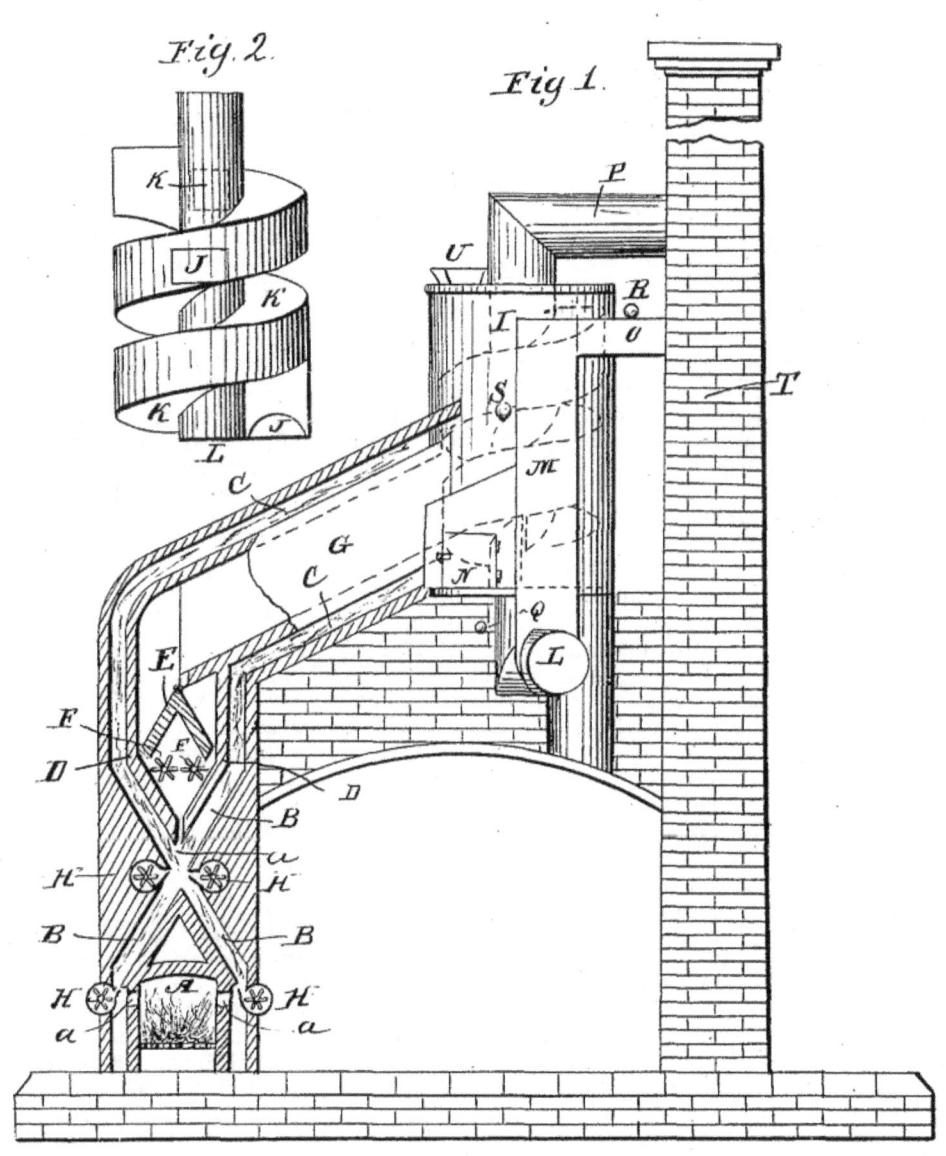

UNITED STATES PATENT OFFICE.

THOS. D. WORRALL, OF CENTRAL CITY, COLORADO TERRITORY.

IMPROVED APPARATUS FOR DESULPHURIZING QUARTZ.

Specification forming part of Letters Patent No. 57,420, dated August 21, 1866.

To all whom it may concern:

Be it known that I, THOMAS D. WORRALL, of Central City, in the county of Gilpin and Territory of Colorado, have invented certain new and useful Improvements in Furnaces for Desulphurizing Quartz Rock, Pyrites, and other metal-bearing substances; and I do hereby declare that the following is a full, clear, and exact description thereof, reference being had to the accompanying drawings, and to the letters of reference marked thereon.

My entire invention relates to a desulphurizing-furnace so arranged that it will not only desulphurize quartz, but also save the gases driven from the pyrites and sulphurets for the purpose of converting them into sulphur, sulphuric acid, bisulphide of carbon, and any other chemical compound of which they may be made to form a part.

In the accompanying drawings, Figure 1 is a vertical section of the desulphurizing-furnace, built in a square form and of any suitable fire-proof material. Fig. 2 is the inside of a spiral furnace with double flue, for the purpose of securing either a double flame, through which pulverized quartz pyrites or other metal-bearing substances may fall while in contact with the flame, or through one of which flame may ascend while through the other quartz descends without coming in contact with the flame.

In Fig. 1, A is a fire-place in the furnace, for generating heat and flame. $a\ a$ are openings in the sides of the fire-place, through which the flame escapes into the flue. B B B B are an X-shaped flue, up which the fire and smoke pass. C C are continuations of said flue. D D are a V-shaped receiver, with an opening at the bottom, (marked d.) E is an inverted-V-shaped distributer suspended by a hinge on the distributing end of a muffle-furnace, or securely fastened in that position. F F are fan-shaped distributers, made to revolve at the base of the distributer E, or in any other part of the furnace in which they may answer the purpose. G is a continuous muffle-furnace surrounded by the flues C C. H H H H are blow-pipes extending across the whole throat of the furnace, designed to operate in the flues B B and to condense the flames upon each other immediately under the opening of the receiver, (marked d.) I is the wall of the furnace, which contains the spiral flues seen on Fig. 2. J J on that figure are openings designed to receive the fire and smoke from the upper and lower flues, C C, in Fig. 1.

K K in Fig. 2 indicate the direction of the spiral flue from which the sulphurous gases escape from the muffle-furnace G in Fig. 1. K' is an opening, through which the gases escape to and down the center of the furnace, passing out of the bottom of the flue at L in Fig. 1 into an ordinary receiving-chamber. (Not shown on the drawings.) M is a flue, built on the outside of the upper part of the furnace, for the escape of the smoke and carbonaceous gases from the spiral flue J, and descending to and joining the other flue at L. N is a small furnace, also connected with the flue M. O is an escape-flue, passing from M into a chimney-stack. P is an escape-flue, passing from the flue K into the chimney-stack. Q R S are gates or dampers to turn both gases and smoke into the chimney-stack when not required for other purposes. T is a chimney-stack. U is a receiving-hopper, through which the pulverized quartz is passed to the furnace.

Having given a description of the different parts of my furnace, I now proceed to describe its operation.

I start a fire in my fire-place at A, from which the flame ascends through the openings on either side at $a\ a$. The drums or air-generators being also set in motion, the blow-pipes operate in the confined flues B B and condense the flames upon each other below d. The flames then continue up the flue B, heating the receiver D, the muffle-furnace G, and the spiral flues J and K, and are either conducted into the receiver through L by closing the valve O or permitted to pass into the chimney-stack T. At the same time the quartz is passed into the hopper U, and enters the spiral flue K, passing over the heated surface which forms the floor of that flue, where it is dried and partly heated. From thence it falls into the continuous muffle-furnace G, and after passing through it is delivered onto the V-shaped distributing-plate E.

The object of hanging the plate upon a pivot or hinge is to secure equal distribution of the quartz.

It will be seen that by this arrangement, should the quartz pass in too great abundance onto and down one valve of the plate, it would so press upon it as to force the upper point under the chute, and thus regulate the exact amount of quartz desired to flow down each valve. By this plate the quartz is delivered onto the diamond-shaped receiver at its widest part D D. Here it falls upon the fan-distributers F F, and by these is delivered into the heated chamber formed by the V-plate. They also serve by their motion to increase the draft in the flue when it is desired to use the flue without any reference to saving and condensing the gases, and will by so doing augment the amount of oxygen used in desulphurizing and oxidizing the quartz, but will simply act as agitators where the draft is cut off, for the purpose of saving the gases. From these revolving agitators or distributers the quartz passes down the walls of the diamond-shaped receiver D D, and through the bottom, at the point where the flames are condensed upon each other, below d, and from thence down the flues B B, where the work of desulphurization is completed.

It will be seen that from the time that the quartz passes into the hopper U until it passes through the bottom of the diamond-shaped receiver at d it has been kept as free as possible from the air, smoke, and flame, only a sufficient amount being admitted to insure that the sulphurous gases pass into the receiver, the object of this being to collect the sulphurous fumes and gases and conduct them, in as pure a form as possible, into a receiver, so as to use them in the manufacture of sulphur, sulphuric acid, bisulphide of carbon, or any other chemical compound in which they can be used. These sulphurous gases are conducted down the flue K', and pass through to L, where they are mixed with the fumes or gases created in the combustion of fuel in the fire-place A, or by the combustion of carbon-oil or any other carbonaceous substances generated in the small furnace n, and thence into any ordinary receiving-chamber, for the purpose of being converted into the chemical compounds above named.

My object in these devices is to introduce metal-bearing ores to gradually-increased heated surfaces and flame, and to keep them in contact with said surfaces a sufficient time to insure that sulphur, arsenic, and other substances that prevent successful amalgamation have been removed before submitting them to that degree of heat at which there may be danger of the sulphur and iron contained in the ores forming a flux, in which the gold and silver may be embedded, as in a matrix, from which they could not be extracted without great difficulty.

I do not desire to confine myself to the combinations shown in this furnace, but wish to use each part of the furnace singly or in any other combination that may be desired; neither do I confine myself to any particular material out of which my furnace or any part of my furnace may be constructed, but propose to use any suitable material.

Having thus described my invention and the mode of carrying it into effect, what I claim, and desire to secure by Letters Patent, is—

1. Operating a blow-pipe in a confined space or flue up which flame is passing, for the purpose of intensifying the heat through which metal-bearing substances in a pulverized or partly pulverized condition are passing, for the purposes set forth.

2. Operating blow-pipes up flues that form a junction, so that when the flames meet they may be condensed upon each other, and thus intensified for the purpose of desulphurizing and oxidizing metalliferous ores passing through said flames, as set forth.

3. An X-shaped flue so constructed that the fire, starting from extreme points at the base, must meet in the center of the flue, and this whether used with or without blow-pipes, for the purpose set forth.

4. The furnace A, with open sides communicating with flues, in connection with the blow-pipes H H H H and the X-shaped flues, substantially as set forth.

5. The V or diamond shaped receiver, with perforated base, for the purpose of heating quartz or other metal-bearing substances when passing over its inner surface while the fire is passing over its outer surface, and of delivering the same either into flues below onto heated plates through simple flame, through flame condensed upon itself by means of two or more blow-pipes playing from opposite directions, or upon a hearth upon which flame has been condensed by blow-pipes.

6. The revolving fan-distributers in the V or diamond shaped receiver in flues in a muffle-furnace or in an open-chimney stack, for the purpose of suspending pulverized quartz and other metal-bearing substances in their downward descent, and of distributing the same in or upon heated surfaces or through flame, for the purposes set forth.

7. In combination with the V-shaped receiver D D and the spiral furnace I, a continuous muffle-furnace of any shape or dimensions—horizontal, semi-horizontal, or perpendicular—through which ores containing sulphur or other volatile agents may pass, for the purpose of simple desulphurization, or for the purpose of driving off sulphur, arsenic, or any other chemical agent which it may be desirable to save for scientific or commercial purposes.

8. One or more inverted-V-shaped plates, either firmly built in the flue or suspended by hinges at the distributing end of a muffle or other furnace or ordinary spout, for the purpose of distributing pulverized quartz falling upon it, in the manner and for the purposes set forth.

9. The V or diamond shaped receiver D D,

in combination with the inverted-V-shaped distributer E, for the purpose set forth, or any other similar purpose.

10. The spiral furnace, with either a double or single flue, for the purpose of securing a slow and gradual descent of pulverized quartz or pyrites while fire is ascending in or under said flues.

11. So constructing said spiral furnace and the conducting-flues connected therewith that while heat and flame are ascending one flue and the quartz, sulphurets, or other metal-bearing substances are descending the other, said substances shall not only be freed from their sulphur for the purpose of metallurgical success, but the sulphurous gases and other volatile agents may be collected and converted into any chemical or commercial agent of which they may be made to form parts.

12. Desulphurizing ores and driving from them arsenic and other chemical agents, for the purpose of securing successful amalgamation and chlorination or smelting, and, simultaneously with this, converting the sulphurous gases, arsenic, or other agents into useful articles for chemical or commercial purposes.

13. Conducting the gases arising from the combustion of carbonaceous substances which have been used to supply heat for the desulphurizing-furnace into a receiver, to be united with the sulphurous gases, for the purpose set forth.

14. The furnace N, connected with the conducting-pipes M and K', for the purpose of supplying any deficiency of carbonaceous gases that may be lacking from furnace A, for the purpose set forth.

15. The use of carbon-oil for the purpose of supplying the equivalents of carbon necessary to the manufacture of the chemical compounds, as set forth.

THOS. D. WORRALL.

Witnesses:
  Jos. L. Coombs,
  Edm. F. Brown.

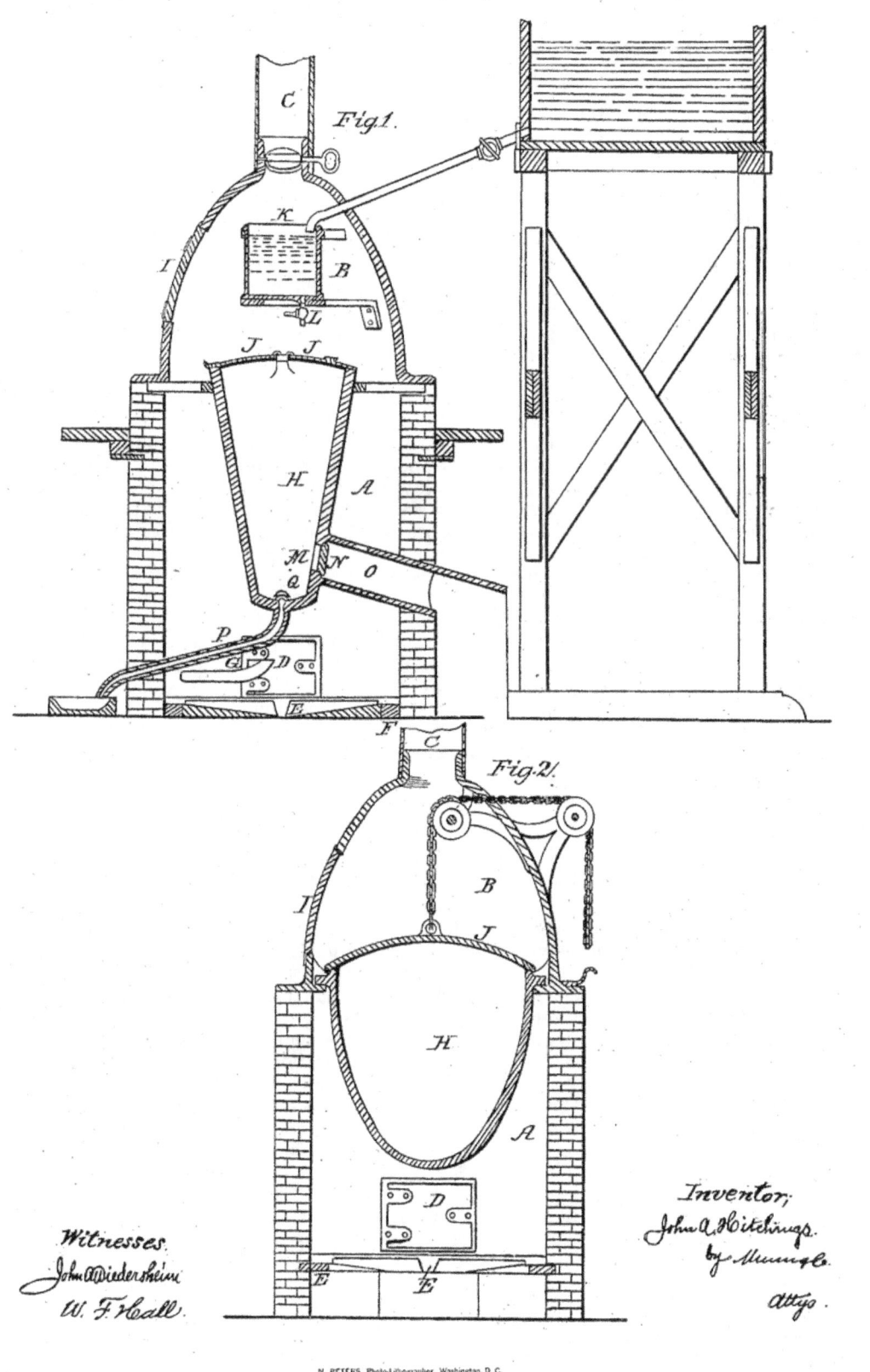

UNITED STATES PATENT OFFICE.

JOHN A. HITCHINGS, OF DENVER CITY, COLORADO.

IMPROVEMENT IN DESULPHURIZING ORES.

Specification forming part of Letters Patent No. **58,100**, dated September 18, 1866.

To all whom it may concern:

Be it known that I, JOHN A. HITCHINGS, of Denver City, in the county of Arapahoe and Territory of Colorado, have made new and useful Improvements in Smelting Furnaces and Crucibles; and I do hereby declare the following to be a full, clear, and exact description of the nature, construction, and operation of the same, sufficient to enable one skilled in the art to which it appertains to construct and use the same, reference being had to the accompanying drawings, which are made part of this specification, and in which—

Figure 1 is a central vertical section through the smelting-furnace, and Fig. 2 is a central vertical section through the crucible and furnace.

The invention consists in the arrangement of the smelting-furnace, which consists of a suspended vessel provided with a discharge-pipe for the removal of the molten metal and a channel for the removal of the slag; second, in the crucible for roasting the tailings with quicksilver, the lid being suspended by a chain from a pulley, to admit of changing and withdrawal of the charge.

In Fig. 1 the smelting-furnace designed for the fluxing process is a circular stone structure, A A, lined with fire-proof brick or gneiss, and with a dome-top, B, and valve-chimney C. It has a door, D, near the bottom for fuel, E being the grate-bars, which rest upon a circular rim, F.

G is a blast-pipe, and H the crucible, which is charged from a door, I, in the dome-covering B.

The crucible may be made of boiler-iron and be of a conical shape, and, if of large size, is to be provided with one or two flues throughout its length. It is to be placed vertically in the center of the furnace, with but a few inches of space around its rim or larger part. Its top has half-section iron covers J J hinged to the rim.

A vessel, K, to contain hot water, is placed above the crucible, with a faucet, L, by which water is drawn into the crucible to detach slag from its sides, as occasion may require.

The crucible has an opening, M, on one side near its bottom, with curved doors N to fit, opening outwardly into the truck or passage O, which, passing through the furnace-walls, affords the means for discharge of the refuse of the charges introduced into the crucible.

A curved iron pipe, P, of an inch or two in diameter, screwed into or riveted to the bottom of the crucible, passes out through the furnace-walls, and serves to draw off the melted ores when sufficiently refined, to be thrown into cold water or cast in molds. The inner opening of the pipe is protected from stoppage by a curved iron plate, Q, scalloped round the edge covering the opening in the roller of the crucible and supported by proper bearings. The pipe P is to be closed by a clay plug externally.

The object of the improvement is the treatment of auriferous and argentiferous ores, which contain sulphurets, &c., for the purpose of removing the sulphur, arsenic, and mineral oils contained therein, after which they may be permeated by the vapor of quicksilver appropriately introduced. The addition of bicarbonate of soda to the extent of one-twentieth of the weight of the material hastens and perfects the process.

The result is treated in an arrastra, and the amalgam retorted, except the button of metal from the crucible, which is broken up and smelted.

The tight chimney and dome carry off the poisonous gases, and the covers of the crucible should fit closely, but not tightly. They may be weighted, but not attached.

The crucible may be arranged, as in Fig. 2, with a lid suspended by a chain and tackle for convenience of manipulation.

Having described my invention, what I claim therein as new, and desire to secure by Letters Patent, is—

1. The arrangement of the crucible, with its dome-covering, sectional lid, and discharge-openings M P, substantially as and for the purpose described.

2. The combination, with the crucible, of the water-supply tank K, as and for the purpose described.

The above specification of my invention signed by me this 1st day of May, A. D. 1865.

JOHN A. HITCHINGS.

Witnesses:
B. HOBBS.
J. M. GALLEMORE.

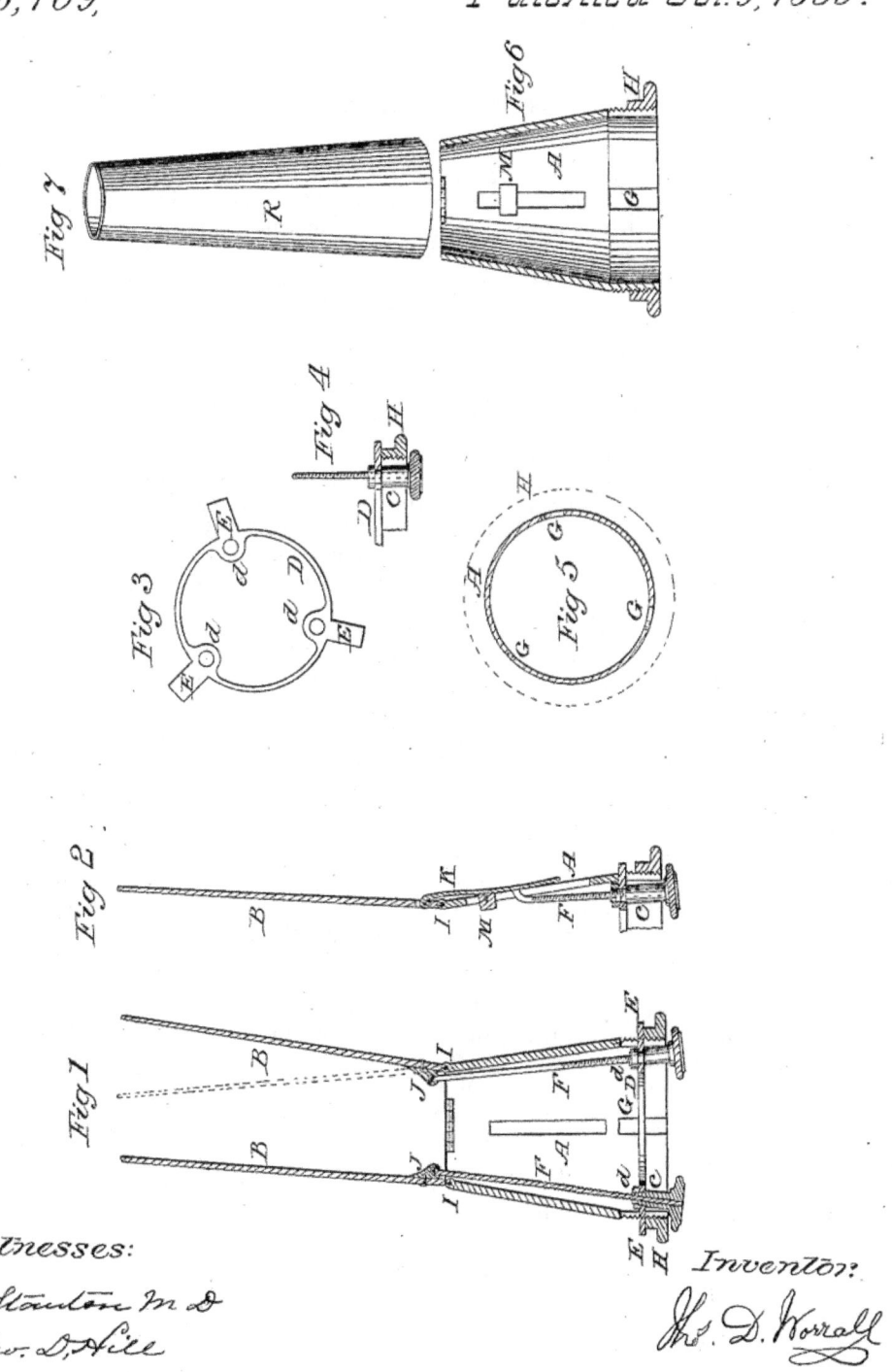

UNITED STATES PATENT OFFICE.

THOS. D. WORRALL, OF CENTRAL CITY, COLORADO TERRITORY.

IMPROVEMENT IN SPECULUMS.

Specification forming part of Letters Patent No. **58,709**, dated October 9, 1866.

To all whom it may concern:

Be it known that I, THOMAS D. WORRALL, of Central City, in the county of Gilpin and Territory of Colorado, have invented certain new and useful Improvements in Vaginal and other Speculums; and I do hereby declare that the following is a full, clear, and exact description thereof, reference being had to the accompanying drawings, and to the letters of reference marked thereon.

My entire invention relates to mechanical contrivances or devices designed to improve that class of surgical instruments known as "speculums," and thereby to remove certain objections to their use as now constructed.

On reference to Ricord's four-valve or any other speculum in common use it will be seen that the expansion commences directly at or near to the outer rim of the instrument, at best in the neighborhood of the labia majora or labia minora; and in order to expand the vaginal walls of the immediate vicinity of the os uteri considerable expansion of the instrument takes place in the neighborhood of the pelvic bones at their junction to form the osseous portion at the base of the pelvic strait, which, in certain condition of the parts well known to professional men, occasions very serious inconvenience to the patient, and sometimes renders the use of the speculum impossible.

To remedy the defect I remove the joint of the valves sufficiently far into that portion of the speculum which passes into the vagina to prevent all possible pressure in the neighborhood of the bones, in a manner described hereinafter.

Another objection to the use of valved speculums consists in the liability of the delicate membrane lining the inner coat of the vagina falling between the valves of the speculum in such a manner that when the valves are being closed, in order to the removal of the instrument, serious mischief is frequently done by pinching the exposed parts between the falling valves.

Serious accidents have sometimes happened in the dropping of caustic preparations from the holder onto the vaginal membrane while engaged in operations requiring their use.

There are also certain flabby or loose conditions of the vaginal walls in which they would obtrude between the open valves of the speculum in such a manner as to preclude the possibility of making correct observations or successfully performing desired operations.

These last three named difficulties are obviated by the use of flexible rubber, as hereinafter set forth.

It is sometimes difficult, in cases where the os uteri has been forced from its normal position by malposition of the uterus, to obtain a view of the cervix by using the ordinary speculum where all the valves move simultaneously, the os uteri frequently falling behind and being hid by one of the valves of the instrument. This difficulty may be obviated by moving one valve at a time, as provided for in my invention.

Having stated the objects of my invention, I now proceed to describe the methods in which I accomplish them.

Figure 1 is a three-valved speculum, in which one valve is seen closed, and one opened, and one detached, and in which the screws and joints are seen inside of the speculum. Fig. 2 is a section of the speculum in which one valve is operated by a screw and nut on the inside moving on a slide on the outside of the valve. Fig. 3 is a ring with flanges on the outside and holes through which the revolving nut passes that operates the valves. Fig. 4 is a section of this ring, showing the manner in which the revolving nut is secured to it, and also the manner in which the ring running round the outer end of the speculum operates upon its flanges. Fig. 5 is the top or outside end of the speculum, within which the ring, Fig. 3, is made to work. Fig. 6 is the body of the speculum with all its valves detached. Fig. 7 is the rubber covering.

The letters of reference on each part are made to correspond in all the figures.

A in Figs. 1 and 6 is a cone-shaped tube with a thread and nut, H, three slots, (marked G,) and three hinges, I.

B are valves, connected with A by the hinges I. C are three nuts tapped to receive and operate on the screws F. They have milled heads, by which they are turned, and are loosely fastened to the ring, Fig. 3, through the holes d.

D is a ring designed to operate up and down

the inside of the tube A for the space of half-inch or more, and contains on its outer edge three flanges, E, to drop into the corresponding slots G on Figs. 1 and 6, and seen also on the end view on Fig. 5 at G.

E are the flanges alluded to above. F are screws connected by joints to the valves at J and with the thumb-nuts G, for the purpose of raising or lowering said valves.

G are three slots cut in A about half-inch deep, and in which the flanges E move up and down. H is a nut with thread cut on the inside and milled on the outside, made to screw on the extreme end of A, and to operate on the flanges E after they have passed through G.

J are studs securely fastened to the valves B, and having joints to connect with the screw F, B being connected with A by the hinges I. The ring, Fig. 3, is placed inside of A, and kept in its place by the flanges E working in the slots G. The screws F are next connected by joints to the stud J and are screwed into the nuts C. After said nuts have been passed through the holes d and are set to the required distance, I next screw the nut H onto the outside of A, the edge of which, pressing upon the flanges E, forces that down with its attached nuts and screws, by which means I force open simultaneously the valves B; but should I desire to operate only one or two of the valves, I should shorten the screws of those I desired to remain down, and thus open one or more at pleasure.

In Fig. 2, K is a joint operating on the outside of the valve B, moved in the same way by the screw F. This joint works by a pulling rather than a pushing motion; and should I adopt this in the place of the joint J, I must place the nut H under the flanges E instead of over them, as in the present drawings.

Before introducing my speculum I draw over it or have securely fastened to it a fine case of rubber or other flexible material, Fig. 7, bringing it over all the joints, so that when I operate the valves the rubber expands with them, making continuous pressure upon all parts of the vagina, affording a protection against possible accidents from the use of caustic, and preventing the folds of the vaginal wall from falling between and being injured by the closing valves.

I do not confine myself to any particular device for operating the valves of the speculum, but will use these or any others that are suitable.

Having described my invention and its operations, what I claim as new, and desire to secure by Letters Patent, is—

1. So constructing a vaginal speculum that the motion of its valves shall be confined exclusively to that portion of the vagina which is inside the pelvic bone.

2. So constructing a speculum that the whole of its valves may be worked simultaneously or one or more separately, at the pleasure of the operator.

3. The use of rubber or other flexible material either securely fastened to or loosely surrounding a valved speculum, and operating with it, for the purposes set forth.

4. The screw F, in combination with the joint J and the nut C, for the purposes set forth.

5. The joint K, in combination with the screw F and the nut C, for the purposes set forth.

6. The ring D, in combination with the tube A, the nut H, the nuts C, the screws F, the joints J and K, and the valves B, for the purposes set forth.

THOS. D. WORRALL.

Witnesses:
J. O. STANTON,
GEO. D. HILL.

A. H. RICHARDSON.
Smelting Furnace.

No. 69,025. Patented Sept. 17, 1867.

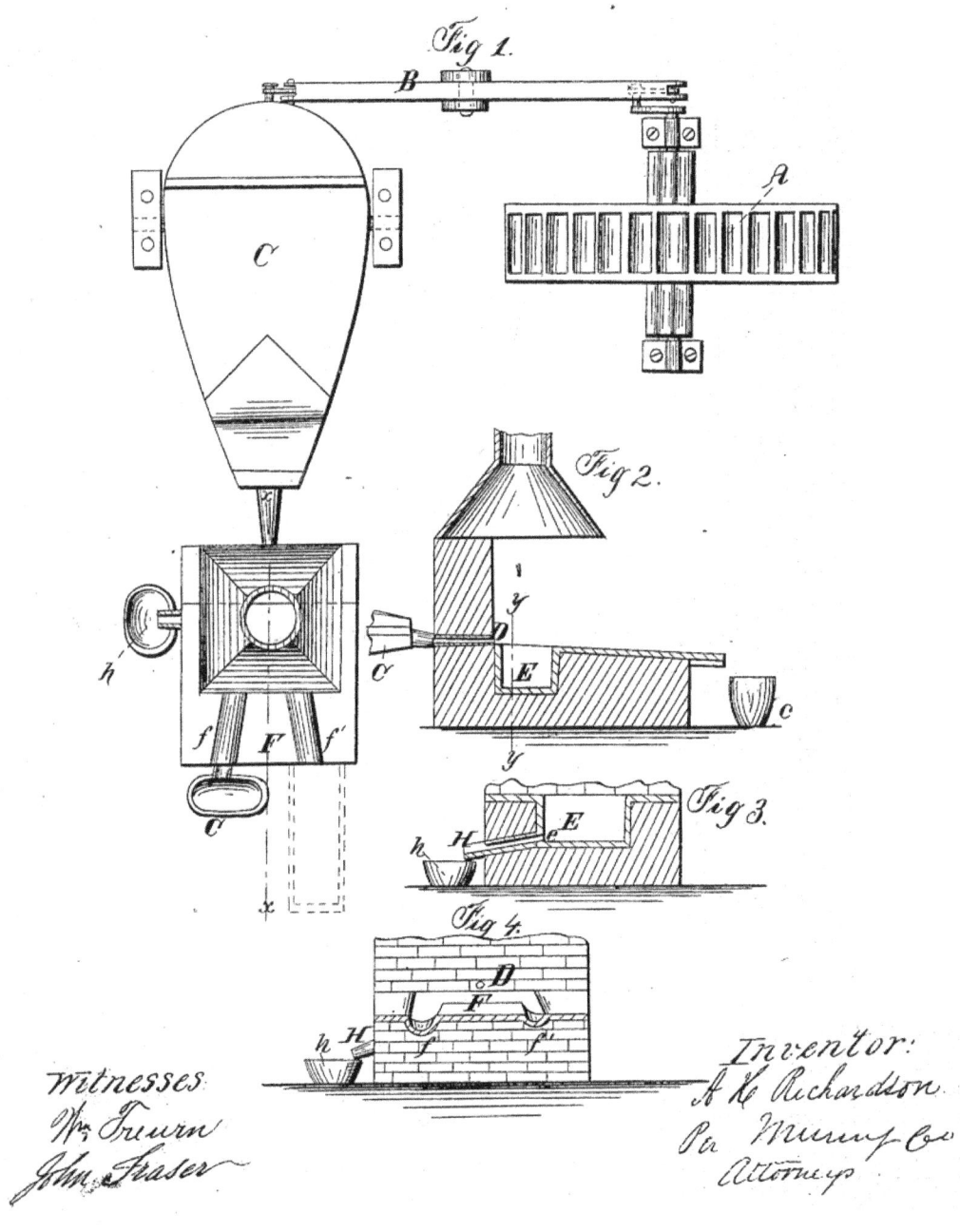

United States Patent Office.

ALFRED H. RICHARDSON, OF DENVER, COLORADO.

Letters Patent No. 69,025, dated September 17, 1867.

IMPROVED FURNACE FOR SMELTING ORES OF SILVER.

The Schedule referred to in these Letters Patent and making part of the same.

TO ALL WHOM IT MAY CONCERN:

Be it known that I, A. H. RICHARDSON, of Denver, in the county of Arapahoe, and Territory of Colorado, have invented a new and improved Furnace for Smelting Ores; and I do hereby declare that the following is a full, clear, and exact description thereof, which will enable others skilled in the art to make and use the same, reference being had to the accompanying drawings, forming part of this specification.

This invention relates to an improvement in furnaces for smelting silver. It consists in directing a blast upon the ores treated with charcoal, in a furnace having three apertures at different levels, for the separation of the slag, silver, and lead by gravitation. In the accompanying drawings—

Figure 1 is a top view of my improved smelting-furnace.

Figure 2 is a vertical section thereof through line $x\,x$.

Figure 3 is a like section through the line $y\,y$, and

Figure 4 is a front view.

Similar letters of reference indicate corresponding parts.

A is a water-wheel, or other source of power; B, the working-beam, attached to the bottom lid of the bellows C. D is the fire, of which the blast is directed upon the ores, which, treated with charcoal, are in the furnace-box E. The box E is furnished with an apron, F, having two grooves, $f\,f'$, at different levels, the slag rising to the top and flowing off at f' into a sluice-box of water, the silver flowing off at f into the pot G. The lead, by its greater gravity, falls through a hole, c, at the bottom of the box E, and flows through duct H into the pot h.

I assert that by treating the ore with charcoal in the furnace, as above described, the silver and lead are effectually and cheaply separated and the antimony desulphurized.

What I claim as new, and desire to secure by Letters Patent, is—

A smelting-furnace, having the blast supplied upon the ores in a furnace-box, provided with an apron, in manner as above set forth, and furnished with three apertures at different levels, in manner and for the purposes substantially as above set forth and described.

The above specification of my invention signed by me this 27th day of May, 1867.

ALFRED H. RICHARDSON.

Witnesses:
H. O. WAGONER,
B. L. FORD.

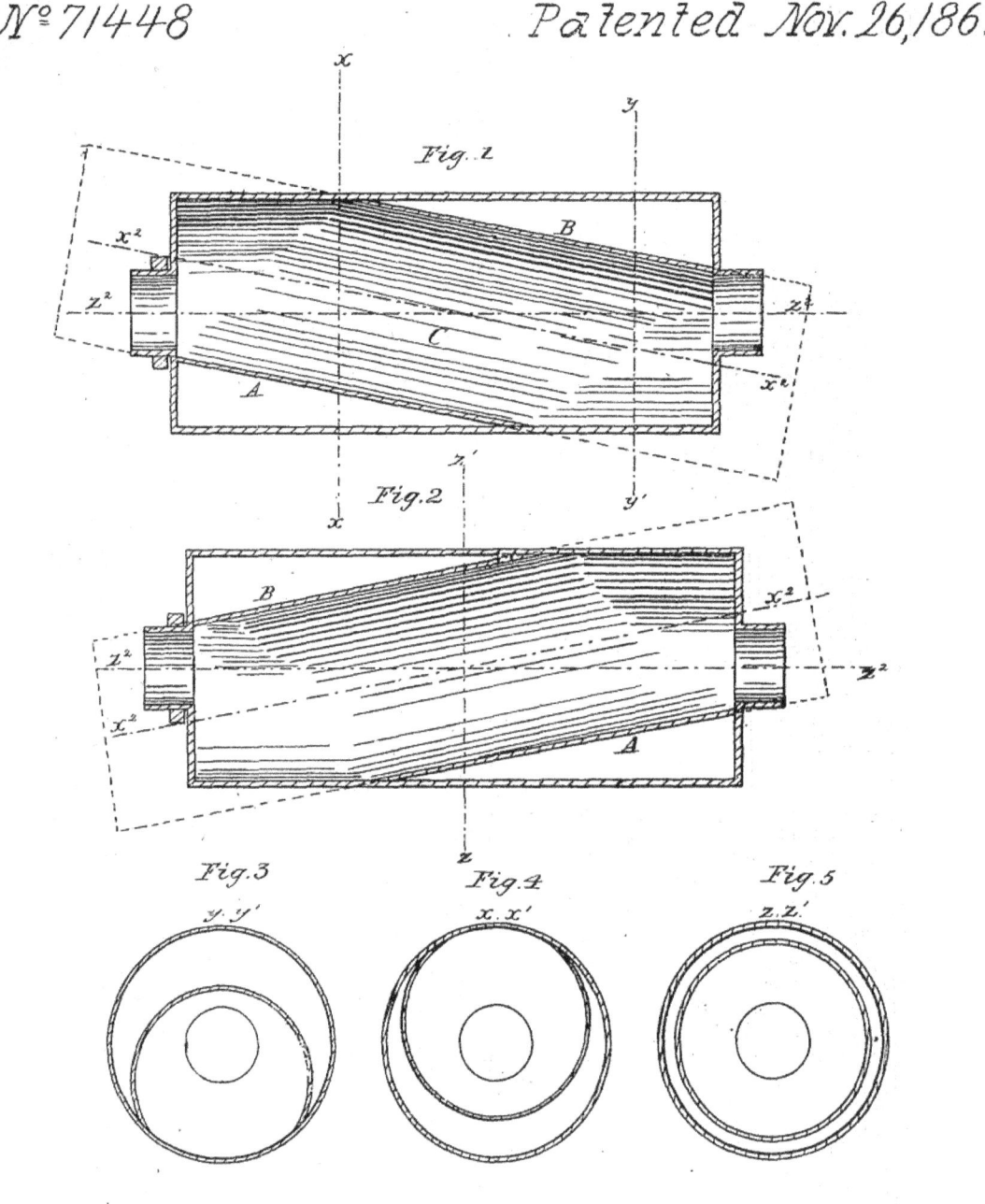

UNITED STATES PATENT OFFICE.

WILLIAM BRUCKNER, OF CENTRAL CITY, COLORADO.

IMPROVEMENT IN FURNACES FOR ROASTING ORES.

Specification forming part of Letters Patent No. **71,448**, dated November 26, 1867.

To all whom it may concern:

Be it known that I, WILLIAM BRUCKNER, of Central City, Gilpin county, Colorado Territory, have invented certain new and useful Improvements in Furnaces for Roasting Ores, &c.; and I do hereby declare the following description and accompanying drawings are sufficient to enable any person skilled in the art or science to which it most nearly appertains to make and use my said invention or improvements without further invention or experiment.

The nature of my invention and improvements consists in making the interior of the box or cylinder, or a portion of it, at an angle of about twenty degrees from the axis of revolution, so that, as the cylinder or box is turned, the ore will, by its own gravity, roll alternately from one end toward the other at every revolution of the cylinder; and in arranging the journals of the cylinder or box diagonally opposite to each other; also, in making openings in the ends of the box or cylinder or hollow journals, for supplying and discharging the ores and for the blaze and heat of the fire to enter and roast the ores or contents of the cylinder.

In the accompanying drawings, Figures 1 and 2 show a cylinder with my improvements cut longitudinally through the center. Fig. 3 is a cross-section on the line $y\,y'$ of Fig. 1. Fig. 4 is a cross-section on the line $x\,x'$ of Fig. 1. Fig. 5 is a cross-section on the line $z\,z'$ of Fig. 2.

In these drawings, C is the outside of the cylinder; and D D the ends, and E E the hollow journals, of the cylinder. A is a wedge-shaped cylindrical incline, on the lower side of the cylinder C, beginning just below the opening in the journal E and extending about two-thirds of the length of the cylinder, at an angle of about twenty degrees to the axis of the cylinder C. A section of this on the line $x\,x'$ is shown in Fig. 4. This incline A, when the cylinder is in the position shown, causes the ores being roasted to roll from the high part of the incline next to journal toward and to the opposite end of the cylinder as the cylinder is turned in the process of roasting the ore. The incline B is similar to the incline A, and arranged diagonally opposite to it in the cylinder C, as shown in the drawings, and Fig. 3 is a cross-section of it on the line $y\,y'$. This incline B causes the ores being roasted to roll in a direction opposite to that they roll on the incline A as the cylinder is turned, so that the ore is kept constantly in motion as the cylinder is turned, rolling or sliding alternately in each direction from both ends of the cylinder.

My improved cylinder may be made of cast or wrought iron, or partly of both, and the inclines A and B may be made of the same materials, or such others as will answer the purpose, as brick or cement, proper brackets or stays being provided to hold the brick and cement in place. This cylinder may be made of iron without the parts represented outside of the inclines A and B, if it is supported by the journals; or, if not supported by the journals, it may be provided with ribs or flanges on the outside concentric with its axis of revolution, which ribs may be grooved for the chains running over pulleys, which turn and hold up the cylinder, which may be steadied by friction-rollers; or the cylinder may be turned by wheels or pulleys arranged under it, which pulleys may have ribs working in the grooves in the ribs on the cylinder, so as to turn it without chains. This cylinder may be provided with a furnace to roast the ores in it and a chimney to conduct off the smoke, such as are shown and described in my Patent No. 60,134, and dated December 4, 1866, or such other kind of furnace or chimney as will answer the purpose. The cylinder may also be provided with a door on the side, for charging and discharging the cylinder, when required; or it may be charged and discharged through the journals or openings in the ends.

In operating this cylinder, a charge is put in, and, as the cylinder is turned, all the ore is caused to roll or slide down the incline A in the first half of the revolution, and in the next half-revolution the ore rolls or slides back again on the incline B, so that all the pieces or particles of ore are kept constantly in motion, backward and forward, and perfectly exposed to the oxidizing influence of the heat and air in the cylinder.

What I claim as my invention and improvement in cylindrical rotary furnaces for roasting ores, &c., is—

1. Making or arranging the interior of the box or cylinder at an angle with or to the axis of revolution, substantially as described, so that, as the cylinder or box is turned, the contents will, by their own gravity, roll or slide alternately from one end toward the other at each revolution of the cylinder.

2. Making the journals at the ends of the cylinder diagonally opposite to each of the inclines or interior working-surfaces of the cylinder.

3. In combination with a box or cylinder having its journals arranged diagonally to its interior inclines or working-surfaces, as described, making openings in the ends or hollow journals for the blaze and heat to enter the cylinder to roast the ores, or for supplying and discharging the ores to be roasted.

WILLIAM BRUCKNER.

Witnesses:
HENRY GRANNIS,
ED. C. PARMELEE.

Jesse H. Harlan & Thos. Pomeroy, Improved GLOVE CUTTER.

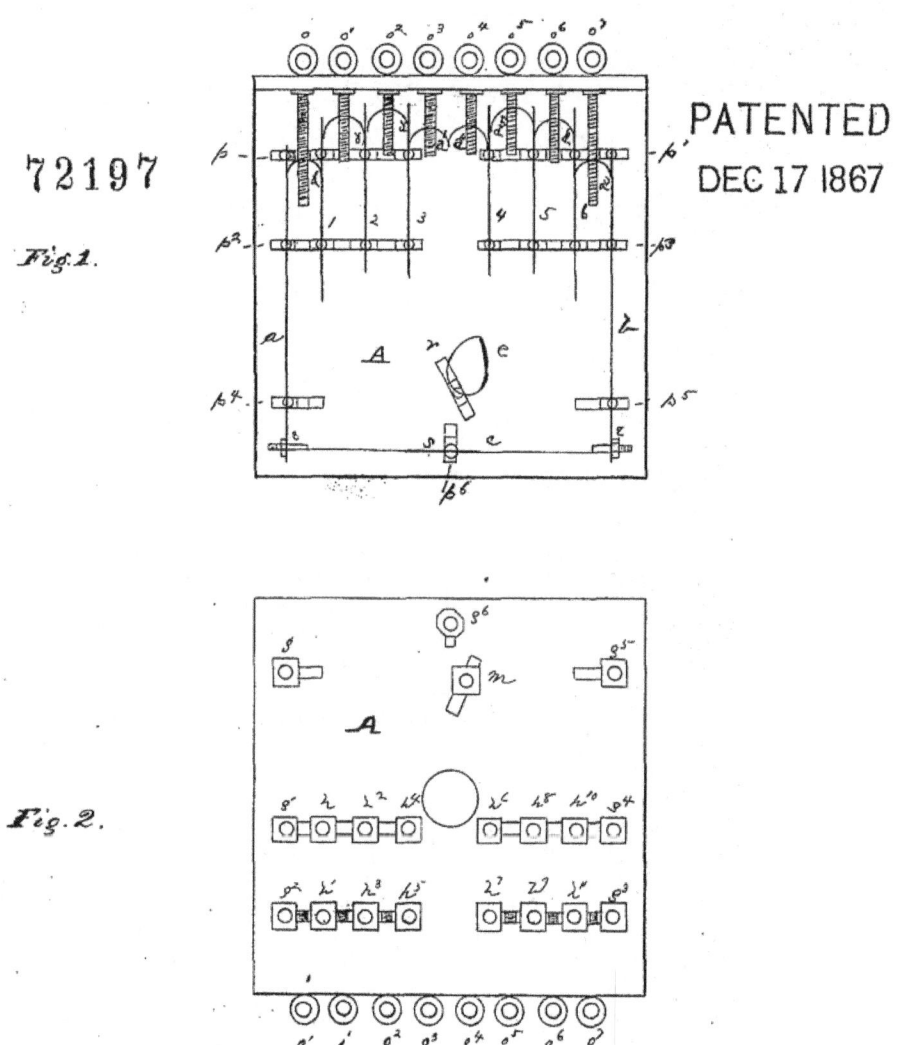

No. 72197 — Fig. 1. Fig. 2.

PATENTED DEC 17 1867

Witnesses.
Saml. S. Boyd
Joseph Dickson

Inventor:
Jesse H. Harlan
Thos. Pomeroy
per Boyd & Co. Attys

United States Patent Office.

JESSE H. HARLAN AND THOMAS POMEROY, OF DENVER CITY, COLORADO, ASSIGNORS TO THEMSELVES AND WILLIAM H. HARLAN.

Letters Patent No. 72,197, dated December 17, 1867.

IMPROVEMENT IN MACHINES FOR CUTTING OUT GLOVES.

The Schedule referred to in these Letters Patent and making part of the same.

TO ALL WHOM IT MAY CONCERN:

Be it known that we, JESSE H. HARLAN and THOMAS POMEROY, of Denver City, Arapahoe county, Territory of Colorado, have invented a new and useful Improved Glove-Cutter, of which the following is a full, clear, and exact description, reference being had to the annexed drawing, making a part of this specification, in which—

Figure 1 represents a bottom view of our invention.

Figure 2 represents a top view of same.

Similar letters indicate like parts.

The object of our invention is to produce a glove-cutter, by which the whole glove may be cut at once from one piece of material, and which may be readily adjusted so as to cut gloves of different size.

It consists of a platen, A, figs. 1 and 2, to the under side of which, as seen in fig. 1, are fixed two parallel knives, a and b, and a third knife, c, at right angles to them, and attached to them at its extremities, the knives a and b being the length of the largest-sized glove, and the knife c twice the width of such glove. Between the knives a and b, and parallel with them, are arranged six knives, 1, 2, 3, 4, 5, 6, their length being equal to that of the respective fingers of the largest-sized glove, the little finger being represented by 1 and 6; the distance between a and 1, 1 and 2, 2 and 3, 4 and 5, 5 and 6, 6 and b, being equal to the width of a finger of the largest-sized glove, while the distance between 3 and 4 is twice that width. Between these knives, at their extremities, are fixed circular knives $d\ d^1\ d^2\ d^3\ d^4\ d^5\ d^6\ d^7$, at a distance from the base of the knives 1, 2, 3, 4, 5, 6, corresponding to the length of the fingers of the largest-sized glove. An oval knife, e, is placed in the position where the thumb of the glove would fall. The knives a, b, and c are held in position by bolts, which, passing through the platen, are fastened by the nuts $g\ g^1\ g^2\ g^3\ g^4\ g^5\ g^6$, while the knives 1, 2, 3, 4, 5, 6, are attached to bolts which are fastened in the same manner by the nuts $h\ h^1\ h^2\ h^3\ h^4\ h^5\ h^6\ h^7\ h^8\ h^9\ h^{10}\ h^{11}$. The oval knife e likewise has a bolt secured by a nut, m, all of which are shown in fig. 2. The circular knives move upon screws, $o\ o^1\ o^2\ o^3\ o^4\ o^5\ o^6\ o^7$, figs. 1 and 2, passing through a projection in the under side of the platen.

The platen being attached to a follower worked by screw, lever, or any other desired power, the bolts being fastened, and the leather from which the glove is to be cut placed beneath the platen, it is brought down upon it forcibly, and being raised, the leather will be cut in such a manner that when turned upon itself it will form a perfect glove, with the exception of the thumb and forjet. The various bolts of the straight knives slide in straight slots $p\ p^1\ p^2\ p^3\ p^4\ p^5\ p^6$, while that of the oval knife slides in an eccentric slot, r, figs. 1 and 2, and the circular knives slide in slots of the straight knives between which they are placed. The knife c is made in two parts, with a double slot, s, and its ends slide in the slots $t\ t'$ of the knives a and b.

Now if it be desired to make a glove of a different size, the nuts being loosened, the knives may be readily adjusted as desired, and then, the nuts being tightened, the glove may be cut as before. The thumb and forjets are cut in the ordinary shape by means of instruments constructed in parts with slots, on the principle already described, and may be fixed to the platen so that the complete glove may be cut at once. We claim this construction as our invention.

The advantages of this invention are obvious, since one machine may be made to do the work of several, by reason of being adjustable to gloves of different sizes.

We do not claim to be the first inventors of a machine cutting the whole glove at once; but

What we do claim as our invention, and desire to secure by Letters Patent, is—

The adjustable knives of a glove-cutter, when constructed and arranged substantially as shown and specified.

JESSE H. HARLAN,
THOMAS POMEROY.

Witnesses:
ALEXANDER DAVIDSON,
ALEX. W. ATKINS.

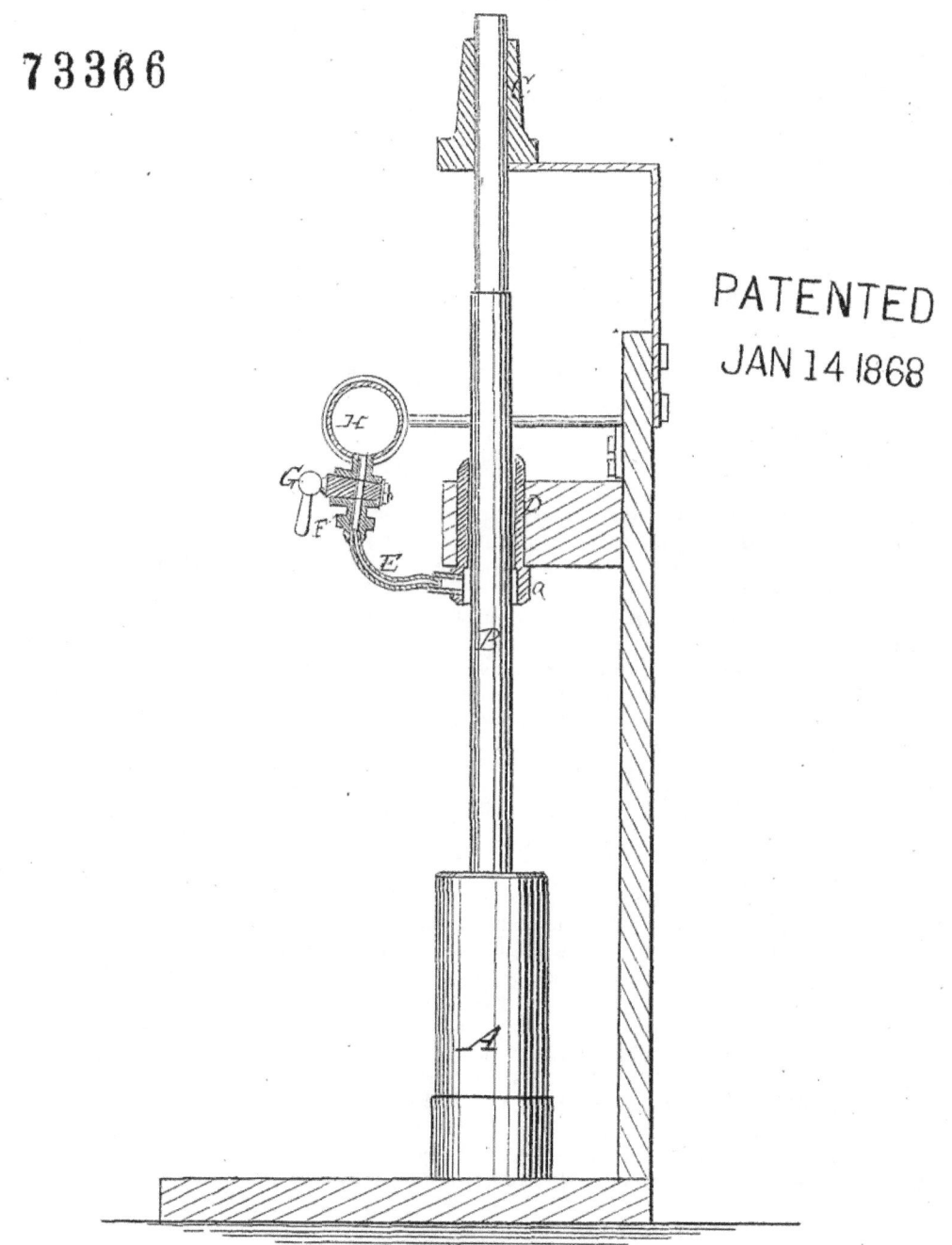

United States Patent Office.

GEORGE R. MITCHELL, OF NEVADA, COLORADO.

Letters Patent No. 73,366, dated January 14, 1868.

IMPROVEMENT IN STAMP-MILLS.

The Schedule referred to in these Letters Patent and making part of the same.

TO ALL WHOM IT MAY CONCERN:

Be it known that I, GEORGE R. MITCHELL, of Nevada, in the county of Gilpin, and Territory of Colorado, have invented a new and useful Improvement in Stamp-Mills for crushing quartz; and that the following description, taken in connection with the accompanying drawing, hereinafter referred to, forms a full and exact specification of the same, wherein I have set forth the nature and principles of my said improvement, by which my invention may be distinguished from all others of a similar class, together with such parts as I claim, and desire to have secured to me by Letters Patent.

The chief difficulty attending the operation of stamp-mills for crushing quartz, consists in the wearing of the stems and the lower boxes of the same, a result due to the adhesion of pulverized rock or quartz to the stems, and the introduction of the pulverized rock or quartz into the boxes, by the elevation or upward movement of the stems. My invention fully obviates this difficulty; and it consists in introducing into the lower boxes of the stems, water from a supply-pipe, and in such a manner as to keep the stems perfectly clean or free from the pulverized quartz, and also keep the stems in a perfectly-lubricated state.

The accompanying drawing represents a side sectional view of a stamp having my improvement applied to it.

A represents a stamp of a stamp-mill, and B the stem thereof, working in bearings C D. The upper bearing, C, may be of usual construction, but the lower one, D, is rather larger in diameter internally, at its lower end, than at any other part, and this enlarged portion forms a water-chamber, a, which communicates, by means of an elastic hose, E, with a metal tube, F, the latter being provided with a stop-cock, G. The tube F is connected to and communicates with a water-supply pipe, H, as shown clearly in the drawing.

It will be seen, from the above description, that the stamp-mill is supplied with water through the lower bearings, D, it being understood that in a stamp-mill a series of stamps is used, and the crushed or pulverized quartz (pulp) carried off by a flow or current of water through the box in which the stamps work. The flow of water from the pipe H is regulated by the cocks G. The water passes from the chambers a down around the stems B, keeping the latter clean, or perfectly free from pulverized rock or quartz, and also keeps the lower bearings in a perfectly-lubricated state while the mill is in operation.

Having thus described my invention, I claim as new, and desire to secure by Letters Patent—

1. The bearing D, having the lower portion enlarged, forming a water-chamber, a, substantially as described.
2. In combination with the above, and with the stem B of stamp A, I claim the water-supply pipe H, tube F, stop-cock G, and flexible hose E, substantially as described and for the purpose specified.

The above specification of my invention signed by me, this 16th day of November, 1866.

GEORGE R. MITCHELL.

Witnesses:
HORACE H. ATKINS,
EDWD. B. STILLINGS.

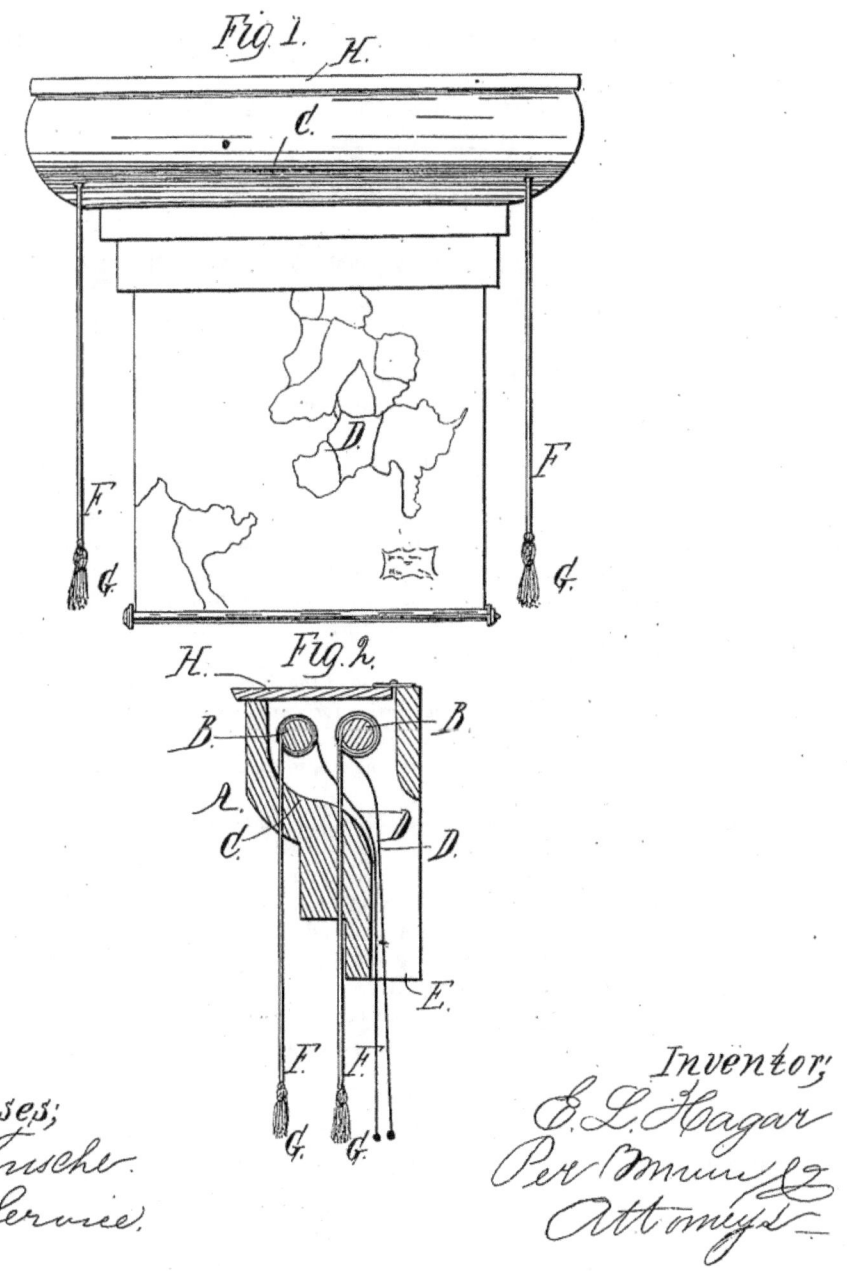

United States Patent Office.

E. L. HAGAR, OF EMPIRE CITY, COLORADO.

Letters Patent No. 77,813, dated May 12, 1868.

IMPROVEMENT IN CHART-ROLLERS.

The Schedule referred to in these Letters Patent and making part of the same.

TO ALL WHOM IT MAY CONCERN:

Be it known that I, E. L. HAGAR, of Empire City, in the county of Clear Creek, and Territory of Colorado, have made and invented a new and useful Improvement in Chart or Map-Roller; and I do hereby declare that the following is a full, clear, and exact description thereof, which will enable those skilled in the art to make and use the same, reference being had to the accompanying drawings, and to the letters of reference marked thereon.

The present invention relates to a roller for maps and other similar charts, and it consists in arranging the roller therefor within a case, that is suitably constructed to allow the map or other chart attached thereto to be rolled up or unrolled at pleasure, through and by means of cords and tassels, or other suitable devices, the said case, when the charts are rolled up, encasing the same, and protecting them from being soiled or injured.

In the accompanying plate of drawings, my improved roller for charts, &c., is illustrated—

Figure 1 being a front view of the same, and

Figure 2 a transverse vertical section, taken in the plane of the line $x\,x$, fig. 1.

A, in the drawings, represents my improved roller-device for maps and other charts, which, in the present instance, consists of two rollers B within a case, C, arranged so as to turn therein, and each roller provided with a map or chart, D, around which they are wound, and passing out, when unwound, through the opening E in the bottom of the said case C.

F, cords attached to rollers B at one end, and at their other passing out of case C, and provided with tassels G, for convenience in manipulating them.

H a cover to case C. This cover is hinged thereto, so as to be susceptible of being opened and closed at pleasure for an inspection and removal or insertion of the rollers B, as may be desired.

Having thus described my invention, I claim as new, and desire to secure by Letters Patent—

The chart-roller constructed as described, consisting of the case C having the hinged lid H, and adapted to receive the chart-rollers B, said chart passing through the curved opening E, their operating-cords F passing through separate openings in front of the charts, as herein shown and described.

The above specification of my invention signed by me, this 10th day of August, 1867.

E. L. HAGAR.

Witnesses:
   GEO. C. MUNSON,
   DAVID J. BALL.

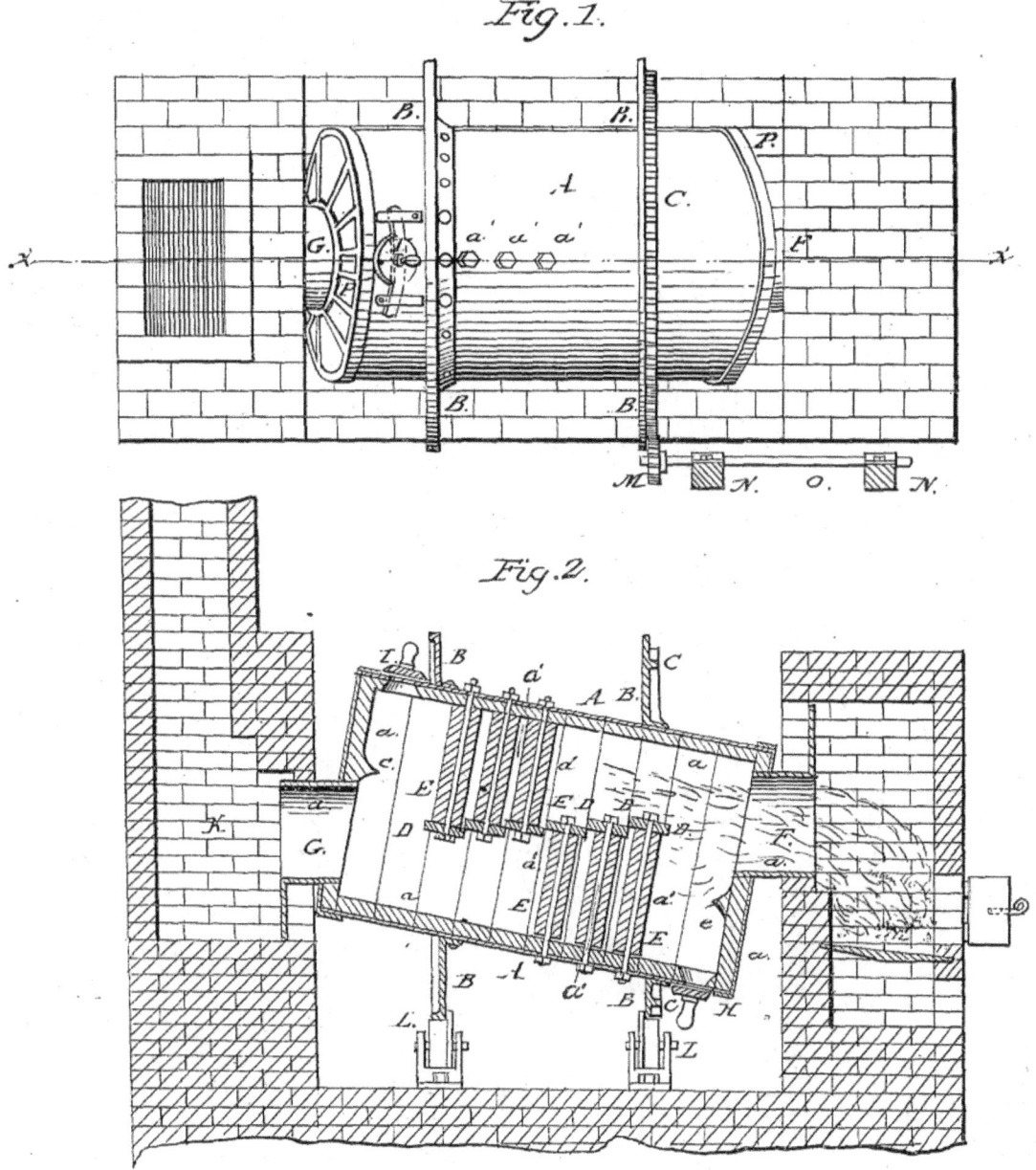

COLLIER, CUSHMAN & FARRELL.
Ore Furnace.

No. 78,928.

2 Sheets—Sheet 2.

Patented June 16, 1868.

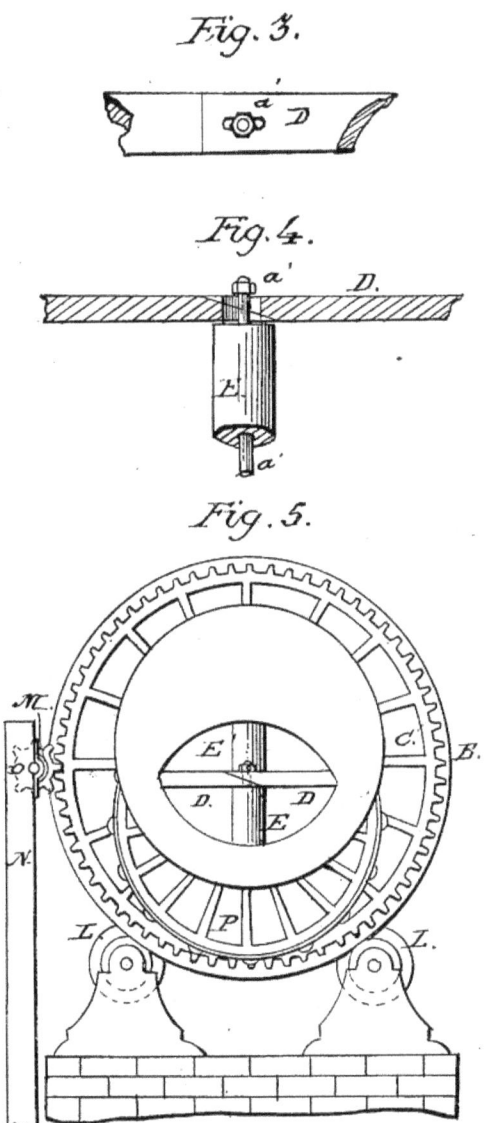

United States Patent Office.

DAVID C. COLLIER, SAMUEL CUSHMAN, AND NEWELL E. FARRELL, OF CENTRAL CITY, COLORADO TERRITORY.

Letters Patent No. 78,928, dated June 16, 1868.

IMPROVEMENT IN ORE-ROASTING FURNACES.

The Schedule referred to in these Letters Patent and making part of the same.

TO ALL WHOM IT MAY CONCERN:

Be it known that we, DAVID C. COLLIER, SAMUEL CUSHMAN, and NEWELL E. FARRELL, of Central City, in the county of Gilpin, Colorado Territory, have invented a new and useful Improvement in Ore-Furnaces; and we do hereby declare that the following is a full, clear, and exact description thereof, which will enable others skilled in the art to make and use the same, reference being had to the accompanying drawings, forming part of this specification.

This invention relates to a new and improved method of constructing furnaces for the wasting and chloridizing of ores, whereby the same is more effectually and economically done.

In the accompanying plates of drawings—

Figure 1 is a side view of our invention.

Figure 2 represents a central longitudinal section of the same, taken in the line $x\ x$, fig. 1.

Figure 3 is a detail view of the partition-tiles, showing the manner of jointing and supporting the same in the centre.

Figure 4 is a detail view of the same, showing also the tiles by which the supporting-rods are protected against the fire.

Figure 5 is an end view of our invention.

Similar letters of reference indicate corresponding parts.

The cylinder A is made of boiler-iron, of the thickness of about three-sixteenths of an inch, and may be of any convenient length, according to the quantity of ore to be treated; but we have found the length of ten feet, or thereabouts, to answer all the requirement, the diameter of the same being about five feet, and is provided with suitable heads P, to which are rigidly attached the tubes F and G.

The cylinder A is lined upon the inside with fire-bricks or tiles, or other suitable material, so as to form a fire-proof lining, a. Said lining a may be of any convenient thickness, as of the thickness of about three inches. Said cylinder A is provided, near one end of the same, on the side further from the tube G, with a man-hole, H, and near the other end of the same, on the opposite side, or the side further from the tube F, with a man-hole, I, by means of which the charge to the cylinder A is both admitted and discharged. Said man-holes H and I are provided with suitable covers, the joints around the same being luted for closing said man-holes.

Extending across the cylinder A, from one side to the other, is a partial partition, formed of iron or other suitable material, or of the tiles D, as shown in the drawing.

The tiles D, commencing at about sixteen inches from one end of the cylinder A, are lapped one upon the other, extend to within sixteen inches of the other end of said cylinder A, as shown in the drawing, fig. 2, and so that said tiles D form a partition in a plane, passing through and coincident with the rotating axis of the cylinder A, and so as to be at right angles to a line drawn from either of the man-holes H and I to said partition.

The tiles D may be made of clay, or other fire-proof substance, in two parts, masoned by one end into the lining a of the cylinder A, and lapped together in the centre of the same, one end of each part of said tiles D being bevelled off for that purpose, or the same may be arranged in any other way, so as to form a partition through the grated part of the cylinder A, as shown in the drawing. The tiles D are supported by the iron bolts a', passing through said tiles D, in the centre of the same, and the outside of the cylinder A; said bolts a' being protected against the heat by a casing of fire-proof tile, E, which said casing E also supports the tiles D.

The tiles E are made of any of the ordinary fire-proof materials for that purpose, are square in form, or may be of any convenient form, provided with a hole through the same longitudinally, to receive the bolts a', and may be formed of one piece, or of any convenient number of pieces, in which latter case they are less liable to be cracked or broken by the unequal expansion of the parts.

The bolts a' are provided on each end with nuts, by means of which the tiles D are firmly held down upon the tiles E; the nuts on the inside of the cylinder A being either protected against fire by clay, or made so large as to resist the influence of the same.

The object of the partition above described is to receive and hold the ore deposited or falling upon the same at each semi-rotation of the cylinder A, so as to receive the full action of the heat upon the same, the flame being divided by said partition, and thereby coming more immediately in contact with the particles of ore held for a time upon said partition, the ore, at every rotation of the cylinder A, by the alternate elevation and depression of each end of the same, hereinafter more fully described, being shifted nearer to the end of the cylinder.

Into each end of the cylinder are firmly bolted cast-iron heads P, in the ordinary way. The heads P are formed of arms or spokes, so as to receive fire-brick or other fire-proof substances to complete the cylinder A.

To the heads P, either a part of the same, or rigidly secured thereto, are short metallic flatted or oval tubes F and G. Said tubes F and G are made of cast iron, and are each provided, upon one side of the same, with a flange, which, with the tube itself, forms a circular plate or ring, whose centre is the centre of rotation of the cylinder A, and which is so far removed from the centre longitudinal line of the cylinder A as to give to each end of the cylinder A an alternate elevation and depression, at each revolution of the same, equal to twice the distance from the said centre of rotation to the said centre line of the cylinder, which will be about fifteen inches or one-fourth of the diameter of the cylinder A; the object of said tubes being to afford a convenient means of opening a communication with the fire in the fire-box J by the tube F, and with the flue K by the tube G, while rotating within the masonry of the same, and so as to prevent the escape of heat from the furnace J except through the cylinder.

The said tubes F and G may be of any diameter sufficient to allow the heat to pass from the fire-box J through the same, as of the longer diameter inside of about three feet, and of the shorter diameter of about two feet.

Said tubes F and G are lined in like manner as the cylinder A with the lining a.

The cylinder A is supported by and rotates upon two wheels B, around the same, as shown. Said wheels B are made of cast iron, and are provided, around the openings to receive the cylinder A, with spokes or arms, which are a part of the same, whereby the same are made lighter and cheaper. The openings to receive the cylinder A are a little larger than the cylinder A, so as that the wheels B may not be injured by the expansion of said cylinder A, and said openings are at one side of the centre of said wheels B.

Said wheels B are secured to the cylinder A by feet or chippings around the openings in the same, through which pass bolts; said bolts also passing through the cylinder A, and are provided with suitable nuts, by means of which said wheels B are firmly secured to said cylinder A.

The wheels B may be of any convenient diameter, as of the diameter of six and a half feet, and are placed at an average distance of one-quarter of the length of said cylinder A from each end of the same, and so that the cylinder A is nearest to the circumference of one of the wheels B, at one end of said cylinder A, and nearest the circumference of the other of said wheels at the other end of said cylinder A; the centre of both said wheels B being in the line of the rotation of said cylinder A, each end of the same will be alternately elevated and depressed by the rotating of the wheels B upon the friction-rollers L.

The wheels B are placed upon the cylinder A, at right angles to the centre of the rotating axis of the same, and are provided with a suitable rim to rest upon the friction-rollers L, and must be of sufficient thickness to give the requisite strength.

Upon any suitable foundation, and rotating in suitable bearings, on any blocks, so situated as to hold the cylinder A in proper position with respect to the furnace J, are the friction-wheels or rollers L, to receive the rims of the wheels B, as shown.

Upon the face of the wheel B, nearer to the fire-box J, or upon either of said wheels which may be more convenient, and upon a suitable flange for that purpose, is the spur-gearing C.

Upon any suitable support, N, and rotating in proper bearings thereon, is the driving-shaft O, and upon said shaft O, at any convenient point, is keyed a pinion, M, so as to fit into the gearing C, by means of which the cylinder A is rotated.

The gearing C upon the wheel B, and the pinion M, are to each other, with respect to their several diameters, and the number of teeth in each, in such ratio as to give the required speed to the cylinder A, which must be very slow, or about one revolution each minute.

Within the cylinders A, upon each of the heads of the same, are the shelves e, made of fire-brick, projecting inwards, so as to prevent the ore from falling out into the tubes F and G when the cylinder is rotating or being charged.

The fire-box J and flue K are constructed in the ordinary way of constructing flues and fire-boxes for treating ores; a suitable chamber being provided in the flue K to receive any ore which, by the rotation of the cylinder A, might fall into the said flue K.

The operation is such that, by placing the ore to be treated in the cylinder A, through the man-holes in each end of the same, a suitable fire burning in the fire-box J, the cylinder A is made to slowly rotate, when, by the alternate elevation and depression of each end of the cylinder A, the ore is carried from end to end of the cylinder, falling upon and retained a short time at each semi-rotation of the cylinder A, passes entirely around the partition in the same, and is thus subjected in every particle to the great heat from the fire-box J, whereby the sulphur and other impurities are driven from the ore.

Having thus described our invention, what we claim as new, and desire to secure by Letters Patent, is—

1. An apparatus for roasting and chloridizing ores, composed of a cylinder, A, rotating on an axis inclined to the true axis of the cylinder, within which, in the line of the rotating axis, is a partial partition for receiving

and retaining the ore for a short time at each semi-rotation of the said cylinder A, in combination with a fire-box, J, and flue K, substantially as shown and described, and for the purposes set forth.

2. The wheels B, in combination with a rotating cylinder, A, substantially as shown and described, and for the purposes set forth.

3. The partial partition, in a plane in the centre of the rotation of the cylinder A, and placed at right angles to a line drawn from the man-hole H or I to said partition, or its equivalent, and in combination therewith, and with any fire-box, J, substantially as shown and described, and for the purposes set forth.

The above specification of our invention signed by us, this   day of   , 1867.

DAVID C. COLLIER,
NEWELL E. FARRELL,
SAM'L CUSHMAN.

Witnesses:
  EUGENE WILDER,
  FRANK HALL.

Johnson & Froggott,

Horseshoe.

No. 82,528. Patented Sep. 29, 1868.

Fig. 1.

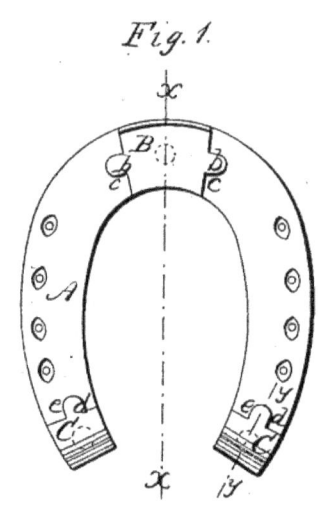

Fig. 2.

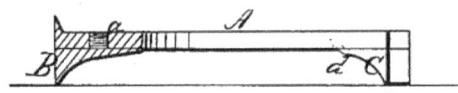

Fig. 3.

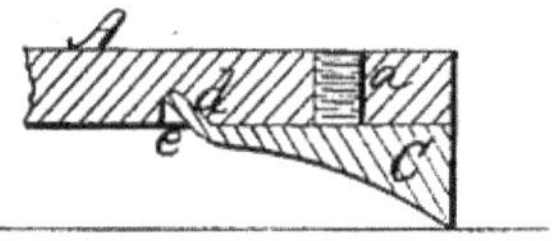

Witnesses;

Wm A Morgan
G C Cotton

Inventor;

P. C. Johnson
E. Fraggott
per Munn & Co
Attorneys

N. PETERS, PHOTO-LITHOGRAPHER, WASHINGTON, D. C.

UNITED STATES PATENT OFFICE.

P. C. JOHNSON AND EDWIN FROGGOTT, OF CENTRAL CITY, COLORADO.

IMPROVEMENT IN THE CONSTRUCTION OF HORSESHOES.

Specification forming part of Letters Patent No. **82,528**, dated September 29, 1868.

To all whom it may concern:

Be it known that we, P. C. JOHNSON and EDWIN FROGGOTT, of Central City, in the Territory of Colorado, have invented a new and useful Improvement in Horseshoes; and we do hereby declare that the following is a full, clear, and exact description thereof, which will enable others skilled in the art to make and use the same, reference being had to the accompanying drawings, forming part of this specification, in which—

Figure 1 is a view of the under side of a horseshoe having calks attached according to our invention. Fig. 2 is a section of the same, taken in the line $x\, x$, Fig. 1. Fig. 3 is a section of a portion of the same, taken in the line $y\, y$, Fig. 1.

Similar letters of reference indicate like parts.

This invention relates to a new and improved mode of securing calks to horseshoes, whereby the former may be very readily applied to and detached from the latter, and a horseshoe always kept supplied with proper calks without the aid of a smith.

In the accompanying sheet of drawings, A represents a horseshoe which is constructed in the usual form, but having a smooth under surface—that is to say, has neither toe nor heelcalks formed on it.

The calks are made separately. B is the toe-calk and C C the heel-calks. These may be constructed in the usual or any proper shape; but each has a screw, a, secured in its upper surface, and of sufficient length to pass entirely through the shoe and be flush with the upper surface thereof.

The toe-calk B is provided at each side with an arm, b, of sufficient length to admit, after the calk is screwed to the bottom of the shoe, of being bent down and fitted in holes $c\, c$ in the under side of the shoe. The heel-calks C C are provided each with an arm, d, projecting from their front ends, and these arms, when the calks are screwed to the bottom of the shoe, are bent down and fitted in holes $e\, e$, made in the under side of the same. (See more particularly Fig. 3.)

The arms of the calks bent down into holes in the shoe prevent the calks from casually unscrewing or turning; and it will be seen that the calks, when worn by use, may be readily detached and replaced by new ones.

We are aware that the use of screws for attaching removable calks to horseshoes is not new, and we therefore do not claim them; but,

Having described our invention, we claim as new and desire to secure by Letters Patent—

The arms $b\, d$, attached to or formed with the calks, and bent down into holes in the bottom or under side of the shoe to form a locking device, in combination with the screws a, substantially as shown and described.

P. C. JOHNSON.
EDWIN FROGGOTT.

Witnesses:
S. P. KENDALL,
W. F. SEARS.

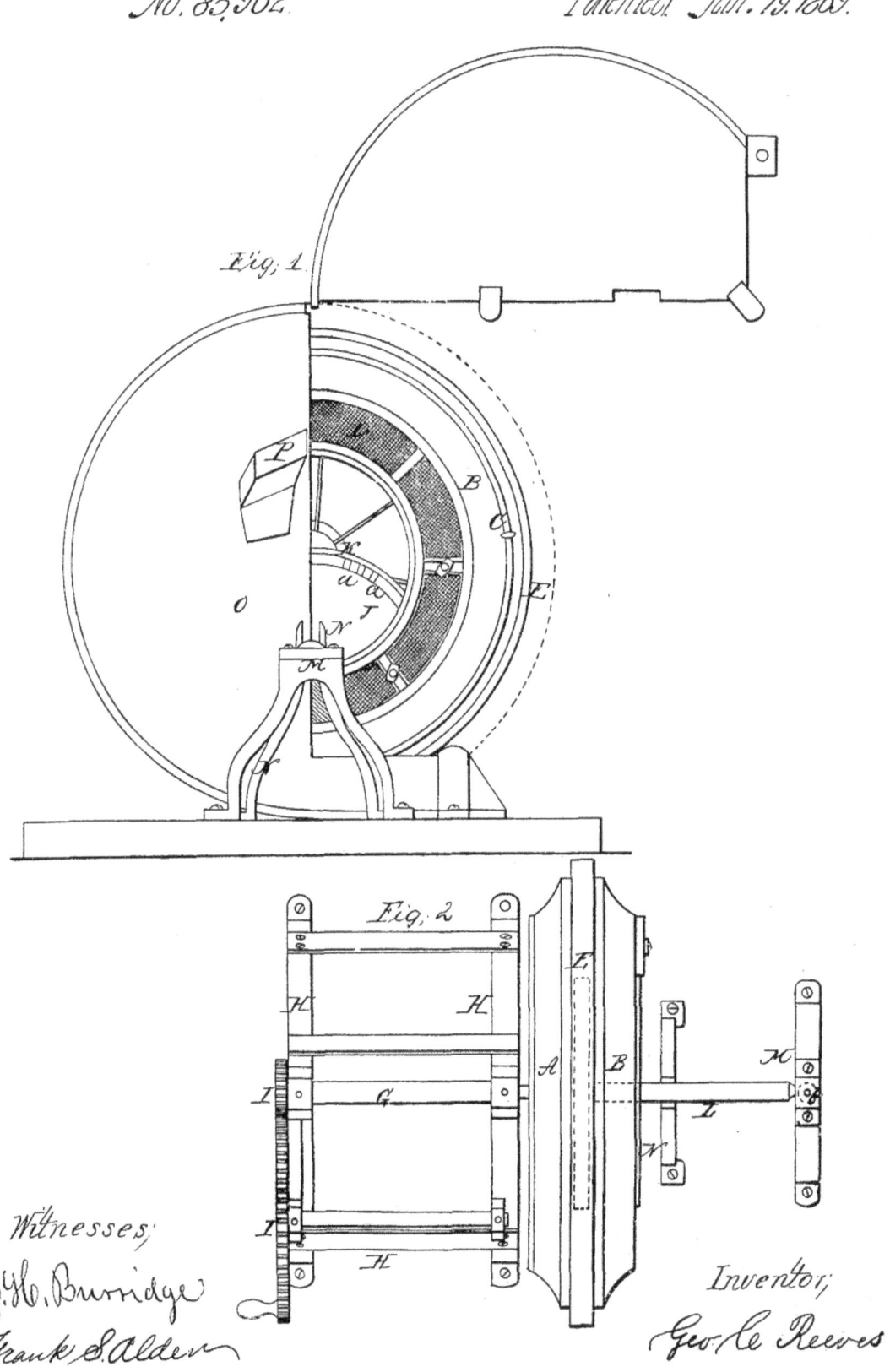

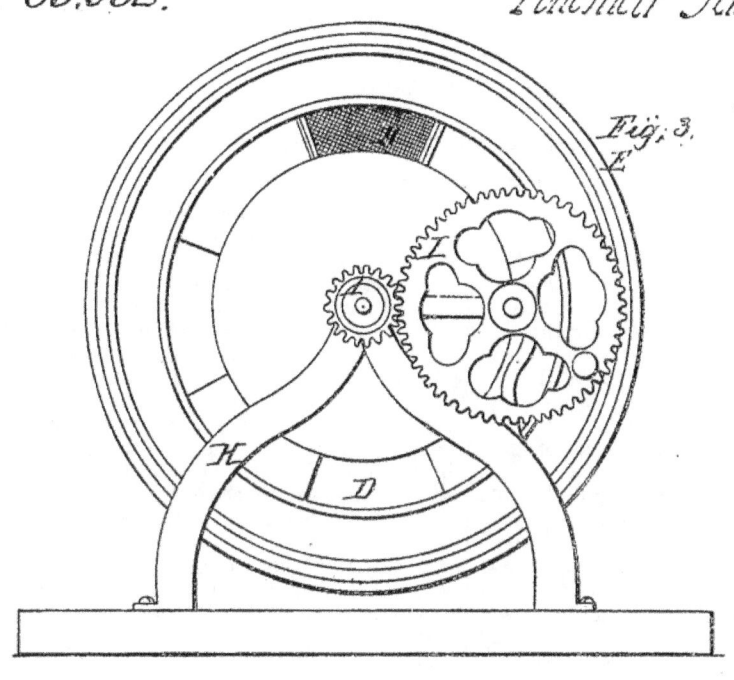
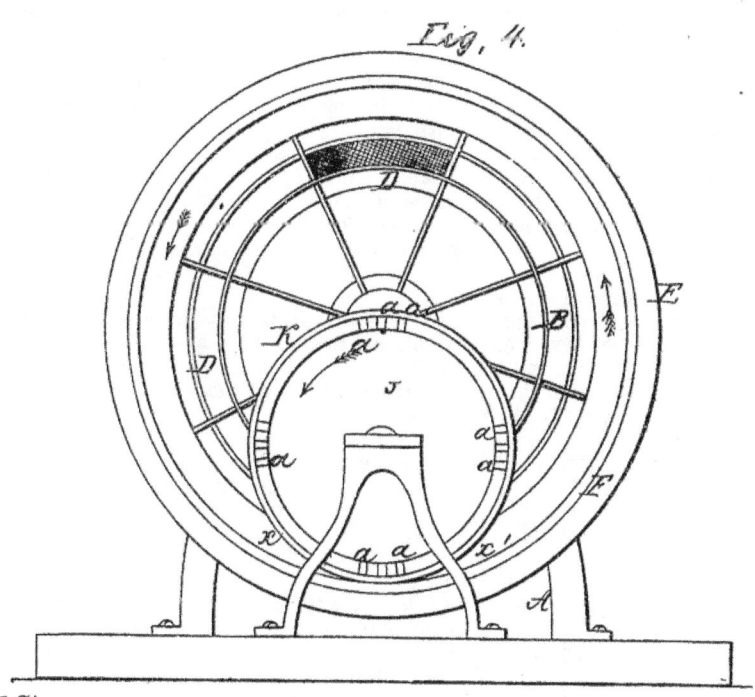

United States Patent Office.

GEORGE C. REEVES, OF BLACKHAWK, COLORADO TERRITORY.

Letters Patent No. 85,962, dated January 19, 1869.

IMPROVED QUARTZ-CRUSHER.

The Schedule referred to in these Letters Patent and making part of the same.

To all whom it may concern:

Be it known that I, GEORGE C. REEVES, of Blackhawk, in the county of Gilpin, and Territory of Colorado, have invented certain new and useful Improvements in Quartz-Crushers; and I do hereby declare that the following is a full and complete description of the same, reference being had to the accompanying drawing, making part of this specification, in which—

Figure 1, plate 1, is a side view of the machine.
Figure 2, a top view.
Figure 3, plate 2, a view of the opposite side of fig. 1.
Figure 4, a vertical section showing the inside.

Like letters refer to like parts in the different views.

This invention relates to a machine for crushing ores by means of a wheel, so constructed and arranged within a revolving shell or battery-wheel, and operating therein in such a way that the periphery of said wheel runs upon the inner surface of the revolving shell, and between which the said ore is continuously fed, by being carried over from one side of the crushing-wheel to the other, by the centrifugal force obtained by the rapid revolution of the shell.

The shell or battery-wheel referred to is constructed in three sections, A B E, fig. 2, secured to each other by means of the hook-bolts C, or by any other suitable device, so that the sections may be easily detached from each other, whereby access is had to the inside, for a purpose hereafter shown.

The side of each section is provided alike with an annular series of openings, D, covered with screens, as shown in fig. 1.

The inner surface of the section E forming a central rim of the battery, and to which section A is permanently secured, is provided with a removable lining, F, of wrought-iron, steel, or hard cast-metal, which, when worn out, can be readily replaced by a new one.

G, fig. 2, is a shaft mounted in the frame H, and to which the battery is keyed, and made to revolve by means of the gearing I.

J, fig. 4, is the crushing-wheel, provided with a removable tire, K, of wrought-iron, steel, or chilled cast-metal, and thereto secured, by means of wooden keys *a*, inserted under the tire, in gains or notches cut in the rim of the wheel.

L, fig. 2, is a shaft, one end of which is supported by the standard M, and in which it is journalled, having a ball-and-socket joint, as indicated by the dotted lines *b*, whereby a vertical movement is allowed to the shaft and wheel J.

To the free end of said shaft is keyed the crushing-wheel J, above described, the periphery of which rests upon and is supported by the inner face of the battery-wheel or shell, as shown in fig. 4, and is retained in this position by the guide N, through which the shaft passes.

O, fig. 1, is an outer covering or case, whereby the battery-wheel or shell is completely enclosed, a section of which is represented as being removed or opened.

Having thus described the construction and arrangement of the machine, the practical operation of the same is as follows, viz:

The ore is thrown into the machine through the chute P, fig. 1. The battery-wheel is now made to revolve, thereby giving motion to the crushing-wheel by friction. As the two wheels revolve in direction of the arrows, the ore is brought under the crushing-wheel at the point X, fig. 4, thence to the opposite side X'. From this point the reduced material is carried over again to X by the centrifugal force obtained by the speed of the battery-wheel passing again under the crusher to X', thence to X, and so on continuously, until the ore is reduced to the degree of fineness necessary.

It will be obvious that a certain velocity must be given to the battery, in order to overcome gravitation, and carry the material over from one side to the other of the crusher, otherwise it would accumulate at X', and therefore not pass under the wheel J but once. In consequence of this rate of velocity, a concussive action is brought to act upon the ore, which is therefore reduced to powder by the combined action of the weight of the wheel J, and the concussion of the same upon it, in consequence of the great velocity of shell or battery.

By this means the reduction of the quartz is rapidly effected, and to any required degree of fineness. Also, by thus giving to the wheels a high velocity, less weight will be required for the crushing-wheel J, which in the ordinary machines is of great weight, the crushing being done solely by the weight of the wheel run at a low speed.

In my machine the crushing-wheel is of much less weight, and run at a high speed, and is therefore more effectual and rapid in the performance of its work, in consequence of the concussion of the wheel upon the ore.

No supplementary device or appliance is required to feed the ore to the wheel, and cause a continuous agitation of the same, this being done by the centrifugal force generated by the velocity of the battery-wheel.

As above said, the shaft of the crushing-wheel J is secured to the standard M by a ball-and-socket joint. By this means the wheel can readily adjust itself to different-sized pieces of quartz in the battery, when rolling therein, and upon the ore, and is therefore unrestrained in the freedom of its vertical motion. It also prevents the wheel from any longitudinal movement, keeping at all times at the centre of the battery-wheel.

The lining F, on the inside of the battery-wheel, and against which all the force of wheel J, in crushing the quartz, is spent, is liable to great and continual wear; hence it is necessary to make it of hard metal, and removable.

The tire K, upon crushing-wheel J, is also removable, and, with my construction, easily taken off from the wheel, when worn, and a new one replaced, which adds materially to the cheapness of the machine, as it does not necessitate the loss of any other part of the machine, and takes but little time to effect the change.

The sides of the battery being connected to each other, as above said, one side can be removed for cleaning up, or for the replacing of the worn-out lining by a new one, or for any other needful repairs.

Another advantage in the construction of this machine is, that when driven by a steam-engine, by a direct connection thereto, it serves as a fly-wheel, thus combining in one a fly-wheel and ore-crushing machine, thereby dispensing with the use of a separate wheel or balance.

I am aware that revolving cylinders, having other cylinders, wheels, or rings revolving within them, and caused to revolve by the outer cylinder, have been used for crushing quartz or ores, but such construction is entirely different from mine, as, in every instance where such devices are used, the outer cylinder or shell revolves slowly, and the inside wheels or rings are corrugated, or have teeth or ridges upon them, which take hold of and are revolved by similar ridges upon the inside of the shell or outer cylinder; or if the faces are smooth, there are two or more inside crushing-wheels, yoked together in such way, that by their weight, the quartz is crushed when between such wheel and the outer cylinder or shell. Further, these inside wheels or rings being free, with nothing to prevent them, would, if the outside cylinder were revolved rapidly enough to overcome their gravitation, be carried around on the inside of and adhering to the shell, and could not produce any result, by reason of the wheels or rings upon the inside, with the quartz being carried continuously around without change of position, with relation to each other, and the inside of the cylinder or shell, while in my mill the crushing-wheel is prevented by shaft and guide from leaving its intended position, however rapidly the outside shell may revolve, but the quartz or substance to be crushed is carried in contact with the shell or battery-wheel successively around, and caused to go between the crushing-wheel J and the shell or battery-wheel, until it is reduced to the proper fineness.

I am also aware that horizontal-revolving wheels, in connection with crushing-wheels or balls, have been used for pulverizing quartz and ores, and such wheels convey the unground quartz to the grinding-wheels or balls by a slow motion or revolution. Such construction or operation I do not claim, as my invention is entirely different, both in construction and operation, being an upright revolving shell upon a horizontal shaft, and having an upright-revolving crushing-wheel within it; and the outer shell revolves so rapidly that it carries the unground quartz, by centrifugal force, along with its inner surface, and continually presents the quartz to the crushing-wheel, at every revolution, until it is reduced to powder, and escapes through the openings in the shell for such purpose; while in a horizontal mill the wheel revolves slowly, and the crushing is entirely done by the weight of the crushing-wheel.

What I claim as my improvement, and desire to secure by Letters Patent, is—

1. The revolving shell or battery-wheel A B E, as the means for feeding the unground quartz to the crushing-wheel J, when operating substantially in the manner described.

2. The wheel J, when constructed with the removable tire K and keys *a*, in the manner and for the purpose described.

3. The combination of the revolving sectional shell or battery, with the crushing-wheel J, shaft, L, ball-and-socket joint, and standard M, arranged to operate in the manner and for the purpose described.

GEO. O. REEVES.

Witnesses:
J. H. BURRIDGE,
E. E. WAITE.

E. Froggat.

Combination Tool.

Nº 88,621.   Patented Apr. 6, 1869.

Fig. 1.

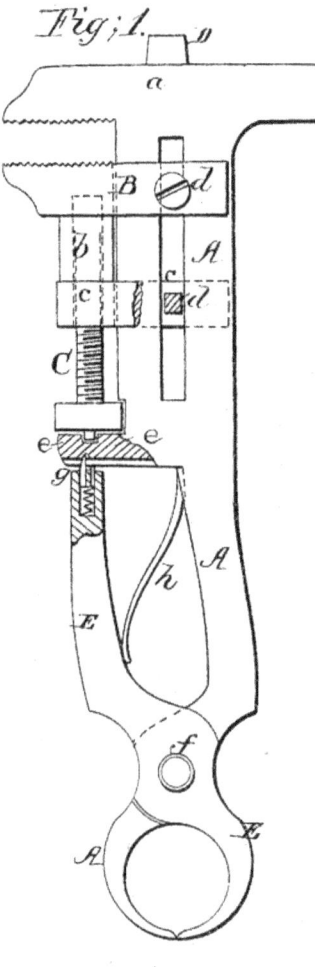

Fig. 2.

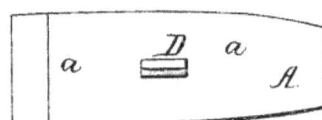

Witnesses:
C. Raettig
John F. Brooks

Inventor:
E. Froggat
pr. Munn & Co.
Attorneys.

EDWIN FROGGATT, OF CENTRAL CITY, COLORADO TERRITORY.

Letters Patent No. 88,621, dated April 6, 1869.

IMPROVEMENT IN WRENCH AND PINCERS.

The Schedule referred to in these Letters Patent and making part of the same.

To all whom it may concern:

Be it known that I, EDWIN FROGGATT, of Central City, in the Territory of Colorado, have invented a new and improved Combination-Tool; and I do hereby declare that the following is a full, clear, and exact description thereof, which will enable others skilled in the art to make and use the same, reference being had to the accompanying drawings, forming part of this specification, in which—

Figure 1 represents a side view, partly in section, of my combined tool.

Figure 2 is a plan or top view of the same.

Similar letters of reference indicate corresponding parts.

This invention relates to a new tool, which is to be used by blacksmiths and mechanics for various purposes, and in which the most important tools, to wit, the hammer, screw-driver, wrench, and pincers, are combined in such manner that either can be used with great facility.

A, in the drawing, represents the shank of my improved tool.

It is made of malleable iron, or other suitable material, and has, on its upper end, formed a head, a, projecting from both sides, as shown.

One end of this head serves as a hammer, the other one, as the upper jaw of a wrench.

The upper half of the shank A is, under the hammer-head a, made flat, and is slotted, as shown.

B is the lower jaw of the wrench. It is forked, so as to straddle the slotted upper part of the shank, and is, by means of a tube, b, connected with a lower guide-arm, c, which also straddles the shank, as shown.

Screws d d are fitted through the forked ends of the parts B c, and through the slot of the shank.

C is a screw, for working the lower jaw. It rests on a step, e, formed on the shank, and fits into the arm c and tube b, as shown. By turning it, the lower jaw will be raised or lowered, at will.

The screw d and the lower arm c serve to steady the motion of the jaw, and make the wrench effective.

The working-faces of the jaws a and B are or may be grooved, or roughened, to increase the effectiveness of the wrench.

D is a tapering metal arm, projecting from the head, a. It serves as a screw-driver.

The lower end of the shank A forms one of the jaws of a pair of pincers, as shown.

The other arm, E, of the pincers is, by a pin, f, pivoted to A, and can, by a spring-catch, g, be fastened to the step e, when the pincers are not to be used.

h is a spring, for forcing the jaws of the pincers apart.

Another form of wrench may be arranged in the same combination with equal effect, and the screw-driver can be omitted, if desired.

The hammer is strengthened by an additional brace, o, as shown, which connects its head with the shank.

The nippers may have steel-faced points, that may be removable, if desired.

Having thus described my invention,

I claim as new, and desire to secure by Letters Patent—

1. The combination-tool, consisting of the wrench, hammer, and pincers, with or without the screw-driver, all operating and arranged substantially as specified.

2. Connecting the movable jaw B of a wrench, by means of a bar or tube, b, with a parallel arm, c, the jaw and arm being bifurcated, so as to straddle the slotted shank A, through which screws d are fitted into the parts B c, substantially as herein shown and described, for the purpose specified.

EDWIN FROGGATT.

Witnesses:
HARVEY M. BURRELL,
F. SCHOENFELD.

4 Sheets—Sheet 1.

R. GEORGE.

MACHINE FOR CONCENTRATING AND SEPARATING ORES AND MINERALS.

No. 89,476. Patented Apr. 27, 1869.

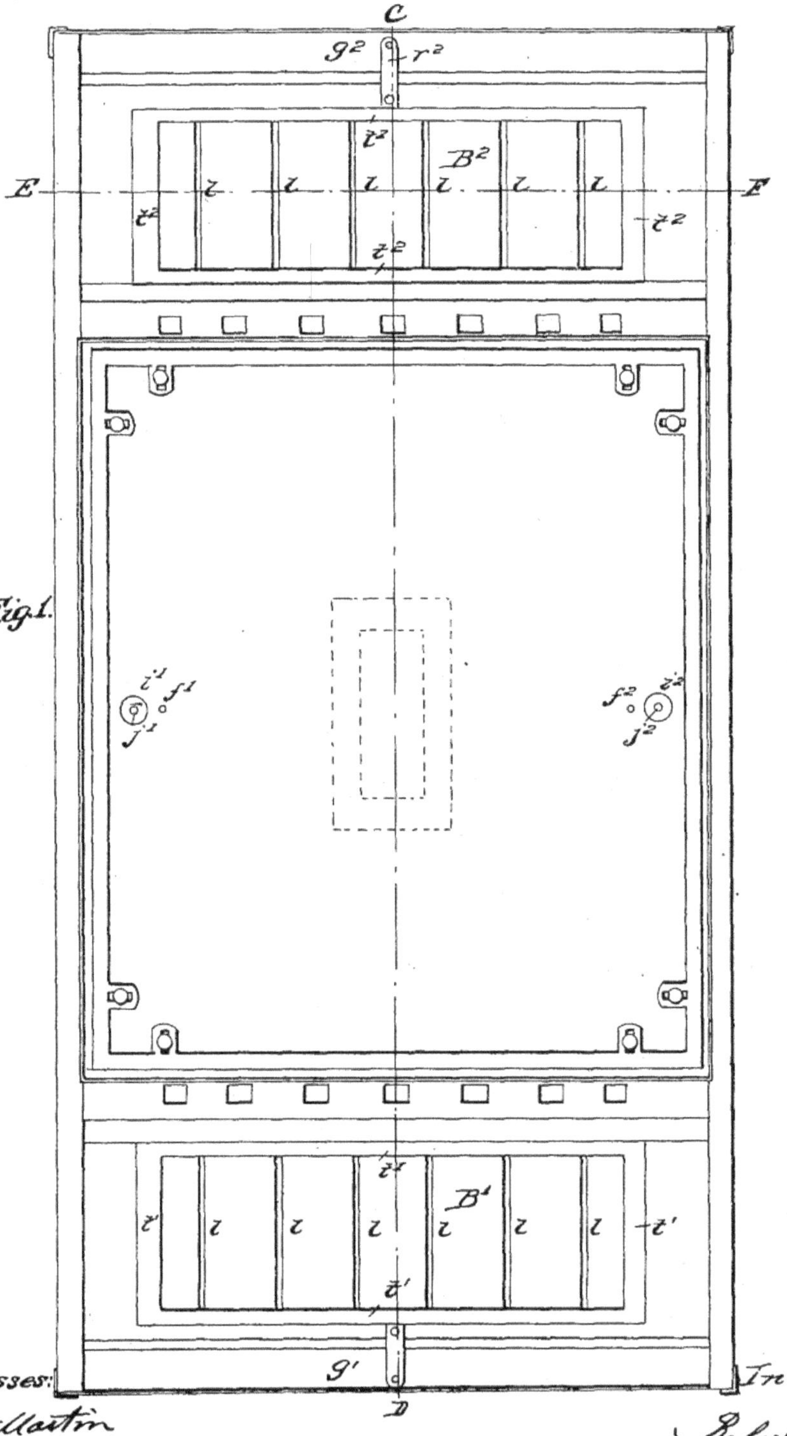

Fig. 1.

Witnesses:
Wm Martin
Wm Cammack

Inventor
Robert George

THE NORRIS PETERS CO., PHOTO-LITHO., WASHINGTON, D. C.

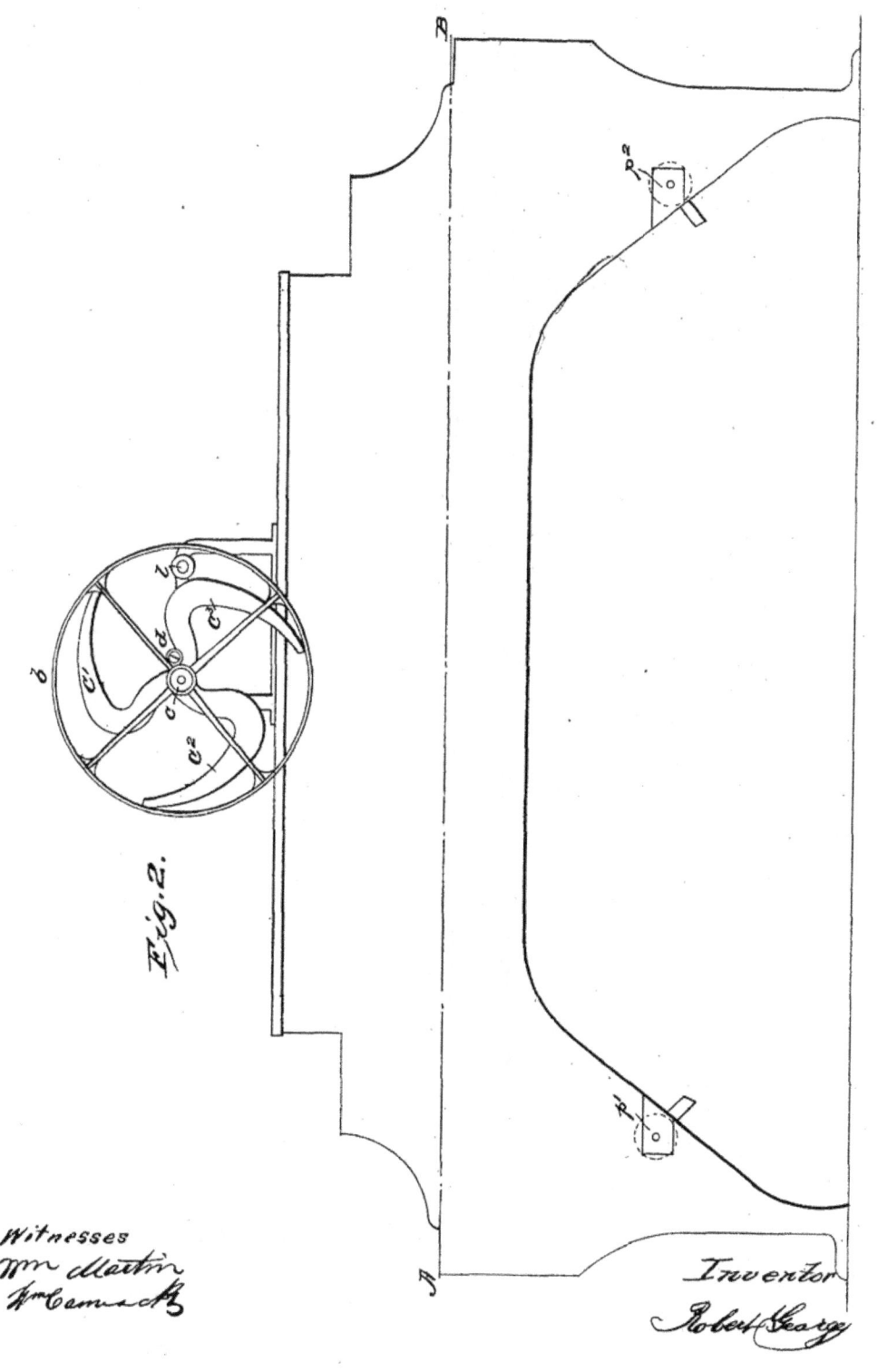

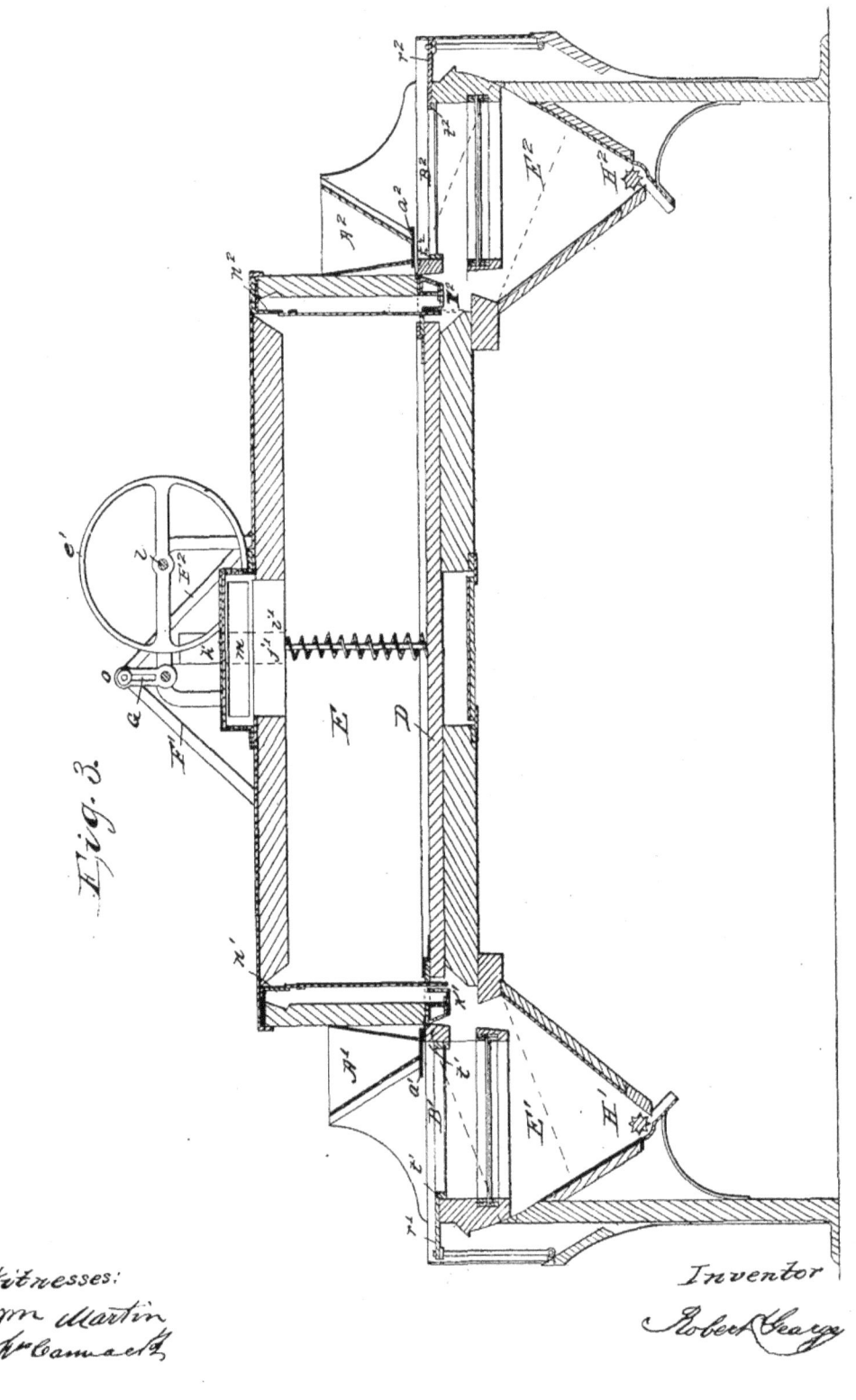

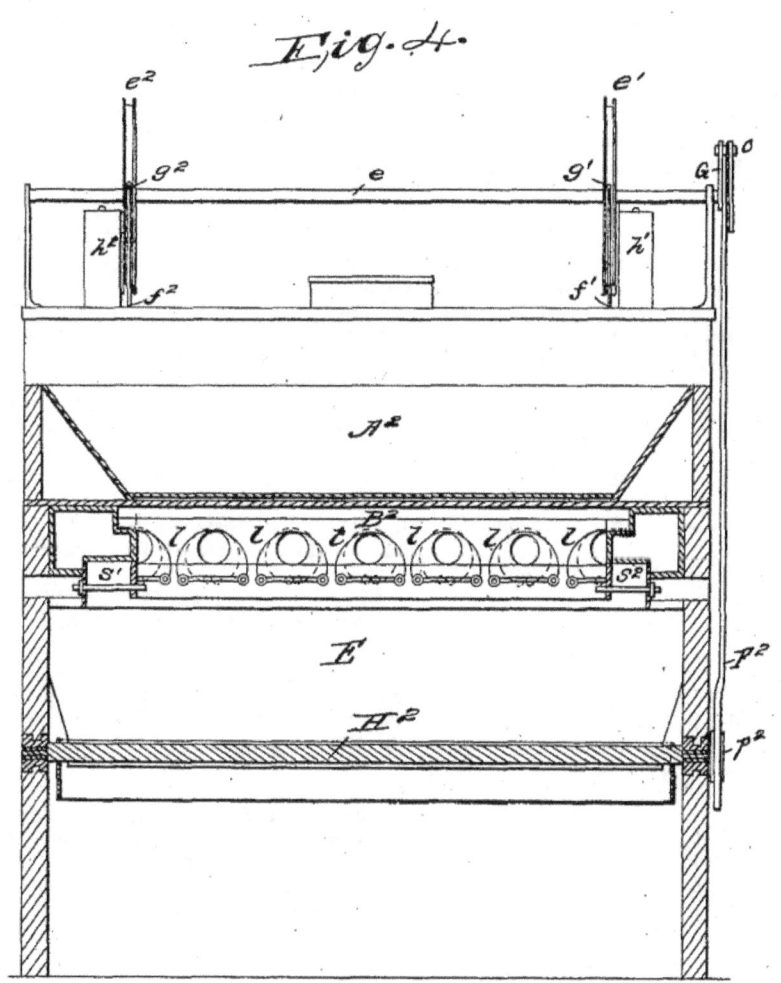

United States Patent Office.

ROBERT GEORGE, OF DENVER CITY, COLORADO TERRITORY.

Letters Patent No. 89,476, dated April 27, 1869

IMPROVED MACHINE FOR CONCENTRATING AND SEPARATING ORES AND MINERALS.

The Schedule referred to in these Letters Patent and making part of the same.

To all whom it may concern:

Be it known that I, ROBERT GEORGE, of Denver City, in the county of Arapahoe, and Territory of Colorado have invented a new and useful Machine for Concentrating and Separating Metals and Mineral Substances from rocks, alluvials, and metallurgical and other products contained in an admixture, or in a natural, or chemical combination; and I do hereby declare that the following is a full, clear, and exact description of the construction and operation of the same, reference being had to the annexed drawings, making a part of this specification, in which—

Figure 1, Sheet I, is a plan view, on the line A B.
Figure 2, Sheet II, is a side elevation.
Figure 3, Sheet III, is a transverse section through line C D.
Figure 4, Sheet IV, is a front view on the sectional line E F.

The sectional lines are indicated by red lines and red-colored capital letters.

The different materials are denoted as follows:
Wood-materials, yellow.
Iron, blue.
Brass, greenish yellow.
Leather, brown.

Similar letters in black ink refer to similar parts throughout the several elevations and sections.

My machine is designed to concentrate and separate the precious metals, especially in such regions where the separation of the same by water can only be accomplished by great cost, or not at all, as is, for instance, the case in the dry placers of Colorado, New Mexico, Arizona, &c.

My object is, further, to save gold, silver, copper, and any valuable metals which are wasted during their treatment in stamp-mills, either by imperfect amalgamation, or where the nature of the minerals which associate or contain the precious metals renders the saving of the same by the old processes impossible. I intend, further, to accomplish the saving of such minute particles of gold, silver, and platinum, which are carried off by the current of water, which is especially the case when the water used for their separation is not pure; and mixed with earthy substances; because it is a fact that the precious metals, in a finely divided state, will condense gases likewise, as platinum-sponge does, to form an atmosphere of such condensed gases around themselves, which causes them to float on water, as is also the case with quicksilver, when in minute particles, whether amalgamated or not, whereby a great loss of the precious metals takes place, when treated in such water.

Furthermore, a great deal of the richest silver and gold-ore is impregnated in the cavities of the associated minerals in a pulverized state of ochre, which cannot be saved by the application of water in the process of dressing or concentrating such ore. A similar difficulty is the case when minerals are to be separated from each other where the difference of their respective specific gravity is only insignificant, as, for instance, by galena and sulphuret of zinc, by iron and copper pyrites. By the hitherto known process of separating such minerals, is always a great loss combined with their concentration, while their separation by technical means remains imperfect and impracticable.

Various machines have been constructed to overcome the above-mentioned difficulties and imperfectness, but they have generally failed to answer in a practical manner, either doing the work insufficiently, or doing too small amount of work in a certain time, or being of no general character for application, answering only to a certain species of minerals, or, when in peculiar circumstances, requiring the utmost equality and minuteness of grain and fracture of the substances to be treated, all circumstances which are practically very difficult to comply with.

I have, therefore, endeavored, with great care, and by manifold expensive experiments, to construct a machine on such principles, and in such a way, that a general application of the same is possible, and the concentration and separation of the precious and other valuable metals are accomplished in great quantities, in shorter time, and by very limited cost, in regard to the price of the machine itself, for the practical working of the same.

The successful result of the working of my machine is accomplished by a variated action of air under and among the particles of the materials to be separated, by accompanied action of concussion, and by simultaneous and continuous carrying off the waste matters and separated valuable substances.

To produce the largest amount of work in regard to quantity and quality, my machine is constructed as double acting in every respect, with the utmost economy of its motive power, and steadiness and durability in the practical use of the same.

The machine consists of the hoppers A^1 and A^2, into which the materials to be treated are charged. The outlet of the same is regulated by the drawers a^1 and a^2. From these drawers the materials pass on the sieves B^1 and B^2, covering all their segments to a desirable thickness. The machine is set in motion by a crank or pulley, b, fastened on the revolving shaft c, with the lifters C^1, C^2, and C^3, which are raising the truck d on the shaft e, with the lever-wheels e^1 and e^2 to the desired distance.

On the lifter-wheels e^1 and e^2 are cords f^1 and f^2, fastened by the regulating-screws g^1 and g^2.

On these cords is the piston D, in the blast-chamber E, attached so when the truck d is raised by lifter C^1, or C^2, or C^3, the same must follow in an upward direction.

To the piston D and the spring tubes h^1 and h^2 are springs i^1 and i^2, connected, which are guided on the rods j^1 and j^2.

As soon as the truck d slides off from the lifter C^1, or C^2, or C^3, the coiled springs i^1 and i^2 will instantly force the piston D downward with great velocity, causing a concussion on the ore, or materials in the hopper A^1 and A^2, as well as on the sieves B^1 and B^2, while the air, having filled the space in the blast-cylinder, from the bottom to the piston D, is forced to pass through the valves k^1 and k^2, lifting up the materials on the segments of the sieves B^1 and B^2. The great velocity of the escaping air will in this moment allow only the larger particles of the separated materials to pass downward through the interstices $l\,l\,l$, &c., into the receiving-chamber E^1 and E^2. By the upward motion of the piston D, the air, having found its inlet through valve m, will be forced through the valves n^1 and n^2, under the sieves, in a similar manner as before, but with the difference that the same will act upon the materials with the regularity of the raising piston D, without the irregular pressure of the springs, and without concussion. In this way the smaller particles will only be agitated, and dust separated in a proper manner.

The separated particles of the metals, or the minerals, will fill up the receiving-chambers E^1 and E^2. As soon as this is the case, the raked pitmen F^1 and F^2 are to be adjusted by the screw o, on the crank G, to act on the wheel p^1 and p^2, fastened on the conveyer H^1 and H^2 in such a manner as to carry off just as much of the separated materials as there will be separated through the sieves into the receiving-chambers.

The conveyers H^1 and H^2 may be either corrugated in the line of their length, or in the form of an endless screw, to facilitate the delivery of the material conveyed thereupon.

In this way all material of a greater specific weight will find its separation through the receiving-chambers, while all waste, or lighter materials, will pass over the sieves into the hoppers q^1 and q^2. If the latter contain some other valuable materials besides the rocky or earthy matters, the same may be separated from the rock or earth by a subsequent treatment, as above explained.

It is evident that a different size of the grain of a substance to be separated, as well as the smaller or larger yield of valuable materials, in regard to quantity, requires different action of the machine, in order to answer in every case. For this purpose, the sieves are so constructed and arranged that the same may easily be changed from a horizontal position to any practical inclination, by the screws r^1 and r^2. Such an inclined position of the sieves will be necessary in the same degree as the waste or earthy matters are predominant to the valuable materials, in order to cause their more speedy passage over the sieves into the hoppers q^1 and q^2. It is further evident that the width of the interstices between the different segments of the sieves which permit the valuable materials to pass into the receiving-chambers, ought to be in proportion to the yield of the materials to be separated. This can be done by means of the screws s^1 and s^2, on the lower frame of the sieves, to any desirable width. The air being forced for the purpose of separating the valuable materials to pass under the sieves B^1 and B^2, will escape partially through the wire gauze of the sieves, and partially through the interstices $l\,l\,l$, &c. The former being divided into small jets by the wire gauze, will promote the separation of the smaller particles of the valuable materials, while the stronger and less divided current of air through the interstices $l\,l\,l$, &c., will especially act on the larger particles. Therefore, in the case where the materials to be separated are of a very minute size, the segments of the sieves may be formed more or less in the shape of tubes, by properly regulating the screws s^1 and s^2 for this purpose, so that all the introduced air is forced to pass through the wire gauze, and cause even the most minute particles of valuable metals to accumulate in the receiving-chambers E^1 and E^2. In such a case, the interstices $l\,l\,l$, &c., will be widened, but the same may be properly decreased by the down-pressing of the frame t^1 and t^2 upon the segments of the sieves, causing the same to assume a less convex surface, so far as desirable.

Finally, the nature and minuteness of the materials to be separated will require a different quantity of air for their treatment. For this purpose the stroke of the piston D may properly be so arranged as to force only the requisite quantity of air through the sieves, by shortening or lengthening either the truck d, or adjusting the connection-cords f^1 and f^2 by the regulating-screws g^1 and g^2, in a proper manner.

Therefore, it may appear evident that, as set forth above, the machine is constructed to be easily regulated for any and every desirable case for practical use, to secure a general application of the same.

What I claim as my invention, and desire to secure by Letters Patent, is—

1. A machine for concentrating and separating metals and mineral substances from rocks, alluvials, and other substances, contained, in combination, in their natural state, or as mats, or other metallurgic products, when constructed and arranged in the manner and for the purpose herein described.

2. The construction and arrangement of the sieves B^1 and B^2, in a machine for concentrating and separating ores and metals, in the manner and for the purpose herein described.

3. The combination of the blast-chamber E with the valves k^1 k^2 n^1 n^2, guide-rods j^1 and j^2, and coil-spring i^1 and i^2, in the manner and for the purpose herein described.

4. The combination of the lifters C^1 C^2 C^3 with the truck d, on the shaft e, and piston D, in the manner and for the purpose herein described.

5. The pitman F^1 and F^2, with the adjustable screw o, crank G, wheels p^1 and p^2, and the conveyer H^1 and H^2, in the manner and for the purpose herein described.

6. The combination of the wheels e^1 e^2, cords f^1 f^2, and the set-screws g^1 and g^2, in the manner and for the purpose herein described.

In testimony whereof, I have signed my name to this specification, in the presence of two subscribing witnesses.

ROBERT GEORGE.

Witnesses:
WM. MARTIN,
WM. CAMMACK.

United States Patent Office.

WILLIAM JOHN LYND, OF GOLDEN CITY, COLORADO TERRITORY.

Letters Patent No. 90,565, dated May 25, 1869.

IMPROVED PROCESS OF SEPARATING IRON AND OTHER METALS FROM POTTERS' CLAY.

The Schedule referred to in these Letters Patent and making part of the same.

To whom it may concern:

Be it known that I, WILLIAM JOHN LYND, of Golden City, Jefferson county, Colorado Territory, have invented a new and useful Process for Removing Iron, Copper, and Other Discoloring-Matter from Potters' Clay and other Argillaceous Substances; and I hereby declare the following to be a full, clear, and exact description of the same.

The object of my invention is to remove the iron, copper, and other discoloring matter from argillaceous substances which are to be used for the manufacture of white and other wares, or for other purposes; and to this end,

My invention consists in subjecting the argillaceous substance in solution to the action of artificial or natural magnets, or of electricity, or of both in conjunction, in the manner herein specified.

In carrying out my invention, I employ a bath, of wood or other suitable material, which contains a solution of potters' clay, (water being usually the solvent,) and one or more artificial magnets, usually plates or sheets of magnetized iron or steel; but these magnets may be bars, rods, balls, chippings or filings of steel, iron, nickel, cobalt, or any composition capable of being magnetized.

In case thin magnetized plates of iron or steel be adopted, they are held a short distance apart from each other in the bath, by ordinary or suitable means, or they may be joined together, with their similar poles in contact.

When the magnets are thus placed in the bath, a thin solution of potters' clay is poured in, so as to partially or wholly cover them, which is allowed to remain for from six to twelve hours.

At the end of this period, the magnets are taken from the bath, and the iron, copper, and other discoloring matters deposited on them from the liquid clay are removed, after which they are again deposited in the solution, and this process is kept up until the clay is purified.

For better and more rapid purification, there may be employed two or more baths, provided with similar or dissimilar magnets, as the case may be.

Under this arrangement, the argillaceous solution is allowed to pass from the first bath to the second, from the second to the third, and so on, before the magnets in the bath from which the clay is withdrawn are removed for cleansing.

In connection with, and in furtherance of the above process, the bath or baths containing the clay in solution may be advantageously lined with magnetized or unmagnetized iron or steel.

In the process as above described, natural or artificial magnets are alone employed to act upon the bath of clay, without the aid of any electrical current or currents.

Yet electricity can be used to advantage in the following manner:

Supposing, for instance, there be a succession of baths. Let the magnets be removed from the first bath, leaving therein nothing but the clay in solution. Then let two wires, leading from a suitable battery and connected with the bath, convey a current of electricity through the clay. This will, in from twenty-four to thirty hours, precipitate the discoloring matter, or cause it to settle at the bottom of the bath.

The upper portion of the clay can now be drawn off into the second bath, and there be acted on by the magnets, as above described.

The poles of the battery are not placed in contact with any of the magnets, nor is the battery used in combination or simultaneously with them; and this use of electricity is not a necessity, since the purification can be effected without it. It is, however, of some advantage, and expedites the operation, by preparing the clay for the subsequent application of the magnets.

Having now described my invention, and the manner in which the same is or may be carried into effect,

What I claim, and desire to secure by Letters Patent, is—

1. The process of removing iron, copper, and other discoloring-matters from potters' clay and other argillaceous substances, by subjecting the clay, when in solution, to the action of one or more magnets, in the manner and for the purposes set forth.

2. The method of precipitating the iron and other discoloring-matter in the clay solution, by passing through the bath containing such solution a current of electricity, as and for the purposes set forth.

3. The mode of preparing potters' clay and like substances from which discoloring-matter is to be removed, by subjecting such substance, in solution, first, to the action of a current of electricity, and afterward to magnetic action, in the manner and for the purposes specified.

WM. J. LYND.

Witnesses:
WM. H. McCABE,
ARTHUR C. HARRIS.

United States Patent Office.

WILLIAM BRÜCKNER, OF CENTRAL, COLORADO TERRITORY.

Letters Patent No. 92,009, dated June 29, 1869.

IMPROVED PROCESS OF ROASTING AURIFEROUS SULPHURETS.

The Schedule referred to in these Letters Patent and making part of the same.

To all whom it may concern:

Be it known that I, WILLIAM BRÜCKNER, of Central, Gilpin county, Colorado Territory, have invented certain new and useful Improvements in the Process for Roasting Auriferous Sulphurets; and I do hereby declare the following description and accompanying drawings are sufficient to enable any person skilled in the art or science to which it most nearly appertains, to make and use my said invention or improvements, without further invention or experiment.

The nature of my invention and improvements consists in the use, in a particular manner, and for special purposes, to be herein described, of common salt, or other substance yielding chlorine and lime, in the roasting of auriferous sulphurets, to prepare them for the process of amalgamation.

Experience has shown, that by the roasting-processes heretofore in use, not more than from fifty to sixty per cent. of the gold contained in these ores has been obtained from them by amalgamation, and that proportion only from the best sort of iron sulphurets, while from the more refractory ores, such as those of Colorado, and particularly those that have not been exposed to the decomposing-action of the atmosphere, often not more than from twenty-five to thirty per cent. of the gold has been obtained.

At the same time there has been a great loss or waste of quicksilver, from its becoming coated, or converted into calomel, or "floured," in which state it has no affinity for gold, and does not combine with it.

Now, the low yield of gold, as above stated, I have found to be owing to two causes: first, a coating formed on the gold in the ordinary process of roasting the ore, and second, the destruction of the amalgamating-capacity of the quicksilver by the sulphates, chlorides, or other products of the roasting-process.

For both these causes, my improvement is found to be an efficient remedy, and so complete, that by using it, nearly all the gold may be extracted from the most refractory ores, or at least eighty or ninety per cent. thereof, by amalgamation.

I will now describe my improved process.

The auriferous sulphurets are to be finely pulverized and the roasting-furnace charged. The ore should be constantly stirred, and the heat raised until the sulphur begins to burn and escape through the chimney, but should then be raised no higher till the sulphur is burned off. After that has been effected, a strong heat should be put on, and charcoal or sawdust may be advantageously added, to deprive the base metals, commonly contained in the ore, of the last atoms of sulphur or sulphur-acid.

This operation is called dead-roasting, and all the gold is now set free, except that it will be found to be more or less coated, according to the amount of copper, lead, or other base metal contained in the ore.

From one-half of one per cent. to five per cent. of the chloride of sodium (common salt) must now be added, according to the richness of the ore and the character of its base metals.

Through the high heat to which it is subjected, in contact with the silicious and other matter in the ore, chlorine is evolved from the salt, and acting on the coating of the gold, forms chlorides of the base metals, and leaves the gold clean and bright, and perfectly susceptible of amalgamation.

For this process or operation, about half an hour is sufficient.

If the ore treated as above was one of the purer sort of iron sulphurets, containing no lead, copper, or other such base metal, or only very small proportions thereof, the ore is now ready for amalgamation, no considerable amount of the chlorides of these metals having been formed, to injure the quicksilver by converting it into calomel, or causing it to "flour."

But if the base metals above referred to were present in the ore in any considerable quantities, which may be ascertained by an examination of the particles of gold before the application of salt, then carbonate of lime, burnt lime, or some equivalent, must be added, to prevent the chlorides of these metals, formed by the use and decomposition of the salt, from acting upon and injuring the quicksilver, as already described.

By this means the lime, or a portion of it, is converted into chloride of lime, and the metals aforesaid into oxides, which have no injurious effect upon the quicksilver.

No more lime should be used than what may be required for the decomposition of the chlorides. From one to three per cent. I have generally found to be sufficient; but if a proper test indicates still the presence of the chloride of copper, or of any other base metal, more lime must be added, till all traces of these chlorides are removed. From half an hour to one hour is commonly sufficient for this part of the process.

I also contemplate the application of chlorine-gas, previously prepared, in place of the compound chloride of sodium.

Having thus described my improved process, it is to be understood that I do not claim as new the use of salt and lime in roasting ores; but

What I do claim, and desire to secure by Letters Patent, is—

The use and application of these materials, in a particular manner, and for special purposes, substantially as set forth in the foregoing specification.

WILLIAM BRÜCKNER.

Witnesses:
  J. DENNIS, Jr.,
  WM. DENNIS.

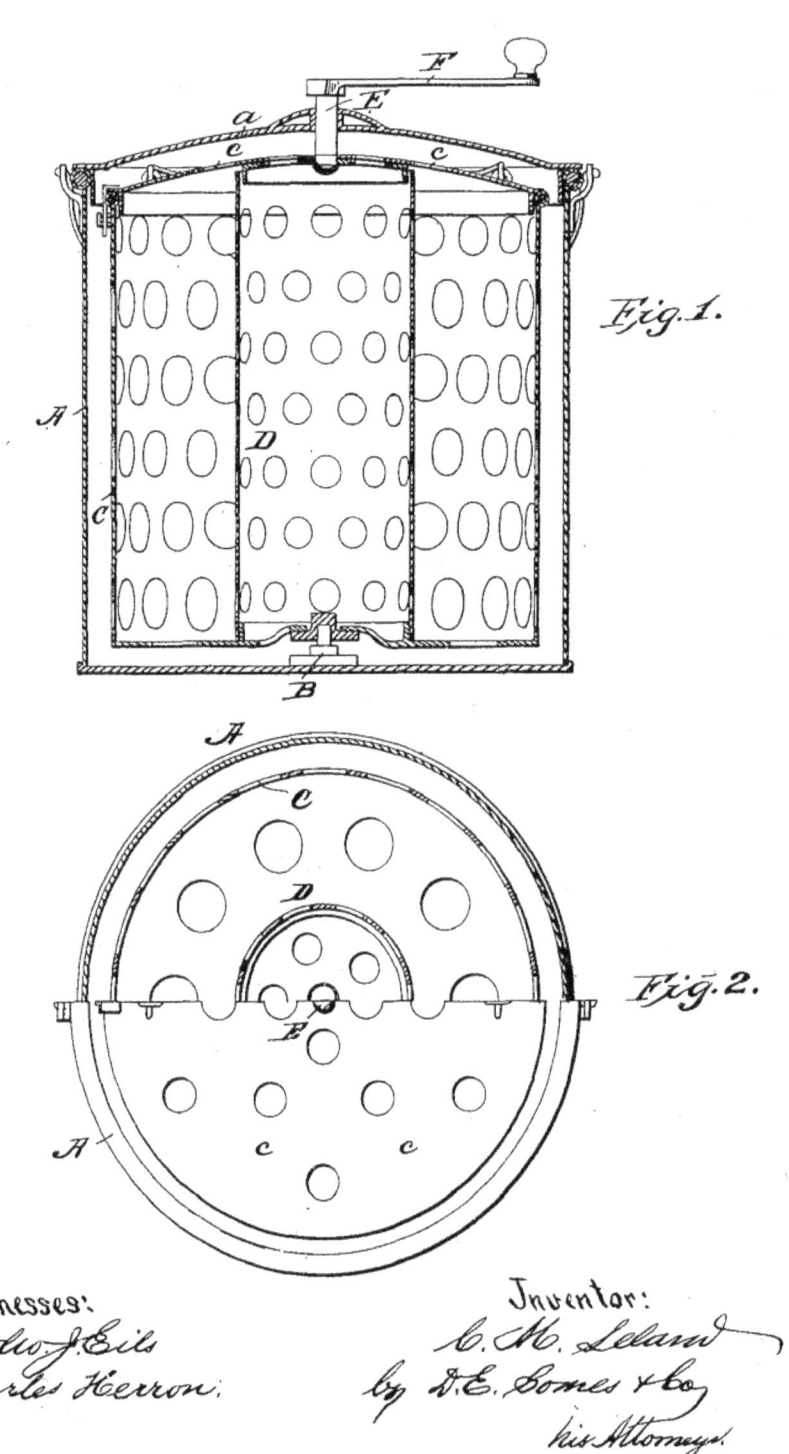

United States Patent Office.

CHARLES M. LELAND, OF CENTRAL CITY, COLORADO TERRITORY.

Letters Patent No. 92,323, dated July 6, 1869.

IMPROVED MACHINE FOR WASHING DISHES, KNIVES AND FORKS, &c.

The Schedule referred to in these Letters Patent and making part of the same.

To all whom it may concern:

Be it known that I, CHARLES M. LELAND, of Central City, in the county of Gilpin, Territory of Colorado, have invented a new and useful Machine for Washing Dishes, Knives, Forks, Spoons, and other Articles; and I do hereby declare that the following is a full, clear, and exact description thereof, reference being had to the accompanying drawings, and to the letters of reference marked thereon.

The nature of my invention consists in providing an apparatus for washing dishes, by passing them swiftly through boiling-hot water, and afterwards drying them by heat, dispensing with wiping.

To enable others skilled in the art to make and use my invention, I will proceed to describe its construction and operation.

I provide a cylindrical kettle, of suitable size, with a removable lid.

In the centre of the bottom of this kettle is a pinion, on which revolves a cylinder or crate, for the reception of dishes, perforated on all sides, and somewhat smaller than the kettle.

The crate has a lid, also perforated, with a pin fastened to it in the centre, pointing upward, and passing through a hole in the lid of the kettle.

On this pin fits a crank, by which the crate is turned. For the reception of knives, forks, and spoons, another smaller, perforated cylinder is inserted in the middle of the crate, and fastened to its bottom.

In the drawings—

Figure 1 represents a vertical section of the dish-washer in full rig.

Figure 2, a half horizontal section and a half plan, with the crank and lid of the kettle removed.

Like letters denote like parts.

A is the kettle for the reception of the water.

a, the lid to it.

B, the pinion on which revolves the crate C, with the lid *c c* and the inner perforated cylinder D.

F, the crank, which turns the crate C, by the pin E.

Its operation is as follows:

The crank and the lid of the kettle are removed. The crate is then lifted out of the kettle, opened, and filled with dishes, standing them on their edges around the sides, in rows, in such a manner that the rows break joints.

The smaller perforated cylinder is filled with knives, forks, and spoons. The crate is now closed, and the lid secured by a bolt.

In the meanwhile, a sufficient quantity of water, with some soft soap, has been heated in the kettle.

The crate is now placed in it, resting on the pinion. The boiling-hot water at once rushes through the perforations of the crate and its inner perforated cylinder, immersing the dishes, knives, forks, and spoons.

The lid is put on the kettle, the crank applied to the pin of the crate, and turned swiftly for about three minutes.

The hot water, and its friction against the plates, knives, forks, and spoons, as they revolve swiftly through it, will clean them thoroughly.

The crank and the lid of the kettle are again removed, the crate lifted out of it, and left to drain for a minute, when it may be placed on a hot stove for a little while, to dry the plates, &c.

These can then be taken out, and put in their proper places without undergoing a wiping.

What I claim as my invention, and desire to secure by Letters Patent, is—

The kettle A, crate C, and perforated cylinder D, when combined, arranged, and operated as and for the purpose specified.

In testimony that I claim the above-described machine for washing dishes, knives, forks, and spoons, I have hereunto signed my name, this 23d day of February, 1869.

CHARLES M. LELAND.

Witnesses:
P. C. JOHNSON,
J. N. WILCOXEN.

United States Patent Office.

WILLIAM JOHN LYND, OF GOLDEN CITY, COLORADO TERRITORY.

Letters Patent No. 92,981, dated July 27, 1869.

IMPROVED METHOD OF EXTRACTING IRON AND OTHER OXIDES FROM CLAY, PORCELAIN-EARTH, &c.

The Schedule referred to in these Letters Patent and making part of the same.

To whom it may concern:

Be it known that I, WILLIAM JOHN LYND, of Golden City, in the county of Jefferson, Colorado Territory, have invented certain new and useful Improvements in the Method of and Means for Extracting Iron, Copper, and other Discoloring-Matters from Potters' Clay and other Argillaceous Substances; and I hereby declare the following to be a full, clear, and exact description of the same.

The importance of a cheap and effective process for removing from porcelain and potters' clay the discoloring-matters, which unfit such substances for potters' uses, has long been felt. Owing to the want of some practicable process of this kind, the clays which are found in this country in such abundance, and which, if properly treated, could be manufactured into wares equalling in quality those of foreign make, are practically of little value.

My object, therefore, is to devise a cheap and efficient method of removing the discoloring-matters from such clays as are fitted for pottery uses, and, at the same time, of rendering them better fitted for subsequent manipulation.

In Letters Patent granted me on the 25th May, 1869, I have described and claimed a mode of removing the iron, &c., from the clay by means of magnets or electricity, or both in conjunction. I have discovered, however, that the purification of the clay may be effected by the employment of iron or steel plates not magnetized or affected by electricity, which are immersed or placed in the clay solution, and upon which the iron and other impurities are deposited.

While these plates thus act as effective purifying-agents, electricity may be employed in conjunction with them, but its action is simply to improve the quality of the clay, and not to take the place of the plates in separating the discoloring-matters from the clay.

In carrying my invention into operation, I employ thin iron or steel plates, the number and size of which will depend upon the quantity of the clay to be purified.

A solution of the clay to be acted on is first formed in a bath or other suitable receptacle, and the plates, after the clay has settled, are let down into this solution, being placed close together, say from one-half inch to one inch apart. I prefer to let them down until they touch the clay that has settled, though this is not essential.

The plates are allowed to remain in this position for from twelve to forty-eight hours, after which they are taken out, and will be found to be covered with a deposit of the red and black oxides of iron, sulphate of iron, &c., the red commonly settling on one side of the plates, the black on the other, and the sulphate above them.

The discoloring-matters deposited upon the plates are removed, and unless the clay be already sufficiently purified, the plates are again placed in the solution, this operation being continued until the requisite purification has been attained.

The plates, though five, ten, or twenty feet in height, will receive the forms of iron present in the clay, provided the water reaches that height. In fact there seems to be no limit to the attraction of the iron from the clay on account of the plates, provided the water above the clay covers them.

By changing the clay from one bath to another, and subjecting it to the same action, or by changing the water without changing the baths, the quality of the clay may be improved.

I am thus enabled to purify the clay by the use of these plates, though unmagnetized, and without the aid of electricity. I can, however, use in conjunction with the plates, wires, carrying a current of electricity through the clay solution. Sulphur and some other ingredients can be thus removed, and the clay is acted on beneficially; but, as above stated, this operation is intended to improve the clay, not to separate the iron from the clay.

In order to aid the action of the plates, and expedite the process, electricity may be employed to advantage, by placing the poles of a battery so as to act on all the plates, or the plates may be made electro-magnets, by the employment of wires coiled around the top of each, or otherwise arranged, through which a current of electricity should be caused to circulate, the plates when thus acting being immersed in the water above the clay in solution, as hereinbefore specified.

I have found it also advantageous in some instances to employ magnets with the plates, the action of the latter being thus rendered more energetic.

Having now described my invention, and the manner in which the same is or may be carried into effect,

What I claim, and desire to secure by Letters Patent, is—

1. The method of removing iron and other discoloring-maters and impurities from potters' clay, and other argillaceous substances, substantially in the manner and by the means herein described, that is to say, by the employment of unmagnetized plates of iron or steel, immersed or placed in a solution of the clay to be purified, substantially as set forth.

2. The employment, with the unmagnetized iron or steel plates, immersed in the bath of clay to be purified, of electricity, substantially in the manner specified, whereby the action of said plates may be rendered more energetic.

3. The use, in combination with unmagnetized steel plates, whether the action of the same be aided or not by electricity, of artificial or natural permanent magnets, substantially as and for the purposes set forth.

In testimony whereof, I have signed my name to this specification, before two subscribing witnesses.

WM. J. LYND.

Witnesses:
WILLIAM ARMOR,
RICHARD H. HARRIS.

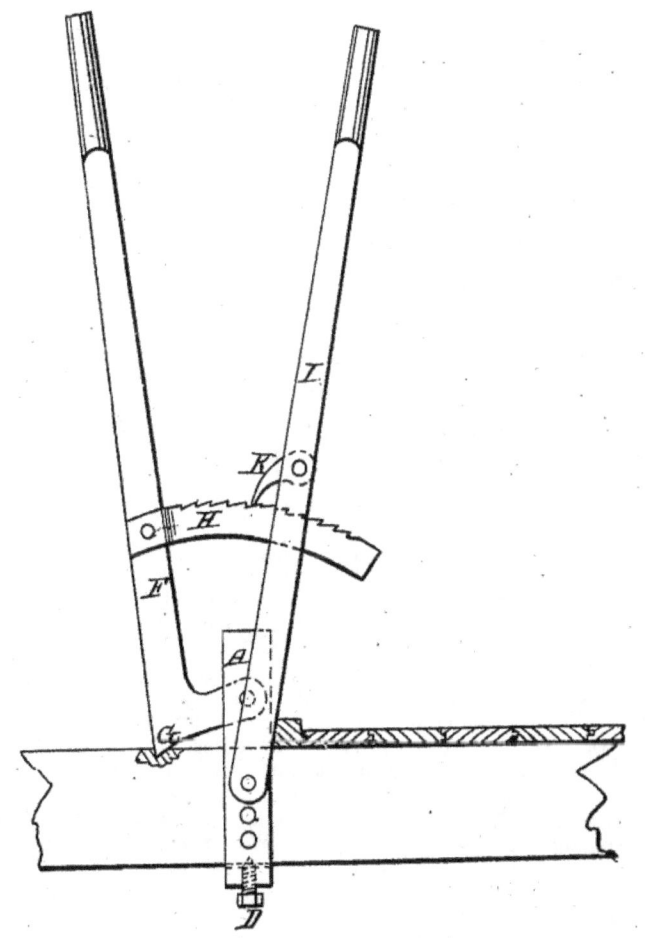
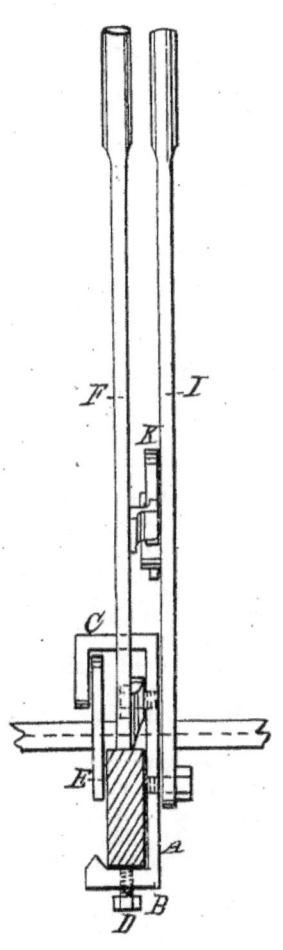

United States Patent Office.

DAVID NEVIN, OF BOULDER CITY, COLORADO TERRITORY.

Letters Patent No. 93,217, dated August 3, 1869.

IMPROVEMENT IN FLOORING-CLAMP.

The Schedule referred to in these Letters Patent and making part of the same.

To all whom it may concern:

Be it known that I, DAVID NEVIN, of Boulder City, Boulder county, Territory of Colorado, have invented a new and improved Flooring-Clamp; and I do hereby declare that the following is a full, clear, and exact description thereof, which will enable others skilled in the art to make and use the same, reference being had to the accompanying drawing, forming part of this specification.

This invention relates to improvements in clamps to be used for clamping the boards of flooring tightly together previously to nailing when laying the floors of buildings.

Figure 1 represents a side elevation of my improved clamp and a sectional view of a floor, showing the position when clamping a floor.

Figure 2 represents a front elevation of the same.

Similar letters of reference indicate corresponding parts.

A represents the stock of the clamp having two right-angled brackets B and C, for taking over and under the joists.

The lower bracket is provided with a set-screw, D, for taking into the wood, to prevent slipping, or a stud will answer as well.

The upper bracket supports a hinged tongue or guard, E, which may be raised to permit the application of the said stock to the joists, and swings down by the side of the joists to prevent the stock from falling laterally.

Near the top of the said stock a cranked lever, F, is pivoted, having a sharp heel, G, for taking into the top of the joists to prevent slipping.

It is also provided with a segmental rack, H, a short distance above the heel and projecting over the stock A.

L represents a clamping-lever, pivoted adjustably at its lower end to the stock A, and provided with a pawl, K, to engage with the said rack.

For operation, a clamping-block, L, is laid on the joists in front of the edge of the board to be clamped and nailed, and the stock A placed on a joist in front of the said block. The sharpened heel of the lever F is then forced into the joist by pulling the set-screw or stud D in the bottom of the joist. Then the clamping-lever is pressed forward against the block and has a powerful clamping action thereon.

When sufficient strain has been applied, the pawl K may be engaged with the notched bar H, to hold the lever I until the board is nailed.

Having thus described my invention,

What I claim as new, and desire to secure by Letters Patent, is—

The flooring-clamp, constructed as described, of the right-angular stock A B C, having the set-screw D and pivoted tongue or guard E, the right-angular pivoted lever F, the adjustable lever I, the rack H, and pawl K, all arranged and operating as described, for the purpose specified.

DAVID NEVIN.

Witnesses:
G. BERKLEY,
ALPHEUS WRIGHT.

P. C. Johnson,
Horse Shoe.
No. 93,447.   Patented Aug 10, 1869.

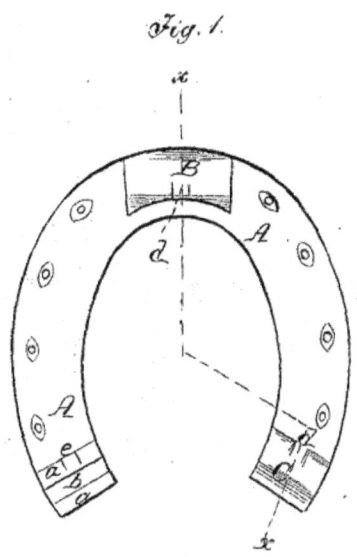

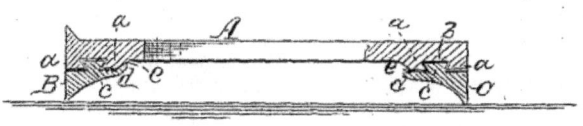

Witnesses
Chas Nida
Wm A Morgan

Inventor
P. C. Johnson
Munn & Co
Attorneys

United States Patent Office.

P. C. JOHNSON, OF CENTRAL CITY, COLORADO TERRITORY.

Letters Patent No. 93,447, dated August 10, 1869.

IMPROVEMENT IN HORSESHOES.

The Schedule referred to in these Letters Patent and making part of the same.

To all whom it may concern:

Be it known that I, P. C. JOHNSON, of Central City, in the Territory of Colorado, have invented a new and useful Improvement in Horseshoes; and I do hereby declare that the following is a full, clear, and exact description thereof, which will enable others skilled in the art to make and use the same, reference being had to the accompanying drawings, forming part of this specification, in which—

Figure 1 represents an inverted plan view of my improved horseshoe.

Figure 2 is a vertical longitudinal section of the same, taken on the plane of the line $x\ x$ of fig. 1.

Figure 3 is a detail perspective view of one of the calks.

Similar letters of reference indicate corresponding parts.

This invention relates to a new manner of constructing the calks of horseshoes, so that they can be readily fastened and removed.

The object of the invention is to provide a horseshoe which can always remain on the hoof, and which may easily receive new calks when the old ones are worn, or when, in winter, sharper toes have to be attached.

The invention consists in making two incisions in one edge of each calk, whereby the portion between the incisions becomes a lug, that may be bent into a recess provided in the body of the shoe. The calk is fitted with a dovetail-tenon into a corresponding groove formed in the shoe, and the aforesaid lug is then bent into the recess. Thereby the lateral displacement of the calk is prevented, while the tenon prevents longitudinal and vertical displacement. When the lug is forced out of the recess, the calk can be removed.

A, in the drawing, represents the body of a horseshoe;

B is the toe; and

C C, the calks.

Where the same are to be fitted upon the shoe, the latter is provided with downward projections, $a\ a$, as shown.

Between the two projections, a, that pertain to one toe or calk, is formed a dovetail-groove, b, shown in fig. 1.

Each calk or toe has a corresponding tenon, c, which can be fitted into the groove, so as to thereby fit the calk or toe to the shoe.

On the inner side, each calk and toe has two incisions, whereby a lug, d, is formed, which may be forced into a recess, e, formed in the part a of the shoe, as is clearly shown in fig. 2.

The calks and toes are thereby securely fastened to the shoe, and cannot spontaneously fall off. But they can be removed when the lug is forced out of the recess.

Having thus described my invention,

I claim as new, and desire to secure by Letters Patent—

The lugs d, when formed by the incisions in the side of the sliding calks, and bent down into recesses in the raised portions, a, of the shoe, to form a locking-device, in combination with the dovetail connections $a\ a\ c$, all constructed, arranged, and operated as described.

P. C. JOHNSON.

Witnesses:
 AMOS W. HALL,
 J. W. CUMINGS.

United States Patent Office.

WILLIAM J. LYND, OF GOLDEN CITY, COLORADO TERRITORY.

Letters Patent No. 93,629, dated August 10, 1869.

IMPROVED PROCESS OF PREPARING COKE FROM COLORADO AND OTHER COALS.

The Schedule referred to in these Letters Patent and making part of the same.

To whom it may concern:

Be it known that I, WILLIAM J. LYND, of Golden City, in the county of Jefferson, and Territory of Colorado, have invented or discovered a new and useful Process of Coking the Different Species of Coals found in Colorado Territory, and in other parts of the United States of America, and at present mined in Jefferson county and in Boulder county of said Colorado Territory, said coals being called by some "glance," by others, "dry bituminous," and by others, "lignite;" and I do hereby declare the following to be a full and exact description of the same.

The coal, to prevent slaking and crumbling by the action of the air, is placed, as soon as possible after it is mined, in a coking-kiln or oven surmounted by a chimney, so arranged as to be hermetically closed or made air-tight, when desired, at the base, where it (the chimney) touches or rises from the kiln or oven. That oven is best which is of the largest practicable size, because the greater the quantity of this coal in ignition together, the better will be the carbonization. A kiln or oven without a chimney will answer, but it should be provided with a covering of suitable material, to close air-tight the aperture allowed for the escape of the aeriform or gaseous products. The covering is better when quite thick, say from three to nine inches. It can be made air-tight by the application of any cement, such as mortar, clay, or wet moulder's sand.

Instead of a kiln or oven, retorts may be used; but the retorts should be provided with doors or valves, to perfectly close the retorts, when the gases or impurities have been expelled, so as to exclude the air, and to confine the heat of the coals in combustion. But the coking of the above-mentioned coals by retorts is not, by any means, so thorough or so certain as by the use of the kiln or oven, and is also more expensive.

The kiln or oven being furnished with coals, the coal is kindled, and, when all the coal is in a state of combustion, the draught is shut off; or, if there be several draughts, to insure thorough and rapid ignition, then the lowest draught is shut off first, and the rest, successively, as the ignition progresses.

The covering at the base of the chimney is closed by degrees as the smoke, gases, or aeriform products escape; and, when the impurities—viz, tar, (a little,) ammonia, bitumen, sulphur, and other fuliginous and volatile products—are nearly or quite removed, the covering is completely closed, and the kiln hermetically shut or made air-tight.

This process will carbonize the above-mentioned coals. But the process is hastened, assisted, and improved by the introduction of carburetted-hydrogen gas or vapor from oil, coal-tar, or other hydrocarbons.

The gas or vapor should be introduced by one or several pipes, so that the gas or vapor may reach all the coals, when the closing is nearly completed.

Instead of the gas or vapor, the hydrocarbon-fluid may be introduced, generating, by contact with the coals, the gas or vapor.

If pipes be used for the gas or fluid, as above specified, they should be closed tightly at the places where they enter the oven.

A little gas or vapor, or hydrocarbon-fluid, may be introduced by one pipe for a short time, after the kiln is elsewhere, or in all other respects closed, and then this last aperture of the pipe be entirely shut where it touches the oven.

By thus proceeding, a coke is obtained from the aforesaid coals which is well adapted for smelting and other metallurgical operations, and all purposes for which an intense heat is required.

Having thus described my said invention, and the manner in which the same is or may be carried into effect,

What I claim, and desire to secure by Letters Patent, is—

The process, substantially as herein described, of making coke from coals, such as herein referred to.

In testimony whereof, I have signed my name to this specification, before two subscribing witnesses.

WM. J. LYND.

Witnesses:
WM. ARMOR,
ARTHUR C. HARRIS.

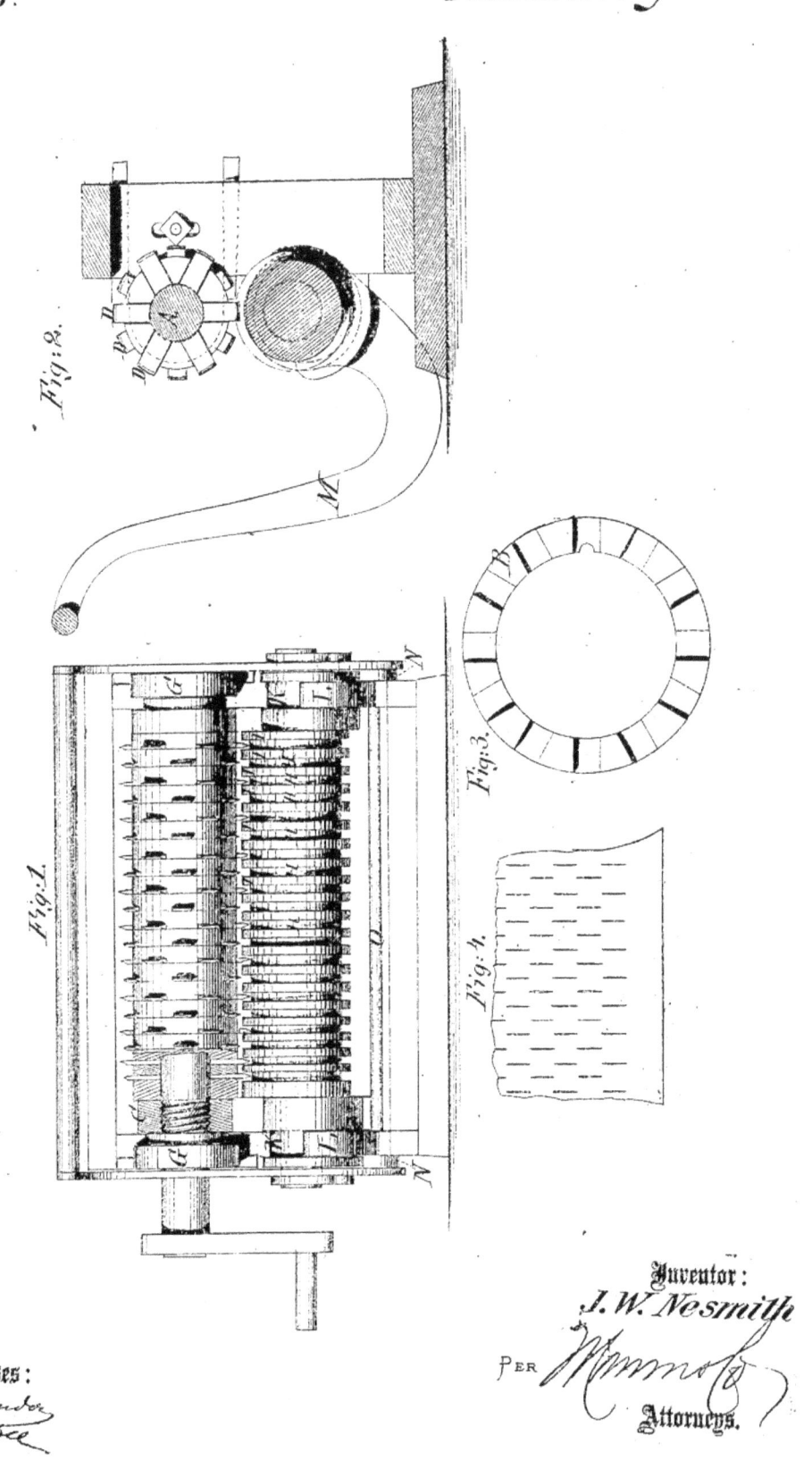

UNITED STATES PATENT OFFICE.

J. WELLINGTON NESMITH, OF BLACK HAWK, COLORADO TERRITORY.

IMPROVED MACHINE FOR PUNCHING METAL SCREENS.

Specification forming part of Letters Patent No. **94,333**, dated August 31, 1869.

To all whom it may concern:

Be it known that I, J. WELLINGTON NESMITH, of Black Hawk, in the county of Gilpin and Territory of Colorado, have invented a new and Improved Screen-Punching Machine; and I do hereby declare that the following is a full, clear, and exact description thereof, which will enable others skilled in the art to make and use the same, reference being had to the accompanying drawings, forming part of this specification.

The object of this invention is to provide a simple and efficient machine for punching sheet metal to make screens, such as are used for screening ores and other substances.

The invention consists of improved arrangements of a punching-roller and grooved roller, between which the sheet is passed to be punched, whereby they may be varied to punch finer or coarser holes, also whereby the sheet may be readily inserted and removed, so as not to punch the border.

The said invention also consists in an improved construction of the punching-roller.

Figure 1 represents a side elevation of my improved machine. Fig. 2 represents a transverse section of the same. Fig. 3 represents an elevation of one of the punch-holding rings of the punching-roller, and Fig. 4 represents a part of a sheet of metal as it appears after punching.

Similar letters of reference indicate corresponding parts.

The punch-carrying roller is composed of a shaft, A, and any preferred number of punch-holding rings or disks, B, fitted to the said shaft, and clamped thereon against a collar at one end by a screw, C, or by other means at the other end. These rings have radial slots or grooves in one side, for the reception of the punches D, which are short flat plates sharpened at the ends, which project from the roller. The said ends project only sufficient to penetrate the sheets to be punched. They are enough thicker than the depth of the radial slots in the rings to be firmly clamped by the rings when screwed up. The journals of this roller are placed in bearings G, arranged in the housings for adjustment laterally, for the purpose of adjusting it exactly to the vertical line of the roller H. They are also adjustable vertically. This roller H is provided with annular grooves, into which the punches project after passing through the sheet metal. The lower roller, H, is journaled in eccentric bearings K, which are arranged to oscillate in their supports L, and they are provided with arms M, preferably forged to them, for turning them when required. These arms are connected at their outer ends by a bar, N, to insure a uniform action of both the said arms, and so bent and connected to the bearings that they may be turned farther between the limits of the floor and the projections of the upper roller than they could be if they were straight, as is clearly shown. They are raised to move the grooved roller away from the other, and vice versa.

N represents eccentric stops placed on a shaft, P, running through the housings, against which the levers strike when moving the grooved roller up to the other, and whereby they are arrested in the said movement. By turning these stops one way or the other, as may be done by a wrench or other means, the distance of the rollers apart may be varied, and thereby the punching will be finer or coarser.

Having thus described my invention, I claim as new and desire to secure by Letters Patent—

1. The combination of the punching-roller, grooved roller, eccentric bearings K, and operating-levers M, when arranged substantially as specified.

2. The combination of the punching-roller, grooved roller, eccentric bearings, levers, and eccentric stops, when arranged substantially as specified.

3. The combination, with the shaft A, having a fixed collar and clamping-nut, of the radially-slotted rings B and punches D, when all arranged substantially as specified.

4. The combination of the punching-roller, grooved roller, and laterally and vertically adjustable bearings G, when all arranged as specified.

The above specification of my invention signed by me this 16th day of June, 1869.

J. WELLINGTON NESMITH.

Witnesses:
G. B. BACKUS,
H. M. OVERHOOD.

M. L. ROOD.
Velocipede.

No. 94,842. Patented Sept. 14, 1869.

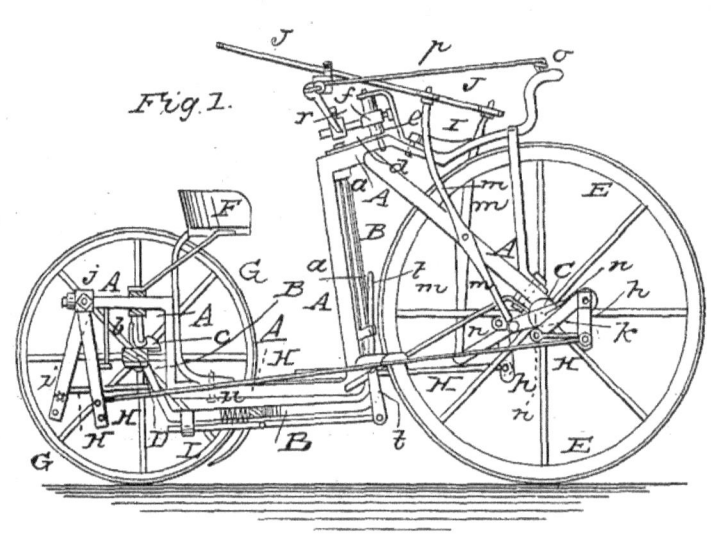

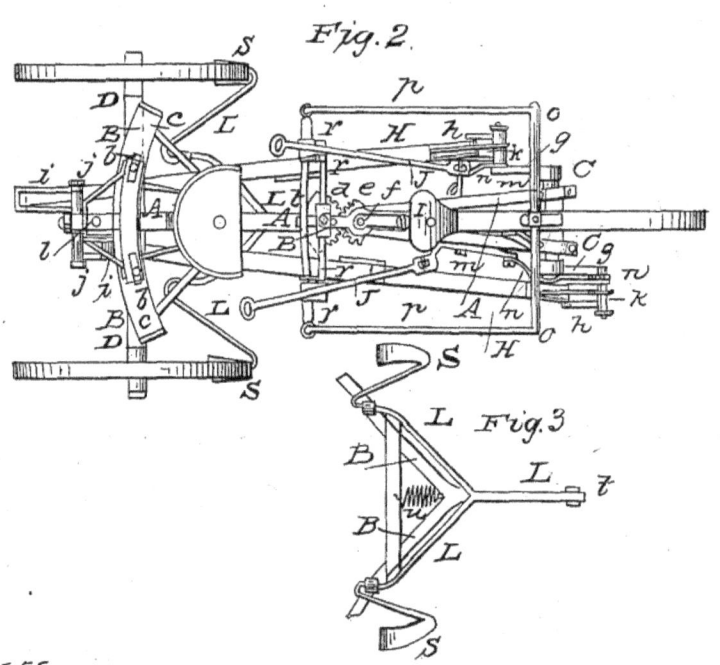

WITNESSES

INVENTOR

M. L. Rood.

United States Patent Office.

M. L. ROOD, OF DENVER, COLORADO TERRITORY.

Letters Patent No. 94,842, dated September 14, 1869.

IMPROVED VELOCIPEDE.

The Schedule referred to in these Letters Patent and making part of the same.

To all whom it may concern:

Be it known that I, M. L. Rood, of Denver, in the county of Arapahoe, and Territory of Colorado, have invented a new and improved Velocipede; and I do hereby declare that the following is a full, clear, and exact description thereof, which will enable others skilled in the art to make and use the same, reference being had to the accompanying drawings, forming part of this specification, in which—

Figure 1 represents a side elevation, partly in section, of my improved velocipede.

Figure 2 is a plan or top view of the same.

Figure 3 is a detail inverted plan view, showing the brake attachment.

Similar letters of reference indicate corresponding parts.

This invention relates to a new three-wheeled velocipede, which is so constructed that it can be propelled by a convenient motion of the feet or hands, readily steered and stopped, and that it will accommodate two riders at once.

The invention consists, first, in a novel construction of jointed reach; secondly, in a new form and arrangement of brake, and also in a novel combination and arrangement of propelling-mechanism.

A, in the drawing, represents the front part of the frame of my improved velocipede.

B is the back part of the frame. The front part extends up from the front axle C, and then down and back, and reaches over the rear axle D. The rear part extends forward from the rear axle, and is close behind the front wheel E, turned up, and has the vertical arm a; thus formed, fitted through the upper part of the frame A, and pivoted therein.

The rear part of the frame A rests on rollers b b, which travel on a segmental plate, c, that is secured upon the rear axle, as shown.

On the upper end of the pin a is mounted a toothed segment or wheel, d, which meshes into a similar wheel or segment, e, which is mounted on a vertical pin, f. This pin is swivelled in the frame A, and is provided with a steering-handle, r, so that by turning said handle, the two parts of the frame will be swung to steer.

The main seat F is supported on the frame A. When steered, the front frame will swing with the front wheel, and the driver's seat will therefore always be in the same direction in which the vehicle is progressing.

The rear axle carries two wheels, G G, which are merely following-wheels, while the front wheel E is the driving and steering-wheel.

On its shaft C are cranks g, from which stirrups h are suspended. These stirrups are, by means of long rods H, connected with stirrups i, which are suspended from a transverse pin, j, that is fitted through the rear end of the frame A, as shown.

On the rods H are pivoted hooks k, which can, as in fig. 1, be locked to the crank-pins, in which case the stirrups h will be locked at right angles to the rods H.

The driver on the seat F may, by means of the feet, alternately depress one of the rods H, and thereby rotate the wheel E, or the hooks k may be uncoupled from the cranks, when the wheel may also be revolved by oscillating the rods H. In this case, however, these rods must be locked together at their rear ends by a pin, l, fitted through their stirrups, i. The device may also be propelled by holding the feet directly upon the cranks g, for which purpose another seat, I, is secured upon the upper front part of the frame A. The device may also be propelled by hand, by means of handles J, which are, by means of levers m and rods n, connected with the cranks. The person on the front seat may also aid in steering by working a front steering-handle, o, which is by rods p p connected with the ends of the handle r.

The brake is in form of a Y-shaped frame, L, shown in fig. 3, with shoes s s at its ends. Its front shank is pivoted to a lever, t, which is pivoted to the front upright a of the rear frame B. A spring, u, serves to draw the shoes of the rear wheels. By swinging the upper end of the lever t forward, the rider on the seat F can at any time apply the brake with one foot.

Having thus described my invention,

What I claim as new, and desire to secure by Letters Patent, is—

1. The frame A B, made of two parts, the front part having its rear end supported on the segmental plate c of the rear part, while the front upright arm a of the rear piece, connects the two parts, substantially as herein shown and described.

2. The arrangement of the jointed frame and steering-device, with respect to the driving-mechanism, in the manner and for the purpose specified.

3. The brake, consisting of the Y-shaped frame L, operated by a lever, t, and arranged substantially as herein shown and described.

4. The combination of the rods H, stirrups h i, cranks g, and shaft C, with the handles J, levers m, and rods n, all connected to form the propelling-mechanism, substantially as herein shown and described.

M. L. ROOD.

Witnesses:
 John D. Roby,
 Wm. B. Davids.

E. Evans,
Land Roller.

No. 94,879. Patented Sep. 14. 1869.

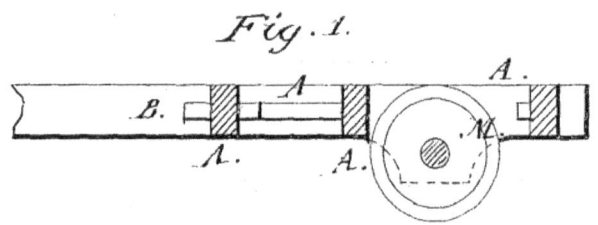

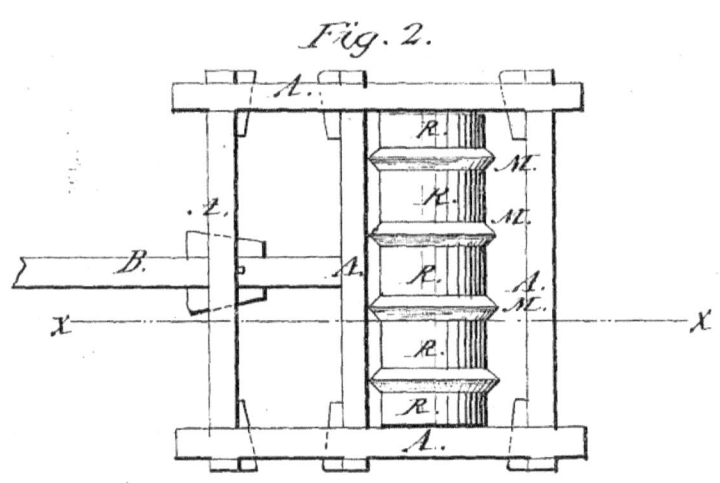

Witnesses:
C. A. Pettit
T. C. Kennon

Inventor:
E. Evans
by Munn & Co
Attorneys.

United States Patent Office.

ELIHU EVANS, OF DENVER CITY, COLORADO TERRITORY.

Letters Patent No. 94,879, dated September 14, 1869.

IMPROVEMENT IN SECTION-ROLLER AND MARKER COMBINED.

The Schedule referred to in these Letters Patent and making part of the same.

To all whom it may concern:

Be it known that I, ELIHU EVANS, of Denver City, in the county of Arapahoe, and Territory of Colorado, have invented a new and improved Combined Section-Marker and Roller; and I do hereby declare that the following is a full, clear, and exact description of the construction and operation of the same, reference being had to the accompanying drawings, making a part of this specification, in which—

Figure 1 is a longitudinal vertical section through line $x\,x$ of fig. 2.

Figure 2 is a top view.

This invention consists in a new arrangement and combination of section-rollers and section-markers in a single instrument, to be employed on plowed ground in rolling the surface and laying off well-defined drills or channels, at any required distance apart, into which the agriculturist can lead water and thereby distribute it uniformly over the field for the purpose of irrigation.

The instrument is designed, and its form and construction has a special adaptation for use on the lands along the eastern slope of the Rocky mountains and Cordilleras, in Colorado and New Mexico, which require irrigation almost every season.

In the drawings—

A is the frame,

B, the draught-pole, and

c, the axle.

R R are section-rollers, each running loosely on the axle, and independently of all the others.

M M are section-markers, interposed between the rollers, and having their sharp wedge-form edges projecting beyond the perimeter of the rollers, as shown in fig. 2, and so constructed as to imprint upon the surface of the ground long well-defined parallel drills or channels, several inches deep, and with pressed and hardened sides and bottom.

These channels may be varied in distance from each other by removing some of the markers, or by substituting longer or shorter rollers between said markers.

By this means, the agriculturist can mark the surface of his ground (which in the country referred to is generally slightly inclined) with series of parallel channels, at any suitable distance, from a few inches to two or three feet apart, and then by introducing water into these channels at their upper end, it will be conveyed to all parts of the field, and brought to every square foot of soil therein.

The means for introducing the water at the upper end of the channels may simply be a small canal or trench running at angles to the drills above described.

When not used thus to lay off the surface of the field into suitable water-channels, the markers may be removed, and the instrument used without them, as an ordinary field or lawn-roller.

The rollers and markers being made in sections, or independent of each other, the instrument is not only adapted to make the channels at different distances apart, as may be required, but it turns more easily at the ends of the field than if the rollers and markers were made in one or two solid pieces; and besides these two advantages, it can be taken apart and packed for transportation into a much more compact and convenient form for handling.

Having thus described my invention,

What I claim as new, and desire to secure by Letters Patent, is—

The section-roller and marker for irrigating-purposes, substantially as above described, having the frame A, draught-pole B, short independent rolls R R, and interposed markers M M, rotating independently of each other and of the rolls, when constructed in the manner herein set forth, and for the purposes specified.

To the above specification of my improvement, I have set my hand, this 13th day of April, 1869.

ELIHU EVANS.

Witnesses:
H. L. BOYD,
J. M. CROSS.

Rice & Van Deren,
Stamp Mill.

No. 95,045. Patented Sep. 21. 1869.

Fig. 1.

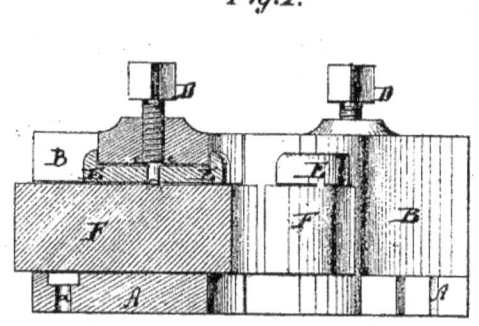

Fig. 2.

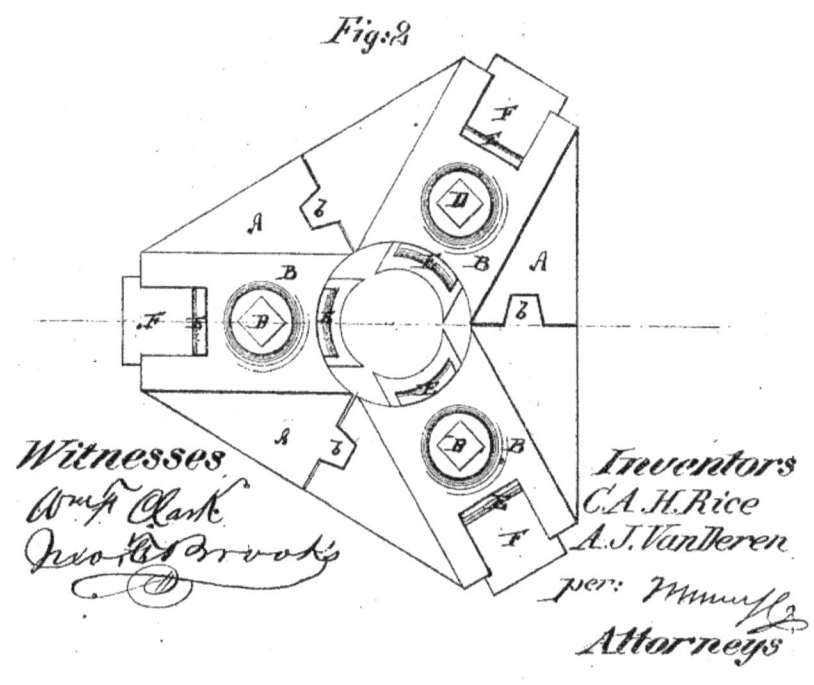

Witnesses
Wm. F. Clark
Jno. R. Brooks

Inventors
C. A. H. Rice
A. J. Van Deren
per: [signature]
Attorneys

United States Patent Office.

CHARLES A. H. RICE AND A. J. VAN DEREN, OF CENTRAL CITY, COLORADO TERRITORY.

Letters Patent No. 95,045, dated September 21, 1869.

IMPROVEMENT IN GUIDES FOR STAMP-MILLS.

The Schedule referred to in these Letters Patent and making part of the same.

To all whom it may concern:

Be it known that we, CHARLES A. H. RICE and A. J. VAN DEREN, of Central City, in the county of Gilpin, and Territory of Colorado, have invented a new and improved Universal Guide for Stamp-Mills; and we do hereby declare that the following is a full, clear, and exact description thereof, which will enable others skilled in the art to make and use the same, reference being had to the accompanying drawings, forming part of this specification, in which—

Figure 1 represents a vertical section of our improved guide for mills.

Figure 2 is a plan or top view of the same.

Similar letters of reference indicate corresponding parts.

This invention relates to a new device for guiding the shafts of stamp-mills; and consists in the general construction of parts whereby the guide-pieces are securely held and readily adjusted.

The whole guide is composed of three or more sections, A A, which are plates carrying boxes for the reception of the guides.

Each plate A has a countersunk hole, a, or equivalent device, to allow its being readily fastened to a supporting-bed.

The various sections are locked together by projecting tenons $b\ b$, which fit into recesses of the adjoining sections, as shown in fig. 2.

The boxes B B, which project from the plates A, are provided with concave inner ends, which together form a circle, as in fig. 1.

Through the top of each box B is fitted a screw, D, which has its lower part turned smaller without a thread, to form a shoulder, c, and which has a concave lower end.

This screw fits, with its shoulder, upon the gib E, which is placed into each box above the wooden guide F. The lower part of the screw fits through the gib, and rests on the guide. The concave end is forced with its sharp edge into the wood, to take a firm hold on the guide while the shoulder presses the gib upon the upper face of the guide.

The inner ends of the guides are also concave, to properly embrace the shaft.

Having thus described our invention,

We claim as new, and desire to secure by Letters Patent—

An adjustable guide for stamp-mills, consisting of the sectional support A, boxes B, screws D, gibs E, and wooden guides F, the screws having the shoulders c and the concave lower ends, when all these parts are arranged together as herein shown and described, for operation as set forth.

CHAS. A. H. RICE.
A. J. VAN DEREN.

Witnesses:
WILLARD SELLER,
WILLIAM R. KENNEDY.

P. C. Johnson,
Clothes Line.
No. 97,409. Patented Nov. 30, 1869.

Witnesses:
A Bonnewendorf
Alex F. Roberts

Inventor:
P. C. Johnson
Per Munn & Co
Attorneys.

UNITED STATES PATENT OFFICE.

P. C. JOHNSON, OF CENTRAL CITY, COLORADO TERRITORY, ASSIGNOR TO MARY JOHNSON, OF SAME PLACE.

IMPROVEMENT IN CLOTHES-LINES.

Specification forming part of Letters Patent No. **97,409**, dated November 30, 1869.

To all whom it may concern:

Be it known that I, P. C. JOHNSON, of Central City, in the county of Gilpin and Territory of Colorado, have invented a new and useful Improvement in Clothes-Lines; and I do hereby declare that the following is a full, clear, and exact description thereof, which will enable others skilled in the art to make and use the same, reference being had to the accompanying drawing, forming part of this specification.

The drawing represents a side view of my improved clothes-line.

This invention has for its object to do away with the props or sticks commonly used to support clothes-lines at or near the middle, to prevent them from hanging too low. Such props or sticks are liable to be broken or blown down, and are, consequently, unreliable and unsafe.

My invention consists in the use of an endless line, hung over two pulleys, and of one or more carriages connecting its two parallel lengths to sustain the lower one, which supports the clothes.

A, in the drawing, represents the endless clothes-line, fitted over two equal-sized pulleys, $a\ b$, which are hung in the posts B and C, that support the line. The post B is the one at which the clothes are to be secured to or removed from the line, and is or may be lower than the other post, C. On the lower length, c, of the line is formed a knot, d, which cannot pass through either one of the pulleys. Between the knot d and the pulley a, on the post B, is fitted, upon both lengths of the line, a carriage, D, which consists of two or more rollers, e, connected by side plates f, and traveling, respectively, on the upper side of the upper length and on the under side of the lower length of line. This carriage can travel on the line, but cannot pass the knot d.

The clothes are hung in the following manner: The carriage D is first drawn against the pulley a, and the knot d against the carriage. The clothes are then hung upon the lower length, c, between the knot and carriage, the knot being gradually moved toward the post C, while the carriage is held against the pulley a. When the line is about half-full—that is to say, when the knot is about in the middle of the line—the carriage is also moved along with the lower length toward the post C, and clothes are hung upon the line between the carriage and the post B until the knob d strikes the pulley b, as in the drawing.

The lower length of the line is now entirely filled, and the carriage is in the middle supporting the weighted line on the stretched upper length, and preventing thereby also the sagging of the lower length.

If desired, two or more such carriages may be used on one line to support the same at different places.

The advantages of this arrangement are that the supporting-posts are dispensed with; that the clothes can all be applied and removed by a person standing at the post B, and that consequently the clothes need not be carried along the entire length of line.

Another advantage is that the line can be elevated to a great height, and that the clothes can therefore be more freely exposed to the air and more rapidly dried. The knot d may, if desired, be dispensed with.

Having thus described my invention, I claim as new and desire to secure by Letters Patent—

The double pulley or carriage D, with its pulleys $e\ e$, in combination with the knot d, cord A, posts B and C, and pivoted holders h, with their pulleys $a\ a$, as shown and described.

The above specification of my invention signed by me this 6th day of October, 1869.

P. C. JOHNSON.

Witnesses:
S. P. KENDALL,
L. W. CHASE.

United States Patent Office.

WILLIAM JOHN LYND, OF GOLDEN CITY, COLORADO TERRITORY.

Letters Patent No. 98,606, dated January 4, 1870.

IMPROVED PROCESS OF PREPARING COAL FOR SMELTING ORES.

The Schedule referred to in these Letters Patent and making part of the same.

To all whom it may concern:

Be it known that I, WILLIAM JOHN LYND, of Golden City, in the county of Jefferson, and Territory of Colorado, have invented or discovered certain Improvements in the Preparation of the Coal of Colorado and similar coal wherever found in the United States, said coal being called by some, dry bituminous, and by others, glance, and commonly called lignite, and said coal being mined in Jefferson county and elsewhere in Colorado Territory, so that said coal can be used in place of coke, or charcoal, or anthracite coal, for smelting, blacksmithing, and other uses to which coke, charcoal, or anthracite is applied; and I do hereby declare that the following is a full and exact description of the same.

The coal is placed in a retort, or other receptacle, large or small, (of any suitable material,) put over, or in, or attached to a furnace or other structure, so as to receive the heat necessary to expel the bitumen, sulphur, and other extraneous or volatile matter. Heat is applied, and when the foreign or volatile matters are driven out, a light charred substance, easily lighted, and giving out intense heat, remains. This will answer for smelting, &c.

Usually, when thus preparing the coal, and converting it into what may be called coke, the pipe or neck of the retort is sealed up, in order to the more perfect carbonization of the mass. But I have also found that coal called "cannel'lignite," and other coals of a like nature, can be coked in a retort, even though not closed altogether from the air, and I therefore contemplate coking the coal, either partially or entirely, in a retort whether sealed up or open. In this preparation of the coal, the retort will require usually to be heated to a cherry-red heat, and maintained for some time at that heat.

An improvement on the above is the following: To the coal in the retort add quick-lime, in quantity about one-sixth of the coal or less. Apply the heat. The carbon of the coal left, after the inflammable parts have been expelled, will be found impregnated with the lime, and so carries the lime-flux in itself. This preparation melts iron readily, and is well adapted for iron-smelting and all metallurgical operations.

An improvement on this last is as follows: Take the coal as prepared with lime, and place it in a furnace, thoroughly ignite it, and then hermetically close it from the air. This gives coke of an extraordinary caloric power.

Another method of preparing the coal is this: Grind the coal to a powder, expel the gases, &c., by heat; then add to the powder, pine-tar or other hydrocarbon; place again in the retort, (after the mixture of coal-powder and coal or pine-tar has been pressed into balls or bricks,) and close the retort, so as nothing may escape. Then apply a gentle heat, until the balls or bricks are hardened. This is excellent fuel for smelting or blacksmithing.

What I claim as my invention, and desire to secure by Letters Patent, is—

1. The mode of coking or preparing Colorado coals, and other coals of a similar kind, in an open or closed retort, substantially in the manner described.

2. The improvements in coking or preparing coals, substantially as above described, for the uses specified.

In testimony whereof, I have signed my name to this specification, before two subscribing witnesses.

WM. J. LYND.

Witnesses:
WILLIAM AMOR,
RICHARD H. HARRIS.

United States Patent Office.

WILLIAM J. LYND, OF GOLDEN CITY, TERRITORY OF COLORADO.

Letters Patent No. 98,607, dated January 4, 1870.

IMPROVEMENT IN USING COLORADO AND SIMILAR COAL FOR METALLURGICAL OPERATIONS.

The Schedule referred to in these Letters Patent and making part of the same.

To whom it may concern:

Be it known that I, WILLIAM J. LYND, of Golden City, in the county of Jefferson, and Territory of Colorado, have invented a new and useful Process of Using Colorado and other Similar Coals in Metallurgical and other Operations; and I hereby declare the following to be a full, clear, and exact description of the same.

The coals which I contemplate using are those known under the names of bituminous glance, dry bituminous, lignite, &c., at present mined in Colorado Territory, and other parts of the United States; and the object I have in view is to employ them, in the place of coke, charcoal, or anthracite, in smelting and other metallurgical operations, and for calcining limestone, burning pottery-ware, brick, &c.

To enable those skilled in the art to understand and use my invention, I will proceed to describe it, having reference, first, to the coking of the coals in connection with metallurgical operations; secondly, to the combination of coking with the calcination of limestone, or preparation of quick-lime; and, thirdly, to the combination of coking with the burning of pottery-ware, brick, &c.

1. *Metallurgical Operations.*

The furnaces, whether reverberatory or otherwise, should have several fire-boxes containing the coal, in number from one to six, more or less, each separated from the other by a partition-wall, and communicating by distinct flues with the basin holding the iron, or ore, or whatever is sought to be reduced.

To insure ignition, the coal when lighted should have a gentle draught for a little while, after which all air should be excluded, except by a long, narrow horizontal opening above the door of each fire-box, to admit air enough to cause the combustion of the bituminous or inflammable part of the coal.

The flames from each fire-box pass through the respective flue into the basin containing the iron, or ore, or other matter, which will thereby attain nearly a white heat, or even more, by the time the inflammable part of the coal has been consumed.

When the inflammable part of the coal has been consumed, I exclude the air from the fire-boxes by tightly closing the horizontal openings above the doors, and close tightly all the flues leading to the basin, except one. Upon the fuel of the box leading to this open flue, let the blast be thrown in any ordinary or suitable manner. During this operation, the fuel in the other fire-boxes is carbonizing.

When the fuel under the blast fails, through consumption, to give the required heat, another flue may be opened, and the fuel of its fire-box similarly operated with. Thus each fire-box in turn will throw its new and intense flame upon the metal, ore, or whatever is sought to be reduced.

Each fire-box in turn can be replenished with coal, and the coking-operation, as above described, go on, so that when the last receives the blast, the first is nearly or quite ready for the renewal of the blast through it. In case it is not ready, some coke can be added to the last to keep up the heat.

The process of coking the coal for the blast and saving the heat, may be carried on without shutting the flues or entirely excluding the atmospheric air from the fuel. The process can be secured by increasing, lessening, or shutting off the draught of air admitted from beneath or elsewhere.

The same process can be similarly performed with furnaces constructed with fire-boxes without partitions, walls, or separate flues, viz, by increasing, lessening, or shutting off the draught of air admitted from beneath or elsewhere to the fuel not subject to the blast.

For some operations, pipes may be added to each fire-box, to carry off the flames, &c., of the replenished coal while coking, so as not to interfere with the blast.

If one fire-box is preferred, a furnace for coking may be placed above, with two pipes, one to let the flames of the bituminous matter, &c., of the coal enter the basin with the flames from the fire-box, the other pipe to let the inflammable matter of the replenished coal in the furnace enter, when desired, the chimney above the basin.

An aperture in the bottom of the furnace, so arranged that the blast will not interfere with the coking, will let the fuel prepared for the blast descend as it is wanted, on the principle of base-burning stoves. In this case, the fire-box may be made more shallow and greater in diameter, thereby allowing the oxygen of the air to unite more freely and completely with the carbon of the coal.

2. *Calcining Limestone.*

The furnaces may be two or more, ten to twenty feet in length, more or less, and three to ten feet in width, more or less, and without compartments, the coal being in one mass in each furnace. When the coal is ignited, the air is entirely excluded, except by a long, narrow horizontal opening above the door of each furnace, or by narrow horizontal openings opposite the series of lateral flues, which, to each furnace, may be in number according to length of furnace, say one flue for each two or three feet.

The flues open into the space occupied by the lime in the lime-shaft, which rises from the sides of the furnaces.

A partition-wall, raised to a proper height, will secure each furnace from derangement of draught.

The heat and flames of the burning extraneous matter given out from the coal, will raise the lime to a white heat, calcining it. When the inflammable parts of the coal are consumed, the flues must be shut closely, and the openings to let in the air hermetically closed. Thus the coal will be coked and the lime calcined.

3. Burning Brick, &c.

The furnaces are like the lime-kiln furnaces, and one or more for each side of kiln, which should have a permanent wall of proper thickness (at least three to four feet) and height, and should be so arranged as to be tightly closed during the burning.

The arches of the kiln should be so arranged as to receive, through the lateral flues, as in lime-burning, the flames from the furnaces, which are operated as those of the lime-kilns.

By the same process, pottery-ware can be well burned. The fuel may be in mass, as above specified, or in separate fire-boxes, as is usual in burning ware.

When the ware has attained a white heat, if more heat is required, instead of closing up the flues and excluding air for completing the coking-process, the apertures above the doors are closed, and a draught let on the fuel from beneath. The draught is increased until the required heat is attained.

In all these cases, the furnace-walls, in order to retain the heat and radiate it, so that all the heat may, as much as possible, go to the metal, or lime, or brick, should be quite thick and massive.

The process above described, of using the coals to obtain heat for burning brick, &c., is applicable, even though it is not desired to obtain coke, though the process described is, however, especially advantageous, for the reason that it affords a means of coking the coal, and at the same time burning the ware, brick, &c.

Having now described my invention, I would state that I do not limit my claim to the precise details herein given in illustration of the manner in which the invention is or may be carried into effect, for it is manifest that the same can be varied in many respects; but

What I claim as new, and desire to secure by Letters Patent, is—

1. The use of coals, such as specified, in smelting and other metallurgical operations, substantially in the manner set forth.

2. The use of coals, such as specified, in the operation of calcining limestone, substantially in the manner set forth.

3. The use of coals, such as specified, for burning pottery-ware, brick, &c., substantially in the manner set forth.

4. The process of coking the coals and smelting, or otherwise reducing metals, calcining limestone, or burning pottery-ware, bricks, &c., simultaneously or by one continuous operation, substantially as herein specified.

In testimony whereof, I have signed my name to this specification, before two subscribing witnesses.

WILLIAM J. LYND.

Witnesses:
WILLIAM ARMOR,
RICHARD H. HARRIS.

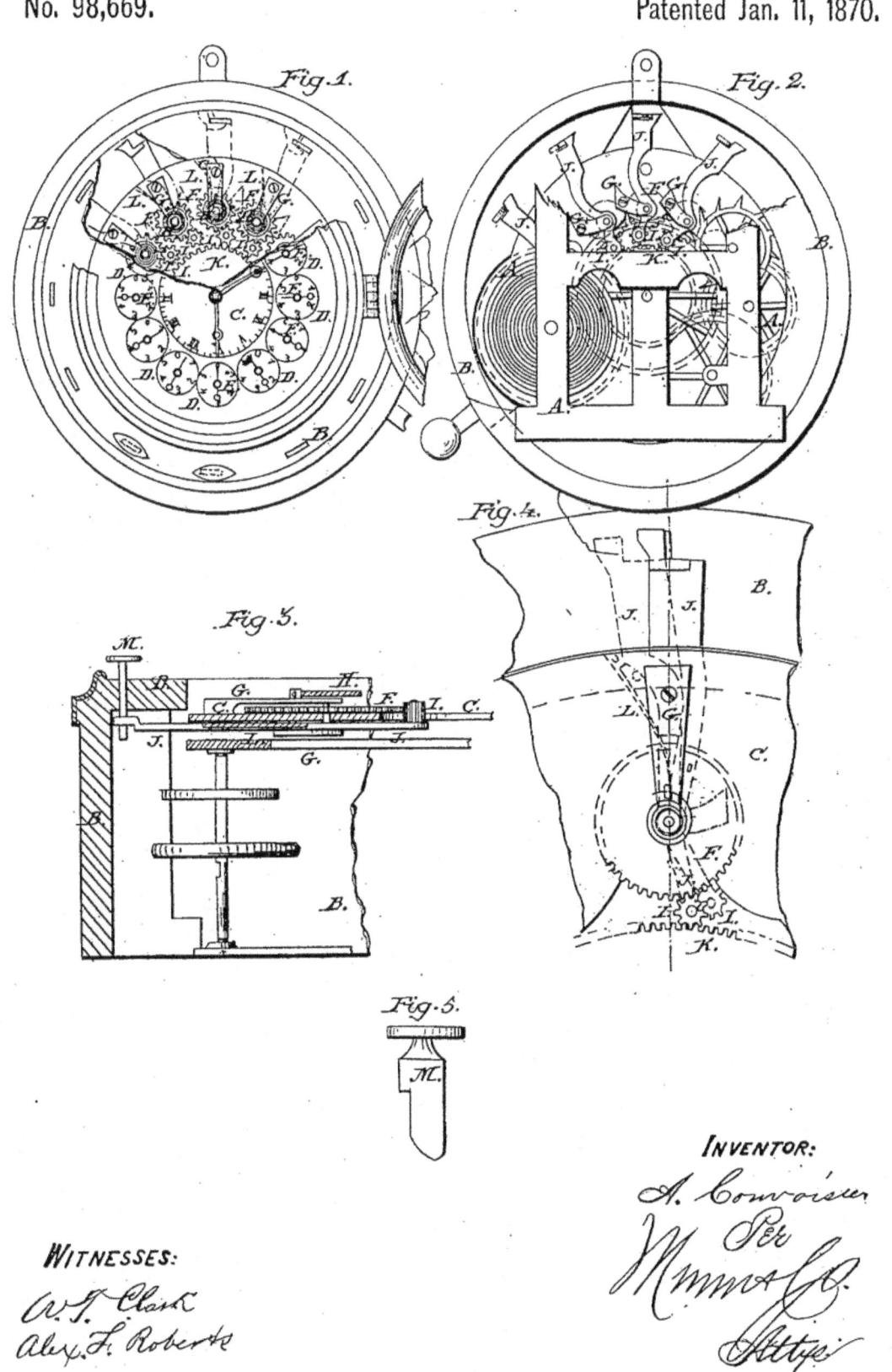

United States Patent Office.

AUGUSTE COURVOISIER, OF DENVER, COLORADO TERRITORY.

Letters Patent No. 98,669, dated January 11, 1870.

IMPROVEMENT IN TIME-REGISTER FOR HIRING-PURPOSES.

The Schedule referred to in these Letters Patent and making part of the same.

To all whom it may concern:

Be it known that I, AUGUSTE COURVOISIER, of Denver, in the county of Arapahoe, and Territory of Colorado, have invented a new and useful Improvement in Time-Register for Velocipedes, &c.; and I do hereby declare that the following is a full, clear, and exact description thereof, which will enable others skilled in the art to make and use the same, reference being had to the accompanying drawings, forming part of this specification.

Figure 1 is a front view of my improved time-register, part of the dial-plate being broken away to show the construction.

Figure 2 is a rear view of the same, the rear plate of the case being removed.

Figure 3 is a detail sectional view of the same.

Figure 4 is a detail view of the same, enlarged.

Figure 5 represents a key for throwing the registering-device into and out of gear with the clock-work.

My invention has for its object to furnish an improved time-register, for use in velocipede-schools, livery-stables, pleasure-boats, billiard-rooms, and other places where articles are rented by the hour, and which shall be so constructed and arranged that the party holding the key can easily know, by reference to the register, how long it has been in his possession; and

It consists in connecting the device with an ordinary clock-work, and in the construction and combination of the various parts of the device, as hereinafter more fully described.

A are the works, B is the case, and C, the dial-plate of a clock.

Around the ordinary dial of the plate C are arranged twelve, more or less, dials D, divided up into hour and minute-spaces, and each provided with a single hand, E.

The hands E are attached to the journals of the small gear-wheels F, which revolve in brackets G, which are attached to the frame of the clock-work.

The wheels F are provided with a stop, which prevents them from making more than one revolution, and stops them, with the hand E upon the zero-mark, when revolved back.

The wheels F are also provided with small coiled springs H, which revolve them back to the zero-mark as soon as they are thrown out of gear with the clock-work.

I are small gear-wheels, attached to the inner ends of the levers J, and the teeth of which mesh into the teeth of the gear-wheels F.

The levers J are pivoted to the journals of the gear-wheels F, or in a line with said journals, so that in whatever direction the levers J be moved, the teeth of the wheels I F will always mesh into each other.

K is a large gear-wheel, attached to the hollow spindle that carries the hour-hand of the clock.

L are springs, attached to the frame of the clockwork, in such positions as to press against the outer parts of the levers J, so that when the said levers are left free, the action of the said springs will throw the wheels I into gear with the wheel K, and the registers will at once begin to record the time.

M are keys, which are passed in through holes in the front plate of the clock-case B, in such positions that their inclined sides may press the free ends of the levers J back, throwing the wheels I out of gear with the wheel K, and allowing the hands E to be carried back to the zero-point by the action of the springs H upon the wheels F.

The keys M and dials D should be numbered with corresponding numbers, so that there can be no question about the dial to which any particular key belongs.

In using the device, when a velocipede or other article is rented to any one, the key of one of the dials is taken out and delivered to the person renting the article. When he surrenders the key, he can read from the corresponding dial the time it has been in his possession. When the key is inserted in its place, the hand E at once moves back to the zero-point, ready to register the time for the next person.

The devices all act independently of each other, and as many of them may be used as can be arranged around the wheel K.

Having thus described my invention,

I claim as new, and desire to secure by Letters Patent—

1. The arrangement of the small gear-wheels F, provided with stops and springs, as specified, the levers J, pinions I, springs L, and keys M, with respect to the journals on which the hands E are placed, and the driving-wheel K, all constructed and operating as and for the purpose specified.

2. The combination of the hands E E, dial D, spring H, gear-wheel F, lever J, spring L, gear-wheel K, and key M, with each other and with the hour-hand, spindle, frame, and case of a clock, substantially as herein shown and described, and for the purpose set forth.

AUGUSTE COURVOISIER.

Witnesses:
HYATT HUSSEY,
J. G. PERRENOUD.

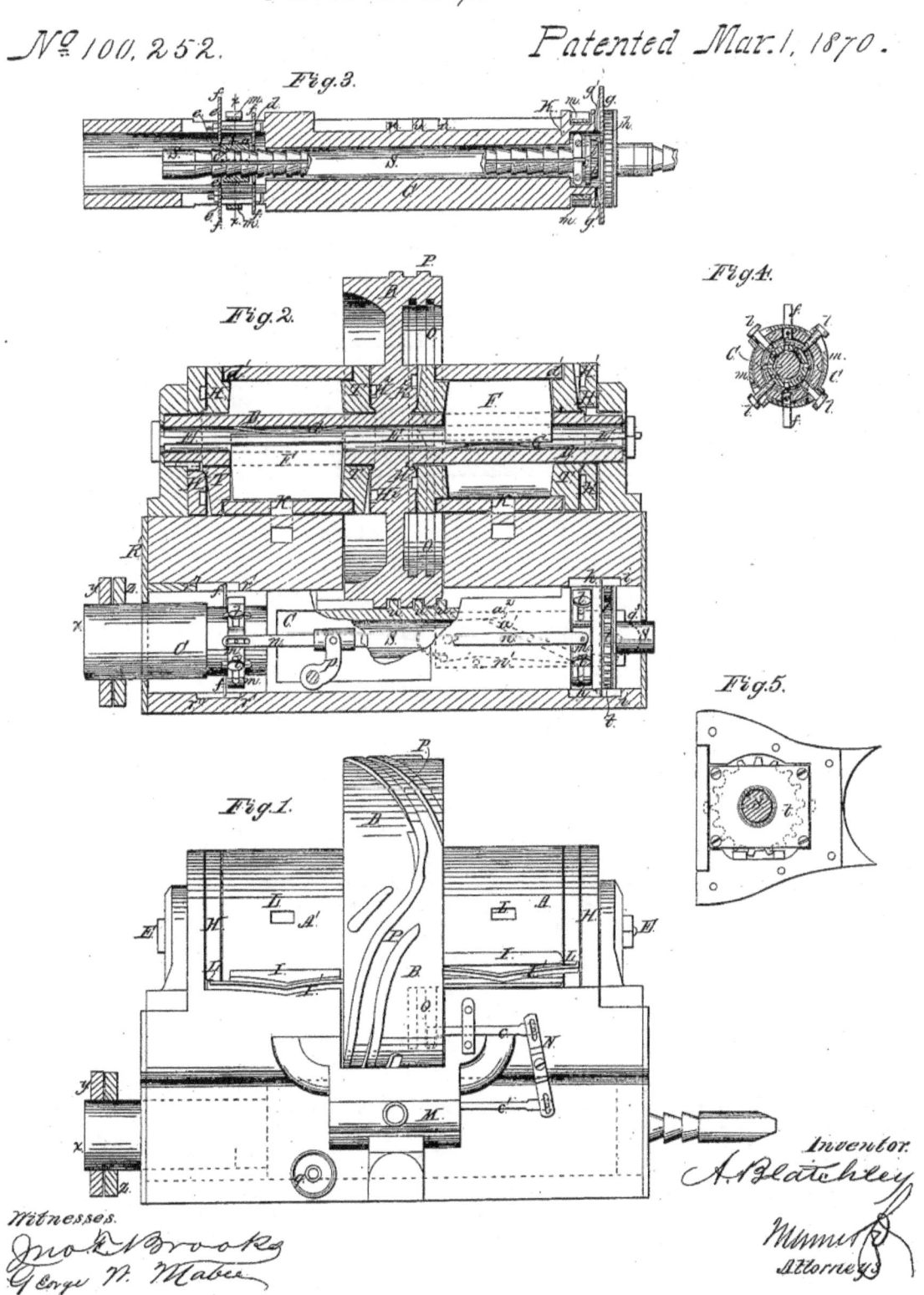

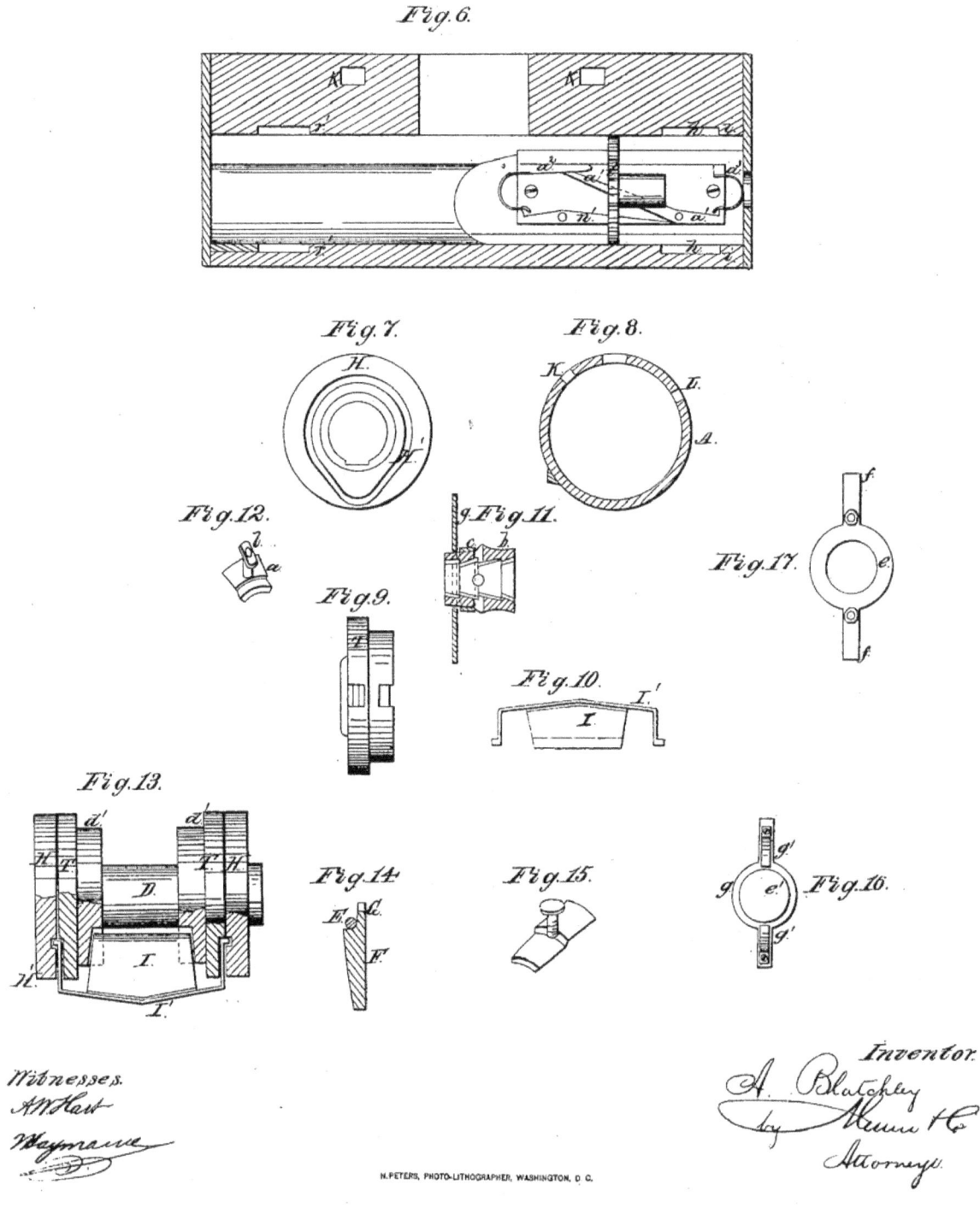

United States Patent Office.

A. BLATCHLY, OF CENTRAL CITY, COLORADO.

Letters Patent No. 100,252, dated March 1, 1870.

IMPROVED ROCK-DRILL.

The Schedule referred to in these Letters Patent and making part of the same

---

To all whom it may concern:

Be it known that I, A. BLATCHLY, of Central City, and in the Territory of Colorado, have invented a new and improved Rock-Drill; and I do hereby declare that the following is a full, clear, and exact description thereof, which will enable others skilled in the art to make and use the same, reference being had to the accompanying drawings forming part of this specification.

This invention relates to improvements in rock-drilling machines, designed to provide an automatically feeding drill, to be actuated by steam power, under a more simple and reliable arrangement than now in use.

The invention consists in certain improvements in the construction of the rotary engines for operating the drill, relating to the valve mechanism, pistons, bridge, or dividing-plates, and to packing the cylinders.

Also, in the combination therewith of a cam-wheel of peculiar construction for communicating a reciprocating movement to the drill-carriage.

Also, in an arrangement for disconnecting the propelling action of the cams with the drill-carriage previous to the blow of the drill.

Also in an arrangement of feed mechanism for the drill, whereby automatic feed is effected;

Also, in an arrangement for imparting an intermittent rotary motion to the drill; and

Also, in an arrangement for disconnecting the feeding mechanism for returning the drill after it has been fed out for the commencement of a new hole; and

Also in an arrangement for rotating the disk.

Figure 1 represents a side elevation of my improved machine;

Figure 2 represents a longitudinal section of the same;

Figure 3 represents a longitudinal section of the drill-carriage, showing the automatic feeding-devices;

Figure 4 represents a transverse section of fig. 3, taken on the line $x\,x$; and

Figure 5 represents a plan of the end of the drill-carriage.

Figure 6, Sheet II, is a central longitudinal section of the bed on which the cylinders rest, and which is recessed to receive the drill-carriage, the same showing the levers and cog-wheel, whereby the drill is rotated.

Figure 7 of said sheet is a face view of one of the cam-grooved disks, arranged at the outer ends of the cylinders.

Figure 8 is a transverse vertical section of the shell of one of the cylinders.

Figure 9 is an edge view of one of the end pieces of the cylinders.

Figure 10 is a plan view of one of the dividing-plates.

Figure 11, Sheet II, represents the inner side of one of the conical spring clamping-jaws, for holding and operating the drill-rod, the spring and clamping-plate being shown in section.

Figure 12, Sheet II, is a perspective view of one of the clamping-jaws and its screw, which are arranged on or near the end of the drill-rod, opposite that on which the conical clamps are placed.

Figure 13, Sheet I, is a side view of the arrangement of parts within each of the cylinders part being broken away, to show the connection.

Figure 14, Sheet I, is a transverse vertical section of one of the pistons, and the rod against which their inner ends abut.

Figure 15, Sheet I, is a perspective view of one of the conical clamping-jaws.

Figure 16, Sheet I, is a face view of the clamping-plate and its springs.

Figure 17, Sheet I, is a face view of one of the two rings, between which one of the sets of clamping-jaws is held.

Similar letters of reference indicate corresponding parts.

I employ a double rotary engine, of which A A' are the cylinders for imparting rotary motion to the cam-wheel B, which imparts reciprocating motion to the drill-carriage C.

For economy of construction, I form the engine-bed into a casing for the drill-carriage.

The cylinders A A' are fixed to the bed in a concavity, and from the said concavity an opening is made through the bed into the chamber, for the cam-wheel to work through for contact with the drill-carriage.

I make the shaft D of the engine hollow, and provide therein a rod, E, running from end to end, by which the ends of the cylinders are kept packed.

F represents the pistons, which are arranged in slots in the shaft, opening into the tubular space therein, and they are provided with springs G, or other equivalent device arranged to force them out against the cylinders.

These pistons are rebated at their bases or inner ends, as shown in fig. 14, to afford a recess for the reception of the rod E.

The effect of the spring G is that of a packing for the outer ends of the pistons, which are constantly in contact with the inner surface of the cylinder, during their revolution with the shaft D and wheel B.

The ends T of the cylinders are concave, and the sides of the pistons fitted thereto, so that no matter how much they wear, the pistons will always fit.

The ends T are rebated at their inner edges d', so as to receive the shell of the cylinder.

H, (see fig. 7,) represents disks, applied to each end

of the shaft, and rotating with it, having cam-grooves H', which, in conjunction with the corresponding grooves, cam-grooves H², in the hub of the wheel B, move the bridges or dividing-plates I into and out of the path of the pistons, for preventing the passage of the steam from the induction-ports K to the exhausts L, the motion being communicated by the yokes I', connected to the dividing-plates, and so bent that their ends project into the grooves H of the plates and the grooves H² of the hubs respectively.

M represents the valve-chest of a common slide-valve, for admitting steam to the ports K.

The said valve is operated by a vibrating arm, N, deriving motion from the cam-groove o, on the interior of the rim of the wheel B.

The connection between said groove and arm is established by means of a rod or bar, c, which has a right-angled end, fitting in the groove, and is provided at its opposite end with a stud or pin working in a slot in the arm N.

The valve-rod e' is similarly connected to the lower end of said arm.

On the face of the cam-wheel are cam-projections P, into which studs u u on the drill-carriage take, and by which the motion is imparted to the carriage.

These cams are so formed that a stroke longer than the face of the wheel may be imparted to the drill-carriage.

They are also so formed that the connection between the wheel and the carriage is broken at the moment the blow of the drill is struck.

This is accomplished by so curving the projections that just previous to the contact of the drill, they recede slightly and allow the drill to continue for a slight distance by its momentum.

The drill-rod S is provided with a series of annular grooves, so formed as to resemble conical sections superposed upon one another, with the bases upward, and by these grooves the drill is suspended by two sets of spring jaws a and b. (See figs. 3 and 15, Sheet I, and fig. 12, Sheet II.)

These spring jaws are made in three or any other preferred number of pieces, having faces fitted to the configuration of the drill, and they are confined to the drill-shank by elastic springs c, or bands of elastic material.

The set a are suspended between a pair of rings d e, (see figs. 3 and 17, Sheet I,) clamped together by means of screw-threaded bolts and nuts, and capable of rising and falling to some extent in a hollow space in one end of the drill-carriage. They are also provided with lateral arms f, projecting through slots in the walls of the drill-carriage.

The set b of clamping-jaws, (see figs. 3 and 15, Sheet I, and fig. 11, Sheet II,) are tapered at one end, and fitted to work into the eye e' of a clamping-plate, g, (see fig. 19, Sheet II,) having two arms projecting into slots in the walls of the casing, as shown at h, fig. 2, just previous to the blow of the drill, whereby the plate is forced back upon the conical jaws, clamping them rapidly to the stem of the drill S, to hold it during the delivery of the blow.

The enlarged ends of the said jaws impart the blow to the drill by the action of the shoulder k of the carriage thereon.

After the blow is struck, the plate g is forced away from the conical jaws by the springs g'.

Before the blow is delivered the arms f of the plate d are arrested in their movement with the drill-rod, by striking against ledges or shoulder formed in the walls of the casing, and which causes the arrest of the jaws a, and they are, therefore, expanded by the force of the drill, and the latter caused to pass through the distance of one notch. On the return movement of the drill-carriage, the arms of the plate e are also arrested at a point sufficiently in advance of that where the drill-carriage stops to force the drill-shank through the jaws b the distance of one notch.

It will thus be seen that the office of the tapered jaws b is to form shoulders or bearing-surfaces for the shoulders K of the drill-carriage, while the office of jaws a is merely to feed the drill.

The jaws b are designed to enter the eye e of the plate g when or an instant before the blow is struck. Without the aid of this plate the jaws b would not bear evenly and firmly on the bases of the cones, in which case, owing to the heavy shock, the outer portions of said bases or shoulders of the cones would be liable to be split or broken off. Other damages might also be caused by the want of this plate, which it is unnecessary to detail.

If the rock being drilled should be so hard that the drill is unable to move the distance of one of the cones or conical sections, there will, of course, be no "feed," as the jaws a do not in that case move back that distance. The "feed" will therefore be effected when the movement of the drill has been repeated often enough to penetrate the rock the distance of one of the conical sections. The latter may be of any preferred length.

For the purpose of opening the jaws to return the drill after it has been fed out, they are connected by screws l to cam-rings m, by passing through slots therein, and these cam-rings are connected to a bar, n, for oscillating them in the direction, to cause the heads of the screws to ride up the inclines on the cam-rings, and thereby draw the jaws outwardly to open them sufficiently to permit the drill-shank to pass freely through them.

The bar n is operated by a key, q, and crank p.

The cam-rings may be operated by other equivalent devices.

For turning the drill, it is provided with a toothed wheel, t, which has a spline-connection with the drill. As the latter is moved out, one of the teeth of the wheel will ride along the under side of the inclined and pivoted spring-lever a^1, thus turning the same, and with it the drill. On the return movement of the latter, the levers a^1 and n' will both be embraced between two of the teeth of the wheel, but so soon as the end of the long arm of the lever a^1 is reached, another tooth of the wheel comes in contact with the under side of the fixed projection or rib a^2, and the same is again ready to make its forward movement.

The end X of the drill-carriage may be weighted by rings y, placed thereon, and between the said rings an elastic collar, Z, may be employed for tempering the shock against the carriage.

Having thus described my invention,

I claim as new and desire to secure by Letters Patent—

1. The combination with the cylinders and wheel B, provided with grooves H² of the rotary cam disks H, yokes I, and bridges, when arranged substantially as specified.

2. The arrangement of the hollow shaft D, packing-rod E, cylinder-head and cam-wheel, substantially as specified.

3. The arrangement of the hollow shaft, tapered pistons F, concave piston-heads and springs G, substantially as specified.

4. The combination with the drill-carriage, having projections u of the cam-projections P, when the latter are formed to discontinue their action upon the carriage previous to the blow of the drill, substantially as specified.

5. The combination with the drill-shank, provided with grooves, as specified, of the spring clamping-

jaws *b*, and clamping-ring *g*, when arranged to clamp and release the said jaws, substantially as specified.

6. The arrangement of the shoulder K of the drill-carriage and clamping-jaws, substantially as specified.

7. The combination with the drill-shank of the feeding-jaws *a*, when arranged substantially as specified.

8. The combination with the drill-shank of the holding-jaws *b* and feeding-jaws *a*, arranged substantially as specified.

9. The combination with the holding and feeding-jaws of the cam-rings, pins, and jaws *l*, substantially as specified.

10. The combination with the cam-rings *m*, of the bar *n*, crank *p*, and key *q*, all substantially as specified.

11. The combination with the drill-shank of the toothed-wheel *t*, projection a^2, and spring-lever a^1, all arranged substantially as specified.

A. BLATCHLY.

Witnesses:
WILLIAM R. KENNEDY,
HENRY S. TAPPAN.

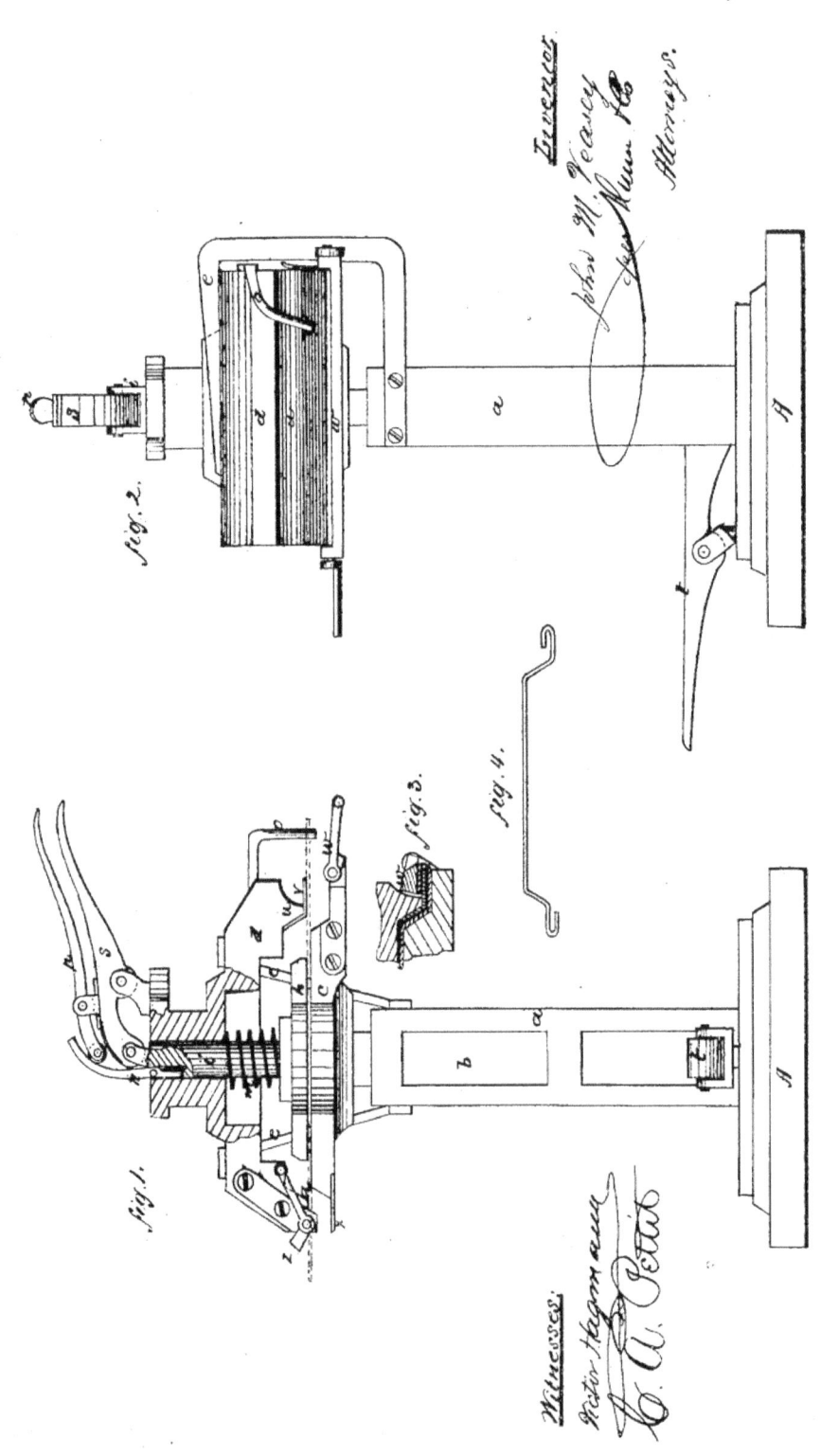

United States Patent Office.

JOHN M. VEASEY, OF DENVER, COLORADO TERRITORY.

Letters Patent No. 101,065, dated March 22, 1870.

IMPROVEMENT IN SHEET-METAL SEAMING-MACHINE

The Schedule referred to in these Letters Patent and making part of the same.

To all whom it may concern:

Be it known that I, JOHN M. VEASEY, of Denver, in the county of Arapahoe and Territory of Colorado, have invented a new and improved Machine for Shaping and Seaming Sheet-Metal for Roofing Purposes; and I do hereby declare that the following is a full, clear, and exact description of the same, reference being had to the accompanying drawings making a part of this specification, in which—

Figure 1 is a sectional,

Figure 2, a side elevation, and

Figure 3 is a detached sectional elevation of one of the seamers.

This invention has for its object to form sections of tin roofing in trough-shape and with reflexed edges, in order to adapt them to convenient use.

The invention consists in certain combinations of the following principal elements, to wit: A vertically-sliding shaper, a mold, a vertically-sliding clamp, between which and the shaper the blank is clasped, and seamers and flange at the sides of the mold and shaper, as will hereinafter more fully appear.

A is the foot-piece.

a, the vertical guide-way.

b, the standard sliding in such guide-way, and bearing the shaper c at its top.

d is the mold, supported on the upper arms of brackets e, which are attached by their lower arms to the vertical guide-way at any convenient point.

h is a clamp affixed to the lower extremity of a vertical stem, i, which passes through the mold, the said vertical stem being surrounded by a spring, m, whose tendency is to force the clamps downward, such tendency being resisted, and the clamp held up out of the way, when not in use, in the recess made for its reception in the mold d, by means of a spring detent, n, placed in a recess in the upper part of the stem i, the lower end of which detent bears on the top of the mold when the clamp is fully elevated.

It is at this time that the sheet of tin is inserted between the clamp and shaper c, the latter being provided with stops at its rear side, and with a flank-guide, o, which insure the placing of the sheet in the proper position.

This having been done, the spring detent is drawn into its recess by lowering the outer end of a lever, p, pivoted in lugs rising from the top of the lever s, by which movement the shorter arm of the lever p throws outward the upper curved part of the detent.

The spring m is thus set free, and draws the clamp h downward until the sheet of metal is clasped firmly between the clamp and the shaper c.

Thereupon the sliding standard b is thrown up into the mold by the pressure of the operator's foot upon the lever t, whose inner end is jointed to the standard, and which has its fulcrum in lugs arising out of the foot-piece A.

This movement of the shaper forms the sheet into a kind of inverted trough, by reason of the ribs $u\ u$ at the sides of the mold, which bend downward the sides of the sheet, leaving such sides at an obtuse angle with the body of the sheet.

One of the ribs u is faced with metal, which is bent under the rib and extends horizontally outward from the mold in the form of the flange v.

To the adjacent edge of the shaper is jointed a seamer, w, provided with a crank-handle, by means of which the edge of the sheet is bent over and folded back upon the flange forming the edge seam, as shown in fig. 3.

A similar flange, x, projects from the opposite side of the shaper—not the mold, as in the case of the flange v—and to the adjacent edge of the mold another similar seamer, z, is jointed, by means of which another edge seam is formed on the opposite side of the sheet, which in this instance is bent under the flange instead of upon it.

The seams having thus been formed, the seamers are turned back, and the shaper c lowered by means of the same lever t which raised it.

The clamp h does not follow the shaper down, for the reason that the same upward movement of the latter which compressed the sheet into mold, so raised the clamp as to release the spring detent n and allow it to fly out over the top of the mold and thus retain the clamp. Hence the sheet is loosened and may be readily removed.

The lever s is pivoted in lugs springing from the top of the mold, and is jointed at its inner end to the top of the clamp-stem i. This lever is the means whereby the clamp may be separately operated.

Having thus described my invention,

What I claim as new, and desire to secure by Letters Patent, is—

1. The clamp h, provided with the stem i moving in a recess in the mold d, in combination with the spring m, detent n, and levers $p\ s$, substantially in the manner and for the purpose described.

2. The combination of the shaper c with the mold d and clamp h, as and for the purpose set forth.

3. The mold d, provided with the ribs $u\ u$, flange v, and seamer z, in combination with the shaper c, provided with the seamer w and flange x, constructed in the manner and for the object specified.

JOHN M. VEASEY.

Witnesses:
CHAS. A. PETTIT,
SOLON C. KEMON.

J. M. VEASEY.
CASTER FOR SEWING MACHINES.

No. 101,328.   Patented Mar. 29, 1870.

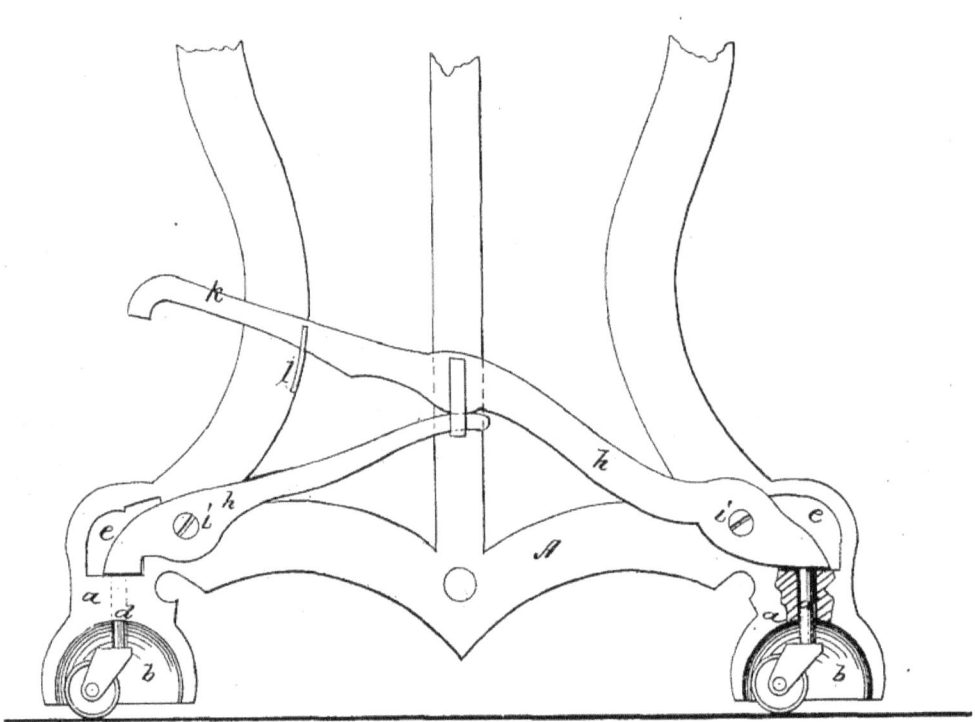

UNITED STATES PATENT OFFICE.

JOHN M. VEASEY, OF DENVER, COLORADO TERRITORY.

IMPROVEMENT IN CASTERS FOR SEWING-MACHINES.

Specification forming part of Letters Patent No. **101,328**, dated March 29, 1870.

To all whom it may concern:

Be it known that I, JOHN M. VEASEY, of Denver, in the county of Arapahoe and Territory of Colorado, have invented a new and Improved Adjustable Caster; and I do hereby declare that the following is a full, clear, and exact description of the same, reference being had to the accompanying drawing, making a part of this specification, in which the figure is a side elevation.

My invention relates to attachments to the legs of sewing-machines, tables, and other similar articles of furniture; and it consists in combining with the casters of the legs levers having curved or bent ends projecting into chambers in said legs and pressing on the pintles of the casters, as hereinafter specified.

In the drawing, A is the end supporting frame of a sewing-machine or other table; $a\,a$, the feet on which the frame rests. $b\,b$ are recesses in such feet. $c\,c$ are casters placed within such recesses, the stems d of the casters being placed in vertical holes in the feet a, instead of being inclosed, as is usually the case, in caps that are themselves attached to the legs of articles of furniture. I dispense entirely with all the usual accompaniments of casters and insert the stems d directly in the feet. This makes a firm connection and one not liable to break. The stems d project upward into recesses $e\,e$ in the upper parts of the feet a, far enough to allow of sufficient play of the casters. The ends of levers $h\,h$ project into the recesses e, so as to act on the tops of the stems. The levers $h\,h$ are pivoted to the frame at the points $i\,i$, and project toward and meet at the center of the frame A, where they are jointed together in any suitable manner. A handle, k, extends onward from the free extremity of one of the levers h and beyond the edge of the frame A, so as to be convenient for manual grasp.

When not in operation the levers h lie nearly horizontal on the inside of the frame A. This is when the table rests solely on its feet and the casters are wholly withdrawn into the recesses b. Previous to moving the table the handle k is raised, bringing the ends of the levers h down upon the tops of the stems d, lowering the casters and raising the table-legs entirely off the floor. A hook, l, is placed on the inside of the frame A to sustain the handle k when the table rests on the casters. When the table has been moved to the required place, on simply lifting the handle k out of the hook l the weight of the table settles it to the floor and raises the casters.

Having thus described my invention, what I claim as new, and desire to secure by Letters Patent, is—

1. The levers $h\,h$, pivoted upon the frame and provided with curved ends projecting into chambers $e\,e$, and pressing on the pintles $d\,d$ of the casters, whose pintles project into the chambers, as shown and described.

2. The combination, with the subject-matter of the above claim, of the hook l, all being arranged as and for the purpose specified.

JOHN M. VEASEY.

Witnesses:
  CHAS. A. PETTIT,
  SOLON C. KEMON.

G. Copeland,
Horseshoe.
No. 102,504. Patented May 3. 1870.

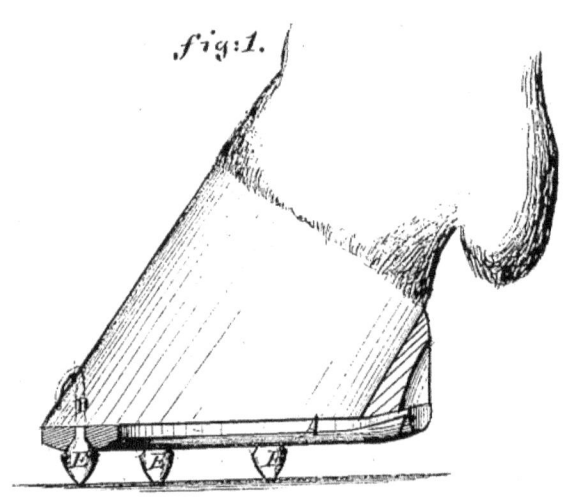

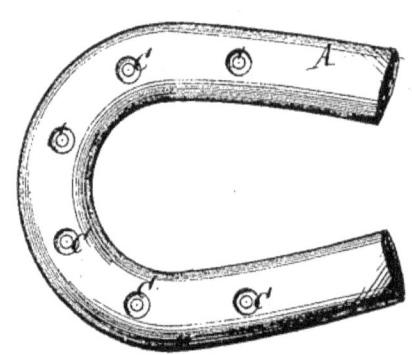

United States Patent Office.

GEORGE COPELAND, OF DENVER, COLORADO TERRITORY.

Letters Patent No. 102,504, dated May 3, 1870.

IMPROVEMENT IN HORSESHOES.

The Schedule referred to in these Letters Patent and making part of the same.

To all whom it may concern:

Be it known that I, GEORGE COPELAND, of Denver, in the county of Arapahoe and Territory of Colorado, have invented a new and useful Improvement in Horseshoes; and I do hereby declare that the following is a full, clear, and exact description thereof, which will enable others skilled in the art to make and use the same, reference being had to the accompanying drawings forming part of this specification.

This invention relates to improvements in horseshoes and the nails for fastening them on the hoofs of animals; and

It consists in making the nails with large double conical heads and the shoes with countersunk sockets around the holes, for the reception of the parts of the enlargements of the heads with which the smaller parts of the heads are joined, all arranged so that the enlarged heads of the nails shall serve as the calks of the shoe, the said heads being made of either iron or steel and hardened or not, as preferred.

Figure 1 is a side view of a hoof with my improved shoe attached, a part being sectional; and

Figure 2 is a plan of the bottom of the shoe.

Similar letters of reference indicate corresponding parts.

A is the plate of the shoe, which may be of any shape in cross section, and may have the ordinary toe and heel calks or not; or, instead of the heel-calks, it may be turned up at the heel, as shown at B, the latter being the arrangement which I prefer.

C represents the countersunk sockets, or the nail-holes.

D represents the nails; and

E, the enlarged heads thereof, which in the example, are represented in the form of double cones united at the base.

These large heads are intended to serve as the calks of the shoe, and constitute detachable calks, which may be very readily removed, for the substitution of others, when worn.

The parts of the heads fitting in the countersunk sockets are designed for strengthening the nails at the junction of the heads with the other parts.

These nails or the heads may be made of steel and hardened or tempered for making them more durable, but they may be made wholly of iron, if preferred.

Having thus described my invention,

I claim as new and desire to secure by Letters Patent—

1. A horseshoe, A B, curved upwardly at the heel, and provided with six conical holes, as shown and described.

2. A horseshoe-nail, having a head formed of two cones whose bases lie in the same central plane thereof, as an improved article of manufacture.

GEORGE COPELAND.

Witnesses:
JOHN M. VEASEY,
JAMES G. TAYLOR.

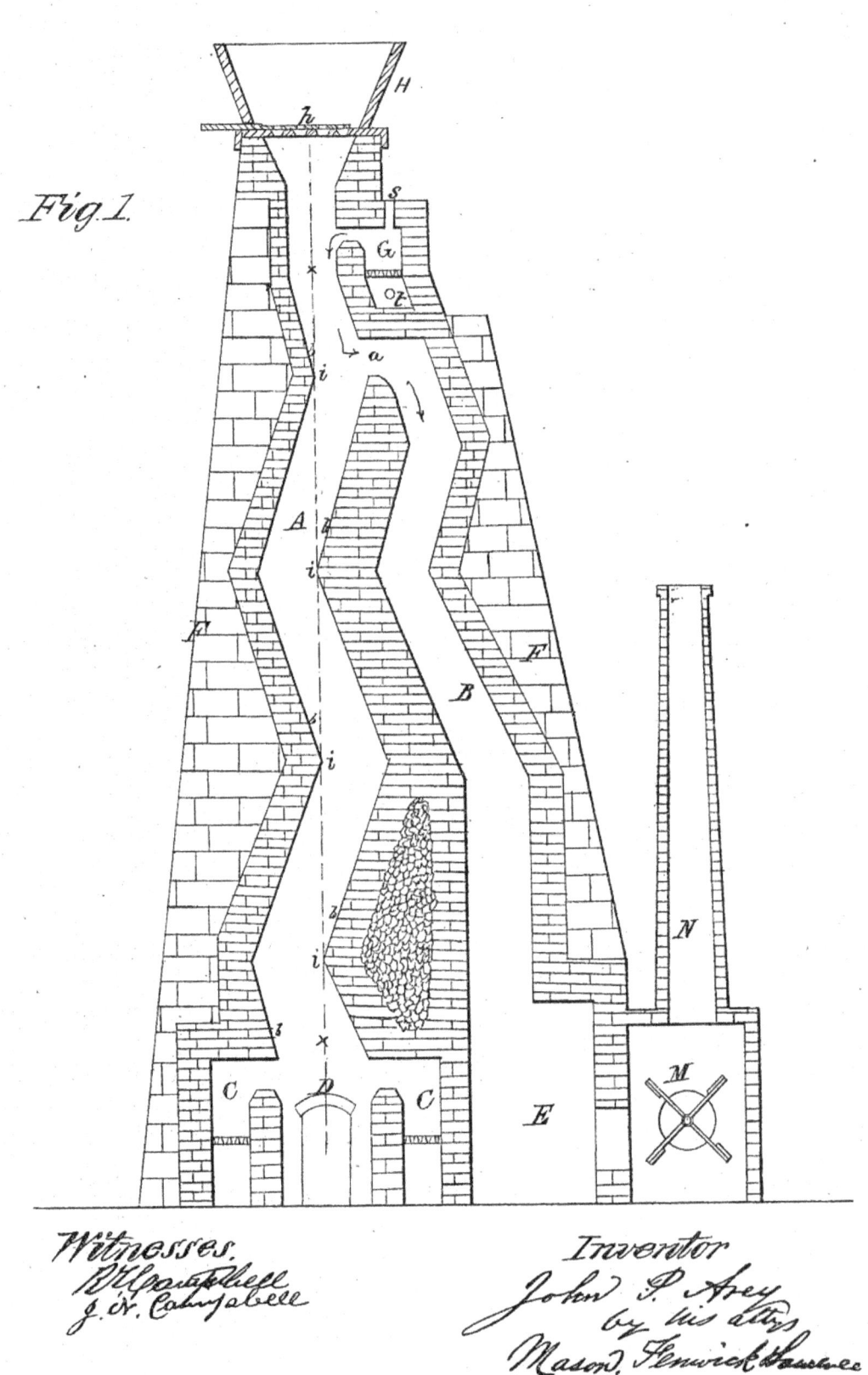

UNITED STATES PATENT OFFICE.

JOHN P. AREY, OF GEORGETOWN, COLORADO TERRITORY.

IMPROVEMENT IN FURNACES FOR ROASTING, OXIDIZING, AND CHLORIDIZING ORES.

Specification forming part of Letters Patent No. **103,006**, dated May 17, 1870.

To all whom it may concern:

Be it known that I, JOHN P. AREY, of Georgetown, in the county of Clear Creek and Territory of Colorado, have invented a new and Improved Furnace for Roasting, Oxidizing, and Chloridizing Ores; and I do hereby declare that the following is a full, clear, and exact description thereof, reference being had to the accompanying drawings making part of this specification, in which—

Figure 1 is a vertical section through the improved furnace.

My invention relates to improvements on furnaces which are designed for roasting, oxidizing, and chloridizing ores and metallic products, and consists, first, in constructing the shaft, or that portion of the flue through which the substance to be treated is dropped, of a zigzag or serpentine form, whereby the heat in the shaft is equalized from wall to wall, and the ascending products of combustion are caused to cross and recross the descending ore or metallic product, and thus, in a comparatively short vertical space, become thoroughly heated and deprived of their foreign volatile matters, as will be hereinafter explained; second, in so arranging an auxiliary furnace or fire-place, with reference to either a serpentine or straight shaft or flue, through which ores or metallic products are dropped, for the purpose of roasting, oxidizing, and chloridizing them, that such products will be subjected to the direct action of the heat of said furnace or fire-place, and thereby partially heated before they are brought under the influence of the heated products ascending from the main furnace in the lower part of said shaft or flue, as will be hereinafter explained; third, in arranging fire-chambers at or near the base of a serpentine flue, and on opposite sides of the receiving-chamber, into which the treated material falls, as will be hereinafter explained.

To enable others skilled in the art to understand my invention, I will describe its construction and operation.

In the accompanying drawings, A represents the shaft of the furnace, which is formed within the walls F, rising in a serpentine or zigzag manner from an accumulating-chamber, D, and terminating at the summit of the furnace, at which latter point the ore is fed into this shaft. B is an escape-flue, which may be of the serpentine form shown, or it may be straight. This flue leads out of the shaft A, near the upper end thereof, and terminates in the dust-chamber E at the base of the furnace. On opposite sides of the chamber D fire-places C C are constructed, the heated products from both of which pass over the bridge walls, meet at the base of the shaft A, and thence rise through this shaft to and through the transverse passage a leading into the upper end of the descending flue B, as shown in the drawings. Near the upper end of the shaft A, and on one side of this shaft, is a fire-chamber, G, the products of combustion from which pass into the shaft A, thence off through the transverse flue a into the main outlet-flue B, as indicated by the arrows in the drawings. This auxiliary fire-place is preferably arranged over the short flue a, so that the heated products will be compelled to descend for a short distance through shaft A before escaping therefrom. I do not, however, confine myself to this arrangement of the fire-place G, as it may be located below or opposite the short flue a, or in any other manner which will compel the heated products rising from it to first enter shaft A before escaping into an outlet-flue. At the upper end of the shaft A I have arranged a feeder, consisting of a hopper, H, having perforations or oblong slots through its bottom, and a correspondingly-perforated slide, h, so applied that, by giving it a reciprocating motion, the ore or the metallic product to be treated will be regularly fed into the shaft. The slide will admit of adjustment, by regulating its length of stroke, for regulating the amount of material fed through at each stroke. I prefer to adopt a feeder substantially as above described, although any other which will answer a good purpose may be employed.

It will be seen by reference to the annexed drawings that the shaft A presents a number of inclined or zigzag planes, and that the prominent angles i of the opposite sides of this shaft, from bottom to top thereof, are in, or nearly in, the same vertical plane which is indicated by the dotted line $x\,x$ in the drawing. Thus it will be seen that the ore, while falling in streams through the shaft, will be crossed and recrossed by the currents of heated products rising from the lower end of the shaft. Also, that the zigzag course of the shaft A will cause the heated currents to circulate freely through the spaces on opposite sides of the descending streams of ore, and uniformly heat the shaft throughout its length. Also, that a great length of shaft is obtained in a comparatively short furnace.

It will also be seen that I employ an auxiliary fire-place near the upper end of the shaft A, which fire-place is furnished with its own draft-passages, and so arranged that the ore crosses the highly-heated products escaping therefrom previous to being brought under the direct influence of the heated currents ascending from the lower part of the shaft, by which means the ore is brought to a condition for being more readily acted upon while falling through the shaft.

Another advantage attending the auxiliary fire-place G is that the flame therefrom, entering the shaft so near the common escape-flue, will pass into this flue along with the dust, which is either too light to pass below or which may be carried into the flue by the draft, and, mingling with the escaping heat and gases, will become thoroughly roasted before it reaches the dust-chamber E. Thus a twofold office is performed by this auxiliary fire-place.

I am aware that Charles Stetefelot shows, in his Letters Patent of the United States, numbered 72,931, and dated December 31, A. D. 1867, an ore-roasting furnace, with supplemental fire-place arranged in the escape-flue, but this is not so arranged that its heated products are caused to impinge upon the body of ore falling through the shaft, as I have above described in reference to the action of the heat from the fire-place G. I do not, therefore, claim as my invention such an arrangement of fire-place as is shown by said Letters Patent; nor do I claim broadly the principle of treating ores by letting them fall through ascending currents of heat; nor do I claim the arrangement of shelves or inclined planes in a vertical shaft, as is shown in Letters Patent numbered 43,129. Such shelves or inclined planes offer obstructions to the free ascending currents of heat, by producing eddies beneath each one of the shelves, while with my zigzag shaft no such obstructions are made. They also tend to clog the shaft.

In order to successfully operate a furnace having the ascending zigzag shaft and the descending flue B, leading into the dust-chamber E, I employ a fan at the base of the chimney M, which will be rotated faster or slower, according to the force of draft required, and to start the fire in the auxiliary fire-place G. draft-dampers may be opened below and above the fire. These dampers are applied in practice opposite the passages s t.

I do not claim roasting or desulphurizing ores by passing them in fine powder through a shaft, together with the products of combustion, in the manner and principle as is described in the patent granted to Whelpley and Storer, January 12, 1864.

Having described my invention, what I claim as new, and desire to secure by Letters Patent, is—

1. The zigzag or serpentine shaft A, in a furnace for roasting, oxidizing, and chloridizing ores or metallic products, constructed substantially as described.

2. In a furnace for roasting, oxidizing, and chloridizing ores or metallic products, the auxiliary fire-place G, arranged above one or more main fire-places, in such relation to the shaft A that the ore falling through this shaft will be subjected to the direct action of the heat passing from said fire-place, as well as that from the main fire-places, substantially as described.

3. In a furnace for roasting, oxidizing, and chloridizing ores or metallic products, the fire-places C, combined with and arranged at or near the base of a zigzag shaft, A, in combination with the fire-place G, which leads directly into the shaft, substantially as described and for the purpose set forth.

4. In a furnace for roasting, oxidizing, and chloridizing ores or metallic products, the relative arrangement of the escape-flue a, the fire-place G, and a feeder, with respect to a shaft, A, or its equivalent, substantially as described.

5. In a furnace for roasting, oxidizing, and chloridizing ores or metallic products, the descending flue B, in combination with the shaft A, receiving-chamber E, and a suction-fan, M, substantially as described.

JOHN P. AREY.

Witnesses:
K. HASKINS,
R. W. CLARKE.

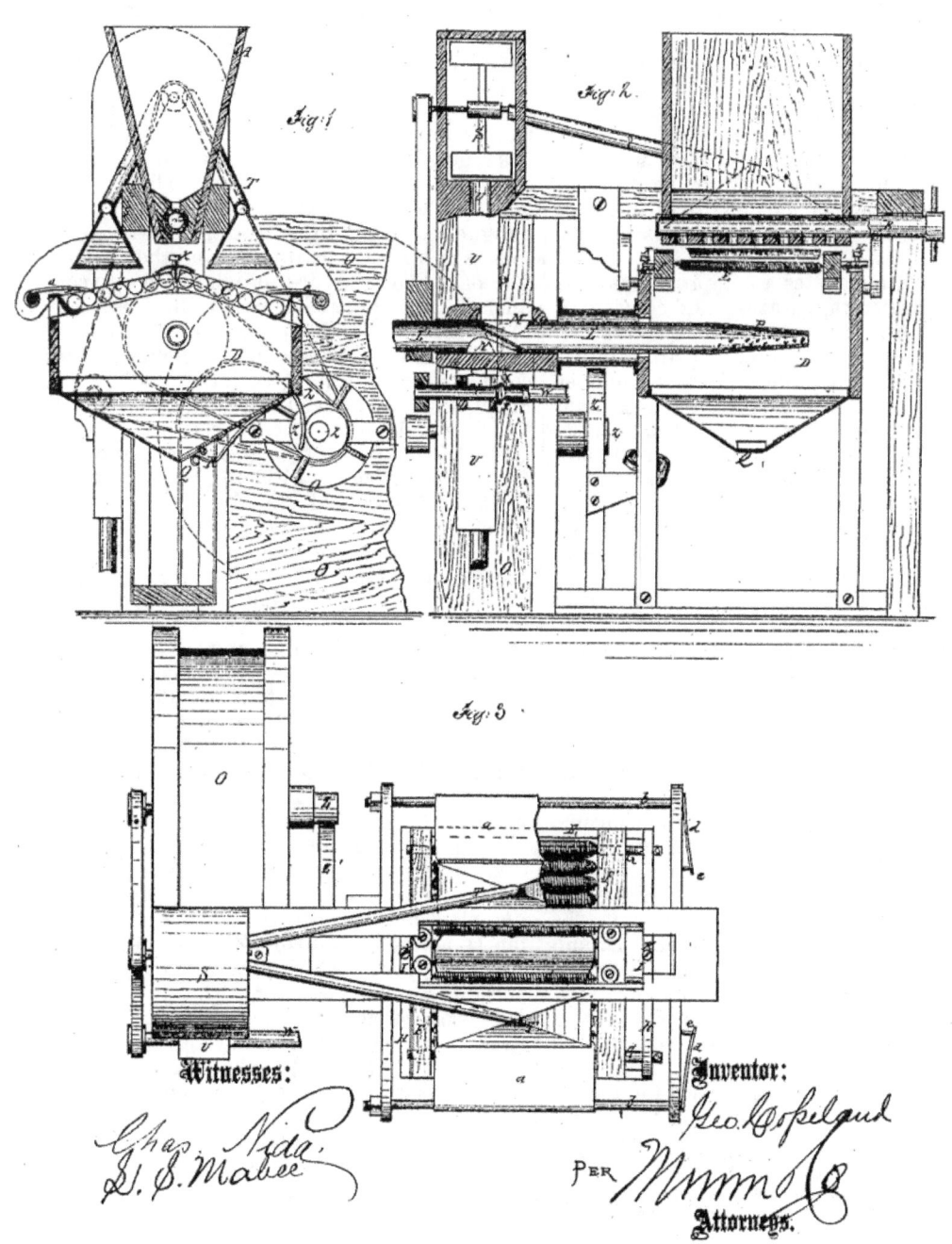

UNITED STATES PATENT OFFICE.

GEORGE COPELAND, OF DENVER, COLORADO TERRITORY.

IMPROVEMENT IN ORE-SEPARATORS.

Specification forming part of Letters Patent No. **103,574**, dated May 31, 1870.

To all whom it may concern:

Be it known that I, GEORGE COPELAND, of Denver, in the county of Arapahoe and Territory of Colorado, have invented a new and Improved Ore-Separator; and I do hereby declare that the following is a full, clear, and exact description thereof, which will enable others skilled in the art to make and use the same, reference being had to the accompanying drawing forming part of this specification.

This invention relates to improvements in dry-ore-separating apparatus; and consists in new and improved means for subjecting the pulverized ore to the action of distributed gusts of air as it falls from a sieve to a hopper below, by which the gangue is prevented from falling with the heavier particles, and is thrown back to be thrown off by skimmers, and the dust is caused to be taken up by suckers, and delivered to water-spray, for being moistened and conducted to a receiver, and retained for further operation, all as hereinafter more fully specified.

Figure 1 is a transverse sectional elevation of my improved apparatus. Fig. 2 is a sectional elevation taken at right angles to the plane of Fig. 1; and Fig. 3 is a top view, partly in horizontal section.

Similar letters of reference indicate corresponding parts.

A is a hopper at the top of the machine for the reception of the pulverized ore, into which it may be conveyed by any suitable means. It has numerous holes along the bottom for the delivery of the ore, and a rotary perforated valve, B, for regulating or stopping the discharge. C represents a sieve placed under the hopper B, and over another hopper, D, and arranged to shed each way from the center line of the delivery-orifices of the hopper above. This sieve is formed of spiral wire coils or springs E, stretched from the end blocks F F' parallel with each other, forming meshes or reticulations, which may be varied for finer or coarser ore, and for varying them the blocks are made adjustable to or from each other by means of the screw-threaded rods G G', by which they are connected, and by which they are supported on the bars H of the frame. The blocks F F' are jointed at the center, and the screw-rods G' thereat rest at the ends on plates I on the tops of the bars H, having adjusting-screws K, by which they may be raised or lowered for varying the angle of the shed. L is a two-way revolving blast-pipe, receiving air alternately through the orifices M N from the fan O, and projecting into the hopper D, where it has a perforated nozzle, P, through which the air is delivered in gusts among the falling particles of heavier matter, and acting on the gangue and other light matters on the sieve, to toss it up and separate it from the heavier. The part L' of the air-pipe is intended to conduct the air admitted through the passage N to another similar hopper at the other side of the blast-fan, to which like attachments are connected, constituting a double-acting machine, whereby the continuous blast from the fan D is delivered to each set in alternate gusts. The hopper D is closed, except at the top, and is provided with an escape-valve, Q, at the bottom, held closed by a spring, R, which will resist the force of the blast, but will yield under the weight of an accumulation of ore sufficiently to let it escape from time to time, and prevent the hopper from filling. S represents a sucker-fan attached to the top of the machine, and having two funnel-mouthed pipes arranged above the sieves to take up the fine light dust, and convey it away through the pipe U to a receptacle. The pipe U receives jets of water from a revolving perforated pipe, V, to which a hose-pipe, W, is jointed at X, and held in contact by a spring, Y, or other suitable means. These water-jets, mixing with the dust, prevent it from being carried away in the air. The sieve has a reciprocating or shaking motion imparted to it by an eccentric wheel, Z, on the shaft of the fan D, acting on a spring, Z^1, connected to the sieve-supports, which are arranged in any suitable way for vibration. The air-blast tube L L' is operated by a blast, Z^2, from the fan-shaft, working over a pulley on it, and the sucker and water-jet tube are also operated by belts from the same shaft; or they may be operated in any approved way. *a* represents skimmers placed at the lower edges of the sieves, and lapping over the upper surfaces a short distance they are arranged on oscillating shafts *b*, having spring-arms *d* and holding-pins *e*, by which they may be raised or lowered, and held at any required position for skimming off the coarse and light particles of gangue, which are floated down over the sieve and above the heavier particles of ore by the action of the sieves and the air.

This apparatus is adapted for the separation of dry quartz of any kind and dry placer-sands. The feed-hopper and valve B may be dispensed with, and the dry pulverized ore may be fed directly to the sieves by hand or other means, as preferred, and other sieves may be used, instead of such as I have described; but I prefer to use these.

Having thus described my invention, I claim as new and desire to secure by Letters Patent—

1. The combination of the air and ore receiving hopper D with the sieves at the top of the air-blast pipe L, and a blower arranged to deliver the air in gusts and in jets, substantially in the manner described.

2. The combination, with the sieves, receiving-hopper D, and air-blast pipe, of a sucker-fan, funnel-shaped sucking-pipes, and a delivery-pipe, substantially as specified.

3. The combination, with the delivery-spout U, for the dust, of a water-jet-distributing apparatus for moistening the dust, substantially as specified.

4. Ore or other sieves composed of the spiral wire springs E, arranged side by side and stretched between end blocks or bars, and either arranged for adjustment by stretching or relaxing the springs or not, substantially as specified.

5. The arrangement of the blocks F F', in two parts, jointed together, and the plates I and adjusting-screws K, with the projecting rods G', for varying the height or pitch of the sieves, substantially as specified.

6. The combination of the blocks F F', spiral wire springs E, and the screw-threaded adjusting-rods G G', substantially as specified.

7. The combination of the skimmers and the sieves, substantially as specified.

8. The combination, with the sieves, hopper D, and air-blast pipe, of the feed-hopper A and revolving perforated valve B, substantially as specified.

GEORGE COPELAND.

Witnesses:
JOHN M. VEASEY,
JAMES S. TAYLOR.

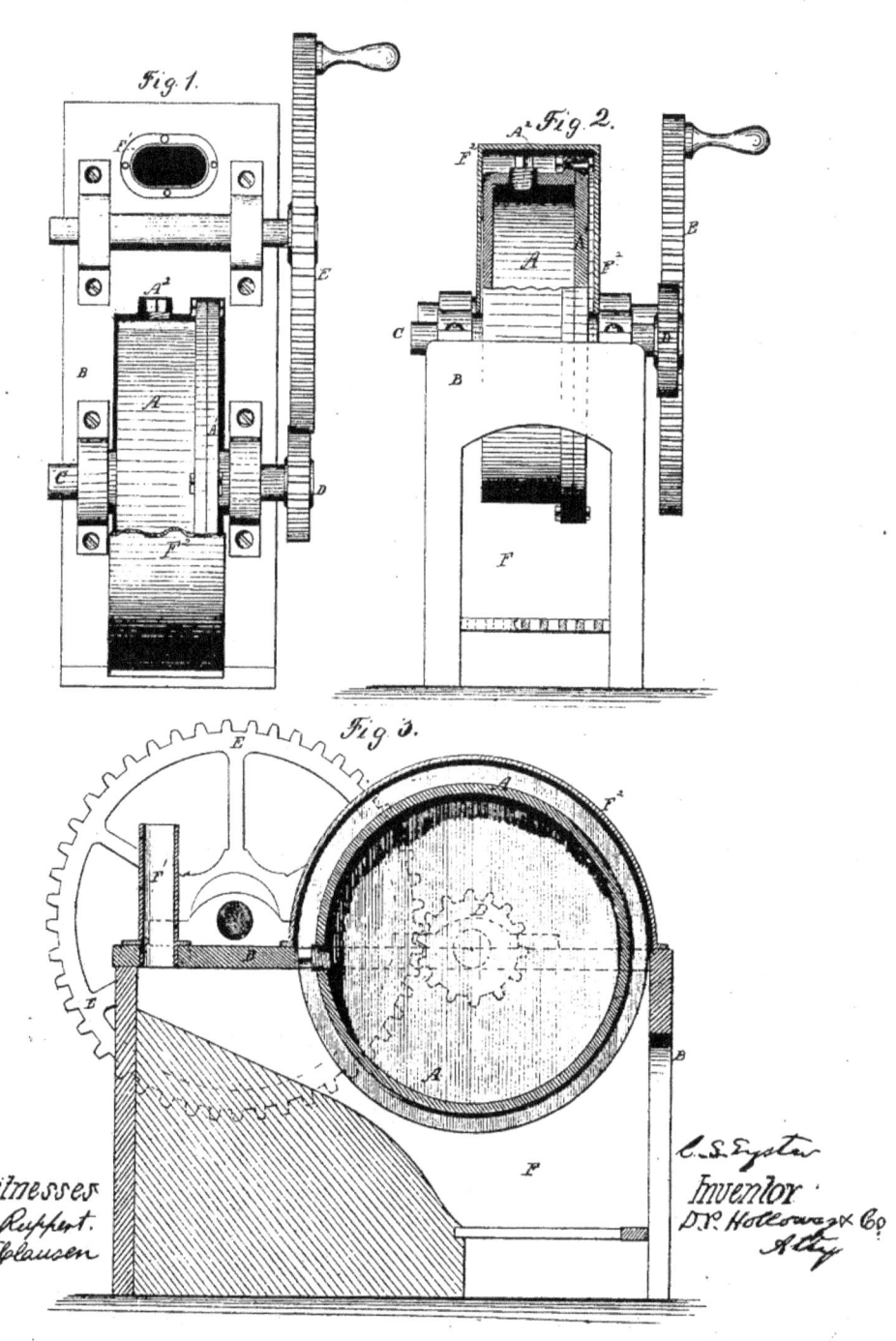

UNITED STATES PATENT OFFICE.

CHRISTIAN S. EYSTER, OF DENVER, COLORADO TERRITORY.

IMPROVEMENT IN SEPARATING AND REFINING METALS.

Specification forming part of Letters Patent No. **104,130**, dated June 14, 1870.

To all whom it may concern:

Be it known that I, CHRISTIAN S. EYSTER, of Denver, in the county of Arapahoe and Territory of Colorado, have invented a new and Improved Process and Apparatus for Concentrating, Separating, and Refining Metals of Different Specific Gravities, when mingled and in a state of fusion or fluidity, and of holding or keeping them in that state of concentration, separation, and refinement until they become solidified, when they may be, by ordinary mechanical means, cut out from each other, according to their respective values; and I hereby declare the following to be a full, clear, and exact description thereof, which will enable those skilled in the art to make and use the same, reference being had to the accompanying drawing, making part of this specification.

Figure 1 is a plan view. Fig. 2 is an end elevation. Fig. 3 is a vertical longitudinal section.

Similar letters have reference to the same parts.

This invention is designed and intended to effect a concentration, separation, and refinement of metals having different specific gravities, when mixed or alloyed and brought into a state of fusion; and my improved process consists in subjecting the fluid-metal mixture or alloy to rapid rotation in a close receiver, turning on its axis, until the different metals of various specific gravities are mechanically concentrated, separated, and refined by the action of the centrifugal force, which will cause the particles or atoms of greatest specific gravity to range themselves on or near the periphery, and those of less specific gravity to arrange themselves in rims or bands concentrically, in the order approximately of their respective specific gravities.

When the metals have thus been concentrated, separated, and refined, they may be gradually cooled by abstracting or taking from the furnace the applied heat necessary for their fused condition while still rotating, until, when solidified, the block may be removed and the metals separated or cut from each other, according to their respective values, by the chisel, tool, or lathe, or in any other analogous manner; and these metals, thus approximately concentrated, separated, and refined, may again be subjected to the same treatment with others before thus treated, and of a like or similar value, until a more perfect, complete, and valuable concentration, separation, and refinement are effected.

The nature of the apparatus will clearly appear from the following description.

It is a metallic chamber, of suitable size and figure, preferably cylindrical or spherical, formed of two parts, so arranged that one of the heads A may be detached for the removal of the ingot when the operation has been completed, to facilitate which the interior of the chamber should have a sufficient draft to conveniently disengage the ingot.

An opening, closed by a plug, A^2, or in other convenient manner, is left in the periphery, to be used for filling the chamber with the melted metals. The chamber A is suspended upon axles C, attached to each head in suitable bearings on the frame B. The caps of these boxes should be so constructed that they may be conveniently removed to permit the cylinder and its axles to be removed. The interior of the cylinder should be smoothed or polished to diminish the adhesion of the ingot.

The chamber is caused to revolve by the pinion D, driven by the spur-wheel E, operated by such driving mechanism as will impart a rapid motion to the chamber in either direction at the will of the operator.

Under the cylinder is a furnace, F, in which a fire may be maintained to keep the cylinder at a temperature as high as that of the fused metals, or higher, if need be, and to keep the metals in fusion.

F^1 is the uptake.

A casing of sheet or other metal, F^2, surrounds the cylinder or chamber A, so as to allow a free circulation of heat entirely around the exterior of the chamber A.

The mode of operating the apparatus is as follows: The cylinder or chamber A being heated to such a temperature as will continue the molten metals in a state of fluidity, the plug A^2 being removed, the mixed or alloyed metals, being reduced to a molten or a fluid state by heat in any suitable and convenient furnace, are poured into the chamber, and the plug A^2 inserted and fastened; or, in some cases, the metals may be put into the cylinder A in a solid form, and then melted. The chamber A is then to be caused to revolve at a high velocity, sufficient to accomplish the intended purpose long enough to permit and force the metals to be separated by the centrifugal force and action, according to their different and respective specific gravities, and arranged in approximate concentric bands within the chamber. The fire should then be removed from the furnace, and the metals within the revolving chamber permitted gradually to cool, the rotation of the cylinder still being kept up until the ingot within is solid enough to be removed, when the cylinder is to be lifted from the frame, the head A removed, and the ingot taken out. It may then be placed in or under a lathe and the metals turned or cut out, according to their respective purity and value, and assorted to be further purified or separated, concentrated, and refined by this same process with others of like or similar kind and value, or by such other ordinary modes as may be in use.

I prefer to arrange the chamber or cylinder to revolve in a vertical plane; but it is obvious that it may be made to produce the same result when revolving in a horizontal plane.

I do not restrict my claim to any particular form or arrangement of the several parts, for these may be varied greatly without departing from the principle of my invention.

The separation of silver from lead may be aided by the addition of a small quantity of zinc.

Having thus described my invention, what I claim, and desire to secure by Letters Patent, is—

1. The mode of separating molten alloys of metals of different specific gravities, by causing them to revolve in a heated revolving chamber, to form, on gradual cooling, an ingot in which the metals are arranged in bands of more or less purity, according to their different densities, substantially as set forth.

2. The chamber A, with a removable head, suspended upon axles C, attached to the heads and arranged to revolve within a furnace, substantially as and for the purpose set forth.

In testimony whereof I have signed my name to this specification in the presence of two subscribing witnesses.

CHRISTIAN S. EYSTER.

Witnesses:
JAMES S. GRINNELL,
S. M. POOL.

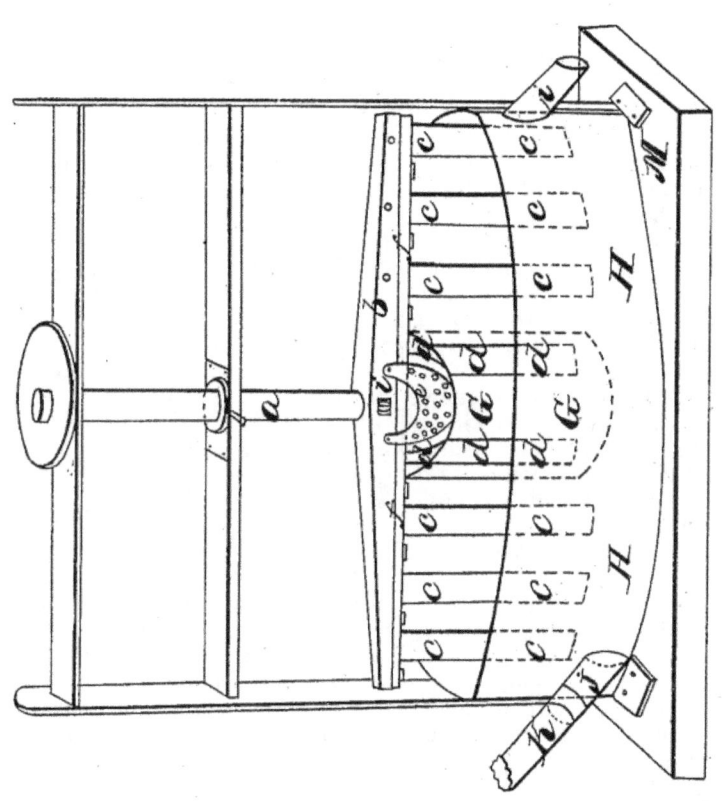
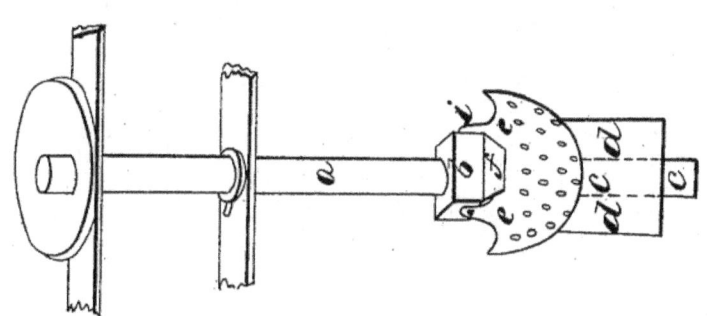

UNITED STATES PATENT OFFICE.

WELLS SPICER, OF SUMMIT COUNTY, COLORADO TERRITORY.

IMPROVED APPARATUS FOR SAVING MERCURY FROM THE WASHINGS OF GOLD AND SILVER ORES.

Specification forming part of Letters Patent No. **105,019**, dated July 5, 1870.

To all whom it may concern:

Be it known that I, WELLS SPICER, of Summit county, in the Territory of Colorado, have invented a new and useful Apparatus for Securing Waste Mercury found in all metallurgical operations where precious metals, such as gold and silver, are extracted from their respective ores by metallic mercury; and do hereby declare that the following is a full, clear, and exact description thereof, reference being had to the accompanying drawings, making a part of this specification, in which—

Figure 1 is a vertical cross-section of said apparatus, and Fig. 2 is a horizontal section of the same on the line $x\,x$ of Fig. 1.

Letters of like name and kind refer to like parts in each of the figures.

My invention consists of a sluice tub or trough, (or several combined,) through which mercury is caused to pass after having been employed in the amalgamation of gold or silver ores, in either tables, stamp-mills, or amalgamating-pans, whereby the contaminated mercury is purified and deposited, together with such precious metals as were not previously separated or amalgamated, the metallic surface of the tub, through which an electric current passes, abstracting and binding the metals when suspended or in solution, according to the well-known electrolytic laws.

In the annexed drawings, A represents a copper sluice-tub from twenty to twenty-four inches in diameter and about eight inches deep. Attached near the bottom and top, and upon opposite sides of the trough, are two spouts, B and C, through the first of which the mercury solution and amalgams enter the vessel, where they are sufficiently agitated, and then discharged through the opposite spout.

The tub A rests upon a platform or bed of timber, D, to which are secured two vertical posts, E E, which are tied together near their upper ends by two cross-bars, F F, forming a support for a vertical shaft, G, working in suitable bearings in said cross-bars. Secured to the lower end of the shaft G is a cross-bar or arm, H, corresponding in length to the diameter of the tub A, placed in a horizontal position immediately over said tub.

I I represent two metallic strips secured to the under side of the arm H, and extending from either end of said arm to within a short distance of its center, and are each provided with three copper rods or plates, K K, &c., which extend downward to within a short distance of the bottom of the tub. A pulley or crank being attached to the upper end of the shaft, and said shaft being caused to rotate, the arm H and strips and plates constitute revolving electrodes.

L represents a copper vessel about six inches in diameter, and somewhat deeper than the tub A, to the bottom of which (in the center) it is secured.

M M represent two zinc plates, connected at their upper ends to the strips I I, and extending downward within the vessel L, forming with it a Daniell battery.

A perforated sack or receptacle for containing solid blue vitriol, U, is secured to the center of the arm H, and extends downward to about one-third of the depth of the vessel L, for the purpose of replacing the same salt in the solution contained in said vessel, as it is decomposed by electrolytic action, and metallic copper deposited upon the walls of said vessel or battery.

The vessel L being now filled with a copper solution containing some free sulphuric acid, an electric current is produced, which flows from the zinc plates M M, through the copper strips I I, into the copper plates K K, &c., down which it passes into the mercurial waste solution, and from thence to the copper surface of the tub A.

The metallic tub, assuming electro-negative polarity, attracts and receives electro-positive elements like mercury, gold, silver, &c.

When the tub A is charged with a solution of mercury, flowered, contaminated, or acidified mercury, metallic mercury is at once deposited at the bottom and upon the sides of the tub, and thus secured and restored to its primitive purity, instead of being wasted. If the solution contains any other precious metals—such as gold, silver, &c.—they are also deposited and amalgamated by the mercury. There should be at least two of these tubs, so placed as that the solution shall pass through each in succession. Said solution, being first thrown upon the bottom of the tubs, is caused to rotate by the motion of the agitators, so as to bring it continually against the galvanized surfaces of said tubs, upon which all of the precious metals are deposited, such as from any cause pass with said solution from the first tub being deposited in the next.

Having thus fully set forth the nature and merits of my invention, what I claim as new is—

1. The metallic sluice-tub A, containing in its center a permanent galvanic battery, L, the zinc plates of which, M M, are in metallic connection with the movable polar agitators K K, &c., substantially as described, and for the purpose set forth.

2. Also, in connection with the above-described apparatus, the saving and securing of waste mercury when in solution, flowered, or amalgamated with precious metals, substantially as and for the purpose shown.

WELLS SPICER.

Witnesses:
  H. J. MODILL,
  J. P. KIRBY.

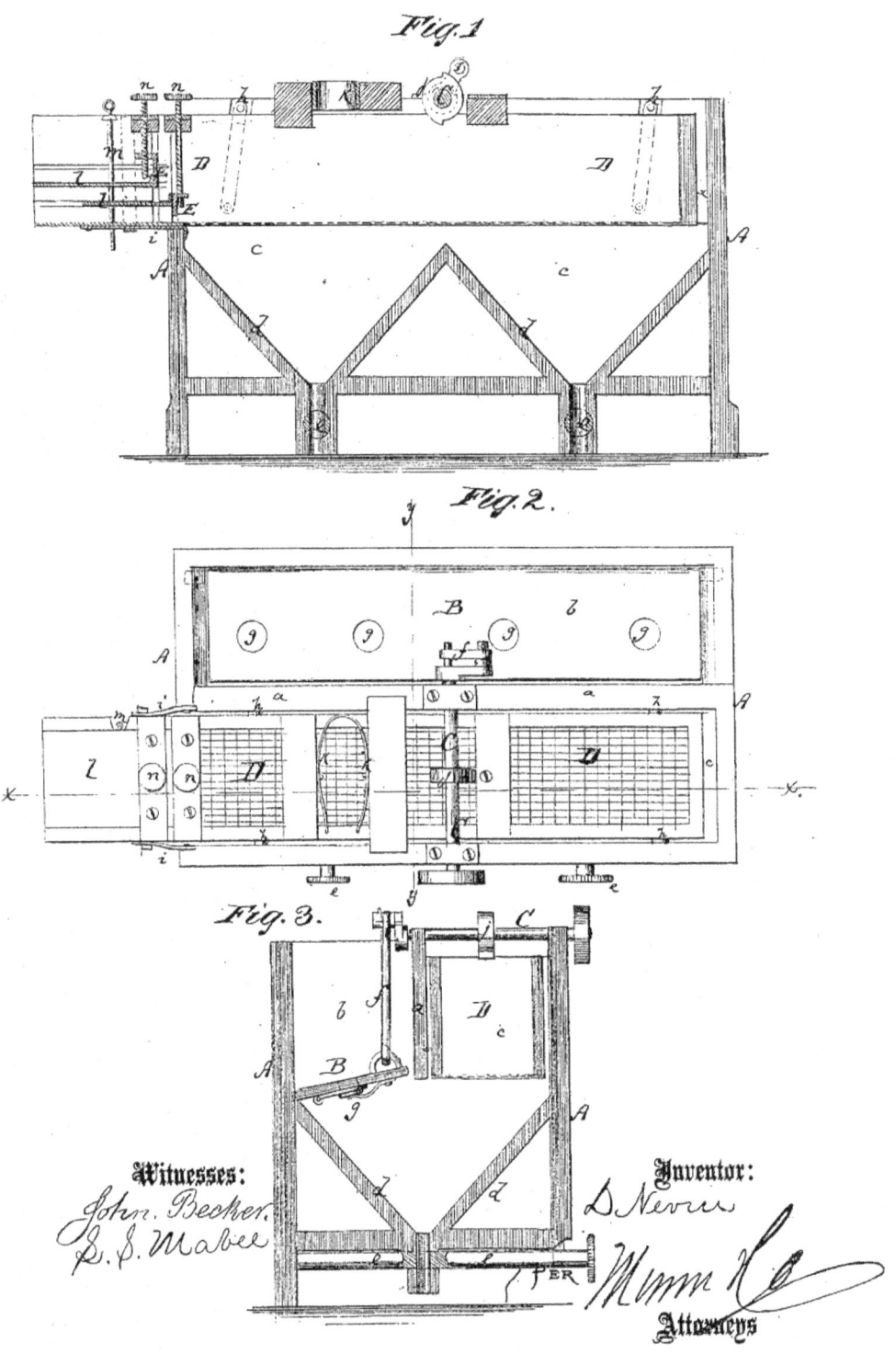

UNITED STATES PATENT OFFICE.

DAVID NEVIN, OF GEORGETOWN, COLORADO TERRITORY.

IMPROVEMENT IN ORE-SEPARATORS.

Specification forming part of Letters Patent No. **105,480**, dated July 19, 1870.

To all whom it may concern:

Be it known that I, DAVID NEVIN, of Georgetown, in the county of Clear Creek and Territory of Colorado, have invented a new and Improved Ore-Separator; and I do hereby declare that the following is a full, clear, and exact description thereof, which will enable others skilled in the art to make and use the same, reference being had to the accompanying drawing, forming a part of this specification, in which—

Figure 1 represents a vertical longitudinal section of my improved ore-separator, taken on the plane of the line $x\,x$, Fig. 2. Fig. 2 is a plan or top view of the same. Fig. 3 is a vertical transverse section of the same, taken on the plane of the line $y\,y$, Fig. 2.

Similar letters of reference indicate corresponding parts.

My invention relates to improvement in ore-separators, and more particularly in that in which an oscillating plunger is employed.

The invention consists in the combination and arrangement of an oscillating plunger with a reciprocating sieve, both simultaneously operated by the revolution of the same crank-shaft, and in the arrangement with the sieve of adjustable separating-plates and sluice-gates, as hereinafter specifically set forth.

A in the drawing represents a tank or other box of suitable size, divided longitudinally by a vertical partition, A, into two compartments, b and c.

The partition does not reach to the bottom of the tank, but allows the two compartments to be united underneath.

The bottom d of the tank is formed into one or more hoppers, as shown, the lower part of each hopper being closed by a stop-cock, e.

The compartment b contains a hinged horizontal plunger, B, which is, by means of a rod, f, connected with the crank of a transverse shaft, C, the said shaft being hung in bearings on top of the tank, as shown.

The plunger B contains a series of apertures, which are closed by downward-opening valves, g, as shown. When the shaft C is revolved it will cause the plunger to oscillate and to agitate the water with which the tank is filled. During the upward stroke of the plunger the valves will open to let the water down, and to prevent suction.

The other compartment c contains a longitudinal sieve, D, which rests on rails or is suspended from swinging bars h, and which projects through one end of the tank, the joints at the end being made tight by leather straps $i\,i$.

A cam, j, on the shaft C, together with a spring, K, serves to impart reciprocating motion to the sieve.

In the front part of the sieve are arranged one or more horizontal plates, $l\,l$, which are to divide the several grades of ore, and to guide them to separate receptacles. These plates are fitted into grooves provided for them in the sides of the sieve, and can be adjusted to any suitable height and distance from each other.

A pin, m, or equivalent fastening may be used to lock the plates l in the desired position. Sluice-gates E E, adjusted vertically by means of screws n, may also be arranged in front of the sieve.

The ore to be separated is thrown into the back part of the sieve, and is, by the agitation of the same, gradually carried forward.

The agitation of the plunger, which forces the water through the sieve, causes the ore and water to pulsate, and allows a more rapid separation and settlement of the heavier ore. The valves in the plunger prevent the ore from packing during the return stroke.

The different grades of ore are separated at the outlet by the arrangement of plates and adjustable sluices, which run them off into different tanks. The ore falling through the sieve is drawn off at the bottom of the tank through the stop-cock e.

Rotary motion is imparted to the shaft C by suitable mechanism.

Having thus described my invention, what I claim as new, and desire to secure by Letters Patent, is—

1. The arrangement of the hinged and valved plunger B, the oscillating sieve D, shaft C, cam j, and rod f, to operate as shown and described.

2. The adjustable plates l, rod m, sluice-gates E, and screw-rods n, arranged in the sieve D, as shown and described.

DAVID NEVIN.

Witnesses:
C. H. MORGAN,
JAMES GUNN.

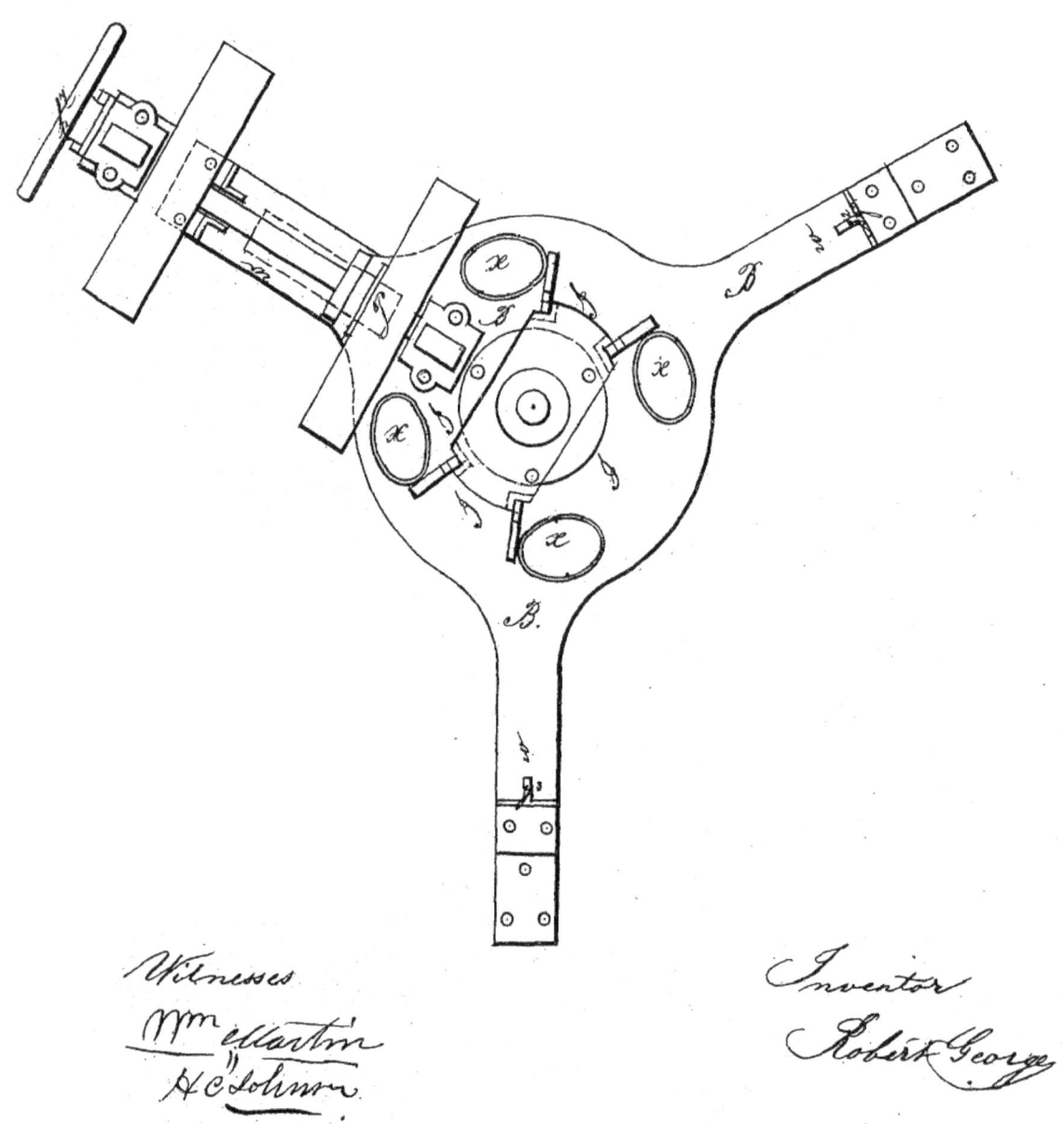

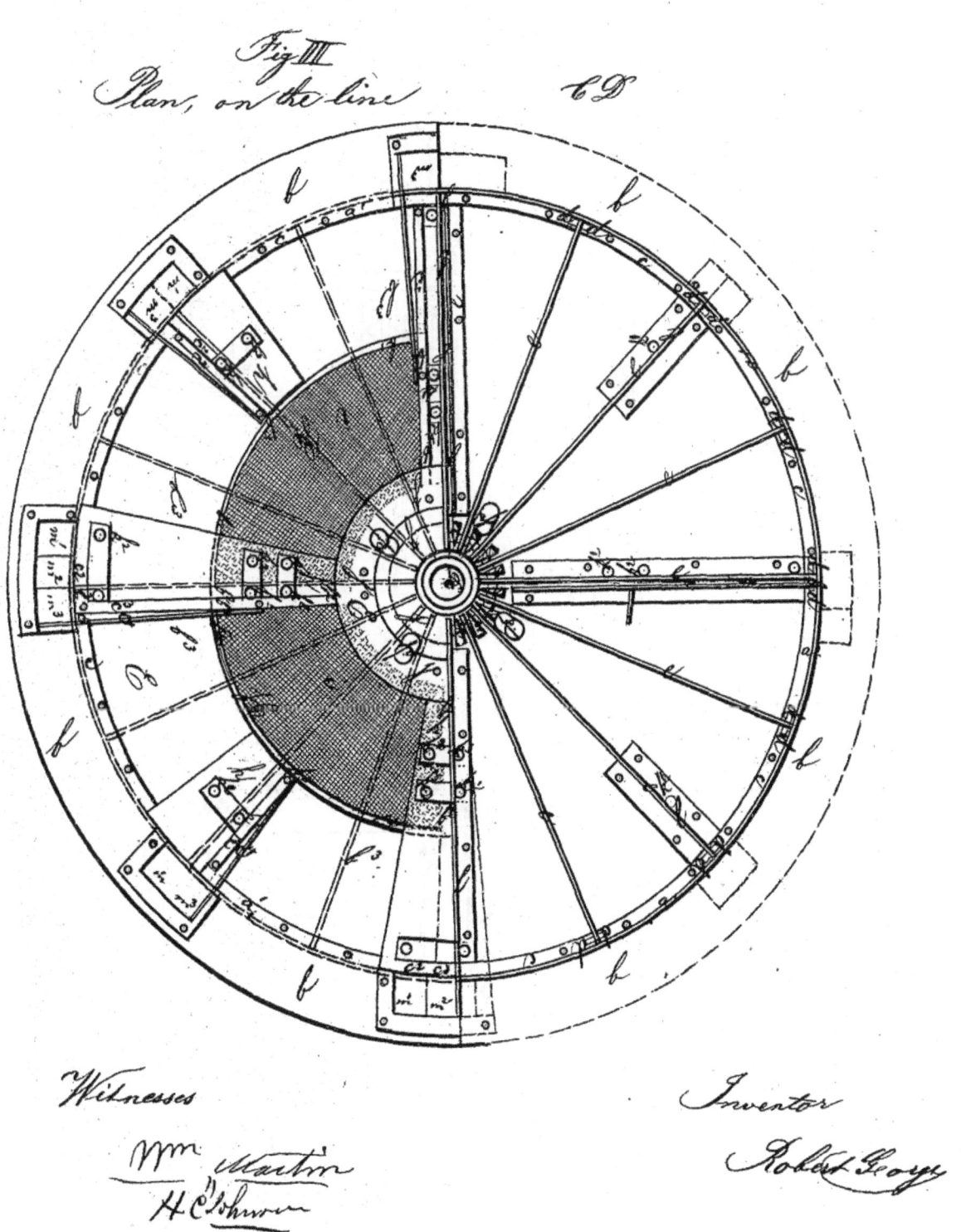

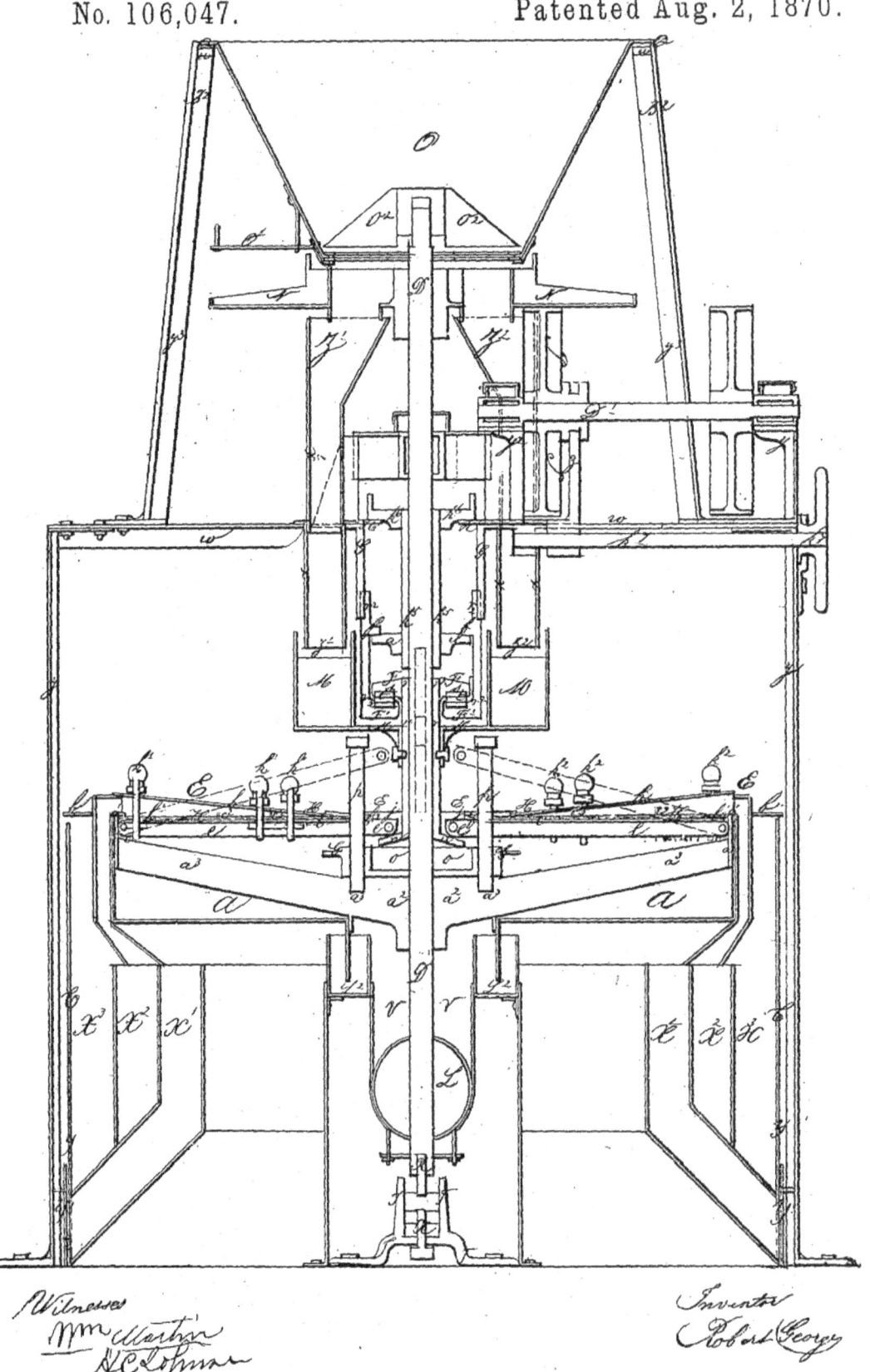

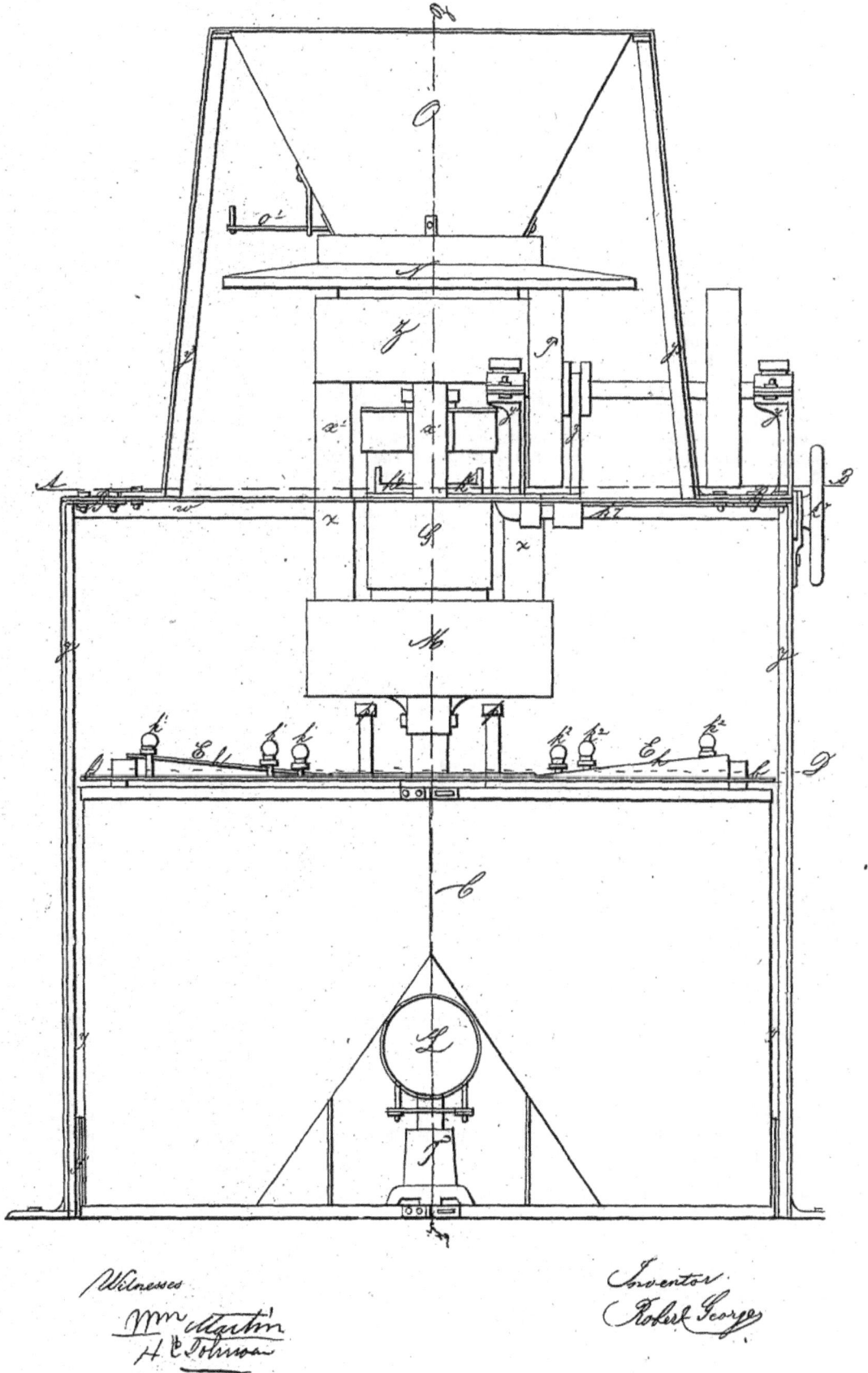

United States Patent Office.

ROBERT GEORGE, OF DENVER CITY, COLORADO TERRITORY.

Letters Patent No. 106,047, dated August 2, 1870.

IMPROVEMENT IN MACHINE FOR SEPARATING MINERAL AND FOSSIL SUBSTANCES.

The Schedule referred to in these Letters Patent and making part of the same.

To all whom it may concern:

Be it known that I, ROBERT GEORGE, of Denver City, in the county of Arapahoe, in the Territory of Colorado, have invented a new and useful Machine for Separating Comminuted Mineral or Fossil Substances, the separation of which, by the machinery heretofore in use, has been, on account of the minuteness of the particles, very imperfect; and I do hereby declare that the following is a full, clear, and exact description of its construction and operation, reference being had to the annexed drawings making a part of this specification.

Figure I, sheet 1, is a plan on the line A B.

Figure II, sheet 2, is a plan on the line C D, the one-half showing it covered with the disk, the other half with disk removed.

Figure III, sheet 3, is a vertical section on the line E F.

Figure IV, sheet 4, is a side elevation.

Similar letters, in blue ink, refer to similar parts in the several sections and elevations.

My machine is a centrifugal separator, and is constructed and designed for the separation of finely-comminuted minerals or fossil substances from dross or other extraneous substances.

The separation of materials of different specific gravity, charged in a sieve through which is forced a current of air or water, will take place if the current of air or water can be forced equally through its meshes, so as to form separate jets, which, passing upward in this manner through the materials, raise and carry the lighter particles off, while the heavier ones settle on the surface of the sieve; the operation will, however, be successful only in so far as these jets of air or water can be kept separate and distinct after having passed through the sieve. Heretofore this has been imperfectly done, and, as a consequence, there was always a great loss of the valuable materials, when the same, being operated, consisted of finely-comminuted or dust-like particles, for the reason that they cohered so closely together, and their minuteness being such, there was no space or interval through which the air or water could pass, and thus, through their cohesive power, presented such a degree of resistance as caused the consolidation of a sufficient number of jets of air or water, whose combined power of pressure was sufficient to overcome the same, and allow the air or water to make its escape, which it done either by raising the cohering mass and pushing it aside, or breaking through the same with a puff, whereby the particles were scattered but not separated.

To overcome this cohesive power I employ centrifugal power, in connection with a vibratory motion, by which the mass being separated is continually agitated by a hopper possessing a rotary and oscillating motion, for the purpose of spreading more regularly and evenly the materials discharged through the same, and which said materials, in their descent, come into collision with a current of air or water separated into distinct jets, to correspond with the meshes of the sieve through which they have passed, the lighter particles being thereby blown or carried off, while the heavier ones fall on the sieve. In this way a partial separation is effectuated; the heavier particles, on striking the sieve, are immediately exposed to the vibratory motion, as well as the continued pressure of the air or water; and by the combined action of which the lighter particles are immediately brought within the influence of the centrifugal power, and by which they are propelled tangentially toward the periphery of the disk, with a velocity in a ratio equal to their weight, which velocity increases progressively as the particles near the periphery, for the reason that the centrifugal power is constantly growing stronger and the cohesion less.

To enable others skilled in the art to make and use my invention, I will proceed to describe its construction and operation.

The machine consists of three main parts:

First, the tripod B;

Second, the chamber C; and

Third, the centrifugal separator A.

The centrifugal separator consists of the rotary sieve and assorter, which is constructed and composed of the following parts, viz:

The large iron wheel a, which is dished, and as the same revolves horizontally, its periphery a^1 is thus raised, so as to form a convex with its nave a^2, which two said parts are connected by the spokes or radii a^3. The periphery a^1 is right-angled, its base being secured to the ends of the spokes a^3, so that the perpendicular of the angle projects outward in a horizontal manner, and forms the water-rim b, which acts as a fly.

The periphery a^1 is furnished on its inside, a little below the vertex, with the circular flange c, extending around on the inside of the same, so as to rest immediately on the spokes a^3. This flange being at right angles with the periphery a^1, is furnished with the sockets d, into which are slipped the supports e, and to which they are jointed by bolts. These supports e consist of two right-angled bars, whose bases are united in a T-shape, so as to leave an interstice in which the blade g folds, and one end of which is pivoted to the same.

On the supports e rests the disk E, which is composed of the four quadrantal plates H. Said plates consist of two parts, viz., the inner rim b^1, which is a quadrantal iron plate with two arms, b^2. In this rim are the interstices l, through which the blade g passes. This inner rim b^1 is fastened to the outer rim b^2 by being sunk into it a little, and then bolted. On the same, and the upper end of b^2, rests the quadrantal-shaped sieve i, and is fastened thereto by compression, by means of bands and bolts.

The disk E is furnished, on its upper side, with the wings h, of different lengths, extending alternately from the plate j over the inner edge of rim b, and from the edge of sieve i to the inner edge of rim b. These wings are fastened to disk E, with which they form an acute angle, by screws k^1 k^2 k^3, and pivots. Screws k^1 k^2 are regulating-screws, by means of which the acuteness of angle formed as aforesaid is governed, and also the interstice l^1, underneath these wings, and securely fastened to disk E are two vertical flanges, c^2 c^3, running parallel with the wing, the shortest and lowest flange being c^2, the longest and highest c^3, which is next immediately in front of the blade g, and prevents any dust or materials getting into interstice l.

Running parallel with the wings h is the pendent trough c^4, resting on the disk E in such a manner that it projects out from under the elevated edge of the wings h. This trough c^4 and the flanges c^2 c^3 open into the conduits m^1 m^2 m^3, being pipes, and cast with the wheel a, as a part of its periphery. The other ends of the supports e are upheld by the conical flange n, which is provided with the niches n^1, into which the supports are slipped, and in which they slide.

The cone n is the base of the wheel F, and rests upon India-rubber or metallic cushions or springs, o, which cushions are kept in position by being sunk in the disk G, which is furnished with a recess for that purpose. The disk G rests on and is supported by the screws p, by which it is also raised or lowered. The screws p rest in pits sunk in the spokes a^3, and extend up through the plate j. This plate j, through which passes the tubed nave of the wheel F, which encompasses the shaft D, overlaps the apex of the quadrantal plates H, and, being securely fastened to the conical flange n, fastens the same, by compression, firmly to the supports e.

The bottom part of the centrifugal separator A is covered with sheet-iron, which forms, at the nave, the pipe v, extending downward, so as to be at right angles with the bottom. In this manner a hollow wheel, composed of the foregoing parts, is constructed, whose axis is the shaft D, and to which it is secured by keying its nave a^2 to the same.

The wheel F consists of the tubed nave r, which terminates in the conical flange n. To the upper part of this tube r is screwed, left-handed, the disk s, the under side of which is provided with a circular groove or recess, into which fits the circular toothed plate t. The teeth of plate t are of an angular shape, and converge toward the nave in a radial manner, and are at right angles with their plane, being disk s, and into which plate t is fastened, by countersunk screws or bolts. The axis of wheel F is the shaft D, to which it is fastened by a spline. The wheel F' is the counterpart of wheel F, excepting it has no conical flange. The tubed nave r^2 of wheel F' fits and works in tube G telescopically, and to which it is keyed, admitting, however, of its telescopic movement. The inside of the tubed nave r^2 is furnished with the two projections f, the under part of which have a recess into which sinks the shoulders u of the tubed male screw k^5, which said screw passes up through plate H', and into which is fitted and fastened the female screw k^6, and terminates in a flat head, furnished with handles at right angles with the periphery, by which it is turned. By turning screw k^5 the shoulders u, sinking in the recess of the projection f, forces them upward, and thereby tubed wheel F' is raised, and as tubed wheel F is in gear with tubed wheel F', it follows that that also will be raised, by the raising of which, with its conical flange or base n, on which rest the supports e, disk E is raised from a plane to an incline; furthermore, by screw p is regulated the pitch line of wheels F and F'.

Wheel F having a rotary motion, and wheel F' being stationary, it follows that, when wheel F rotates, on account of being in gear with wheel F', it will also have an oscillating motion, by which the disk E, which rests on it, as aforesaid, will be constantly oscillating.

Tube G is a part of disk I, fig. I, which said disk I rests upon and is securely fastened to the arms w of the tripod B.

This disk is perforated by four circular holes, in which slide the pipes x, which are regulated by screw-nuts.

These pipes fit telescopically pipes x^1, which pipes x^1 are united in a circular manner, forming four convex mouths, which are surrounded by the rims z^1 z^2, and are supported by uprights sitting on disk I.

Immediately below disk I is the hopper m, consisting of two cylindrical plates, the one encompassing the other, and joined by spiral strips, which also form the interstices at the bottom of the hopper, through which the materials pass onto the sieve i.

This hopper is keyed or otherwise fastened to tube r of wheel F, and has, therefore, as oscillating and rotary motion.

Immediately over the mouths Z is the horizontal friction-wheel n, whose short spokes or radii form intervals, between which the materials pass from the hopper O into mouth Z. The axis of friction-wheel N is shaft D, to which it is keyed. Wheel N is also furnished with two rims, the one below and the other on top, and, being at right angles with its plane, these prevent the materials passing through from being wasted or lost by passing over its side.

The wheel N, at its periphery, rests on the vertical friction-wheel P, revolving on its own axis, and which is supported by the extended upright y and the support y^2.

Running parallel with the arm w, on which rests wheel P, and being underneath, is a long male screw, k^7, which governs and regulates the clutch z, and by means of which wheel P is forced from the periphery toward the nave of wheel N, or *vice versa*. In this manner is regulated the speed or velocity of the whole apparatus.

The hopper O is of a funnel-shape, its bottom being provided with a rotary damper, O', wherewith is regulated the discharge of materials into the apparatus.

The hopper rests in the circular plate Q, which plate rests on the arms of the small tripod B'.

The shaft D extends up through hopper O, and it is squared at the top, to which is fitted the scraper O², which revolves with the shaft, and by means of which the materials in hopper O are being continually agitated and forced through the apertures in regular quantities.

The tripod B consists of three uprights, y, and three arms, w, to which is fastened the disk I, and upon which arms rest the tripod B', consisting of three uprights, y^2, and three arms, w^1, to which the plate Q is fastened.

As will have been seen, the shaft D extends the entire length of the machine, and, forming its axis, the upper end terminating in the hopper O, the lower end rests on the steel pin R, which is sunk and rests in a circular plate fitted into the cup of the step T, so that it can slide up and down, and is regulated by the screw U, and by means of which the shaft D is raised or lowered.

The receiving-chamber C consists of two semi-circular parts, each part being divided into three semi-circular chambers, X^1 X^2 X^3, which are so formed that the bottom part of the innermost chamber X^1 extends in an inclined manner underneath the chambers $X^2 X^3$, and X^2 underneath X^3.

In this manner the bottom of each chamber faces the outside wall Y, which is provided with slides y^1, or such similar contrivance, through which the chambers discharge their contents.

Into these chambers the conduits $M^1 M^2 M^3$ open.

By constructing the bottoms of the chambers $X^1 X^2 X^3$ in this manner, there is formed in chamber C a triangular opening, into which extends the pipe L, which is a long pipe furnished with an elbow, which elbow is surrounded by the circular rim L^2.

Over the elbow is slipped pipe V, resting in the rim L^2, which is filled with mercury, making an air-tight joint.

As the shaft D passes through the elbow of pipe L, I provide the bottom part of it with a packing-box, so as to prevent the escape of any air or water therethrough.

The manner of operating my machine is as follows:

To the axis of wheel P is connected the motive power by which the apparatus is worked. Pipe L is in connection with a blowing-machine, so that a current of air is forced up through it, into the separating-chamber A, and from which it makes its escape through the interstices l and the sieves i. The materials to be separated are placed into hopper O, through which they are forced by the rotary scraper O^2, and fall through, between radii or spokes of wheel N, into the mouthed pipes x and x^1, by which they are conducted into the oscillating and vibrating hopper M, by which they are evenly distributed over sieve i, when separation begins. When the particles of the mass to be separated have been agitated and exposed to the centrifugal power, as aforesaid, those particles of equal weight will move in a sliding or rolling manner from the center toward the periphery of the separator, and, as they move in a tangential direction, they come in contact with the wings h. As the particles of greatest specific gravity are least in bulk, they immediately pass through the interstice l', which, being regulated by screw k^2, will admit of any size desired. Those particles being of an equal weight, but less specific gravity, will be of the greatest bulk, and, as a consequence, cannot pass through the interstice l', and will be forced to rise and slide over the wing, as particles of a greater bulk are more easily carried off by the centrifugal power, whose power of action is dependent on the circumference which the particles expose to its action. The current of air or water which is continually issuing on each side of the blade g, up through the interstice l, prevents the choking of interstice l', or of the flanged troughs $c^2 c^3$. Of those particles raised and forced over the wing, the heavier ones will drop down on arriving at the elevated edge of the same, whereas the latter ones, having an inclined direction, will pass away over those dropping down at the edge of the wing, are caught in the trough c^4, and the current of air exuding up through interstice l, and which has been divided by blade g, upon which rests the wing h, will prevent any but those particles of a greater specific gravity from falling into trough c^4, as the power of its pressure forces the others over the sieve. The shorter or alternate wings operate in the same manner, excepting they have but one trough, c^2, besides trough c^4, and are designed to gather and collect those particles falling on the center of the graduated plates, and which otherwise would be carried off tangentially by the centrifugal power before coming in contact with the longer wings, and, as these consist of larger particles, only trough c^2 is dispensed with.

What I claim as my invention, and desire to secure by Letters Patent, is—

1. The process of separating minerals and valuable fossil substances from extraneous substance by centrifugal apparatus, operating with a jet of air or water.

2. The centrifugal separator, constructed and operating as described.

3. The disk E, with sieves, plates, wings, blades, and flanges, in manner as constructed and described, together with its mode of operation and manner of fastening.

4. The tube-wheels F and F^1, their peculiar construction, together with their attachments and appendages.

5. The process by which the disk E is raised and lowered, so as to be either on a plane or an incline, together with the screw k^5, with its manner of construction and attaching.

6. For the manner of attaching the friction-wheels N and P, so as to regulate the velocity or speed of the apparatus.

7. The process of forcing air or water through materials, and thereby separating them, in the centrifugal separator A.

8. For the manner of constructing rim L^2, whereby joint of the pipe V and the pipe L are rendered airtight by the mercurial or water-packing.

In witness whereof I have, this 14th day of July, A. D. 1870, hereunto set my hand in presence of—

ROBERT GEORGE.

Witnesses:
E. P. WEBER,
LOUIS SCHULZE.

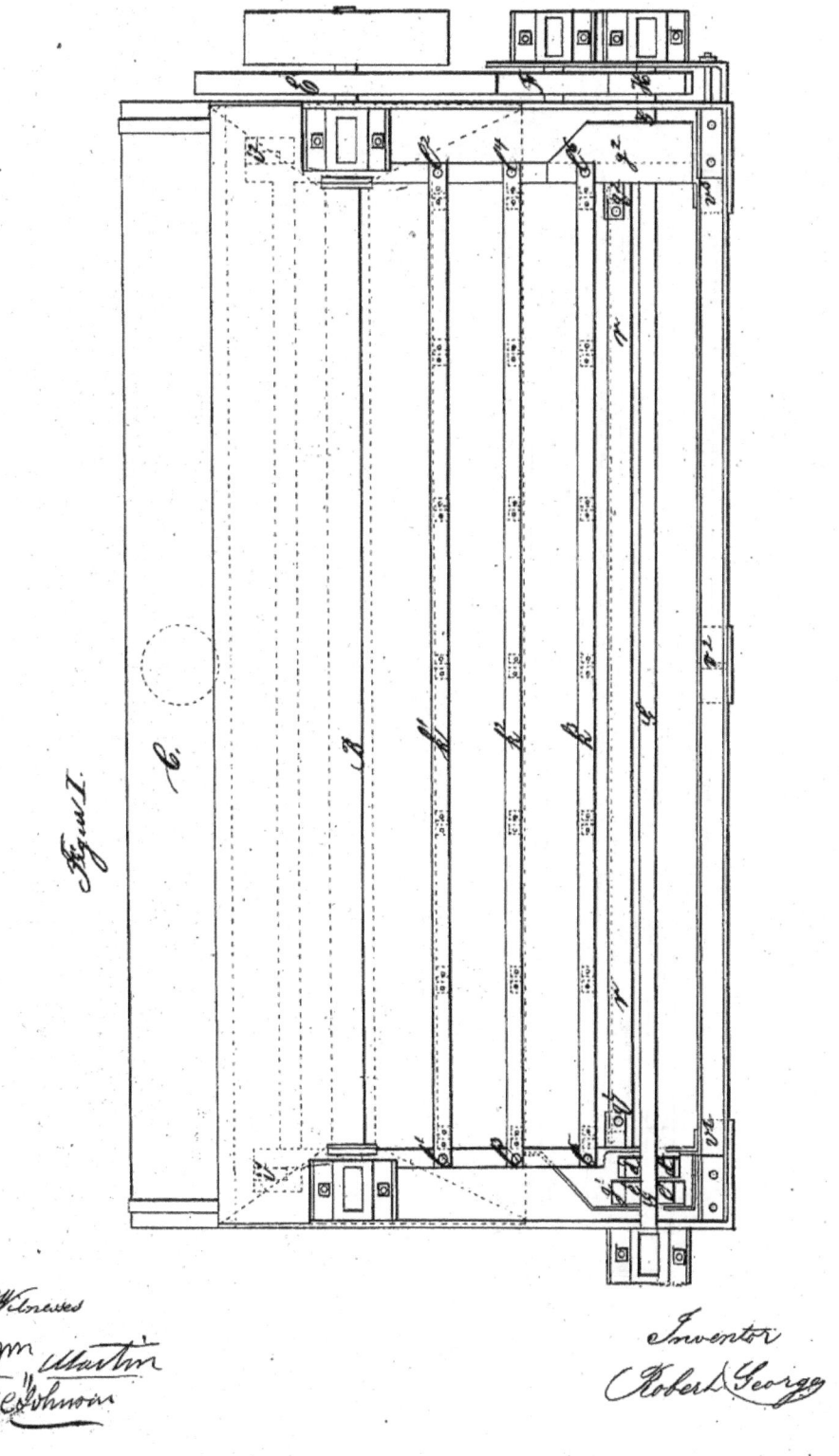

R. GEORGE.
MACHINE FOR SEPARATING AND CONCENTRATING ORES AND OTHER MATERIALS OF DIFFERENT SPECIFIC GRAVITIES.

No. 106,048. Patented Aug. 2, 1870.

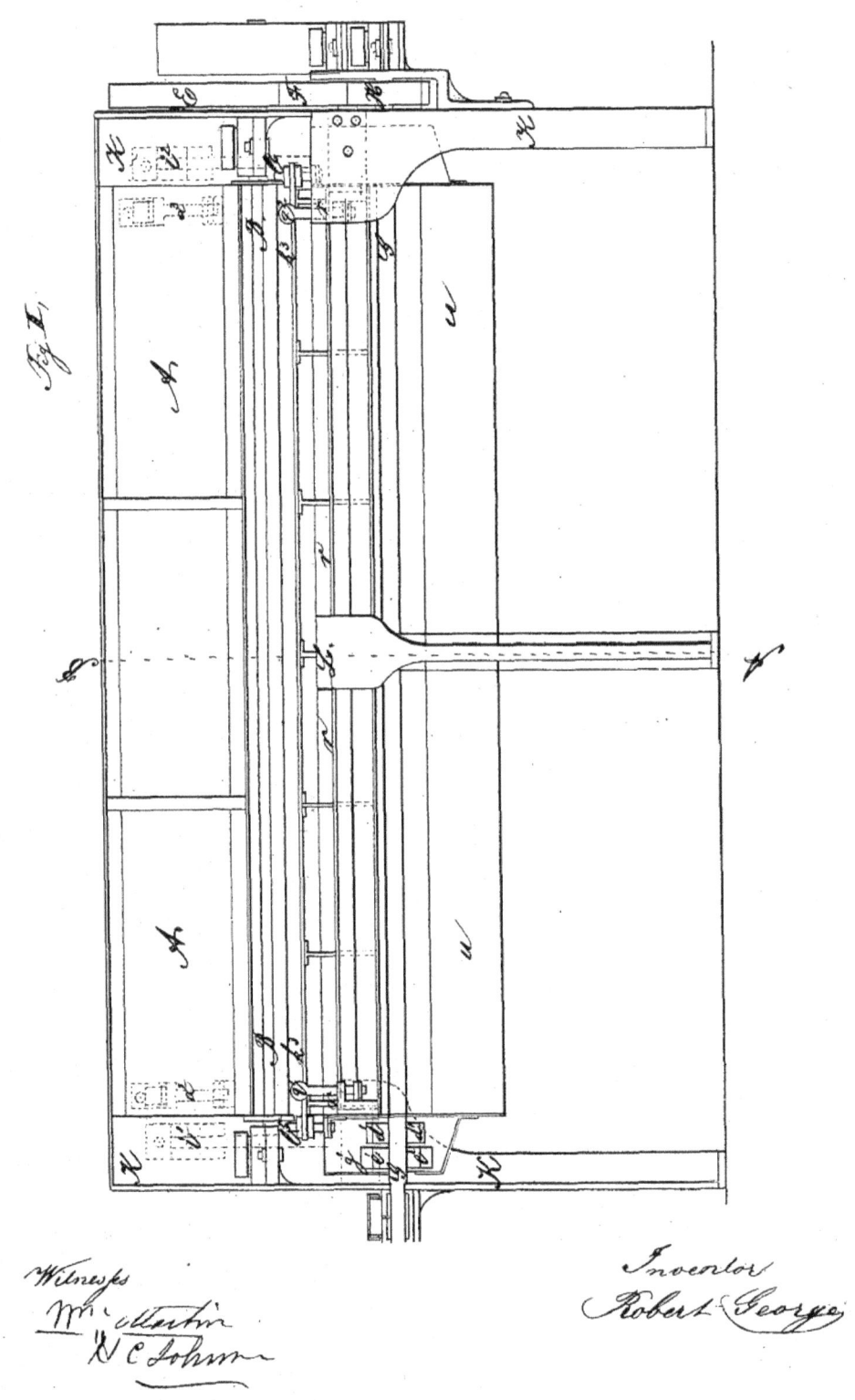

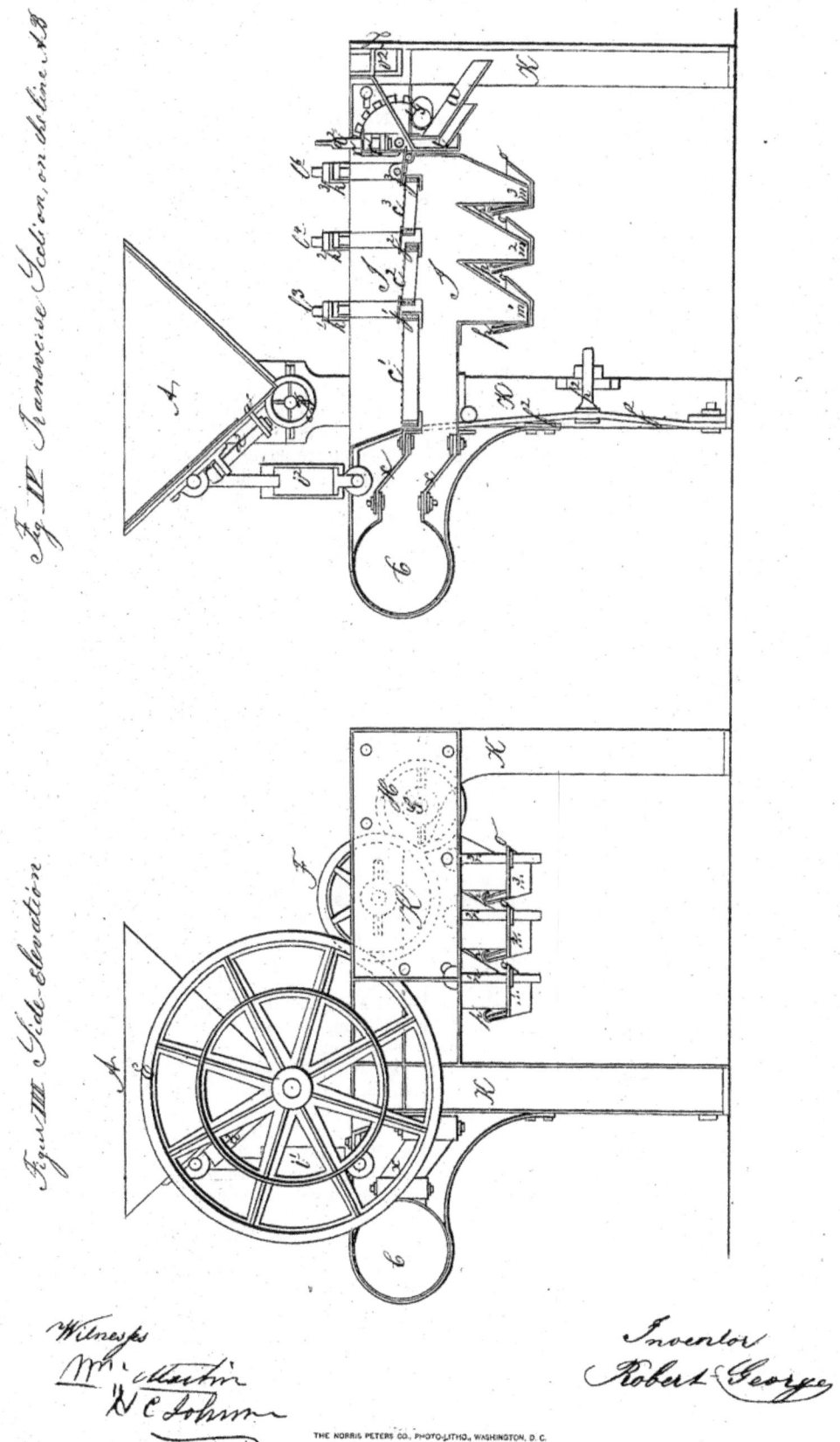

United States Patent Office.

ROBERT GEORGE, OF DENVER CITY, COLORADO TERRITORY.

Letters Patent No. 106,048, dated August 2, 1870.

IMPROVEMENT IN MACHINE FOR SEPARATING AND CONCENTRATING ORES AND OTHER MATERIALS OF DIFFERENT SPECIFIC GRAVITIES.

The Schedule referred to in these Letters Patent and making part of the same

---

To all whom it may concern:

Be it known that I, ROBERT GEORGE, of Denver City, in the county of Arapahoe and Territory of Colorado, have invented a new and useful Machine for Separating and Concentrating Materials of Different Specific Gravity, metals, rocks, alluvials, and any metallurgical and organic fossil substances contained in an admixture or natural strata, or in a chemical combination; and I do hereby declare that the following is a full, clear, and exact description of the construction and operation of the same, reference being had to the annexed drawings making a part of this specification, in which—

Figure I, sheet 1, is a plan.

Figure II, sheet 2, is a front elevation.

Figure III, sheet 3, is a side elevation.

Figure IV, sheet 3, is a transverse section on the line A B.

Similar letters, in blue ink, refer to similar parts throughout the several elevations and sections.

The nature of my invention consists in the construction of a machine possessing the following properties, and designed—

First, to simplify the process of concentrating and separating all kinds of useful and valuable ores and mineral substances, during the process of dressing (separating) from rocky matters, and other injurious or extraneous substances, for the purpose of their subsequent metallurgical treatment.

Secondly, to save, unaided by any other apparatus or appliance whatsoever, all of the precious metals or other useful and valuable mineral substances undergoing the process of crushing and separation in stamp-mills, or any other grinding machinery, and prevent the great loss accruing by the use of the amalgamating apparatus of mercury and the other appliances heretofore used, to save and concentrate the useful and valuable minerals for their subsequent metallurgical treatment.

Thirdly, to save the precious metals contained in alluvials, or so-called dry placers.

Fourthly, to separate mineral coal, graphite clay, and minerals for paints, &c., from injurious and extraneous substances, as iron pyrites, slate, sand, &c.

To enable others skilled in the art to make and use my invention, I will proceed to describe the construction and operation of my machine.

The machine consists of two main parts, viz., the outside frame-work K and the separating-chamber I.

In order to charge the machine with materials to be separated, it is necessary to assort and classify them according to their size; if they consist of rocky matters in large lumps, they ought to be crushed either in jam-crushers, rollers, or stamps, and then passed through a series of sieves, to render them fit for charging. When the materials to be separated are found in alluvials, as is frequently the case of the precious metals, in dry placers, &c., it will suffice to separate the larger rock or gravel by merely screening it.

The material thus assorted is charged into the hopper A, and spread evenly.

The damper a^1 is then opened, by the screws $a^2 a^3$, a sufficient width to fill the flutes of the roller B.

The motive power to work the machine may be applied either to the shaft of the roller B, or to the shaft G; in either case, the intermediate wheel F will transmit the motion from B to G, or G to B.

To the shaft G are fastened and attached the lifting-wheels d^1 and d^2, the cam-wheels e^1 and e^2, and the spur-wheel H.

The frame-work of the separating-chamber I rests on its front part on India-rubber cushions or metallic springs, marked $v^1 v^2 v^3$, which said cushions or springs are kept in position by boxes fastened to and supported by the front bar L, of the main frame-work K.

The rear part of the separating-chamber is suspended by the swivels $i^1 i^2$, attached to the main frame-work K.

When the machine is set in motion, the roller B, revolving, discharges the contents at about the center of the raised back of the separating-chamber I, whereby the same are evenly spread over the rear side of the sieve C', at the same time the separating-chamber I is lifted by the wheels $d^1 d^2$, which causes the charged materials to oscillate vertically on the sieves, while the cam-wheels $e^1 e^2$ move the separating-chamber horizontally backward, until the prolongations $g^1 g^2$ slide off from the engaged tooth of the wheels $e^1 e^2$, at which moment the springs $f^1 f^2$ reverse the motion of the separating-chamber I, and force it to the front bar L, producing thereby a horizontal concussion of the charged materials, which forces the same from sieve c^1 to sieve c^2 and c^3, in order to facilitate the forcing or sliding of the charged materials, more speedily toward the front of the machine. The separating-chamber I may be raised in the rear by the swivels $i^1 i^2$, in such a manner that the sieves $c^1 c^2 c^3$ will be placed on an incline toward the front of the machine.

The velocity of the stroke of the springs $f^1 f^2$ is regulated by the screws $h^1 h^2$.

The separating-chamber I is connected with the slotted pipe C by means of leather, rubber, or metallic packing x, sufficiently pliable, so as not to interfere with the oscillating and rising movements of the separating-chamber.

If the machine is charged with materials in a dry state, air is forced in under sieves $c^1 c^2 c^3$ by a bellows fan, or other blowing apparatus, connected with the pipe O. The continuous oscillations of the materials on the sieves $c^1 c^2 c^3$ will facilitate the passing upward of the air through the charged materials, whereby the particles of greater specific gravity accumulate on the bottom of the sieves, while the lighter ones are raised to the surface of the agitated materials.

To separate the heavier particles from the overlying lighter ones, in a continuous manner, the sieve c^1 is overlapped by the metallic strip j^1, which said strip, at the same time, forms a rim over the edge of c^2; in like manner c^2 is overlapped by j^2, and c^3 by j^3. The overlaps $j^1 j^2 j^3$ are securely fastened to the bars $k^1 k^2 k^3$ which said bars $k^1 k^2 k^3$ are fastened and attached to the separating-chamber by the screws $l^1 l^2$, by means of which screws the said bars $k^1 k^2 k^3$ can be raised and lowered, thereby widening and narrowing the interstices formed by the strips $j^1 j^2 j^3$ and the sieves $c^1 c^2 c^3$, as may be required for the admission of the particles of greater specific gravity into the troughs of the separating-chamber, which said troughs, marked $m^1 m^2 m^3$, are provided with a movable and detached bottom, suspended scale-like, as seen by p', and which said bottom can be raised or depressed by means of the regulating-screws $n^1 n^2$, to such a degree as to form an orifice sufficient to allow the separated materials to make their exit at the edge o; while, in this manner, the valuable or heavier particles make their exit through the troughs $m^1 m^2 m^3$, as above described, the lighter or exhausted materials have to pass over the damper r. The latter is so constructed that it can be easily raised or lowered in a curvilinear manner, as the nature of materials on the sieves $c^1 c^2 c^3$ may require, for a perfect separation. If the damper r is raised by the regulating-screws $q^1 q^2$, with which it is provided, so far as to form a small interstice between it and the overlap j^3, through which the particles from the undermost of the materials sliding over the damper r can pass, this will afford the operator a criterion to determine whether all useful and valuable materials are exhausted and sieved or not. If there are any passing therethrough, the same will be saved by passing over the apron t, while the exhausted and extraneous materials are carried off over the apron u.

If the charge is in a wet state, as, for instance, the tailings from stamp-mills, water may be introduced, instead of air, or water and air together, in a similar manner as that stated for the introduction of air alone, through the pipe O.

The velocity of the fluted roller B for charging is calculated to be fifteen revolutions per minute, and, as the roller is provided with four flutes, with a depth of an inch each, and being six feet long, the capacity for charging will be 333.84 cubic inches per minute.

Supposing that the charge consists of common gold-bearing quartz or alluvial, the machine will separate eight tons and fourteen hundred pounds in one hour, or in ten hours, the gold contained in eighty-seven tons of quartz or alluvial, a capacity almost higher than practicable operation will require in any of the aforesaid cases. The applicability and utility of my machine are evident from the foregoing.

What I claim as my invention, and desire to secure by Letters Patent, is—

1. A machine for separating, concentrating, and saving the precious metals, and other valuable and useful minerals or fossil substances, as the same exist and are found, either in a crude state or artificially produced by chemical combinations or technical admixtures, arranged, constructed, and operated in the manner and for the purposes hereinbefore described and set forth.

2. The sieves $c^1 c^2 c^3$, together with their arrangements and connections to form the adjustable interstices.

3. The troughs $m^1 m^2 m^3$, with their movable and detached bottoms o.

4. The damper r, as arranged and described.

5. The lifting-wheels $d^1 d^2$, for causing the oscillation, and the cam-wheels $e^1 e^2$, to promote the discharge of the materials, together with their attachments and manner of operating.

6. The fluted roller B and the hopper A, together with their fastenings and manner of construction and application.

7. The cushions, being either India rubber or metallic spring, marked $v^1 v^2 v^3$, and the boxes, whereby they are secured and kept in position.

8. The slotted pipe O, with the leather, rubber, or metallic connections, which are sufficiently pliable to admit of the free and the unimpeded motion of the separating-chamber I, and its manner of attachment, as described and set forth.

9. The springs $f^1 f^2$, together with their appliances, mode of regulating, and manner of operation.

10. The swivels $i^1 i^2$, together with their application, as described and set forth.

In witness whereof I have hereunto set my hand and subscribed my name this 7th day of July, A. D. 1870.

ROBERT GEORGE.

Witnesses:
  E. P. WEBER,
  LOUIS SCHULZE.

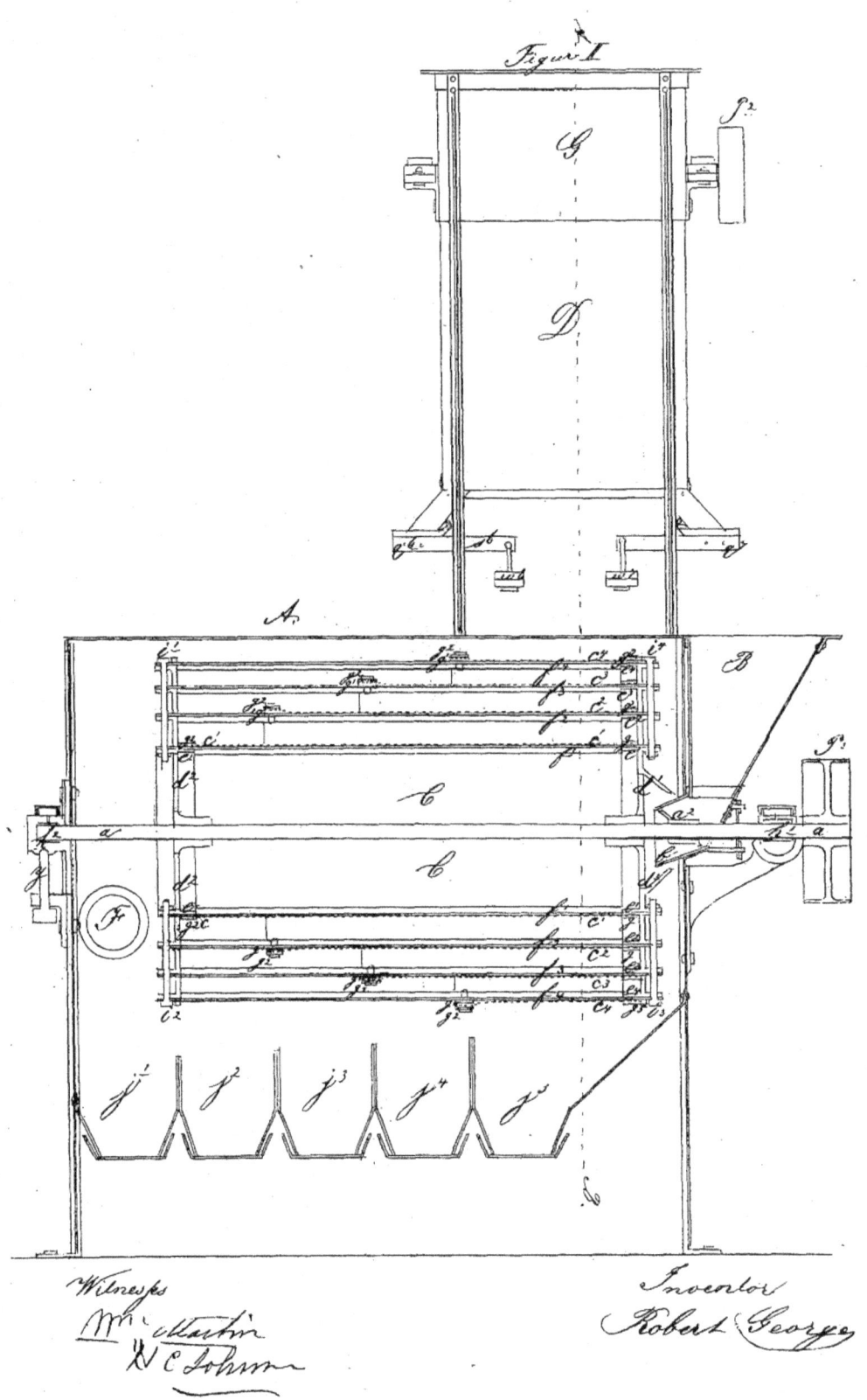

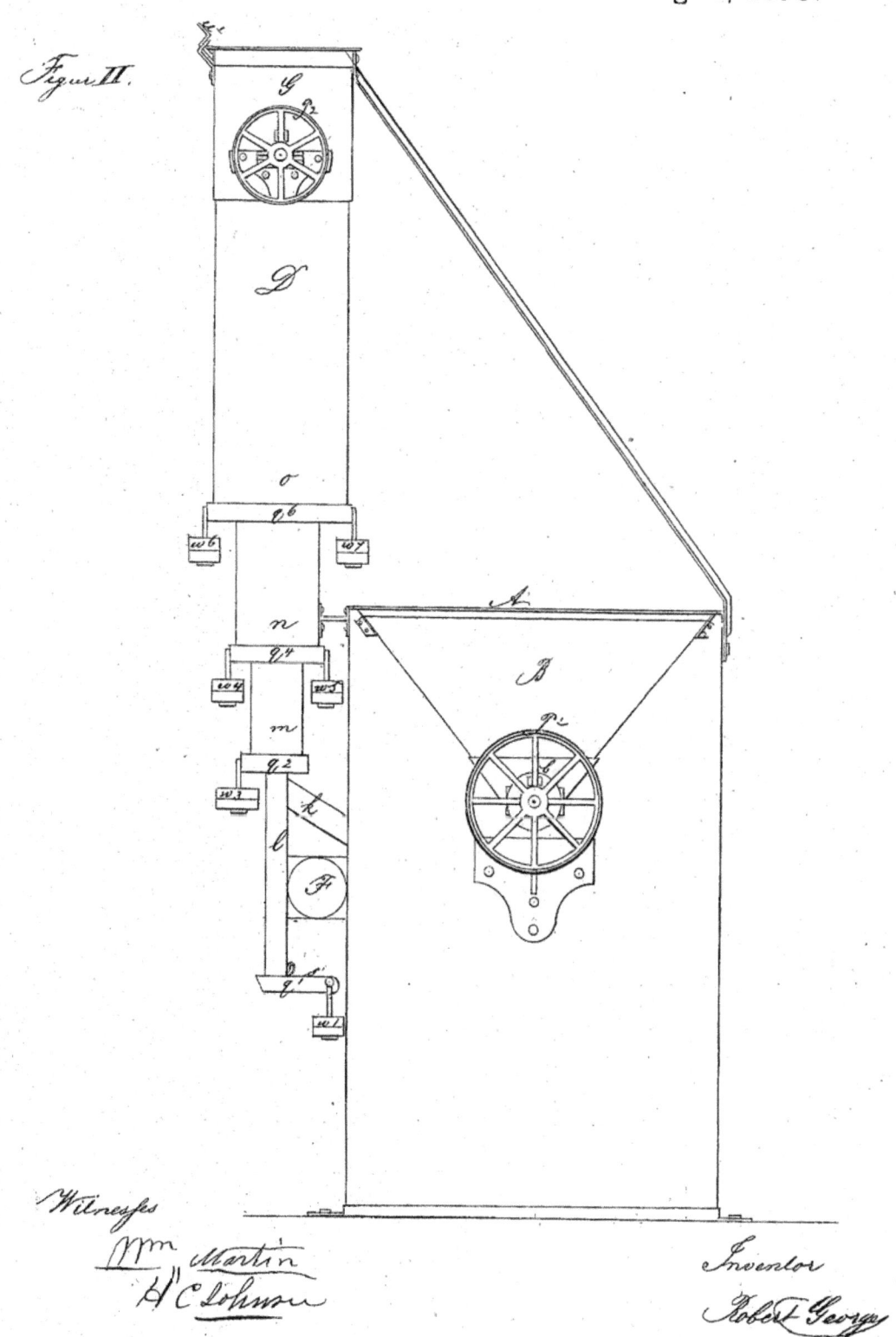

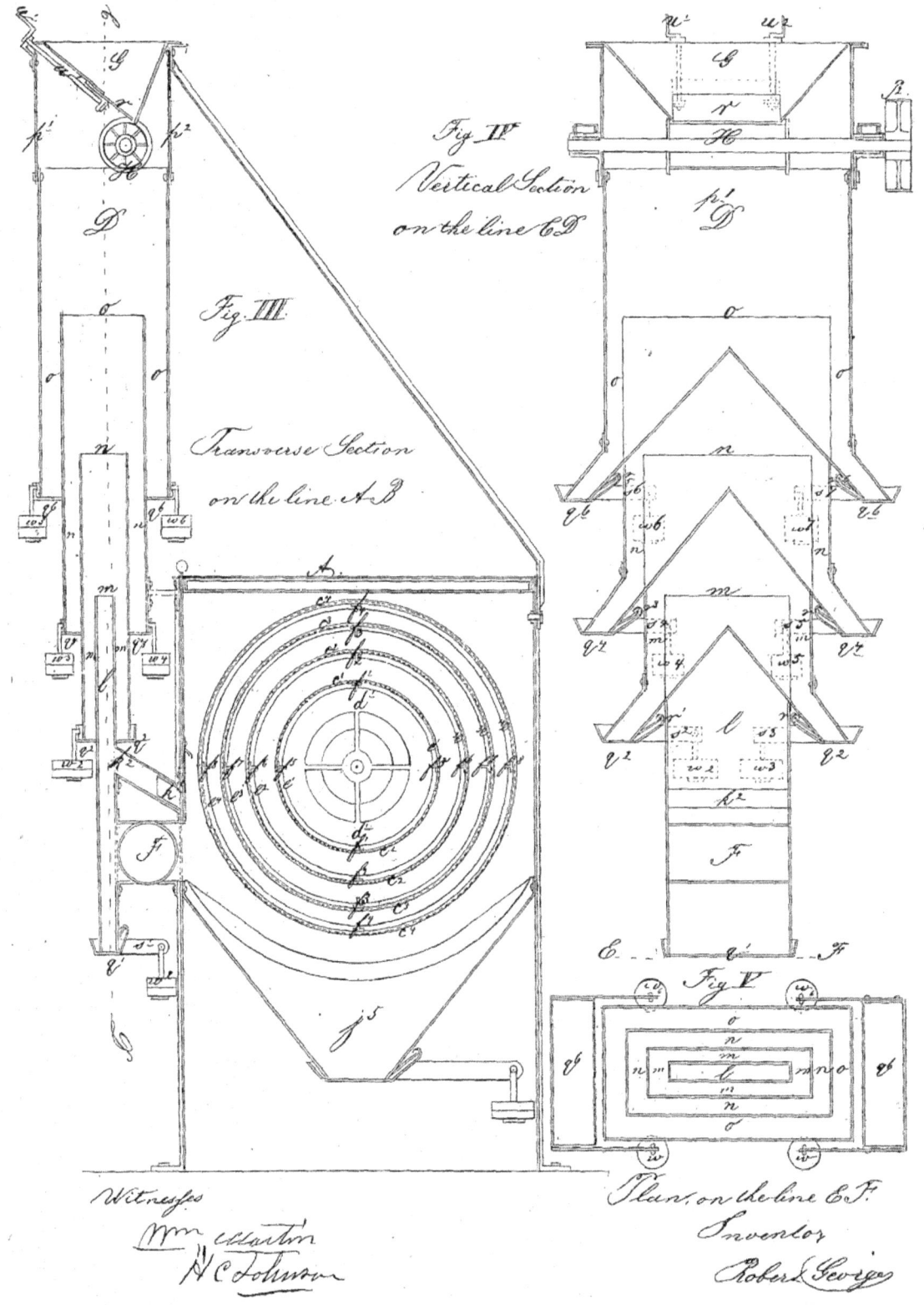

United States Patent Office.

ROBERT GEORGE, OF DENVER CITY, COLORADO TERRITORY.

Letters Patent No. 106,049, dated August 2, 1870.

IMPROVEMENT IN APPARATUS FOR SEPARATING AND CONCENTRATING ORES.

The Schedule referred to in these Letters Patent and making part of the same.

To all whom it may concern:

Be it known that I, ROBERT GEORGE, of Denver City, in the county of Arapahoe, in the Territory of Colorado, have invented a new and useful Machine to Sift, Assort, Separate, and Size Useful and Valuable Minerals and Fossil Substances; and I do hereby declare that the following is a full, clear, and exact description of its construction and operation, reference being had to the annexed drawings making a part of this specification, in which—

Figure I, sheet 1, is a longitudinal section and side view.

Figure II, sheet 2, is a front elevation.

Figure III, sheet 3, is a transverse section on the line A B.

Figure IV, sheet 3, is a vertical section on the line C D.

Figure V, sheet 3, is a plan on the line E F.

Similar letters, in blue ink, refer to similar parts throughout the several elevations and sections.

My machine is a combined sifter and separator, and is designed and constructed to sift, separate, and size minerals and fossil substances, in a comminuted state.

When materials are to be sifted or assorted, in order to gather and collect the particles of a uniform size, or separate them from dross, dust, or other extraneous matter, they have been heretofore charged either on plane, curved, or cylindrical sieves of wire-gauze, or perforated sheet metals, and the promiscuous mass, to be operated as above, was, in all cases, spread or charged first on the finest sieve, and the portion remaining unsifted, being the greatest bulk of the materials, was then successively run through sieves of increasing and varying coarseness, until the whole mass was sifted and assorted.

To this mode of operation is consequent the practical difficulty that thereby the finest sieves are overloaded, and subjected to the greatest weight and bulk of the materials to be sifted, and, as a consequence, they wear out very fast, especially when the materials to be sifted are of a considerable specific gravity, as, for instance, metals, and mineral substances, or when they are of a sharp-edged fracture. Furthermore, by the charging and overloading of the finest sieves first with the bulk of the materials, the separation is imperfect, as the larger particles not only settle on the surface of the sieve, and thereby prevent the finer ones from passing through, but, being also possessed of a greater cohesive power, they attract the smaller particles, and carry the same with them. Especially is this the case when the larger particles are of an amorphous, porous, or irregular form, from all of which the operation is not only rendered defective, but also impracticable. Especially is this the fact when mineral substances of great fineness are being treated.

In the construction and operation of my combined sifter and assorter, I have endeavored to remove and cure all of the above difficulties and imperfections, and thus secure a perfect operation.

To enable others skilled in the art to make and use my invention, I will proceed to describe its construction and operation.

The machine consists of three main parts, viz:

First, the square box A, with the hopper B.

Second, the cylindrical sieves C.

Third, the separator D.

The materials which it is intended to assort, sift, and size, are charged into the hopper B, through which the shaft a extends longitudinally along the bottom part, which is there furnished with and encompassed by the endless screw a^2, whose office is to convey the materials to be sifted over the spout b, in regular quantities, into the cylindrical sieves C, which said cylindrical sieve C consists of the shaft a, the inlet-plate d^1, the exit-plate d^2, the sieves c^1 c^2 c^3 c^4, and the rectangular bars f^1 f^2 f^3 f^4, &c., and is constructed as follows:

The inlet-plate d^1 is an iron circular plate, provided, on the inside, (facing the sieves,) with the circular flanges e^1 e^2 e^3 e^4, projecting rectangularly, and, on the outside part, with a conical flange, whose base is the plate, sufficiently large to admit of the insertion of the spout b from the hopper B, without friction. The exit-plate d^2 is the counterpart of the inlet-plate d^1, with the exception of the flanges, it being provided with only one corresponding flange, viz., e^5. Both plates have corresponding perforations, through which pass the rectangular bars f^1 f^2, &c. The exit-plate d^2 is also provided, on the outside, with an extended conical flange, through which the materials from sieve c^1 are discharged.

The sieves c^1 c^2 c^3 c^4 are cylindrical in form, and are made either of wire or perforated sheet metals, and are of different sizes and dimensions, decreasing in coarseness and size from the center, the innermost sieve being the coarsest and longest, the outermost the finest and shortest. These sieves are fastened to inlet-plate d^1 by slipping them over the flanges e^1 e^2 e^3 e^4, and are then securely fastened in position by means of hoops g^2 driven over the sieves, and so compressed and fastened between the hoops and flanges. In like manner sieve c^1 is fastened to exit-plate d^2. The other sieves, not extending to exit-plate d^2, rest on the rectangular bars f^2 f^3, &c., which not only act as a support, but also prevent the sieves from bending or bulging out. The unfastened edges or ends of the sieves are placed between the iron bands or hoops g^1 g^2, which bands or hoops are securely fastened to the rectangular bars by means of bolts, whereby the end of the sieves is securely and immovably fastened. The bars f^1 f^2 f^3,

&c., are of iron, and are made of a rectangular shape or form, so as to provide a base or support for the sieves, which rest upon and are fastened to them, as aforesaid, and also to form a wall, to which a parallel bar is bolted, and between which the longitudinal ends of the wire or perforated metal, forming the sieve, are passed, and, by the compression, securely fastened, whereby its cylinder form is given it. These rectangular bars are deprived of an angle at their ends, forming thus a shoulder, which rests against the inlet and exit-plates d^1 d^2, while the other angle is passed through the perforation in said plates, as heretofore mentioned, and securely bolted by bolts i^1 i^2. In this manner, a solid, compact cylinder, of four sieves, or more, as necessity may require, is formed, the axis of which is the shaft a, which passes through the center of the inlet and exit-plates d^1 d^2, and is thereto securely fastened by keys or set-screws.

The shaft a is supported by and rests on the journal-boxes h^1 h^2, and is moved by a crank or pulley, P.

Journal-box h^2 is attached and fastened to the outside frame-work A in a slide, which is regulated by the adjusting-screw y, whereby the cylinder C can be raised or lowered, so that the sieves will be either in a plane or incline, and thereby a speedy or slow discharge of the materials being sifted is secured by this process. The bulk of the materials being sifted is constantly diminishing, in a ratio proportionate to the sizes of the sieves through which it alternately passes, and, as a consequence, overloading of the finer sieves cannot take place, and thus the usual wear and tear of the same are prevented and obviated, especially as now the materials may be selected for the construction of the sieves in proportion to the work required, and the bulk and weight of materials to which they will be subjected.

Where the materials to be sifted are in a very comminuted or pulverized state, the dust thereof will inevitably mix in with the assorted mass. As this may be objectionable, especially when it is necessary to have the assorted particles of a uniform clean grain, I overcome and prevent this by introducing a blast of air into the box A, containing the cylindrical sieve C, by means of the pipe F, which, connected with a blowing-machine, the current of air introduced, as above, prevents the settling of the dust on the box A, but forces it out, through the slot k^1, either into a chimney, or into the dusting separator D, if attached, which last-mentioned machine consists of a series of four rectangular chambers, of successive and increasing dimensions, the smallest of which is partially inserted into the next largest, and are both fastened together laterally by means of iron strips placed in an equilateral triangular manner, the base of which terminates in the buckets marked q^1 q^2, &c., and which also form the shafts m n o. To these is fastened the next largest chamber, and then the largest chamber, in like manner. The largest chamber is furnished on the top with a cap, which has two apertures in the sides, for the egress of the dust, air, &c.

This cap is furnished on the top with a hopper, G, into which the materials are placed, and from which they pass through an interstice governed by a damper, and pass onto a corrugated roller, H, from thence to be emptied down through the chambers above mentioned.

The construction of this apparatus is based upon the principle that air, steam, water, or any fluid, when forced through a pipe, will exert a power of pressure in a ratio equal to the velocity of its force. This power of pressure will be exerted on all bodies that obstruct or impede its passage or exit.

When the obstructing or impeding bodies consist of particles in an undetached or loose state, the same will be forced along by this pressure until their resistance, being their weight, overcomes the same. This pressure is diminished and lessened in proportion to the increasing width of the pipe, until wholly lost in the counteracting atmospheric pressure, or until its force and power are expended.

A great many ores, especially silver, are deposited in the cavities of the quartz rocks in a state of pulverization equal to that of ocher, or in such minute particles, and when these rocks are crushed these ores are to be found only in a finely pulverized state, which is also the case with argentiferous, galena, and other ores, when crushed with the accompanying quartz rocks. Therefore it is that, even by the best European methods for dressing and separating the variable ores, more than twenty-five per cent. is wasted and carried off with the refuse of rocky matters, as dust. If this dust containing these valuable metals is forced into the apparatus D by a strong current of air through the slot k^2 as aforesaid, those particles whose specific gravity is not sufficient to overcome the pressure of this current of air will be raised to the top of the pipe l, into the chamber m, whereas the heavier particles will have fallen down into the bucket q^1.

As chamber m is considerably wider than l, the pressure of the current is a lessened accordingly, and therefore the next heavier particles drop into the shafts m and into bucket q^2. The balance will be forced up chamber m into chamber n, which, being still larger, the pressure is still less proportionately. Consequently, the next heavier particles fall into shafts n, and from thence into buckets q^3 and q^4. The rest is forced up through chamber n into chamber o, whose dimensions are still greater, and wherein the pressure exerted is still less; and the next heavier particles are deposited in shafts o, through which they fall into the buckets q^5 and q^6. The remainder is forced up through chamber o, and out of the apertures p^1 p^2 with the escaping current, and lost in the atmosphere as dross.

The buckets q^1 q^2 q^3 q^4 are secured at the bottom of the shafts l, m, n, and o in a balancing manner, hanging suspended from the rear side of the same on pivots r^1, r^2, r^3, &c.

To these buckets is attached, lengthwise, a lever, s^1, s^2, &c., in a rectangular manner. As these buckets are evenly balanced, it is evident that, as soon as any materials whatsoever fall into them, they will open and discharge the same. To keep them shut, the weight w is attached to the long arm of the lever, whereby they are prevented from opening until such a certain quantity of materials shall have accumulated, whose weight is sufficient to overcome and raise this weight so attached, upon which the bucket will open and empty its contents, or so much thereof as is necessary to restore the equipoise, when the weight immediately closes it again.

The bottom of the sifting-box A terminates in a trough extending throughout its entire length, which is divided into various compartments, forming the respective chambers j^1 j^2 j^3 j^4 j^5, the bottoms of which are movable and detached, and are secured and operate in a like manner as the buckets q^1, &c. By this contrivance the filling up of the same is prevented, at the same time there is always such an amount of material retained as is sufficient to render them air or water-tight.

When mineral substances are in a very comminuted state, it is in most cases very difficult to size and assort them by sifting, as the required minuteness of the meshes of the sieve renders them very easily clogged and unendurable, inasmuch as the fineness of wire-gauze necessary for their construction is easily corroded. Therefore, in these cases, the materials to be assorted should be first treated in apparatus D, which is done in the following manner:

The comminuted particles are charged into the hopper G, the bottom of which is governed by the damper r, which is regulated by the screws w^1 w^2, and by means of which the aperture is widened or narrowed in so far as is necessary to insure a sufficient discharge of materials therethrough to fill the corrugations of the roller H, or such quantities as may be required for successful operation.

The roller H discharges its contents in such a manner that the same fall in a direction perpendicular with the center of the chamber l, the air, or whatever agent is made use of, being introduced into the apparatus D through the pipe k^2, being forced upward, comes into contact with the falling particles, and those particles whose weight is sufficient to overcome the pressure of this current continue in their descent and fall into bucket q^1; whereas, the next heavier particles will be separated from the mass and forced into chamber m, from thence into shafts m, where they drop into bucket q^2; while the next heavier ones, find their way into shafts n, and the next into shafts o, while the lightest particles are forced out through the apertures p^1 p^2, in the manner already fully described and set forth.

It is apparent, from the foregoing operation, that particles are separated according to their weight, and, as a consequence, the assorted particles, though of a uniform weight, will vary and differ in their dimensions and size. To instance, if the current of air in the chamber l has a pressure sufficient to carry with it particles weighing one grain, particles of this specific gravity would be deposited in buckets q^2, for the reason that the increased dimensions of the chamber m would lessen the pressure in a proportionate degree, and therefore would be insufficient to force the particles of one grain weight any higher.

Now, if the particles deposited in bucket q^2 consist of quartz rock, whose specific gravity is about 2.6, and iron pyrites, whose specific gravity is about 5, the particles of quartz will be about double the size of the iron pyrites, though both particles weigh one grain.

Thus it will be seen that, by the use of my combined sifter and assorter, a separation of minerals and fossil substances, according to their nature or quality, as, for instance, quartz from iron pyrites, galena, copper, &c., different in their specific gravity, can be had without the aid or application of any other machinery.

The degree of pressure exercised by the introduced current of air, or whatever agent is made use of, can be ascertained and measured by the manometer, or by a water-gauge attached to the several chambers.

What I claim as my invention and desire to secure by Letters patent, is—

1. The process of assorting minerals or fossil substances of different specific gravity, according to their nature or quality, by means of a pressure brought to bear on them by forcing a current of air through a pipe, tube, or series of chambers, into which the particles to be assorted are dropped.

2. The process of separating mineral or fossil substances, and assorting them according to their weight, and then size them, or to size them first, and then assort them according to their weight, substantially in the manner described.

3. A combined sifter and assorter, constructed and operated in the manner hereinbefore set forth.

4. The cylindrical sieve C, consisting of a series of four or more cylindrical sieves, the one encompassing the other, and graded, so that the coarsest and longest sieve will be the center or inside one, and the shortest and finest the outside one, together with the manner of constructing inlet-plate d^1 and exit plate d^2 and their appendages; also the rectangular bars f^1, f^2, &c., with their manner of fastening; also, the mode of fastening and securing sieves c^1 c^2 c^3 c^4 to inlet-plate d^1, to exit-plate d^2, and to the rectangular bars f^1, f^2, &c.

5. The manner of putting the cylindrical sieve C together and fastening it to shaft a.

6. The construction of the box A, with its trough divided into the compartments j^1 j^2 j^3 j^4 j^5, together with their movable and detached bottoms n, constructed and operating in manner described and set forth, together with the hopper B, its method of operation and manner of attachment and construction, and also the mode of attaching journal-box h^2, so as to allow it to slide, thereby regulating the cylindrical sieve C, and placing it either on a plane or incline, and also the slot k.

7. The process of introducing a current of air, water, or any other fluid into the box A, and forcing the same through the sieves c^1, &c., thereby separating and carrying off the dust from the sifted materials, and forcing the same through the slot k^1 into the dust-separator D.

8. The construction of the dust-separator D, as explained and set forth, consisting of a series of four or more chambers of increasing dimensions, and fastened together by inserting the end of one into the other, and fastening them laterally together by strips placed to form an equilateral triangle, and opening into the buckets q^1 q^2 q^3 q^4, also, for the manner of constructing and operating the said buckets q^1, &c.

9. The manner of constructing the cap covering the largest chamber, so as to form the aperture p^1 p^2, the hopper H, and providing the same with the damper r, regulated by the screws U^1 U^2, and for the corrugated roller B, its manner of attachment and mode of operation.

10. The process of operating the separator D, that is, charging the ore in regulated quantity from above to meet a current of air from below.

In testimony whereof I have hereunto set my hand this 11th day of July, A. D. 1870.

ROBERT GEORGE.

Witnesses:
E. P. WEBER,
LOUIS SCHULZE.

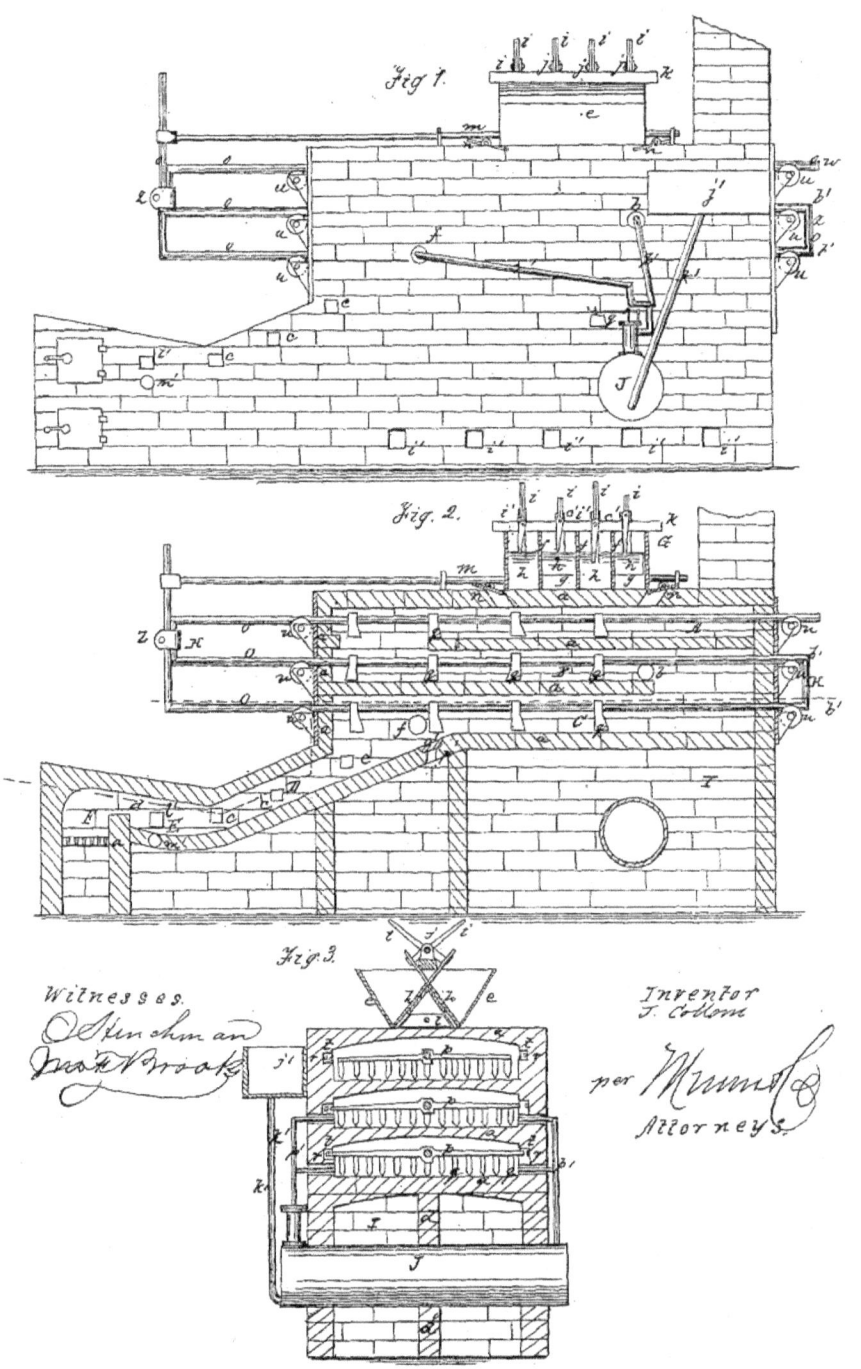

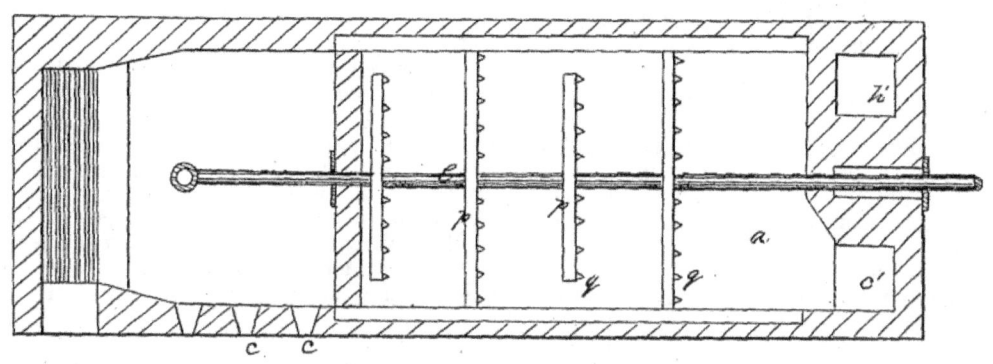

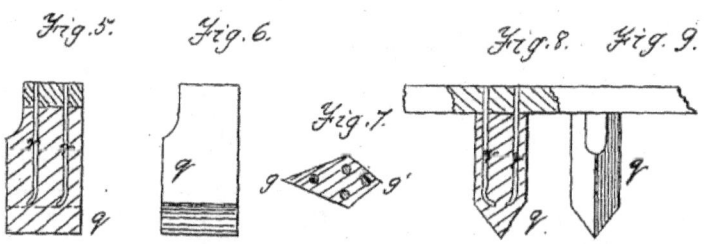

UNITED STATES PATENT OFFICE.

JOHN COLLOM, OF EMPIRE CITY, COLORADO TERRITORY.

IMPROVEMENT IN ROASTING-FURNACES FOR ORES.

Specification forming part of Letters Patent No. **106,553**, dated August 23, 1870; antedated August 15, 1870.

To all whom it may concern:

Be it known that I, JOHN COLLOM, of Empire City, in the county of Clear Creek, Colorado Territory, have invented a new and useful Improvement in Metallurgic Furnaces; and I do hereby declare that the following is a full, clear, and exact description thereof, which will enable others skilled in the art to make and use the same, reference being had to the accompanying drawings, forming part of this specification.

The nature of my invention relates to improvements in furnaces, whereby the perfect desulphurizing, oxidizing, chloridizing, and smelting of metallic ores and metallurgical products are effected in larger quantities and at less cost for manual labor, fuel, tools, and repairs of furnace than has hitherto been the case.

In the accompanying drawings, Figure 1 represents a side elevation of a furnace provided with my improvements. Fig. 2 represents a longitudinal sectional elevation of the same. Fig. 3 represents a transverse sectional elevation. Fig. 4 represents a horizontal section. Figs. 5 to 9 represent details.

Similar letters of reference indicate corresponding parts.

The general arrangements of the furnace consist of three desulphurizing, oxidizing, and chloridizing chambers, A, B, and C, an inclined reaction-bed, D, a smelting-bed, E, fire-place F, mixing and feeding apparatus G, stirring-machine H, condensing-chamber I, and a steam-generating apparatus, J.

The chambers are formed by the sides and ends of the furnace and the four arches a, a, a, and a, which have each an open space at one end, but on alternate sides of the furnace. These may be built of common brick when it is not intended to melt refractory ores in the fusing-bed. On each side the chambers are provided with holes $b\ b$ to introduce air, steam, chlorine and other gases, and to examine the charge. The reaction-bed D is built of firebrick or other suitable material, and on its side has doors $c\ c\ c$ to allow working the charge. The melting-bed is also built of fire-brick, and its peculiar construction and its relation to the fire-place F has for its object the production of the greatest heat immediately behind the bridge d.

The mixing and feeding apparatus G consists of a **W**-shaped box, e, divided by the partitions $f\!f$ into several compartments, each provided with an aperture, g, and a valve, h, to be raised and lowered by the handles $i\ i$, which latter are supported by the check-bolts $j\!j$, secured to the beam K, a scraper, l, worked by means of the rod m, and the valves $n\ n$. The arrangement is such that the scraper will rake certain regulated quantities of each kind of ore contained in the separate compartments.

The stirring-machine H consists of the pipes O O O, which may be ordinary gas-pipe, or round, square, or oblong iron tubes. In wide furnaces more than one tube to carry and cool the rakes in each chamber would be required.

The rakes $p\ p$ may be of cast or wrought iron, and provided with the flukes $q\ q$, made of clay or other fire and sulphur proof material, and attached to the rake-beams by the rods $r\ r$, slightly bent at their lower end to firmly hold the clay. The ends of the flukes are pointed to prevent the ore from accumulating under them, and their section above the taper is represented in Fig. 7. Figs. 5 and 6 show the side and longitudinal section, and Figs. 8 and 9 end and transverse section, of the flukes.

The angle s is made more acute than s', for the purpose of causing the ore to pass slowly in the direction of s'. The obtuse angle s' being set toward the fire-place F in the chambers A and C and toward the chimney in chamber B, the ore will pass through the furnace, as desired. The rakes are of two lengths, and the flukes of the longer ones set so as to pass between and fill up the grooves made by those of the shorter. The ends of the longer rakes enter the metallic guides $t\ t$, by which they are kept in their proper position, and the tubes O o o are supported by the rollers $u\ u$.

For the purpose of cooling the tubes and rakes a stream of water (or air when water cannot be had) enters the pipes O at v and escapes at w, from whence, when necessary, it is conveyed into a tank. (Not shown.) The water will be conveyed to the pipes at v, and from them at w, by flexible hose; and the guides $t\ t$, which are hollow, are cooled by water entering at $x\ x$.

The stirring-machine has a reciprocating motion, which may be imparted to it by any suitable application of power at z and z, and the length of its stroke is equal to twice the distance from center to center of the rakes, so that the set of grooves made by the one in the ore may be filled by the other, and thus be constantly exposing a new surface of the ore to the influence of the heat and gases. The ends a' a' a' of the roasting-chambers A, B, and C are temporarily closed by brick after the stirring-machine has been set in its place, and can be opened by the removal of the brick when the rakes need to be withdrawn for repairs. The pipes are put together by suitable connections, so that they may be separated at the angles b' b' to be withdrawn when necessary.

From the chamber A the gases pass down the flue c' into the condensing chamber I, divided by the partition d', where, owing to their diminished velocity and temperature, they deposit much of the fine ore and volatilized metals—lead, silver, and gold—which they bear. From the condensing-chamber the gases escape into the air through the chimney h', and the deposited dust is drawn out through the holes i' i' i' i'.

The steam-generating apparatus J, placed in the condensing-chamber and heated by the gases, is for the purpose of generating steam to be introduced into the roasting-chambers to facilitate the removal of the sulphur and the oxidation and chlorination of the ores and to regulate the temperature. Steam having a pressure of three or four pounds per square inch is very suitable for this purpose, and the boiler holding steam of this density may be supplied with water already hot from the tank j and through the pipe k', thus avoiding the expense and labor of providing a feed-pump and economizing a part of the heat held by the water used in cooling the stirring-machine.

The amount of heat to be absorbed by the water and steam may be regulated by partially covering the upper part of the boiler with sand supported by an iron frame, and the pressure of the steam in the boiler may be regulated by the safety-valve q'.

This furnace is designed especially to treat ores of lead, copper, silver, and gold, but may be used for other purposes. The great length of the three roasting-chambers, together with that of the reaction and melting beds and their relative position, constitutes an important feature. It enables the maintenance of a high temperature in the melting and reacting beds and a moderate heat in the upper chambers, and consequently the subjection of the ore to a gradually-increasing temperature from the time it enters the furnace until it is withdrawn therefrom. By this means the chemical reactions necessary to the reduction of most kinds of ore may be going on in different part of the furnace simultaneously, but successively, as the ore passes through the furnace and is exposed to the various degrees of heat, so that the fusible sulphides of antimony, silver, lead, copper, and iron may be safely roasted in the chambers, while their oxides and sulphates are being treated at a high heat in the reacting and smelting beds. By this arrangement the roasting and smelting of metals can be carried on continuously in the same furnace by the same fire, and with my complete mode of mixing, feeding, and stirring the ore, at the very smallest cost for labor, fuel, tools, and repairs. The said mode of stirring the ore by flukes of the shape represented is very thorough, as the ore on the top of the ridges falls to the bottom of the grooves, and is next pressed outward, and finally rises to the surface again, thus causing all the ore to pass repeatedly from the surface to the bottom of the layers. The arrangement of one chamber above another tends to economize heat, as that which passes through the roof of one chamber is taken up by the ore above it; and much of the valuable metals volatilized in the melting-bed will be condensed in passing over the cold ore in the upper chamber. The melting-bed, on account of the high heat prevailing there, will require to be repaired occasionally, which may be done without disturbing the rest of the furnace.

The following are some of the ways in which this furnace may be used in treating different kinds of ores.

Galena should be roasted in the chambers, so as on reaching the head of the reaction-bed most of the lead should be converted into oxide and sulphate, then the increased temperature would cause the oxide and sulphate to react upon each other and upon the undecomposed sulphide, producing sulphurous acid, metallic lead, and a slag containing oxide of lead. The latter should be reduced to metallic lead by throwing into the furnace and mixing with the ore a suitable quantity of charcoal. In carrying out this mode of smelting it is essential that the oxidation in the chambers should be carried so far that after the reactions have taken place oxide, and not sulphide, of lead should remain in the slag, as the former can readily be reduced by charcoal, while the latter would require to be reroasted, or to be reduced by metallic iron. All ores while on the reaction and smelting beds would need to be stirred with a hand-rake through the holes or working doors c c c.

In treating lead ores associated with a silicious gangue, the roasting in the chambers would be continued until nearly all the galena had been changed into sulphate and oxide of lead; then on the reaction-bed the high temperature there prevailing would cause the silica present to react upon the sulphate and oxide, resulting in the dislodgment of sulphuric acid and the formation of silicate of lead, together with the silicates of lime, baryta, and iron, when such bases occur in the ore.

The silicate of lead may be treated in the melting-bed with charcoal and metallic iron, giving as a product metallic lead and silicate of iron and an impoverished slag, all of which may then be drawn off into a suitable receptacle. Or, when circumstances are favorable, the partially-fused silicates may be drawn from the furnace, allowed to cool, broken into fragments, and smelted, with iron or iron ore, in a cupola-furnace.

As it is important that as much as possible of the sulphuric acid should be expelled before the mass becomes fused, it is intended by a judicious regulation of the fire, and admission of air and steam through the holes at the head of the inclined hearth, to cause the commencement of the reactions at the upper end of the bed, that they may be continued until the mass reaches the melting-bed and there becomes fused.

The various kinds of ores, matts, &c., of which the charge had to be compounded, on being put into the compartments of the mixing and feeding apparatus, could, by a proper attention to the valves $h\ h$, be intimately mixed in the exact proportions desired, and fed into the furnace with a regularity and precision unattainable by manual labor; and the rate at which the ores pass through the furnace can be nicely governed by a proper regulation of the speed of the stirring-machine, and by the depth of the ore in the furnace.

Copper pyrites and other sulphureted copper ores should be roasted in the chambers and reach the head of the reaction-bed as soon as only sufficient sulphur remained to draw all the copper into a matt, and enough iron oxidized to form a fusible slag with the silica present, and then, on being exposed to the heat of the reaction-bed, the silica would combine with the oxide of iron, and the copper with the sulphur, and on reaching the higher heat of the melting-bed the perfectly-fused matters would separate into a substratum of sulphides or matt, and a superstratum of silicates or slag. The latter would be drawn out at the door l' and cast away as useless, and the matt run out through the hole m' into a tank of water, to be granulated, and afterward returned to the furnace, to undergo a similar roasting and smelting to remove the remaining sulphur, iron, and other impurities. In working ores of this class, the introduction of steam through the holes $b\ b$ would facilitate the removal of sulphur and oxidation of metals.

Silver ores may be treated in this furnace by being mixed with the silicious lead ores, and roasted and smelted, as has already been described, the silver concentrated in the lead and afterward separated by cupellation; by being mixed with copper and iron pyrites the silver concentrated in a matt and separated therefrom by a process of liquation, amalgamation, or precipitation; or by a chlorination roasting preparatory to amalgamation. In roasting for amalgamation the silver ore, pyrites, and salt would be put into the compartments of the mixing and feeding machine, and mixed and fed into the furnace in the usual way, roasted under a moderate heat in the chambers A and B, and then under the higher temperature of chamber C, to cause a reaction of the sulphuric acid of the metallic sulphates upon the sodium of the salt, resulting in an evolution of the chlorine, which would immediately combine with the silver, forming a chloride of silver readily decomposed by iron and taken up by mercury in the process of amalgamation.

In treating silver ores containing only a small quantity of base-metal sulphides—such as zinc, copper, lead, antimony, &c.—the chlorination of the silver and the decomposition of the sulphates would be thoroughly accomplished on reaching the head of the reaction-bed, and would not need to pass through the reaction-bed, but would be discharged through the aperture n' by the removal of the brick stopper o; but when the ore abounds in base-metal sulphides the latter part of the roasting should be effected under the higher heat of the reaction-bed, in order to decompose the sulphates and chlorides of zinc, copper, lead, &c., as these remaining in the ore would seriously interfere with the amalgamation. The decomposition of the base-metal sulphates and chlorides will be greatly facilitated and the use of salt economized by allowing a suitable quantity of steam to pass into the furnace from the boiler J through the pipes $p'\ p'$.

Gold ores, whether sulphurous or quartzose, can be successively treated in this furnace by being mixed, roasted, and smelted with silicious lead ores or with sulphureted copper ores, as already mentioned.

Auriferous iron pyrites could be partially roasted in the chambers and then melted in the fusion-bed, by which the gold would be concentrated in an iron matt, from which it could be readily separated by being melted with lead ores, or by an amalgamation, or a precipitation process; or the sulphurous ores could be well roasted in the chambers and then in the reaction-bed to decompose the sulphates of iron and copper, and then be withdrawn from the furnace to be treated by the amalgamation or chlorination process.

Having thus described my invention, what I claim as new, and desire to secure by Letters Patent, is—

1. The combination of the inclined reaction-bed D and melting-hearth with a mechanical roasting-furnace, all arranged as and for the purpose specified.

2. The combination of scraper, scraper-rod, and regulating-valves, each constructed and operated as described.

3. The improved stirring-rakes $p\ p$, having tapering flukes $q\ q$ thereon to prevent an accumulation of the roasting ore beneath them, and having angles $s\ s'$, of different acuteness, so that when reciprocated they will stir the ore at each half-stroke and cause it to pass slowly in the direction of the larger angle.

4. As an improvement in metallic furnace-rakes, the construction of the flukes q, in the manner shown and described.

JOHN COLLOM.

Witnesses:
J. H. YENLEY,
WILLIAM LIGHT.

J. W. Treadway,

Gang Plow.

№. 108,214.   Patented Oct. 11. 1870.

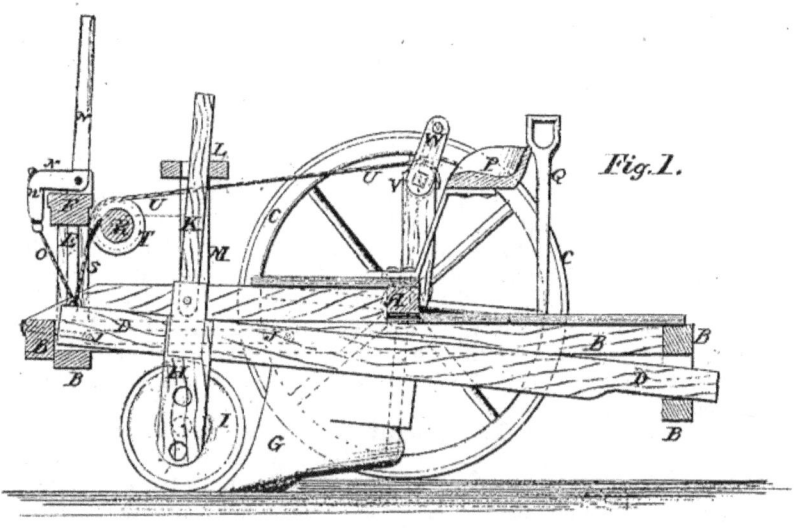

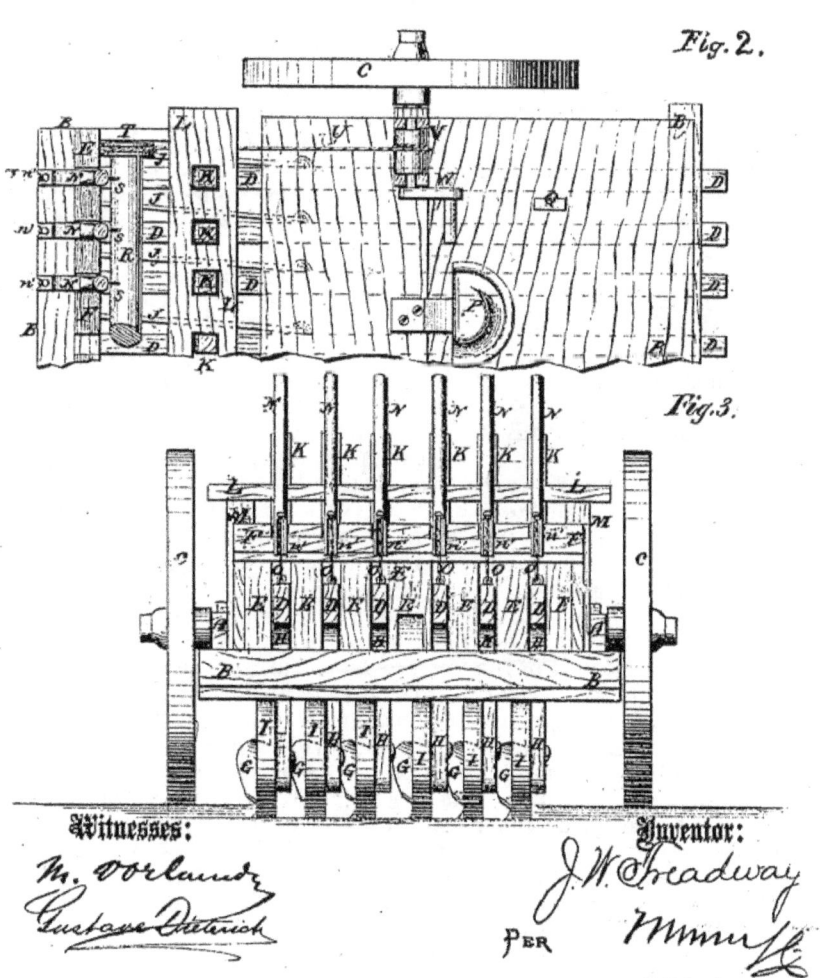

Witnesses: Inventor:

UNITED STATES PATENT OFFICE.

JAMES W. TREADWAY, OF CROWN POINT CENTRE, NEW YORK, ASSIGNOR TO OLIVER A. WHITTEMORE, OF DENVER, COLORADO.

IMPROVEMENT IN GANG-PLOWS.

Specification forming part of Letters Patent No. 108,212, dated October 11, 1870.

To all whom it may concern:

Be it known that I, JAMES WILLSON TREADWAY, of Crown Point Centre, in the county of Essex and State of New York, have invented a new and useful Improvement in Gang-Plows; and I do hereby declare that the following is a full, clear, and exact description thereof, which will enable others skilled in the art to make and use the same, reference being had to the accompanying drawings, forming part of this specification.

Figure 1 is a vertical longitudinal section of my improved plow. Fig. 2 is a top view of a portion of the same. Fig. 3 is a front view of the same.

Similar letters of reference indicate corresponding parts.

My invention has for its object to furnish an improved gang-plow, simple in construction and effective in operation, and which shall be so constructed that the plows will adjust themselves to the surface of the ground, so as to work at the same depth upon uneven and level ground, and so that the plows may be raised from the ground independently or all together, as may be required; and it consists in the construction and combination of the various parts of the machine, as hereinafter more fully described.

A is the axle-tree, to which the frame B of the machine is attached.

C are the wheels, the right-hand one of which I prefer to place upon a crank axle or horn, so that it may be adjusted to run upon the unplowed land in front of the plows or upon the furrow in the rear of the plows, as may be desired.

D is a set of parallel beams, the rear ends of which work in holes in the rear part of the frame B, as shown in Figs. 1 and 2. The forward ends of the beams D work between uprights or posts E, and are prevented from dropping down too far by a cross-bar of said frame passing beneath the said ends. The upper ends of the uprights E are connected and held in their proper relative positions by a cross-bar, F, to which said upper ends are attached.

G are the plows, which are made without landsides, and which are securely attached to the middle parts of the beams D.

To the beams D, in front of the plows G, are attached standards H, to the lower parts of which are adjustably pivoted the gage-wheels I, by which the depth at which the plows work in the ground is regulated. When plowing sod land or stiff soil, cutters may be attached to the sides of the gage-wheels I to cut through said sod or soil in front of the plows G. The draft-strain upon the beams D is sustained by the rigid bars or rods J, the rear ends of which are pivoted to the sides of the beams D, and the forward ends of which are pivoted to the forward part of the frame B or to the uprights E. The bars J also enable the plows to be backed out of the ground when required by "backing up" the machine.

K are guide or supporting bars or rods, which are pivoted to the upper side of the forward part of the beams D in such a way as to allow the said beams to have a free movement in the plane of their length, but no lateral movement. The upper ends of the bars K pass up through holes in the cross-bar L, the ends of which are screwed to the upper ends of the posts or standards M, the lower ends of which are secured to the side bars of the frame B. The bars K are designed to prevent the beams D from being inclined laterally by side pressure upon the plows, and thus guard against the possibility of the forward ends of the beams D being made to bind in the spaces between the uprights E by the said side pressure of said plows.

N are right-angled levers, which are pivoted at their angles to the cross-bar F, so that their short arms may rest upon a shoulder or rabbet of the said bar F, and their long arms may project vertically upward. The ends of the short arms of the levers N that project in front of the bar F are curved downward or have grooved cams or segments of pulleys n' formed upon them, as shown in the drawings.

To the levers N are attached the upper ends of the cords or chains O, which pass down along the grooves of the cams n', and the lower ends of which are attached to the forward part of the beams D. By this construction each of the plows may be raised from the ground independently of the others by operating the lever N, connected with that plow. This may be done by the driver from his seat P by means of the bar Q, which has a hole in one end, that may be passed over the upper end of either of the levers N. The bar or handle Q, when not in use, may be placed in a socket in the platform of the machine in such a position that it may be conveniently reached by the driver.

R is a shaft, the journals of which revolve in bearings in supports attached to the forward parts of the side bars of the frame B.

To the shaft R is attached one end of the short ropes or chains S, the other ends of which are attached to the forward parts of the beams D, so that by turning the said shaft to wind up the ropes or chains S the plows will all be raised from the ground at the same time.

To one end of the shaft R is attached a pulley or drum, T, to which is attached and around which is wound a rope or chain, U, the other end of which is attached to the short shaft or drum V, the journals of which work in bearings in supports attached to the frame-work of the machine in such a position that the driver from his seat P may reach the crank W, attached to the inner journal of said shaft or drum V, and operate it, and thus raise the plows from the ground all at the same time.

Having thus described my invention, I claim as new and desire to secure by Letters Patent—

1. The combination of the beams D, plows G, adjustable gage-wheels I, pivoted draft-bars J, uprights E, pivoted guard-bars K, and perforated bar L with each other and with the frame B, axle-tree A, and wheels C, substantially as herein shown and described, and for the purpose set forth.

2. The cam-levers N n', ropes or chains O and U and S, crank-drum V, drum T, and roller R, with the plow-beams D, all arranged substantially as shown and described, whereby said beams may be singly or collectively elevated.

JAMES WILLSON TREADWAY.

Witnesses:
 GEORGE BROWN,
 W. C. GUNNISON.

H. Bolthoff,
Shoe Flask.
No. 108,556. Patented Oct. 25. 1870.

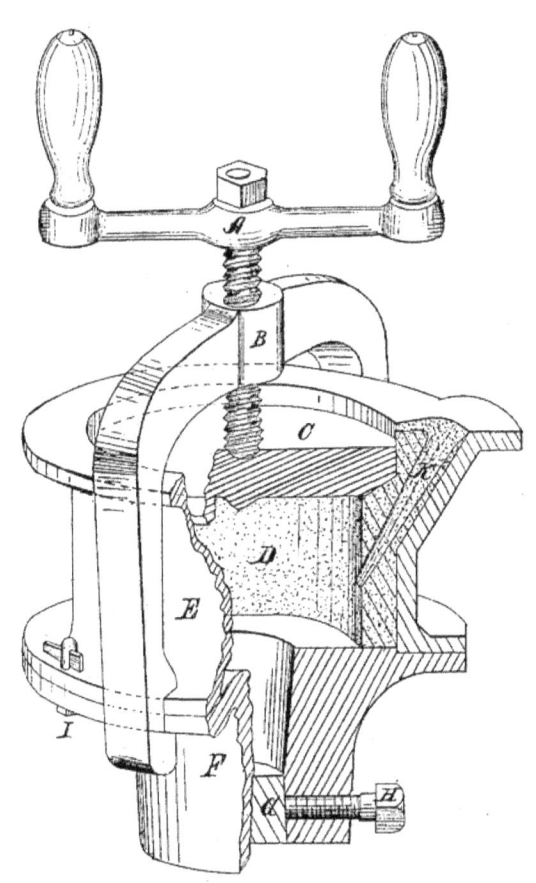

Witnesses Inventor.

United States Patent Office.

HENRY BOLTHOFF, OF CENTRAL CITY, COLORADO TERRITORY.

Letters Patent No. 108,556, dated October 25, 1870.

IMPROVEMENT IN FLASKS FOR CASTING STAMP-SHOES FOR CRUSHING-MILLS.

The Schedule referred to in these Letters Patent and making part of the same.

To all whom it may concern:

Be it known that I, HENRY BOLTHOFF, of Central City, Gilpin County, Colorado Territory, have invented a new and Improved Molding-Flask for the Manufacture of Stamp-Shoes and Dies for Stamps or Crushing-Mills, by means of Screw-Pressure; and I do hereby declare that the following is a full and exact description thereof, reference being had to the accompanying drawings, and to the letters of reference marked thereon.

The nature of my invention consists in exerting screw-pressure upon the iron when in a molten state, by means of a screw, as shown at A in the accompanying drawings. This pressure is continued until the iron becomes chilled or hard.

By means of this pressure, the iron of the shoe or die is rendered much more dense and durable than by the ordinary mode of casting.

The screw is held in position by means of the clasp B, which clasp may be made so as to be adjusted to either the upper or lower rim of the molding-flask.

The lower end of the screw is adjusted in a concave in the upper service of the upper "chill" or cover to the flask at C. The inside of the flask E is packed with sand, represented by D, which sand serves the double purpose of supporting the cover C when the pattern is withdrawn, and also for facilitating the removal of the shoe or die when cast.

The upper portion, E, of the flask is secured to the lower portion or chill, F, of the flask, by means of the key at I.

G is a movable plug, which can be easily raised or lowered for the purpose of lengthening or shortening the neck of the shoe, to any length required. This plug is fastened at any given point, by means of a thumb-screw, H.

The iron is poured into the flask through the groove or spout at K

On the under side of the cover C, and at D, by reference to the drawings, is a teat, or prominence, which is designed to produce a concave on the bottom of the shoe, which will prevent the shoe from wearing to a point when placed on an old die having an irregular surface.

A shoe manufactured in this flask will be perfectly smooth and regular in form, making it easily and perfectly adjustable to the stem, thus diminishing the liability of breaking on account of imperfect adjustment. Besides, these shoes and dies will wear nearly twice as long as the ordinary shoes and dies on account of the greater density given to the iron by screw-pressure exerted in the manner above described.

What I claim as my invention, and desire to secure by Letters Patent, is—

A flask, constructed and arranged as described.

Witnesss: HENRY BOLTHOFF.
WESLEY CRITCHEL,
JOSEPH W. KENNEDY.

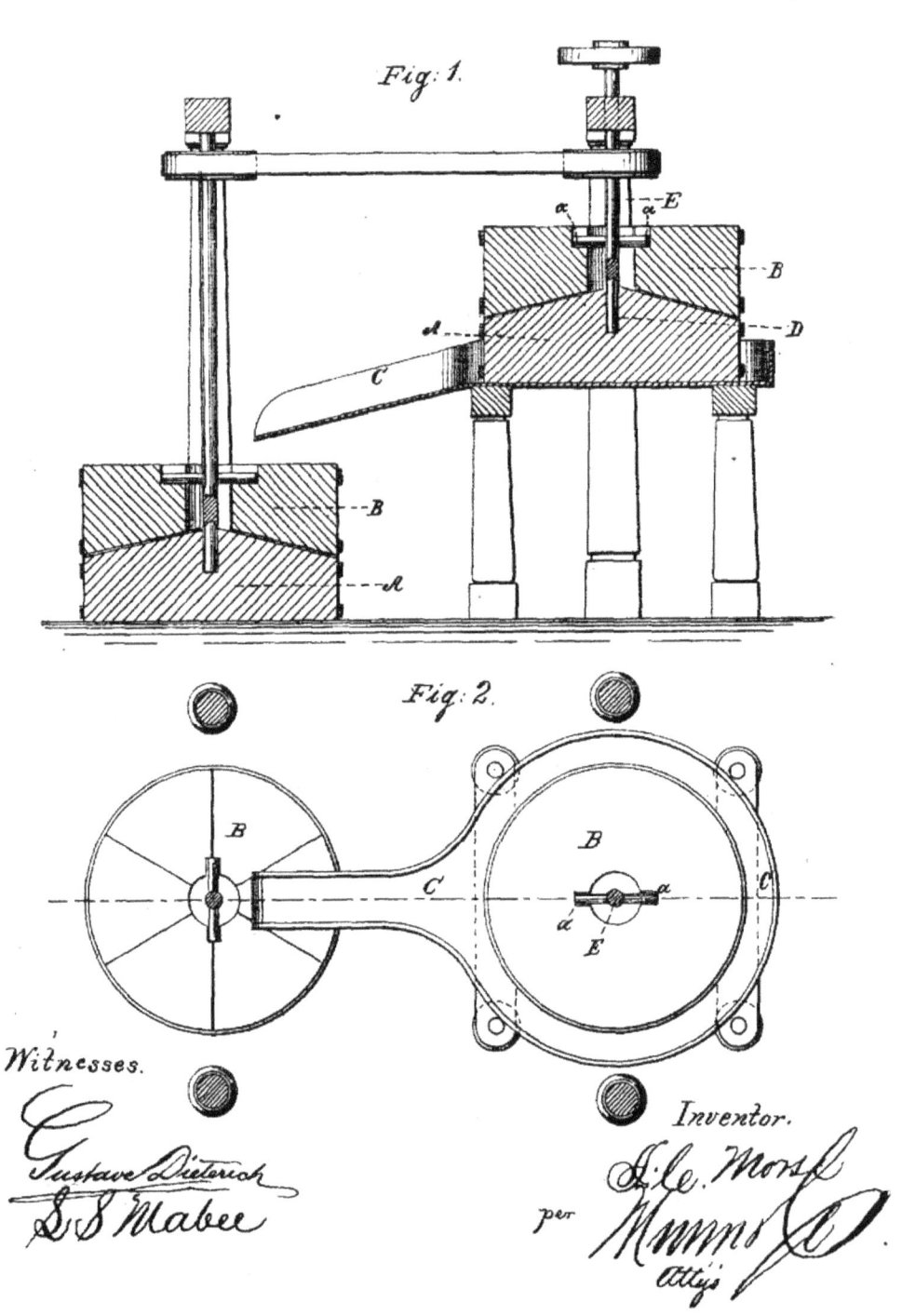

United States Patent Office.

FREDERICK C. MORSE, OF BUCKSKIN, COLORADO TERRITORY.

Letters Patent No. 108,617, dated October 25, 1870.

IMPROVEMENT IN ORE-PULVERIZERS.

The Schedule referred to in these Letters Patent and making part of the same.

To all whom it may concern:

Be it known that I, FREDERICK C. MORSE, of Buckskin, in the county of Park and Territory of Colorado, have invented a new and improved Ore-Pulverizer; and I do hereby declare that the following is a full, clear, and exact description thereof, which will enable others skilled in the art to make and use the same, reference being had to the accompanying drawing forming part of this specification.

Figure 1 represents a vertical longitudinal section of my improved ore-pulverizer.

Figure 2 is a plan or top view of the same.

Similar letters of reference indicate corresponding parts.

This invention relates to an improved arrangement of the grinding-stones in an ore-pulverizer, or a new method of hanging them, and consists in providing the convex bedstone with a step, on the end of which the driver of the upper or rotary concave stone is placed.

A and B in the drawing are the two grinders, which constitute my pulverizer. They are made of stone or other suitable material, and their grinding surfaces may be burred in the usual manner or otherwise prepared at will.

The lower fixed grinder A is made with a conical grinding surface so as to be higher in the middle than at the edges, as shown.

The upper rotary grinder B, which may be made of one or more pieces, as desired, has its grinding surface concave to correspond with the shape of the lower grinder.

The ore to be pulverized is inserted between the grinders through a central opening of the upper grinder.

D is a step inserted in the stone A at its center. On this the driver E is set, its lower end being recessed for the purpose. At the upper end it is arranged in suitable supports, and its horizontal arms $a\ a$ project into recesses or notches in the stone B; thus motion being imparted to the driver by means of a band and pulley, or other means, the stone B will be rotated.

This arrangement is simple, inexpensive, and adapted to facilitate removal of the upper stone to receive a new dressing, or for other purposes.

The apparatus is intended more particularly for gold ores, and will give an opportunity of removing the small particles of gold from the pulp as soon as they become separated, preventing their being ground any finer than natural size.

On the ordinary flat grinders the ore is exposed for too long a time to the action of the grinders, and its metallic contents are therefore ground or crushed.

I propose to arrange two or more sets of grinders on one apparatus, each set being somewhat higher than the other, as indicated in fig. 1.

The ore is first ground by the highest pair of stones, and is then carried to the next lower pair in a trough, C.

The separated metal is retained by the amalgamating plates immediately after leaving the grinders.

In this manner complete separation without unnecessary labor is produced.

Another advantage of my invention is the scouring and burnishing of the metal and the consequent cleaning of the same.

Having thus described my invention,

I claim as new, and desire to secure by Letters Patent—

The arrangement with the stationary convex bedstone A and rotary concave stone B, of the step D and driver E, provided with arms $a\ a$, all as shown and described.

FREDERICK C. MORSE.

Witnesses:
ASSYRIA HALL,
J. R. FOSTER.

A. SMITH.
GRAIN SCOURER.

No. 110,301.   Patented Dec. 20, 1870.

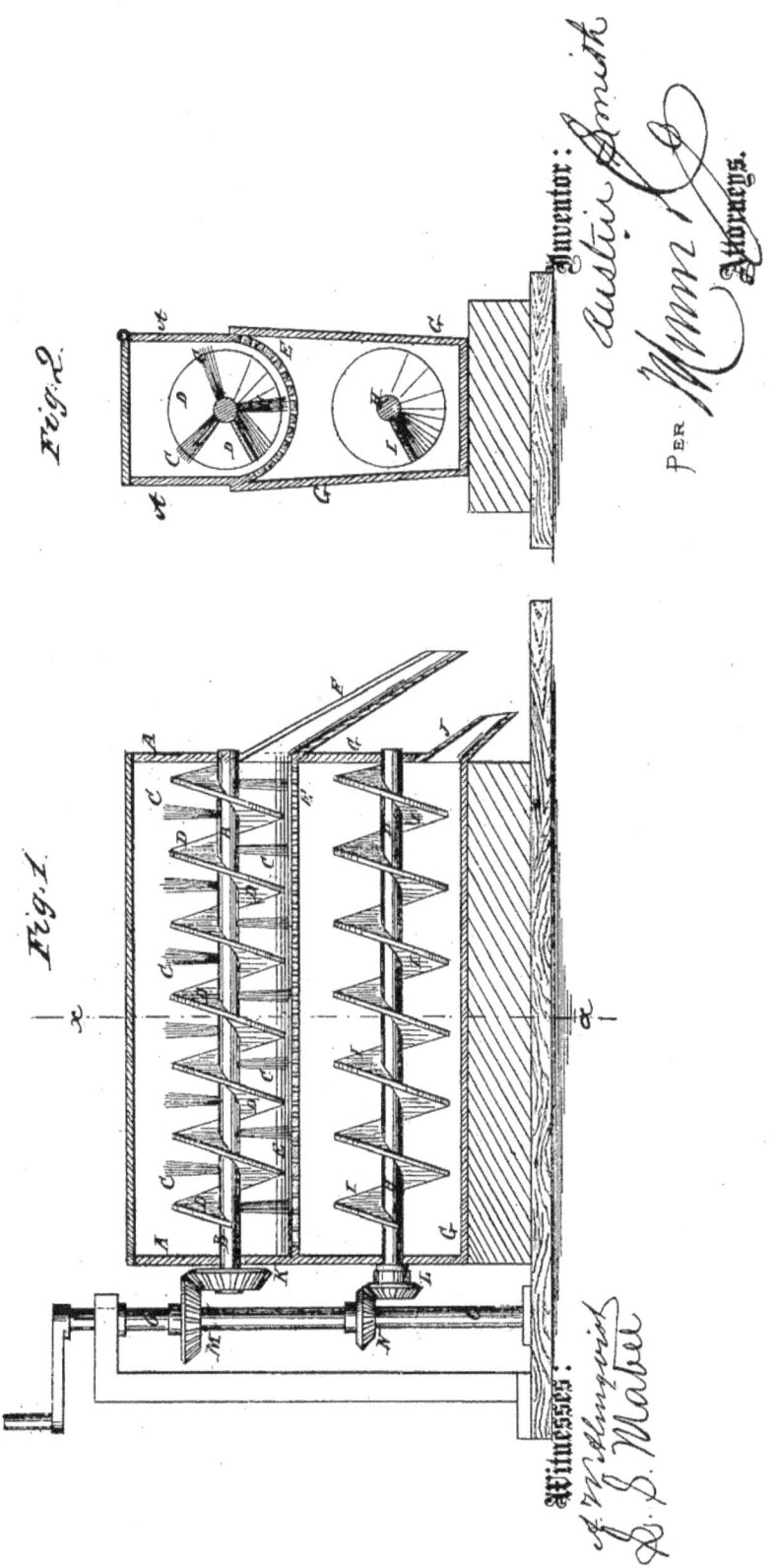

United States Patent Office.

AUSTIN SMITH, OF VALMONT, COLORADO TERRITORY.

Letters Patent No. 110,301, dated December 20, 1870.

IMPROVEMENT IN GRAIN-SCOURERS.

The Schedule referred to in these Letters Patent and making part of the same.

To all whom it may concern:

Be it known that I, AUSTIN SMITH, of Valmont, in the county of Boulder and Territory of Colorado, have invented a new and useful Improvement in Grain-Scourer; and I hereby declare that the following is a full, clear, and exact description thereof, which will enable others skilled in the art to make and use the same, reference being had to the accompanying drawing forming part of this specification, in which—

Figure 1 is a vertical longitudinal section of my improved machine.

Figure 2 is a vertical cross-section of the same, taken through the line $x\,x$, fig. 1.

Similar letters of reference indicate corresponding parts.

My invention has for its object to furnish a simple, convenient, inexpensive, and effective machine for cleaning and scouring wheat for grinding; and

It consists in the construction and combination of the various parts of the machine as hereinafter more fully described.

A is the frame-work, box, or casing of the machine.

B is a shaft, the ends of which revolve in bearings in the ends of the frame-work or casing A.

To the shaft B is attached a spiral brush, C, of broom-corn or other suitable material.

The shaft B may also have a spiral thread or flange, D, attached to it if desired, but generally this will not be necessary.

E is a semi-cylindrical sheet-metal bottom, which is perforated with numerous holes for the dust scoured from the grain to escape through.

The holes in the bottom E I prefer to make with a square punch diagonally with the shaft B, and with their rough edges upward.

The cleaned grain escapes from the machine through the spout F, by which it is conducted to the burs or to some suitable receiver.

The dust may be allowed to fall to the floor into some suitable receiver, or into a box, G, placed beneath the perforated bottom E, and in which works a shaft, H, having a spiral thread or flange, I, attached to it, by which the dust is conveyed into the spout J, by which it is conducted to some suitable place or receiver.

To the ends of the shafts B and H are attached small bevel gear-wheels, K L, respectively, the teeth of which mesh into the teeth of the bevel gear-wheels M N, attached to the vertical shaft O, which may be driven by any convenient power.

It may be observed that the rough edges of the perforated bottom E tend to prevent the grain from being carried around by and with the spiral brush C, and thus facilitate the operation.

Having thus described my invention,

What I claim as new, and desire to secure by Letters Patent, is—

1. The spiral brush C and concave screen E, combined with the spiral flange D, arranged as and for the purpose described.

2. The rotating-scouring brush and concave screen, combined with a spirally-flanged shaft H I, arranged thereunder, in the receiving-chamber, as and for the purpose described.

AUSTIN SMITH.

Witnesses:
JEROME THOMAS,
JESSE HARTLEY.

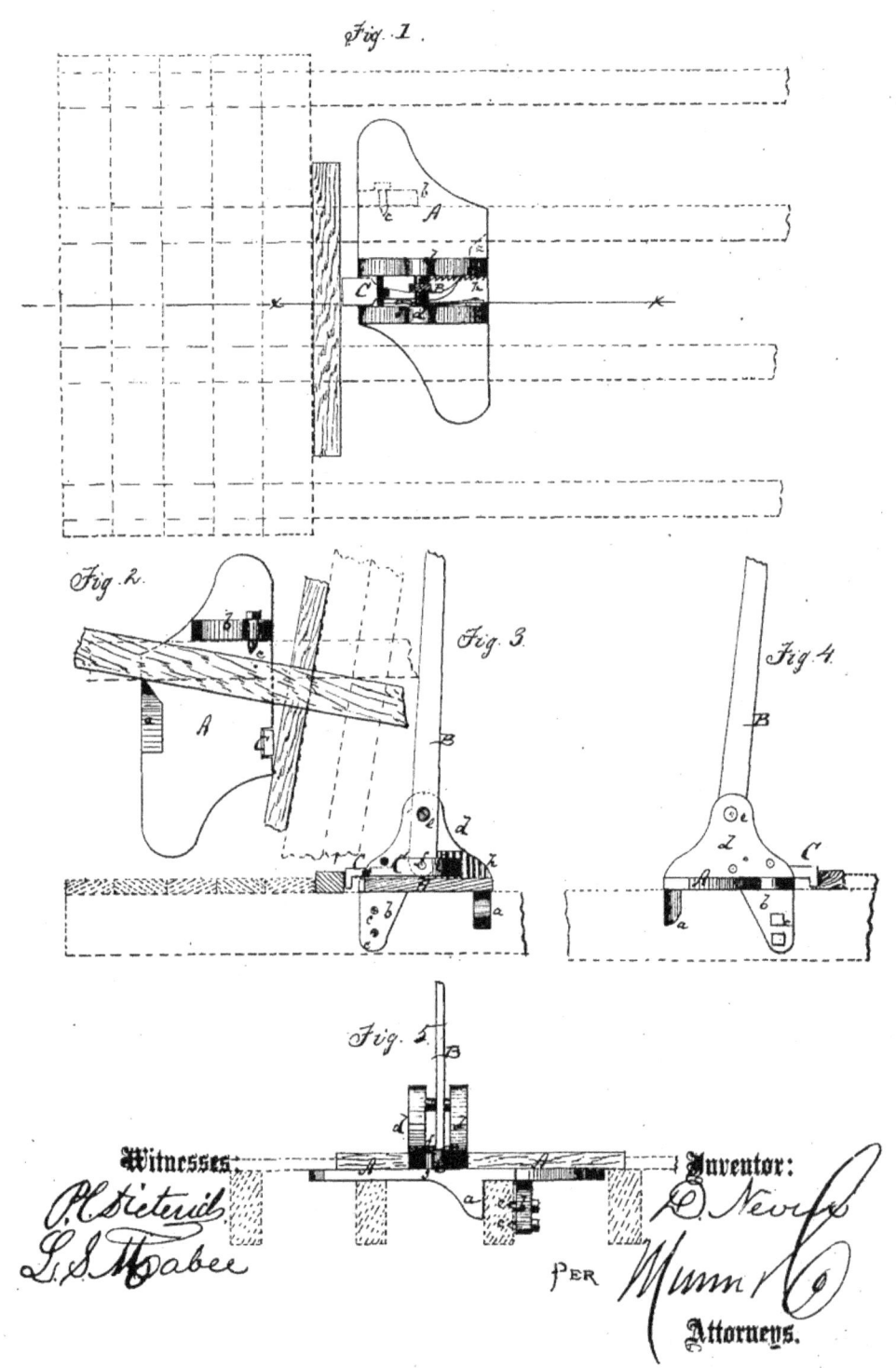

UNITED STATES PATENT OFFICE.

DAVID NEVIN, OF GEORGETOWN, COLORADO TERRITORY.

IMPROVEMENT IN FLOOR-CLAMPS.

Specification forming part of Letters Patent No. **111,560**, dated February 7, 1871.

To all whom it may concern:

Be it known that I, DAVID NEVIN, of Georgetown, in the county of Clear Creek and Territory of Colorado, have invented a new and Improved Flooring-Clamp; and I do hereby declare that the following is a full, clear, and exact description thereof, which will enable others skilled in the art to make and use the same, reference being had to the accompanying drawing, forming part of this specification, in which—

Figure 1 represents a plan or top view of my improved flooring-clamp. Fig. 2 is an inverted plan view of the same. Fig. 3 is a vertical section through the same, taken on the plane of the line $x\,x$, Fig. 1. Fig. 4 is a side view, and Fig. 5 a front view, of the same.

Similar letters of reference indicate corresponding parts.

This invention relates to a new implement for pressing boards together before nailing the same to the floor-beams.

The invention consists in a new construction of stock, which is made self-fastening to the beams, and in the connection therewith of a sliding spring-clamp and operating-lever, all arranged as hereinafter more fully set forth.

A in the drawing represents the stock of my improved flooring-clamp. It is made of cast metal, in form of a plate, of suitable shape. From its under side project two lugs, a and b, of which one, a, is parallel with the straight front edge of the plate A, while the other, b, is at right angles thereto. The lug a is arranged under the back portion of the plate A, and has that edge which is faced by the lug b sharpened, as in Fig. 2. The lug b contains one or more set-screws, c, which are fitted through it, as shown, and pointed at their inner ends.

From the upper face of the plate A project two ears, $d\,d$, between which the clamping-lever B is pivoted by a pin, e.

The lower end of the lever B is, by a pin, f, connected with the clamping-jaw C, which is a bar placed between the ears d upon the plate A.

A spring, g, is placed against one side of the jaw C, and holds its inner end against a rack, h, which is formed at one ear, d, as in Fig. 1.

The lever B is so pivoted that it may have a slight lateral play to throw the jaw C clear of the rack.

The operation is as follows: The plate A is placed upon a beam to straddle the same with the lugs a and b. The screws c are so set that their points are in a plane nearer to that of the edge of a than the beam is wide. The device will, therefore, be applied to the beam obliquely, as in Fig. 2. But as, by the lever B, the jaw is forced against the flooring, it will, since it is in line with the lug a, at first shift the plate A on the beam, by forcing the edge of a into the same until the motion of the jaw is parallel to the direction of the beam. The clamp is then firmly established, and acts solely against the flooring. By the screw c the device can be adjusted to beams of different width.

Having thus described my invention, I claim as new and desire to secure by Letters Patent—

The flooring-clamp consisting of the plate A, lugs $a\,b$, screw c, lever B, and jaw C, all applied to operate substantially as herein shown and described.

DAVID NEVIN.

Witnesses:
LEMUEL F. YATES,
CHAS. W. POLLARD.

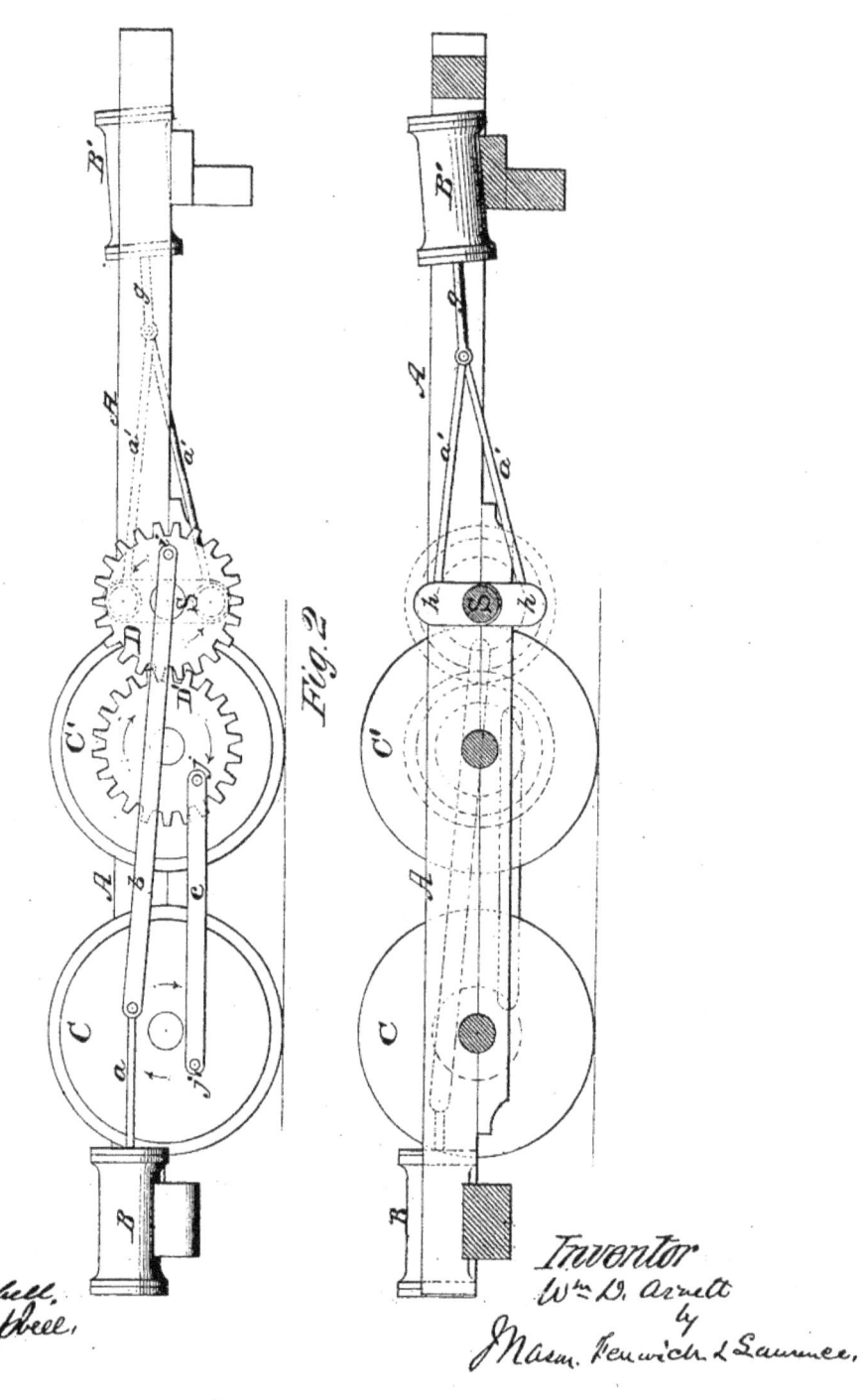

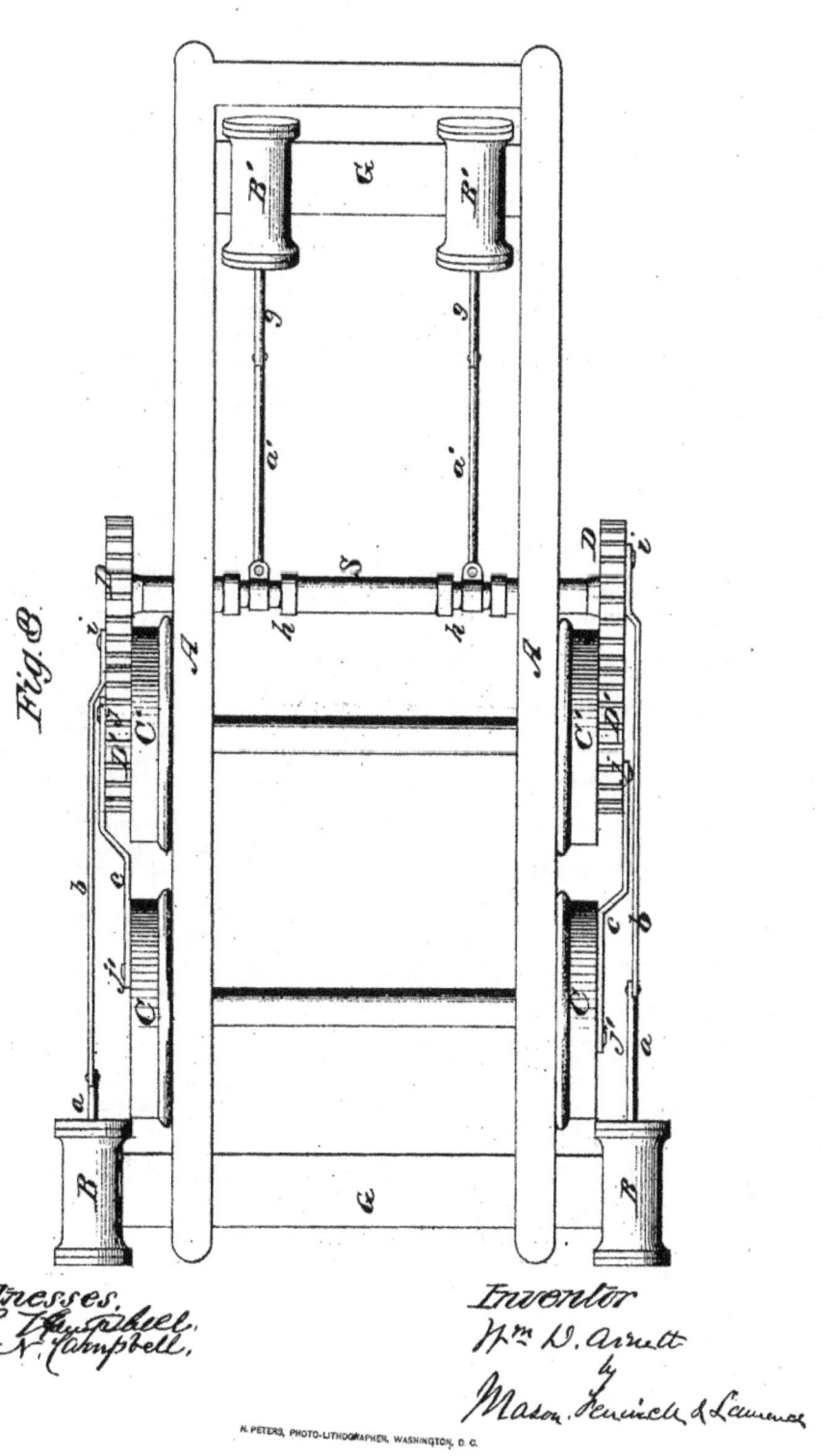

United States Patent Office

WILLIAM D. ARNETT, OF DENVER, COLORADO TERRITORY.

Letters Patent No. 111,603, dated February 7, 1871.

IMPROVEMENT IN DRIVING-POWER FOR LOCOMOTIVES.

The Schedule referred to in these Letters Patent and making part of the same.

To all whom it may concern:

Be it known that I, WILLIAM D. ARNETT, of Denver, in the county of Arapahoe and Territory of Colorado, have invented a new and improved Driving-Power for Locomotives; and I do hereby declare that the following is a full, clear, and exact description thereof, reference being had to the accompanying drawing making part of this specification, in which—

Figure 1, plate 1, is a side elevation of a locomotive-carriage having my invention applied to its wheels.

Figure 2, plate 1, is a longitudinal section through the same.

Figure 3, plate 2, is a top view of fig. 1.

Similar letters of reference indicate corresponding parts in the several figures.

This invention relates to an arrangement of the steam-cylinders, the pitman-rods, and cranks upon the frame of a locomotive, whereby the power is more equally and advantageously distributed to the driving-wheels than hitherto.

The following description of my invention will enable others skilled in the art to understand it and carry it into effect.

The frame A of the locomotive may be constructed in the usual well-known manner, and the driving-wheels C C' applied thereto in a manner which is well understood by builders.

At or near each end of this frame A a cylinder-bed, G, is applied, on which two steam-cylinders are applied, which may receive steam from the boiler in any suitable manner.

The piston-rods $a\ a$ of the rear cylinders B B are connected to pitman-rods $b\ b$, which extend forward, and are applied to wrist-pins $i\ i$ on the surfaces of two spur-wheels D D.

The wheels D D are keyed on the ends of a crank-shaft, S, having two cranks $h\ h$, to which the pitman-rods $a'\ a'$ of piston-rods $g\ g$ are connected.

The piston-rods $g\ g$ are applied to pistons B' B' at or near the front end of frame A.

The points of attachment of the pitman-rods $b\ b$ and $a'\ a'$ are so arranged relatively to each other that the shaft S is taken hold of and power applied to it by the four cylinders at four points, in a circle or at quarter strokes, so that, practically, the shaft S has four cranks, which are equidistant from the axis of said shaft.

The spur-wheels D D engage with the teeth of spur-wheels D' D', which are keyed on the end of the axles of the front drivers C' C'. Thus motion is transmitted from the crank-shaft S to said drivers.

The wheels C' C' communicate rotary motion to the rear drivers C C through the medium of two connecting-rods $c\ c$, which are applied to wrist-pins $j\ j$ on spur-wheels D' D', and to wrist-pins $j'\ j'$ on the wheels C C.

The wrist-pins on wheels D' D' C C have the same length of strokes as the wrist-pins $i\ i$ and cranks $h\ h$, so that all the wheels rotate at the same degree of speed.

The wrist-pins $j\ j$ and $j'\ j'$ are so, relatively to one another and to the wrist-pins $i\ i$ and cranks $h\ h$, that there are four impulses on each side of the frame A, operating at different points of a circle to propel the carriage; that is to say, by dividing a circle into eight equidistant points, and distributing these points as described, we have the arrangement above described.

By this arrangement the locomotive will not act against itself nor against traction, the forward pressure is counterbalanced by the backward pressure, and power is applied uniformly to the crank-shaft; hence, it will be seen that there is a very rapid application of the propelling impulses to the wheels, which will greatly assist in ascending grades, as well as in the propulsion generally.

If desirable, the spur-wheels may be located inside of the frame A; but I prefer to have them outside thereof, for convenience of access and repairs.

Having described my invention,

What I claim as new, and desire to secure by Letters Patent, is—

The relative arrangement of the wrist-pins $i\ i\ j\ j\ j'\ j'$ and cranks $h\ h$, in combination with the connecting-rods, the spur-wheels D D', and steam-cylinders B B', substantially as described, and for the purposes set forth.

WILLIAM D. ARNETT.

Witnesses:
WM. RAYMOND,
M. L. HORR.

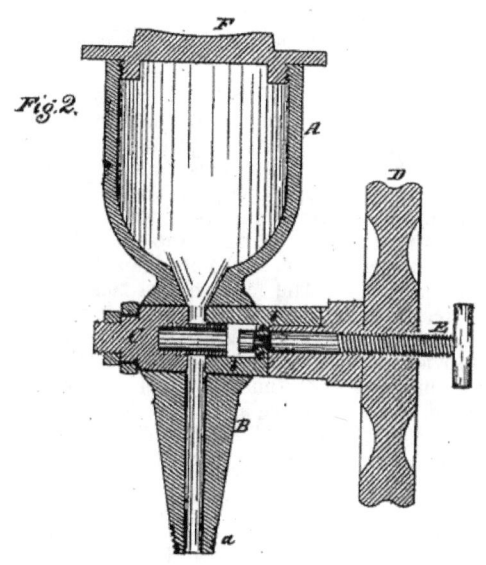
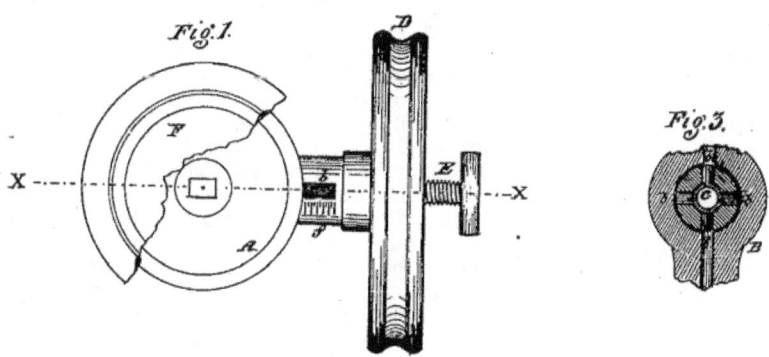

United States Patent Office.

GEORGE C. MUNSON, OF EMPIRE CITY, COLORADO TERRITORY.

Letters Patent No. 111,669, dated February 7, 1871.

IMPROVEMENT IN FEEDING QUICKSILVER TO STAMPS AND AMALGAMATORS.

The Schedule referred to in these Letters Patent and making part of the same.

To all whom it may concern:

Be it known that I, GEORGE C. MUNSON, of Empire City, Clear Creek county, and Territory of Colorado, have invented a new and improved Apparatus for Feeding Quicksilver to Stamps and Amalgamators; and I do hereby declare that the following is a full and exact description thereof, reference being had to the accompanying drawing, forming a part of this specification, and to the letters of reference marked thereon.

My invention has for its object to provide an apparatus for feeding quicksilver to stamp-mills and amalgamators, which may be readily adjusted so as to supply a larger or smaller quantity of quicksilver, as may be desired, to the mill or amalgamator, and by means of which the quantity so fed or supplied may be accurately measured and determined.

Hitherto, the usual mode employed has been to throw in by hand a small quantity of quicksilver at certain intervals; but it is evident that by such means the quantity fed would be irregular, even with the greatest care.

By my invention, however, the quantity supplied can be regulated with the greatest nicety and precision.

This invention is also well adapted for supplying oil to machinery for lubricating purposes.

The nature of my invention consists in the employment or use of a cup provided at its lower extremity with a hollow stem, through which the quicksilver is conducted into the stamp or amalgamator.

Within the said stem is fitted and works a horizontal tapering shaft, having an equal bearing through the said stem, which said shaft is provided with one or more longitudinal slots, within each of which said slots is fitted a sliding plug, operated by a set-screw located and working within the shaft.

Secured to the outer end of this shaft is a pulley, by which the shaft is operated, and, as the shaft rotates, the slots already mentioned receive a charge of quicksilver from the cup, and deliver it into the opening in the stem, from whence it passes into the stamp or amalgamator, the size of the charge being regulated at will by means of the set-screw above mentioned.

To enable others skilled in the art to make and use my invention, I will proceed more particularly to describe its construction and operation.

Figure 1 is a top plan view of my apparatus.

Figure 2 is a vertical section, taken through the line X X.

Figure 3 is a transverse section of the shaft to show the position of the sliding plugs.

Letters of like name and kind indicate like parts in each of the figures.

A represents the cup, which may be made of any proper material and of suitable dimensions, and is provided at its lower extremity with a hollow stem, B, through which the quicksilver is conducted from the cup A to the amalgamator.

The lower end of this stem is fitted into the shell or covering of the amalgamator on which it is to be used, either by means of a screw-thread, as seen at *a*, or by any other suitable and well-known means.

Within the stem B is closely fitted a horizontal tapering shaft, C, which has an equal bearing through the said stem, and is made to rotate therein by means of a pulley, D, attached and secured to its outer end.

The shaft C is provided with one or more longitudinal slots, which, as the shaft rotates, receive the quicksilver from the cup A, and deposit it within the hollow stem B, from whence it passes into the amalgamator.

Within each of these slots is fitted a sliding plug, *b*, for the purpose of regulating the quantity or size of the charge of quicksilver received from the cup and deposited within the amalgamator.

Each of the said plugs is provided with a gib, *c*, that fits and works in an annular groove on a shaft attached to a set-screw, E, located and working within the shaft, by which means the said plugs are made adjustable, so that the quantity of quicksilver received into the slots at each charge may be increased or diminished as may be desired.

One of these plugs is made longer than the others, and extends outside of the stem, so that its end comes opposite to a scale, *f*, marked upon the shaft, by which means the quantity of quicksilver received into the slots from the cup and deposited in the amalgamator is accurately measured.

F represents the lid or cover of the cup, which does not require particular description.

It will be understood that the pulley D may be either turned by hand or driven by a belt, as may be desired.

The operation is simple and readily understood.

When the shaft C is made to rotate, each of the slots in its turn comes directly underneath the opening in the bottom of the cup A, and receives its charge, which it deposits in the hollow stem B, from whence it passes into the amalgamator, the quantity or size of the charge being regulated by means of the sliding plugs fitted in the slots on the shaft, which said plugs are adjusted by means of the set-screw E, so that the recess will hold just the quantity wanted; and, the shaft being closely fitted within the stem, the charge of quicksilver received from the cup into the recess is cut off and retained in the latter, until, by the rotation of the shaft, it is brought to the open space in the lower part of the stem, when it falls out and passes into the amalgamator.

Having thus described my invention,

What I claim as new, and desire to secure by Letters Patent of the United States, is—

1. The adjustable plugs b, operated by means of a set-screw, and constructed and arranged in connection with the shaft C and cup or reservoir A, to cut off and deliver to the stamp-mill or amalgamator any desired quantity of quicksilver, substantially as herein shown and described.

2. In combination with the plugs b and shaft C, the scale or indicator f, substantially as described, and for the purposes set forth.

GEORGE C. MUNSON.

Witnesses:
JOHN S. THORNTON,
WM. VENTZ.

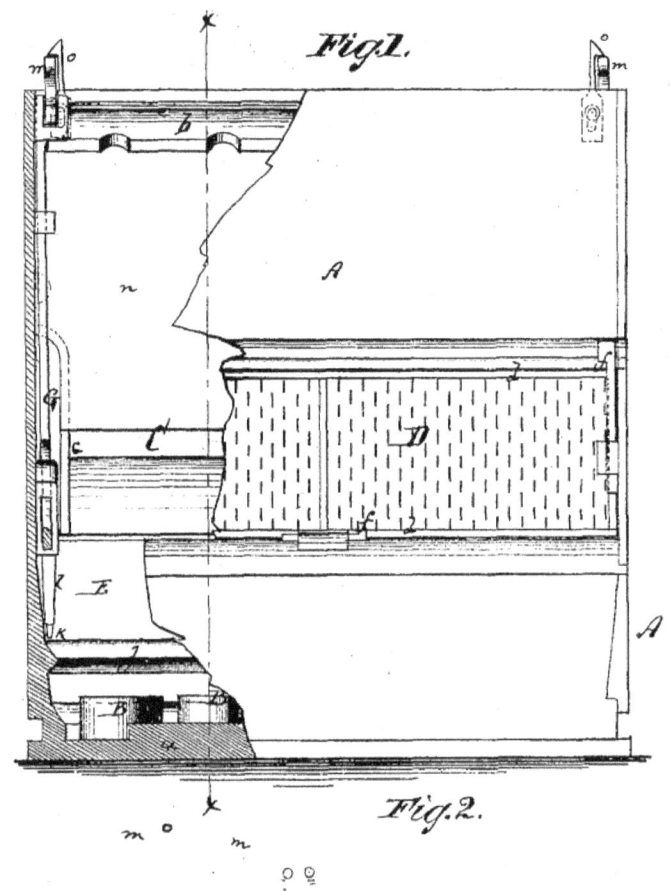

United States Patent Office.

LYMAN GRISWOLD, OF DENVER, COLORADO TERRITORY.

Letters Patent No. 112,804, dated March 21, 1871.

IMPROVEMENT IN COMBINED ORE-CRUSHERS AND AMALGAMATORS.

The Schedule referred to in these Letters Patent and making part of the same.

To all whom it may concern:

Be it known that I, LYMAN GRISWOLD, of Denver, in the county of Arapahoe, Colorado Territory, have invented a new and improved Combined Ore-Crusher and Amalgamator; and I do hereby declare that the following is a full, clear, and exact description thereof, which will enable others skilled in the art to make and use the same, reference being had to the accompanying drawing forming part of this specification.

Figure 1 represents a side elevation, partly in section, of my improved crusher and amalgamator.

Figure 2 is a vertical transverse section of the same, taken on the plane of the line $x\,x$, fig. 1.

Similar letters of reference indicate corresponding parts.

My invention relates to ore-crushers and amalgamators, and consists in certain improvements, which will be first described in connection with all that is necessary to their full understanding, and then clearly pointed out in the claim.

A in the drawing represents the case or box within which the crusher-dies B B are set up on the bottom a of the same.

The punches are secured to rods that pass through the trough-shaped cover b of the case, said punches and rods being not shown in the drawing.

The cover b of the case A is made double inclined, so that it is deeper along the middle than at the sides, and serves as a trough for the water, by which the rods are lubricated and the ore moistened.

The holes in said trough for the rods are larger than the rods, to permit the water to enter the case.

The middle portion of the case A is somewhat enlarged, as shown in fig. 2, so as to constitute the chute C for inserting the ore, and opposite to said chute, to receive the screen D.

The chute is formed in shape of a longitudinal hopper, extending from end to end of the case, and has its inner side open near the bottom, to discharge its contents into the case.

The bottom of the chute is inclined for guiding the ore properly to the dies.

The ends of the chute are, by plates $c\,c$, kept a distance off the ends of the case, so that the ore may be kept from the frames or levers used for clamping the amalgamating-plates, which are hereinafter described.

The screen D is secured in place by a frame, d, which is fastened by means of keys or wedges.

E E' are the amalgamating-plates. They are secured in inclined positions to the inner sides of the case A, and extend from end to end of the same. They are preferably made of copper.

Quicksilver is used in the case during the crushing process.

The plate E under the bottom of the chute is connected with a longitudinal strip or plate, F, which is, by means of swinging yokes g and wedges h, secured against the opening in the side of the case A.

By swinging aside the yokes the strip F, with its plate E, can, by means of handles i, be readily removed.

The other plate E' slants off the inner face of the screen, and can be taken out by removing said screen.

The lower edges of both plates E E' rest in grooved ribs $j\,j$, as shown, the said ribs forming V-shaped projections for protecting the plates and preventing them from "scouring."

The plates E E' are held down by rubber pads K, that are secured in or to the inclined arms l of vertically-adjustable frames G, the said frames being arranged at the ends of the case, and connected at their upper ends to pivoted levers $m\,m$, by which the pads can be lifted off the plates.

Spring-catches o serve to hold the levers $m\,m$ in the lowered positions.

The plates c in the chute are for protecting the arms l, frames G, and pads k from the ore.

That side of the case A which is above the chute is made in form of a removable plate, n, which is held in place by means of wedges and bolts. By its removal ready access can be had to the interior of the case.

The chute C is also made removable and secured in similar manner. The interior of the apparatus can thus be readily reached.

Similar devices heretofore made could not be opened at the sides, except by the removal of the screen, which is frequently insufficient to allow the clearing up and removal of broken dies, shoes, &c.

Having thus described my invention,

I claim as new and desire to secure by Letters Patent—

1. The elastic pads $k\,k$, secured to the sliding frames G, and connected with the levers m, substantially as herein shown and described.

2. The chute C, having its inner side open and bottom inclined, and the plates $c\,c$ combined as described with case A, for the purpose specified.

3. The plate E, combined as described, with strip F, yoke g, wedge h, and handle i, for the purpose of securing or detaching the said plate, as set forth.

LYMAN GRISWOLD.

Witnesses:
FREDERICK CRAMER,
JOHN I. HASTINGS.

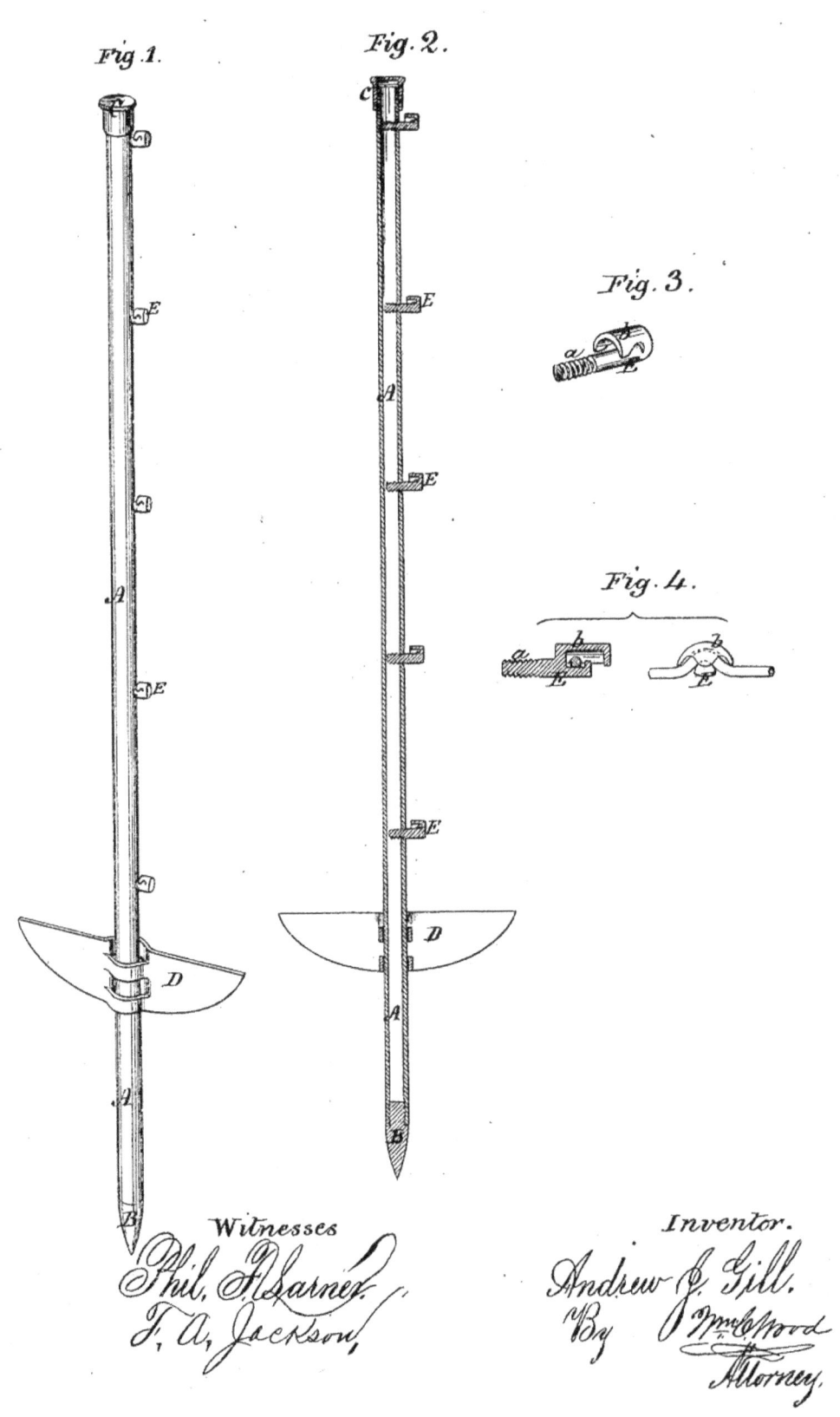

United States Patent Office.

ANDREW J. GILL, OF DENVER, COLORADO TERRITORY.

Letters Patent No. 113,872, dated April 18, 1871.

IMPROVEMENT IN FENCE-POSTS.

The Schedule referred to in these Letters Patent and making part of the same.

To all whom it may concern:

Be it known that I, ANDREW J. GILL, of Denver, in the county of Arrapahoe and Territory of Colorado, have invented certain new and useful Improvements in Metallic Posts for Fences, Telegraphs, &c.

My invention is designed as an improvement in posts intended more especially for the construction of wire fences, and the same consists in constructing the post of metallic piping provided with a cap at the top and a solid point at the base.

My invention further consists in the combination with a fence-post of a bladed flange-support and certain wire-holding studs of peculiar construction; and I do hereby declare the following specification, taken in connection with the drawing furnished, to be a full, clear, and exact description thereof.

Figure 1 represents in perspective a view of one of my improved fence-posts complete;

Figure 2 represents a vertical section of the same; and

Figure 3, a view in perspective of one of the holding-studs.

Figure 4 represents a modification of the holding-studs.

In the drawing—

A represents the hollow fence-post. It is constructed of metallic piping, and arranged to be driven into the ground, having a solid point, B, attached to its base. It is also provided with a screw-cap, C. The point B may be secured by a screw-thread, or swaged in a well-known manner.

D is the flanged support or brace. It is constructed of a single piece of metal provided with a central tubular neck, which is loosely fitted to the post A, and also provided with a sharp-bladed edge, which renders it easy to be driven into the ground when attached to or used in combination with a post. By the use of this flanged support D the post A, when driven into the ground, is firmly secured in an upright position. When it is found necessary to drive the posts into the ground at different depths the flange-support, being loosely attached to them, may be raised or lowered, and then driven into the ground after the post shall have been placed in position.

E in each case represents a holding-stud. They are arranged to securely hold the wire, and at the same time protect the points of contact therewith.

The peculiar construction of the holding-stud is shown more clearly in fig. 3. It consists of a pin, a, provided at one end with a screw-thread, affording a means of attachment to the post.

The opposite end of the pin is enlarged, and rises in the form of a hood, b.

The wire, when placed in the stud, is passed over the pin a and directly under the hood b, which effectually shields its point of contact therewith thereby in a great measure preventing rust.

In fig. 4 I have shown a modification of my improved holding-stud. The stud therein represented is made of an angular form. The wire is held in position by the hook formed on the end of the stud.

This construction of the holding-stud will also be found very desirable, as the points of contact with the wire are fully protected, as shown in fig. 4. Posts substantially as described would be desirable for ordinary telegraphic purposes.

Having thus described my invention,

I claim as new and desire to secure by Letters Patent—

1. The improved iron post herein described, formed of piping, and provided with a fixed cap, C, and solid point, B, as and for the purposes specified.

2. The holding-stud E, arranged to hold the wire, and provided with the cap or hood b to protect the points of contact therewith, as described.

3. In combination with a drive-post A, and loosely connected thereto, the bladed flange lateral support D, substantially as described

ANDREW J. GILL.

Witnesses:
J. B. CASS,
J. B. WOODWORTH.

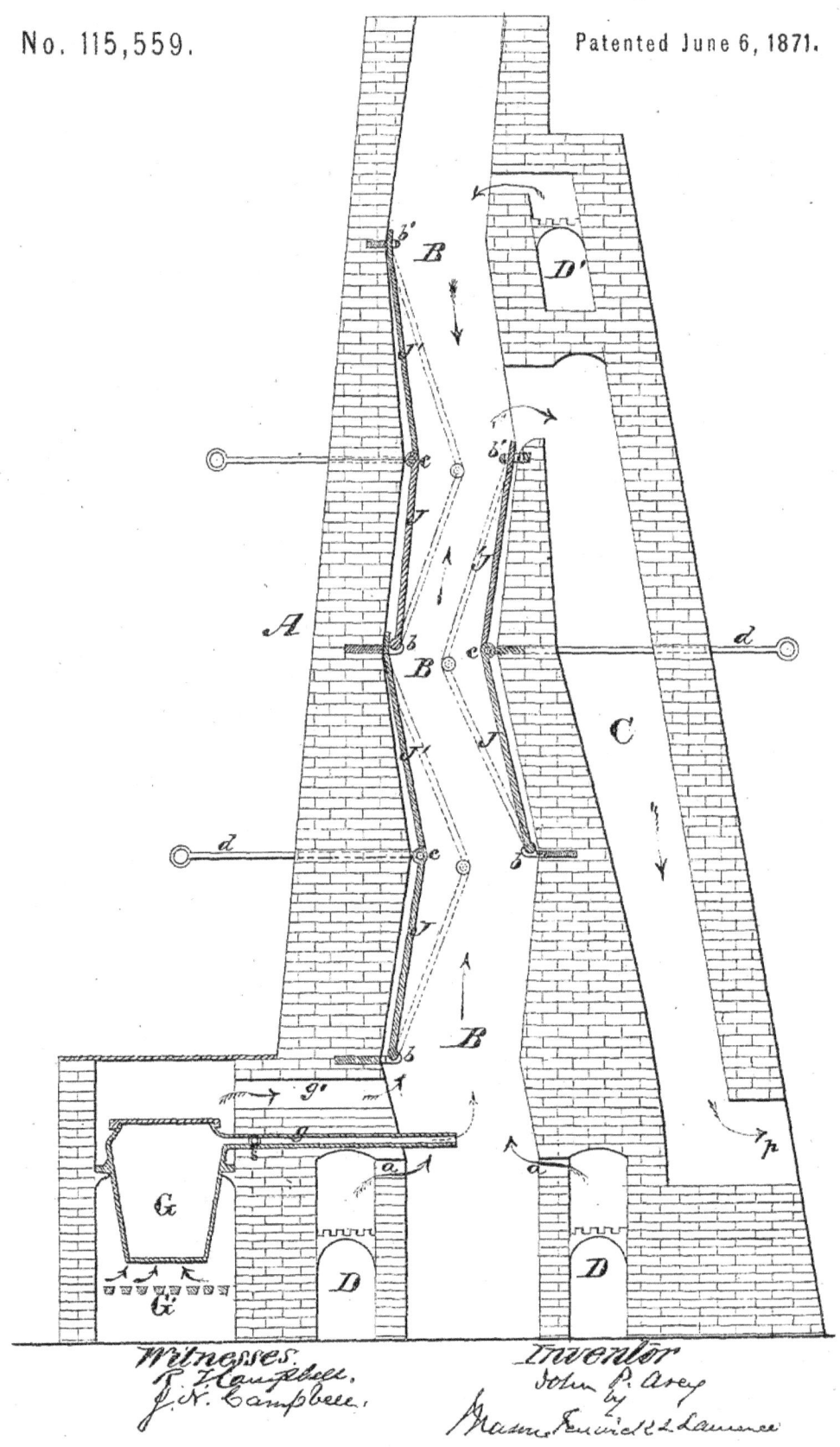

UNITED STATES PATENT OFFICE.

JOHN P. AREY, OF GEORGETOWN, COLORADO TERRITORY.

IMPROVEMENT IN FURNACES FOR ROASTING ORES.

Specification forming part of Letters Patent No. 115,559, dated June 6, 1871.

To all whom it may concern:

Be it known that I, JOHN P. AREY, of Georgetown, in the county of Clear Creek and Territory of Colorado, have invented certain Improvements in Furnaces for Roasting, Oxidizing, and Chloridizing Ores; and I do hereby declare that the following is a full, clear, and exact description thereof reference being had to the accompanying drawing, which represents a vertical section through a furnace having my improvements applied to it.

This invention relates to improvements which are applicable to the furnace for roasting ores described in the schedule annexed to my Letters Patent of the United States numbered 103,006, and dated on the 17th day of May, 1870. The object of the first part of my invention is to improve the shaft or stack of a roasting-furnace by the arrangement therein of hinged plates, and providing such plates with means which will allow them to be conveniently adjusted and set at different angles or planes, thereby obtaining a zigzag or serpentine passage in the shaft, which can be contracted or enlarged according to the condition of the ore under treatment, as will be hereinafter explained. The object of the second part of my invention is to chloridize the metals by subjecting them, while passing through the flue or flues of a roasting-furnace, to the action of chlorine gas, which is generated in a retort or in retorts suitably combined with the furnace, thereby obtaining greater economy of chloridizing material than is the case where such material is mixed in the solid form of the ore, as will be hereinafter explained.

The following description will enable others skilled in the art to understand it.

In the annexed drawing I have represented a furnace which in many respects resembles the furnace described and shown in my Letters Patent numbered 103,006, above referred to. I prefer to employ a furnace thus constructed in carrying out my invention; but I do not confine myself thereto.

A represents the shaft or stack of the furnace, through which rises in a serpentine manner a flue-space, B. At the base of this flue-space, and on opposite sides of the same, are the main fire-chambers D D, constructed with outlets $a\ a$, for the escape of the heated products into the flue B. Near the top of the stack, and communicating with the main flue B, is a secondary or oxidizing-furnace, D', the products from which, and also from the furnaces D D, pass off into a descending flue, C, and finally escape therefrom at p. The sides of the main flue B may be made zigzag, as shown, or they may be made straight or flat. I prefer to have this flue made of the zigzag form shown in the drawing, although it may be made straight and the zigzag form obtained in the following manner: On opposite sides of the flue B are hinged plates J J', which are supported in pairs upon lugs b, and connected together in pairs by hinges e. The upper end of each plate J' is received through a suitable guide, through which its upper end can slide freely. Each pair of plates J J' has connected at the points e an adjusting-rod, d, which passes through the furnace-wall, as shown, and which should be provided with an adjusting-screw or some equivalent device which will securely hold the plates at any desired angle. It will be seen from the above description that the flue-space B can be contracted or enlarged according to the nature of the material which it is desired to treat in the furnace. The dotted lines in the drawing indicate the plates J J' adjusted so as to leave quite a narrow flue-space of a zigzag form between them, and at the points c, where the plates are hinged together. The full lines indicate the plates J J' adjusted against the masonry walls of the flue, so as to present the greatest possible space and less prominent angles at c. Thus the flue-space is adjustable according as it may be desired to subject the descending material a longer or shorter time to the action of the ascending heat and gases. The surfaces of the plates J J' may be coated with some suitable cement which will protect the plates from rapid destruction.

In the process heretofore practiced in chloridizing metallic substances in shaft-furnaces, the salt or other materials from which the chlorine was obtained, was either mixed intimately with the pulverized ore before the same was fed into the furnace, or was fed simultaneous with the ore, and the whole mixture being subjected to the heat of the furnace, the chlorine generated during the descent through the shaft of the furnace. This method is objectionable from the fact that it necessitates a great waste of salt, owing to the difficulty of determining the exact proportion of salt to use with a given amount of ore, or the per cent. of chlorine which will be evolved during the descent of the material through the furnace. To safely avoid any material loss of the precious metals an extra amount of chloridizing material is always used. To obviate these objections I manufacture the chlorine gas in a retort, G, arranged in a furnace, G', and inject the gas thus generated into the flue B at or near the bottom thereof by means of a pipe, g. The furnace G may have an outlet at g' for conducting its products of combustion into the flue B. For the purpose of regulating the amount of chlorine gas which it is required to discharge into the flue B a valve, s, may be applied to the pipe g. In this way I introduce pure chlorine gas into the furnace-flue and bring it in contact with the descending stream of ore, and in this way a greater or lesser amount of gas can be employed, according to the requirements of the case, and there will be little or no waste.

I do not confine myself to the introduction of chlorine gas at the bottom of the flue B, as gas may be led into this flue as well as into the descending flue C, at different points. By admitting this gas into the flue C the fine metallic dust which escapes the action of the chlorine in the main flue B, and which is carried off by the strong draft, will be thoroughly chloridized.

I do not claim a furnace with a vertical shaft and stationary inclines, as shown in the patent of F. A. W. Partz, dated June 14, 1864, as such construction presents obstructions to the ascending currents, and besides does not admit of a variation of the size of the flue; neither do I claim a shaft-furnace such as is shown in Charles Stetefeldt's patent, dated December 31, 1867, as such furnace is not constructed with means for varying the size of the flue, nor is it constructed with a chlorine-gas generator and injector; neither do I claim furnaces constructed as described in patents of Henry Tindall, dated October 13, 1868, and of H. H. Eames, dated February 2, 1869, as in such furnaces powdered ore is not flowed down through a shaft and subjected in all of its particles to the ascending fumes of chlorine gas; but

I claim as new and desire to secure by Letters Patent—

1. The employment of adjustable plates in the shaft or stack of a roasting-furnace, whereby the flue-space can be contracted or enlarged and at the same time given a zigzag or serpentine form, substantially as described.

2. The combination of a chlorine-gas generator and injector, in combination with a roasting-furnace, through the stack of which the powdered ore falls, and in its fall is treated by fire and said chlorine gas, substantially as described.

JOHN P. AREY.

Witnesses:
J. N. CAMPBELL,
R. T. CAMPBELL.

2 Sheets--Sheet 1.

A. H. TOWNSEND.

Improvement in Repeating Ordnance.

No. 115,659. Patented June 6, 1871.

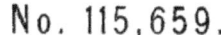

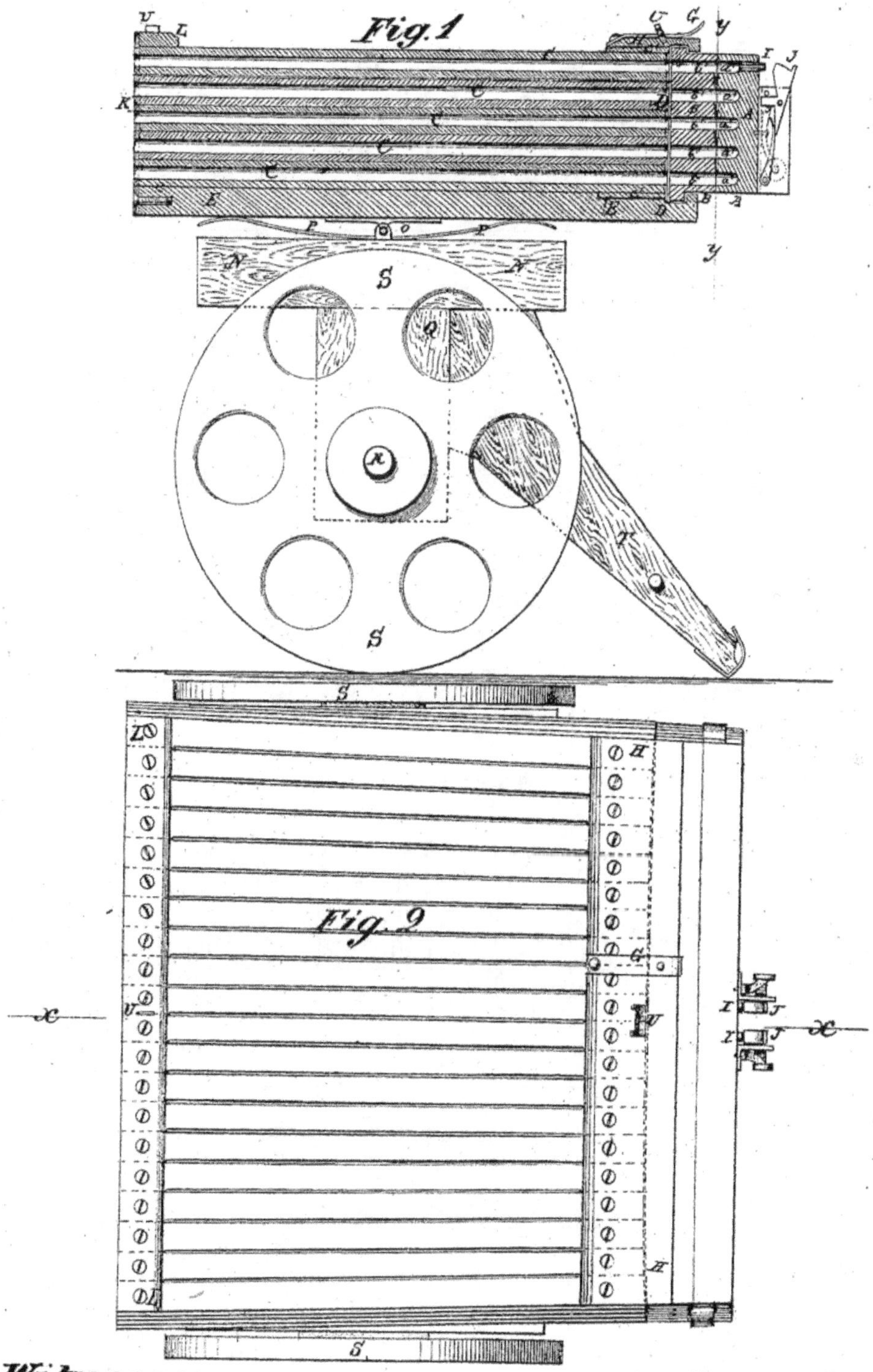

Witnesses:
A.W. Almqvist
Wm. H. C. Smith.

Inventor:
A. H. Townsend,
Per
Attorneys.

AM. PHOTO-LITHOGRAPHIC CO. N.Y. (OSBORNE'S PROCESS.)

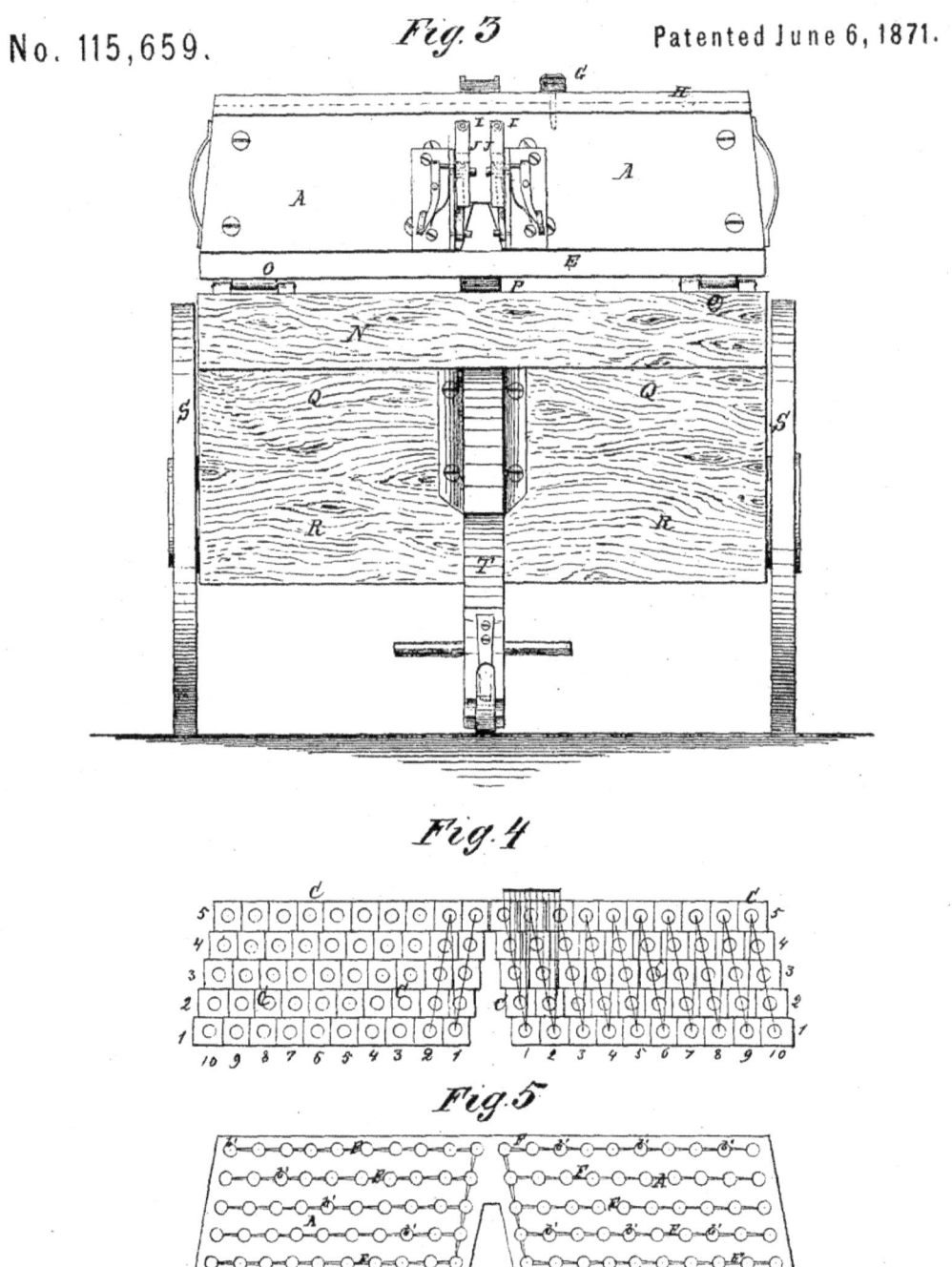

UNITED STATES PATENT OFFICE.

ALFRED H. TOWNSEND, OF GEORGETOWN, COLORADO TERRITORY.

IMPROVEMENT IN REPEATING-ORDNANCE.

Specification forming part of Letters Patent No. 115,659, dated June 6, 1871.

To all whom it may concern:

Be it known that I, ALFRED H. TOWNSEND, of Georgetown, in the county of Clear Creek and Territory of Colorado, have invented a new and Improved Gun; and I do hereby declare that the following is a full, clear, and exact description thereof, which will enable others skilled in the art to make and use the same, reference being had to the accompanying drawing forming part of this specification, in which—

Figure 1, Sheet I, is a side view of my improved gun, partly in section, through the line $x\ x$, Fig. 2. Fig. 2, Sheet I, is a top view of the same. Fig. 3, Sheet II, is a rear view of the same. Fig. 4, Sheet II, is a detail view of the rear ends of the barrels, showing their diagonal arrangement. Fig. 5, Sheet II, is a detail sectional view of the breech-piece taken through the line $y\ y$, Fig. 1.

Similar letters of reference indicate corresponding parts.

My invention relates to that class of guns which is constructed to throw numerous balls from different barrels, and either simultaneously or in quick succession.

I will first describe my improvements in connection with all that is necessary to a full understanding thereof, and then clearly point them out in the claim.

A and B are two parts, which form the breech-piece of the gun. $a'\ b'$ are corresponding perforations, made to register with each other, and to receive the cartridge. At the point of junction or joint formed by these plates are apertures F, connecting the several chambers, in order to communicate the fire from one to the other. These apertures may be uniform in size or graduated diminishingly from first to last. C are the barrels, formed independently and arranged one upon another in diagonal planes. D is a plate between the breech-piece and the barrels, and having perforations correspondent thereto. The barrels are placed in two divisions, one on each side of a central line, and each obliqued reversely thereto. E is the plate which supports the barrels; K, a muzzle-plate, to assist in holding them firmly in position; and H L plates to receive the sights U U. The plates H E are grooved to receive tongues on the breech-piece A B, by which the latter may be made readily removable. G is a spring, having a pin which enters a perforation in plate H and piece B, in order to hold the breech-piece detachably. I is a cap-tube, connecting with one of the cartridge-chambers, and J the hammer which strikes upon it. The gun thus constructed is supported upon the carriage N Q R S T. N is a platform, on the center of which the gun is hinged; Q, a shoulder projecting from the axle; and T, a trail thrown out obliquely from the shoulder Q to support the gun in a horizontal position. The platform N likewise serves to regulate the amount of deviation allowable on each side of the hinge O. Upon this hinge the gun is turned in sighting it, and a spring, P P, is fixed centrally thereunder, but unfastened at either end.

The mode of operation is as follows: The breech-piece A B being loaded with cartridges, fixed in position, and aimed at the object, the hammer is brought down upon the nipple. The cartridge in the first chamber is thus ignited, and in quick succession thereafter, but not simultaneously, all the rest. A momentary interval is required to impart ignition through the channels F to the succeeding chambers, and this prevents the shock and recoil so objectionable in guns of this character. The cartridges exploding, the balls follow each other from the gun in quick but imperceptible succession, and in lines slightly divergent from and directed centrally to the object. The breech-piece is immediately withdrawn and a duplicate thereof substituted.

This slight lapse of time in changing the breech-pieces is sufficient for a circulation of air through the barrels, an expulsion of fouling gases, and an absorption of much heat.

Having thus described all that is necessary to a full understanding of my invention, what I esteem to be new and desire to protect by Letters Patent, is—

1. A breech-piece, formed of two pieces, A B, with perforations $a'\ b'$ and converging apertures F at their joint or junction, as and for the purpose specified.

2. A tongued breech-piece, A B, grooved plates H E, and detachable pin and spring G, combined as and for the purpose specified.

3. The independent sectional barrels C, the perforated plates D K, and the bottom plate E, combined, constructed, and put together as described.

4. The arrangement of spring B B and hinge O beneath the barrel, as and for the purpose specified.

ALFRED H. TOWNSEND.

Witnesses:
 JAMES W. DRIPS,
 WM. SPRUANCE.

William D. Arnett. Impt. in Locomotives.

117031 Fig. 1

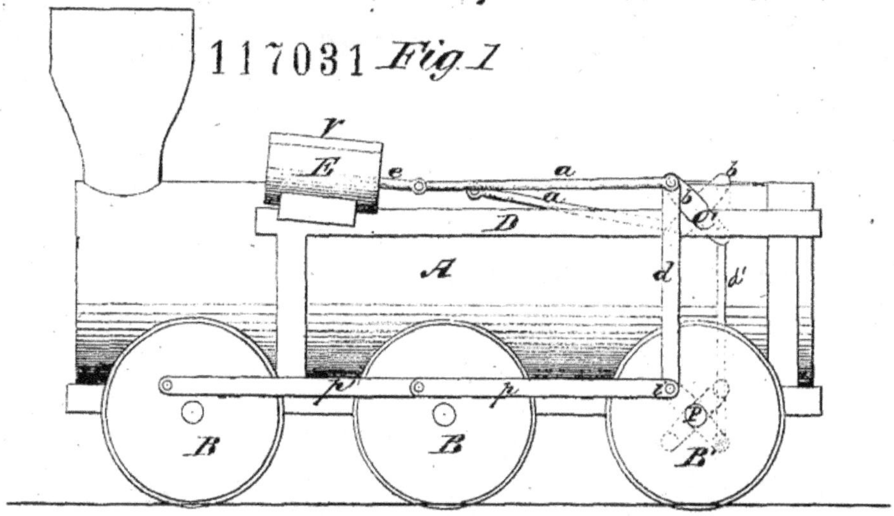

Fig. 2

PATENTED JUL 18 1871

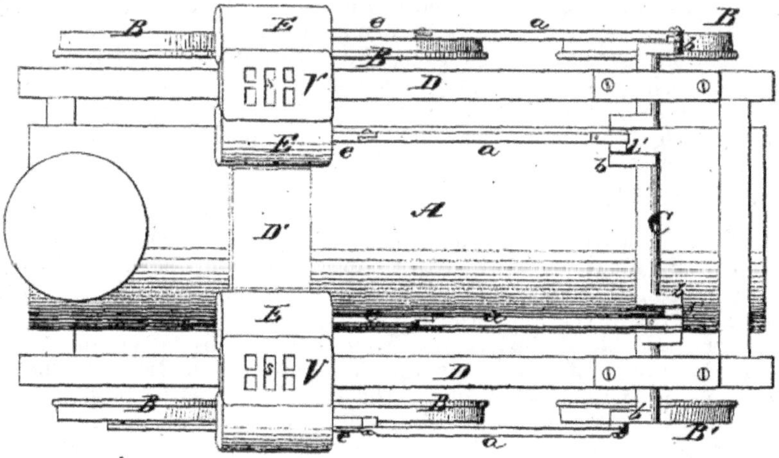

Fig. 3

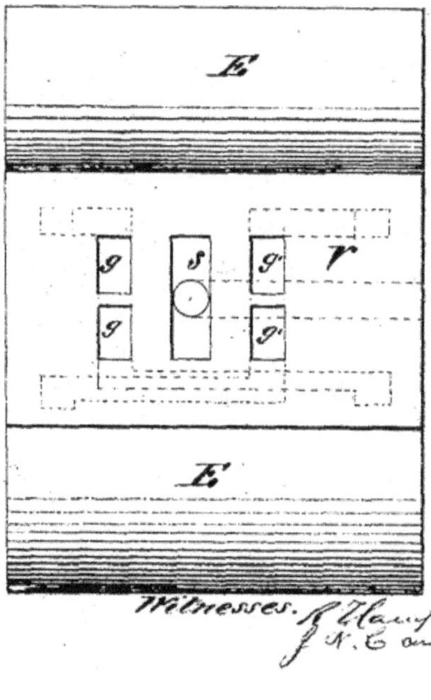

Fig. 4

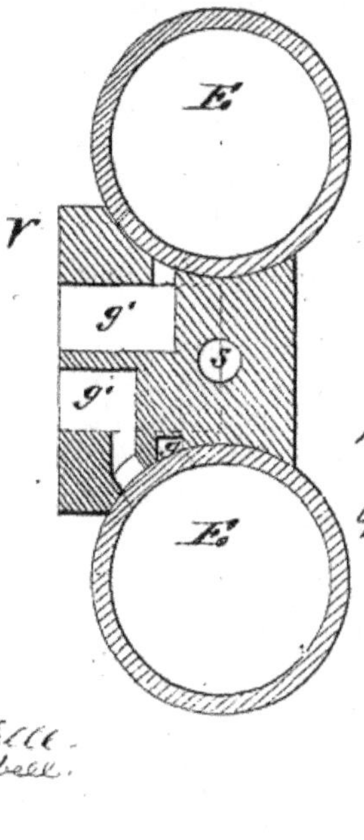

Inventor
William D. Arnett
by
Mason Fenwick Lawrence
Atty

Witnesses. R. Campbell.
J. K. Campbell.

UNITED STATES PATENT OFFICE.

WILLIAM D. ARNETT, OF DENVER, COLORADO TERRITORY.

IMPROVEMENT IN LOCOMOTIVES.

Specification forming part of Letters Patent No. 117,031, dated July 18, 1871.

To all whom it may concern:

Be it known that I, WILLIAM D. ARNETT, of Denver, Arapahoe county, Territory of Colorado, have invented a new and useful Improvement in Locomotives; and I do hereby declare that the following is a full, clear, and exact description thereof, reference being had to the accompanying drawing making part of this specification, in which—

Figure 1 is a side view of a locomotive having my improvement applied to it. Fig. 2 is a top view of the same. Figs. 3 and 4 are views representing the combination of two steam-cylinders with a valve-seat adapted therefor.

Similar letters of reference indicate corresponding parts in the several figures.

This invention relates to certain improvements on the invention set forth in the schedule annexed to my Letters Patent bearing date on the 7th day of February, 1871. The nature of this invention consists in the arrangement, on each side of the locomotive and upon a suitable frame, of two steam-cylinders, both communicating with a single valve-chest, and both connected, through their piston-rods and pitmen-rods, with a crank-shaft, which latter is connected by four pitmen-rods to the crank-axle and faces of the rear driving-wheels, as will be hereinafter shown.

The following is a description of my invention, which will enable others skilled in the art to understand it.

In the accompanying drawing, A represents the boiler of the locomotive, which is suitably mounted in a frame, D, which is supported upon the axles of driving-wheels B B B'. At the front end of this frame D, and supported upon a horizontal transverse beam thereof, are four steam-cylinders, E, arranged on each side of the frame in pairs. These cylinders are inclined, as shown in Fig. 1, so that their longitudinal axes intersect the axis of a horizontal transverse crank-shaft, C, which is located over and in the vertical plane of the axle P of the rear driving-wheels B', and which is supported on the top of the frame D. Each pair of steam-cylinders E E is supplied with steam through ports $g \, g \, g' \, g'$, and exhaust through ports S, which are made through a valve-bed, V, on which a single slide-valve works. In this way two cylinders, E E, on each side of the locomotive, are supplied with steam at the same time, and through a single valve-chest, and exhaust through a single port in the valve-seat bed V. The piston-rods e of the two pairs of steam-cylinders E E are connected to the front ends of pitmen-rods a, which are connected at their ends to cranks b on the shaft C. Each pair of cranks $b \, b$ is arranged at quarter-stroke, or, in other words, each pair is arranged at right angles, as indicated in Fig. 1, so that while one pair of pistons is pushing, the other pair is pulling. The cranks b on the outer ends of the shaft C are connected to wrist-pins i on the outer faces of the rear driving-wheels by means of pitmen-rods $d \, d$; and to the same wrist-pin i rods p are connected, which are also connected to wrist-pins on the next forward wheels B. These latter wheels B are connected to the front wheels B by means of rods p', as shown in the drawing. In this way the piston-rods of the outer cylinders on both sides of the locomotive are connected indirectly to the rear driving-wheels. The rods a' of the inside steam-cylinder are connected to cranks on the axle P of the rear driving-wheels.

By this arrangement the force is applied in a vertical or nearly vertical direction to turn the rear driving-wheels of the locomotive, while the steam-cylinders through which this force is transmitted are arranged near the forward end of the locomotive and operate alternately in pairs.

Having described my invention, what I claim as new, and desire to secure by Letters Patent, is—

The arrangement, on each side of a locomotive, of a pair of steam-cylinders, which receives steam through a single slide-valve bed, V, and whose piston-rods $e \, e$ communicate motion to the crank-shaft P of the rear driving-wheels through pitmen-rods $a \, a$ and $d \, d'$, substantially as described.

WILLIAM D. ARNETT.

Witnesses:
GEORGE W. LEAS,
JOHN W. WEBSTER.

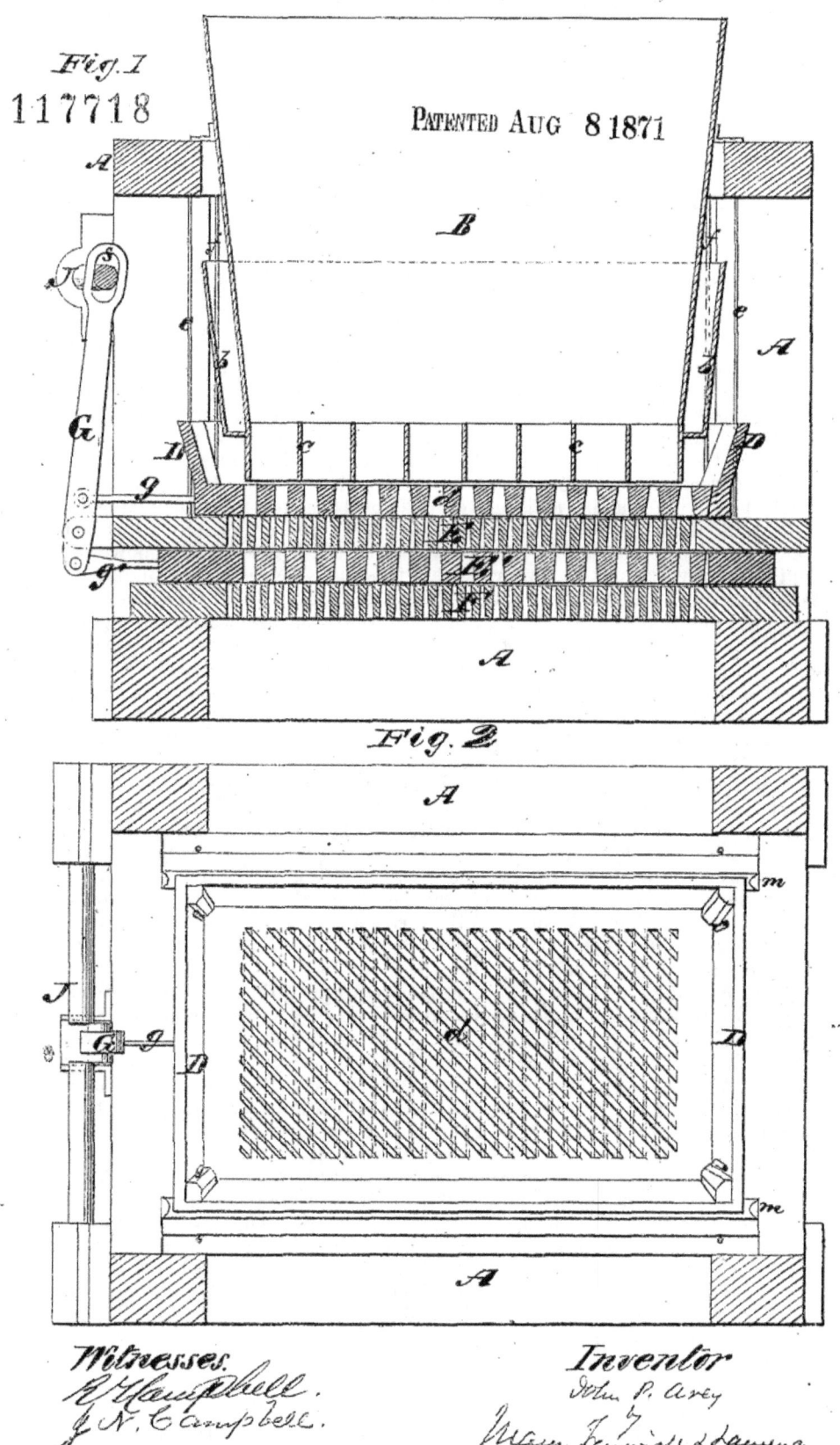

UNITED STATES PATENT OFFICE.

JOHN P. AREY, OF GEORGETOWN, COLORADO TERRITORY.

IMPROVEMENT IN FEEDERS FOR ORE-ROASTING FURNACES.

Specification forming part of Letters Patent No. 117,718, dated August 8, 1871.

To all whom it may concern:

Be it known that I, JOHN P. AREY, of Georgetown, in the county of Clear Creek and Territory of Colorado, have invented a new and Improved Feeder for Ore-Roasting Shaft-Furnaces; and I do hereby declare that the following is a full, clear, and exact description thereof, reference being had to the accompanying drawing making part of this specification, in which—

Figure 1 is a sectional view of the feeder taken longitudinally and vertically through its center. Fig. 2 is a horizontal section through the frame of the feeder with the frame removed.

Similar letters of reference indicate corresponding parts in the several figures.

This invention relates to a novel device which is applicable to the furnace for oxidizing and chloridizing ores, for which Letters Patent of the United States were granted to me on the 17th day of May, 1870, and which is used on top of the shaft or stack through which the ore is dropped. The invention relates to a mode of keeping the feed-funnel cool; and also to a mode of uniformly distributing the powdered ore while it is being fed into the stack of the furnace.

The following description will enable others skilled in the art to understand my invention and one practical mode of carrying it into effect.

In the accompanying drawing I have not represented any feeder applied to a furnace, as it is applicable to stack or shaft-furnaces for oxidizing, chloridizing, and desulphurating ores, and especially to my improved furnace referred to above. A represents the frame of the feeder, which may be made of cast-iron, and which is adapted to fit upon the top of the stack or shaft into which the ore is introduced. B represents the funnel or receiver for the ore, which has a grated bottom, c, and which is surrounded below by a tank, b, through which water is made to flow for keeping the receiver cool. Below this receiver is a pan, D, which has a grated bottom, d, the bars of which are arranged obliquely. This pan, with its grated bottom, is hung from frame A by wires f, and is guided between two ribs, $m\ m$, which rise from a grate, E. The grate E has bars which extend transversely across it at right angles to its length, and this grate is rigidly fixed to the frame A. Beneath the grate E is another grate, E', the bars of which are obliquely arranged, and beneath the last-named grate is still another grate, F, the bars of which are transversely arranged, like the grate E. The grates D and E' are longitudinally movable, and are moved by means of a lever, G, the shortest arm of which is connected to the grate E' by a rod, g', and the shortest arm of which is connected to the pan D and its grate d by means of a rod, g. The lever g has a loop, s, on the upper end of its longest arm, through which passes the crank of a shaft, J. This crank-shaft J has its bearings on frame A, and it is rotated by power applied to one of its ends. The feeder hereinabove described is subjected to the influence of the heat in the shaft or flue of the furnace on which it is supported, and for this reason the grates will become highly heated. I prevent the receiver B from becoming unduly heated by means of water, which may be kept running through the tank B.

It has been shown that the grates are composed of oblique and transverse bars, and that two movable grates, d E', are employed in combination with two stationary grates, E F. The object of this arrangement I will now explain. The ore is in a state of fine powder, and in order to properly subject it to the roasting, oxidizing, and chloridizing processes it should be discharged into the shaft of the furnace in a shower rather than in a compact stream. A single screen or grate will not do this, as the material will naturally collect at and near its center, while at the ends there will be very little discharge. By the employment of a grate with oblique bars, in combination with a grate whose bars are transverse, the action of the crossing-spaces when one of the grates is moved will be to distribute the powder uniformly over the surfaces of the grates and prevent its collection at one point more than at another.

I do not confine myself to the number of grated distributers represented in the drawing, as any required number of them may be employed.

The tendency of the powdered ore is to pack at the bottom of the hopper B; but this is prevented by the narrow transverse strips c, which will allow the powder to pass between them as it is removed by the highest grate d.

In carrying my invention into effect I shall apply a cone-pulley on the crank-shaft J, so that by changing the driving-belt from one of the surfaces of such pulley to another the movements imparted to the grates can be made faster or slower, as may be required.

It will be seen from the above description that,

by the employment of grates or slotted distributers which will spread the powdered ore uniformly over a given surface, I am enabled to feed fast or slow, as circumstances require. Both plates of a pair may have diagonal bars, but, of course, the bars must cross each other. Both bars may be movable, but in reverse directions.

I am aware that it is not new to move a wire screen over a stationary sheet-metal screen, the latter mounted upon stationary bars at the top of a shaft-furnace. This is shown in Charles Stetefeldt's patent of March 1, 1870. I also am aware that a circulation cooling-chamber has been constructed upon the top of a shaft-furnace, in close proximity to the hopper. This also is shown in said patent of Stetefeldt. I am not aware that a hopper with grated bottom has ever been arranged above reversely-moving grated plates, the bars of one plate crossing the bars of another plate; nor am I aware that several pairs of such plates for grinding and agitating or diffusing the ore in its passage to the furnace from the hopper have ever been devised previously to my invention; neither am I aware that the ore has been subjected to a shearing action in its passage from the hopper to the furnace; neither am I aware that a hopper mounted above the feeder has ever had combined directly with it a cooling and circulation-chamber, the chamber being portable with the hopper and feeder. Therefore, while I do not claim anything shown in said patent of Stetefeldt,

What I claim as new is—

1. A feeder for an ore-roasting furnace, which is composed of grated plates which have a shearing feeding operation, substantially as described.

2. The hopper B, provided with a subdivided bottom and arranged over grated distributers, substantially as described.

3. The combination of a hopper, B, and a circulating cooling-tank, b, substantially in the manner described.

JOHN P. AREY.

Witnesses:
J. N. CAMPBELL,
R. T. CAMPBELL.

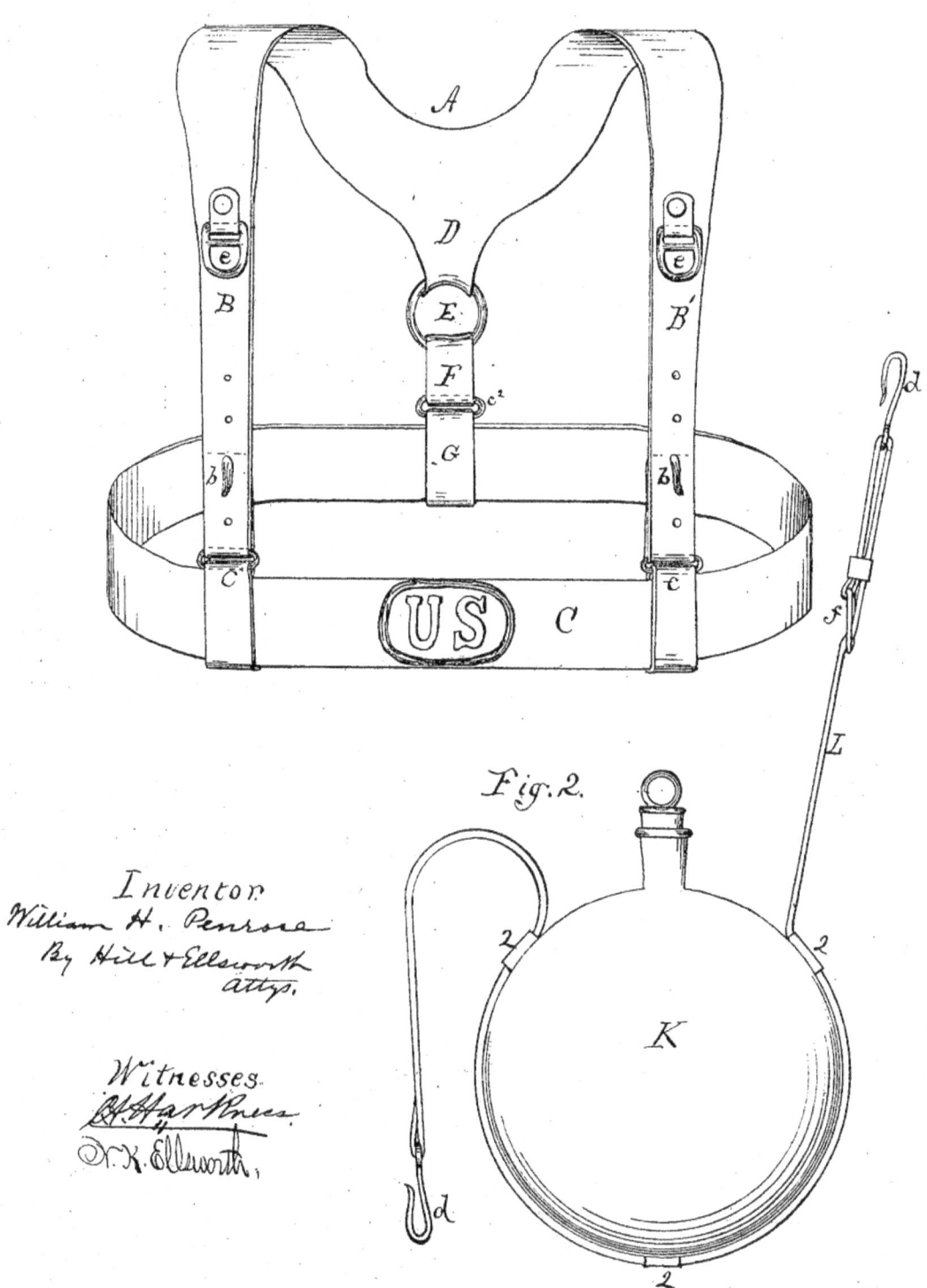

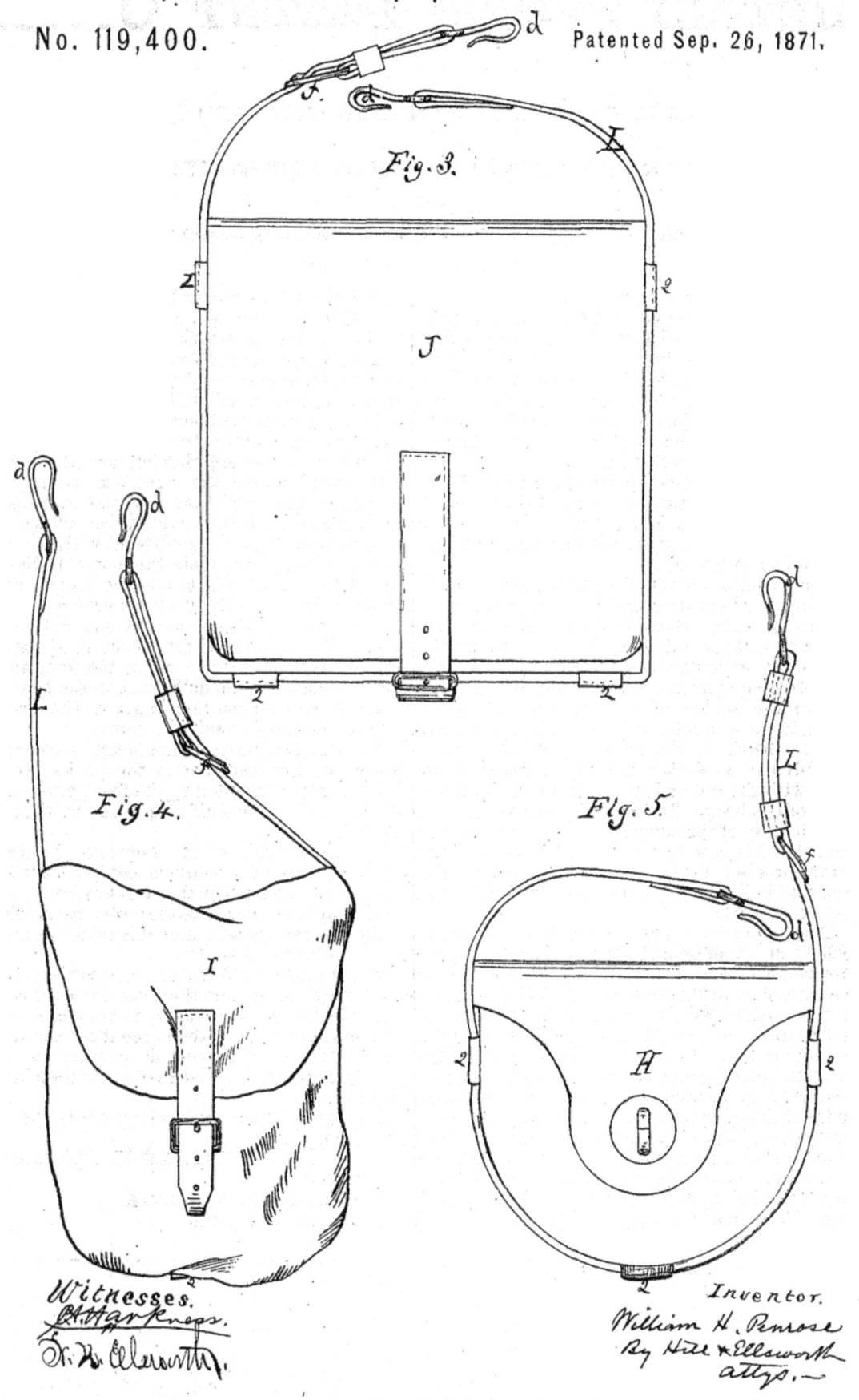

UNITED STATES PATENT OFFICE.

WILLIAM H. PENROSE, OF FORT LYON, COLORADO TERRITORY.

IMPROVEMENT IN MILITARY EQUIPMENTS.

Specification forming part of Letters Patent No. 119,400, dated September 26, 1871.

To all whom it may concern:

Be it known that I, WILLIAM H. PENROSE, of Fort Lyon, in the county of Bent, in the Territory of Colorado, have invented certain Improvements in Soldiers' Equipments; and I do hereby declare the following to be a full, clear, and exact description of the same, reference being had to the accompanying drawing forming part of this specification, in which—

Figure 1 represents a perspective view of the supporting apparatus, and Figs. 2, 3, 4, and 5 the adjustable connecting-straps adapted to a canteen, haversack, knapsack, and cartridge-box or pouch, respectively.

Similar letters of reference in the accompanying drawing indicate corresponding parts.

This invention relates to the means employed for supporting a soldier's canteen, haversack, knapsack, cartridge-pouch, blanket, overcoat, and other equipments, and has for its object to relieve the soldier of the pressure across his chest, in the arm-pits, and around the abdomen, and to distribute the necessary weights more equably and in such a way as to interfere the least with the full and free exercise of the functions of the body. To this end it consists in the combination of the supporting apparatus, represented in Fig. 1, with the adjustable connecting-straps or slings for the various equipments represented in Figs. 2, 3, 4, and 5, as I will now proceed to describe.

The supporting apparatus consists of a waist-belt, C, and a bifurcated yoke, A B B' D, the two front ends of which extend down through loops $c\ c'$, attached to the waist-belt, and thence back upward behind the front part of the strap a sufficient distance to enable them to adjust the belt higher or lower by means of hooks $b\ b$. The yoke extends down behind in curved lines to the middle of the wearer's back, where the two parts unite at D and support a ring, E, which is connected to a loop, c^2, by means of a strap, F. The loops $c\ c^1\ c^2$ are attached to the waist-belt by means of straps G, the rear strap and one of the front ones being movable and the other stationary. Each shoulder-strap or brace B B' is provided with a half-ring or button, $e\ e$. The slings by which the canteen, haversack, &c., are connected to the supporting apparatus consist of leather straps L, provided with spring-hooks $d\ d$ and adjusting-buckles $f\ f$, as fully shown in the several figures, numbered 2, 3, 4, and 5.

In applying the supporting apparatus unclasp the waist-belt plate; place the yoke upon the shoulders by passing the left arm through the left brace B; then the right arm through the brace B'; take care that the yoke A rests well upon the neck; hook the waist-belt plate; slide the movable loop c^1 equidistant with the other from the belt-plate; slide the loop c^2 to the center of the back, and adjust the length of the shoulder-braces B B' by the hooks $b\ b$.

In putting on the canteen K and clothes-haversack J attach one of the hooks d to the ring E; then bring the other end to the front and attach its hook d to the half-ring e on the shoulder-brace B, and adjust the length of the straps L by the buckles f to suit the person.

In putting on the cartridge-pouch H and ration-haversack I connect one of the hooks d to ring E; bring the other end to the front, and connect the hook d to the half-ring e on the shoulder brace B'.

The application of the improved devices to other articles of a soldier's equipment will be understood without further description.

Having thus described my invention, what I claim as new therein, and desire to secure by Letters Patent, is—

The adjustable bifurcated yoke, combined with a waist-belt to support the necessary equipments from the breast and back of the wearer in the manner described, each equipment being attached by a strap, L, with suitable connections from the front and rear of said yoke, for the purpose specified.

This specification signed by me this 19th day of January, 1871.

WILLIAM H. PENROSE.

Witnesses:
 ALFRED A. WOODHULL,
 SAML. F. HATCH. (114)

H. Bolthoff, Stencil Cutter.

No. 119,737.

Fig. 1

Patented Oct. 10, 1871.

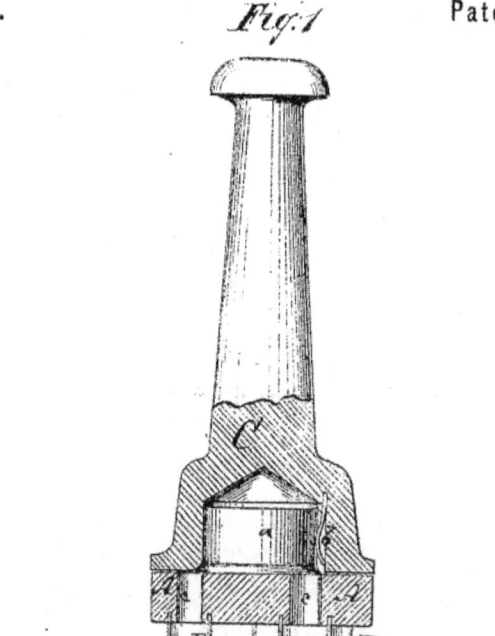

Fig. 2.

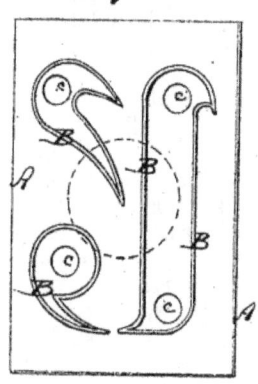

Witnesses:
C. Raettig
Wm. H. C. Smith.

Inventor:
H. Bolthoff

Per Munn & Co
Attorneys.

UNITED STATES PATENT OFFICE.

HENRY BOLTHOFF, OF CENTRAL CITY, COLORADO TERRITORY.

IMPROVEMENT IN DEVICES FOR CUTTING STENCIL-PLATES.

Specification forming part of Letters Patent No. 119,737, dated October 10, 1871.

To all whom it may concern:

Be it known that I, HENRY BOLTHOFF, of Central City, in the county of Gilpin and Territory of Colorado, have invented a new and Improved Stencil-Cutter; and I do hereby declare that the following is a full, clear, and exact description thereof, which will enable others skilled in the art to make and use the same, reference being had to the accompanying drawing forming part of this specification, in which—

Figure 1 represents a side view, partly in section, of my improved stencil-cutter. Fig. 2 is an end view of the same.

Similar letters of reference indicate corresponding parts.

My invention consists in an improvement upon the construction of stocks for stencil-cutters, as hereinafter fully described and subsequently pointed out in the claim.

A in the drawing represents the block or body of my improved stencil-cutter. It is made of brass or other suitable material, cast of rectangular or other form and suitable size. B is the cutter. It is made of cast-steel or equivalent material, and so formed as to produce the aperture for the desired letter or mark when applied to the material to be cut. The cutter is affixed to the plate by fitting its upper part into the mold wherein the plate is cast, so that eventually the two will be firmly united by casting. In this manner the cutter is cheaply made of best material, it being unnecessary and too expensive to use steel for the body A, while the blade must be made of the hard substance. From the plate A projects a tenon, a, of cylindrical or other form, into a corresponding socket of the handle C. Within the handle is, at the side of the socket, a clamping-spring, b, which serves to retain the block in place. The block is also perforated, as at $c\ c$, over each mark or letter, in order to facilitate the removal of the cut-out pieces.

In using the cutter the block is secured in the handle, placed upon the article to be cut, and forced down by a hammer blow. The next cutter to be used is then readily substituted in the handle for the first, placed in position, and applied by hammering.

The cutting-blades for every set of type are of equal length and height, in order to produce uniform letters. The width of the several blocks is preferably such that when the material is ruled into equal spaces and one block applied to the middle of each space the letters will all be equally far apart.

Having thus described my invention, I claim as new and desire to secure by Letters Patent—

The brass plate A, having tenon a and perforations $c\ c$ constructed, as described, to serve as a stock for cutters B and to fit handle C, as set forth.

HENRY BOLTHOFF.

Witnesses:
JOSEPH S. UPDEGRAFF,
LEWIS V. WILCOX.

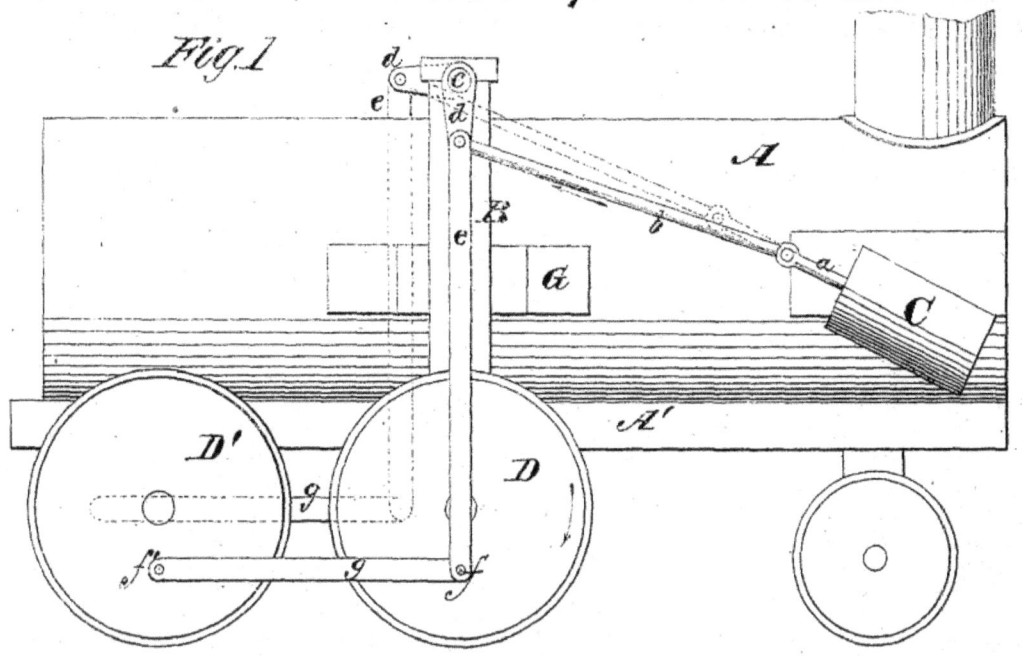
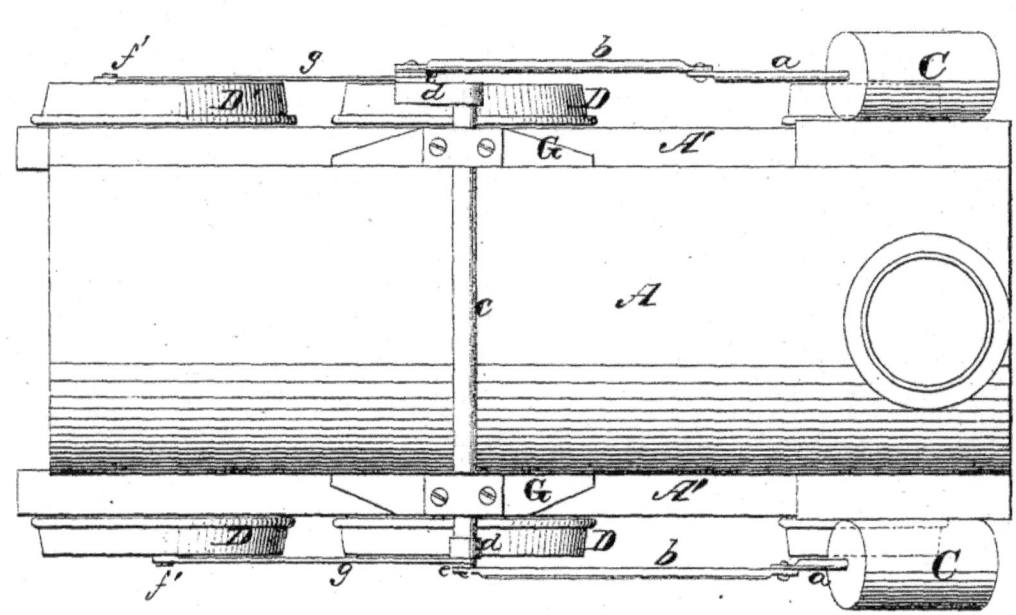

UNITED STATES PATENT OFFICE.

WILLIAM D. ARNETT, OF DENVER CITY, COLORADO TERRITORY.

IMPROVEMENT IN LOCOMOTIVES.

Specification forming part of Letters Patent No. 120,180, dated October 24, 1871.

To all whom it may concern:

Be it known that I, WILLIAM D. ARNETT, of Denver City, in the county of Arapahoe and Territory of Colorado, have invented an Improvement in Locomotives; and I do hereby declare that the following is a full, clear, and exact description thereof, reference being had to the accompanying drawing making part of this specification, in which—

Figure 1 is a side view of a locomotive having my improvement applied to it. Fig. 2 is a top view of the same.

Similar letters of reference indicate corresponding parts in both figures.

The object of this improvement is to interpose pitmen-rods and a two-throw crank-shaft between inclined steam-cylinders and the driving-wheels, and so arrange said parts that the power will be transmitted vertically to the rear driving-wheels through the medium of toggles operating alternately on opposite sides of the locomotive, as will be hereinafter explained.

The following description of my invention will enable others skilled in the art to understand it.

In the accompanying drawing, A represents the boiler of a locomotive, and A' the frame thereof, which are supported upon six wheels, four of which, D D', are the driving-wheels. Directly above the axle of the forward driving-wheels D D standards B B are erected upon the frame A' on opposite sides of the boiler, and securely attached to this boiler by means of brackets G G or in any other suitable manner. The upper ends of the standards B B are provided with journal-boxes for a horizontal transverse crank-shaft, c, carrying cranks $d\ d$ on its ends, which are arranged at quarter strokes. To the wrist-pin of each crank two pitmen-rods, b and e, are connected. The pitmen-rods $e\ e$ are connected at quarter strokes to wrist-pins f on the outer faces of the driving-wheels D D, which latter are connected to the rear driving-wheels D' D' by means of rods $g\ g$ and wrist-pins $f\ f$. The pitmen-rods $b\ b$ are connected to piston-rods $a\ a$, the pistons of which work in steam-cylinders C C, whose axes if extended backward would intersect the axis of the crank-shaft c.

It will be seen from the above description that my improvement can be applied to well-known forms of locomotives by changing the position of the steam-cylinder beds and by addition of the crank-shaft c, the standards B B and the pitmen-rods $e\ e$. It will be seen that during the down strokes of the cranks $d\ d$ these cranks, in combination with the pitmen-rods $e\ e$, form toggle-joints and afford an advantageous mode of applying power to turn the wheels.

Having described my invention, what I claim as new is—

The combination of the pitmen-rods $e\ e\ b\ b$, crank-shaft c, frame B, and inclined cylinders C C, all arranged and operating on the driving-wheels D D, substantially as described.

WILLIAM D. ARNETT.

Witnesses:
VINCENT D. MARKHAM,
JOHN W. WEBSTER.

(94)

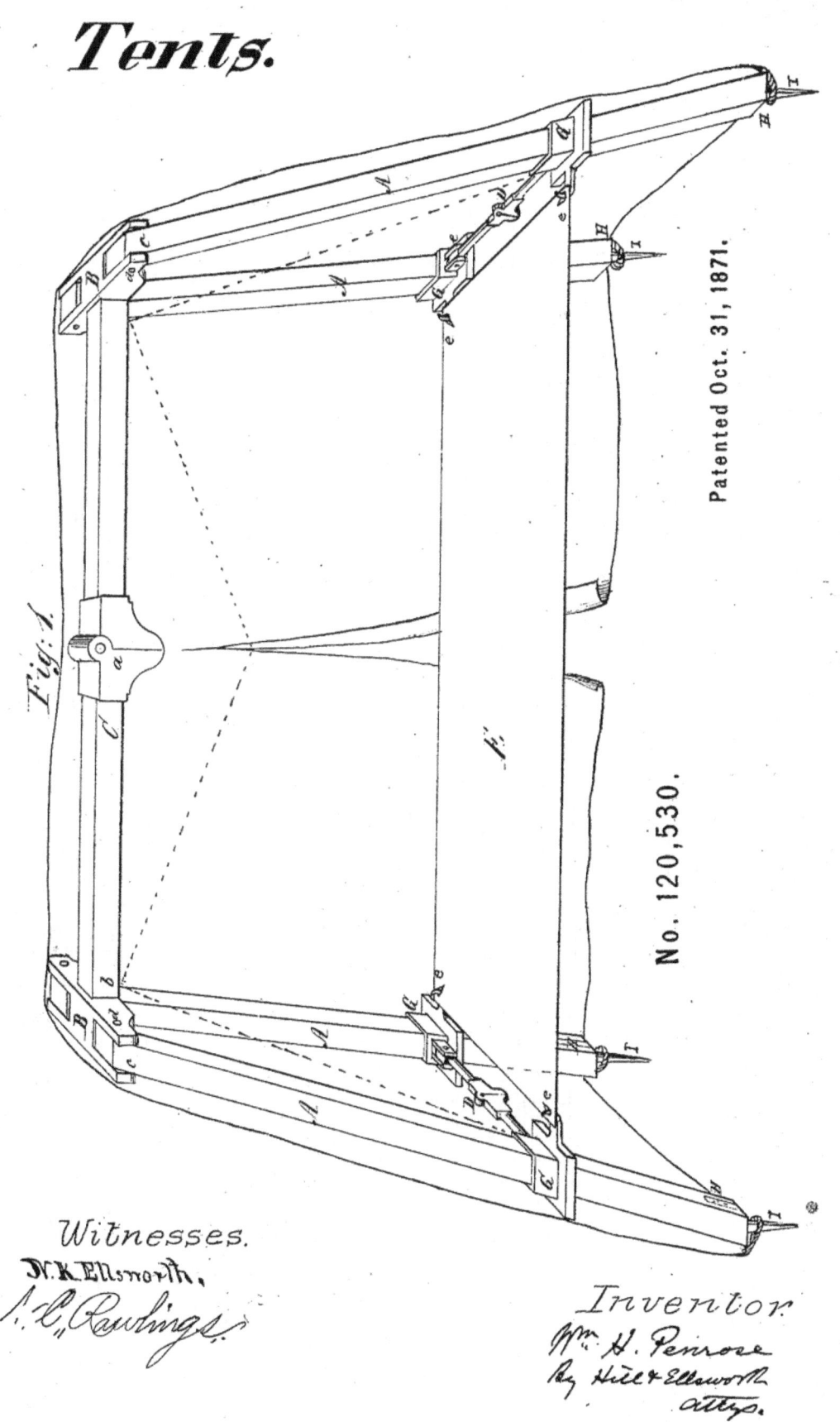

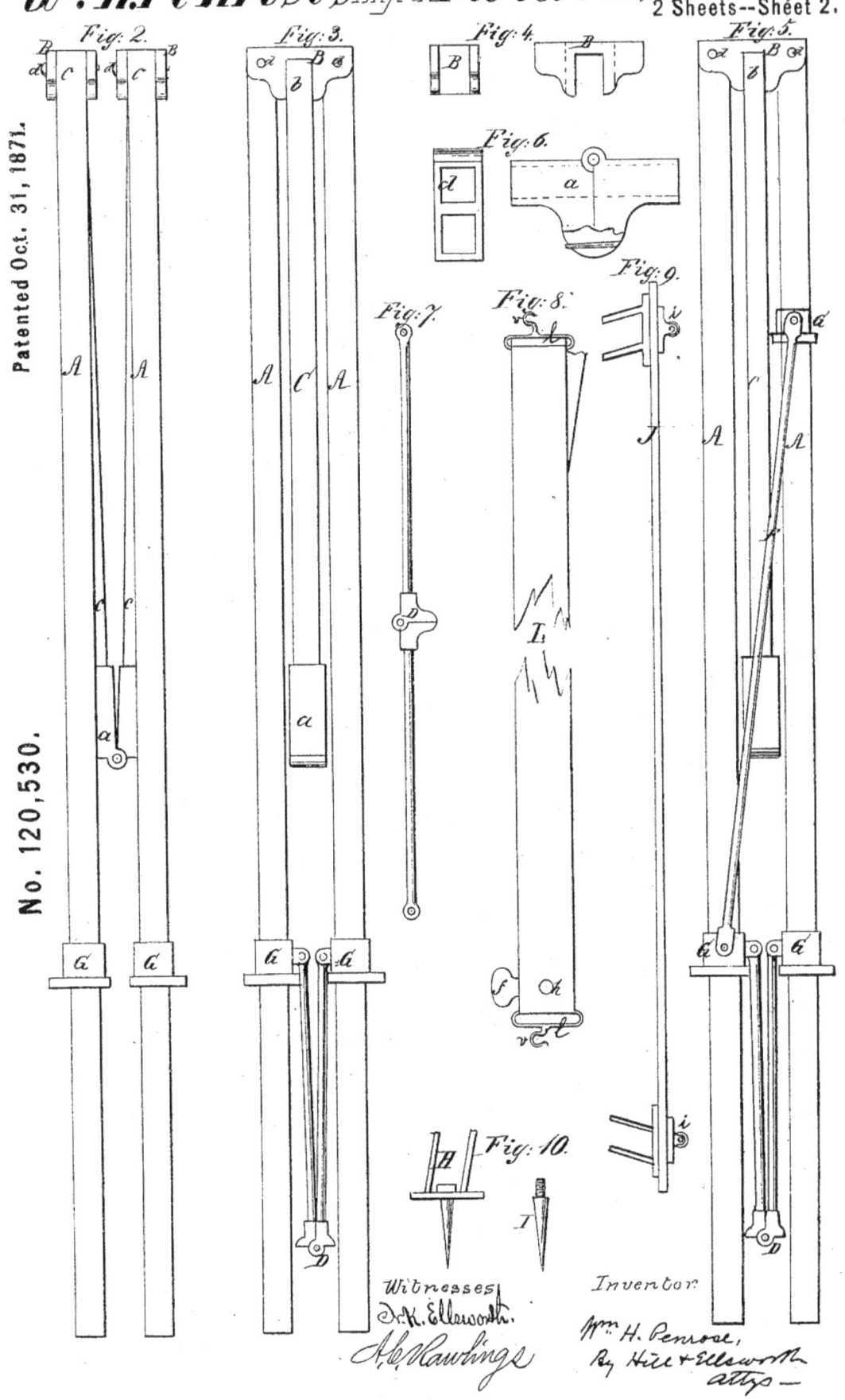

UNITED STATES PATENT OFFICE.

WILLIAM H. PENROSE, OF FORT LYON, COLORADO TERRITORY.

IMPROVEMENT IN COMBINED TENTS AND COTS.

Specification forming part of Letters Patent No. 120,530, dated October 31, 1871; antedated September 30, 1871.

To all whom it may concern:

Be it known that I, WILLIAM H. PENROSE, of Fort Lyon, Bent county, Colorado, have invented certain Improvements in Cots and Tents, of which the following is a specification, reference being had to the accompanying drawing forming part of this specification, in which—

Figure 1 is a perspective view, representing the bunk set up for use, the dotted lines indicating the position of the bipod before the bar C is extended. Fig. 2 is a side view of the bipod and the bar C folded. Fig. 3 is an end view of the same, with the bar D folded. Fig. 4 is a side view and an end view of the head-plate B. Fig. 5 is an end view of the bipod, with solid extension-bar F and jointed extension-bars C D. Fig. 6 is an end view and a side view of the hinge of the extension-bar C. Fig. 7 is a view of the extension-bar D. Fig. 8 is a section, showing each end of the air-sack, with the pillow, bellows, and air-tube. Fig. 9 is a view, showing the structure of the foot-bar and sockets when employed; and Fig. 10 is a view of the foot-socket with the pin inserted and also pin detached.

Similar letters of reference in the accompanying drawing indicate corresponding parts.

My invention consists in the construction of a combined portable field-cot and tent, and the adaptation of an air-cushion mattress for use in connection therewith, substantially as hereinafter described, the object of the whole being to promote the comfort, convenience, and health of the soldier, and to economize space, weight, material, and cost. To this end the invention consists in the several devices composing the cot, the tent, and the air-mattress, which I will now proceed to describe in detail.

The cot, bunk, or bedstead consists of four uprights, A A A A; two horizontal hinges or head-plates, B B, to which the uprights are articulated, as shown in Figs. 1, 2, 3, and 5; two lateral braces made to fold as shown at D, or in one rigid bar, as represented at F; one longitudinal folding-bar, C, provided with a locking-hinge, *a*; four or more thimbles, G G G G, fitting upon the standards A; and one sacking-bottom, E, of canvas or other suitable material, with eyes *e* adapted to catch over hooks upon the thimbles in order to hold the bed-bottom E, as shown in Fig. 1. In addition to these necessary parts there may be four foot-sockets, H I, constructed as shown in Fig. 10, to hold the feet of the standards A A in place, each one being composed of a socket, H, to receive the foot, and a pin, I, screwed into it to project down into the ground and keep the whole rigidly in position; or, instead of such arrangement, two foot-supporters, constructed as shown in Fig. 9, may be used, each consisting of a long bar, J, with a foot-socket, H, attached near each end; and, if preferred, a caster, *i*, underneath. The former construction is adapted to the field and the latter to the house.

The details of construction of all these parts will be readily understood from the drawing, which represents the apparatus, in Fig. 1, as set up and ready for use; and in Figs. 2, 3, and 5 as folded and ready for transportation or packing away. The hinges *a* are so constructed that when the bar C is extended the plates or leaves of the hinge will lock and hold the bar in that position. This result is easily effected by attaching a spring-catch to one leaf, adapted to hook over a shoulder on the other whenever the bar is fully extended; and preferably I construct the snap so as not to lock until the bar is arched a little, as seen in Fig. 1, in which case the bar supports the weight to better advantage, and has a tendency to press out the upper ends of the standards and keep the bottom E more tightly strained. The bars D, when employed, are jointed to fixed thimbles G, and are constructed very similarly to the bar C except that they may be made much smaller, and the snap-catch may be omitted. When the rigid bar D is substituted for the folding-bar F one end of it is pivoted to a fixed thimble and the other to a loose thimble sliding on the opposite leg of the bipod, so that, although the bar itself is inflexible, the legs can be folded up with it attached, as represented in Fig. 5. All the parts referred to may be made of any suitable materials, and molded or otherwise ornamented as the fancy may suggest. The tent is constructed as represented in Fig. 1, the frame being put together as above described, and a tent-cloth of suitable shape being thrown over it and secured at the corners by means of loops passing around the pins I. The air-mattress L is made of canvas covered with vulcanized rubber or otherwise rendered air-tight, and is about four inches thick, its length and width being adapted to the size of the occupant. The sack is furnished with an air-pillow, *f*, at one end connected internally with it, and also an escape-tube, *h*, and a bellows, *g*, for the purpose of readily and conveniently filling it. Thus constructed, it is supported by links *l l* at each end, terminating in hooks *v v*, adapted to secure the corners of the sack to the thimble G, leaving the whole body of the mattress clear of contact with anything beneath. Suitable hooks attached to the standards or the bar C by thimbles or otherwise, may be provided for gun-racks, and to hold knapsacks, clothing, &c., when in the field.

It is evident that the canvas bottom E or the air-sack L may be employed at pleasure, and that with either of them the apparatus may be used in the field as a tent or tent and bunk combined, while it can be used in-doors, in hospital buildings and elsewhere, simply as a bunk or bed, with or without curtains, as may be preferred by the occupant.

Having thus described my invention, what I claim as new therein, and desire to secure by Letters Patent, is—

1. The combination of the uprights A A, jointed to cap-plates B, with the folding-bar C, the thimbles G G, and the extension-bars articulated to the thimbles, and connecting the lower ends of the uprights, when constructed to operate substantially in the manner and for the purposes set forth.

2. The combination of the frame, above described, consisting of the parts A, B, C, D or F, and G with a bed-bottom supported by the thimbles G, substantially as described.

3. The combination of said frame with the bed-bottom E or L and the tent-cloth covering the whole, substantially as described.

WILLIAM H. PENROSE.

Witnesses:
SAMUEL T. HATCH,
CHARLES B. ADAMS.   (162)

(3.)

H. Bolthoff, Stamp Guides.

No. 121,985.

Patented Dec. 19, 1871.

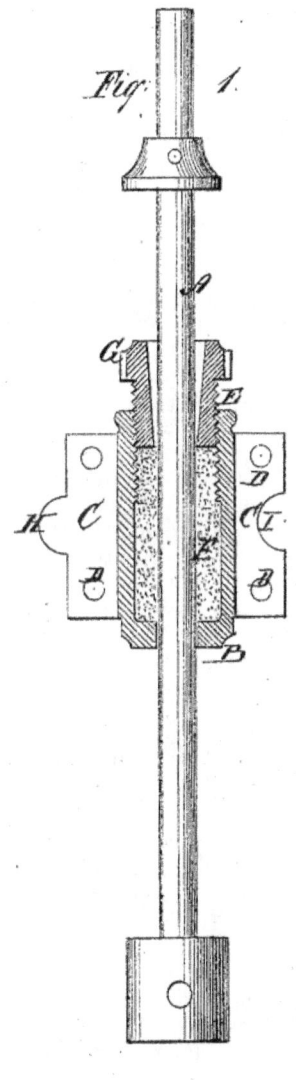

Fig. 1

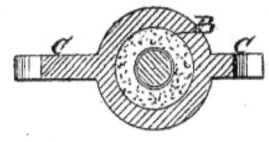

Fig. 2

Witnesses:
C. Raettig.
Wm. H. C. Smith.

Inventor:
H. Bolthoff.
per Wmm C.
Attorneys.

UNITED STATES PATENT OFFICE.

HENRY BOLTHOFF, OF CENTRAL CITY, COLORADO TERRITORY.

IMPROVEMENT IN STAMP-GUIDES.

Specification forming part of Letters Patent No. 121,985, dated December 19, 1871.

To all whom it may concern:

Be it known that I, HENRY BOLTHOFF, of Central City, in the county of Gilpin and Territory of Colorado, have invented a new and useful Improvement in Stamp-Guides; and I do hereby declare that the following is a full, clear, and exact description thereof, which will enable others skilled in the art to make and use the same, reference being had to the accompanying drawing forming part of this specification.

My invention consists in a new way of preventing the friction and expensive wear of stamp-stems upon their ordinary metal packing by interposing between the stem and guide any cheap elastic packing; by adjusting a follower to take up the wear; and by enabling them to mutually support one another, when arranged horizontally in a series by a peculiar construction, as hereinafter described and pointed out in the claim.

In the accompanying drawing, Figure 1 represents a longitudinal section of the guide with the stem and stamp in place. Fig. 2 is a cross-section of the guide.

Similar letters of reference indicate corresponding parts.

A is the stem. B is the guide, with wings C C projecting therefrom for bolting the guide to the timbers. D represents holes through the wings for the bolts. The body of the guide B is chambered out or made tubular for containing hemp or other elastic packing, and on its upper portion on the inside a screw-thread is cut, as seen in the drawing. E is the follower, which has a screw-thread which engages with the thread within the guide. F represents the packing, which is compressed around the stem by means of the screw-follower. G is a collar around the upper portion of the follower, which collar may be in any form for allowing the follower to be turned down by a wrench or otherwise. The inner portion of the follower is in the cup-form to allow of the introduction of oil or other lubricating material. The stem passes through the bottom of the chamber and through the follower loosely, so that the full bearing of the stem will be upon the packing.

When the packing is worn so that the stem has become loose, the follower is screwed down so as to compress the packing around it. New packing may be introduced from time to time, as occasion may require.

By this improvement on the guides for stems of stamping-mills the stems are protected from wearing against metallic surfaces, and are, consequently, rendered more durable than they have heretofore been.

It will be observed that one of the wings C has a projecting ear, H, and the other a cavity, I, of corresponding size and shape. This is for the purpose of having the wings fit into each other and be made self-supporting when a number of stamps are placed side by side.

Having thus described my invention, I claim as new and desire to secure by Letters Patent—

1. The combination of the stamp-guide B, filled with elastic packing F, with the threaded follower E, when constructed and arranged as and for the purpose set forth.

2. The combination, with the stamp-shaft A, of the guide B, having projection H and corresponding cavity I on the opposite sides of wings C C, as shown, and for the purpose specified.

HENRY BOLTHOFF.

Witnesses:
D. D. LAKE,
T. T. STOKES.

(3)

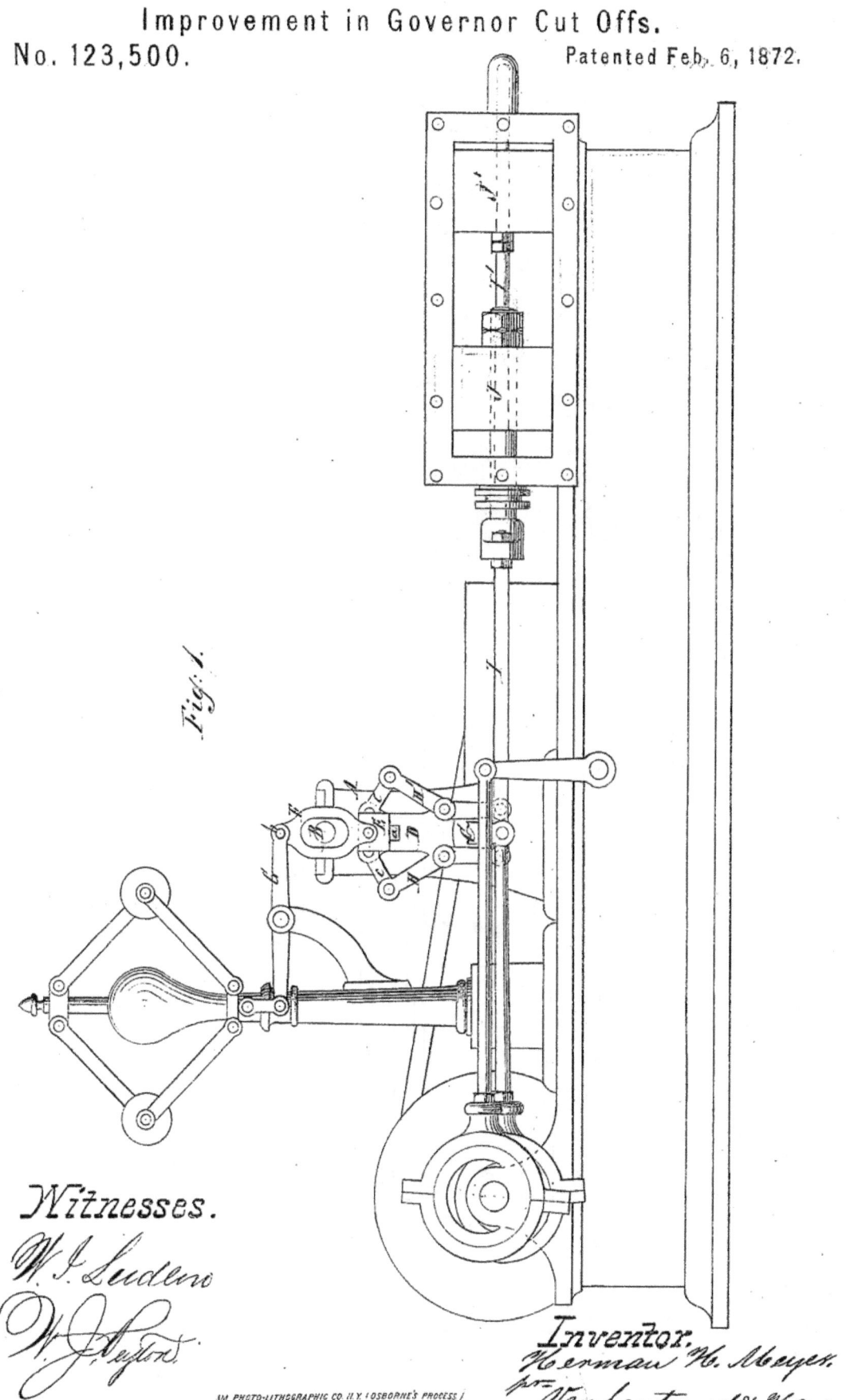

3 Sheets--Sheet 2.

H. H. MEYER.

Improvement in Governor Cut Offs.

No. 123,500. Patented Feb. 6, 1872.

Fig: 2.

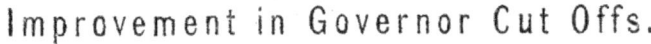

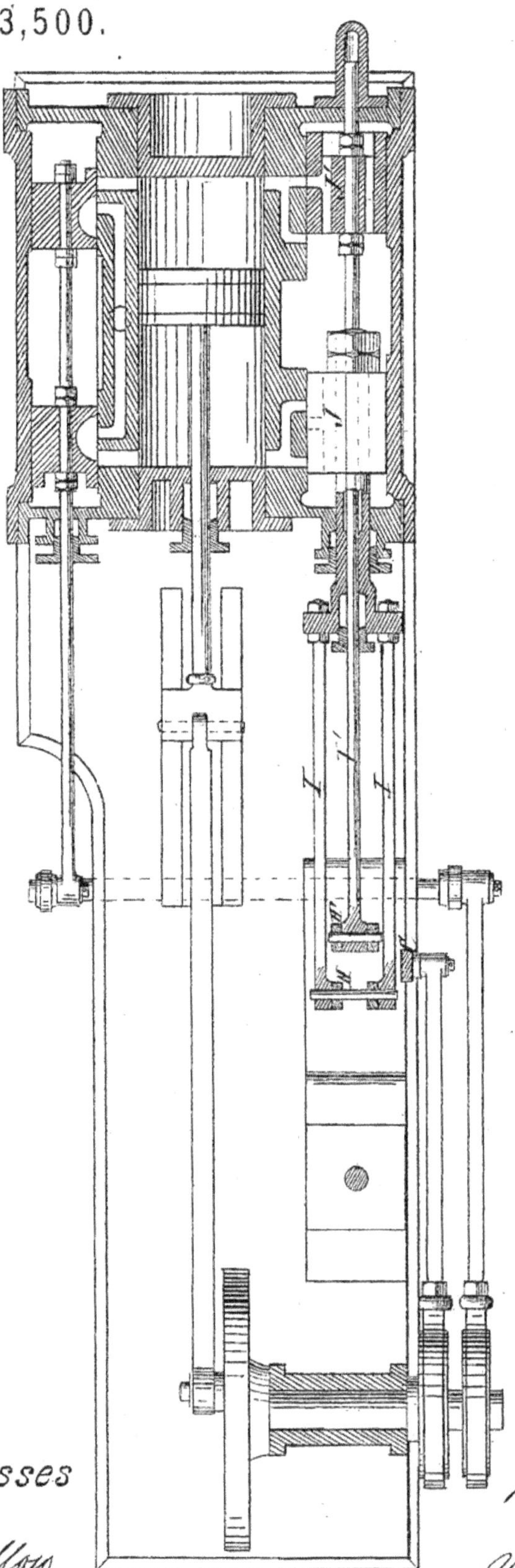

Witnesses

W. J. Ludlow

W. J. Peyton.

Inventor:

Herman H. Meyer.

per.

Van Santvoord & Hauff

Attys.

AM. PHOTO-LITHOGRAPHIC CO. N.Y. (OSBORNE'S PROCESS.)

H. H. MEYER.
Improvement in Governor Cut Offs.
No. 123,500. Patented Feb. 6, 1872.

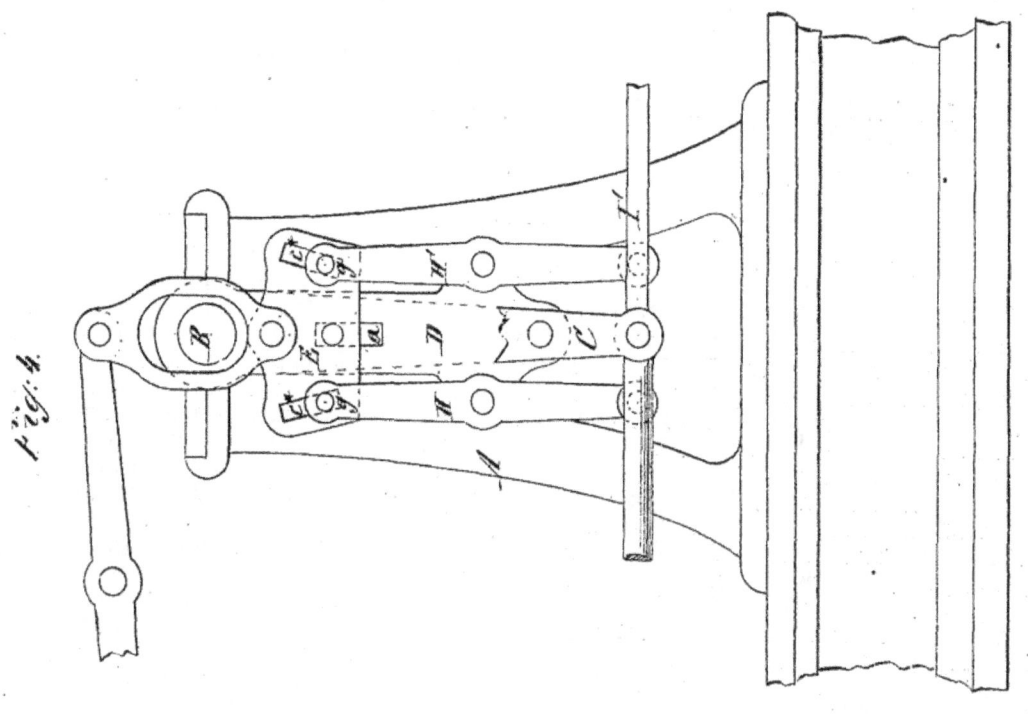

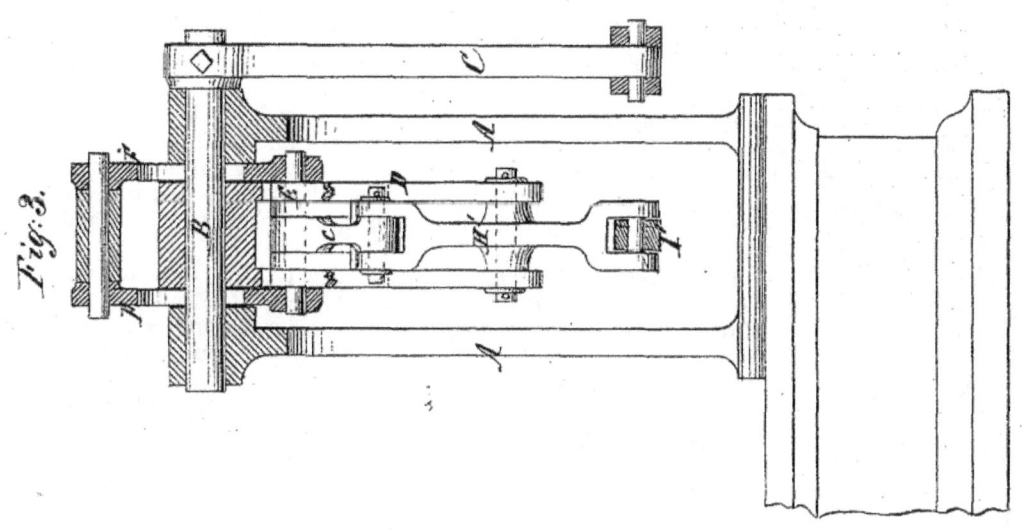

UNITED STATES PATENT OFFICE.

HERMAN H. MEYER, OF DENVER, COLORADO TERRITORY.

IMPROVEMENT IN GOVERNOR CUT-OFFS.

Specification forming part of Letters Patent No. 123,500, dated February 6, 1872.

To all whom it may concern:

Be it known that I, HERMAN H. MEYER, of Denver, in the county of Arapahoe, in the Territory of Colorado, have invented a new and useful Improvement in Governor Cut-Offs; and I do hereby declare the following to be a full, clear, and exact description thereof, which will enable those skilled in the art to make and use the same, reference being had to the accompanying drawing forming part of this specification, in which drawing—

Figure 1 represents a sectional front view of my cut-off mechanism, showing its connection with the governor and with the steam-valves of an engine. Fig. 2 is a sectional plan or top view of the same. Fig. 3 is a detached sectional rear view of my cut-off mechanism. Fig. 4 is a side view of a modification thereof.

Similar letters indicate corresponding parts.

This invention consists in the arrangement of a slide moving in guide-slots in a frame which is suspended from a rock-shaft, and which forms the bearings for the fulcrum-pins of two levers, connecting at their upper ends with the slide, and at their bottom ends with the steam-valve of an engine in such a manner that, by imparting to the rock-shaft an oscillating motion, the steam-valves receive the required motion to admit steam alternately at one and then at the opposite end of the cylinder, and by connecting the slide with the governor the steam-valves are moved toward or from each other, according to the speed of the engine, and steam is cut off sooner or later, as the governor dictates.

In the drawing, the letters A A designate two standards, which are secured to the frame of a steam-engine, as indicated in Fig. 1, and which form the bearings for a rock-shaft, B, on the end of which is mounted an arm, C, that connects with an eccentric on the crank-shaft, so as to impart to the rock-shaft the required oscillating motion. On this rock-shaft is also secured a pendent frame, D, the two side pieces of which are provided with slots a to receive a slide, E, which connects, by straps F, pivot b and lever G with the governor, as indicated in Fig. 1. The slide E connects, by links c, with levers H H', which have their fulcrums on pivots d, secured on opposite sides in the pendent frame D; and from the lower ends of these levers extend rods I I' to the steam-valves J J' of the engine. These steam-valves are situated on one side of the cylinder, while the exhaust-valves are situated on the opposite side thereof; and motion is imparted to said exhaust-valves by a separate eccentric.

This arrangement of the steam and exhaust valves forms no part of my present invention; but I prefer to use valves of such a construction that the pressure of the steam acting on them is balanced as near as practicable, so that said valves can be moved with the least possible friction.

The steam-valves J J', being connected to the levers H H', receive a reciprocating motion by the action of the eccentric, which imparts motion to the rock-shaft B, and said valves are so arranged that when the same are caused to close up steam is cut off from the cylinder at an earlier part of the stroke than when said valves are moved apart.

By referring to Figs. 1 and 3 of the drawing it will be seen that whenever the slide E is depressed the steam-valves are caused to close up, and when said slide is raised the steam-valves are moved apart.

The connection between the slide E and the governor is such that, when the balls of the governor fly out, the slide is depressed, and since, by this motion, the steam-valves are caused to close up, steam is cut off at an earlier part of the stroke than it is if the balls of the governor sink down, and, consequently, an automatic cut-off is obtained which regulates itself according to the changes in the speed of the engine.

In Figs. 1, 2, and 3 I have shown levers H H', which are connected to the slide E by means of links c; but the connection between the slide and said lever may be effected in different ways—such, for instance, as shown in Fig. 4, where the slide is provided with oblique slots c^* to act on pins g, which are secured in the upper ends of the levers H H'— and, by the action of these oblique slots on said pins, an oscillating motion is imparted to the levers H H' whenever the slide E is raised or depressed, and the steam-valves are closed up or moved apart, as previously explained.

What I claim as new, and desire to secure by Letters Patent, is—

The slide E, connected to the governor of a steam-engine and moving in a pendent frame, D, mounted on a rock-shaft, B, which receives an oscillating motion from the main shaft of the engine, in combination with levers H H', which have their fulcrums in the pendent frame D and connect with the steam-valves and with said slide, substantially in the manner and for the purpose herein shown and described.

HERMAN HENRY MEYER.

Witnesses:
JOHN W. WEBSTER,
F. JENSEN.

A. J. GILL.

Improvement in Hooks for Wire Fences.

No. 124,349.   Patented March 5, 1872.

124,349

UNITED STATES PATENT OFFICE.

ANDREW J. GILL, OF DENVER, COLORADO TERRITORY, ASSIGNOR TO F. A. CLARK, OF SAME PLACE.

IMPROVEMENT IN HOOKS FOR WIRE-FENCES.

Specification forming part of Letters Patent No. 124,349, dated March 5, 1872.

To all whom it may concern:

Be it known that I, ANDREW J. GILL, of the city of Denver, in the county of Arapahoe and Territory of Colorado, have invented a certain new and useful Improvement in Wire-Hooks for Fences.

My invention consists in providing the ends of the arms of the hook upon each side with a projection, around which the wire is bent; and I do hereby declare that the following specification, taken in connection with the drawing furnished, to be a full, clear, and exact description thereof.

Referring to the drawing, the figure represents a perspective view of one of my improved hooks with the wire in position.

A represents the body or shank of the hook proper. B and B′ are the two arms of the hook. Upon the outer end of each of these arms there is formed a double projection, C C′. The shank of the hook is also provided with a pin, D, by means of which it may be attached to the fence-post.

It will be perceived that, by reason of the projections C C′ upon the ends of the arms, the hook may properly be termed a "double hook." It is attached to the post in a horizontal position; and when the wire is fastened it is passed either from above or below the arms B B′, and bent around the projections in the manner shown in the drawing.

Before my invention numerous hooks and studs have been devised for holding the wire of fences, but, in almost every instance, after a wire has been once tightened, the hook has failed to prevent it from sliding back and forth on the shank, and consequently the wire is frequently loosened. To remedy this defect it has been found necessary to employ various wire-tightening devices in connection with the studs. With a hook provided with the double projections C C′, as shown, the wire is held firmly, and it is impossible for it to slide upon the shank.

Having thus described my invention, I claim as new, and desire to secure by Letters Patent—

A wire hook for fences, the arms of which are provided with the double projections C C′, substantially as and for the purpose described.

ANDREW J. GILL.

Witnesses:
E. G. MATTHEWS,
EDWARD A. RESOR.

JOHN EVANS.
Improvement in Ships' Berths.

No. 125,729. Patented April 16, 1872.

Fig. 1.

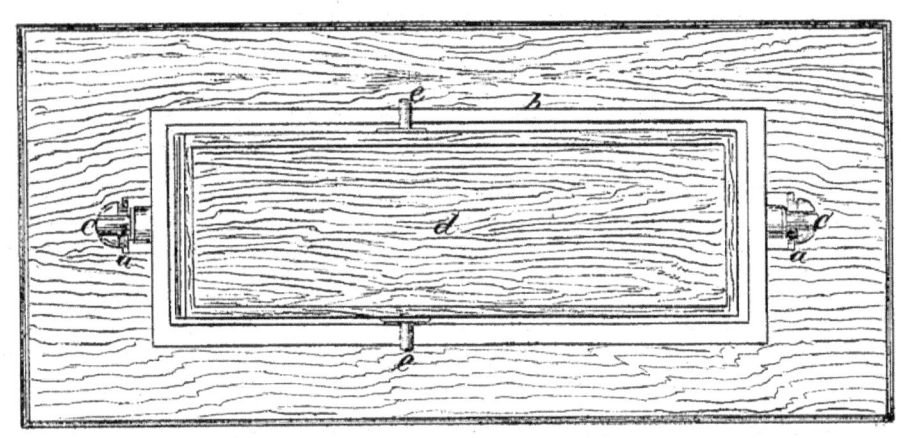

Fig. 2.

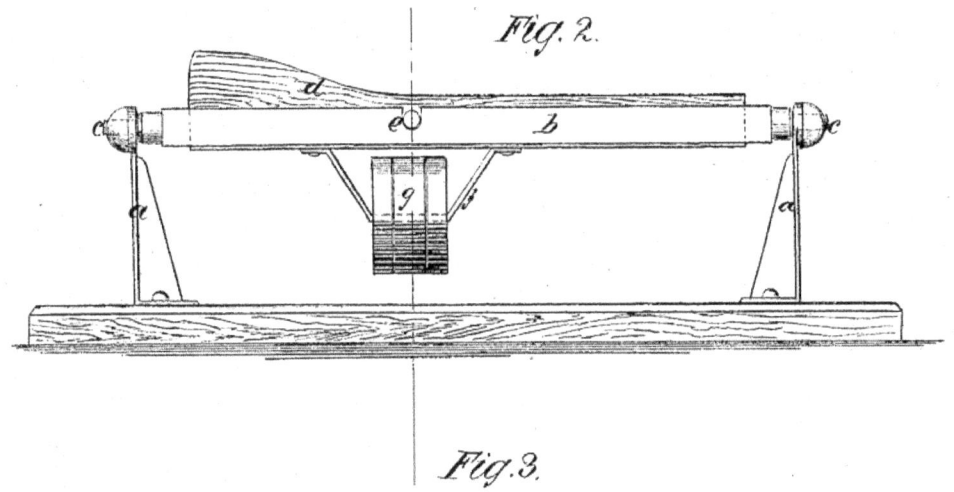

Fig. 3.

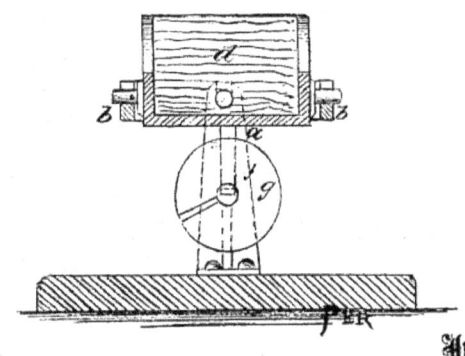

Witnesses:
John Becker.
Alex F. Roberts

Inventor:
John Evans
Attorneys.

UNITED STATES PATENT OFFICE.

JOHN EVANS, OF DENVER, COLORADO TERRITORY.

IMPROVEMENT IN SHIPS' BERTHS.

Specification forming part of Letters Patent No. 125,729, dated April 16, 1872.

Specification describing a new and useful Improvement in Apparatus for Supporting Beds, Couches, and Chairs in Steam-Ships and other vessels, invented by JOHN EVANS, of Denver, in the county of Arapahoe, Colorado.

The invention will be first fully described and then clearly pointed out in the claim.

Figure 1 is a plan or top view of a bed supported by my improved apparatus. Fig. 2 is a side elevation of the same. Fig. 3 is a transverse section on the line $x\,x$, Fig. 1.

Like letters indicate the same parts throughout the drawing.

$a\,a$ are two upright frames or standards, of iron or other suitable material, which may be screwed or otherwise securely attached to the floor or other convenient part of the vessel. These standards form a convenient means for supporting my apparatus; but I may sometimes use brackets, attached to the sides of the room, or other suitable means of support. b is a metal or other frame, provided at its ends with trunnions or journals c, which support the said frame in the standards a. The said frame b, at or near its center, supports the box or case d, which is also provided with trunnions or journals e for this purpose. The length of the frame b must be so adapted to that of the box or case that, without occupying unnecessary space, the latter will have room to swing freely in the said frame. This box or case, which is preferably made of wood, (although other materials may be used, if found more convenient,) contains the bed; and it will be seen, by reference to Figs. 2 and 3, that the occupant of the same will be nearly level with the four points of suspension, and will, therefore, as the vessel rolls or pitches, simply rise and descend with very slight, if any, oscillating motion. The said case or box has projecting down from its bottom a ballast-holder, f, in which I place any required number of weights, g. To effect the desired object—viz., the maintenance of the horizontal position of the bed without swinging the same below the points of suspension of the apparatus—the weight of the ballast must be sufficient to bring the center of gravity of the entire apparatus, with its occupant, considerably below the said points of suspension; and the proper amount of ballast to do this, without rendering the apparatus unnecessarily heavy, may be readily ascertained by adding to the ballast till the required stability of the apparatus is obtained. Then, throughout all the movements of the vessel in the roughest weather, the bed will remain horizontal, or nearly so, and the occupant will enjoy a rest and relief which would otherwise be unattainable.

I am aware that tables and compasses have been adjusted on shipboard upon the same principle as that employed by me—namely, by hinge-joints at right angles to each other; but my object has been, while availing myself of this principle, to get a compact and simple device which would economize the space that is now so important a matter on vessels and steamers. I also provide for adjustable weights, by which, if a child or light person occupies the berth, some weight may be taken off; otherwise there would be an unnecessary swing and an unpleasant vibration.

Having thus described my invention, what I claim as new, and desire to protect by Letters Patent, is—

The berth or bed supporter of a ship or steamer, consisting of the frame b, having trunnions $c\,c$ resting in standards $a\,a$; the case d, having journals $e\,e$ arranged in bearings upon the frame b; and the series of weights g, suspended, as and for the purpose set forth.

JOHN EVANS.

Witnesses:
T. B. MOSHER,
GEO. W. MABEE.

JAMES W. CUMINGS.

Improvement in Ore-Crushers.

No. 126,034. Patented April 23, 1872.

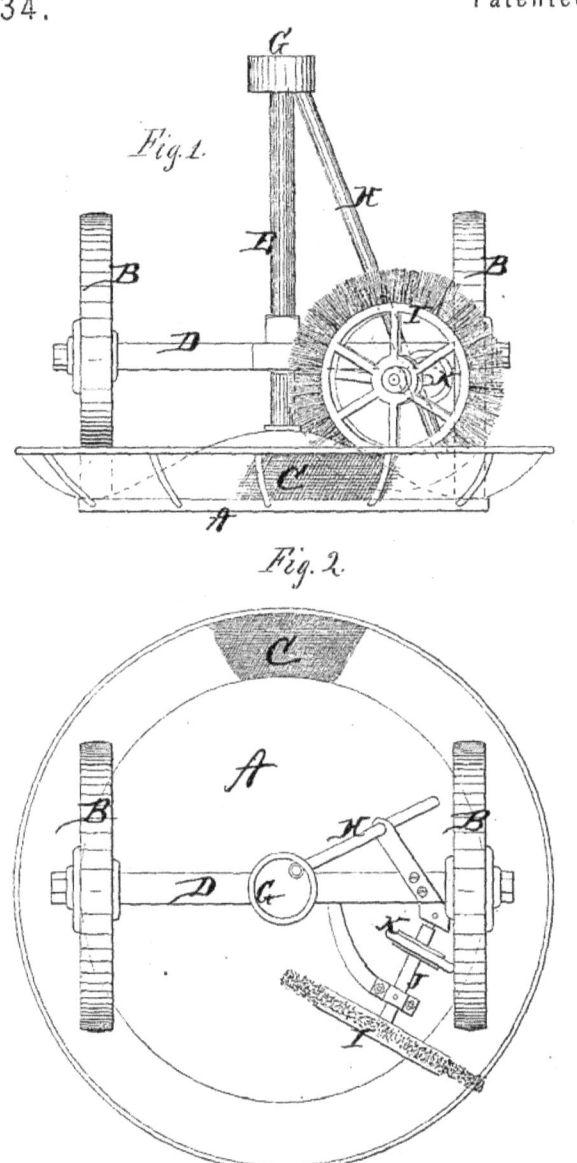

126,034

UNITED STATES PATENT OFFICE.

JAMES W. CUMINGS, OF GEORGETOWN, COLORADO TERRITORY.

IMPROVEMENT IN ORE-CRUSHERS.

Specification forming part of Letters Patent No. 126,034, dated April 23, 1872; antedated April 10, 1872.

To all whom it may concern:

Be it known that I, JAMES W. CUMINGS, of Georgetown, in the county of Clear Creek and Territory of Colorado, have invented certain new and useful Improvements in Machines for Pulverizing Ores and other substances; and do hereby declare the following to be a full, clear, and exact description thereof, reference being had to the accompanying drawing and to the letters of reference marked thereon.

My invention is intended as an improvement on a mill known as the "Chillian quartz-mill;" and it consists, first, in adding one or more feed-pipes, one end of each of which shall be attached to a rotary-feed hopper placed over and attached to a perpendicular or upright driving-shaft, and the other end extending down immediately in front and partly under a crushing or grinding wheel, in such a manner that it travels around with the shaft, and continually distributes material to be ground directly in front of said wheel, and on the concave surface of the pan; second, in a revolving wheel furnished with brushes or scrapers set nearly at right angles with said crushing or grinding wheel, and adjusted in such a manner that it may follow said wheel around the circle, and continually sweep or scrape the pulverized material from the concave surface of the pan on to a screen, as will be hereinafter described; third, in a concavo-convex screen extending around the outside periphery of the pan, and set or adjusted to the part of a circle corresponding with the circle traveled by the rotary brush, in such a manner that it may screen the material swept on by the brush, by allowing the part which is sufficiently fine to pass through the meshes, and at the same time furnishing a sufficient incline to allow the coarse or unground portion to roll back by the force of gravity on to the concave surface of the pan to be reground.

In order to enable others skilled in the art to which my invention appertains to make and use the same, I will now proceed to describe its construction and operation, referring to the annexed drawing which forms a part of this specification, and in which—

Figure 1 is a side elevation, and Fig. 2 is a plan view of a mill with my improvements attached.

A represents a circular pan, having a raised convex center, and along the outer edge it is concave, forming, as it were, a circular trough, in which the crushing-wheels B B move. Along the outer edge of the pan A is attached a concave screen, C, of suitable fineness to allow only the ore crushed sufficiently fine to pass through. This screen, though concave, is raised upward from the point of attachment to the pan, so that the coarse part of the ore coming on the same will be enabled by its gravity to fall back into the trough or track for the crushing-wheels. These wheels B B are mounted upon the ends of a horizontal axle, D, which is attached in the center in any suitable manner to an upright shaft, E, rising from the center of the pan A. On top of this shaft is placed a feed-hopper, G, which revolves with the shaft. From this hopper one or more feed-pipes, H, extend down in front and partly under the crushing or grinding wheel B. These feed-pipes being suitably braced or connected with the axle D, travel around with the same, and continually distribute material to be crushed or ground directly in front of the wheels, and on the concave surface of the pan. I represents a wheel provided with brushes or scrapers, and mounted upon a shaft, J, having its bearings in braces or arms attached to the axle D, in such a manner that the wheel I will be set nearly at right angles with the crushing-wheel, and follow said wheel around the circle. The wheel I is revolved by a friction-wheel, K, upon the shaft J, bearing against the side of the crushing-wheel, whereby said wheel I will continually sweep or scrape the pulverized material from the concave surface of the pan A to the screen C.

Having thus fully described my invention, what I claim as new, and desire to secure by Letters Patent, is—

1. The revolving feed-pipe or pipes, H, in combination with the rollers B and revolving brush I, in a mill for pulverizing ores or other substances, substantially as set forth.

2. The rotating wheel I provided with a

brush or scraper, in combination with the concavo-convex screen C and crushing-rollers B, arranged to operate as and for the purposes set forth.

3. The concavo-convex screen C extending around the outside of the pan, as shown, in combination with the crushing-rollers B B, arranged to operate substantially as herein set forth.

JAMES W. CUMINGS.

Witnesses:
 EDWIN GRIBBLE,
 C. D. WILLIAMS.

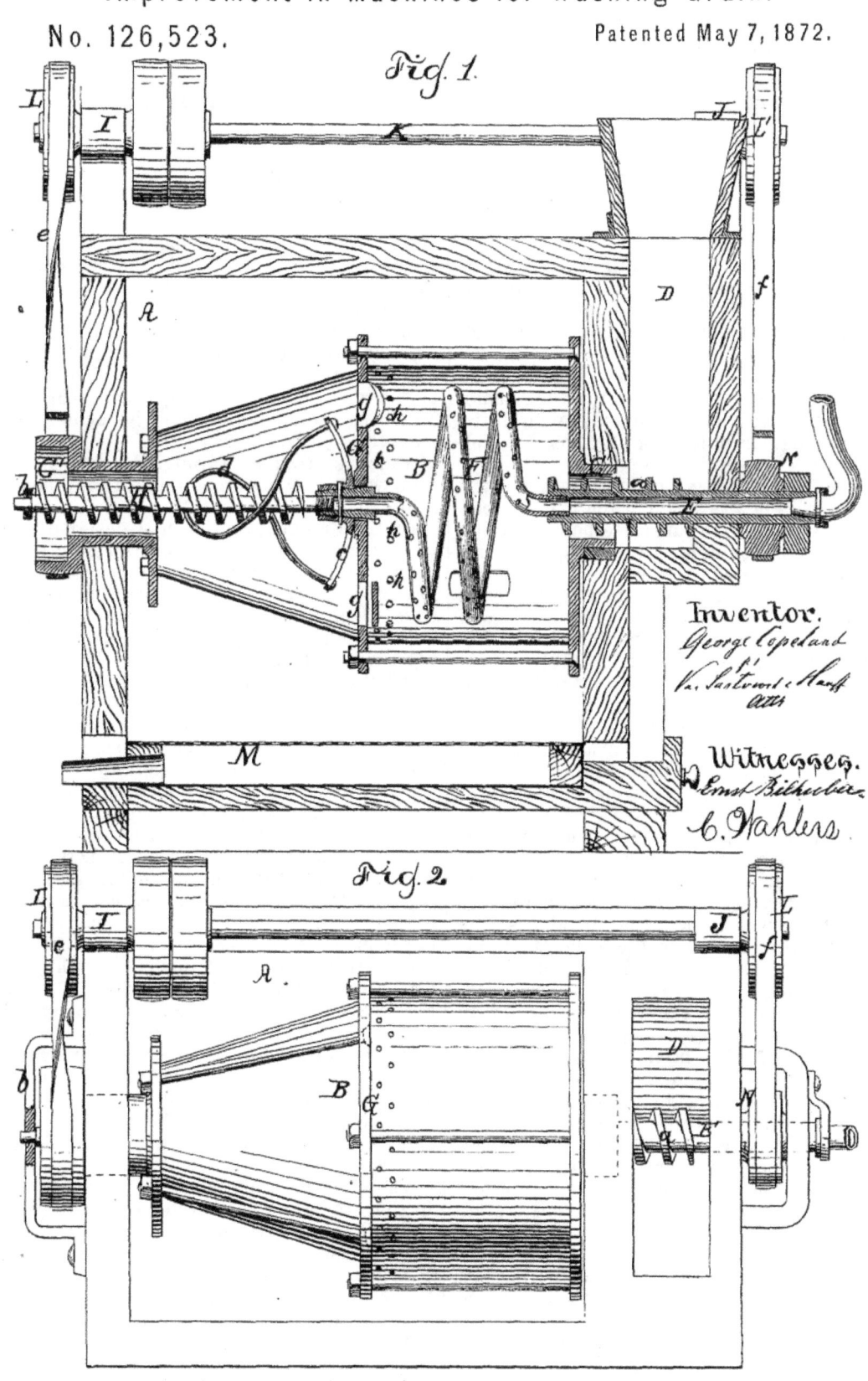

UNITED STATES PATENT OFFICE.

GEORGE COPELAND, OF DENVER, COLORADO TERRITORY.

IMPROVEMENT IN MACHINES FOR WASHING GRAIN.

Specification forming part of Letters Patent No. 126,523, dated May 7, 1872.

To all whom it may concern:

Be it known that I, GEORGE COPELAND, of Denver, in the county of Arapahoe, Territory of Colorado, have invented a new and Improved Machine for Washing Grain; and I do hereby declare the following to be a full, clear, and exact description thereof, which will enable those skilled in the art to make and use the same, reference being had to the accompanying drawing forming part of this specification, in which drawing—

Figure 1 is a vertical central section of my machine. Fig. 2 is a plan or top view thereof.

Similar letters indicate corresponding parts.

This invention relates to an apparatus for thoroughly cleaning grain, and especially wheat, just before grinding, so as to free it from all impurities, and to produce a good quality of flour from an inferior wheat. My invention consists in a cylinder, revolving in a box or frame on hollow gudgeons or journals, through which the grain is forced into the cylinder by means of a spirally-wound blade or flange arranged on a hollow shaft within said gudgeon, and directly beneath the hopper or supply-opening of the machine. From said hollow shaft, and within the cylinder, extends a perforated coiled pipe, into which water is passed through said shaft, and which is caused to revolve in an opposite direction to that of the cylinder, so as to agitate and thoroughly scour the wheat by means of the water issuing from the perforations in the same, the water being permitted to pass off through perforations in the cylinder. The cylinder has a partition or diaphragm through the center, with two or more openings, through which the grain passes after having been thoroughly washed, said openings being provided with gates to open and close them for the purpose of controlling the flow of its contents, as some grain needs more washing than others. The partition forms a bearing for the coiled pipe, which extends through the same and connects with a discharge-screw which serves to force the grain through the hollow gudgeon on the delivery end of the cylinder, which tapers down toward its delivery end in the form of a truncated cone. The water issuing from the coiled perforated pipe within the cylinder is thrown in among the grain by centrifugal force, the pipe revolving in an opposite direction to that of the cylinder, and receiving its motion from a belt connected with a pulley on one end of the driving-shaft of the machine, on the opposite end of which is mounted a similar pulley, from which extends a belt which passes over a pulley formed on the outer end of the hollow gudgeon of the cylinder on the discharge end of the machine, so as to impart to said cylinder the required motion. The cylinder is mounted in a box or frame, in the lower part of which is arranged a trough to receive the dirty water flowing from the perforations of said cylinder.

In the drawing, the letter A designates a box or frame, in which is mounted horizontally a cylinder or drum, B, by means of hollow gudgeons or journals C C' arranged on the ends of the same. Through the hollow gudgeon C, and beneath the hopper D, passes a pipe, E, to which is connected a hose, from which it receives water. On the pipe E I have wound spirally a blade or flange, a, which serves to carry the grain entering through the hopper D into the cylinder B. To the inner end of pipe E is secured a perforated spiral pipe, F, which coils around within the cylinder B, and thence passes through a partition or diaphragm, G, arranged within the same, and it connects with a discharge-screw, H, which extends through the hollow gudgeon C', and has its bearing in a bridge, b, secured to the end of the frame A. From that portion of the pipe F which passes through the partition G extends a curved blade, c, to which is attached a curved or twisted wire, d, which aids in discharging the grain. On the top end of the frame A are mounted the journals I J, which form the bearings for the driving-shaft K, on one end of which is mounted the pulley L, which imparts motion to the cylinder by means of a belt, e, and on the opposite end a similar pulley, L', which connects with a pulley, N, on the pipe F by means of a belt, f.

The grain entering the hopper D is taken up by the screw a and carried into the cylinder D, where it is subjected to the action of the water issuing from the perforations in the coiled pipe F, which revolves in an opposite direction to that of the cylinder B, and thereby throws the water in among the grain with great force. Having been thoroughly washed, the grain passes through openings g in the diaphragm

G (which are formed by punching up the metal, and provided with gates so that they can be opened or closed as desired,) into the delivery end of the cylinder, where it is thrown forward by the curved wire d, and taken up by the discharge-screw H, and thence passes out of the machine.

The dirty water discharges from the cylinder B through perforations $h\ h$, or by any other desirable means, such as, for instance, a wire-gauze or a continuous wire round the cylinder. In the lower part of the box or frame A I have provided a trough, M, which receives the dirty water issuing from the cylinder.

It is obvious that the cylinder may be placed either in a vertical or horizontal position, as desired.

What I claim as new, and desire to secure by Letters Patent, is—

1. The cylinder B, mounted on the hollow gudgeons C C' within the box or frame A, and provided with perforations h for discharging the water, in combination with the spiral water-pipe F, substantially as described.

2. The partition or diaphragm G, arranged within the cylinder B, and provided with gates g which can be opened or closed, as described.

3. The spiral blade a on the water-pipe E for carrying the grain into the cylinder B, in combination with the discharge-screw H for discharging the grain, substantially as set forth.

4. The combination of the driving-shaft K with the hollow gudgeon C', pulley N, cylinder B, coiled pipe F, and discharge-screw H, substantially as described.

5. The combination of the box A, cylinder B, hopper D, and trough M with the feed-screw a, coiled pipe F, and discharge-screw H, as set forth.

GEORGE COPELAND.

Witnesses:
  PERCY B. SMITH,
  GILBERT STANLEY.

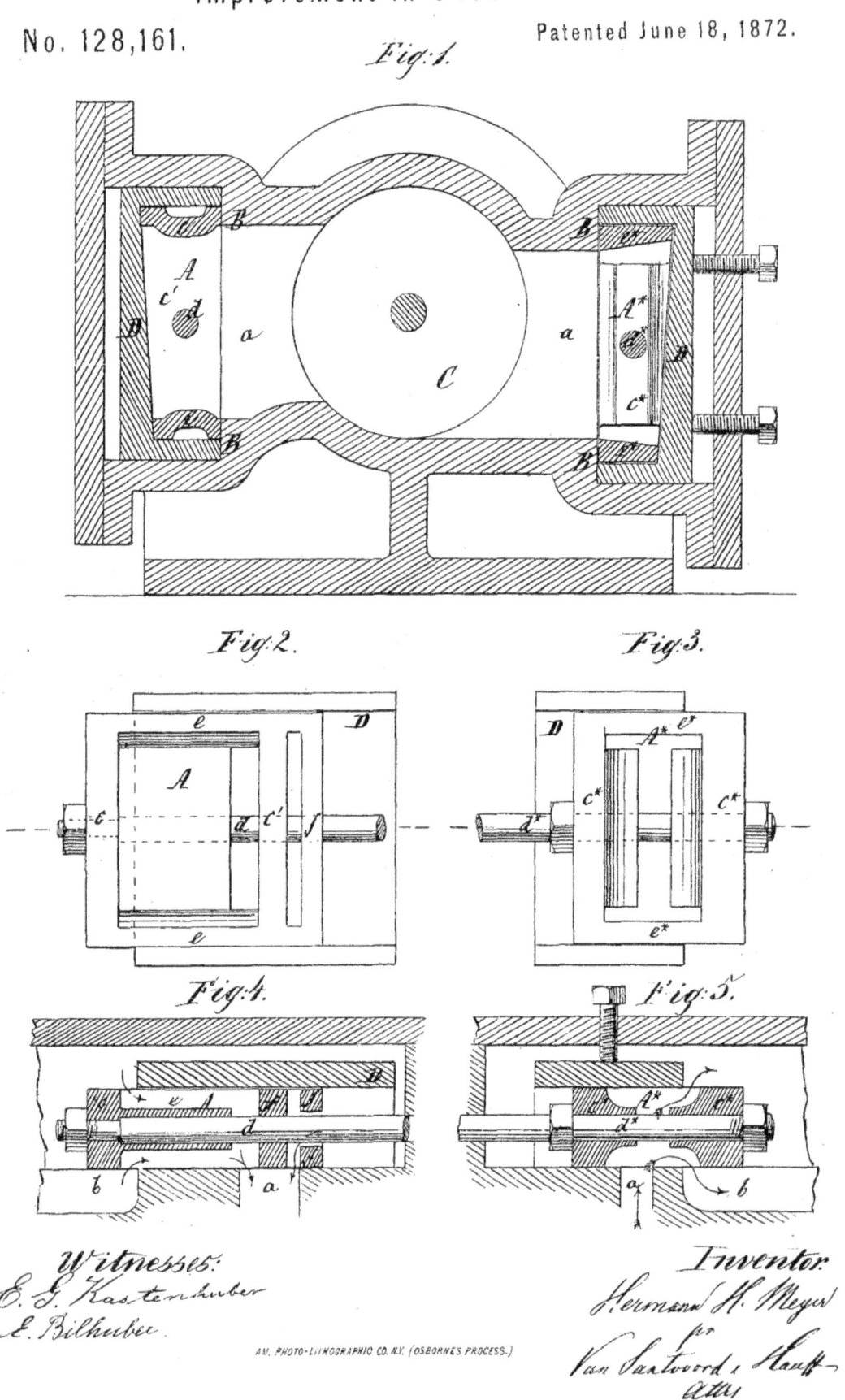

UNITED STATES PATENT OFFICE.

HERMAN H. MEYER, OF DENVER, COLORADO.

IMPROVEMENT IN SLIDE-VALVES.

Specification forming part of Letters Patent No. 128,161, dated June 18, 1872.

To all whom it may concern:

Be it known that I, HERMAN H. MEYER, of Denver, in the county of Arapahoe and Territory of Colorado, have invented a new and useful Improvement in Steam-Valves; and I do hereby declare the following to be a full, clear, and exact description thereof, which will enable those skilled in the art to make and use the same, reference being had to the accompanying drawing forming part of this specification, in which drawing—

Figure 1 represents a transverse section of a steam-cylinder, showing two modifications of my valve, one being used as the steam-valve, and the other as the exhaust-valve. Figs. 2 and 3 are inverted plan views of said two modifications of my valve. Figs. 4 and 5 are longitudinal sections of the same.

Similar letters indicate corresponding parts.

This invention relates to a steam-valve which opens two or more passages to one port, and which is wedge-shaped, and provided with a correspondingly wedge-shaped cover, fitting closely to the valve on three sides in such a manner that by my valve the freedom of the passage of the steam to or from the cylinder is insured; and, furthermore, by the wedge-shaped cover the valve is relieved from the pressure of the steam on its back, and if the valve wears it wears tight, the wedge-shaped cover having a tendency to keep the same close up to its seat.

In the drawing, the letter A designates a valve, which is set edgewise, as shown in Fig. 1, and which moves on the vertical seat B. In this seat is a port, a, which leads into the cylinder C; and said seat is also provided with a depression, b, (see Figs. 4 and 5,) so that when the valve is brought to the position shown in these figures steam passes through the body of the valve to or from the port a in the manner indicated by the arrows. The body of the valve A consists of two heads, c c', through which extends the valve-rod d, and which are connected by the sides e, (see Fig. 2.(These sides extend somewhat beyond the head c', and between them are secured two cross-bars f, f, Fig. 4, whereby the bearing-surface of the valve is increased without reducing the area of its steam-passages.

My valve may, however, be also constructed as shown at A* in Figs. 1, 3, and 5. By referring to Figs 3 and 5 it will be seen that this valve A* is composed of two heads, c^* c^*, in which is secured the valve-rod d^*, and if this valve is brought in the position shown in Fig. 5 the steam passes through the same, as indicated by the arrows.

The valve A or A* is made wedge-shaped, (see Fig. 1,) and over it is fitted a cover, D, fitting the same closely on three sides, the top of said cover being inclined to fit the back of the valve. By these means the valve is relieved from back pressure, and as it wears downward the inclined top of the cover will keep it at all times close up to its seat, so that it will work steam-tight for a long time.

In constructing my valve I first plane and scrape its back and both edges; then I plane the three inner sides of the cover, and fit it over the valve; and, finally, the cover and valve are planed and scraped together on the face to fit on the seat. The cover is held in position by set-screws or in any other desirable manner.

What I claim as new, and desire to secure by Letters Patent, is—

The wedge-shaped valve A, composed of two heads with cross-bars or strips, f f', in combination with an adjustable cover, D, fitting the same closely on three sides, constructed and arranged substantially as shown and described.

HERMAN H. MEYER.

Witnesses:
F. JENSEN,
JOHN W. WEBSTER.

W. D. ARNETT.
Improvement in Spark-Arresters for Locomotives.
No. 128,841. Patented July 9, 1872.

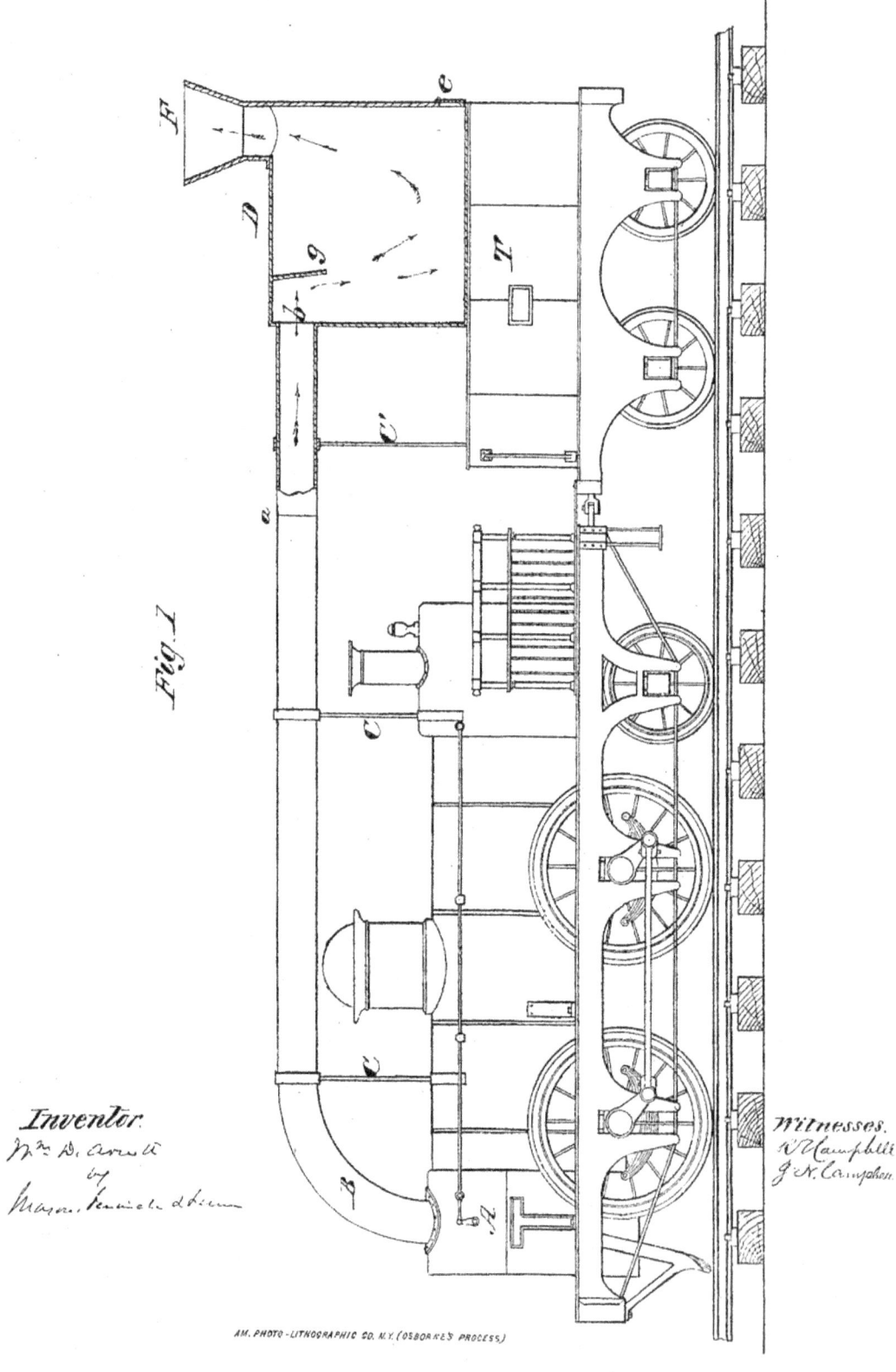

UNITED STATES PATENT OFFICE.

WILLIAM D. ARNETT, OF DENVER, COLORADO TERRITORY.

IMPROVEMENT IN SPARK-ARRESTERS FOR LOCOMOTIVES.

Specification forming part of Letters Patent No. 128,841, dated July 9, 1872.

To all whom it may concern:

Be it known that I, WILLIAM D. ARNETT, of Denver, in the county of Arapahoe and Territory of Colorado, have invented a new and Improved Spark-Arrester for Locomotive-Engines; and I do hereby declare that the following is a full, clear, and exact description thereof, reference being had to the accompanying drawing making part of this specification, in which—

Figure 1 is a side elevation of a locomotive and tender, showing my improved spark-arrester, partly in section.

The following description of my invention will enable others skilled in the art to understand it.

In the accompanying drawing I have represented a spark-arresting trap or receiver, D, arranged upon a locomotive-tender; but this trap may be supported upon the locomotive or upon trucks of its own. From the smoke-box A of the locomotive a pipe, B, extends backward and communicates at b with the interior of the trap D. This pipe B is supported upon the locomotive by means of rods C C, and upon the tender T by means of a rod, C'. This pipe B should be jointed at a so as to afford it all the flexibility required, and to allow the separation of the tender from the locomotive when this is necessary. The spark receiver or trap D may be rectangular or of any other desirable shape. It is provided with a smoke stack, F, a deflecting-plate, g, and also openings e, which latter are closed by means of doors or slides. The smoke-stack F will afford all the draught required for the locomotive-furnace, it being aided by the exhaust steam which escapes into the smoke-box A. The deflecting-plate g is arranged opposite the rear terminus of the pipe B, and directs the sparks and cinders down upon the bottom of the trap, from which they can be removed from time to time through the openings e. Instead of allowing the steam from the cylinders to exhaust into the smoke-box A, as is usual, the exhaust may be made directly into the receiver D.

I do not claim a spark-arrester constructed as shown in the patent granted to Charles B. Keyes June 19, 1866, nor one constructed as shown in the application of H. Fairchild, rejected September 12, 1866; but

What I do claim as my invention, and desire to secure by Letters Patent, is—

The combination of the pipe B, rising from the fire-box and running back above the engine, with the water tank or box D, which has the deflector g near to the front of the box and directly opposite the passage of said pipe B, and has the smoke-stack arranged in rear of said plate above the said passage, all in the manner shown and described, whereby the sparks are effectually deflected into the tank and at the same time a powerful draught maintained, as set forth.

WILLIAM D. ARNETT.

Witnesses:
WM. M. B. SARELL,
EDWARD L. BERTHOUD.

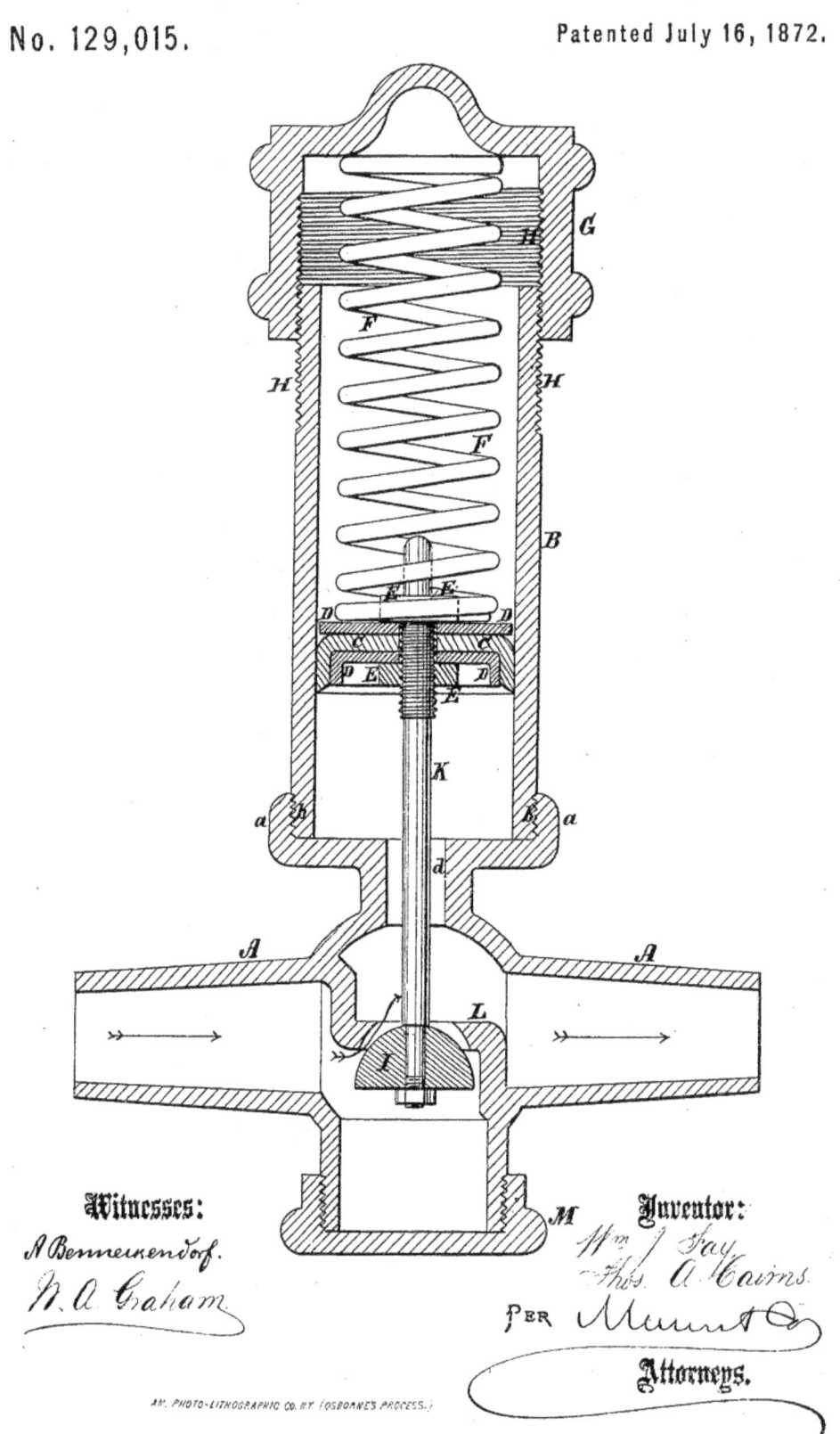

UNITED STATES PATENT OFFICE.

WILLIAM J. FAY AND THOMAS A. CAIRNS, OF DENVER, COLORADO TER.

IMPROVEMENT IN FLUID-PRESSURE REGULATORS.

Specification forming part of Letters Patent No. 129,015, dated July 16, 1872.

Specification describing a New and Improved Fluid-Pressure Regulator, invented by WILLIAM J. FAY and THOMAS A. CAIRNS, of Denver city, in the county of Arapahoe and Territory of Colorado.

Our invention consists of a hollow cylinder attached to a globe or other like valve, and communicating at one end with the chamber or pipe into which the water flows through the valve, and in this cylinder is a piston, whose rod is connected to the valve, and a coiled spring is placed behind the piston under such tension as to hold the valve open until the pressure becomes too great for the pipes beyond the valve, when the water-pressure on the piston will close the valve and keep it closed until the pressure on said piston and in the pipes to be protected falls below the power of the spring, which will then open said valve again.

The drawing represents a sectional elevation of our apparatus for regulating the flow of water, and for shutting off the water at certain pressures, so that the pressure in pipes of houses situated in the low districts may be regulated to a point suitable for the location of the house, or to shut the water off when there is an excess of pressure—as, for instance, in the case of fire, when the Holly Water-Works are in operation, thus preventing the bursting of hot-water apparatus and the weak pipes of the house.

A A is made in the form of the ordinary globe-valve, having soldered or screwed ends, and having a socket, a, cast on the upper end to receive the cylinder B, to which it is made fast by a thread at the point $b\ b$. C is a cupped leather packing, which, expanding with the pressure, prevents leakage into the upper part of the cylinder B. D D are brass cup and plate to keep the leather in form. E E are nuts to hold all on stem. F is a spring, which is compressed to the proper point by means of the cap G, turning on the screw-threads at H. I is a rubber, leather, or metal valve attached to stem K, and filling the water-way in the diaphragm L, when raised, as shown in drawing. M is a cap screwed on to admit the valve I to be screwed on stem K.

The operation of the machine is as follows: The valve being open, water is admitted from the main pipe, as indicated by the arrows. It finds a passage to the under side of the piston-leather C through the opening d for the stem. If the outlets be closed, the pressure, acting on the piston C, will raise it up against the force of the spring F, thereby shutting the water-way with the valve I; then, when an outlet is opened on the pipe in the house, or at any point of the pipe leading from A, the pressure on the lower side of the piston is reduced, so that the spring F is able to force it down and open the valve I, thereby allowing the water to flow at any pressure that may be desired. The cylinder, piston, and spring are proportioned to each other in such a manner as to admit of the nicest adjustment of pressure.

We propose to use a piston in this manner in preference to the diaphragm heretofore used, because it admits of greater motion of the valve, and that the valve is or can be made conical or parabolic in form, thereby closing the opening gradually until it arrives at the entirely-shut point, producing no concussion in the pipes. The diaphragm admits of but little motion of the valve, thereby necessitating the use of a nearly flat valve, which, on closing, produces concussion in the pipes, and a disagreeable noise when the force of the spring and the pressure of the water on the diaphragm are nearly equal.

After repeated trials of the diaphragm in many ways it has been considered practically a failure, particularly when used to regulate the flow of gas. The piston is also superior to the diaphragm, in that it will last for years, while the diaphragm soon wears out.

Having thus described our invention, we claim as new and desire to secure by Letters Patent—

In a pressure-regulator for fluids the combination of a cylinder and piston with the regulating valve and spring, substantially as specified.

WILLIAM J. FAY.
THOMAS A. CAIRNS.

Witnesses:
T. B. McCORMIC,
M. W. LEVY.

J. M. VEASEY.
Improvement in Sewing-Machine Casters.
No. 129,629. Patented July 16, 1872.

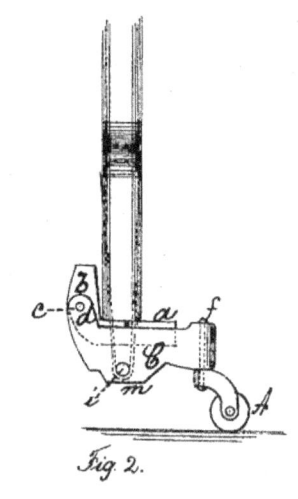

Fig. 1

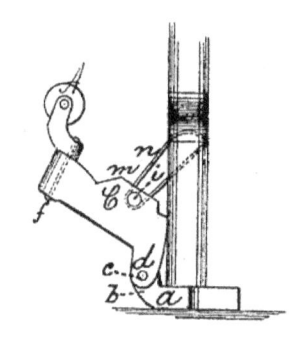

Fig. 2

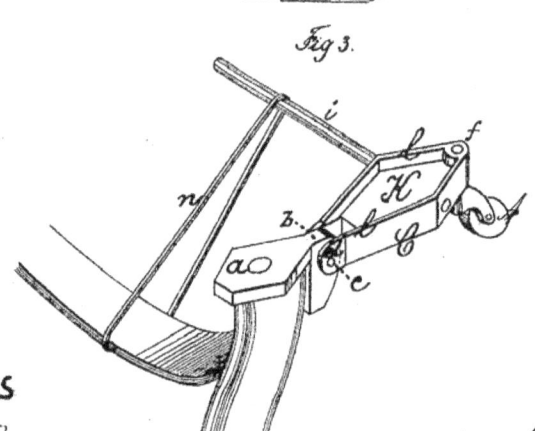

Fig. 3

WITNESSES

INVENTOR:
J. M. Veasey.
By Geo. E. Brown, Atty.

129,629

UNITED STATES PATENT OFFICE.

JOHN M. VEASEY, OF DENVER, COLORADO.

IMPROVEMENT IN SEWING-MACHINE CASTERS.

Specification forming part of Letters Patent No. 129,629, dated July 16, 1872.

Specification describing an Improvement in Sewing-Machine Casters, invented by JOHN M. VEASEY, of Denver, Arapahoe county, Colorado.

This invention consists of a plate having a caster at one end and at the other end hinged to a foot permanently attached to the leg of a sewing-machine, said plate having a recess in its upper side, into which the foot fits, and said plate being, by means of a hinge, rendered capable of being turned back when the leg is raised, so as to allow the foot to be placed directly on the floor, and thus steady the machine while in operation.

Figure 1 is a side elevation, showing the plate under the leg; Fig. 2, a side elevation, showing the plate turned back; and Fig. 3 is a perspective view of the plate turned partly back and inverted.

C is the plate, having a hole at one end to receive the caster-shank f of the caster A, flanges l at the sides, and lugs d at the other end. The foot a is attached to the bottom of the machine-leg. Said foot has a projection, b, at one end, which, when the foot is placed in the recess K within the flanges l, enters between lugs d and is connected therewith by a pivot, c, so as to form a hinge. A rod, i, passing through lugs m extending downward from the plate C, connects the plates in pairs, so that two of them can be worked together. When the sewing-machine is to be used it must be lifted high enough to enable the plate C to be turned back from under each leg, so that when the machine is lowered the feet a rest directly on the floor. On raising the machine the plates can be turned under the feet again. A spring, n, or elastic cord, or other suitable material, connecting the rod i and leg or any attachment to the leg, serves to facilitate the movement of the plate C when turned either backward or forward.

I claim as my invention—

1. The plate C, provided with flanges l and lugs d, in combination with the caster A and the foot a, having projection b, all constructed, arranged, and operating as and for the purpose described.

2. The combination of the subject-matter of the first claim with the rod i and elastic cord or spring n, in the manner and for the purpose explained.

JOHN M. VEASEY.

Witnesses:
JOHN F. KIRBY,
HENRY B. HINE.

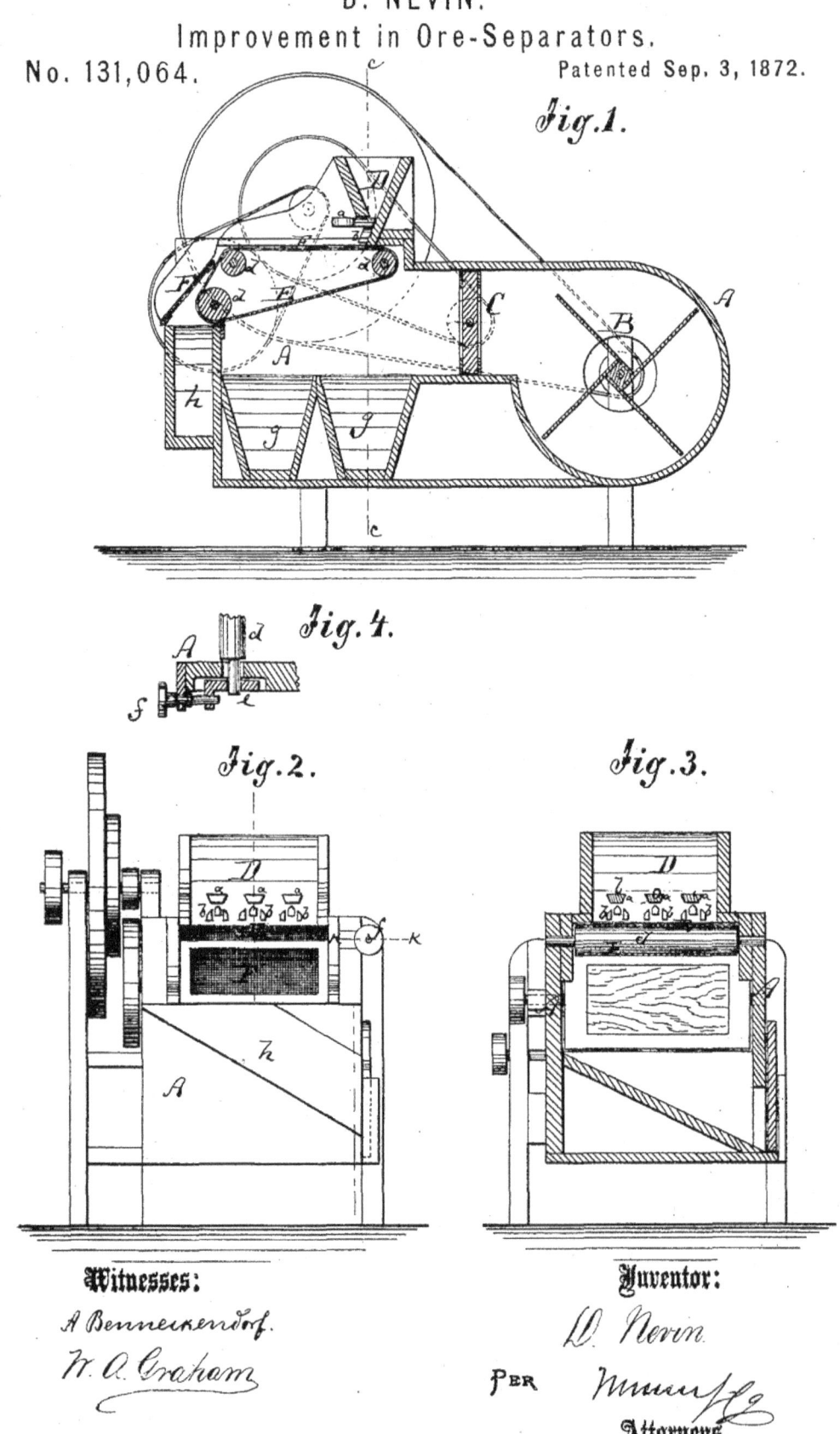

UNITED STATES PATENT OFFICE.

DAVID NEVIN, OF GEORGETOWN, COLORADO TERRITORY.

IMPROVEMENT IN ORE-SEPARATORS.

Specification forming part of Letters Patent No. **131,064**, dated September 3, 1872.

Specification describing a new and Improved Ore-Separator, invented by DAVID NEVIN, of Georgetown, in the county of Clear Creek and Territory of Colorado.

In the accompanying drawing, Figure 1 represents a vertical longitudinal section of my improved ore-separator. Fig. 2 is a front elevation of the same, and Fig. 3 a vertical transverse section on the line $c\,c$, Fig. 1. Fig. 4 is a detail horizontal section on the line $k\,k$, Fig. 2.

Similar letters of reference indicate corresponding parts.

This invention relates to a new ore-separator, in which air currents, or rather puffs, are used to effect the desired separation of the heavier from the lighter metals.

The invention also consists in the use of a continuous rotary wire-screen under the hopper, in the use of a screw for regulating the same, and of a stationary tail-screen, as hereinafter more fully described.

A in the drawing represents the frame or case of my improved separator. B is the rotary fan, hung in one end of the same, to produce a continuous air-current. C is a rotary blade covered with leather or otherwise made practically impervious to air. It is placed in the air-channel directly in front of the fan, and of such size as to fill said channel when in the position shown in Fig. 1. While being revolved the blade C interrupts the air-current whenever it thus closes the channel and then opens it again, thereby causing the air to be blown in puffs toward the forward part of the machine and not in a continuous current. D is the feed-hopper, into which the dry ore, reduced to proper fineness, is placed. One or more slide-gates, $a\,a$, in the bottom of the hopper serve to regulate the escape of ore therefrom. Lugs $b\,b$, sharp-edged on top, are placed against the side of the hopper, under the gates a, and serve to spread the ore so that it will be supplied across the entire width of the movable screen E, or the hopper may be used with one gate the whole width, and without the lugs for spreading the ore. The screen E is of wire-gauze of the requisite fineness, and is placed around rollers $d\,d$, whereby and whereon it is moved continuously and regularly, so that its upper part moves forward. One of the rollers, d, hangs in sliding bearings e, which can be adjusted lengthwise by means of a screw or screws, f, with the object of imparting to the wire-screen a suitable degree of tension, and true direction between the sides of frame. The driving-rollers are to be covered with leather or other material.

In operation, the puffs of air blown from below through the traveling screen E cause the ore on the latter to bound up and drop down alternately, the heavier falling lower and passing through the meshes of the screen E into lateral discharge-spouts g. The lighter ore reaches the tail-screen, through which some passes into a spout, h, while the very lightest material falls over the edge of the tail-screen. The several shafts and rollers are revolved by means of belts or other suitable mechanism.

Having thus described my invention, I claim as new and desire to secure by Letters Patent—

1. The rotary wire-screen E arranged under the feed-hopper of an ore-separator, as specified.

2. The tail-screen F placed against and combined with the rotary wire-screen E, to operate as set forth.

DAVID NEVIN.

Witnesses:
 HENRY C. HARRINGTON,
 WM. N. HUTCHINSON.

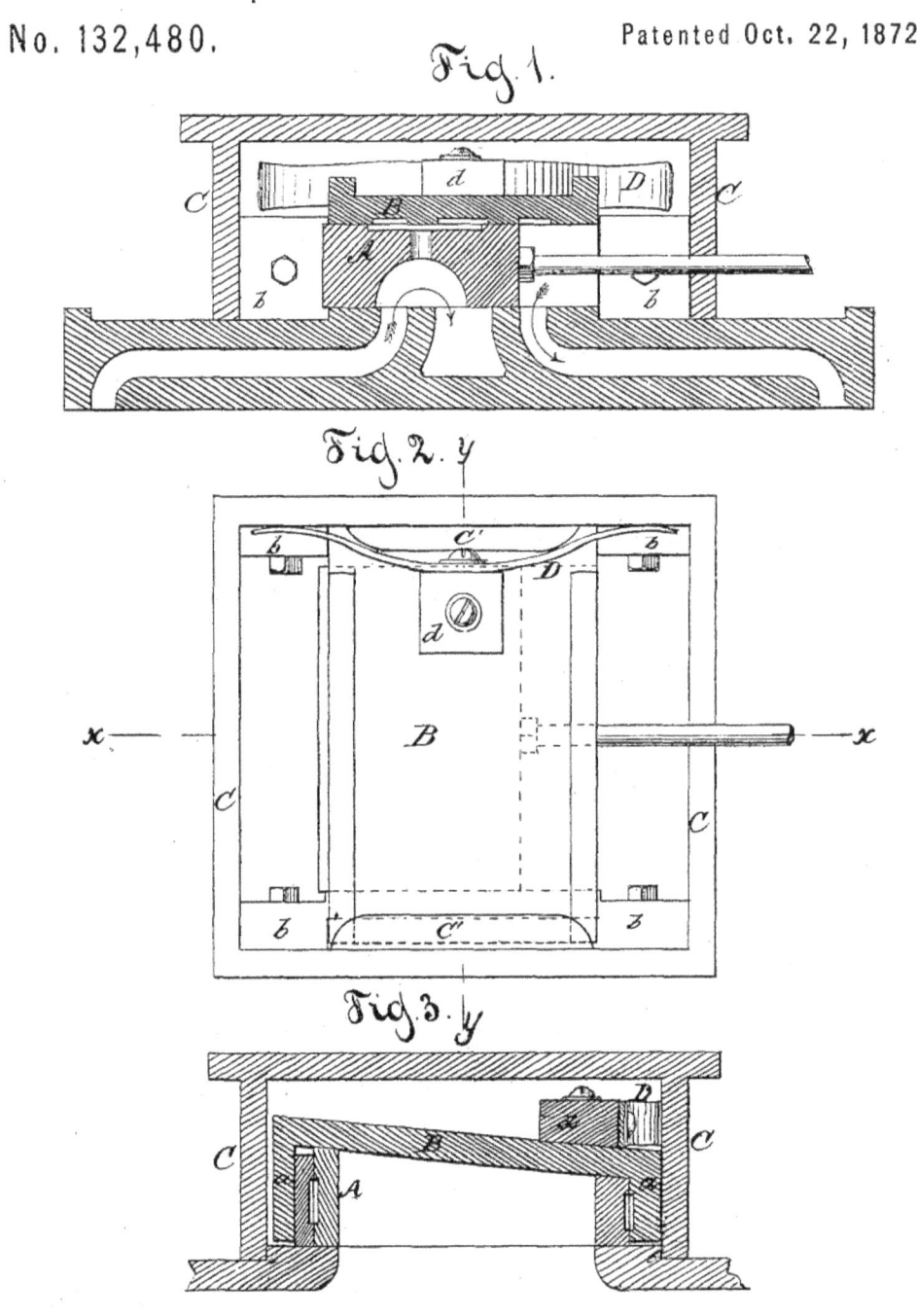

UNITED STATES PATENT OFFICE.

HERMAN H. MEYER, OF DENVER, COLORADO TERRITORY.

IMPROVEMENT IN SLIDE-VALVES.

Specification forming part of Letters Patent No. **132,480**, dated October 22, 1872.

To all whom it may concern:

Be it known that I, HERMAN H. MEYER, of Denver, in the county of Arapahoe, in the Territory of Colorado, have invented a new and useful Improvement in Slide-Valve; and I do hereby declare the following to be a full, clear, and exact description thereof, which will enable those skilled in the art to make and use the same, reference being had to the accompanying drawing forming part of this specification, in which drawing—

Figure 1 is a vertical section in the plane of the line $x x$ of Fig. 2; Fig. 2 is a plan view, the top of the steam-chest being removed; and Fig. 3 is a vertical section in the plane of the line $y y$ of Fig. 2.

Similar letters indicate corresponding parts.

This invention relates to slide-valves; and consists in the combination, with a slide-valve, of a cover, which holds the valve down to its seat, and which is so constructed and arranged as to compensate for wear of the valve, the cover closing against the back of the valve so as to prevent it from wearing leaky.

The letter A designates a slide-valve; and B, a cover placed over its back within the valve-chest C. Both the valve and the cover are made wedge-shaped in cross-section, (see Fig. 3,) and the ends $a\ a$ of the cover overlap the sides of the valve, as shown in Fig. 3; but space is left between its ends $a\ a$, and the walls of the steam-chest to allow it to advance to compensate for the wear of the valve. The ends $a\ a$ of the cover are guided and prevented from moving lengthwise of the valve by guide-pieces $b\ b\ b\ b$ in the corners of the steam-chest, but they do not prevent motion of the cover crosswise of the valve. The ends of the cover extend under ears $C'\ C'$, which are secured to the side of the steam-chest, and which serve to keep the cover in place and prevent it from rising off its place over the valve. The face of the cover, which comes next to the back of the valve, is inclined so as to correspond to the wedge-shaped or inclined back of the valve, and at its thicker end I apply a spring, D, which is, in this example, flat, and is so arranged that its ends bear against one side of the steam-chest while its center bears against a shoulder, d, on the cover. This arrangement causes the cover to advance over the valve and compensate for wear, and thereby prevent leakage.

One advantage of my invention is found in locomotives, which, when running on a down grade, have their steam shut off, and while in this condition their valves keep on moving and wear on their seats, so that at length the wear forms a space between the back of the valve and the cover, and in such cases the cover would be of no benefit. In order to obviate this difficulty, I have provided a spring to bear upon the cover and feed it along across the back of the valve, as described, the cover being made in length less than the width of steam-chest inside, so as to allow it to be moved along by the spring as the wear of the face of the valve proceeds.

What I claim as new, and desire to secure by Letters Patent, is—

A cover, B, arranged over the back of a slide-valve, as described, in combination with a spring to move the cover on the back of the valve and compensate for the wear of the valve, substantially as described.

HERMAN H. MEYER.

Witnesses:
ADOLPH L. REICHARD,
F. JENSEN.

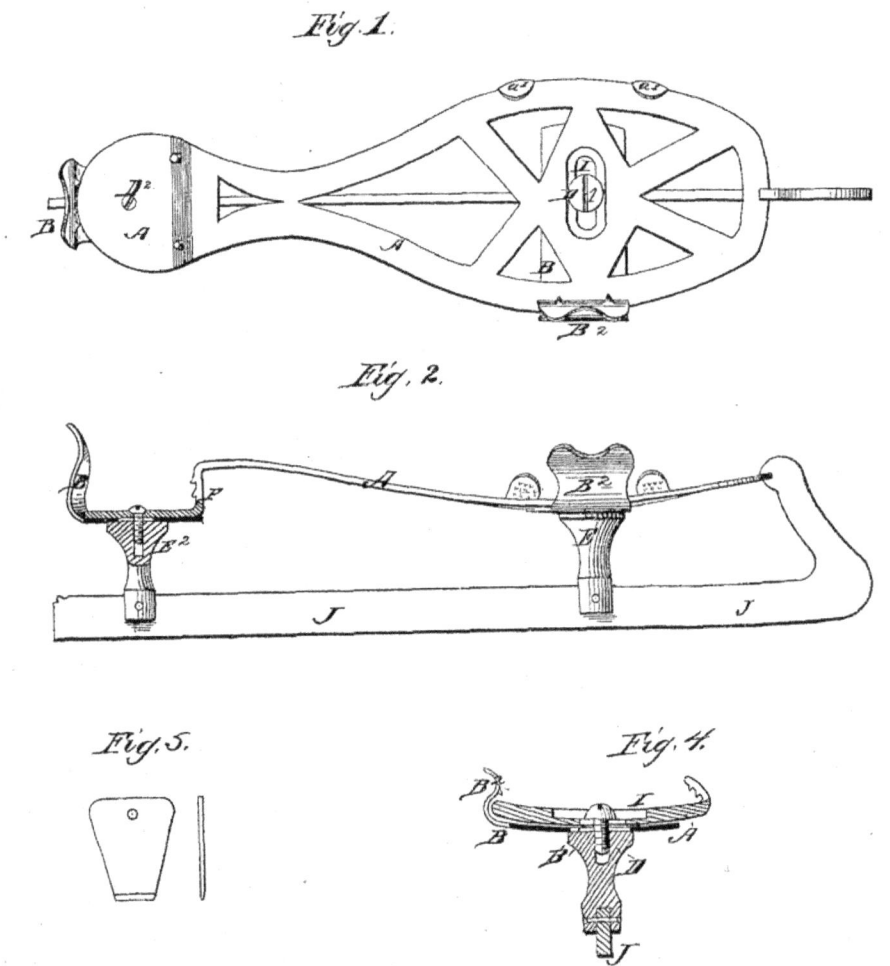

UNITED STATES PATENT OFFICE.

JOHN HUNTER AND JOEL T. CHENOWETH, OF DENVER, COLORADO TER.

IMPROVEMENT IN SKATE-FASTENINGS.

Specification forming part of Letters Patent No. **133,314**, dated November 26, 1872.

To all whom it may concern:

Be it known that we, JOHN HUNTER and JOEL T. CHENOWETH, both of Denver, county of Arapahoe, in the Territory of Colorado, have invented a new and useful Improvement on Skate-Fastenings; and we do hereby declare that the following is a full, clear, and exact description thereof, which will enable others skilled in the art to make and use the same, reference being had to the accompanying drawing forming part of this specification.

Figure 1 is top view of skate. Fig. 2 is side view. Fig. 4 is sectional view. Fig. 5 is view of screw-driver.

A, sole of skate, with flanges a' a' turned upward and curved inward to clasp the edge of the sole of the boot. B is spring, with slot B^1 and curved end B^2. The spring is secured under the sole A and on top of the stand E by screw D, which passes through sole A and slot B^1 and into stand E, as shown in Fig. 4. The spring B is fitted to the bottom of sole A, turned upward and curved inward, which presses the sole of the boot against and under the flanges a' a'. The spring can be moved out or in, according to the width of boot-sole, by loosening the screw D. The curved flanges a' a' and curved spring B^2 have rough or rasp surfaces to prevent slipping of sole of boot, and to increase the gripe of flanges a' a' and spring B^2. Spring B on rear end of skate is fastened under the heel-plate a and on top of stand E, Fig. 2. The spring B can be adjusted to suit the size of heel of boot by loosening the screw D^2 and moving the spring back the required distance. The spring B is turned upward and curved forward, which forces the heel of the boot forward and against the heel-front F; the curved end of spring B and heel-front F have toothed and rough surfaces, which secure the heel in proper position on the heel-plate a. The sole A can be moved to the right or left by loosening the screw d' and moving the sole A, with slot I, so as to bring the iron runner into the position desired.

We claim—

1. An improved skate-fastening, which will be light, strong, and simple in construction, inexpensive in manufacture, and reliable in operation, and which shall be so constructed that it may be firmly secured to the boot by a simple pressure of the boot against the springs.

2. We claim the skate-fastening, constructed and arranged as and for the purpose described.

JOHN HUNTER.
JOEL T. CHENOWETH.

Witnesses:
 MORITZ BARTH,
 WILLIAM BARTH.

A. M. OLDS.
Washing-Machines.

No. 134,609. Patented Jan. 7, 1873.

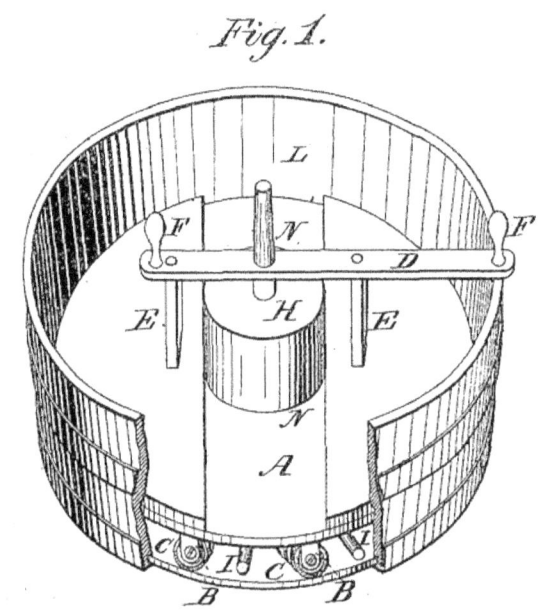

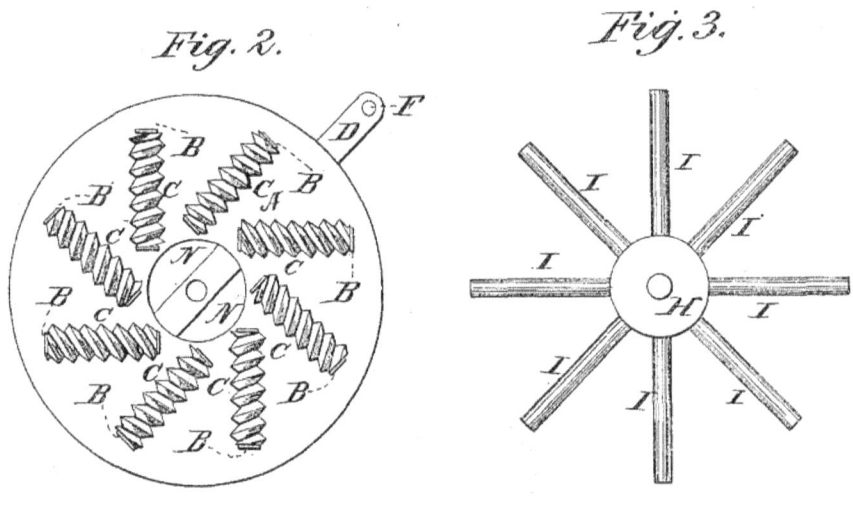

Witnesses.
Wm H. Post.
Fred M. Brush.

Inventor.
A. M. Olds.

UNITED STATES PATENT OFFICE.

AMANDRIN M. OLDS, OF GREELEY, COLORADO TERRITORY.

IMPROVEMENT IN WASHING-MACHINES.

Specification forming part of Letters Patent No. **134,609**, dated January 7, 1873.

To all whom it may concern:

Be it known that I, AMANDRIN M. OLDS, of the town of Greeley, county of Weld, and Territory of Colorado, have invented a new and Improved Washing-Machine; and I do hereby declare that the following is a full and exact description thereof, reference being had to the accompanying drawing and to the letters of reference marked thereon.

In said drawing, Figure 1 is a sectional perspective view of my invention with a portion of a tub in connection, showing its position when ready for operation; Fig. 2 is a view of the under side of the upper or movable portion of the machine; and Fig. 3 is a plan view of the lower or stationary portion of the same.

Similar letters of reference indicate like parts.

This invention consists in so constructing and arranging rollers that when revolutions are made in contact with clothes washing may be accomplished with great ease and rapidity.

A is the upper portion of the machine, on the under side of which are secured, in bearings B, screw-rollers C, the position of said rollers being placed so that the line of the thread of the screw is at right angles with the diameter of the circular portion A. D is an arm connected with the part A by standards E. On either end of the arm D are handles F for operating, one being further from the axis of the machine than the other, so as to give more purchase when operated with one hand. H is a circular post provided with bars I at its base, which rest in the bottom of the tub L, the upper portion A being held in position by said post passing through corresponding openings N N.

The clothes being placed on the bars I and the rubbing portion A above, the handle of the long end of the arm D may then be moved right and left; and if clothes are very dirty, a slight pressure may be made upon the other handle at the same time; or if a greater change of position of the clothes should be desired, a few complete revolutions in either direction may be made. Thus the rubbing-surfaces of the screw-rollers gradually and directly move longitudinally against the clothes, requiring less power to produce the desired result through this transverse movement by these revolutions.

This machine may be operated in any ordinary-sized wash-tub, doing its work with ease and rapidity, and be within the means of any family, as they can be manufactured cheaply.

What I claim as my invention, and desire to secure by Letters Patent, is—

An attachment for wash-tubs, consisting of the circular disk A, screw-rollers C, and radial arms I and handles D, when combined to operate substantially as set forth.

A. M. OLDS.

Witnesses:
W. H. POST,
FRED. M. BRUSH.

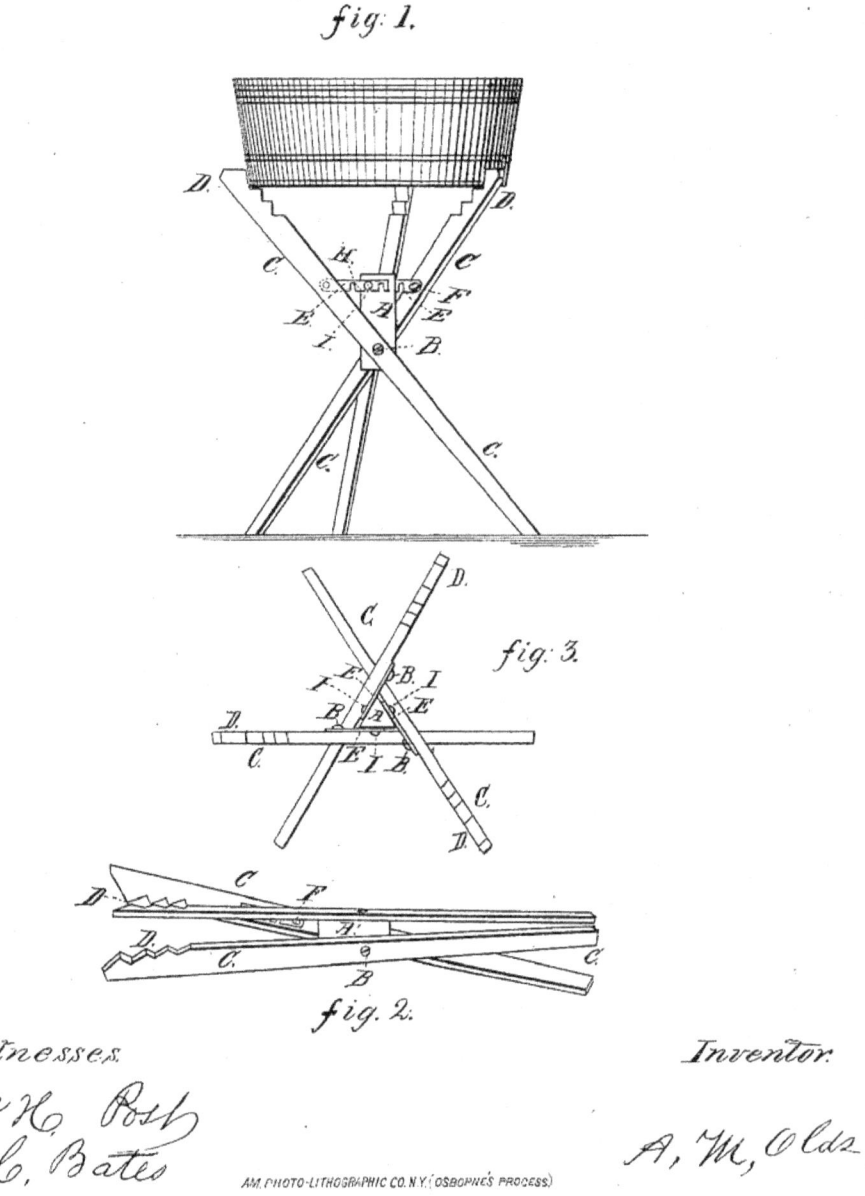

UNITED STATES PATENT OFFICE.

AMANDRIN M. OLDS, OF GREELEY, COLORADO TERRITORY.

IMPROVEMENT IN WASH-TUB HOLDERS.

Specification forming part of Letters Patent No. **137,473**, dated April 1, 1873; application filed December 30, 1872.

To all whom it may concern:

Be it known that I, A. M. OLDS, of the town of Greeley, in the county of Weld and Territory of Colorado, have invented a new and Improved Adjustable Wash-Tub Holder; and I do hereby declare that the following is a full and exact description thereof, reference being had to the accompanying drawing and to the letters of reference marked thereon, which form part of this specification.

In said drawing, Figure 1 is a front elevation of my invention, showing it as adjusted and in use. Fig. 2 is a view of the same in a compact form when not in use.

Similar letters of reference indicate like parts.

This invention consists in a suitable device being provided for holding wash-tubs of various sizes at any desired height, and readily adjusted to conform to the height of the person using, and when not in use be folded up, so as to only occupy an economical space.

A is an oblong triangular center-piece, near the lower end of which are pivoted, by screws B, legs C, said legs or pieces, on their inner upper portion, having notches D provided, in which tubs of various sizes may securely rest. E are short flat pieces of iron, one end of which is pivoted, by screws F, to the pieces C, the other ends having openings or notches H formed on the under side, suitable for hooking onto screws or pins I when adjustments are made, thus holding it firmly in position at any height required.

Wood may be used in place of these iron pieces, and answer a very good purpose; or the whole arrangement may be constructed having four legs instead of three, or the connection for holding in position be made from leg to leg instead of with center-piece, but would not be as desirable.

The holder is considered very desirable for private or family laundries, being compact and easily adjusted to any required height for use, and so cheap that every family may avail themselves of its convenience.

What I claim, and desire to secure by Letters Patent, is—

The leg-pieces C, provided with suitable bearings or notches D, whereby tubs may be securely held in position, when arranged in combination with the adjustable pieces E and center-block A, substantially as described.

AMANDRIN M. OLDS.

Witnesses:
WM. H. POST,
A. C. BATES.

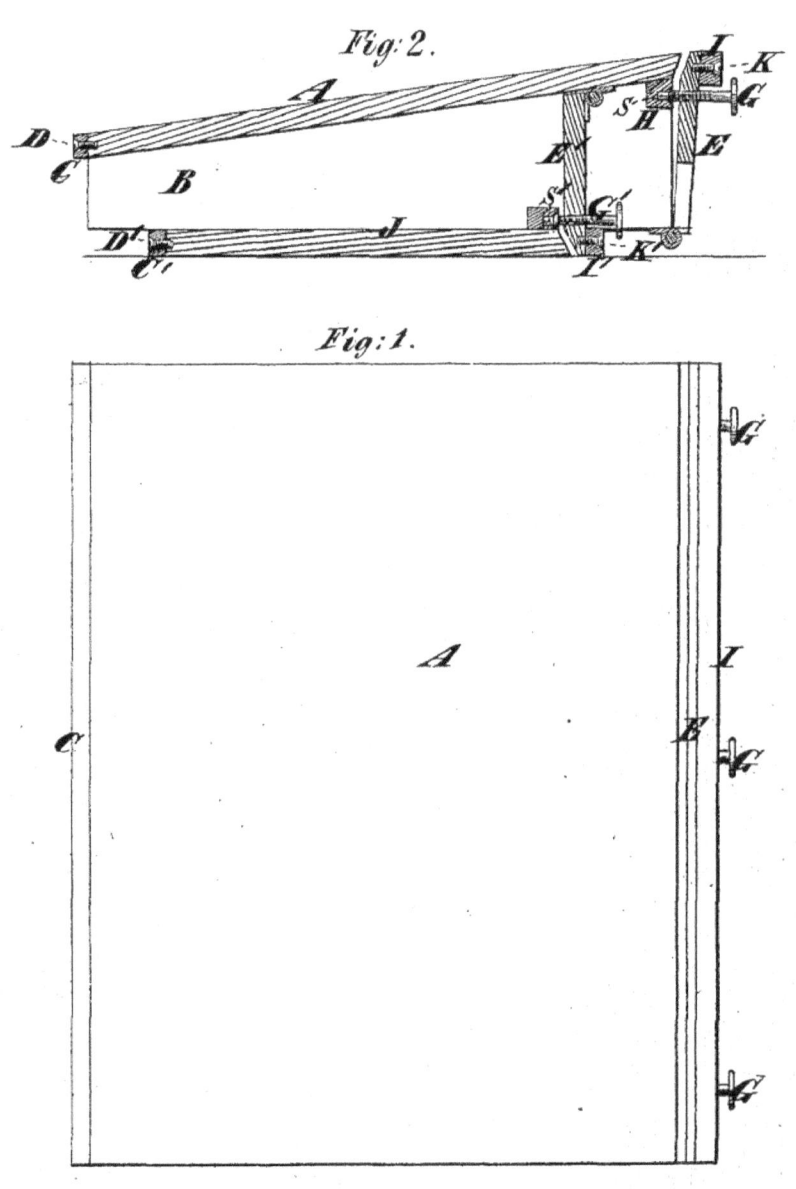

UNITED STATES PATENT OFFICE.

HERMAN H. MEYER, OF DENVER, COLORADO TERRITORY.

IMPROVEMENT IN DRAWING-BOARDS.

Specification forming part of Letters Patent No. **139,411**, dated May 27, 1873; application filed February 17, 1873.

To all whom it may concern:

Be it known that I, HERMAN H. MEYER, of Denver, in the county of Arapahoe and Territory of Colorado, have invented an Improved Drawing-Board, of which the following is a specification:

This invention consists in a novel construction of the board, including hinged stretching-pieces, whereby paper may not only be secured without the use of tacks, paste, or glue, but may also be stretched throughout its whole length or at different points, and be made to present a smooth surface without puckering.

In the accompanying drawing, Fig. 1 is a top view of a board made according to my invention, and Fig. 2 is a transverse section of the same.

Similar letters of reference indicate corresponding parts in both figures.

The board proper, A, is erected on two taper side-strips, B B, and is of the usual rectangular shape. Along its bottom edge there extends a clamping-strip, C, for holding the paper. It is secured in place and operated by screws D D. E is a stretching-piece, which is hinged to the fore-ends of the side-strips B B. In its upper portion are a series of thumb-screws, G G, whose ends abut against metal buttons or plates s s, on a strip of wood, H, arranged under the edge of the board. The piece E is furnished at the upper edge with a clamping-strip, I, operated by screws K K, in the same manner as the strip C, before described. As this board is only suitable for paper of one length, I provide on the under side of the side strips another board, J, for shorter paper. Like the board A, it is provided with a clamping-strip, C′, for securing the bottom edge of the paper, and with a stretching-piece, E′, hinged to the board A, for straining or stretching the paper.

Whichever board is to be used is turned uppermost, and the top edge of the paper is secured between the stretching-piece E or E′, and clamping-strip I or I, by means of the screws K or K′. The other edge of the paper is drawn tight over the board by the hand and fastened between the clamping-strip C or C′ and the bottom edge of the board. When the paper is thus secured the thumb-screws G or G′ are screwed up to abut against the buttons s or s' in the strip H or H′, and force the stretch-piece out and thereby stretch the paper. One or more of the screws just mentioned may be screwed up to stretch out a pucker, or all may be operated.

Often paper becomes all puckered after a change in the weather, and with an ordinary board it is difficult to smooth it out, but with my board the puckers may be all stretched out.

This board is specially advantageous for securing paper having a glossy surface, which is injured by the usual method of damping and stretching.

I claim—

1. The combination of the board furnished with a clamping-piece, C, the swinging stretch-piece E, likewise furnished with a clamping-strip and the thumb-screws G G, substantially as and for the purpose set forth.

2. The side strips B B, in combination with the boards A and J, the clamping-pieces and stretch-pieces, essentially as and for the purpose set forth.

HERMAN H. MEYER.

Witnesses:
S. G. COLLINS,
J. L. McNEIL.

J. M. McFARLAND.

Stamps for Crushing Ores.

No. 140,425. Patented July 1, 1873.

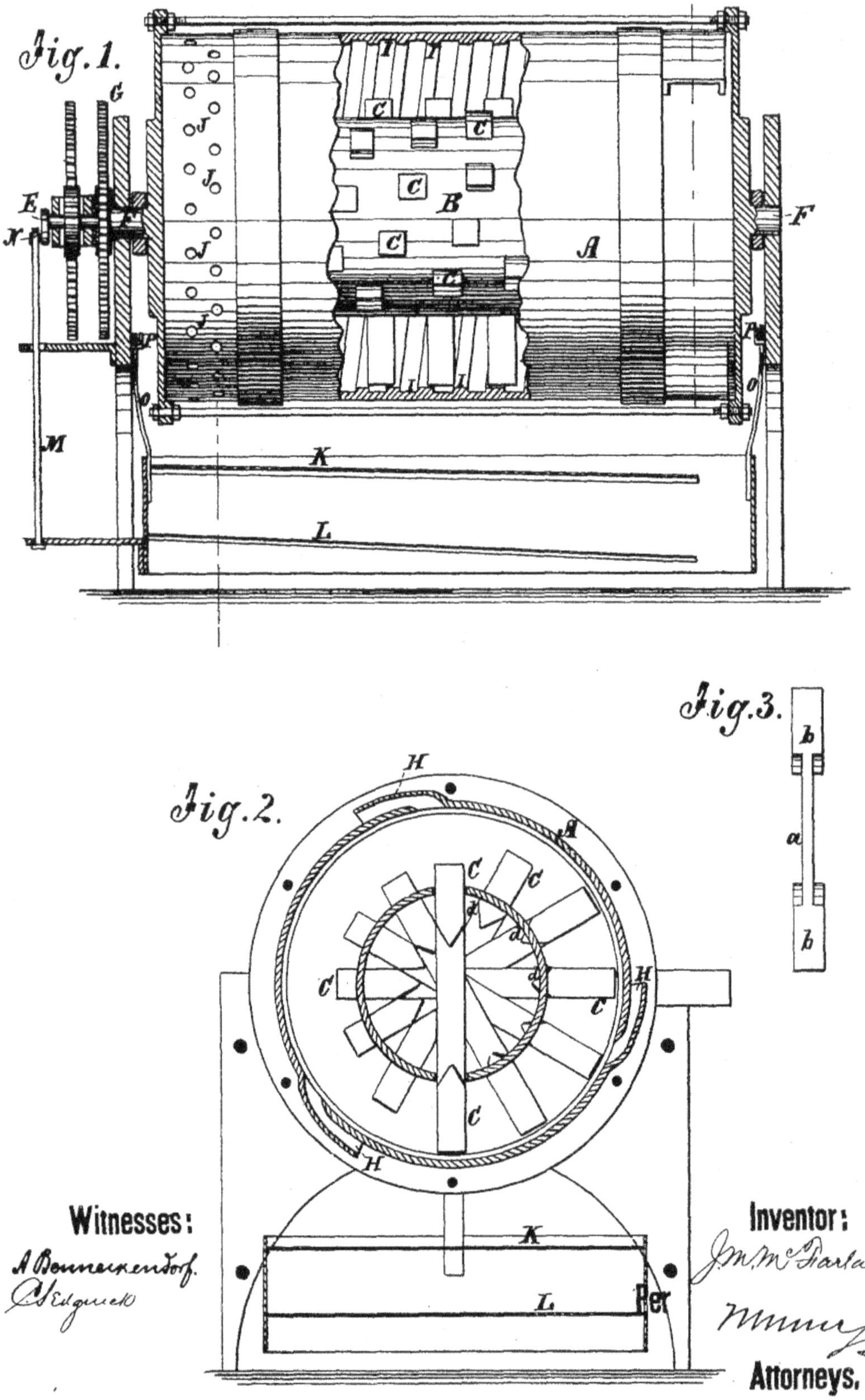
Fig. 1.
Fig. 2.
Fig. 3.
A
B
C
E
F
G
H
I
J
K
L
M
a
b
d
o

Witnesses:

A Bonnerkendorf.

C Sedgwick

Inventor:

J. M. McFarland

Per Munn & Co

Attorneys.

AM. PHOTO-LITHOGRAPHIC CO. N.Y. (OSBORNE'S PROCESS.)

UNITED STATES PATENT OFFICE.

JAMES M. McFARLAND, OF GOLDEN CITY, COLORADO TERRITORY.

IMPROVEMENT IN STAMPS FOR CRUSHING ORES.

Specification forming part of Letters Patent No. **140,425**, dated July 1, 1873; application filed May 31, 1873.

To all whom it may concern:

Be it known that I, JAMES MAXEY MCFARLAND, of Golden City, in the county of Jefferson and Territory of Colorado, have invented a new and Improved Ore-Crusher, of which the following is a specification:

The most essential part of my invention consists of a novel mode of operating stamps for crushing and pulverizing ores, &c., by a horizontal revolving cylinder, through which a series of bars, with a stamp-head at each end, are arranged diametrically, so that they can slide endwise a short distance. The cylinder is arranged a suitable distance above the bottom of the bed containing the ore, and caused to revolve slowly; the stamps, as they approach the vertical line, slide in the cylinder and strike a blow on the ore, and are then forced around by the cylinder, and have a grinding or crushing effect. They strike two blows at each revolution. They are arranged as close together, both lengthwise and circumferentially, as they can be and work well, and they strike a great number of blows to each revolution.

Another part of my invention consists of a hollow cylindrical rotating ore-holder, into which the ore is fed at one end and caused to work along slowly to the other end during the progress of the work, and discharge through holes onto a screen, which is arranged to separate the fine particles and carry the coarse portion back to the head of the ore-holder to be delivered into it again for reworking it. Another part of the invention consists of spiral ribs in the hollow revolving ore-holder, to work the ore along the cylinder as it is gradually reduced by the stamps.

Figure 1 is partly a side elevation and partly a sectional elevation of my improved ore-crusher. Fig. 2 is a transverse section taken on the line $x\,x$ of Fig. 1, and Fig. 3 is a side elevation of one of the stamps.

Similar letters of reference indicate corresponding parts.

A is the outside cylinder or case for holding the ore. B is the inside stamp-carrying cylinder, and C represents the stamp. These stamps consist of bars a with steel heads b, the bars and heads being considerably longer than the diameter of cylinder B, and arranged in diametrical mortises or holes in it, so as to project from the surface as close together throughout the whole surface as they can and be free to slide for striking the blows. They slide endwise and fall onto the ore in the bottom of the holder whenever they approach the vertical line, so as to slide down on the walls of the holes in which they work. The end, sliding down and striking the ore, remains until it arrives near the top of the cylinder, when the bar slides again, and the other end falls on the ore, and so on. These stamps are arranged close together in the lengthwise direction of the cylinder, and, circumferentially, they are as close together as the shoulders d will allow, and, at the same time, let the stamp-heads fall to the bottom of the ore-holder. This cylinder B is turned by the shaft E. The outside cylinder A is mounted on the journals F, and is turned by the wheel G; it receives the ore through the spouts H at one end, conveys it along slowly to the other end, by the spiral ribs or corrugations I, at the same time that it is subject to the stamps, and delivers the crushed ore at the other end through the holes J upon a coarse screen, K, through which the fine portions pass onto the screens L to be again separated, and the coarse portions are carried by said screens back to the head of the crusher to be passed through it again. The screens are vibrated by the rod M and crank N; they are suspended by the rods O from hooks P in the frame, to allow them to be shaken.

Having thus described my invention, I claim as new and desire to secure by Letters Patent—

1. The mode of operating stamps by a revolving cylinder, in which a series of stamps are arranged in radial mortises, substantially as specified.

2. The combination, with a series of stamps and an operating-cylinder, as described, of a

revolving case inclosing the stamps and holding the ore to be crushed, substantially as specified.

3. The said revolving ore-holder, having spiral ribs or corrugations, in combination with the stamps for passing the ore along toward the discharge as the crushing progresses, substantially as specified.

4. The combination, with the rotating case and ore-holder, of the screens K L, arranged substantially as specified.

JAMES MAXEY McFARLAND.

Witnesses:
L. J. SMITH,
EDWARD D. COE.

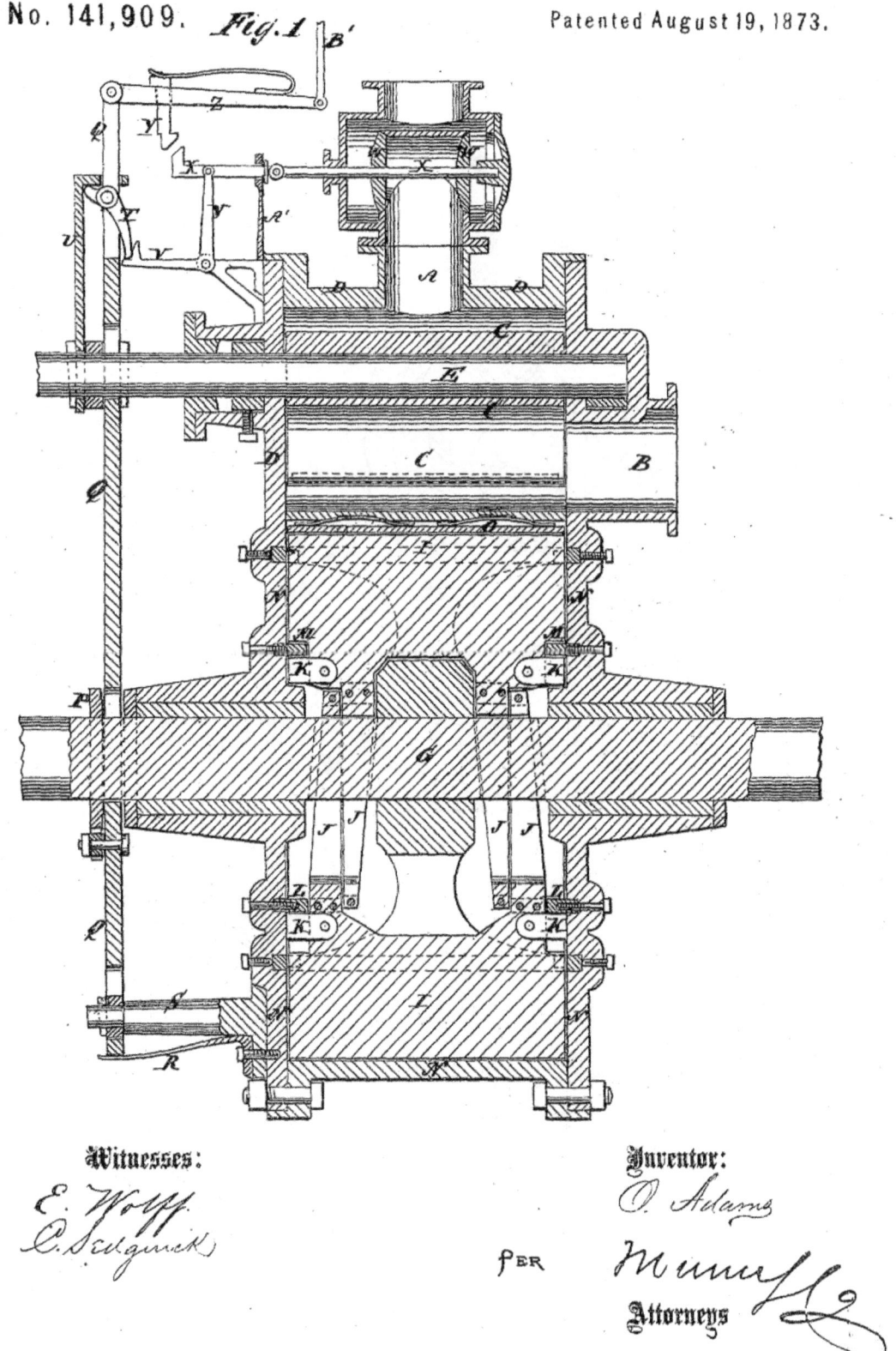

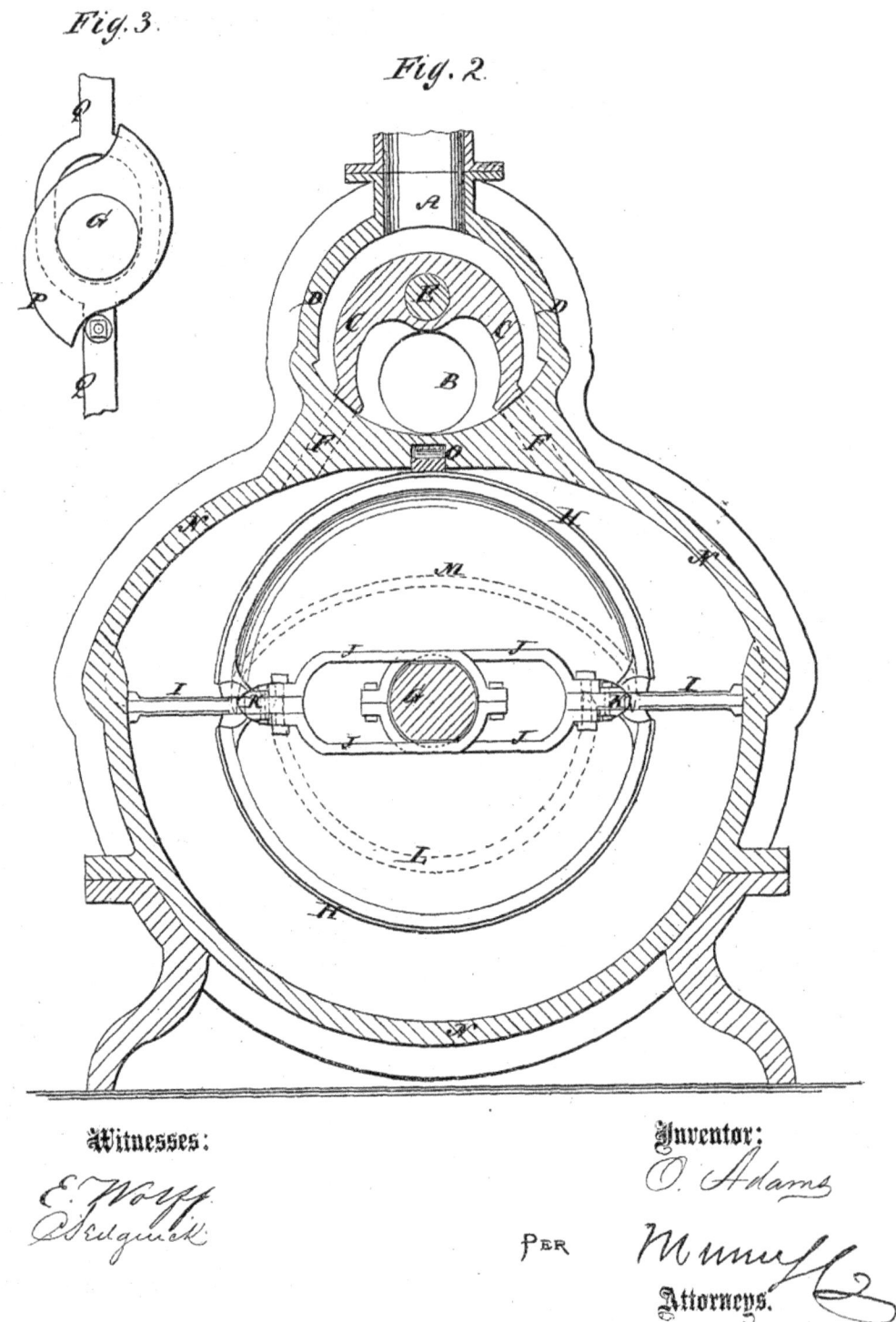

UNITED STATES PATENT OFFICE.

ORWIN ADAMS, OF BLACK HAWK, COLORADO TERRITORY.

IMPROVEMENT IN REVERSIBLE ROTARY STEAM-ENGINES.

Specification forming part of Letters Patent No. **141,909**, dated August 19, 1873; application filed March 8, 1873.

To all whom it may concern:

Be it known that I, ORWIN ADAMS, of Black Hawk, in the county of Gilpin and Territory of Colorado, have invented a new and useful Improvement in Reversible Rotary Steam-Engine, of which the following is a specification:

Figure 1, Sheet I, is a detail vertical longitudinal section of my improved engine. Fig. 2, Sheet II, is a detail vertical cross-section of the same. Fig. 3, Sheet II, is a detail view of the cam.

Similar letters of reference indicate corresponding parts.

My invention has for its object to furnish an improved rotary steam-engine, simple in construction and effective in operation, working with little friction, and which may be readily reversed, and will enable the steam to be cut off at any desired point of the stroke. The invention consists in the combination of circular and elliptical guides with the pistons and shaft, and in the arrangement of mechanism for operating the cut-off valve.

A represents the induction-pipe, and B the exhaust. C is the throttle or reverse valve, which is placed in the valve-chest D, and is keyed to the shaft E. The shaft E works in bearings secured to the heads of the steam-chest D, with set-screws to relieve the pressure upon the valve-seats. F are the induction and exhaust ports. G is the main shaft, to which is keyed the drum H, through slots in the face of which the pistons I move in and out. The shaft G works in cast-steel bearings twice as long as the diameter of the said shaft, and made adjustable with keys and gibs. The pistons I are bolted to yokes J, which work upon the shaft G, the said shaft being slightly flattened to receive them. To the pistons I and yokes J, at or near their point of intersection, are secured slides K, which move along the outer or convex surface of the circular guide L to force and hold the pistons I out, and along the inner or concave surface of the elliptical guide M to force and hold the pistons I in. The steel circular rings working against the metallic packing in edge of the drum, are let into the heads of the cylinder or case N, and are adjusted by set-screws. The part of the cylinder N above the points of intersection of the guides L M is recessed, as shown in Fig. 2, to allow the exhaust steam to escape freely around the edge of the pistons, as soon as they have completed their stroke. The steam is prevented from passing directly from one port, F, to the other by a packing, O, set in the cylinder N, and held against the drum by springs, as shown in Figs. 1 and 2. To the shaft G, at one end of the cylinder N, is secured a cam, P, which moves the bar Q downward by striking against a pin and friction-roller attached to the said bar Q. The bar Q is moved upward gradually, as allowed by the cam P, by a spring, R, which presses against its lower end. The bar Q is slotted to receive and slide upon the spindle S and the shafts G E, and to its upper part is attached a dog, T, which as the said bar Q moves upward gradually, strikes against a bar, U, looped around the shaft E, and sleeved around the bar Q, and is thrown out upon the toe of the bell-crank lever V, which operates the balanced valve W, so that as the bar Q is moved quickly downward by the cam P the dog T will operate the lever V, and open the valve W suddenly at the beginning of the stroke. As the valve W opens the valve-stem X is caught and locked by the tappet or catch Y attached to the lever Z. The lever Z is connected with the upper end of the bar Q, so that as the said bar again gradually rises the tappet Y will be raised from the valve-stem X at the end of the stroke, when the valve W will be instantly closed by the action of a stiff spring, A'. The long arm of the lever Z is attached to the governor-rod B', so that the valve W may be released at some point between the beginning and end of the stroke, depending upon the speed of the engine. By placing a cut-off in the ports F the steam may be cut off at one-fifteenth or any other desired point of the stroke.

To reverse the engine, the valve-works are thrown out of gear, and the cut-off is thrown open by a lever, not shown in the drawing. The engine, when reversed, works at full stroke, and is regulated by the throttle-valve. The cut-off may also be made reversible by an extra cam, friction-pulley, and lever arrangement.

In engines not requiring a governor the cut-off can be regulated by the engineer, and in any case the governor-valve to regulate the engine is done away with, which is important where steam is used expansively.

Having thus described my invention, I claim as new and desire to secure by Letters Patent—

1. The circular guide L and the elliptical guide M, in combination with the slides K, yokes J, pistons I, drum H, and cylinder or case N, substantially as herein shown and described.

2. In combination with the valve-stem X, the spring A′, bell-crank lever V, dog T, trip-bar U, and reciprocating rod Q, as specified.

ORWIN ADAMS.

Witnesses:
  HAL. SAYR,
  J. N. NICHOLS.

H. H. MEYER.

Governor Cut-off Gears.

No. 142,491. Patented September 2, 1873.

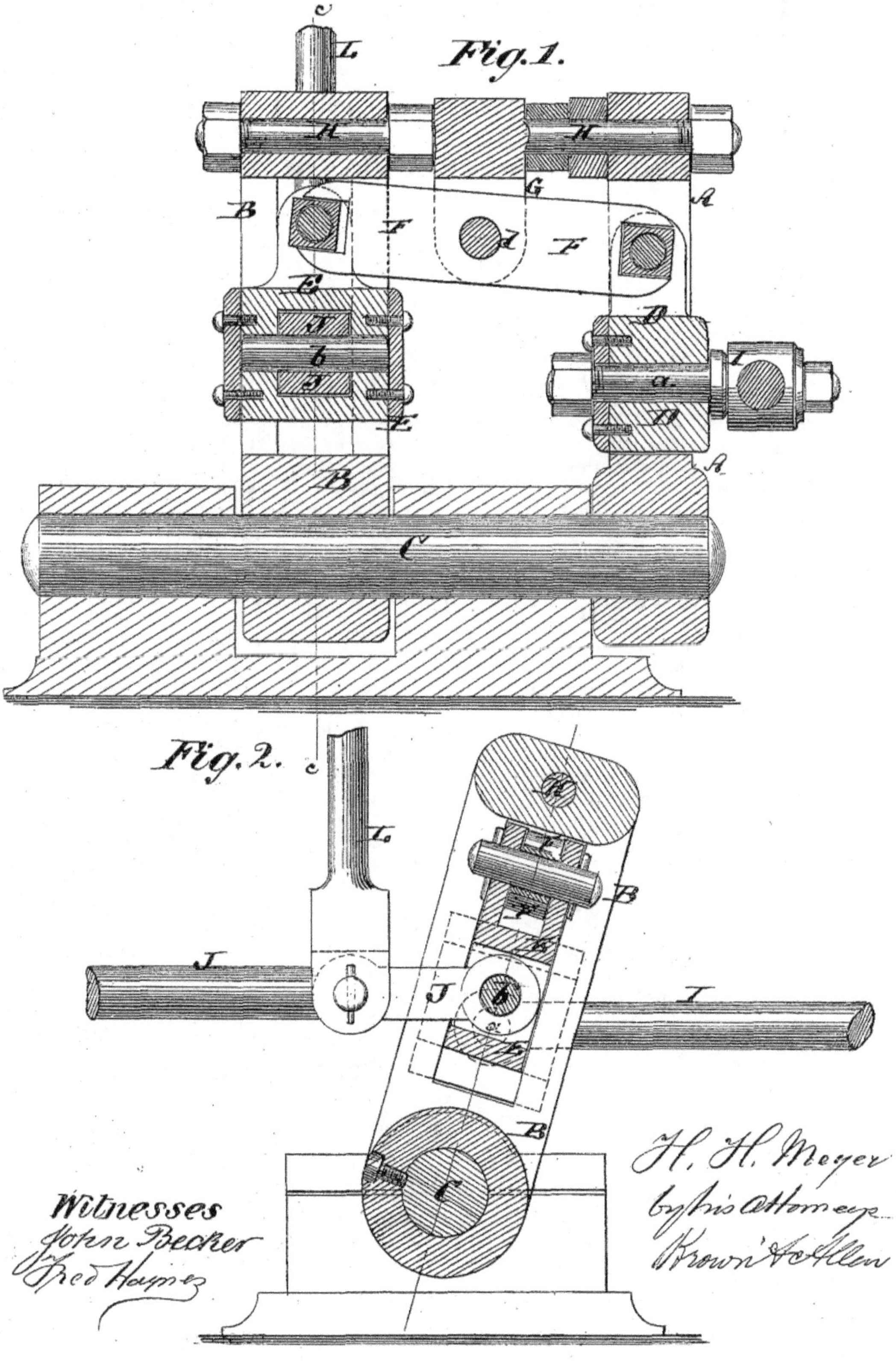
Fig.1.
Fig.2.
Witnesses
John Becker
Fred Haynes
H. H. Meyer
by his Attorneys
Brown & Allen

A.M. PHOTO-LITHOGRAPHIC Co. N.Y. (OSBORNE'S PROCESS)

UNITED STATES PATENT OFFICE.

HERMAN H. MEYER, OF DENVER, COLORADO TERRITORY.

IMPROVEMENT IN GOVERNOR CUT-OFF GEARS.

Specification forming part of Letters Patent No. **142,491**, dated September 2, 1873; application filed April 9, 1873.

To all whom it may concern:

Be it known that I, HERMAN H. MEYER, of Denver, in the county of Arapahoe and Territory of Colorado, have invented a certain new and Improved Governor Cut-Off Gear, of which the following is a specification:

Figure 1 is a sectional side elevation of my improved cut-off gear, and Fig. 2 a vertical transverse section of the same on the line C C, Fig. 1.

Similar letters of reference indicate corresponding parts.

The object of this invention is to produce a very simple, positive, and quick cut-off gear for steam-engines; and the invention consists in connecting the eccentric-rod of the engine and the valve-rod of the same with opposite ends of a vibrating beam, with which the governor is also connected, and which is hung in a frame that is vibrated by the action of the eccentric-rod, so that, when the governor raises or lowers its connection with said beam, the vibratory motion imparted to the valve-rod will thereby be varied in the desired manner by moving the connection of the valve-rod and eccentric-rod nearer to or farther away from the pivot of the aforementioned vibrating frame. In this manner the weight of the eccentric and valve rod is caused to rest on the bearing of the beam, and is thereby balanced to the action of the governor, and, by connecting the two rods to the aforementioned beam, but very little force from the governor is required to advance the cut-off, as the distance through which the governor has to move the valve-rod is but small and the apparatus consequently very sensitive.

In the accompanying drawing, the letters A and B represent two slotted posts or arms secured to a rock-shaft, C, which has its bearings in the bed-plate of the engine, about midway between the cylinder and main shaft. The upper ends of the slotted arms are connected by a rod, H. The eccentric-rod I from the engine-shaft is, by a pin, a, pivoted to a slide or block, D, that is vertically movable on the slotted arm A. The valve-rod J connects in a similar manner by a pivot-pin, b, with a sliding-block, E, which is up and down movable on the arm B. The two blocks D and E are connected by a beam, F, the center of which works on a pin, d, hung in arms G, that are extended from the rod H, as clearly shown in Fig. I. The valve-rod or eccentric-rod may, either one of them, be connected to the governor-rod L, or such governor connection may be directly obtained with one of the slides D E. If the speed of the engine changes, the governor raises or lowers its connection, and thereby carries the valve-rod and block E, when connected therewith, nearer to or farther away from the center of the rock-shaft C, thereby varying the stroke of the valve in the desired manner, and, at the same time that the governor pushes down or raises the valve-rod, the eccentric-rod is moved farther away from, or nearer to, the center of the rock-shaft, thus varying the stroke of the valve still more effectively. The object of the invention is thus fully attained.

What is here claimed, and desired to be secured by Letters Patent, is—

The combination of the eccentric-rod I, slide D, beam F, and slide E with the valve-rod J and governor-connection L, when the beam F, connecting with the slides D E, is hung in a vibrating frame, A B, for operation, substantially as described.

HERMAN H. MEYER.

Witnesses:
F. JENSEN,
JOHN W. WEBSTER.

W. E. MUSGROVE.
Machines for Clearing Streets of Snow.

No. 143,176. Patented September 23, 1873.

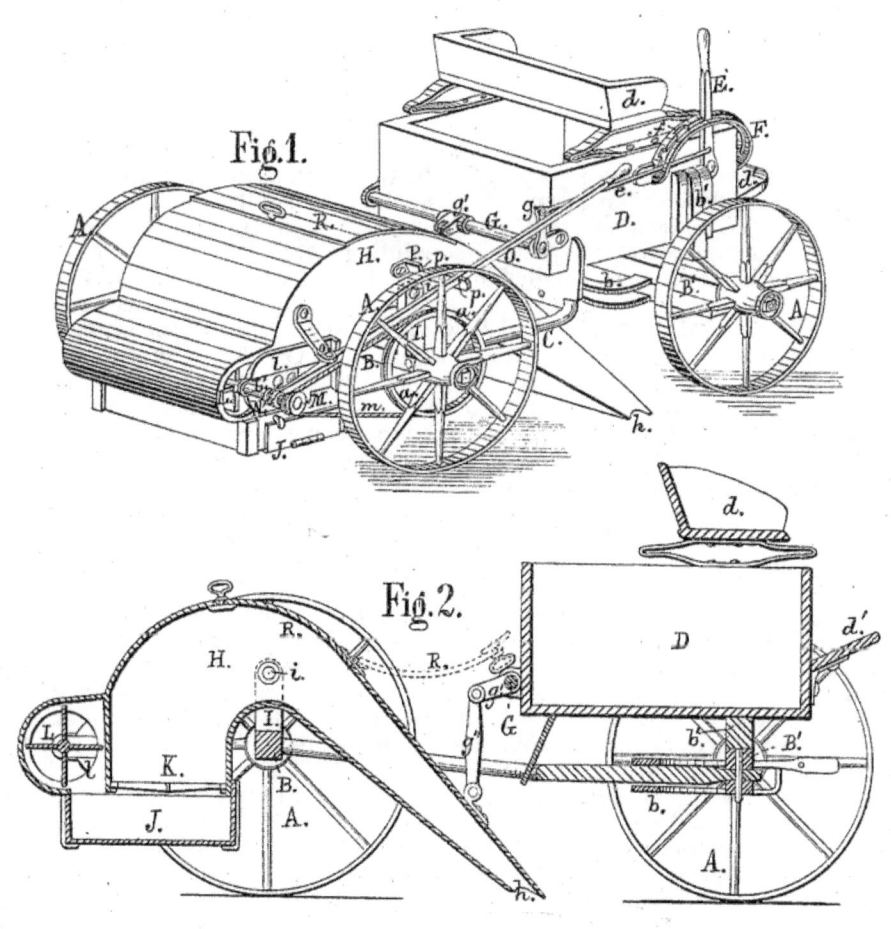

ATTEST:
W. H. Pearce
Walter Allen

INVENTOR:
William E. Musgrove
By Knight Bros
Attys.

UNITED STATES PATENT OFFICE.

WILLIAM E. MUSGROVE, OF FAIR PLAY, COLORADO TERRITORY.

IMPROVEMENT IN MACHINES FOR CLEARING STREETS OF SNOW.

Specification forming part of Letters Patent No. **143,176,** dated September 23, 1873; application filed February 17, 1873.

To all whom it may concern:

Be it known that I, WILLIAM E. MUSGROVE, of Fair Play, in the county of Park and Territory of Colorado, have invented a Machine for the Removal of Snow and Ice from Streets, Roads, &c., of which the following is a specification:

My invention consists of an apparatus supported on wheels, and having a case in which is placed a furnace supplied with an air-blast by a blower, the case ending at front near the ground in a long and narrow opening, through which the heated air and smoke are projected against the snow and ice covering the ground.

Figure 1 is a perspective view. Fig. 2 is a longitudinal section of my machine.

A are the wheels on rear and fore axles B and B', connected together by a forked reach, C. b is the fifth-wheel and tongue-hounds. b' is the fore bolster, supporting a box, D, on which is the seat d and foot-board d'. This box may contain fuel to feed the fire, and its rear end is supported on the reach C. E is a lever running in guides F, having notches f to hold the lever in any position in which it may be placed. The lever E is connected by a rod, e, to a crank, g, upon a rock-shaft, G, carrying also a crank, g', whose outer end is connected by a rod, g'', to the fore end of the case H. The case H is supported on gudgeons i having bearings on standards I arising from the rear axle B. The front part of the case H consists of a chute that increases toward the mouth in transverse breadth, and becomes narrower in the opposite direction, ending forward and downward in a long and narrow mouth, h, whose proximity to the ground is regulated by the lever E. J is the ash-pan; K, the furnace. L is a rotary blower forcing air through the fire, the blast being regulated by sliding dampers l. The shaft L' of the blower carries a loose pulley, M, connected by a belt, m, with a pulley, a, upon the rear wheel, so that the pulley M turns with said wheel, but with a much greater rate of speed. N is a sliding clutch, by which the loose pulley M is clutched to the shaft L', so as to cause the said blower-shaft to turn with the pulley M when desired. The clutch is operated by a forked lever, O, fulcrumed at o, and resting on a bracket, P, having notches p, in which the lever rests to hold the clutch either in or out. R is a door, which is folded back, as shown by dotted lines in Fig. 2, to allow the supply of fuel to the fire.

The inside of the case H, or at least the parts thereof subjected to the greatest heat, would be preferably lined with fire-clay or some analogous substance for the protection of the metal and to prevent escape of heat.

I claim as my invention—

1. The machine for the removal of snow, ice, &c., having the adjustable wide-mouthed case H, furnace K, and blower L, constructed to operate in the manner and for the purposes herein set forth.

2. The combination of the case H supported on gudgeons i, the lever E, and connecting mechanism e g g' g'', for the adjustment of the mouth h in relation to the surface of the ground.

3. The combination of the case H, blower L L', pulley and clutch M N, and lever O, as and for the purpose set forth.

4. The combination of the furnace K, case H, blower L L', pulley M, clutch N, and pulley a attached to the wheel, all substantially as and for the purpose set forth.

WILLIAM E. MUSGROVE.

Witnesses:
SAML. KNIGHT,
ROBERT BURNS.

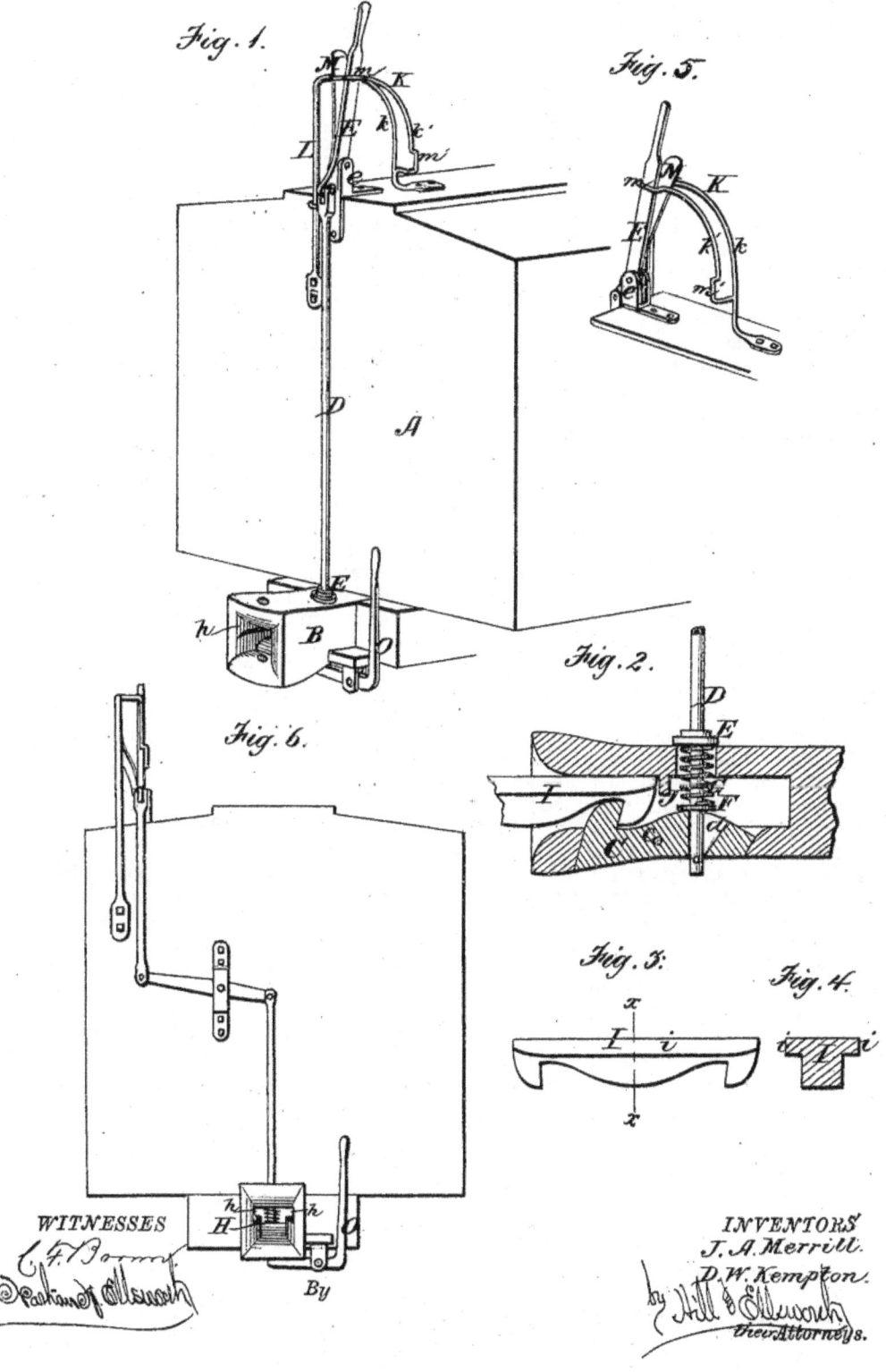

UNITED STATES PATENT OFFICE.

JAY A. MERRILL AND DAVID W. KEMPTON, OF DENVER, COLORADO TER.

IMPROVEMENT IN CAR-COUPLINGS.

Specification forming part of Letters Patent No. **143,524**, dated October 7, 1873; application filed August 8, 1873.

To all whom it may concern:

Be it known that we, JAY A. MERRILL and DAVID W. KEMPTON, both of Denver, in the county of Arapahoe and Territory of Colorado, have invented a new and Improved Car-Coupling; and we do hereby declare the following to be a full and exact description of the same, reference being had to the accompanying drawing forming part of this specification, in which—

Figure 1 is a perspective view of a freight-car provided with my invention. Fig. 2 is a section of the draw-head. Fig. 3 is a side elevation of the double coupling-hook. Fig. 4 is a section through line $x\ x$ of Fig. 3. Fig. 5 is a detached perspective view of the device for holding the lever on the top of the car; and Fig. 6 is a front elevation of a car, showing a different arrangement of levers.

Similar letters of reference in the accompanying drawings denote the same parts.

This invention relates to car-couplings employing a hook in the draw-head in place of the common pin; and has for its object to provide for the public a self-coupling device, adapted principally for freight-cars, which shall be simple in its construction, sure and efficient in its operation, and obviate the necessity of an attendant going between the cars to couple or uncouple the same. To these ends the invention consists in the peculiar construction of the draw-head and coupling devices, as I will now proceed to describe.

In the drawings, A represents a freight-car, and B the draw-head, in the lower side of which is pivoted, at c, the coupling-hook C. D is a vertical rod extending from the lever E at the top of the car, and passing through an enlarged orifice in the draw-head B and a tapering orifice, d, in the rear end of the hook C, as shown in Fig. 2, its lower end being provided with a suitable pin, so that when raised it will elevate the rear end of the hook. The rod D is provided, near the upper surface of the draw-head, with a fixed collar, E, and on the upper surface of the hook C with a loose washer, F. Between the collar E and washer F is a spiral spring, G, which bears down on the rear end of the hook, and holds its forward end up to its work. The front end of the chamber H of the draw-head is somewhat T-shaped, as shown in Fig. 6, in order to hold firmly and keep from sagging the correspondingly-shaped double hook I, which slides freely in the chamber H, but fits it sufficiently close to be held in a nearly horizontal position. The grooves $h\ h$ in the sides of the chamber H are widened at the mouth of the latter, as shown in Fig. 1, their lower sides tapering downward, while the lower sides of the corresponding flanges i of the hook I taper upward at each end, as shown in Fig. 3. The entrance of the hook into the chamber is thus facilitated when the hook happens to be slightly inclined, or when there is some variation between the heights of the draw-heads, and any sharp concussion between the end of the hook and the draw-head is prevented. J represents a stop in the chamber H to prevent the end of the hook I from coming in contact with the spring G and rod D. The lever E is curved outward at its lower end, and is pivoted between ears e on the roof of the car, as shown, the rod D being jointed to its lower end. The upper end of the lever D works in a curved guide, K, composed of two parallel curved pieces, $k\ k'$, supported at the end of the car by a vertical rod, L. The lever E is provided on one side with a curved spring, M, attached to its lower end, and inclined outward at the upper end, where it bears against the part k of the guide K, and presses the lever against the opposite part k', which is provided with recesses $m\ m'$, adapted to hold the lever, which has sufficient lateral play to enable the spring M to force it into said recesses.

It will be seen that when the double hook I is in its place in the draw-head of one car its outer end projects horizontally, and on being forced into the draw-head of an adjacent car its projecting hook passes over the pivoted hook C, the latter yielding to allow it to pass, and afterward returning to place, where it is held by the spring G.

To uncouple, the attendant on the roof of the car throws back the upper end of the lever E, first pressing the latter inward to disengage it from the recess m. This operation raises the rod D, and with it the rear end of the hook C, thus disengaging its forward end from the coupling-hook I. If it is desirable or necessary to hold the hook C in this position—that is, out of connection with the coupling-hook I, the lever E is engaged with the lower orifice m, where it is held by the spring M. This feature is of importance when a car is to be uncoupled from another not in motion, as the brakeman can leave the lever in the proper position, and is not obliged to remain on the roof until the train starts in order to uncouple the car.

For operating the coupling by a person standing on the ground or on the platform, I provide a bell-crank lever, O, which is pivoted at one side of the draw-head, as shown in Figs. 1 and 6, so as to press upward against the bottom of the hook C at its rear end. This, however, is designed for use only in exceptional cases.

In Fig. 6, I have shown a modification of the device for operating the hook C, in which the lever E is located at one side of the car instead of in the center. This arrangement leaves unobstructed the "runway" or passage along the center of the car.

The whole arrangement of parts is simple, and the operation is certain and effective. The pivoted hook C is held up to its work by the spring G, and is not liable to become disengaged, while at the same time it can be held out of connection as long as desired, as before mentioned. The front of the draw-head is provided with orifices for the reception of the ordinary pin, which can be used, if desired, with a link. The stop J protects the spring G from the hook I, which otherwise might enter the chamber sufficiently far to damage the spring.

We claim as our invention—

1. The hook C, provided with the tapering slot or orifice d, in combination with the vertical rod D and spring G, substantially as described.

2. In a draw-head containing a pivoted hook to be operated by a spring-rod passing through the chamber, the stop J, adapted to protect the spring G from the coupling hook or link, substantially as described.

JAY A. MERRILL.
D. W. KEMPTON.

Witnesses:
NATHAN K. ELLSWORTH,
MELVILLE CHURCH.

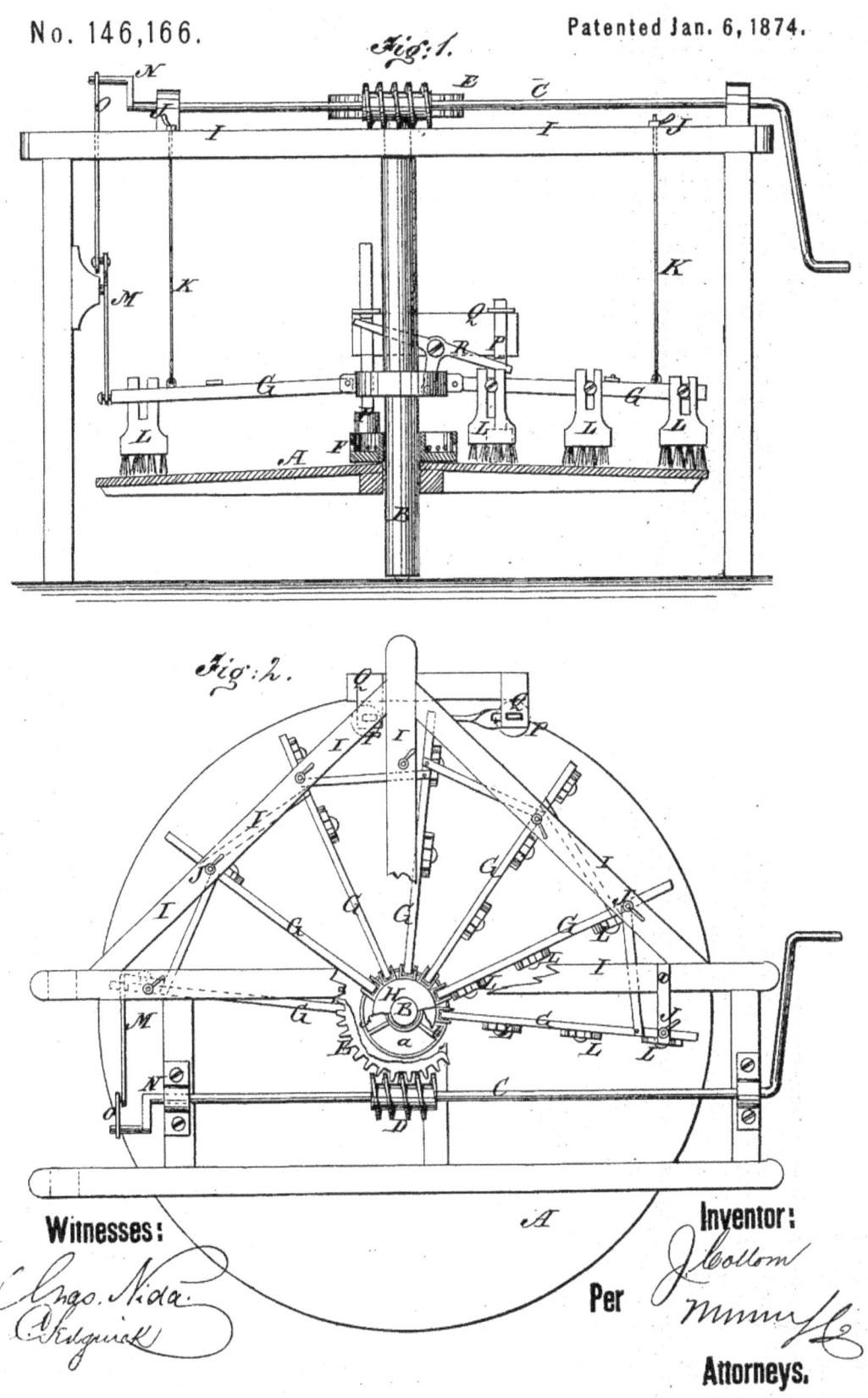

UNITED STATES PATENT OFFICE

JOHN COLLOM, OF IDAHO SPRINGS, COLORADO TERRITORY.

IMPROVEMENT IN ORE-WASHERS OR BUDDLES.

Specification forming part of Letters Patent No. **146,166**, dated January 6, 1874; application filed July 19, 1873.

To all whom it may concern:

Be it known that I, JOHN COLLOM, of Idaho Springs, in the county of Clear Creek and Territory of Colorado, have invented a new and Improved Buddle, of which the following is a specification:

My invention relates to improvements in that class of machines known as revolving buddles, and is designed to provide such machines whereby the separation of ores and other substances of different specific gravities may be effected more completely in less time and at less cost than has hitherto been done. The first part consists of an oscillating and adjusting arrangement of the brooms employed, in connection with the table, and the water-currents for stirring and distributing the pulverized ore on the table. The second part consists of a partitioned distributing-box for regulating and controlling the application of the water; and the third part consists of a pounding apparatus combined with the table for jarring it, as an additional element in the process of separating and distributing the different kinds of ores.

Figure 1 is a transverse sectional elevation of my improved buddle, and Fig. 2 is a plan view with some parts broken out.

Similar letters of reference indicate corresponding parts.

A is a large table or disk arranged on a horizontal plane on a vertical shaft, B. It is constructed so as to descend from the center to the periphery—say, about half an inch to the foot—and it is caused to revolve slowly by a horizontal driving-shaft, C, worm D, and wheel E, or any other suitable means. F is the distributing-box. It is suspended over the center of the disk so as not to revolve, and contains, say, five compartments, a, b, d, e, and f, one for the crude ore, and one for water for each class or grade of ore to be made. G represents the brush-arms. They radiate from a hub, H, on the shaft, a little above the distributing-box, and are arranged to oscillate horizontally. The arms are pivoted to this hub, and near their outer ends they are suspended from an overhead frame, I, by rods K and adjusting-nuts J, by which they can be raised or lowered. These brush-arms are, in this example, seven in number, and they are about equally distributed over one-half of the disk. L represents the brushes, which are suspended from the arms, so as to brush the surface of the disk with more or less force, as required by the case in hand, being attached so as to be adjusted. They are arranged about as far apart on the arms as their breadth, and those on one arm are opposite the spaces of the next, or in any equivalent order, whereby the separation and distribution are better than if the brushes were continuous on the arms, or arranged in concentric circles. The number is diminished on the rearmost arms of the series, and those retained are near the periphery of the disk. The brushes are arranged so as to gradually work the substance under treatment from the center to the periphery of the disk, first the finer portions, and then the coarser parts. The oscillatory motion of the brushes is effected by the bell-crank M, crank N, and connecting-rod O. P represents the pounders, of which, in this example, there are two. They are arranged to drop alternately on the margin of the disk at about the middle of the series of brush-arms, said pounders being provided with any suitable supporting-frame, Q, and apparatus for lifting them, which, in this example, consists of a rock-lever, R, which is actuated by one of the brush-arms. The pounding apparatus is for causing a more rapid settling of the heavier minerals after being stirred by the brooms, so as to leave the lighter particles to be carried off by the water.

The manner in which minerals are separated and concentrated by this improved buddle is as follows: The finely-crushed ore, consisting, say, for instance, of quartz, copper pyrites, iron pyrites, and galena, is conveyed by water through a suitable spout into the compartment a of the distributing-box, from which it passes through the small holes, and spreads itself uniformly upon the surface of the table, the heavier minerals settling mostly near the center, and the lighter near the periphery, but still in a mixed condition, as the separation caused by the running water only is very imperfect. As the table revolves the minerals are subject to the combined action of the clear water from the distributing-box, and the stirring of the brooms, which causes the quartz and other light earthy matter to pass to the periphery of the disk, and then to fall into a suitable receptacle, while, owing to the jarring action of the pounders and the greater density of the other minerals, the latter still remain on the buddle; but the copper pyrites, and then the iron pyrites, being subjected to the action of the other brooms and larger quantities of clean water, are each passed to the circumference, and deposited in separate receptacles. The galena still remaining on the table may be removed by other brooms or scrapers, or be washed off by strong jets of water. I prefer the latter method.

The intensity of the action of the brooms upon the minerals under treatment is increased or diminished by lowering or raising the broom-arms by turning the nuts on the upper end of the suspending-rods. By attention to this, together with a proper regulation of the quantity of water that enters the several compartments of the distributing-box, finely-crushed ores of different specific gravities can be separated more perfectly and with greater economy than by such revolving buddles as have hitherto been in use, some of which have no brooms or partitioned distributing-boxes, and others have stationary brooms, whose slow dull action tends rather to collect and push the various minerals together into ridges than to cause their separation, as the rapid strokes of my oscillating brooms do.

Having thus described my invention, I claim as new and desire to secure by Letters Patent—

1. The combination, with the rotating table or disk, of oscillating brushes, arranged substantially as specified.

2. A partitioned distributing-box, in combination with the rotating table, substantially as specified.

3. A pounding or jarring apparatus combined with the rotating table, substantially as specified.

JOHN COLLOM.

Witnesses:
THOS. J. DEAN,
W. A. ROSS.

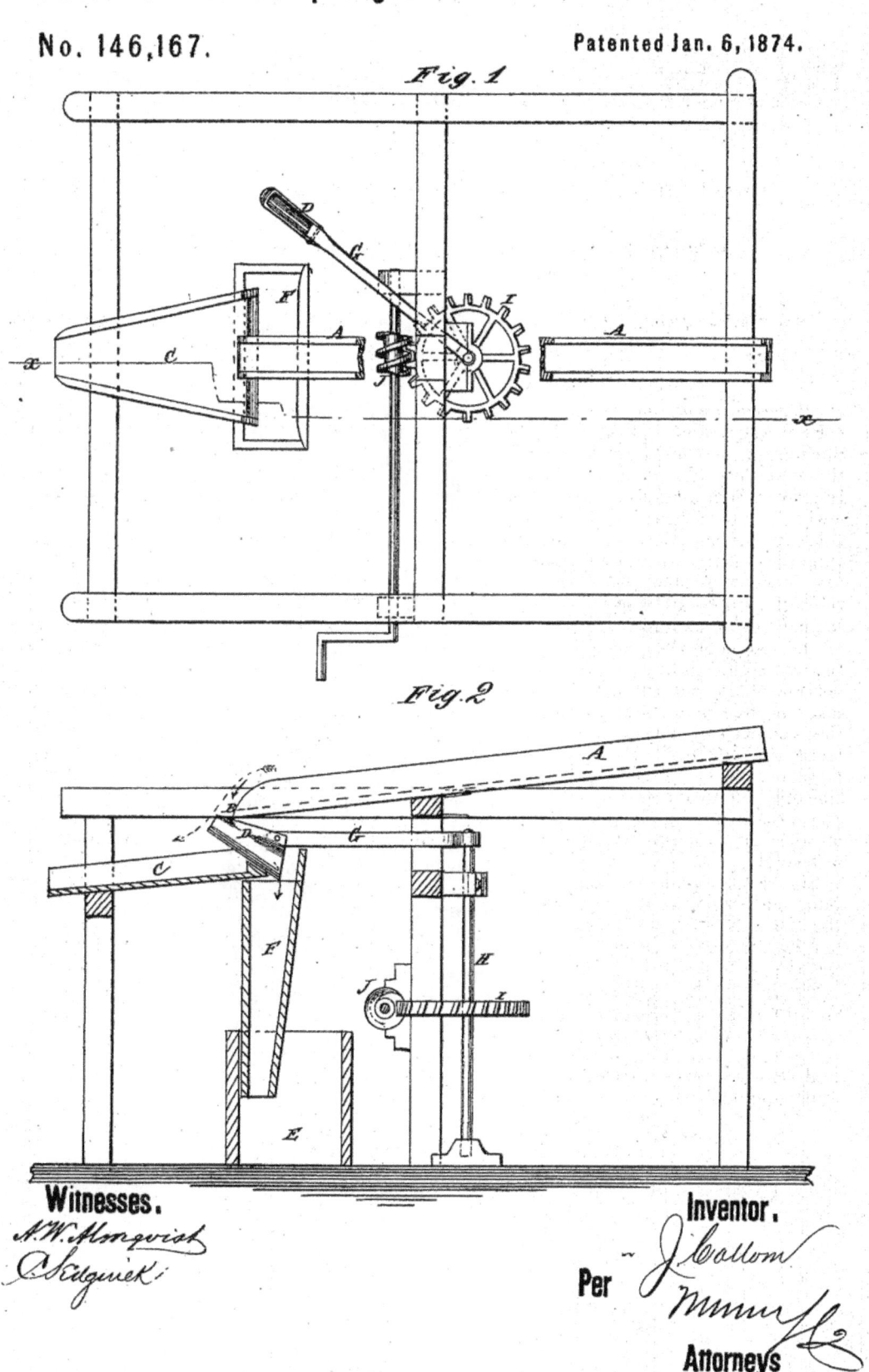

UNITED STATES PATENT OFFICE.

JOHN COLLOM, OF IDAHO SPRINGS, COLORADO TERRITORY.

IMPROVEMENT IN MACHINES FOR SAMPLING ORES AND OTHER MATERIALS.

Specification forming part of Letters Patent No. **146,167**, dated January 6, 1874; application filed July 19, 1873.

To all whom it may concern:

Be it known that I, JOHN COLLOM, of Idaho Springs, in the county of Clear Creek and Territory of Colorado, have invented a new and Improved Sampling-Machine, of which the following is a specification:

My invention consists of a small short spout, which is slowly and regularly moved at intervals under the mouth of a spout or trough, through which the substance to be sampled is caused to run, and receives a certain portion of the said substance, and diverts it from the regular course into a sample-box. The proportion of the substance taken to the whole mass is determined by the proportion which the said short spout or receiver bears to the length of the circuit it travels, in the greater portion of which it is not passing the spout. The object is to obtain from crushed ore, grain, and other substances, samples representing an average as to quality, and the proportionate weight.

Figure 1 is a plan view of my improved sampling-machine, with a part broken out to show the parts below more distinctly. Fig. 2 is a longitudinal sectional elevation taken on the line $x\ x$ of Fig. 1.

Similar letters of reference indicate corresponding parts.

A is the spout through which the substance to be sampled, say crushed ore, is to be carried, and discharged, at the mouth B, into another spout, C, to conduct it away again. D is the short sampling spout or receiver for moving past the mouth B, to receive a small portion while passing, and divert it to the sample-box E, through the spout F. This sampling spout or receiver is mounted on the end of an arm, G, projecting from a revolving shaft, H, which is turned slowly by the wheel I and worm J, the latter being on a shaft, which is turned by any competent power.

The proportion which the width of the receiver bears to the whole circle through which it travels determines the proportion taken of the substance to be sampled.

When crushed ore is to be sampled, it will be run with water through a comparatively flat spout, but for grain, sand, and other dry substances, the descent will be steeper.

Having thus described my invention, I claim as new and desire to secure by Letters Patent—

The combination of the sampling spout or receiver D with a conducting-spout, A, when provided with a revolving shaft and arm, and arranged in a predetermined proportion to its circuit, and also arranged for diverting the substance received by it from the conducting-spout from the regular course into a sample-receiver, substantially as specified.

JOHN COLLOM.

Witnesses:
THOS. J. DEAN,
W. A. ROSS.

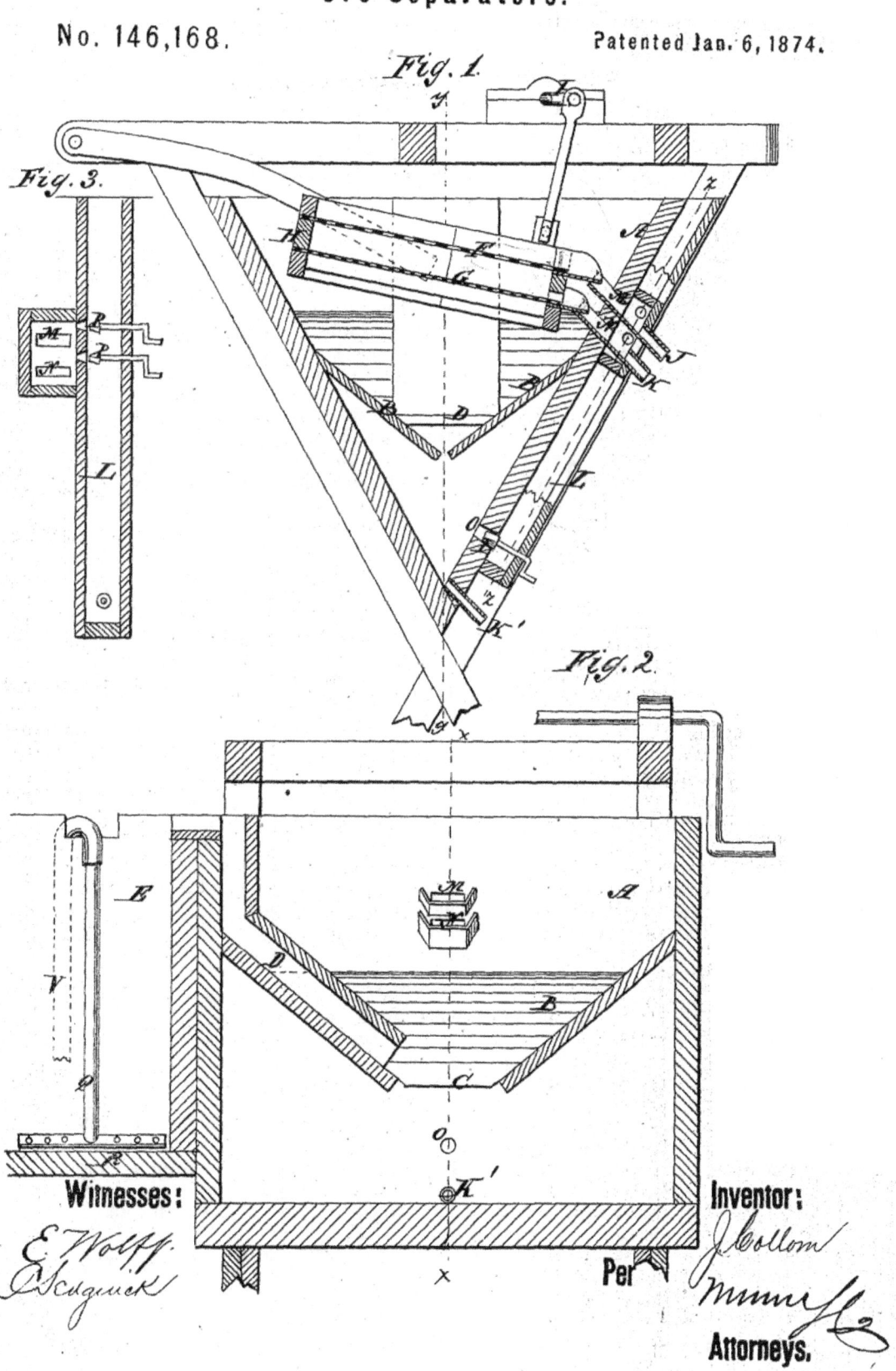

UNITED STATES PATENT OFFICE.

JOHN COLLOM, OF IDAHO SPRINGS, COLORADO TERRITORY.

IMPROVEMENT IN ORE-SEPARATORS.

Specification forming part of Letters Patent No. **146,168**, dated January 6, 1874; application filed July 19, 1873.

To all whom it may concern:

Be it known that I, JOHN COLLOM, of Idaho Springs, in the county of Clear Creek and Territory of Colorado, have invented a new and Improved Ore-Grading Machine, of which the following is a specification:

My invention consists of two or more grading-sieves in the upper portion of a tank of water having appropriate discharge-passages for different grades of material escaping from the sieves, which are actuated in the water by suitable mechanism, and also having a washing attachment so arranged that currents of water are caused to flow upward against the descending currents of ore and separating the "slime" water from the coarser particles, and causing it to flow with the fine particles of ore into another tank, in which is a siphon-pipe adapted to collect that which is sufficiently heavy to settle to the bottom of the water in said tank and convey it to the receptacle for it.

Figure 1 is a transverse sectional elevation of my improved ore-grading machine taken on the line $x\,x$ of Fig. 2. Fig. 2 is a sectional elevation taken on the line $y\,y$ of Fig. 1, and Fig. 3 is a sectional elevation of Fig. 1 on the line $z\,z$.

Similar letters of reference indicate corresponding parts.

A represents a water-tank, which is preferably made with two inclined sides and vertical ends, and has a hopper, B, inside, with a narrow slotted opening, C, at the bottom; also, an inclosed escape-passage, D, leading from the opening C at the bottom of the hopper up over the top of the hopper A into another hopper, E. F and G represent a couple of grading-sieves mounted on a shaking shoe, H, in the upper portion of the hopper A, which is actuated by a crank-shaft, I. The crushed ore is discharged, together with a stream of water, upon the upper end of the upper sieve. The coarse matters escaping off the lower end of sieve F pass out through the side of the hopper by the spout J, and those from sieve G escape by the spout K, while those falling through sieve G, also through the opening C, escape by the spout K'. In order to separate the slime-water and the lighter particles, I attach a washing apparatus, consisting of the water tank or box L, into the top of which a supply of fresh water is caused to flow, and from which the water is caused to flow into tank A through the passages M N O, against the streams of ore, so as to separate the fine particles and slime-water from the larger and heavier grains, and carry them up through passage D into tank E. The water which enters at O encounters the falling ore at the passage C, and there separates the light matters. All these passages for admitting water to the tank A are provided with a regulating valve, P, by which the currents are regulated, as required.

In practice the spouts J, K, and K' discharge into water-tanks in which the water-level is kept about as high as that in tank A, so that the streams flowing into tank A are not carried off with the ore. Any number of grading-sieves may be employed in a gang, and any number of grades can be made.

In the tank B, to which the slime-water and light particles of ore are carried, there is a siphon-pipe, Q, connected with a long perforated pipe, R, in the angle at the bottom of the tank, which collects the particles which are heavy enough to settle, and the siphon carries them out of the tank into the proper receptacle. The part V of the siphon outside of the tank E is made of flexible substance, so that it can be put inside of the tank to be filled for setting the siphon in operation.

Having thus described my invention, I claim as new and desire to secure by Letters Patent—

1. The combination of a set of inclined submerged grading-sieves, a water-tank, and apparatus for actuating the sieves, substantially as specified.

2. The combination of means for injecting currents of fresh water, and the escape-passage D with the submerged sieves, substantially as specified.

3. The inverted T-shaped siphon-pipe, combined with a V-shaped receiving-tank, E, for the slime-water, substantially as specified.

4. The said siphon-pipe, provided with a flexible portion, V, substantially as specified.

JOHN COLLOM.

Witnesses:
 THOS. J. DEAN,
 W. A. ROSS.

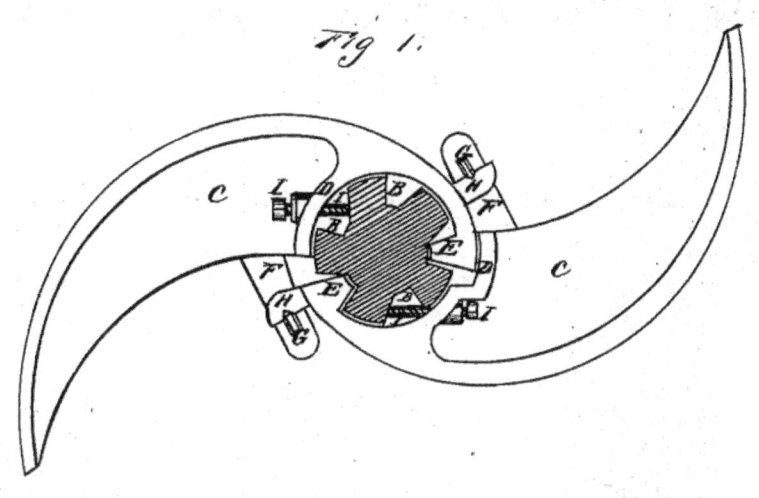
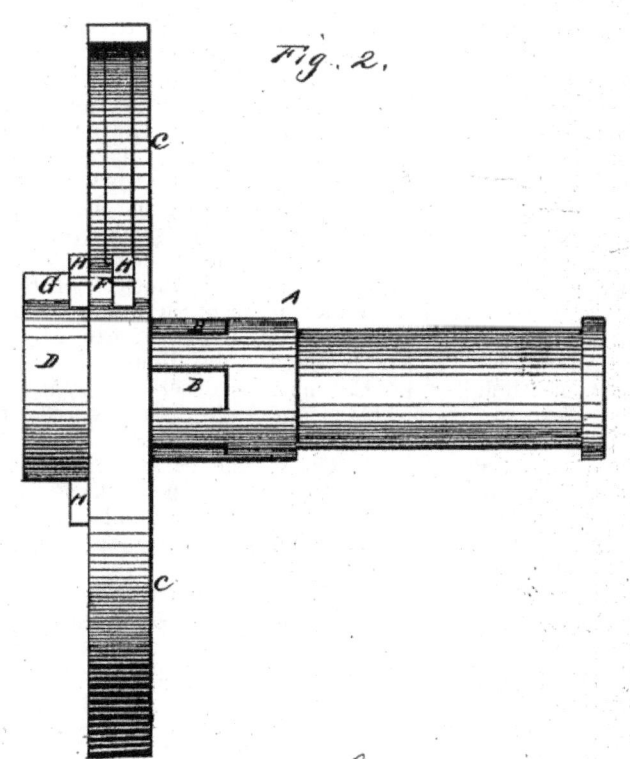

UNITED STATES PATENT OFFICE.

JOHN F. MALLINCKRODT, OF MIDDLE BOULDER, COLORADO TERRITORY.

IMPROVEMENT IN SECTIONAL CAMS.

Specification forming part of Letters Patent No. **146,193**, dated January 6, 1874; application filed July 3, 1873.

To all whom it may concern:

Be it known that I, JOHN F. MALLINCKRODT, of Middle Boulder, Boulder county, Territory of Colorado, have invented a Sectional Cam; and I do hereby declare the following description and accompanying drawings are sufficient to enable any person skilled in the art or science to which it most nearly appertains to make and use my said invention or improvement without further invention or experiment.

The object of my invention is to provide an improved sectional cam which can be easily taken from and readjusted to the shaft upon which it is secured, and thus avoid the difficulties which are met with when one of the old style of entire cams breaks, or when it is necessary to change the relative positions of a number of cams upon the same shaft. My invention consists, principally, in a novel and simple mode of constructing the two parts of the cam, so that they can be effectually secured to their place upon the shaft, in which key-seats are set.

Referring to the accompanying drawings for a more complete explanation of my invention, Figure 1 is a transverse section of the cam-shaft, showing a side view of the cam. Fig. 2 is an edge view of the cam upon its shaft.

A is the shaft, upon which any number of cams are to be secured. This shaft has the key-seats B cut in it longitudinally, and into these seats the hooks from the cams are placed. The cam is divided into two parts, C C, each having a section of a long stout hub, D, cast or otherwise formed with it. From the ends of each of these sections, which form the inner extension of the backs of, or lifting-faces of, the cams, a hook, E, projects inward, and this hook fits into one of the key-seats B. From the inside of the web of the cam a lug, F, projects, and this is slotted, so as to admit a wedge or key, G. Two similar lugs, H, arise from the hub, just behind the hook E, and the lug F of each section passes between the lug H of the opposite section. The key G, being then driven through the slot in the lug F and behind the lugs G, holds the whole cam firmly to its place. As the hooks do not fit absolutely tight in the key-seats B, the cam might move backward a little upon the shaft. In order to prevent this, I employ a set-screw, I, which passes through the hub of each half of the cam and enters one of the key-seats, so that, when drawn tight, its force is exerted against that of the hooks. This holds the cam strongly in its place, and at the same time renders it a short operation to change the position of or renew a cam. The lifting-face of the cam is formed by bending upon it a plate of spring-steel, which can be renewed at any time.

Having thus described my invention, what I claim, and desire to secure by Letters Patent, is—

1. The sectional cam composed of the two parts C C, having the hooks E, fitting into the key-seats of the shaft, and secured by the lugs F and H and the key G, substantially as herein described.

2. In combination with the sections C C of a cam with other hooks E, the set-screw I, substantially as and for the purpose described.

In witness whereof I hereunto set my hand and seal.

JOHN F. MALLINCKRODT. [L. S.]

Witnesses:
  C. E. BONNEL,
  CHARLES H. HOOK.

J. H. ROWLAND.
Mitering-Machines.

No. 146,403. Patented Jan. 13, 1874.

UNITED STATES PATENT OFFICE.

JOHN HENRY ROWLAND, OF DENVER, COLORADO TERRITORY.

IMPROVEMENT IN MITERING-MACHINES.

Specification forming part of Letters Patent No. **146,403**, dated January 13, 1874; application filed November 8, 1873.

To all whom it may concern:

Be it known that I, JOHN H. ROWLAND, of Denver, in the county of Arapahoe and Territory of Colorado, have invented a new and Improved Mitering-Machine, of which the following is a specification:

This invention consists of a saw-guide and plane-guide for controlling the saw and plane in cutting off and smoothing the wood sticks, with which there are a couple of shifting-stops and a scale for a guide, by which to adjust the stops against which the wood pieces are held for sawing bevels of any angle, right or left, and the support for said stops is jointed to the saw and plane guide so as to be adjusted around its major axis, and at right angles to the direction in which the shifting-stops change the angles of the miters for making "splayed" miters.

Figure 1 is a front elevation of my improved mitering-machine. Fig. 2 is a plan view. Fig. 3 is a sectional elevation taken on the line $x\,x$ of Fig. 2; and Fig. 4 is an end elevation.

Similar letters of reference indicate corresponding parts.

A is a bed piece to be bolted or otherwise fastened to the work-bench; B and C, the saw and plane guide, supported above the front edge, at right angles to its surface, the part C being on the metal bars D, which are secured to the front edge of the bed, so that they can be shifted up or down to adjust said part C as far above the part B as required by the width of the plane and the stuff to be sawed, the latter being presented from the left-hand side, so as to project through the space between the two parts far enough to be sawed off and planed by the saw and plane running alongside of the saw-guide, the plane being turned over on one side, and its bottom placed against the guide, outside of the plane-bit, so that the latter does not come in contact with the guide. D' represents metal plates attached to the ends of the bed, and projecting beyond the saw and plane guide to the left, about as far as the width of the table E, which holds the work, and having a curved slot, F, near the left end, which is considerably widened to make sufficient breadth for the required length of the slot, in which works a binding-screw, G, which screws into the end of the work-table E, which is pivoted at H in the plane of the saw and plane guide, so as to swing down below the horizontal plane to any degree that may be required for making splayed miters. The table has two adjustable stops, I, against which the wood pieces are held for sawing and dressing them to make the miters, one for right and the other for left hand bevels, said stops being pivoted at J, near the saw and plane gage, and having a binding-screw, K, working in a curved slot, L, in the table, for holding the stops fast. A scale, M, is provided for the stops I, and another at N for the vertical adjustment of the table. The stops I swing around to a right angle to the saw and plane gage, and meet there against a stationary stop, O, for which said stops I are each notched at P, so that they are not arrested until they meet together, and come to a right angle with the saw and plane guide.

Thus I have contrived a more simple and efficient machine for sawing and smoothing ordinary miters of any angle, also splayed miters, than any heretofore made, as I believe.

Having thus described my invention, I claim as new and desire to secure by Letters Patent—

1. The combination of the bed A, saw and plane guide B C, work-table E, and adjustable stops I, for sawing and smoothing miters, substantially in the manner described.

2. The work-table E, jointed to the bed, and the saw and plane guide, and having the fastening-screws G, substantially as specified.

JOHN HENRY ROWLAND.

Witnesses:
GILBERT STANLEY,
JAMES STAPLES.

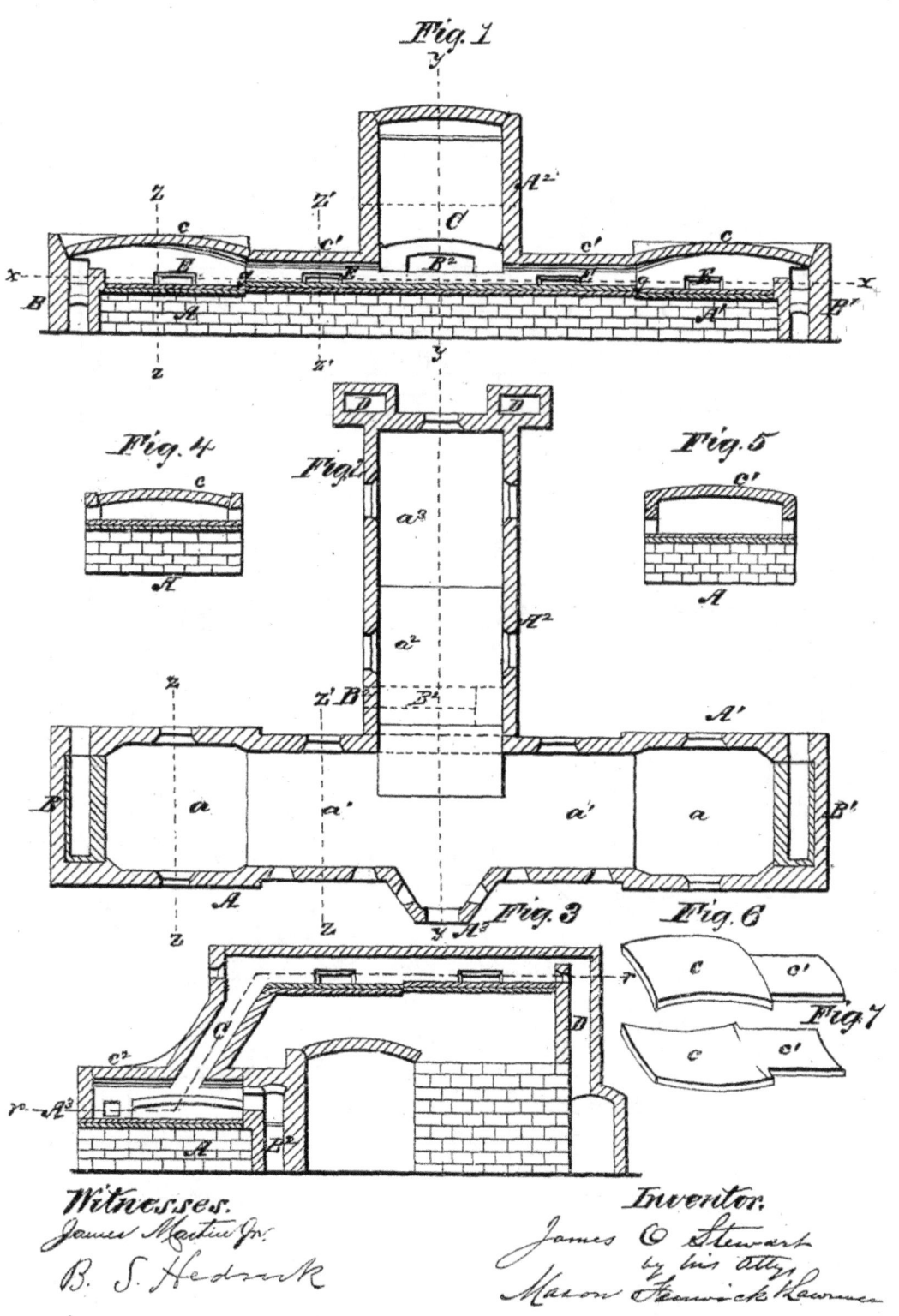

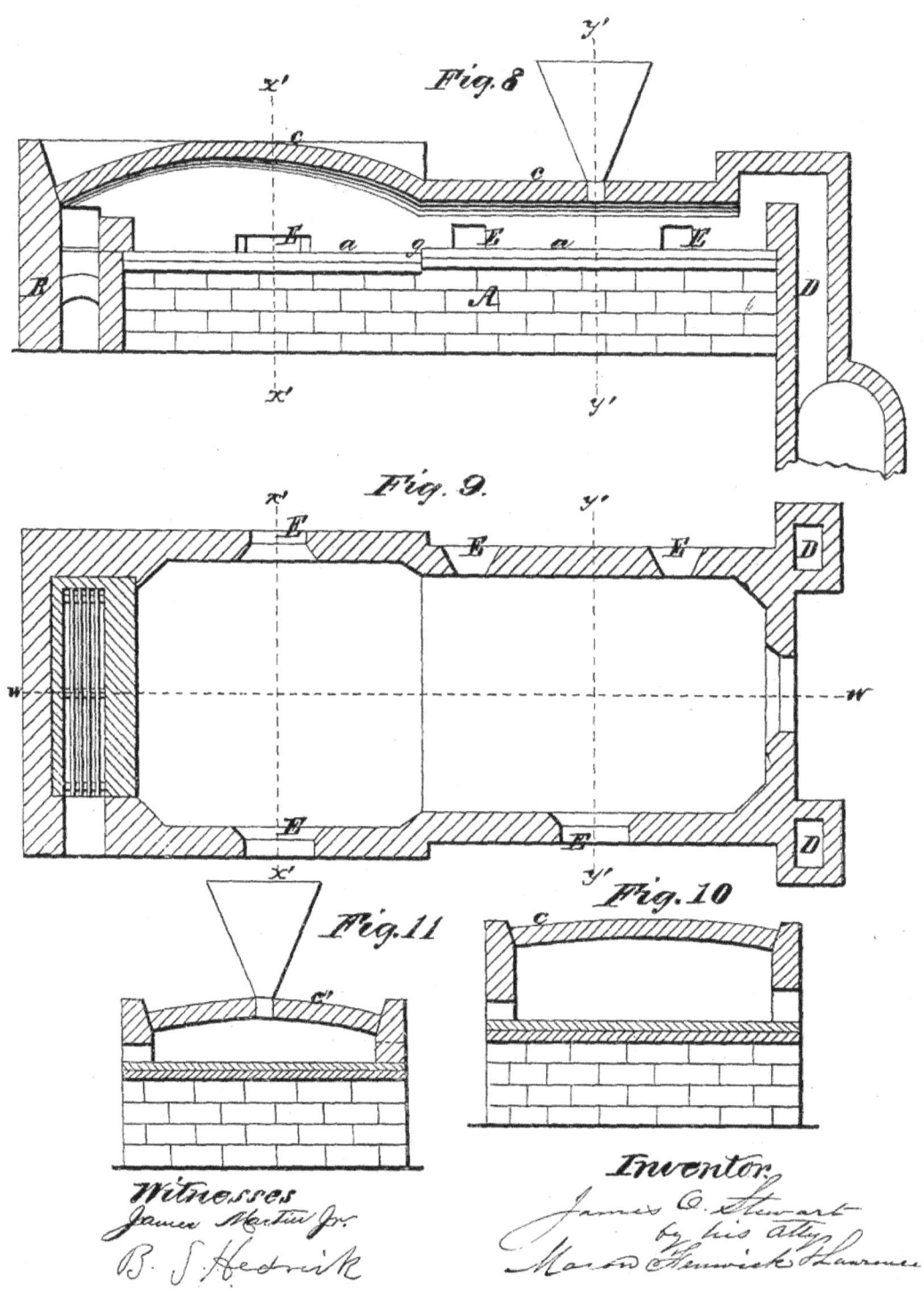

UNITED STATES PATENT OFFICE.

JAMES O. STEWART, OF GEORGETOWN, COLORADO TERRITORY.

IMPROVEMENT IN REVERBERATORY FURNACES FOR ROASTING ORES, &c.

Specification forming part of Letters Patent No. **148,096**, dated March 3, 1874; application filed January 15, 1874.

To all whom it may concern:

Be it known that I, J. OSCAR STEWART, of Georgetown, county of Clear Creek, Territory of Colorado, have invented a new and useful Improvement in Reverberatory Furnaces for Roasting, Desulphurizing, or Chloridizing Ores and Minerals or metallic products; and I do hereby declare that the following is a full, clear, and exact description thereof, reference being had to the accompanying drawings, making part of this specification, in which—

Figure 1, Plate I, is a vertical longitudinal section of my improved furnace, constructed with three roasting or treating chambers in communication with one another. Fig. 2 is a horizontal section of the same in the line $x\ x$ of Fig. 1. Fig. 3 is a vertical transverse section in the line $y\ y$ of Figs. 1 and 2. Fig. 4 is a cross-section in the line $z\ z$ of Fig. 1. Fig. 5 is a similar section in the line $z'\ z$ of Fig. 1. Figs. 6 and 7 are perspective views of the upper and under sides of the combined cylindric and spherical top or arch of the roasting or treating chambers. Fig. 8 is a longitudinal section of my improved combined cylindric and spherical top applied to a furnace with a single roasting or treating chamber, the section being in the line $w\ w$ of Fig. 9. Fig. 9 is a horizontal section of the same. Fig. 10 is a cross-section in the line $x\ x'$ of Figs. 1 and 2. Fig. 11 is a similar section in the line $y\ y$ of Figs. 8 and 9.

My invention is designed for that class of reverberatory furnaces which is adapted for roasting, desulphurizing, or chloridizing ores, minerals, or metallic products.

The nature of my invention consists, first, in varying the length and width of the roasting or treating chambers of each furnace relatively, and combining with the same an arch or crown, which is in form of a segment of a hollow sphere, where it overhangs or covers the first hearth of the roasting-chamber, and in form of a segment of a cylinder where it overhangs or covers a second, or a second and third, hearth of said chamber. This construction, as will hereinafter be made to appear, enables the operator to utilize the heat in a more proper manner and to a greater extent than can be done with other forms of furnace tops or crowns in use. It consists, second, in combining an elevated furnace in a peculiar manner with one or more low-down furnaces, so that an auxiliary fire-box is employed, from which heat passes over a hearth, which is underneath the flue which connects the lower furnace with the upper furnace.

By this arrangement, as will hereinafter be made to appear, a fresh supply of heat to the ore is provided at a point where the main-furnace heat is losing its temperature, and this fresh heat, combining with the heat from the main furnaces, heats the charge of ore which is on the hearth directly adjoining the auxiliary fire-box, and, passing through the flue to the upper furnace, is sufficient to ignite and keep the sulphur burning in the ores of said furnace. Thus all the heat is utilized to the best advantage, and hence the expense for fuel reduced. Labor is also saved, inasmuch as the ore can be very expeditiously handled or moved from hearth to hearth.

The construction of the crowns, together with the combination of furnaces, enables the operator to roast a greater number of tons of material in a given time than has heretofore been accomplished with furnaces with which I am familiar.

To enable others skilled in the art to understand my invention, I will proceed to describe it.

$A\ A^1$ represent two furnaces on a plane (for instance) with the horizon. A^2, a furnace elevated above this plane. $B\ B^1$ are the fire-boxes of the furnaces $A\ A^1$, and B^2 is the fire-box of the furnace A^2. The furnace B^2 is placed at right angles to the furnaces $A\ A^1$, and the side walls of its front end are carried over to the front wall of said furnace, and also made to unite with an extension or bulging front portion, A^3, of said furnaces, as shown. The portion of the furnace A^2 which extends over the meeting ends of the furnaces $A\ A^1$ forms a flue, C, which connects with the fire-box B^2, which is just in rear of the meeting ends of the furnaces $A\ A^1$, as shown. The furnaces $A\ A^1$ have hearths $a\ a^1$, and the furnace A^2 hearths $a^2\ a^3$, as shown. The hearth a is considerably broader than the hearth a^1, and consequently the walls upon which the crowning portion of this hearth rests are set farther apart. The hearth a is nearly square, while that of a^1 is oblong. The part a of the furnace is crowned with an arch, c, which presents the form of a segment of a hollow sphere, while the part a^1 is crowned with an arch, c^1, which is in the form of a segment of a cylinder. This combination crown is shown clearly in Figs. 6 and 7 of the drawings. At the point where the flue of the auxiliary fire-box is employed the bulged-out portion of the front wall of the main furnace or furnaces is connected to the flue-wall by means of a crown, c^2, which is a segment of a hollow sphere. D D are the draft-flues, and E E E the work-doors to the hearths of the furnace, and g steps between the hearths.

In Figs. 8 and 9 the same construction of furnace in all respects to the one just described is maintained, except that only one roasting-chamber, A, with its own fire-box and draft-flues D, is adopted in the erection and working of the furnace. This single furnace may have three hearths like those a a^1, and in that case the cylindric portion of the crown will be double the length of the spherical portion, and another step like g will be constructed between the two hearths which come under this cylindric arch.

To facilitate the description, I will first describe the operation of the single furnace, Figs. 8 and 9, and I shall speak of it as having three working hearths instead of two. A charge of ore being placed upon the third hearth which is nearest the draft-flue, the sulphur begins to ignite, and, after about three hours' stirring, is moved upon the hearth a^1, or No. 2, by means of spades or hoes through the back and front side work-doors. Another charge of ore is now placed upon the vacated hearth just referred to. The ore on both hearths is stirred for about three hours more, when it is found that ore on hearth a^1 is nearly desulphurized—that is, the raw sulphur has been burned out, and the metals, having taken up oxygen from air admitted to the furnace through the fire-box and work-doors, are formed into sulphates, so that the ore has changed its color, and gives off a light sulphurous-acid odor. This charge of ore, then, on the hearth a^1 is moved forward, as before stated, to hearth a, or No. 1, and the ore on hearth No. 3 (not shown) is moved to hearth a^1, or No. 2, and a new charge of ore takes its place. As soon as these manipulations are ended, about four to ten per cent. of common salt is thrown in and intimately mixed with the ore on the hearth No. 1, and, as the sulphuric or sulphurous acid present does decompose the salt, the chlorine is liberated from the salt, which chlorine, in part, is absorbed by the metals present, such as gold, silver, and a portion of lead, zinc, and iron, formed into chlorides of these metals. Just for this reason the ore must be at a good heat, above a high red heat, but not to a white heat, and at the same time it is of the utmost importance that a large supply of fresh undecomposed air be admitted to this ore on this hearth a, in order to get rid of the last traces of sulphurous acid; and to accomplish this chemical reaction I have found the arch, with the peculiar combination of spherical and cylindric form, to be very important, because it admits (by being highly curved over the hearth a) of a large full fire, so that plenty of cold air can be used and still not chill the charge on the hearths beyond this first charge; and, at the same time, while such heat under any other shaped crown to the hearth a would sinter or bake and spoil the ore on hearth a; this allows the heat to pass along this crown to the transverse or cylindric crown, with which it is combined and united, where the heat is depressed down upon hearth a^1 and the hearth No. 3 (not shown) without being chilled by the admission of so much air to the ore on the hearth a. When all the charges of ore are stirred about three hours from the time of moving the ore on hearth a, it is found that this last-mentioned ore has become chloridized, having changed its color again and become spongy or woolly, and it gives off a sweet chlorine smell. It is now withdrawn from the furnace and the manipulation continues as before stated.

The relative proportions of the hearths of the furnace, whose operation has been just described, may be as follows: Hearth a, 9 x 9 in clear; hearth a^1, 8 x 10 in clear; and hearth referred to as No. 3, but not shown, 8 x 12 in clear.

The operation of the combined furnace, Figs. 1, 2, and 3, is as follows: The ore is admitted on the last hearth a^3 of the elevated furnace; it is stirred for an hour or an hour and a half; the sulphur here ignites as on hearth No. 3 of single furnace; the charge is then moved forward to the hearth a^2, and a new charge takes the place of it. Both charges are stirred about one hour and a half, or less, and the charge on this second hearth is drawn down upon the hearth in the lower furnace where the auxiliary fire is located, and the charges in the elevated furnace proceed as before. The charge which is under the auxiliary fire having lost a large portion of its sulphur before it reached the hearth, requires an increased amount of heat to keep its remaining sulphur ignited or burning, and for this purpose this auxiliary fire at this point is very essential. This charge of ore, after stirring about one and a half hours, is moved upon either one of the intermediate hearths a^1 of the furnaces A A¹, and is in a short time ready to take salt, as heretofore stated, and be treated in all respects the same as in the operation of the single furnace. Other charges of ore constantly taking its place, it in due time is finished by chloridizing it under the high curved crown, when it is withdrawn from the furnace.

What I claim as my invention, and desire to secure by Letters Patent, is—

1. The furnace for roasting, desulphurizing, or chloridizing ores, as described and shown, with a roof constructed as at $c\ c'$, and with the

part c of said roof nearest to the fire-box B and the part c' farthest therefrom, substantially as described.

2. The chamber of the furnace A^2 constructed on a higher plane than the chamber of furnace A, combined with the fire-box B and B^2 and connected with the chamber of the furnace A by flue C, substantially as and for the purpose described.

3. The elevated furnace A^2, with its flue C and fire-box B^2, as described, in combination with the furnaces A A^1, constructed with the roofs c c' and fire-boxes B B^1, substantially as described.

JAMES O. STEWART.

Witnesses:
ANTHONY J. AUGUST,
JERRY G. MAHANY.

R. C. MOWBRAY.
Door-Securers.

No. 148,574. Patented March 17, 1874.

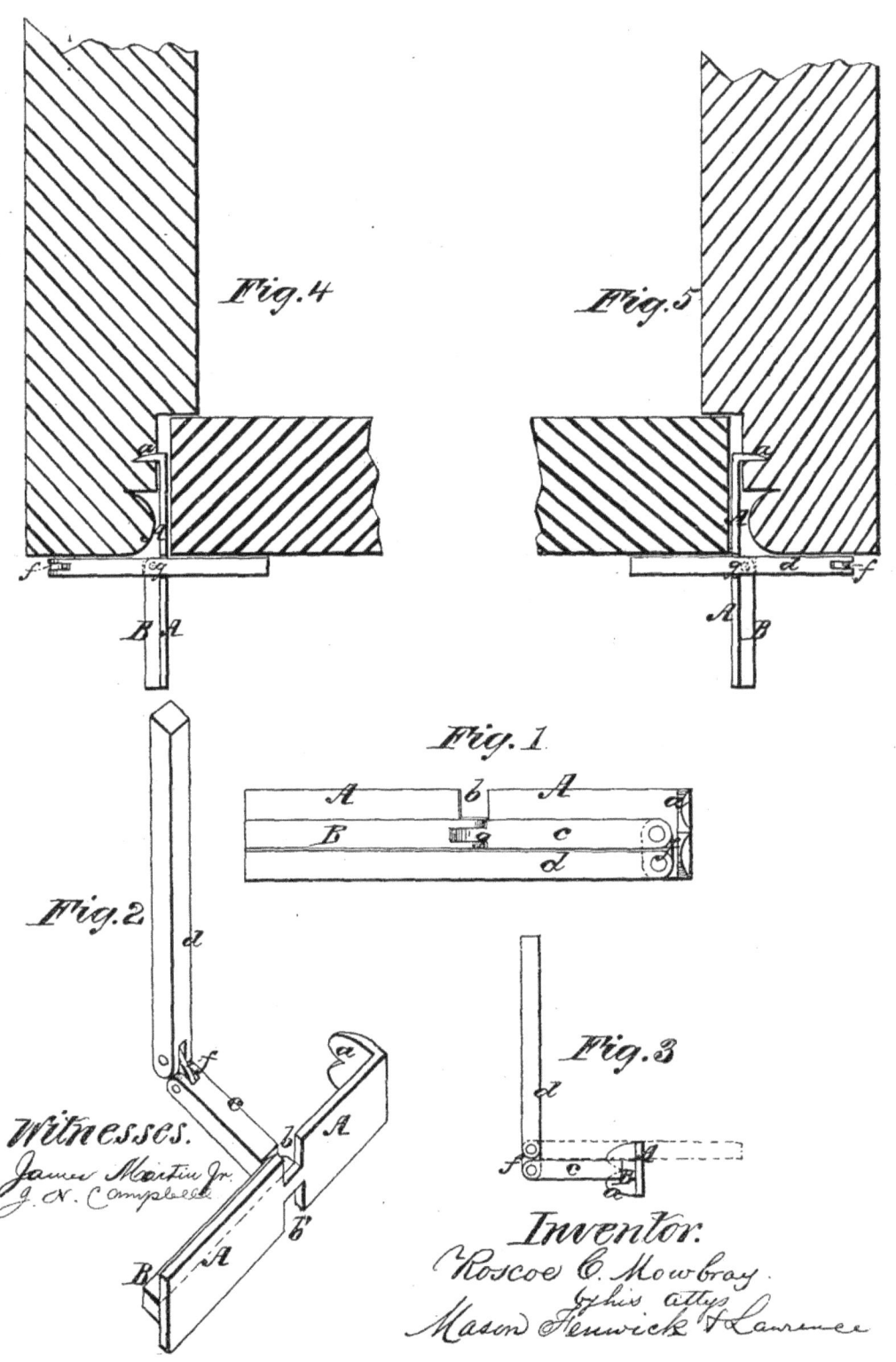

UNITED STATES PATENT OFFICE.

ROSCOE C. MOWBRAY, OF DENVER, COLORADO TERRITORY.

IMPROVEMENT IN DOOR-SECURERS.

Specification forming part of Letters Patent No. **148,574**, dated March 17, 1874; application filed February 14, 1874.

CASE B.

To all whom it may concern:

Be it known that I, ROSCOE C. MOWBRAY, of Denver, Arapahoe county, Territory of Colorado, have invented a new and Improved Portable Door-Fastening; and I do hereby declare that the following is a full, clear, and exact description thereof, reference being had to the accompanying drawing making part of this specification, in which—

Figure 1 is a back view of my fastening as folded to be carried in the pocket or other place. Fig. 2 is a perspective view of the same as unfolded and ready for application to a door. Fig. 3 is an end view of it in the same condition as in Fig. 2. Fig. 4 shows a horizontal section of a left-hand door and jamb, with the fastening applied between the jamb and door. Fig. 5 is a similar section of a right-hand door and jamb with the fastening applied to it.

My invention consists, first, in the combination, with a supporting-plate which has one of its ends bent over at right angles to its face, and notched on its edge about midway of its length, of a hinged and jointed stay-bar. This combination is such that the bar can be folded against the back of the supporting-plate, and also can be unfolded, and again partly folded, so as to enter the notch in the edge of the plate on either edge, and stand across the crack which is between the door and jamb. My invention consists, second, in a plate provided with a notch on each edge, in combination with the hinged and jointed bar, whereby the fastener can be readily used on a right or left hand door-jamb.

To enable others skilled in the art to understand my invention, I will proceed to describe it.

A is a supporting-plate, with one of its ends bent over at right angles to its face. This bent-over end a is cut so as to present sharp entering-points, as shown. In each edge of the plate, about midway of its length, rectangular notches $b\ b'$ are cut. B is a narrow rib, formed or placed in the center on the back of the plate A, at the opposite end from the entering-points. This rib terminates at the notches $b\ b'$. To the inner end of this rib a bar, c, equal in length to the distance between the notches and the end a, is hinged, as at g; and to the free end of this bar another bar, d, double the length of the bar c, is connected and hinged by means of a short double-joint link, f, as shown.

In Fig. 1, it will be seen that the plate A is broad enough to allow the bar d to be folded against its back. It will also be seen that the short link f allows it to be so folded that its edge will be on the outside of and parallel with the edge of the rib B and short bar c. The plate thus serves as a sort of protection and case to it when not in use.

To use the invention in a left-hand door-jamb, the traveler only has to unfold it, as in Fig. 3, introduce the plate between the edge of the door and the face of the jamb, and close the door hard enough to drive the points of the end a into the jamb, and then turn down the bar d across the door-crack into the rectangular notch, as shown in Fig. 4.

To use it on a right-hand door-jamb, he must turn the fastener so as to bring the points of the end a toward the jamb, and bring the bar d to the top, and proceed just the same as when using it in a left-hand door-jamb.

What I claim as my invention, and desire to secure by Letters Patent, is—

1. The combination of the jointed and hinged bars $c\ d$ with the rib B and the plate A, notched on its edge, as at b, substantially as and for purpose set forth.

2. The notches $b\ b'$ of the plate, in combination with the hinged bars and rib, thus giving reversibility, and permitting attachment to either a right or left hand door-jamb, substantially as described and shown.

3. The short double-joint link f between the long bar and the short bar in the construction of the fastener, as and for the purpose herein described.

ROSCOE C. MOWBRAY.

Witnesses:
G. I. STEBBINS,
A. ARNOLD.

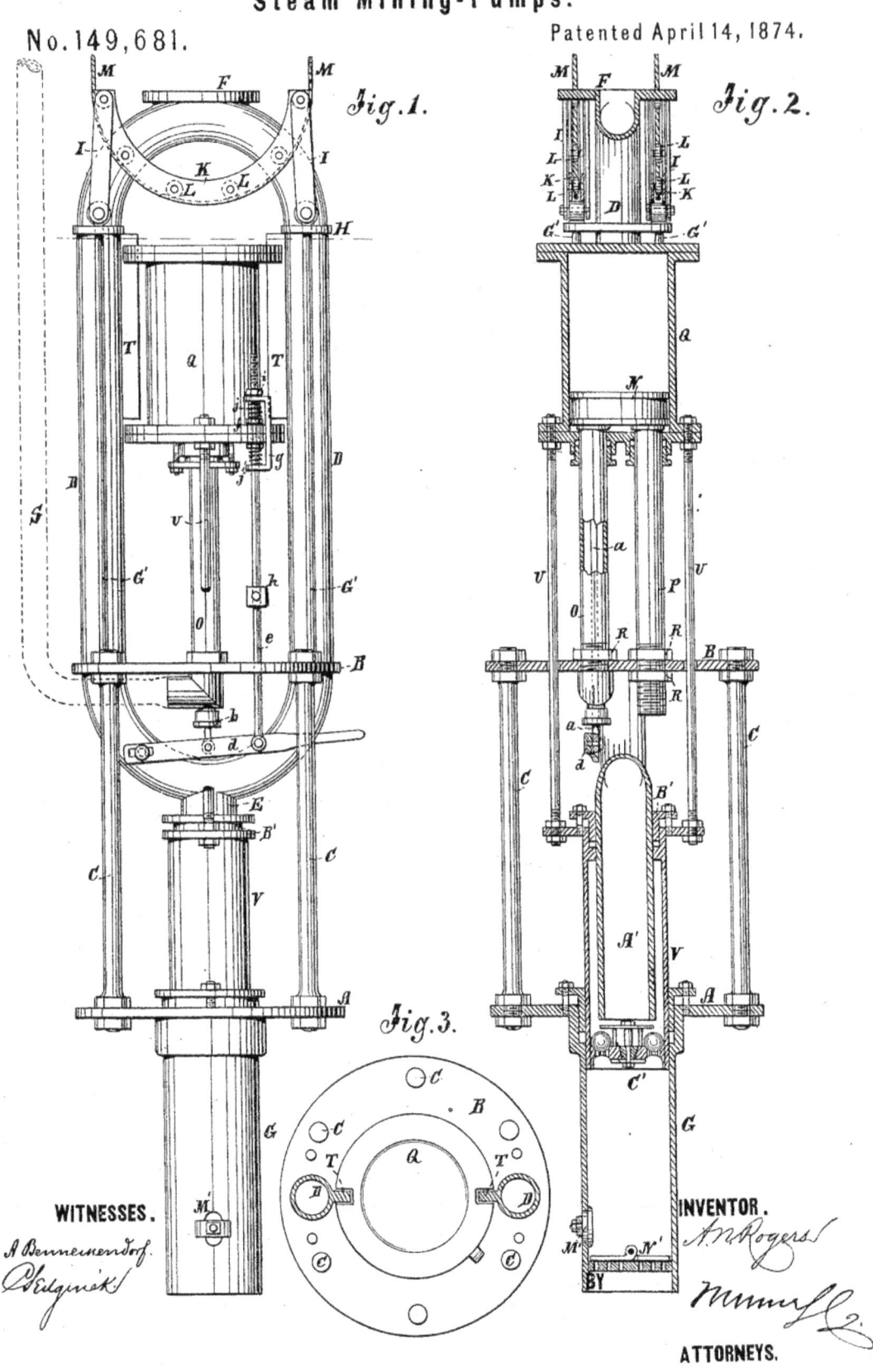

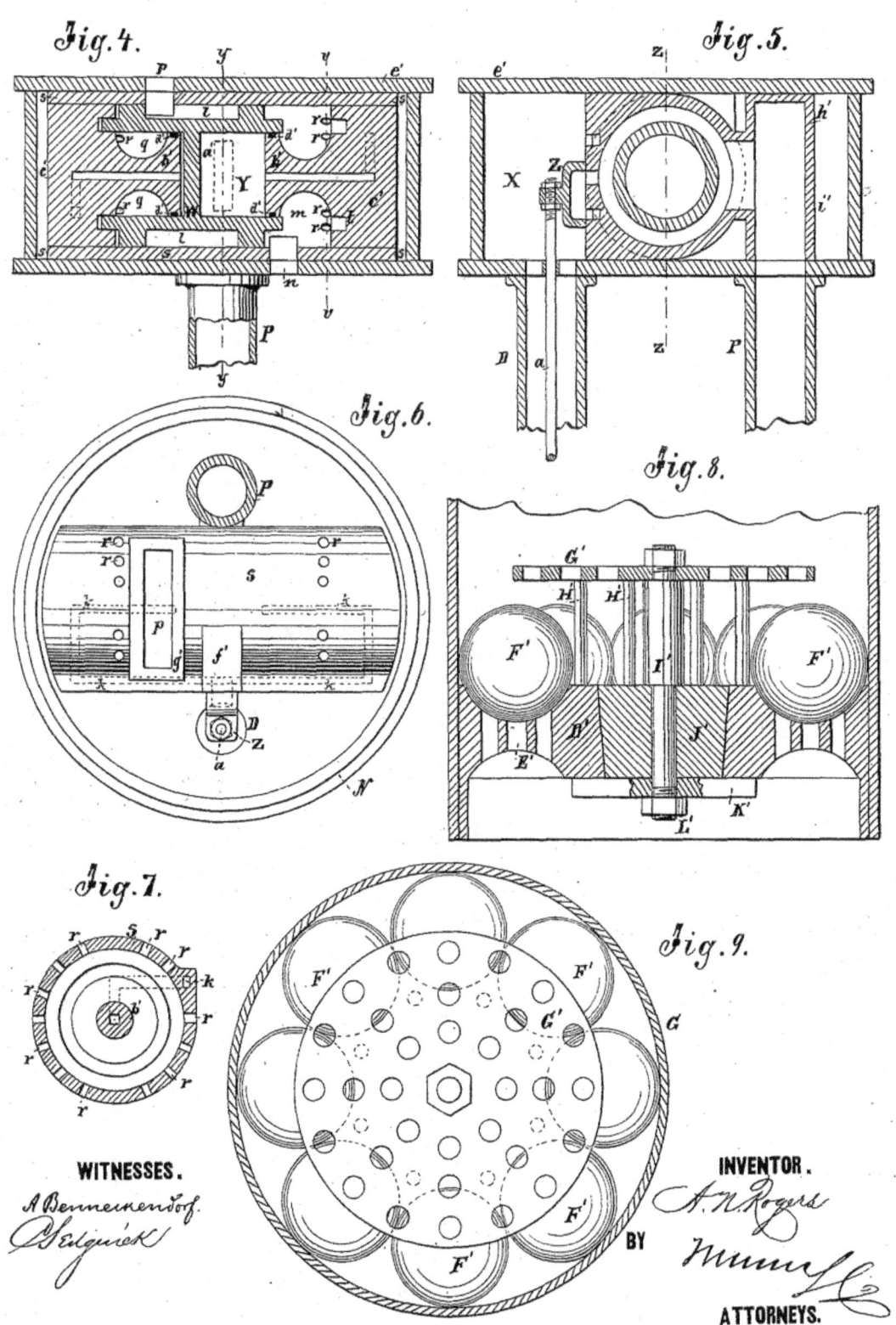

UNITED STATES PATENT OFFICE.

ANDREWS N. ROGERS, OF CENTRAL CITY, COLORADO TERRITORY.

IMPROVEMENT IN STEAM MINING-PUMPS.

Specification forming part of Letters Patent No. **149,681**, dated April 14, 1874; application filed February 14, 1874.

To all whom it may concern:

Be it known that I, ANDREWS N. ROGERS, of Central City, in the county of Gilpin and Territory of Colorado, have invented a new and Improved Steam Mining-Pump, of which the following is a specification:

The object of this invention is to furnish a new and improved form of steam mining-pump adapted to the progressive work of sinking a water-shaft, or of freeing from water any mines, quarries, or other cavities that may be submerged. The invention consists of a reciprocating steam-cylinder with a stationary piston and a continuous acting force-pump in a light strong frame, having apparatus by which it can be conveniently suspended by ropes and pulleys, so as to be conveniently adjusted as the work progresses, the steam being conducted down to the engine by pipes, and the water forced up by other pipes, of which sections will be added on as the engine descends. The invention also consists of certain improvements in the construction of the engine and the pump to adapt it for the use for which it is intended, which will be particularly described and claimed.

Figure 1 is a side elevation of my improved pump. Fig. 2 is a sectional elevation. Fig. 3 is a section of Fig. 1 on line xx. Fig. 4 is a sectional elevation of the steam-piston taken on the line zz of Fig. 5, which is a section of Fig. 4, on the line yy. Fig. 6 is a plan of the steam-piston with top removed. Fig. 7 is a section through the valve on line vv of Fig. 4. Fig. 8 is a sectional elevation of the pump-valve, and Fig. 9 is a horizontal section of the working-piston of the pump and a top view of the valve.

Similar letters of reference indicate corresponding parts.

A and B represent a couple of metal disks firmly connected together a short distance apart, one above another, by the rods C; the upper one is also connected firmly to the two branches D of a large pipe, E F, for conducting the water up from the pump, and the lower one is also connected to pump-cylinder G. Disk B also has suspending-rods G' attached to it, which extend along up the sides of the branches D through the ears H near the upper ends, and are jointed to links I, which depend from the yokes K, whereon rollers L are mounted, around which the ropes M, for suspending the machine in the mine, pass. These devices constitute the frame whereon the working parts are mounted, as follows: The steam-piston N is fixed in a stationary position a suitable distance above the disk B on the top of two hollow piston-rods, O and P, within the reciprocating cylinder Q, said rods being fastened to the disk by clamping-nuts R, and projecting through it to the lower side. The rod O is for conducting live steam to the engine from a pipe, S, (shown dotted,) from the mouth of the mine, and rod P is for the exhaust. It may discharge at the end of its extension below the disk, or it may have a pipe attached for conducting the steam away. The cylinder works on guides T on the branches D of the water-pipe, and connects by rods U with the working-plunger V of the pump. The valve for the steam-engine is at W. Within the piston N steam enters to it from the hollow rod O at the chest x, and is let into and exhausted from the cylinder y, in which valve W works by the slide-valve Z, which is worked by a rod, a, extending down through the steam-pipe O and the stuffing-box b to the lever d, from which a rod, e, extends up through the flanges f of the cylinder and through the bent bar g, said rod having a stop, h, below the flanges, another, i, above, and a coiled spring, j, between each end of the bar and said flanges. The bar g, striking the stops just before the cylinder stops, shifts the valve Z, and the springs j allow the bar g to shift a little, so that the cylinder can move onto the end of its stroke after shifting the valve. The dotted lines k, Fig. 6, and the dotted and full lines k, Fig. 4, show the course of the steam in entering the cylinder y from the ports of the valve Z. The steam exhausts from said cylinder into the annular space l. The valve n opens chamber m to the cylinder Q below the piston by uncovering port n, when it shifts to the left, and at the same time opens the exhaust from the upper part of said cylinder to the hollow piston P, by uncovering port p to the annular space l. When it goes the other way it opens chamber q and admits live steam to the upper part of the cylinder Q through port p, at the same time opening port

n to the exhaust. Steam enters chambers m and q from chamber X, through the perforations r in the shell or case s containing said chambers and the valve. At the outer end of each chamber is an annular groove, t, coinciding with the end of the valve, and receiving it at the end of its stroke in that direction to cushion it by the steam shut into said groove when the piston enters. The valve W is a hollow movable cylinder with only one head, a', which is in the middle, and works between the two stationary pistons b' formed on the heads c' of the valve-cylinder s. These heads, together with the pistons b', are fitted in the cylinder s, so as to be taken out and put in readily to adjust the valve; also, the packing d'. The case s will, in practice, be cast together with head e'. It drops down into its place in the piston N from the top when the head e' is put on, and is held fast by said head when screwed on. In practice a ground joint will probably be required between the case s at port n and the head of piston N, also at the lower end of the joint i' of the exhaust-tube within the case. The working-piston V is hollow, and has a valve, C', where the water enters its lower end, and it receives another stationary piston, A', into it through the stuffing-box B' in its upper end, said stationary piston being the lower portion of the pipe E, through which the water escapes. It extends as low as the valve C' will allow when the piston V is raised. The pump-barrel G' is of about twice the capacity of the stationary piston A', and receives about twice as much water into it, when the piston rises, as is forced through the stationary piston during the same time, which, being forced through valve C' into the piston on its downstroke, from which only half the quantity was emptied on the upstroke, causes a continuous discharge as well when the piston goes down as when it goes up with only two valves. Moreover, the flow is not only continuous and uninterrupted, but it is in one direction, and therefore free from the shocks and jars due to the frequent and sudden stops and changes of the flow in the ordinary continuous or double-acting pumps. The valve C' is composed of a plate or disk, D', with numerous perforations, E', in a circle, each having a small seat and a ball, F', to close it. Said balls are kept in place by a disk, G', supported by rods H' a sufficient distance above the disk D' to allow the balls to play, and held fast by a rod, I', passing down through a center plug, J', in the disk D, and a bridge, K', by which, and a nut, L', the plug and the disk G' are held in place. The object of this arrangement is to enable the balls to be put in place and taken out through the disk D' from the bottom by removing the nut L' and raising the plug J', rod I', and disk G. A hand-hole is made in the lower part of the pump-barrel at M' for introducing the arm to adjust the balls. N' is the valve at the bottom of the pump-barrel.

Having thus described my invention, I claim as new and desire to secure by Letters Patent—

1. The combination of the disks A B, pump-rods C, pipes D E F, and pump-barrel G, in the manner herein described, to constitute the frame-work for the operative parts of a mining-pump to be suspended by ropes, as set forth.

2. The combination of suspending-rods G', links I, yokes K, and pulleys L, with the pump for suspending it by ropes, as described.

3. The stationary piston N, reciprocating cylinder Q, hollow piston-rods O P, the steam-valves W, and slide-valve Z, substantially as specified.

4. The valve W having a chamber, y, in each end, in combination with stationary heads b', chambers m q, ports n p, and the inlet-orifices r, substantially as specified.

5. The valve cylinder or case, fitted in the chamber of piston N, and secured by and between the heads, as described.

6. The combination of bar g and springs j, with the rod e and its stops, and the flanges of the cylinder for shifting valve Z before the cylinder-stops, substantially as specified.

7. The disk G', standard H', rod I', plug J', and bar K', with the valve-disk D', and the balls F', substantially as specified.

ANDREWS N. ROGERS.

Witnesses:
A. P. THAYER,
T. B. MOSHER.

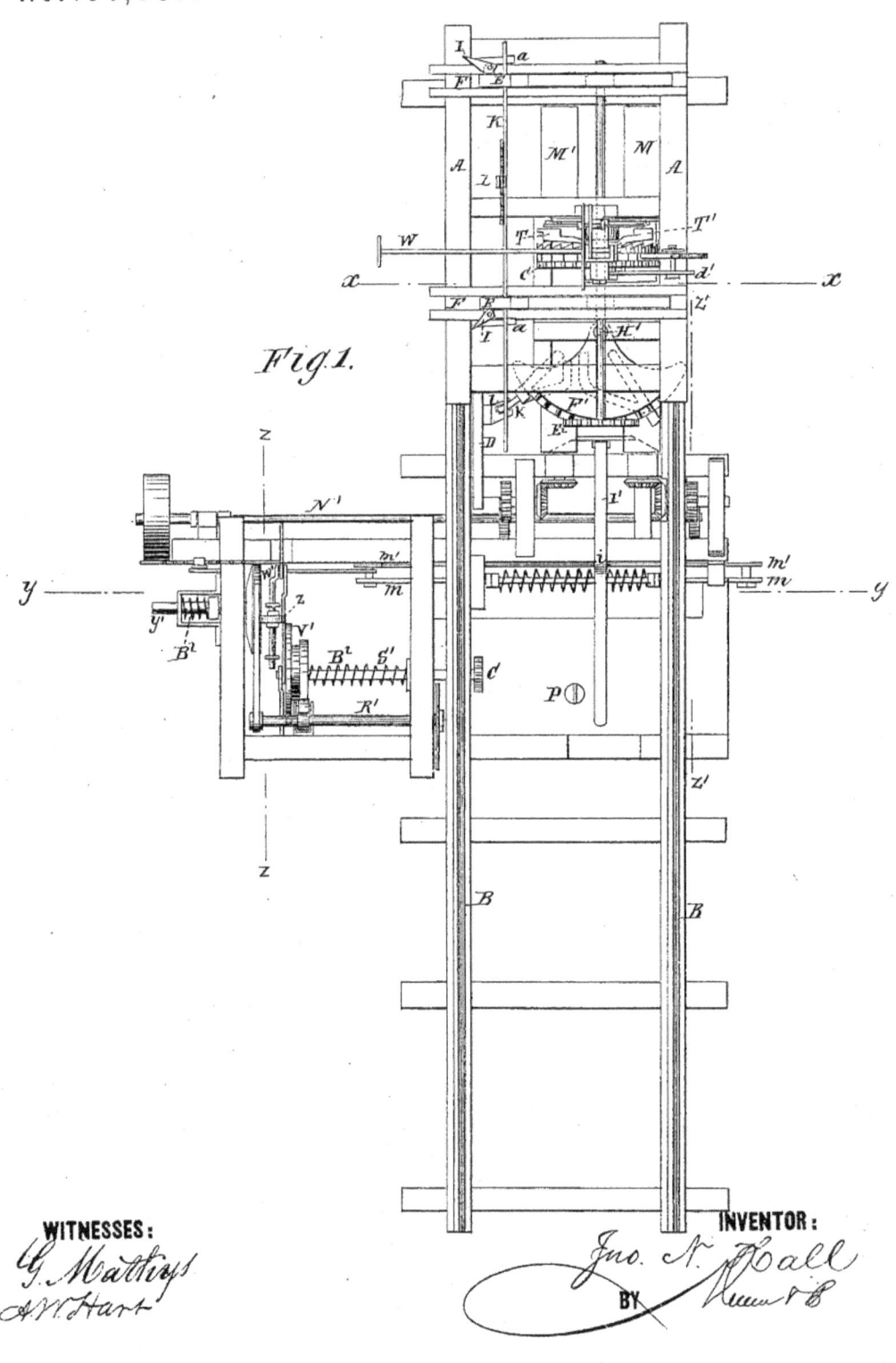

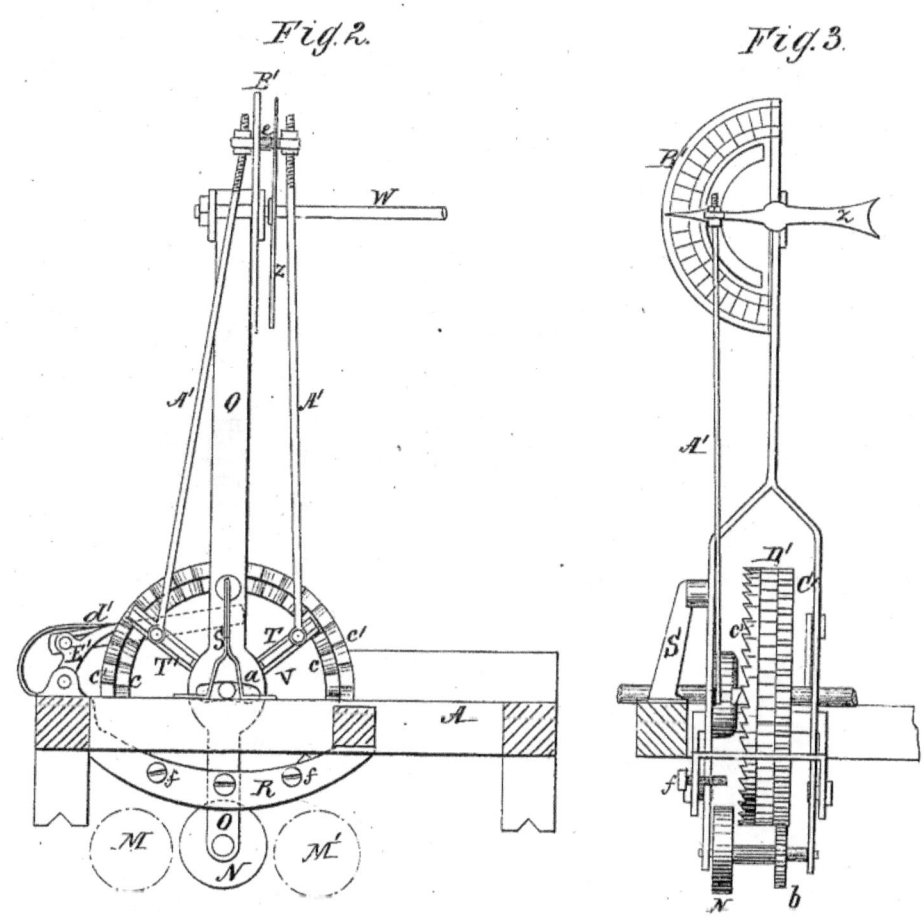
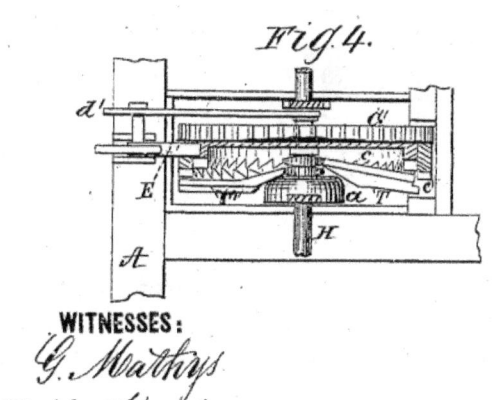

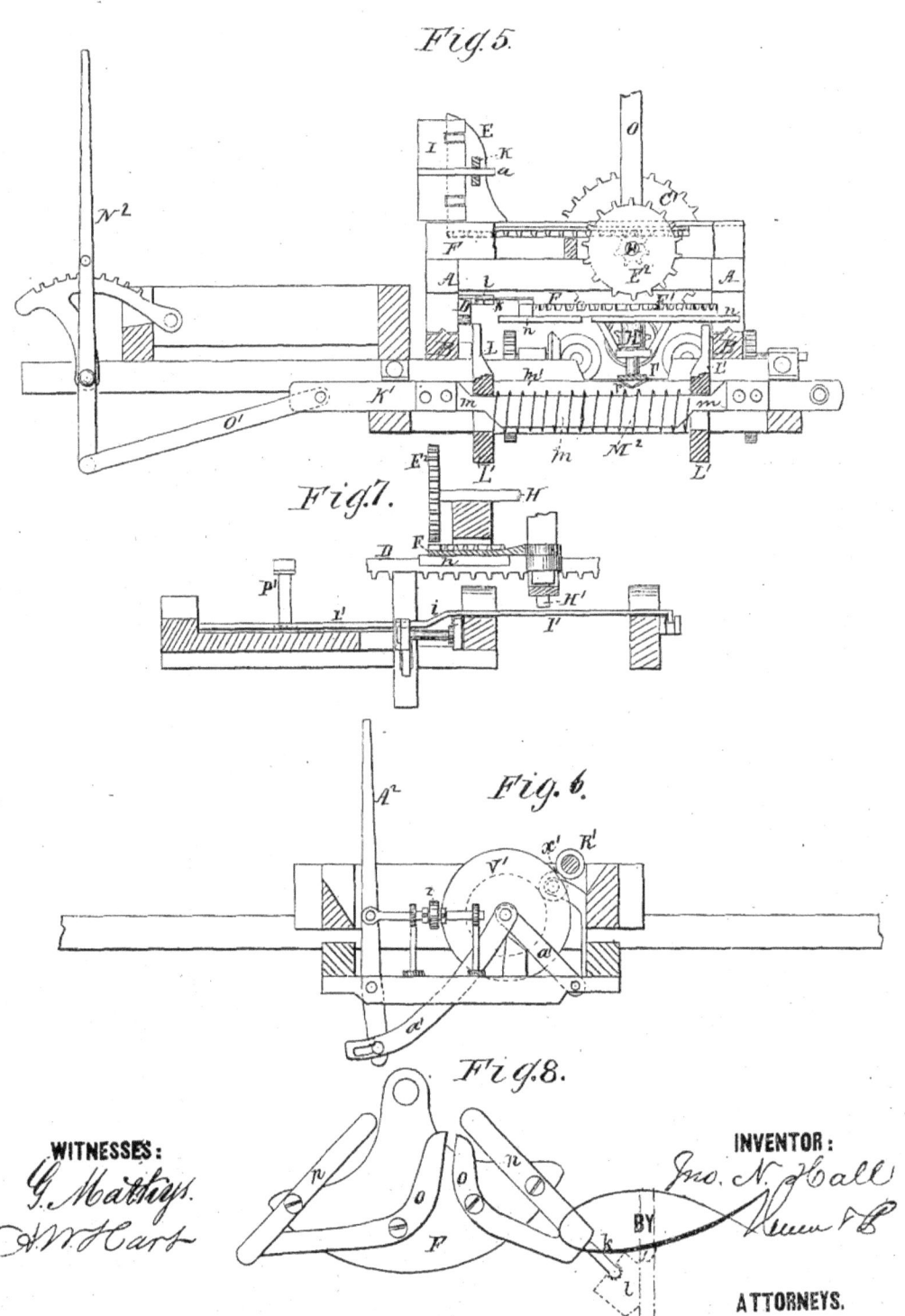

UNITED STATES PATENT OFFICE.

JOHN N. HALL, OF CENTRAL CITY, COLORADO TERRITORY.

IMPROVEMENT IN CIRCULAR-SAW MILLS.

Specification forming part of Letters Patent No. **150,567**, dated May 5, 1874; application filed April 4, 1874.

To all whom it may concern:

Be it known that I, JOHN N. HALL, of Central City, in the county of Gilpin, Colorado Territory, have invented a new and useful Improvement in Circular-Saw Mills; and I do hereby declare that the following is a full, clear, and exact description of the same, reference being had to the accompanying drawing forming a part of this specification, in which—

Figure 1 is a top plan view of the whole apparatus. Fig. 2 is a cross-section of the carriage on the line $x\ x$ of Fig. 1, showing the ratchet and adjusting mechanism; and Fig. 3 a side elevation of the same, the fragment of the carriage proper being in section. Fig. 4 is a section of the ratchet, showing the arrangement of the spring-pawl. Fig. 5 is a cross-section on the line $y\ y$ of Fig. 1, showing part of the automatic log-setting mechanism. Fig. 6 is a section on line $z\ z$, Fig. 1, showing the friction apparatus for operating the log-carriage. Fig. 7 is a longitudinal section on the line $z'\ z'$ of Fig. 1. Fig. 8 is an under-side view of the segment forming part of the automatic mechanism.

The features of my invention are, first, an improved apparatus for adjusting the ends of the log as it rests upon the head-blocks; second, for adjusting the log for slabbing; third, for automatically moving the log laterally toward the saw after each cut, or from the saw when necessary; fourth, for operating the log-carriage, as hereinafter described.

In the drawing, the log-carriage A is reciprocated on ways B by means of a pinion, C, which meshes with its rack D, and the knees E of the head-blocks F are arranged for reciprocation by means of a rack-and-pinion connection with shaft H, as usual or well known in machines of this class. The means for adjusting the ends of the log on the head-blocks consist of levers or plates I, which are pivoted vertically to the knees, and have projecting-arms a, which work in slots of a bar, K. Said bar is adjusted or thrown in either direction lengthwise by a lever, L, which has a well-known form of locking-mechanism, rack, and spring-lever pawl for holding it in any adjustment. At each throw of said bar one of the plates I is turned away from the log, while the other pushes against it; hence the log is moved laterally and simultaneously at each end, and thereby quickly adjusted in the desired position for slabbing, &c. The means for adjusting the knees, and thereby the log preparatory to slabbing, (or at any other time when the automatic setting mechanism cannot be used,) consist in part of two long rollers, M M¹, Figs. 1 and 2, which are arranged between and parallel to the ways B, and constantly rotated in opposite directions by suitable gear connection with the driving-shaft N', (Fig. 1,) which is in this instance arranged at right angles to the ways B and rollers aforesaid. The secondary function of the rollers is to move the knees E in one direction or the other, according as a plain-faced wheel N, Fig. 2, is brought in frictional contact with one or the other of them. This wheel has its bearings in the lower end of the forks of a lever, O, which is pivoted in a frame, R, beneath the carriage, and held vertical by a plate-spring, S, attached to the carriage on the upper side. One fork of the lever O has a boss, a, where the shaft H passes through it, and the aperture therein is elongated horizontally to allow the lever to vibrate on its fulcrum. The boss (which is preferably beveled on its inner side or edge) acts on the inclined shoulders of ratchet-pawl T T', which are pivoted on shaft H, and adapted to engage, one with the inner, the other with the outer, row of ratchet teeth $c\ c'$, on the wheel V. The teeth $c\ c'$ are inclined in opposite directions, and the pawls are correspondingly beveled. The latter are used to limit the movement of the ratchet-wheel V, and thereby determine the adjustment of the knees E. To set the pawls, I employ the long handle W, which projects laterally from the upper end of lever O, and is adapted to rotate to adjust the pointer Z, which is connected with the pawls by rods A', so that they move together. The pointer moves over an arc, B', which is graduated from one inch to six or more, (commencing at the lower side,) and is slotted to permit suitable connection of the rods A' by means of a short bar or wrist, e, as shown. The adjustment of the index Z on the graduated arc determines the adjustment of the knees E for slabbing the log, since if it be set at any number—say, three inches—on the arc the pawls will be raised correspondingly, and then the lever being pulled over toward the right, in Fig. 2, (i. e., toward the knees,) the boss a causes the pawl T to engage with the inner ratchet c, and simultaneously also the wheel N is brought into contact with roller M. The rotary movement of this wheel is communicated to the shaft H, and the knees E thereby reciprocated through the medium of a pinion, b, Fig. 3, which is fast on the same axis as N, and meshes with the large spur-gear C' that is fast on said shaft. If the lever O be pushed in the opposite direction—i. e., toward the left, as seen in Fig. 2—the other pawl, T', will engage the ratchet c' and the wheel N with the roller M¹, so that the knees will be moved back. A ratchet-faced wheel, D', Fig. 3, is arranged between the wheels V and C', and a pivoted pawl, E', engages it. This pawl and wheel hold the knees E steady against the log during the sawing operation. A slotted bar, d', connects it (the pawl) with lever O, so that the pawl is always thrown out of the ratchet when the lever is tilted toward it—i. e., to the left, Fig. 2. The slot permits the lever O to tilt toward the right. It will be understood that in this operation of adjusting the log for slabbing, the pawl T or T', which is locked into its ratchet, is carried around with it or with the wheel V as the latter revolves, and continues thus locked as long as the lever O is being pulled or pushed toward it, (the pawl.) The downward movement of the pawls is arrested by pins or stops f on the frame when the lever O is released, and resuming the vertical position by the action of spring S the pawl is also released.

I will now proceed to describe the automatic log-setting mechanism. It has no operative connection with the rollers M M¹ or ratchet mechanism above described, but acts on the knees E of the log-carriage (to reciprocate them in one direction or the other, as required) through the medium of a spur-gear, E'', Figs. 1, 5, which is fixed on the end of shaft H, and meshes with a toothed segment, F', as the log-carriage is moved back after a board has been cut off. This segment is arranged horizontal, but fixed on a vertical axis, H', Figs. 1 and 5, which has its bearings in a frame at the end of the log-carriage, and is adapted for slight endwise movement. When the log-carriage is jigged back the lower end of the shaft H' moves over and in contact with the long bar I', the latter being raised at the inner end by means to be shortly described. The shaft thus rides up a short incline, i, Figs. 1, 6, formed on said bar, which lifts the locking-arm k out of the notched plate l, thus freeing the segment and causing it to mesh with the spur-gear E''. They are held in mesh during the further backward movement, and the knees thus moved to the desired extent. When the log is again fed up to the saw the segment is restored to its normal central position and locked as before. The means for elevating the bar I' and turning the segment on its axis are a double bar, K', and dogs L' L'. The latter are slotted and arranged to slide on one part, m, of the double bar K', being held apart by a spiral spring, M². The part m has inclined shoulders on the upper and under side at each end, which, when the bar K' is reciprocated by the hand-lever N² and connecting-rod O', cause the one or the other of the dogs to rise vertically, and move laterally, toward the other dog. The position thus assumed by one of the dogs enables it to turn the segment F' on its shaft by coming in contact with and acting on one of the projecting bars n attached to its under side, Figs. 1, 5, 7. When the log-carriage is fed forward the segment is returned to its normal central position by a fixed standard, P', Figs. 1, 6, whose thin upper end enters between the curved bars o. The other part, m', of the double bar K' has a central notch, r, in which a projection on the under side of bar I' rests when the hand-lever is in the vertical position—i. e., when the automatic mechanism is not set for operation. The moving of the bar K' in either direction causes the projection to rise out of the notch, and thus elevate the bar I', as above described.

It will be understood that the dogs are set when the carriage is ready to be jigged back, and, until the thickness of cut requires change, the adjustment may remain the same, the segment returning each time to its place, and being successively turned to move the knees, and thereby the log, up to the saw.

The saw-shaft R' is constantly rotated in one direction by a band from the shaft, and the counter-shaft S', on which the pinion is mounted, is rotated alternately in one direction or the other to feed or jig the log-carriage, it being only necessary to bring the friction-disk V', which is on the inner end of shaft S', alternately into or out of contact with the idler x', as usual in machines of this class. A like friction-disk, W', is mounted on a short shaft, Y', in the same horizontal plane, and in such proximity to shaft S' that one disk overlaps the other about one-third of its diameter. A small friction-wheel, z, is arranged for adjustment between the two disks, so as to bear against the face of both when in use for forward motion, and to be out of contact with both, or with disk V', when the log-carriage is at rest. The shaft of the friction-wheel z is slid in its bearings by the hand-lever, whose jointed rods a' a' form the bearing for the inner end of shaft S'. Thus said shaft S' is elevated, and the friction-wheel z simultaneously adjusted, by the same movement of the lever. A cross-belt passes from disk W' to a pulley on saw-shaft R'. They hence rotate reversely. When the wheel is moved to the right, Figs. 1, 8, or in the direction of the arrow, the log-carriage is fed up to the saw, that movement continuing so long as said wheel and the disks are in contact, and increasing as the wheel is carried nearer the axis of disk. When the lever is thrown to the left the wheel is drawn back out of contact with disk V', which latter is then brought in frictional contact with the idler x' and the carriage jigged back. A spiral spring, B'', is applied to each of the disk-shafts to cause them to press against the friction-wheel z with sufficient force to create the desired degree of friction.

It is evident a weight or other device might be used in place of the springs.

What I claim is—

1. The combination, with the knees of the head-blocks, of pivoted log-adjusting plates or levers, and a connecting-bar and lever mechanism for operating them, substantially as shown and described.

2. The combination, with the sliding knees of the head-block and a shaft, H, of a ratchet-wheel, a pawl, a pivoted lever for acting on said pawl, and a mechanism for adjusting it, the friction-gear N, a roller, a pinion, b, and spur-gear C', substantially as shown and described.

3. The lever O, carrying the friction-wheel N, and provided with the elongated transverse slot to receive the shaft H, and adapt it to vibrate on its fulcrum in the frame R, and the spring S, combined as shown and described, for the purpose specified.

4. The combination of the slotted bar d', lever O, pivoted pawl E', and ratchet-wheel D' with shaft H and sliding knees E, as shown and described.

5. The combination, with the sliding knees, of the head-blocks and shaft H, of spur-gear e^2, toothed segment F' having bars $n\ n$, dogs L L', and adjustable bar K' m, substantially as shown and described.

6. The double bar K, having notch r in one part thereof, the bar I', in combination with segment F', its adjustable shaft H', and the spur-gear e^2 on shaft H, as shown and described.

7. The standard P', in combination with the pivoted segment F', having curved bars o on its under side, as shown and described.

8. The combination of friction-wheel z, with disks V' W', saw-shaft R', and adjusting mechanism, as shown and described.

9. The combination, with the shafts S' Y', and their disks V' W', and wheel z, of springs B', as shown and described.

10. The rollers M M¹, rotated in opposite directions, and arranged parallel to the ways B and to each other, to operate the knees of the head-blocks through the medium of wheel N, and suitable intermediate apparatus, substantially as shown and described.

JOHN N. HALL.

Witnesses:
  EDWARD V. BENTON,
  A. W. HART.

W. J. LYND.
Coking Fossil Coals or Lignites.

No. 150,872. Patented May 12, 1874.

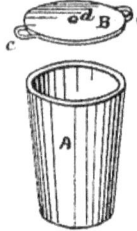
Fig. 1.

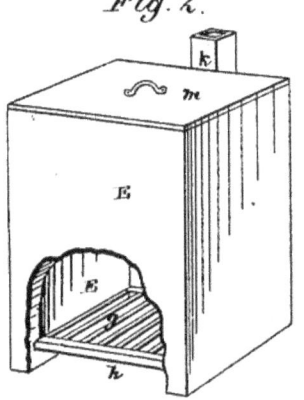
Fig. 2.

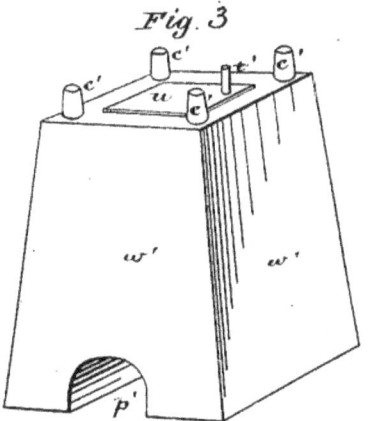
Fig. 3.

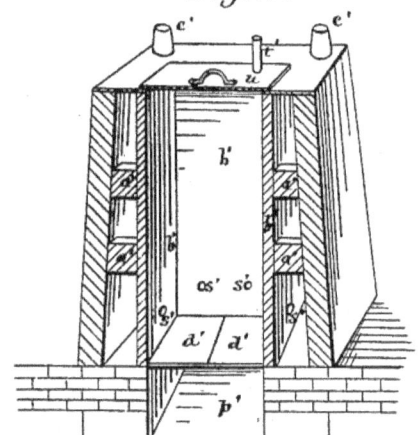
Fig. 4.

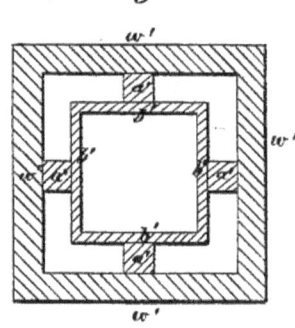
Fig. 5.

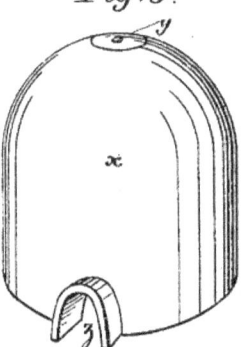
Fig. 6.

Witnesses.
Ewell Dick
Wm. E. Chaffee

Inventor.
Wm. J. Lynd
by atty Hollok

UNITED STATES PATENT OFFICE.

WILLIAM J. LYND, OF DENVER, COLORADO TERRITORY.

IMPROVEMENT IN COKING FOSSIL COALS OR LIGNITES.

Specification forming part of Letters Patent No. **150,872**, dated May 12, 1874; application filed April 20, 1874.

To all whom it may concern:

Be it known that I, WILLIAM JOHN LYND, of Denver, Colorado Territory, have invented new and useful Improvements in Coking certain Fossil Coals; and I do hereby declare the following to be a full and exact description of the same.

That it may be more clearly known what are the coals understood by certain fossil coals, I specifically designate as such the coals found in the Territories of Colorado, Wyoming, Utah, and New Mexico, and all similar coals wherever found in the United States. Some of these coals are at present mined near Cañon City, in Fremont county, at or near Trinidad, and elsewhere in Colorado Territory; at Rock Springs and elsewhere in Wyoming Territory; at Evanston and elsewhere in Utah Territory; at Coos Bay and elsewhere in Oregon Territory; at Bellingham Bay and elsewhere in Washington Territory; at Monte Diablo and elsewhere in California. These fossil coals are reported by geologists to be of the eocene formation. In the geological survey of Ohio, vol. 1, page 83, is the following statement: "It should also be mentioned that in North America the cretaceous was a great coal-making period, as rocks of this age in the far west contain, at various points, important beds of lignite, some of which are from thirty to fifty feet in thickness. The coals of Vancouver's Island, Bellingham Bay, Monte Diablo, those of New Mexico and Arizona, as well as some of the most valuable beds in Utah, Colorado, and Wyoming, are of cretaceous age. These, with some tertiary lignites, comprise all the so-called coals of the far west." In Professor Hayden's report of 1870, page 186, is the report of the Omaha Gas Company: "Residue, after coking in retort, twelve bushels of earthy breeze in small cubes, which, when put in the furnace fires, smothered them. The coke is worthless for heating purposes. Coal from Rock Springs, Wyoming, was also treated, and is also precisely similar." These coals are commonly called and recognized as lignites; yet, as other names are given, I prefer to denominate them as fossil coals, and to specify localities at which some of them are found and are mined, that they may be definitely known. From these coals I make a serviceable coke, useful for all heating purposes. I coke them on a principle founded on the admitted fact that no fossil coals contain bitumen, while all fossil coals do contain bituminous organic matter—in other words, the elements or constituents from which bitumen is formed. These constituents are hydrogen and carbon, and sometimes oxygen combined with them. I here subjoin a careful analysis of European coals:

	Carbon.	Hydrogen.	Oxygen and Nitrogen.	Ashes.
Brown coal	71.71	4.85	21.67	1.77
Hard bituminous coal	82.92	6.49	10.86	.13
Cannel	83.75	5.66	8.04	2.55
Coking coal	87.95	5.26	5.41	1.40
Anthracite	91.98	3.92	3.16	.94

From this table it is evident that the brown coal has about five times more oxygen and nitrogen than hydrogen, and the other coals contain hydrogen, and oxygen, and nitrogen in nearly the same quantities.

Now, as coals require, in order to coke or fuse together, about or more than four parts free or disposable hydrogen, and less than two parts hydrogen combined or fixed to one hundred parts carbon, and as eight per cent. oxygen holds in combination one hydrogen, it is evident that the coals which have little oxygen and the requisite or more than requisite free hydrogen, and which are called, on this account, hydrogenous coals, will coke or fuse, when, on the contrary, those which have an excess of oxygen, and less than the requisite hydrogen, will not coke or fuse by the ordinary processes. The fossil coals specifically designated above differ in the quantity of oxygen and free hydrogen they contain. Nearly all have been analyzed, and one of the superior sort gives the following analyses: Oxygen and nitrogen, 17.63; phosphorus, 0.00; sulphur, .07; carbon, 76.00; hydrogen, 4.75; ash, 1.55; specific gravity, 1.25. According to the report of Professor Mees, of Columbus, Ohio, this coal gives dust for coke. According to Professor Hayden's report, as above, the coke was an earthy breeze in small cubes, and worthless for heating purposes. This will not coke or fuse in slack form, but I have found that by finely pulverizing it, it will coke and make a superior coke, when treated as hereinafter described.

One of the inferior grades of these fossil coals gives the following average of five analyses: Water, 16.00; volatile substances, 38.00; ash, 4.50; fixed carbon, 41.50. This coal will not, under ordinary conditions, coke or fuse, whether in slack or pulverized state. But with the addition of a powder of coal sufficiently hydrogenous, it will make a first quality of coke, if treated as described below.

Now, as almost all the above-designated and similar fossil coals carry oxygen in excess over what the coking coals hold, we must, in case of some, disengage the hydrogen, so that its full virtue can be exerted; and, in case of others, add sufficient of hydrogenous coal to effect the desired end. But I have discovered that a less percentage of hydrogen is necessary to be present in coal to effect fusing than is usually thought requisite, because, by minute pulverization, all the hydrogen present can be made effective.

I am aware that asphaltum, coal-tar pitch, and hydrocarbons in general, can be used to aid in coking; but, aside from the expense of pulverizing the asphaltum, the still greater expense, and almost utter impossibilty, of commingling it evenly and in just proportions with the coal, and the inferior quality of coke thus produced, make all attempts to coke by this means unavailing.

In carrying out my invention, I use coal, either in the slack or finely-pulverized state; but I prefer to use the powdered coal. I have discovered that the more finely powdered coal is the better it is adapted by these processes for making good coke. When the coke is finely powdered, and the heat is properly applied thereto, as hereinafter described, the constituents of bitumen will be more readily disengaged, and will combine so as to draw the particles of the coal and make them cohere, and form a uniform, compact, dense coke.

In practicing my invention I can employ several kinds of apparatus, as, for instance, a covered crucible, the cover having a hole in it for the escape of gases, as seen in Figure 1 of the accompanying drawings.

A is a crucible. B is the cover, with handles c and an aperture, d.

Fig. 2 represents a furnace to receive the crucible. E is the furnace or crucible-chamber. g is the grate. h is the ash-pit; k, the chimney; m, the cover.

In order to make the coke of a uniform texture, compact, dense, and without the lumps usually visible in coke from slack, the coal should be reduced to a fine powder or flour. The crucible is charged with the coal powder, and covered and placed in the furnace E, in which a fire is burning. The entire crucible is raised to a high degree of heat. The burning of the gases which escape by the aperture d assist in heating the cover and upper part of crucible, and the coal is thus bituminized and coked. When coked a blue flame appears at the aperture d, and the crucible should then be taken out and cooled and its contents removed. The above indicates one simple form of apparatus for carrying out my process, from which it will be noted that said process may readily be practiced with any furnace so arranged or constructed that its heat can be applied to the exterior of the vessel, retort, or kiln containing the coal to be coked, in such manner as to produce bituminization and consequent coking of the coal.

A second kind of furnace is that of a vertical retort fixed within walls, and having apertures for the escape of gases, which are burned by air or steam that enters through apertures in the outer walls, the gases thus burned increasing the heat of the retort, which is first heated to a high degree before charged with finely-powdered coal. An apparatus for this purpose is shown in Figs. 3, 4, and 5.

Fig. 3 is a perspective view of said apparatus. Fig. 4 is a vertical central section, and Fig. 5 a horizontal section, of the same.

a' a' a' a' are fire-tiles built into walls for braces to retort. b' b' b' are walls of retort. s' s' s' s' are apertures for the escape of gases. t' is a pipe attached to cover u. This pipe is for the escape of such gases as may be in excess, and not able to find vent through apertures s' s'. d' d' are two heavy iron doors, which swing on hinges, and are kept in place by a horizontal transverse bar which is movable, and can be taken out or removed from under said doors, when the latter are to be dropped. w' w' are outer walls. p' is the arched opening for cars to enter to receive the coke when discharged from the retort, and c' c' c' c' are the chimneys. The chimneys connect with space between the retort and outer walls. The coal is put into the retort, first heated to a red or white heat, and the gases evolved from the coal burned outside the retort by air or superheated steam which enters through apertures in the outer walls, and by the gases so burned the first heat of the retort is maintained or increased. Bituminization is effected in this way, and, as a consequence, the charge of coal is coked. The charge is withdrawn after the retort is cooled a little, and another charge is introduced and proceeded with in like manner. I can use this form of retort, whether single or in cluster, as in the case of the Appolt oven, with apertures in any part of retort for escape of gases, near the top, or near the bottom, or near both top and bottom of retort, whether with single or double outer walls; or I can use any kiln or retort constructed on a similar plan to burn the gases which escape from the coal being coked for heating the vessel or inclosure containing the coal, whether horizontal, vertical, or otherwise.

Another form of apparatus adapted to carry out my process is represented in Fig. 6.

x is a circular oven, arched in the form of a dome. y is aperture for escape of gases. z is doorway for introducing coal and discharging coke. The oven is heated to a high temperature, and then charged with coal. It is better to tamp it a little, or, in the case of some coals, to dampen a little. The door is closed, or only one or two small apertures left open for the introduction of a very little air, and the aperture in dome is partly closed. The coal is thus heated by the radiation of the oven and the constituents of bitumen evolved and combined. As the process of bituminization progresses the particles of coal are drawn together and made to cohere. When the bituminization has sufficiently progressed, the gases escaping are set on fire, and, by increasing the heat of interior or lining of furnace, cause the particles to fuse and cohere more strongly. When the whole mass has been subjected to this increased heat and the gases cease to evolve, the coal is coked. The oven can be closed awhile to cool sufficiently, and the coke may then be withdrawn. Air for the burning of the gases in this kind of oven may be supplied by pipes running from the bottom of outside walls upward, and circling round the dome and radiating to the interior of kiln like spokes of a wheel. The entrance of air can thus be easily controlled and the door be entirely closed. If this kind of kiln be furnished with one or more chimneys, so that the escape of gases can be controlled, then the aperture of dome may be closed. The openings into the chimneys will be in the dome. In lieu of this particular form of kiln, I can use any other kiln in which the gases are burned within the kiln, and in which the radiation of the heat caused by the gases so burned effects completely bituminization and consequent coking of these fossil coals.

I do not, therefore, confine myself to the use of any one class of ovens, but use every sort of oven in which bituminization and consequent coking, as above described, can be effected.

As above stated, I prefer, when coking in the above manner, to have the coal in a pulverized condition, in which condition it is possible and practicable to coke coals whose slack is not cokable by ordinary processes. In the case of coals which will not coke even when pulverized, I mix with the powder of such coals the powder of a largely hydrogenous coal, whereby bituminization and consequent coking of the whole mass may be effected.

Having described my invention, and the manner in which the same is or may be carried into effect, what I claim, and desire to secure by Letters Patent, is—

The process herein described of treating fossil coals, such as above designated, by reducing the coal to a finely-divided or powdered state, and then subjecting the same, whether mixed or not with a powdered or finely-divided hydrogenous coal, to the coking operation, as set forth.

In testimony whereof I have hereunto signed my name this 20th day of April, A. D. 1874.

WM. J. LYND.

Witnesses:
  EWELL DICK,
  HENRY R. ELLIOTT.

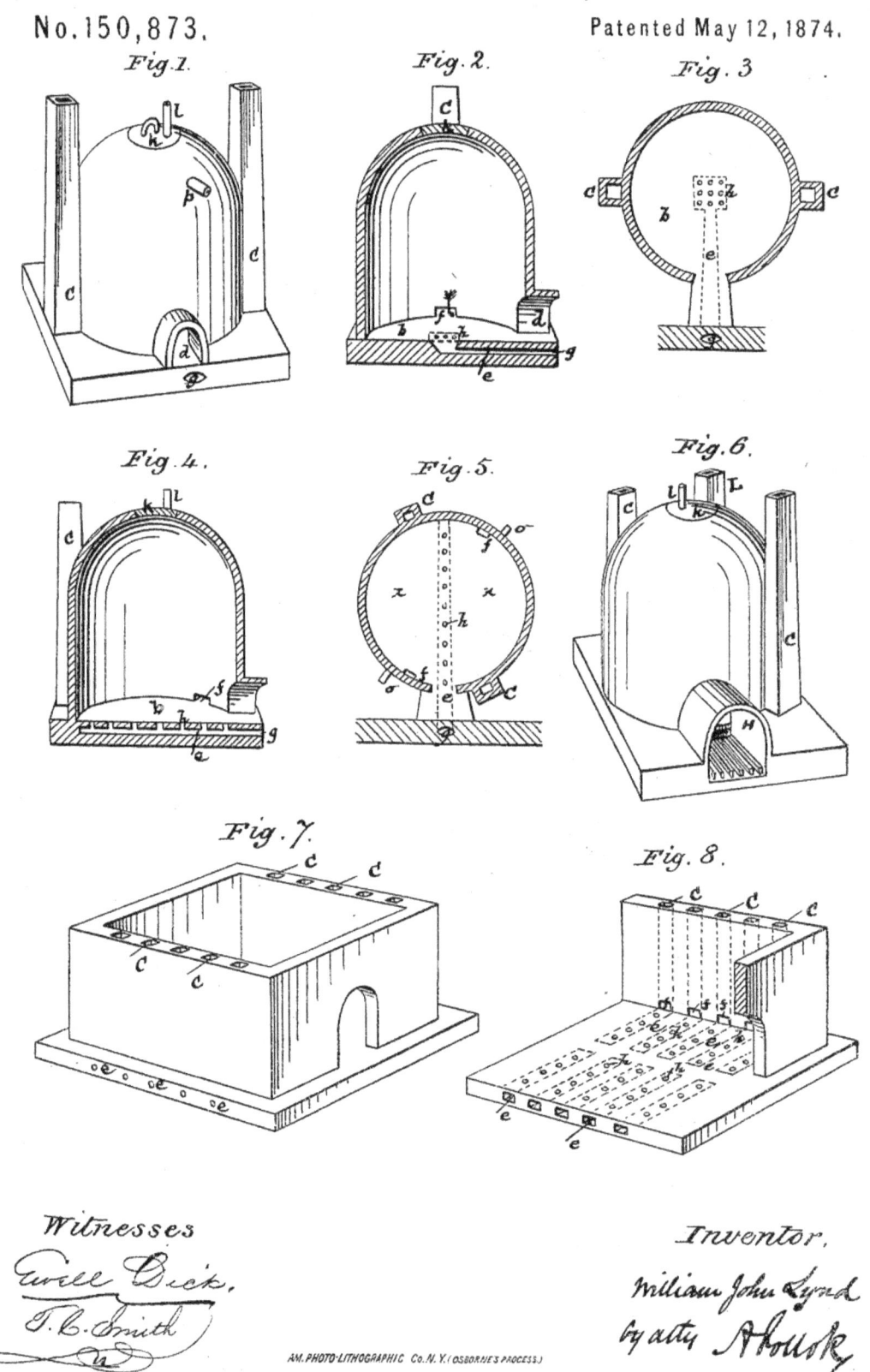

UNITED STATES PATENT OFFICE.

WILLIAM J. LYND, OF DENVER, COLORADO TERRITORY.

IMPROVEMENT IN COKING FOSSIL COALS OR LIGNITES.

Specification forming part of Letters Patent No. **150,873**, dated May 12, 1874; application filed April 17, 1874.

To all whom it may concern:

Be it known that I, WILLIAM JOHN LYND, of Denver, in the Territory of Colorado, have invented certain new and useful Improvements in Coking Fossil Coals, of which the following is a specification:

This invention is particularly directed to the manufacture of good merchantable coke from the fossil coals, commonly known as lignites, of the far west, such as are found and mined near Trinidad, and elsewhere in Colorado Territory; at Rock Springs, and elsewhere in Wyoming Territory; at Monte Diablo, and elsewhere in California, &c.

I coke the mass from the bottom upward, and carry off the gases and volatile products evolved from the coal in a direction opposite to that in which the coking proceeds. The fire is started by draft-openings in the floor or hearth. When started, said openings are closed, and a small quantity of air is admitted from above the coal to get the mass well ignited. When thus ignited, the air is shut off, and the coking is continued and completed by the radiant heat of the mass. The ordinary methods of admitting air until the coking is complete I have found, by careful experiment, to be practically unavailable and inoperative in treating lignites, which, by such methods, are reduced mainly to ash and breeze; and I prefer to carry on my process in close kilns, having, in the top, a small damper-regulated air-admission opening, and a chamber or space above the coal for receiving the gases which first rise into that space, and then descend and pass down through the coal and escape from chimney-openings at the bottom of the oven or kiln. I provide two or more of such draft or escape openings, having corresponding chimneys located at different points in the surrounding walls of the oven or coking apparatus, so that, by opening one and closing the other alternately, or by opening one series and closing the other series alternately, the coking can be carried on with regularity, and evenly throughout all portions of the mass. As before stated, this process is mainly applicable to coals in the lump, and by it such coals can be thoroughly coked without disintegration or losing their original form. This is a feature of special importance with most of the varieties of the lignites, which, when in the condition of slack, or when once disintegrated, cannot, by the ordinary processes, be again caused to cohere and coke.

My invention may be carried into effect in many ways. In the accompanying drawing I have represented several forms of apparatus in which the process can be carried on.

Figure 1 represents a perspective view of one form of oven; Fig. 2, a vertical central section of the same; Fig. 3, a ground plan.

The interior walls or lining of the oven should be composed of fire-brick, or other suitable material; and they may be oval, circular, or elliptical, or take any other form. The oven has doorway d; in this case arched, though the ceiling or top of doorway may be horizontal. C C are chimneys, which are vertical, and built alongside of the inner wall of oven, leaving a space between the chimneys and the outer wall. It has not been deemed necessary here to represent more than the inner walls or lining of the oven. The outer walls, which are not shown, surround and stand at a distance of from two to two and a half feet from the oven proper, the space between the two being filled usually with sand. Two chimneys are here delineated, but three or more may be used, and should be placed equally distant from each other. The openings from the oven into the chimneys are about on a level with the floor, as seen at f, Fig. 2. The chimneys need not rise higher than the top of the oven, where they are supplied with covers to close them alternately while coking is going on, and to close them both and altogether when the coking is completed; but chimneys which rise several feet above the oven are preferable. The ground plan in Fig. 3 shows the position of the openings f, that lead to the chimneys, and also the direction and shape of passage e under the floor or hearth, for the admission to the oven of air entering through opening g in the outer wall of foundation. The ground floor or hearth b is composed, preferably, of fire-brick, and rests on a bed of concrete or small stones, or sand or other material. At the center of the floor are apertures h, lined with iron, and opening into passage e below the floor. A cover, k, closes the aperture at top of oven.

This cover has a pipe, *l*, which conveys air to the oven from above. A pipe, *p*, extending from the oven through the outer wall, may also be used for the same purpose, although this is not essential.

The coking operation with this oven is conducted as follows: The oven may be either cold or heated. The air-flues are opened and some burning coals, or other fire-kindlings, are placed at or near the apertures *h*. The oven is charged, and the doorway *d* is then tightly closed. The cover *k* is not put in its place for a short time. The air descends through the open top of the oven, and passes through the coal and mingles with gases in combustion, and passes with them into the chimneys, as shown by arrows. When the coal is enough ignited the cover *k* is put in place, and the air for supporting combustion passes through the pipe *l*. One of the two chimneys C C is open at a time. This alternate opening and closing takes place every hour, or every two hours. This is continued until smoke ceases to issue and carbonic-acid gas only is expelled. All the apertures of the oven are now closed and made air-tight. After the oven cools, the coke is removed, and the oven again charged and operated in the same way. The pipe *p* in this operation is not essential, though useful, as by it, when insufficient air is admitted through pipe *l*, the proper supply can be obtained without removing the cover. In case it is desired to have the oven heated when charged, the coke should be removed as soon as it can with safety, so that the oven may be already heated for the next charge. The pipe or aperture *l* in the top of the oven is an important adjunct in the operation. After a considerable body of the coal is ignited—say one-third of the mass—the quantity of air admitted by the pipe may be gradually diminished until two-thirds, or thereabout, of the coal is ignited, after which the pipe may be closed entirely. The ignition of the remaining one-third of the coal will be secured by radiation from the mass below. The gradual limitation of air admitted may be effected by means of a slide-valve at the mouth of the pipe or aperture *l*, or by means of a series of perforated stoppers formed to fit in nest, and with apertures gradually diminishing in size; or other devices for the purpose may be used.

In Figs. 4 and 5 I have represented a vertical section and ground plan of an oven, resembling the oven shown in the preceding figures, except in the construction and arrangement of the ground floor or hearth and the openings for escape of gases. The ground floor or hearth *b* has under it two arched spaces, *x x*, and an air-passage, *e*. This air-passage runs under the floor of the kiln from front to rear of the interior wall of the oven, and has openings into oven, lined with iron. This air-passage separates the two arched spaces *x x*. The openings *f* for the escape of gases are on a level with the floor, as seen in Fig. 4, and they communicate with the spaces *x*, which in turn communicate with the chimneys C. Into the spaces *x* extend passages or pipes *o*, through which air can pass to spaces *x* under the floor. The operation of this oven is like the other, except in the passage of the gases into spaces under floor, and burning there by the air admitted at *o o* to said spaces. The unconsumed gases pass from the spaces to the chimneys, which, together with the openings *o*, are opened and closed alternately and in succession, as before described.

In Fig. 6 is represented an oven resembling that shown in Figs. 1, 2, and 3, with the exception that there is no flue *e* or apertures *h*; but in lieu thereof there is an open space or chamber beneath the hearth, and a fire-box, H, of suitable construction communicating with said space, so that the flames from the coal in the fire-box will pass under the hearth and heat it. At the end of the space opposite to the fire-box is a chimney, L, for carrying off the smoke from the fire-box. The main oven is charged, and the charge ignited, and then the heat at the bottom (caused by the products of combustion from the fire-box passing under the floor or hearth) is maintained and kept up until the coking is complete. Under this arrangement no air need be admitted through pipe *l*, but at the same time a little air admitted through the pipe will aid the operation.

To the spaces below the floors or hearths of the ovens represented in Figs. 4, 5, and 6, superheated steam may be supplied to burn the gases with more intensity.

In Figs. 7 and 8 is represented another form of oven or kiln.

Fig. 7 is a perspective view, and Fig. 8 is a like view with a portion of the walls broken away.

This oven is in form a parallelogram. It may be of any length, and from four feet to fourteen feet wide. As the coal is carried into the kiln and there piled up, the doorways are high and wide enough for men to pass in and out with cars on a movable railroad. These doorways are to be closed (after the charging of the kiln) with movable brick plastered over with mud. The air-flues *e* in the floor of the kiln may run all the way across, or to a partition under the center of oven, so that the air from either side will not go beyond the partition. This last method is exhibited in the drawing. The dotted lines show the position of air-passages under the floor. Each air-flue is in line with a chimney, and admits air through apertures *h*, lined with iron. Grates may be used. The chimneys C are vertical and about two feet apart. In a furnace twenty-four feet long there would be about nine chimneys on each side. The walls of oven may be six to eight feet high, and three to three and one-half feet thick, but well abutted at base. The chimneys open into oven at about the level of the floor, as seen at *f*.

This oven is operated as follows: Proper

kindling material is distributed over the floor. The first layer of coal is placed so that a draft can occur from the air-flues and insure ignition of kindling material. The oven is filled to within two feet of the top, when small coal is used for a covering, and slack is placed over the small coal. The slack need not be put on until the coal is ignited, as it otherwise would hinder the descent of air to assist the combustion of kindling material. The chimneys on one side of the kiln are now closed by tiles or iron covers. The chimneys on the other side are left open. The escaping gases will ascend these chimneys. When the process has gone on in this way for two hours, then open the chimneys which have been closed and close the chimneys which have been open. This alternation is repeated as often as desired, until the whole mass is coked. This becomes known when smoke ceases to be given out. The chimneys should then be closed and the mass covered with a heavy coat of slack or coke-dust, to prevent the burning of coke while the mass is cooling. It is evident that this kiln may be arched and apertures be provided in the arch for supplying the air. When the kiln is thus constructed the trouble and expense of covering the charge with coke-dust when the coking operation is completed will be saved, since the air can be effectually excluded by closing tightly the apertures of the arch. For some coals this form of kiln is preferable.

As in making gas the defects of one kind of coal are counterbalanced by the properties of another kind of coal, so in coking a mixture of coals is attended at times with decided advantage. I may, therefore, mix different coals in whatever condition they may be, whether in lump, slack, or powdered state. I coke the coals either without mixture or with it, and in the proportions found to be most economical and effective.

I do not broadly claim coking coals from the bottom upward and carrying off the air and gases in the opposite direction; but

What I do claim is—

1. The mode herein described of coking coals commonly known as lignites by coking the mass from the bottom upward and carrying off the gases in the opposite direction, the same being effected by the admission of air from above in small quantity at first, and the gradual diminution and final cutting off of said air-supply as the coking proceeds and before it is terminated, the coking of the upper part of the mass being effected by radiation from the lower ignited portion, as set forth.

2. The combination, with the charge-chamber and the chimneys communicating therewith at or near the level of the floor or hearth, of one or more air-supply pipes or apertures, located in the top or arch of the oven, and communicating with said chamber, substantially as and for the purposes shown and set forth.

3. The air-flues beneath the oven floor or hearth for conveying air to the interior of the charge-chamber, as and for the purposes set forth.

In testimony whereof I have hereunto signed my name this 17th day of April, A. D. 1874.

WM. J. LYND.

Witnesses:
 EWELL DICK,
 HENRY R. ELLIOTT.

N. LARSEN.
Miners' Candle-Holders.

No. 151,297. Patented May 26, 1874.

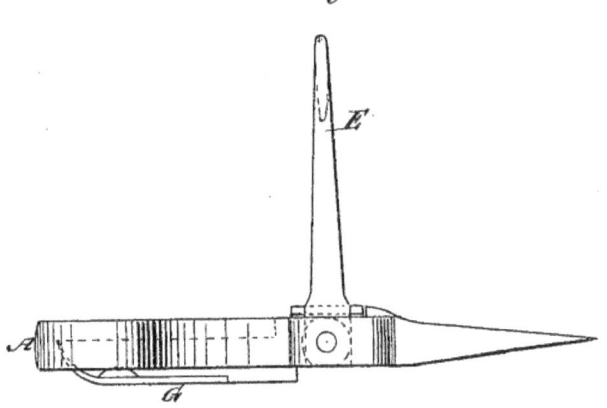

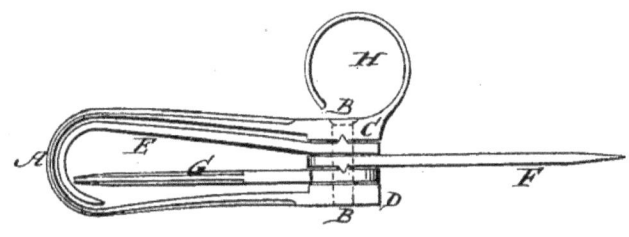

UNITED STATES PATENT OFFICE.

NEILS LARSEN, OF MILL CITY, COLORADO TERRITORY.

IMPROVEMENT IN MINERS' CANDLE-HOLDERS.

Specification forming part of Letters Patent No. **151,297**, dated May 26, 1874; application filed March 7, 1874.

To all whom it may concern:

Be it known that I, NEILS LARSEN, of Mill City, in the county of Clear Creek and Territory of Colorado, have invented a new and useful Improvement in Miner's Candle-Holder, of which the following is a specification:

The invention will first be fully described, and then pointed out in the claim.

In the accompanying drawing, Figure 1 is an edge view, showing the hook extended as when hung on the wall for supporting the candle. Fig. 2 is a plan view, showing all the parts in their proper position.

Similar letters of reference indicate corresponding parts.

A is a bow-spring. B is a pin, riveted to the side C, and made fast therein. The other end of the pin passes through the other part D of the bow-spring, so that that part of the spring can spread or move outward on the end of the pin. E is the hook by which the candle-holder is hung up, as seen in Fig. 1. F is an awl, which can be stuck in the wall, or in any wooden fixture, for supporting the candle-holder. G is a blade similar to a pocket-knife blade. This blade is convenient for many purposes in the mine. All these parts (the hook, the awl, and the blade) are attached to the pin B, and are held in position (as they may be wanted when in use) by means of ribs and recesses. (Seen in Fig. 2.) The spring of the bow A holds the ribs in the recesses, but the ends of the spring are allowed to spread on the pin when either part is turned outward from the bow A, as before mentioned. H is the ring for the candle, formed by an elongation of the end C of the spring.

This candle-holder may be carried in the pocket, the awl being then folded down within the bow, as seen in Fig. 2. Provided with this combined device, the miner enters the mine feeling prepared for all the contingencies which are likely to occur.

Having thus described my invention, I claim as new, and desire to secure by Letters Patent—

The combination, with bow A, provided with the rivet B, hook E, and sticker F, of the candle-holder H, as and for the purpose specified.

NEILS LARSEN.

Witnesses:
OTHELLO R. OSTRANDER,
CALEB W. CHURCHILL.

UNITED STATES PATENT OFFICE.

JAMES DOUGLAS, JR., OF QUEBEC, CANADA, THOMAS S. HUNT, OF BOSTON, MASS., AND JAMES O. STEWART, OF GEORGETOWN, COLO. TER.

IMPROVEMENT IN EXTRACTING SILVER, GOLD, AND OTHER METALS FROM THEIR ORES.

Specification forming part of Letters Patent No. **151,763**, dated June 9, 1874; application filed February 23, 1874.

To all whom it may concern:

Be it known that we, JAMES DOUGLAS, Jr., of the city and Province of Quebec, in the Dominion of Canada, THOMAS STERRY HUNT, of the city of Boston, in the State of Massachusetts, one of the United States of America, both British subjects, and JAMES OSCAR STEWART, of Georgetown, Colorado, one of the Territories of the United States, a citizen of the United States, have invented certain new and useful Improvements in the Art of Extracting Silver and Gold from their Ores, constituting a general method for the treatment of silver ores, whether with or without gold, of which the following is a specification:

The mode of procedure differs somewhat, according as the silver ores are associated with much ore of the base metals, zinc and lead, or are free from such admixture. In the first case—that is to say, if ores of zinc and lead are present in considerable quantity, and copper be not present—we add of copper pyrites, or of a mixture of other copper ores, with iron pyrites, so much as shall be found by experience to result in the most thorough extraction of silver. Even a very small percentage is of advantage, and a large excess is in no way objectionable. The ground ore or ores is then calcined with common salt or other chlorides in a suitable furnace, as is usual in the chlorination of silver ores. The charge, when withdrawn is to be treated by agitation or lixiviation in any suitable vessel with a bath consisting of a solution of protochloride of iron and common salt, as in the Hunt and Douglas patent copper process.

The acid fumes from the roasting of pyrites or other sulphureted ores must be passed over or otherwise brought in contact with the bath during its action upon the roasted ore to prevent the loss of protochloride of iron otherwise resulting from the action of the oxides of lead and zinc present. The bath in this part of the process dissolves the copper, besides the zinc and the greater part of the silver, which has been chloridized in the furnace, while the copper in the solution chloridizes silver, which escapes chloridization in the furnace.

After digestion for four or eight hours at a temperature which is best from 120° to 200° Fahrenheit, the solution is drawn off and the silver precipitated by allowing it to remain for some time in contact with sheet-copper, or, better, to filter through two or three boxes with perforated bottoms filled with cement copper. In either case the copper is dissolved and the silver separated in the metallic state. When, however, copper regulus, gray or purple copper ore, copper pyrites, or magnetic iron pyrites can be obtained, it is advantageous to allow the solution holding silver and copper to pass, before going to the metallic copper, through filter-boxes charged with one of these sulphurets—preferably ground copper regulus or a rich copper ore. In this way the protochloride of copper in the solution is converted into dichloride at the expense of the copper in these sulphurets, thereby greatly reducing the consumption of metallic copper in subsequent precipitation of the metallic silver, as above described. At the same time the copper is extracted from such ores or regulus, and, in case these are argentiferous, the silver also, without the cost of furnace treatment.

In this part of the process it must be remembered that an elevated temperature and a considerable excess of common salt or other chlorides are required to keep the dichloride of copper in solution. From the copper solutions, freed from silver, the copper is readily precipitated by scrap iron, less than one part of iron being required to separate two parts of metallic copper.

After the copper has been precipitated the solution will contain, besides chloride of sodium, protochloride of iron and chloride of zinc, provided this metal was present in the ores. By evaporating, out of contact of air as much as possible, till it crystallizes out, the greater part of the salt may be recovered from the solution and used in the furnace, with the addition of a further portion of chloride of sodium, for chloridizing a second charge of ore, as before, while the mother-liquor from the salt containing the protochloride of iron is to be used to form, with the addition of common salt, a bath for its treatment after roasting.

The pulp or residue remaining, after the roasted ore has been treated with the chloride bath, will probably, if the ore was rich in this metal, contain some undissolved chloride of silver. This may be extracted by lixiviation with hot brine, or with a solution of hyposulphite of soda, and any gold, if present, subsequently removed by chlorination, or the pulp or residue may be at once treated by mercury, and the gold and silver obtained together in the form of an amalgam.

In the second case mentioned—that is to say, when the silver ores to be treated contain little or no base metal ores, such as blende or galena—the chlorination in the furnace may be dispensed with if a solution of either or both of the chlorides of copper can be obtained, since these readily chloridize and make soluble silver and its ores.

We prefer to prepare these chlorides by treating oxidized copper ores with a bath of protochloride of iron and common salt, as in the Hunt and Douglas copper process; but when copper ores are not to be had we obtain such a solution by dissolving sulphate of copper and common salt in water. In either case the pulverized silver ores are to be digested for some hours at a heat approaching boiling with frequent agitation, when the silver is chloridized and the copper wholly converted into dichloride, and at length precipitated as a sulphuret with the residues, from which it may be separated by calcining in the air, and subsequently treating with a bath of protochloride of iron and common salt, as directed above for oxidized copper ores, by which means a solution of chloride of copper is got to treat a fresh portion of silver ore.

Both the solutions containing chloride of silver and the residues are to be treated as already described. In this method of extracting silver, the only reagent consumed is the protochloride of iron.

The advantages which we claim for the system above described, are, first, that in chlorinating in the furnace silver ores containing base metals, such as zinc and lead, a more perfect chlorination is effected by mixing them with ores holding copper and iron, and subsequent treatment with the bath of protochloride of iron; second, that all the copper in the charge is recovered at a slight cost; third, that as much copper is extracted from unroasted copper ore or regulus as is contained in the state of protochloride in the solution from the roasted ore, and, moreover, that unroasted silver-bearing ores or regulus may be decomposed by this solution containing chlorides of copper; fourth, that metallic silver perfectly free from base metals is obtained by the precipitation with copper, and, moreover, that the silver left undissolved in the residues will yield a much purer amalgam than if the roasted ore had not been previously treated with the bath; fifth, that gold, if present in the ore, is left in the best condition either to be chlorinated, or to be amalgamated with the chloride of silver remaining in the residues; sixth, that by the removal of the base metals before amalgamation a saving of mercury is effected; seventh, that a great saving of salt is effected through the recovery, by evaporation, of the chlorides usually thrown away in the waste liquors; eighth, that in treating simple ores of silver, or ores of silver containing but little base metal, as lead or zinc, the costly operation of roasting with salt may be dispensed with, and the inexpensive protochloride of iron may be used to produce the chloride of copper necessary for their treatment.

The bath formed of protochloride of iron and chloride of sodium will dissolve the copper and silver from ores mixed or unmixed with other metals, and will eliminate gold, silver, or copper from mixed or unmixed ores, whether the ordinary amalgamation process is employed or not.

Having thus described our invention, what we claim is—

The process of eliminating copper or silver from ore by immersing the ore in a bath of protochloride of iron and chloride of sodium.

J. DOUGLAS, Jr.
THOMAS STERRY HUNT.
JAMES OSCAR STEWART.

Witnesses as to J. DOUGLAS, Jr.:
JAS. B. LLOYD,
I. L. DAWSON.
Witnesses as to THOMAS STERRY HUNT:
G. M. CROCKER,
R. W. RAYNER.
Witnesses as to JAMES OSCAR STEWART:
D. H. MITCHELL,
JERRY G. MAHANY.

R. TEATS.
Apparatus for Conveying and Cooling Roasted Ores.
No. 152,532. Patented June 30, 1874.

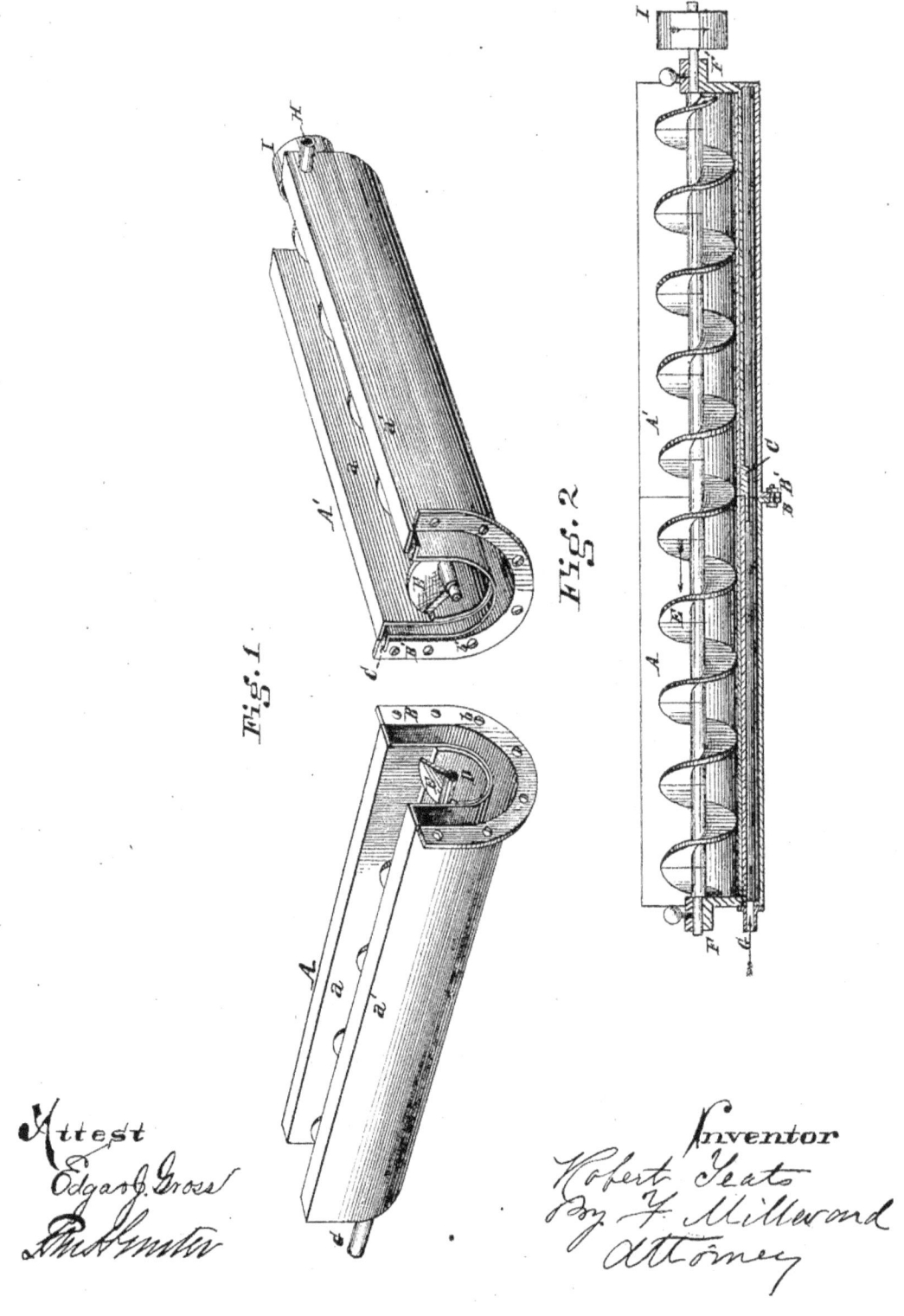

UNITED STATES PATENT OFFICE.

ROBERT TEATS, OF CENTRAL CITY, COLORADO TERRITORY.

IMPROVEMENT IN APPARATUS FOR CONVEYING AND COOLING ROASTED ORES.

Specification forming part of Letters Patent No. **152,532**, dated June 30, 1874; application filed June 9, 1874.

To all whom it may concern:

Be it known that I, ROBERT TEATS, of Central City, Gilpin county, Colorado Territory, have invented certain new and useful Improvements in Apparatus for Conveying and Cooling Roasted Ores, of which the following is a specification:

My invention relates to that class of conveyers which act by means of a screw or worm, the thread or flange of which revolves in close proximity to the inner surface of a semi-cylindrical trough, and thus presses the ore through said trough; and my invention consists, in connection with said screw-conveyer, of a cooler formed below the screw-conveyer, the bottom of the conveyer being a part of the same, into which, at one end, cold water under pressure is introduced through a pipe near the bottom, and gradually rises under said pressure around the inner plate of the trough until it is forced out at a pipe near the top of the other end, the object of this being twofold: First, owing to the cold water entering and surrounding the trough, the inclosed heated ore from the roasting-furnaces is deprived of heat; and, second, in the same action, this liberated heat gradually heats the water as it passes to the other end of the trough, which it reaches in a fit state for use in amalgamating the ore, thereby saving steam, which has been heretofore used for that purpose. This same heated water, as it comes from the trough, may also be used for boiler-feeding, if required, thus doing away with the customary heater.

Figure 1 is a perspective view, representing disconnected sections of a conveying-trough (with the inclosed screw broken apart) embodying my invention. Fig. 2 is a sectional elevation of trough, showing inclosed screw entire.

A A' are sections of a hollow semi-cylindrical cooling and conveying trough, with inner and outer shells a a', respectively. The outer shells, a', of the two sections have flanges B B', while one of the inner shells a has a projecting lip, C, thus making an impenetrable water-tight joint when joined together with gaskets and secured by bolts passing through apertures b. Inside of the inner shell a, and fitting snugly against it, I provide a false cast-iron shell, D, to protect the trough from the wearing tendency of the passing ore. I prefer to use this cast-iron lining because it is cheaper and more convenient to replace (when worn out) than the shell proper, while it does not materially hinder the process of cooling. E is the worm, which is made of cast-iron and put together in sections. It rests upon bearing F F' at each end of the trough, secured to the bottom of the same, and I prefer to introduce a bearing also at the point of connection between the sections A A', which will relieve the inner false shell D of the weight of the screw, and also support the latter. G is the supply-pipe for cold water; and H is the escape-pipe for this water, which, while passing through the space between the shells in the opposite direction to the ore, becomes charged with the heat from the passing ore, and is adapted, while thus heated, to be used for amalgamating the ore or to feed the boiler. I is a pulley revolved by steam-power; or, if the trough is one of a series, I use bevel-gearing and a line of shafting.

The ore to be operated upon in my apparatus is that received from a roasting-furnace, and it has been customary heretofore to spread this ore on extensive floors, and by manual labor, subjected to the poisonous gases, it has been stirred up and slowly cooled.

With my apparatus the ore can be taken directly from the furnace and fed through a hopper into the end of the conveyer and cooler, and it is, in transit from one end to the other, thoroughly cooled, the water which cools it being heated in the manner before explained, the water and ore moving in opposite directions, as shown by arrows.

I claim—

In combination with the screw-conveyer E, the hollow cooling-trough A A', constructed to operate substantially in the manner and for the purpose specified.

In testimony of which invention I hereunto set my hand.

ROBERT TEATS.

Witnesses:
FRANK MILLWARD,
R. M. HUNTER.

UNITED STATES PATENT OFFICE.

JOHN P. DYER, OF PUEBLO, COLORADO TERRITORY.

IMPROVEMENT IN MEDICAL COMPOUNDS OR SALVES.

Specification forming part of Letters Patent No. **152,833**, dated July 7, 1874; application filed May 22, 1874.

To all whom it may concern:

Be it known that I, JOHN P. DYER, of Pueblo, Colorado Territory, have invented a certain Compound of Medicines, to be used in the case of cancerous affections, ulcers, and malignant sores, of which the following is a specification:

This invention relates to those remedies used in the cure of the above-named diseases.

To prepare this remedy, take twenty-five pounds of red-oak bark ground in an ordinary bark-mill; take eight pounds of sarsaparilla. Then put the bark and sarsaparilla in nine gallons of water; boil down to one gallon; then remove the bark and strain the decoction through a coarse cloth; then take the decoction thus obtained and put it in a brass kettle; add to it two ounces of belladonna and two ounces of hyoscyamus, (solid extracts of each;) then add one pint of strained honey, two ounces of gum-turpentine, three ounces of mutton or beef suet, and two ounces of beeswax; then simmer all these ingredients in the brass kettle over a slow fire until it becomes of the consistency of very thick tar; then add two ounces of gum-camphor, (powdered,) stirring until it is well mixed.

This remedy is used in the following manner: Cleanse the affected part thoroughly with warm water and castile-soap; spread the remedy on a linen cloth, and apply it to the affected part. Let it remain twenty-four hours; then put on a fresh application, cleansing again with castile-soap, and so continue the use of the remedy until a cure is effected. This remedy will in all cases be found to be very soothing to the patient, and will effectually eradicate the entire disease and effect a permanent cure.

What I claim as my invention is—

The compound herein described, composed of red-oak bark, sarsaparilla, belladonna, hyoscyamus, honey, spirits turpentine, camphor, bees-wax, and mutton or beef suet, in about the proportions specified.

J. P. DYER.

Witnesses:
R. H. WARD,
CHS. H. LYNCH.

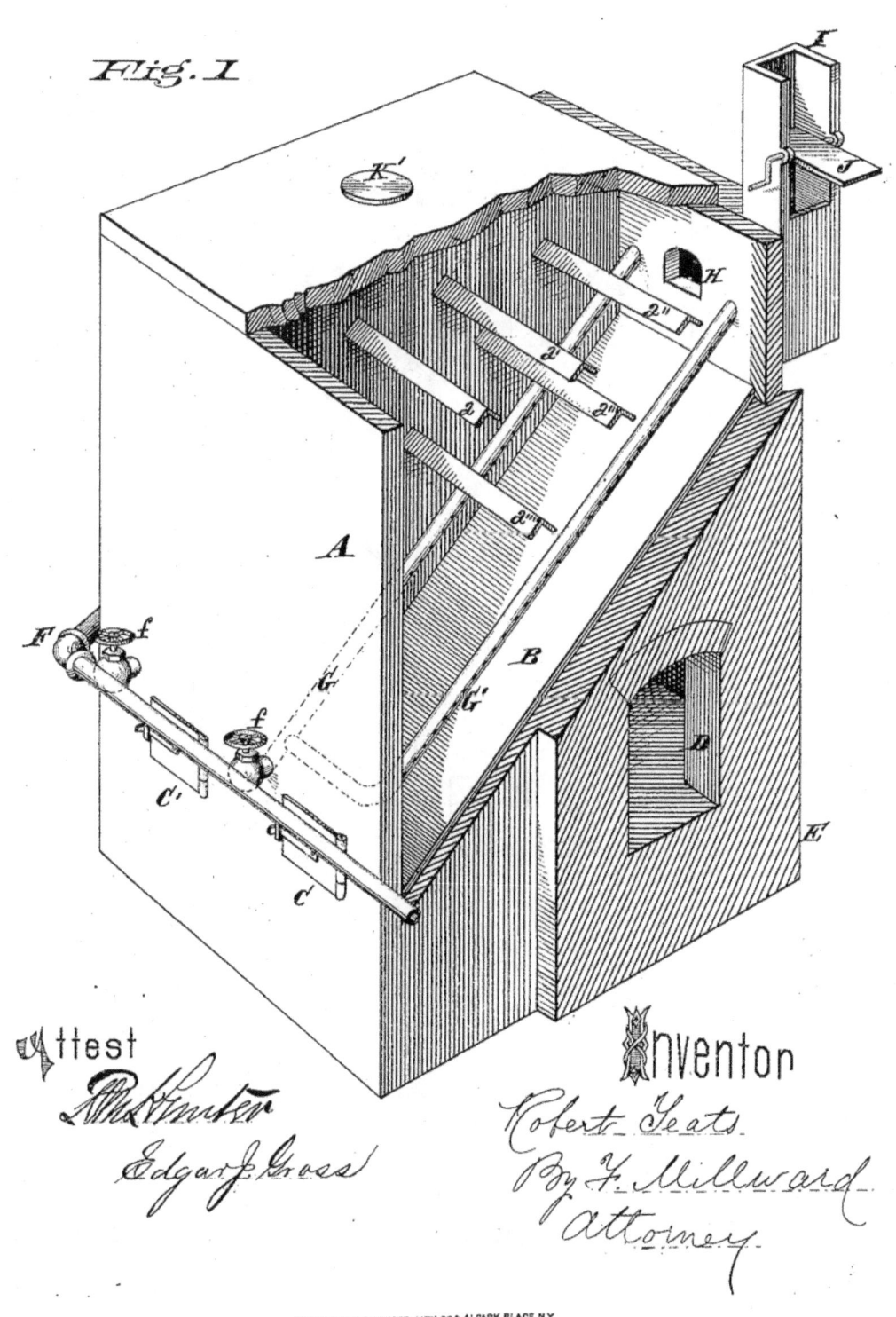

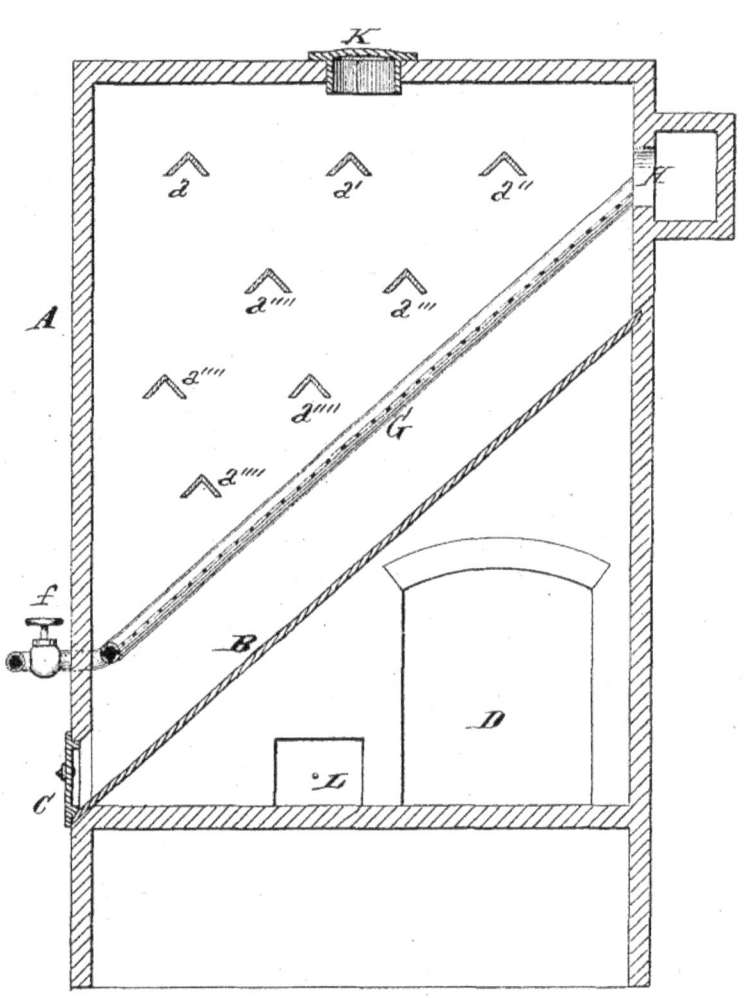

UNITED STATES PATENT OFFICE

ROBERT TEATS, OF CENTRAL CITY, COLORADO TERRITORY.

IMPROVEMENT IN DRYING ORES.

Specification forming part of Letters Patent No. **153,397**, dated July 21, 1874; application filed June 22, 1874.

To all whom it may concern:

Be it known that I, ROBERT TEATS, of Central City, Gilpin county, Colorado Territory, have invented certain new and useful Improvements in Devices for Drying Ores, of which the following is a specification:

My invention relates to the class of dry-kilns intended for drying ore received wet from the mine or crusher, having a chamber or series of chambers with inclined iron floors or chutes; and my invention consists, in the first part, in connection with said kiln, of devices by which a blast of air is introduced into said chambers, for the purpose of rapidly taking up and carrying away the moisture, and thus drying the ore deposited therein; and my invention consists, in the second place, of transverse perforated pipes for more effectually distributing the blast, and a regulator-vent for escape into the flue of the mill of said blast, after being spent. My invention consists, in the third place, of transverse bars or angle-irons to prevent the ore from becoming packed, and also causing the blast to eddy, thereby utilizing to the fullest extent the drying quality of the blast.

Figure 1 is a broken perspective view of a dry-kiln, having my improvements attached. Fig. 2 is a vertical section through one chamber of the kiln.

A is the body of the kiln, having, in this instance, two separate chambers. B is the iron floor of one of the chambers. C C' are doors for the exit of the ore after being dried. D is the opening from the space under floor B to the chimney E, (shown in section,) and forms part of the connection from the boiler of the mill. F is the supply-pipe for air, hot or cold, leading, if hot air is wanted, from a coiled pipe in the flue leading from the boiler, and is fitted with valves $f f'$, connecting with the perforated escape-pipes $g g'$. These escape-pipes have perforations, one or more rows, on the sides or bottoms. The air being introduced under pressure, it leaves the perforations and penetrates through the ore in the chamber, which has been fed through aperture K. $a\ a'\ a''\ a'''\ a''''$ are wood or iron bars or angle-irons, resting in the walls of kiln A to prevent the ore from packing, and also to cause the ejected blast to eddy among the particles. H is an exhaust-port for the escape of the blast, either to a chimney connected below the butterfly-valve J, the escape then being below the valve, as seen in Fig 1, or, when the valve is vertical, through flue I into the open air. When it enters from the damper to the chimney it acts as a blower, the force whereof is regulated by amount of opening of valve J. The air, as before stated, may, if preferred, be charged with caloric, and this may be done in a coiled pipe in the flue leading from the boiler, and then forced by a blower through supply-pipe F, regulated by valves $f f'$ into vent-pipes G G', leaving which at the orifices, it permeates the surrounding ore, drying it, and then passes through port H. The ore may be partially heated by vapors from the fire-box passing on their way to chimney E through passage D, under the floor B. The ore is introduced through apertures K K' into the chambers A, directly from the crusher or mine, and after having been dried is taken out at door C C'. If it is thought necessary to dry ore when the mill is not running, fire may be introduced under floor B at the door L, in place of the blast of air.

I claim—

1. In combination with the kiln A, the blast-pipes F f, connected and operating substantially as and for the purpose specified.

2. The combination of kiln A, blast-pipes F f, and perforated distributing-pipes G, operating substantially in the manner and for the purpose specified.

3. In combination with the kiln A, and blast apparatus F f G, the bars $a\ a'$, &c., operating substantially as described, for the purpose specified.

4. In combination with the kiln A, and blast apparatus F f G, the escape-flue regulating-valve J, operating as and for the purpose stated.

In testimony of which invention I hereunto set my hand.

ROBERT TEATS.

Witnesses:
EDGAR J. GROSS,
J. L. WARTMANN.

F. W. FREUND.
Breech-Loading Fire-Arms.

No. 153,432.   Patented July 28, 1874.

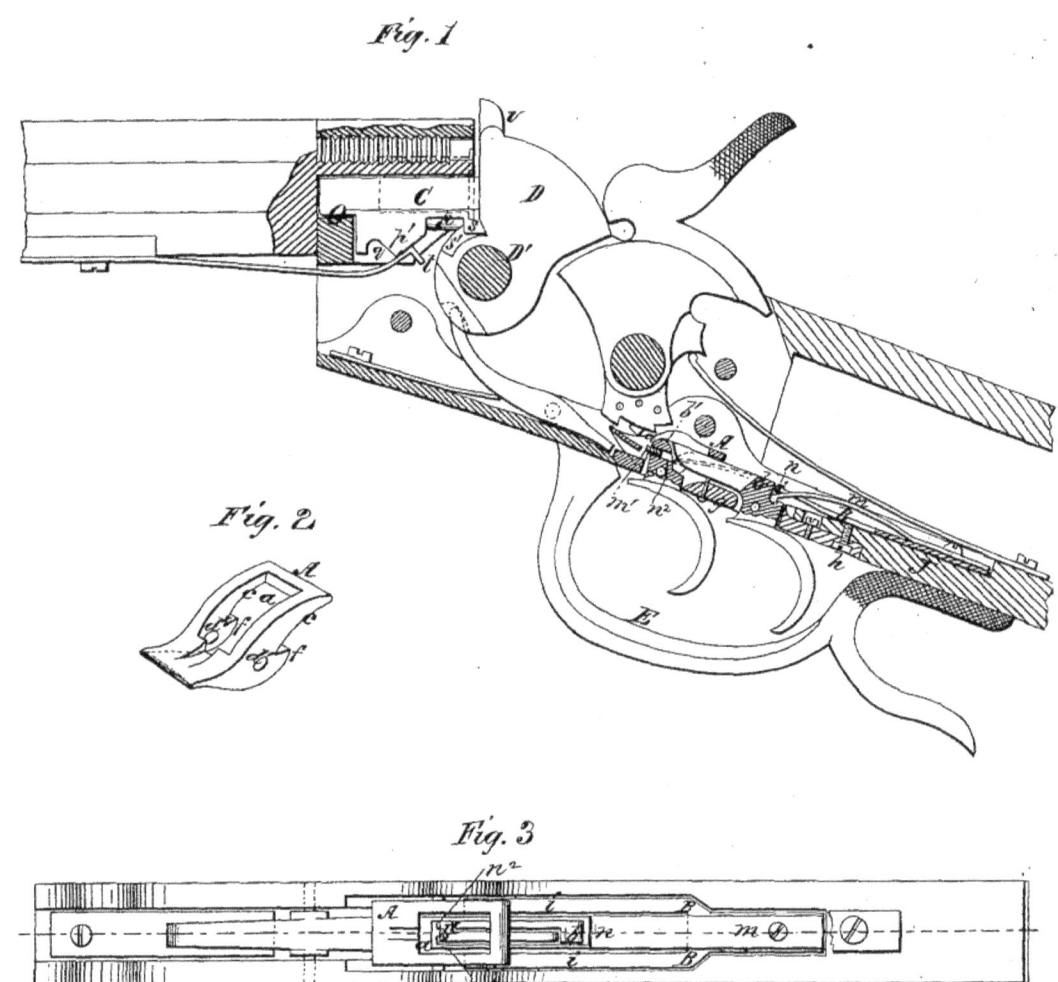

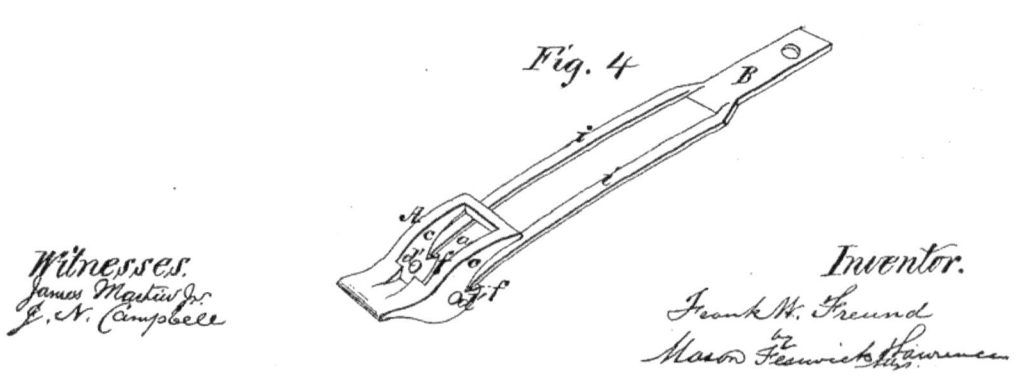

UNITED STATES PATENT OFFICE.

FRANK W. FREUND, OF DENVER, COLORADO TERRITORY.

IMPROVEMENT IN BREECH-LOADING FIRE-ARMS.

Specification forming part of Letters Patent No. **153,432**, dated July 28, 1874; application filed October 13, 1873.

To all whom it may concern:

Be it known that I, FRANK W. FREUND, of Denver, Territory of Colorado, have invented certain new and useful Improvements in Breech-Loading Fire-Arms; and I do hereby declare that the following is a full, clear, and exact description thereof, reference being had to the accompanying drawings, making part of this specification, in which—

Figure 1 is a side view, showing a portion of the arm in section in the line $x\,x$, Fig. 3, and a portion in elevation. The fire-arm appears not cocked. Fig. 2 is a perspective view of my improved sear. Fig. 3 is a top view of the trigger-box or bottom piece of the stock with the improved sear and sear-spring and other trigger mechanism, the main spring of the hammer being broken away in order to not have it hide the said mechanism. Fig. 4 is a perspective view of the improved sear and forked spring in proper relation to one another, but detached from the arm.

To enable others skilled in the art to understand my invention, I will proceed to describe the same with reference to the drawing.

My improvements relate to an improved slotted sear and forked sear-spring, whereby I am enabled to put double-set triggers in breech-loading guns which have the lock in the center and a low hammer.

In the accompanying drawings, A represents the sear. It is made of one solid piece of steel cut out at the center, as at a, to allow the set-triggers $b\,b'$ to work in between the inner sides formed by cutting out the metal to form the opening a. The sides of the sear are shaped like the rocker of a cradle, and the rear under portion of each is cut away to form a detent, f, for the end of the sear-spring, as shown at c. This sear is fastened to the trigger-box or bottom piece J of the stock, so as to vibrate, by two screws, $d\,d$, one on each side, in order that it may work with an equal bearing on each side as the set-triggers $b\,b'$ strike at points between these screws. The sear is also made so that the set-triggers are independent of it; these triggers therefore can be and are attached to the trigger-plate g, and this plate being confined by only one screw, h, great convenience for taking these triggers out for oiling, or any other purpose, is afforded, it not being necessary, as in many cases, to take the whole lock apart for this purpose. B represents the sear-spring. It is forked as at $i\,i$, and its respective forks i fit above the respective detents f, which are near the screw-pivot holes d' of the sear, as shown. The opening between the forks of the spring B allows room for the set-triggers to work up and down, and it also permits the spring m of the rear trigger b to be placed above it, and its front end to pass down between its forks behind the detent n of said trigger; and it also permits the angular spring m', which operates upon the forward trigger b', to be extended to the detent n^2 of said trigger, and to play up and down without obstruction between its forks. This sear-spring, by being set in detents near the pivots of the sear, is not subject to great leverage strain, and therefore is not liable to be broken easily.

It has long been a serious complaint against the single-set trigger of the most approved arms that when it is set fine it is not safe, and if constructed to be set otherwise it is too hard to operate for fine shooting. This complaint my improvement entirely obviates without altering the approved style of the arm.

What I claim as my invention, and desire to secure by Letters Patent, is—

1. The sear A, open at its center, as at a, and constructed with independent detents $f\,f$, whereby it is adapted for use with a forked spring, the set-triggers $b\,b'$, and the hammer, substantially as and for the purpose described.

2. The sear-spring B, forked as at $i\,i$, in combination with the sear A, whereby these parts combined are adapted for use with the set-triggers $b\,b'$ and the hammer, substantially as and for the purpose described.

FRANK WM. FREUND.

Witnesses:
H. M. HALE,
L. C. CHARLES.

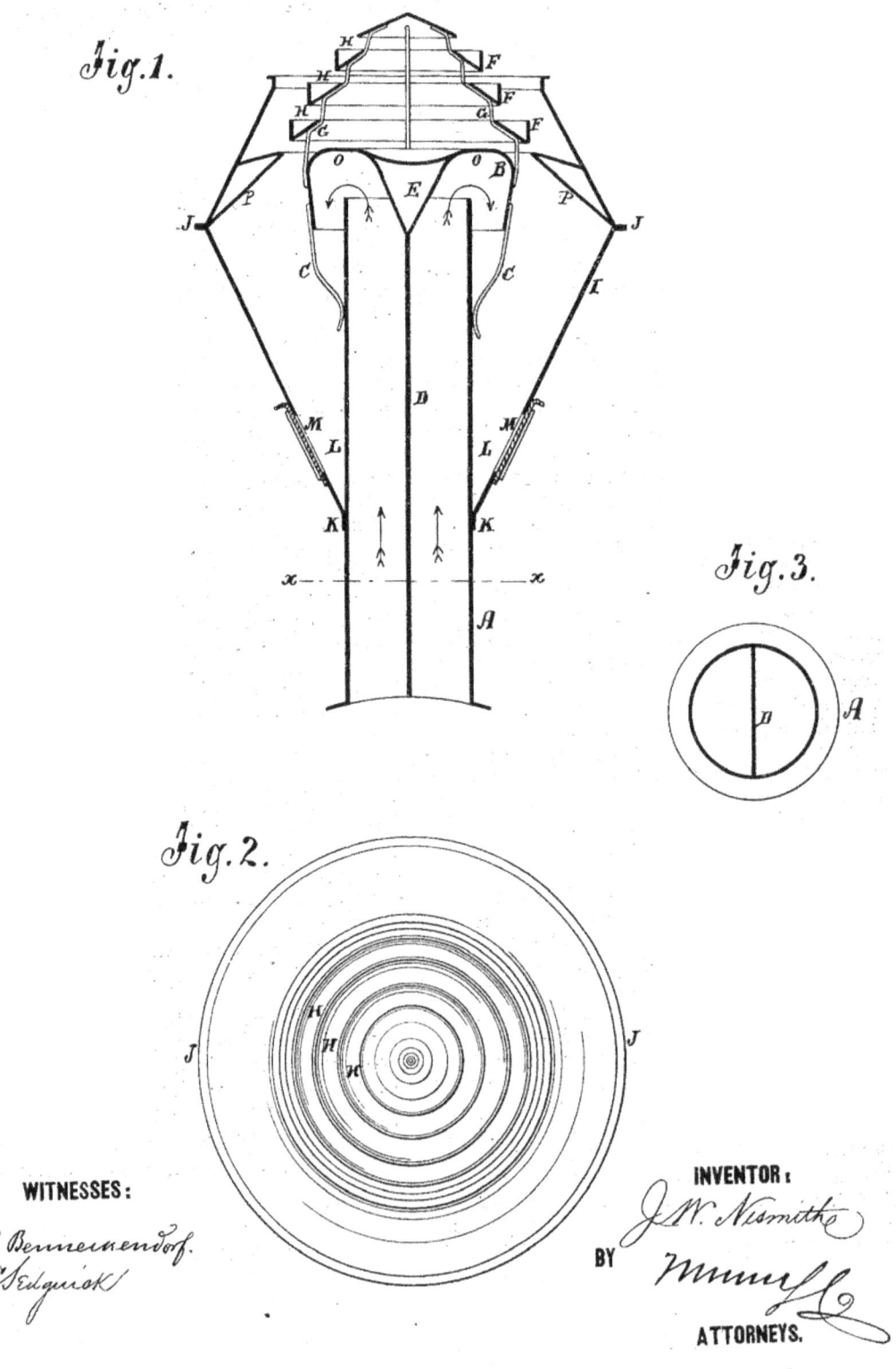

UNITED STATES PATENT OFFICE.

J. WELLINGTON NESMITH, OF GOLDEN, COLORADO TERRITORY.

IMPROVEMENT IN SMOKE-STACKS AND SPARK-ARRESTERS.

Specification forming part of Letters Patent No. **154,412**, dated August 25, 1874; application filed May 1, 1874.

To all whom it may concern:

Be it known that I, J. WELLINGTON NESMITH, of Golden, in the county of Jefferson and Territory of Colorado, have invented a new and useful Improvement in Smoke-Stacks and Spark-Arresters, of which the following is a specification:

The object of this invention is to furnish a smoke-stack and spark-arrester for coal-burning locomotives which will not only prevent the escape of sparks, but economize fuel. Ordinary smoke-stacks (when the coal which is used on western roads is being burned) throw a stream of sparks, which endangers everything combustible which is exposed. By the present improvement the sparks are arrested and drop by their own gravity into a receptacle provided for them.

The invention consists of an inverted pot over the top of the flue, confined in any substantial manner, having attached thereto a series of concentric flanges or rings, forming (together) an open pyramid, surmounted by a cap, all in combination with the diamond-shaped bulge or head of the smoke-stack.

In the accompanying drawing, Figure 1 is a vertical central section of the improved smoke-stack. Fig. 2 is a top view. Fig. 3 is a cross-section of Fig. 1 on the line $x\ x$.

Similar letters of reference indicate corresponding parts.

A is the smoke-flue. B is the inverted pot, supported over the top of the flue by the vertical springs C, or by any other suitable means. The flue is divided into two parts by the vertical partition D, which meets the apex of the inverted cone E within the pot B. F represents one or more flanges above the pot, and attached thereto by the straps G. These flanges diminish in diameter from the lower to the upper one, as seen in the drawing, with space H between for the discharge of the smoke. I is the head of the smoke-stack, consisting of the frustums of two cones, connected at their bases J. This head is attached to the outside of the smoke-flue at K, forming (with the flue) a V-shaped annular space, L, for receiving the sparks. $m\ m$ are apertures in the head near the connection K, closed by the slide N, through which the sparks are removed. The course of the sparks and products of combustion is indicated by the arrows. As they ascend they are driven upward by the blast till they strike the curved surface O of the pot. The sparks, being thus arrested, drop by their own gravity into the V-shaped receptacle L, from whence they are removed. The smoke and gases pass out and upward, and escape without carrying any fire. The partition D is not an indispensable feature, and the smoke-stack may be made either with or without it, to produce the same or a similar effect.

It will be seen that the entire products of combustion, as well as the exhaust-steam, are discharged into the inverted pot, and from that downward; the sparks falling, and the smoke, steam, and gases rising, as described. With this smoke-stack and spark-arrester, combined and arranged as shown, fuel is economized and the "spark nuisance" is entirely abated.

By dividing the smoke pipe or flue A and the cap B correspondingly into two or more parts, the products of combustion are separated and driven out in separate currents, being thus able more readily to lose their heat and deposit their sparks in the troughs F H, to which they are guided by the inner flange or cone P.

Having thus described my invention, I claim as new and desire to secure by Letters Patent—

The combination, with flue A, cap B, and stack-head I, of the guiding-cone P and the series of troughs F H, growing gradually smaller as they arise above the cap, and having open intervals between them, as and for the purpose specified.

J. WELLINGTON NESMITH.

Witnesses:
 JAS. M. MANAHAN,
 W. C. ARMOR.

M. McCARTY.
Current-Wheels.

No. 155,035. Patented Sept. 15, 1874.

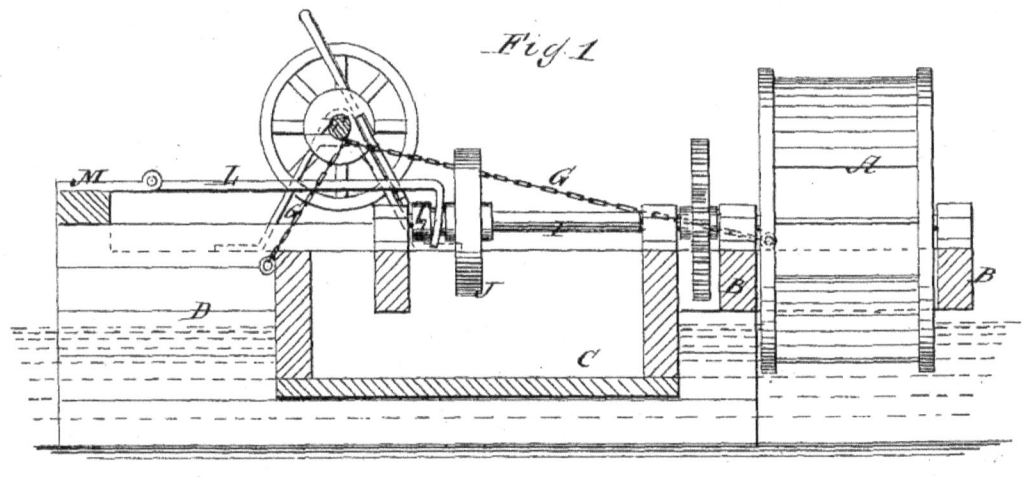

Fig. 1

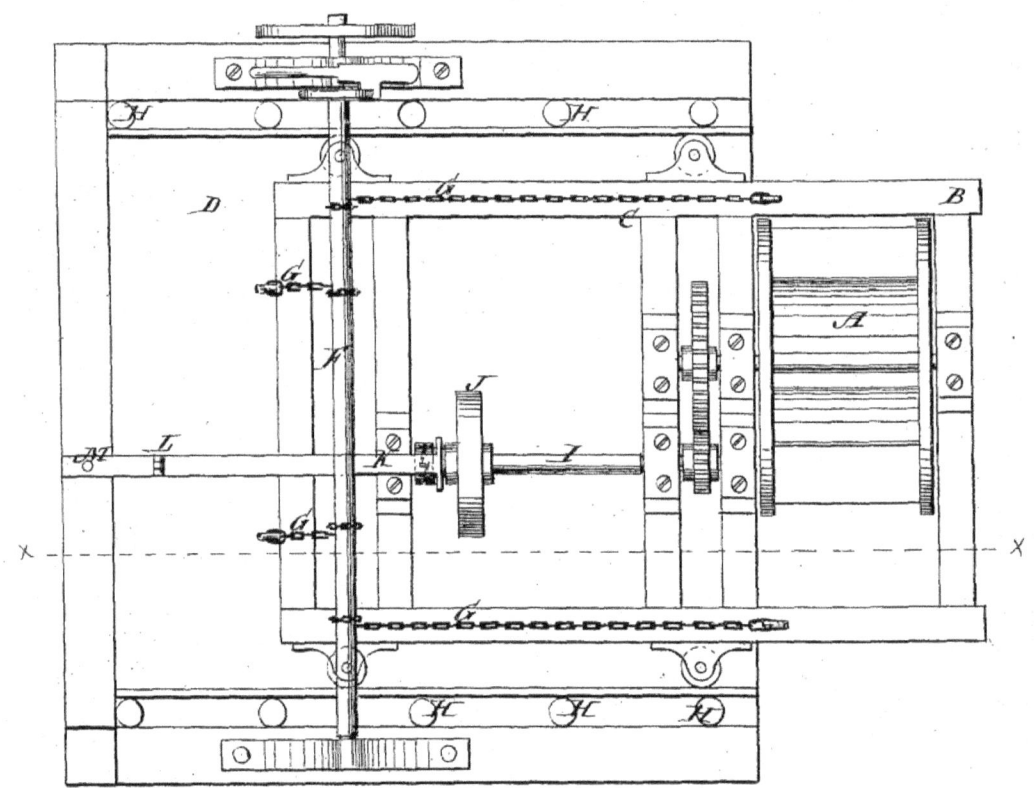

Fig. 2

WITNESSES:
E. Wolff
A. F. Terry

INVENTOR:
M. McCarty
BY Munn & Co.
ATTORNEYS.

UNITED STATES PATENT OFFICE.

MICHAEL McCARTY, OF PUEBLO, COLORADO TERRITORY.

IMPROVEMENT IN CURRENT-WHEELS.

Specification forming part of Letters Patent No. **155,035**, dated September 15, 1874; application filed August 15, 1874.

To all whom it may concern:

Be it known that I, MICHAEL McCARTY, of Pueblo, Pueblo county, Colorado Territory, have invented a new and Improved Current-Wheel, of which the following is a specification:

My invention consists of a current-wheel arranged at the outside of a float which is arranged in a slip or basin in the river-bank, or between two piers at right angles to the current, so that it can be floated out to extend the wheel into the current, and back to withdraw it therefrom, for stopping and starting the wheel, and regulating it to the force of the current; and the shaft of the wheel is made to slide forward and backward through the wheel for transmitting the power, the wheel being confined in the place for gearing with the counter-shaft to be driven by it.

Figure 1 is a longitudinal sectional elevation of a current-wheel arranged according to my invention, taken on the line xx, Fig. 2; and Fig. 2 is a plan view.

Similar letters of reference indicate corresponding parts.

A represents the wheel, which is mounted in the frame B, which projects from the float C, so as to overhang said float. The float is arranged in a slip, D, made in the bank, or between projecting piers at right angles to the current of the stream, so as to move the wheel out into the current at the mouth of the slip, or back within the protection of the slip, the slip being deep enough for the float to ride on the water. F represents a windlass, with chains G, for moving the float out and in; and H represents rollers or wheels at the sides of the float, bearing against the walls of the slip to lessen the friction between the float and the walls of the slip. The walls of the slip are to guide the float, the slip being only wide enough to allow it to move freely, but not so as to allow any unnecessary play. The shaft I for transmitting the motion is arranged to slide forward and backward through the driving-wheel J, which is held in its place by the bar K, which is jointed at L to rise and fall with the float, while the end M is held by a fixed object to which it is made fast.

This construction enables the wheel to be easily managed for setting it in motion and stopping it, and also for protecting it from floating objects or too great force of water in time of floods.

Having thus described my invention, I claim as new and desire to secure by Letters Patent—

A current-wheel mounted on a float arranged in a slip at right angles to the current, and provided with means to shift it out into the current and back into the slip, substantially in the manner described.

MICHAEL McCARTY.

Witnesses:
JOHN D. MILLER,
WM. J. BUCKLAND.

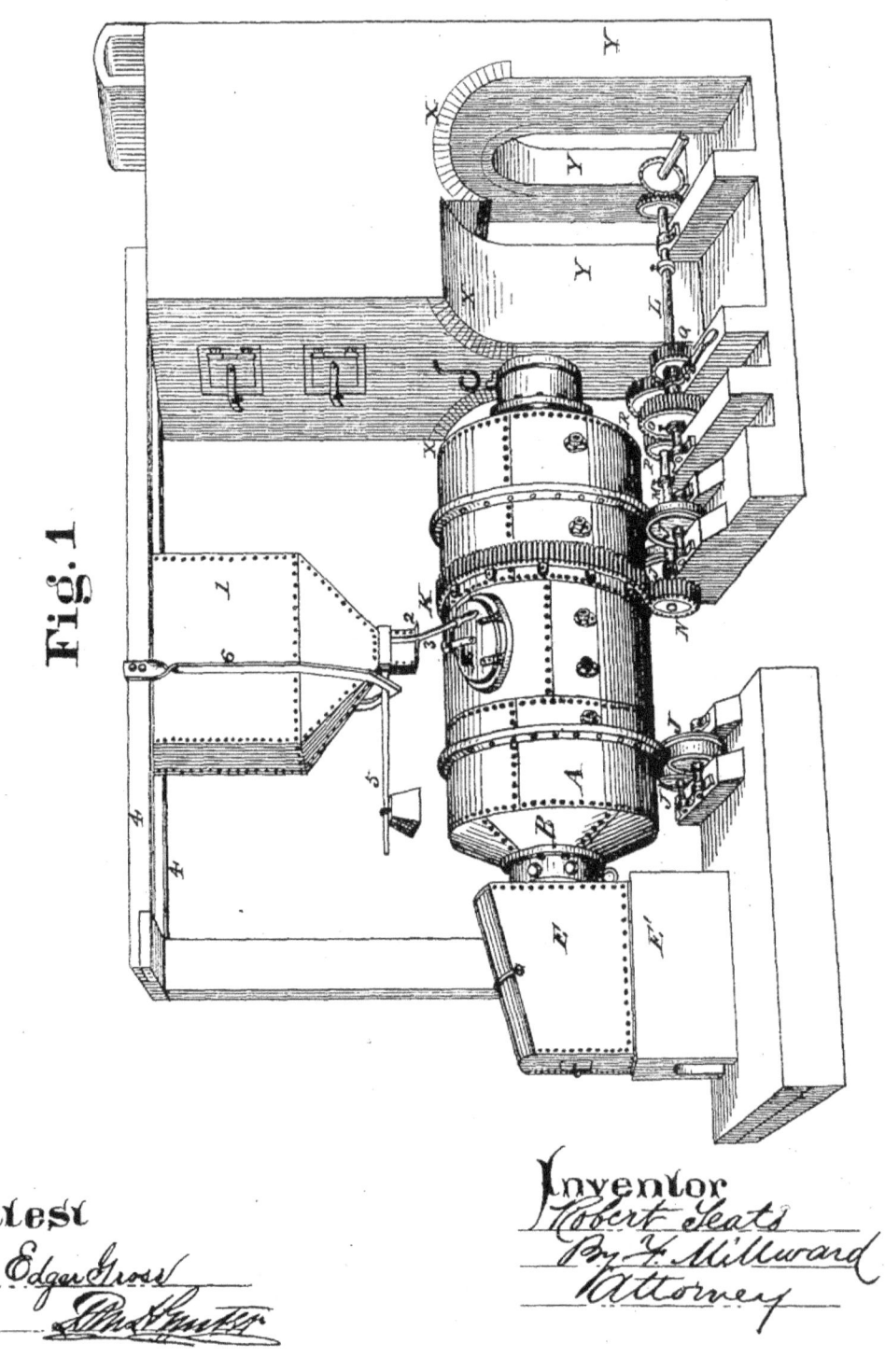

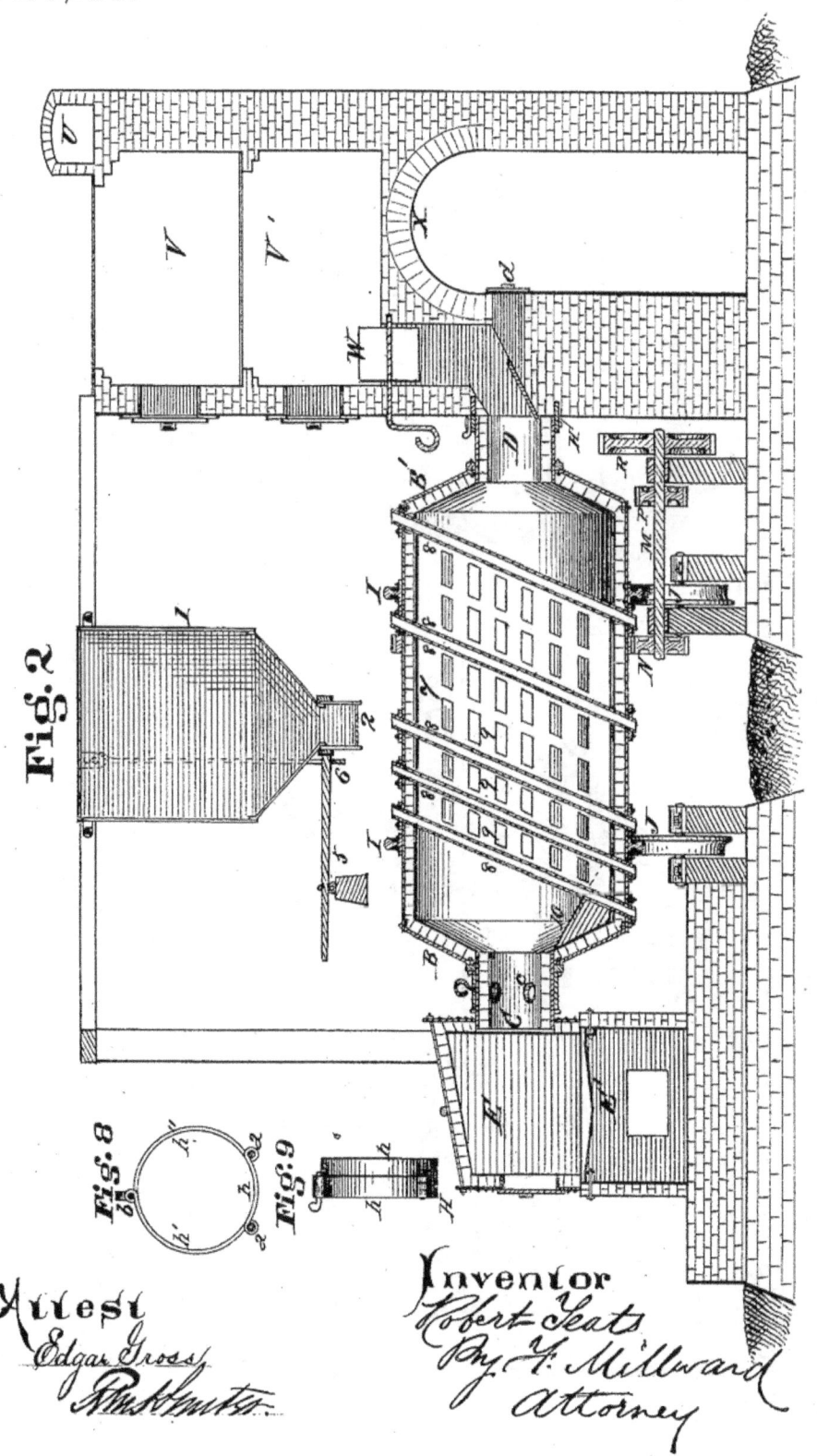

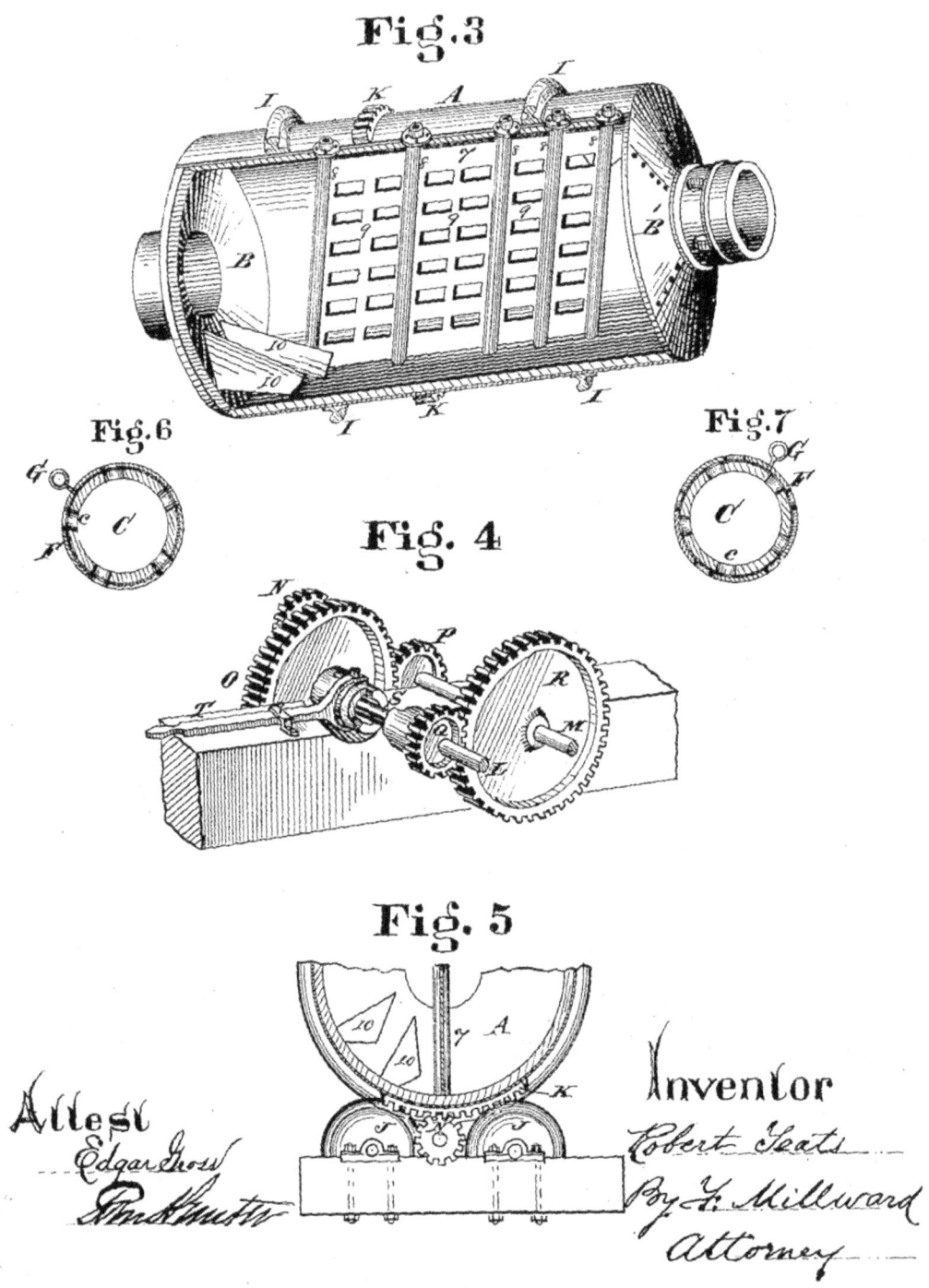

UNITED STATES PATENT OFFICE.

ROBERT TEATS, OF CENTRAL CITY, COLORADO TERRITORY, ASSIGNOR TO HIMSELF AND ABEL D. BREED, OF NEW YORK, N. Y.

IMPROVEMENT IN REVOLVING ORE-ROASTERS.

Specification forming part of Letters Patent No. **155,123**, dated September 15, 1874; application filed March 21, 1874.

To all whom it may concern:

Be it known that I, ROBERT TEATS, of Central city, county of Gilpin, Territory of Colorado, have invented a certain new and useful Cylinder-Furnace for uniformly mixing, chloridizing, roasting, and desulphurizing gold, silver, and other ores and substances, of which the following is a specification:

My invention consists, first, in the provision, in connection with the peculiarly-formed furnace and conveyer, of angle-pieces which act in conjunction with the parts named to uniformly mix the ores in the revolution of the furnace; second, in the provision and construction of a series of apertures around the throat of the furnace, governed by a ring-door for admitting and graduating a supply of air to the furnace; third, in connection with the back throat of the furnace, of a hinged neck or rim, which, by opening, will admit of the removal of the furnace without the disturbance of the brick-work.

Figure 1 is a perspective view of an apparatus embodying my improvements. Fig. 2 is a vertical section of the same. Fig. 3 is a sectional perspective view of the revolving furnace, with its conveyer and angular pieces. Fig. 4 is a perspective view of the gearing or mechanical movement for operating the revolving furnace. Fig. 5 is a section through the furnace, showing the supporting-wheels of the furnace and a portion of the driving-gear. Figs. 6 and 7 are cross-sections of the front throat of the furnace, with its air-passages and governing-rim in the open and closed positions, respectively. Fig. 8 is a cross-section of the hinged rim of the back throat, the opening of which permits the removal of the furnace, a side view of the same being shown in Fig. 9.

A is the revolving furnace, constructed of boiler-plate, substantially as shown, and lined with brick, as shown in the sections. It is made with conical ends B B', for the purpose of dispensing with square corners in which the ore would be likely to collect and remain undisturbed. The ends of the furnace are formed with hollow throats C D. The throat C revolves within an iron front in the stationary furnace E. The furnace E is in two parts, E E', the lower part of which incloses the ash-pit and supports the grate-bars. The part E is supported upon an angle-iron bottom, (which is made a part of it,) which simply rests on the part E', so that it is adapted to move backward and forward to a slight degree to permit of the removal of the revolving furnace A without the disturbance of any brick-work in the apparatus. Through the throats C a number of apertures, c, are made for the admission of air to the furnace A, the said apertures being governed by an exterior ring, F, correspondingly perforated, as shown in the sections, Figs. 6 and 7. The ring F, by means of handle G or otherwise, can be moved around the throat so as to open or close the apertures, and thus govern the supply of air to the furnace A.

The admission of air at the throat C, between the furnace E and the revolving furnace A, provides for a greater supply of oxygen than is possible when the air is admitted only through the furnace E E'. The other throat, D, revolves within the ring H, which, as shown in Figs. 8 and 9, is made in three parts, $h\ h'\ h''$, the part h being at one point the full width of the ring, half of which width is inclosed in the brick-work, as shown in Fig. 2. The parts $h'\ h''$ are hinged, at points a, to the part h, as shown in Fig. 8, so as to be capable of opening and closing, to admit of the removal of furnace A without disturbing the brick-work, the parts being, when closed, secured together at point b by any suitable fastening.

It will be seen that when it is necessary to remove the furnace A, (which cannot be moved endwise, owing to its connection with the wheels that support it,) it is simply necessary to move forward the furnace E a short distance and then open out the hinged parts $h'\ h''$, when the furnace is left free for lateral movement and removal.

The exterior of the furnace A is fitted with circular rails I, which rest on and between the flanged supporting-wheels J J J J, as shown in Figs. 1 and 2, and a circular gear-wheel, K, is also secured to the periphery of the furnace A, by which it may be rotated.

In order that the furnace A may be revolved

and governed in the manner before indicated, I provide the following mechanical gear-movement:

L is the driving-shaft, operated by the motive power of the apparatus, and M the driving-shaft of the revolving furnace A, a pinion, N, being secured to this shaft, which gears into the wheel K and drives it. The two shafts L M are connected together by gear-wheels O P Q R. The large and small wheels alternate on the two shafts L M, so that each large wheel gears into a small wheel upon the opposite shaft, as shown. The wheels P R are fast upon the shaft, and the wheels O Q revolve loosely on the shaft L.

A revolving clutch, S, sliding upon a groove and feather in shaft L, is arranged by sliding (moved by lever T) to connect with and drive either of the gear-wheels O Q. When placed midway between these wheels the clutch revolves, but imparts no motion to the gear-wheels, and, consequently, the furnace A remains stationary. When the clutch S is brought in connection with the pinion Q a slow motion is given to the furnace A, and, on the contrary, when the clutch S is moved into connection with the wheel O, a high velocity is given to the furnace A. This change of motion or stoppage can be conveniently accomplished by the operator at any time during the process of roasting the ores.

U is the flue from the furnace to the chimney connecting with the dust-chambers V V′, which, with the damper W, are of the customary construction.

I prefer that the dust-chambers shall be supported by arches X, resting on the columns Y Y Y, in place of the customary framework of timber used heretofore for this purpose. This provision affords ample space for the occupancy of the driving-shafts and gearing.

The furnace A is provided with one or two doors, Z, through which it may be charged or discharged, and the furnace is charged from a hopper, 1, the mouth of which is fitted with a sliding door, 2, opened or closed by a handle, 3.

When the ore is not being weighed the weight of the hopper rests on angle-iron flanges upon the bars 4, between which it is inclosed. When, however, it is necessary to weigh the ore in the hopper, the weight is taken up by the weighted lever 5 and yoke 6, the location of the weight indicating by proper graduations the weight of the ore in the hopper, as the short end of the lever then supports the entire weight of the ore and hopper.

The dividing conveyer 7 is diametrically located in the furnace A, and is in the plane of the axis its entire length. It is composed of cast-iron inclined pipes 8 and perforated or slotted plates 9, fitting into grooves in the pipes 8. The plane of the plates 9 being in line of the axis no obstruction is offered to the free passage of the currents of heated air through the furnace and the pipes 8, in connection with the conical heads B B, and angle-pieces 10 serve to convey the ore backward and forward from end to end of the furnace, and thoroughly mix it, the angle-pieces throwing the ore from the conical ends of the furnace onto the conveyer 7 at opposite ends.

The operation is as follows: The furnace is heated with wood or coal, (light wood is preferable,) and after the furnace E and the revolving furnace A are hot the ore is introduced by stopping the revolution of the furnace and opening one of the doors Z, this door being stopped immediately under the mouth of the hopper. By means of the slide 2, which is opened after the ore is weighed, the ore is dropped into the furnace A in sufficient quantity to form a charge. After the door Z has been closed the furnace is revolved very slowly until the sulphur commences to burn, so as to raise as little dust as possible, then the speed can be increased to the fastest speed. After the sulphur is removed, salt may be thrown through the door d. For low grades of ores from four to five per cent. of salt is sufficient, and for rich ores some of them requiring a much larger per cent. of salt. After the salt has been thoroughly mixed, which will be in a few revolutions of the furnace, the speed of the furnace should be changed to a slow motion, and occasionally allowed to stand still for several minutes at a time until the ore is thoroughly chloridized. This can be ascertained at any time by taking a test with a long-handled spoon from the door d in the rear. After this a car may be run under the furnace A, and the door Z should be opened and a fast motion given to the furnace A, which will result in the discharge of the ore from the furnace in a very few minutes, and the furnace is then ready for another charge.

In a furnace having a capacity of two tons, (the cylinder A being for this capacity about twelve feet long, exclusive of the throats, and five and one-half feet in diameter outside,) the time of roasting a charge of silver ore, having very little base metals, is from three to five hours — ores containing a large proportion of zinc, lead, and other base metals, requiring as high as eight hours.

It requires but one man upon each watch to run from five to eight furnaces, he tending the furnaces, firing the same, and charging and discharging.

A man of ordinary ability can be taught to tend the same in a very few days.

It requires from three-fourths to one cord of wood for twenty-four hours for one furnace.

I claim—

1. In combination with the cylinder A and conveyer 7, located as described, the angle-pieces 10, operating in connection with the conveyer and cylinder, substantially as and for the purpose specified.

2. The furnace E E′ and cylinder A, in combination with the register F, encircling

the perforated throat C *c*, connecting the furnace and cylinder, substantially as and for the purpose specified.

3. In combination with the cylinder A and the sliding furnace E, the hinged ring H *h h' h''*, substantially as and for the purpose stated.

In testimony of which invention I hereunto set my hand.

ROBERT TEATS.

Witnesses:
　FRANK MILLWARD,
　H. M. HUNTER.

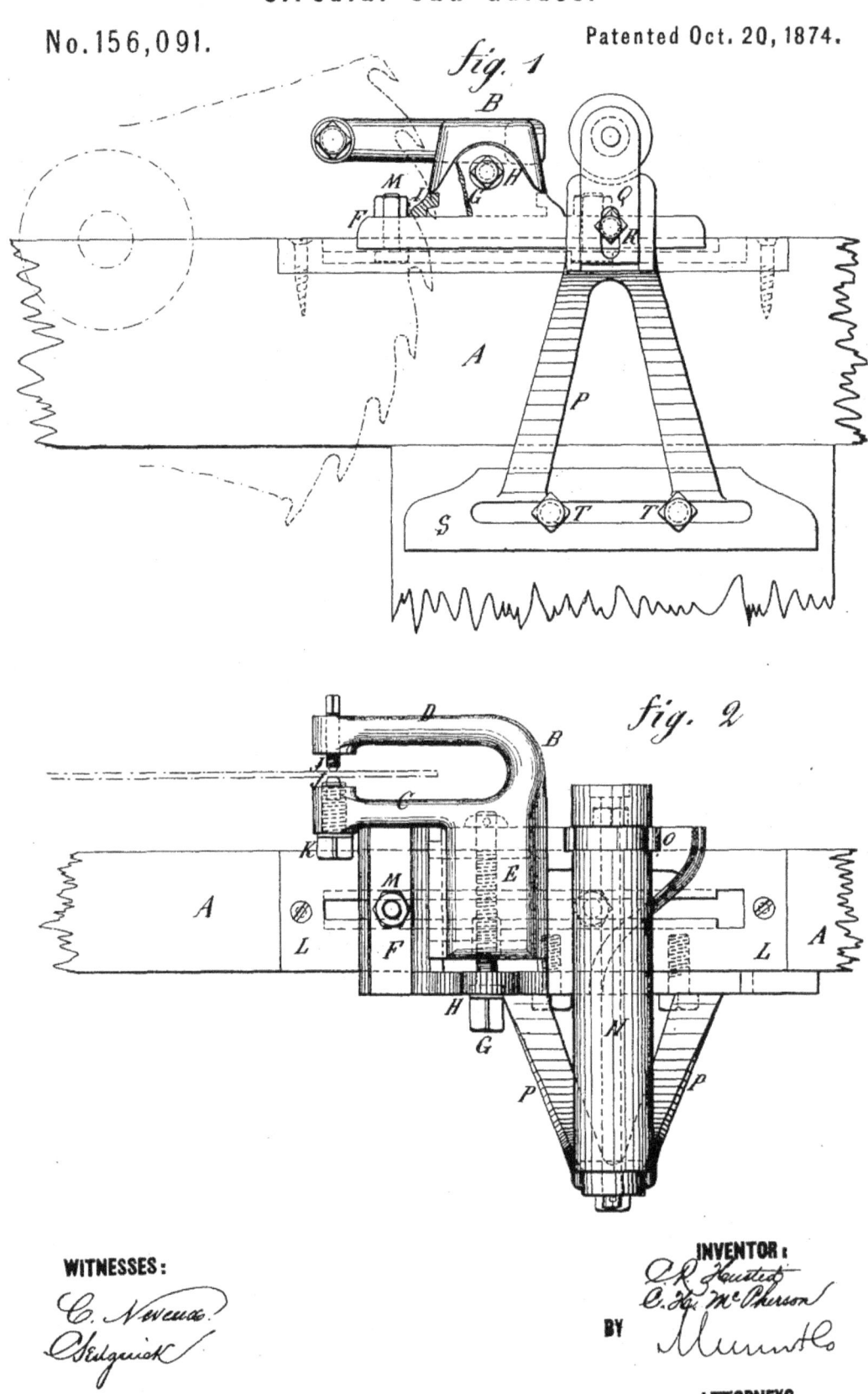

UNITED STATES PATENT OFFICE.

CALVIN R. HUSTED AND CHARLES H. McPHERSON, OF SOUTHWATER, COLORADO TERRITORY.

IMPROVEMENT IN CIRCULAR-SAW GUIDES.

Specification forming art of Letters Patent No. **156,091**, dated October 20, 1874; application filed August 1, 1874.

To all whom it may concern:

Be it known that we, CALVIN R. HUSTED and CHARLES H. McPHERSON, of Southwater, in the county of El Paso and Territory of Colorado, have invented a new and useful Improvement in Circular-Saw Guides, of which the following is a specification:

The invention will first be fully described, and then pointed out in the claim.

In the accompanying drawing, Figure 1 is a side elevation. Fig. 2 is a top or plan view.

Similar letters of reference indicate corresponding parts.

A is a portion of the saw-frame, to which the guide and roller are attached. B is the guide, consisting of two arms, C and D, and guide-plate E, which latter is made to slide transversely on the adjusting-plate F by means of the screw G through the projecting ears H. This guide-plate is kept in position by the removable cleat I, which is fastened, by screws, to the plate F. The guide-plate E slides on planed bearings, so that it moves easily and true to adjust the arms to the saw. The adjusting-points J J are wood, made adjustable in the ends of the arms C D. One or both of these wood points J may be confined in a hollow metallic screw, as seen at K, if desired. The saw in both these figures is seen in dotted lines. The adjusting-plate F rests on the bed-plate L. The bed-plate is slotted, so that the adjusting-plate F can be moved longitudinally with the saw-frame. M are screws, by which the slide F is held to the bed-plate. On the outer sides of the adjusting-plate F are lip-flanges, which guide the plate F on the bed-plate. N is the supporting-roller. This roller is for the purpose of supporting the overhanging portion of the log, and its upper surface is on a level with the lower surface of the log. This roller is connected with the adjusting-plate F, and, by means of a slotted flange, O, in which it revolves, it is made adjustable as to height, and may be entirely detached from the adjusting-plate F and saw-guide. The other end of this roller is supported by the double brace P. This end of the roller is adjusted vertically by means of the slotted pivot-slide Q on the upper end of the brace, held in position by the screw R. The lower end of the brace is attached to the slotted piece S, which is adjustable horizontally on the frame, and held in position by the screws T.

This saw-guide may be adjusted to the saw with perfect accuracy and with entire safety when the saw is running as well as when it is at rest, and it is done easily and expeditiously at all times.

Having thus described our invention, we claim as new and desire to secure by Letters Patent—

The combination, with saw-frame, of the sliding guide B, slide-plate F, and horizontal roller O, as shown and described, for the purpose specified.

CALVIN R. HUSTED.
CHARLES HENRY McPHERSON.

Witnesses:
H. H. PLATT,
FRED. SCHUYLER.

H. BOLTHOFF.
Slide-Valves for Steam-Engines.

No. 156,270. Patented Oct. 27, 1874.

Fig. 1.

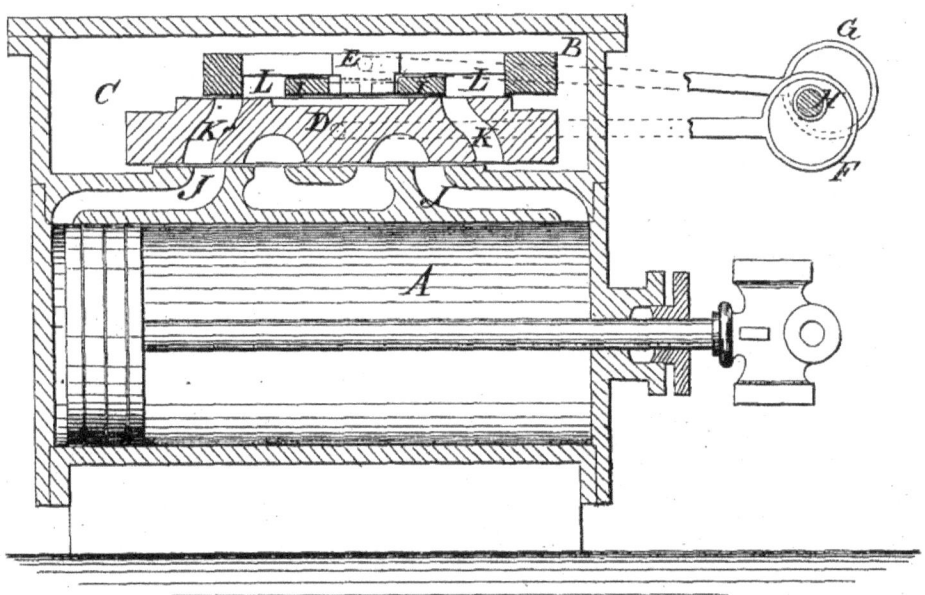

Fig. 2.

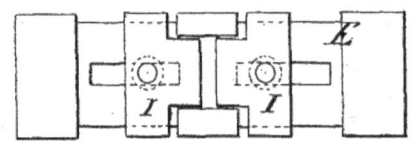

UNITED STATES PATENT OFFICE.

HENRY BOLTHOFF, OF CENTRAL CITY, COLORADO TERRITORY, ASSIGNOR TO HIMSELF AND JAMES CLARK, OF SAME PLACE.

IMPROVEMENT IN SLIDE-VALVES FOR STEAM-ENGINES.

Specification forming part of Letters Patent No. **156,270**, dated October 27, 1874; application filed August 1, 1874.

To all whom it may concern:

Be it known that I, HENRY BOLTHOFF, of Central City, in the county of Gilpin and Territory of Colorado, have invented a new and useful Improvement in Slide-Valves for Steam-Engines, of which the following is a specification:

The invention will first be fully described, and then pointed out in the claims.

In the accompanying drawing, Figure 1 is a vertical longitudinal section of a steam-engine, showing the slide-valve arranged to operate according to my invention. Fig. 2 is a top view of the upper part of the valve.

Similar letters of reference indicate corresponding parts.

A is the main cylinder. B is the steam-chest. C is the slide-valve. This slide-valve is composed of two parts, D being the lower part and E the upper part. These parts are connected with the two eccentrics, F and G, which are on the main shaft H. The eccentrics are so arranged on the shaft that the parts D E are simultaneously moved in opposite directions. The valve is so set as to about half open the main port, more or less, as the case may require, when the crank is on the center. This half-opening is made preparatory to the opening of the port above. The upper part E is moved in an opposite direction, consequently the full opening is made in less than the usual time required by the ordinary valve. This result cannot be obtained except with a double valve. It requires both movements to produce the result and obtain the opening for admitting steam to the cylinder. The part E is constructed with steam-ports, the same as the part D. This part E has on the inside of each port an adjustable jaw or block, I, for the purpose of increasing and decreasing the size of the ports for cutting off steam at any point of the stroke that may be desirable. J are the steam-ways to the cylinder; K, the ports or ways through the parts D of the valve; L, the ports of the part E of the valve.

The two parts D E thus perform the duty of the main valve of ordinary steam-engines, but in a superior manner—that is, by moving the parts in opposite directions, and thereby increasing the speed of the opening of the port one-half. At the point of taking steam these parts move at their greatest speed. This is accomplished by the direct action of the eccentrics alone.

In ordinary engines "lead" is generally given for obtaining an increased opening at the time the piston begins to travel, thereby causing friction at a point where the crank is without leverage, and is moved by the acquired momentum, causing a loss of power at that point.

By my improvement this difficulty is obviated, as the steam is not admitted until the piston is on its stroke.

The increased speed of the opening supplies the piston with steam at the proper time, thereby avoiding the invariable loss sustained by the action of the ordinary valve.

It will be seen that with this double valve, for quickly admitting steam to the cylinder, I have combined a variable cut-off, which is readily adjusted to the duty required of the engine.

I am aware that there is nothing new in the idea of two valves arranged one upon the other and moving in opposite directions, and serving the purpose of cut-off and main valves, respectively, and I therefore do not wish to be understood as making claim to such invention; but

Having described my invention, what I claim as new therein is—

1. The combination, with cylinder having ports J J, of the valve D, having ports K K, and the valve E, having ports L L, said valves moving simultaneously in opposite directions, as and for the purpose described.

2. The two-part slide-valves D and E adapted to move in opposite directions, in combination with the adjustable blocks I I, as and for the purpose specified.

HENRY BOLTHOFF.

Witnesses:
HENRY M. SELLERS,
C. C. WELCH.

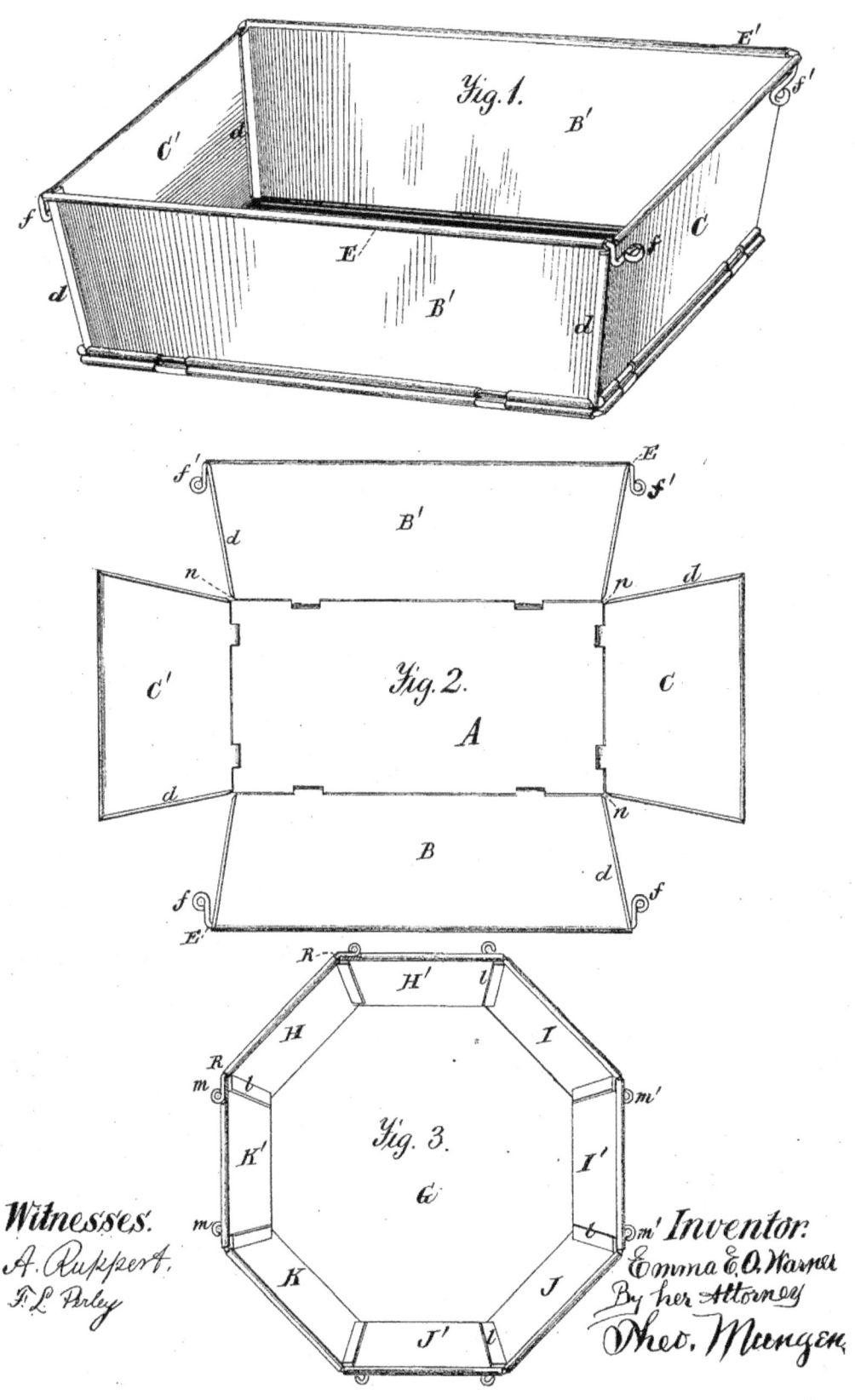

UNITED STATES PATENT OFFICE.

EMMA E. O. WARNER, OF DENVER, COLORADO TERRITORY.

IMPROVEMENT IN BAKING-PANS.

Specification forming part of Letters Patent No. **156,470**, dated November 3, 1874; application filed September 7, 1874.

To all whom it may concern:

Be it known that I, EMMA E. O. WARNER, of Denver, in the county of Arapahoe and Territory of Colorado, have invented a new and useful Improvement in Baking-Pans; and I hereby declare the following to be a full, clear, and exact description of the same, reference being had to the accompanying drawings, making a part of this specification, in which—

Figure 1 is a view, in perspective, of a pan embodying my improvements. Fig 2 is a plan view of the same when opened out, and Fig. 3 is a plan view of a modification of my improvement.

This invention relates to an improvement in baking-pans for baking cake, bread, &c.; and it consists of a pan having the portion surrounding the bottom to form the sides and ends or circumference constructed in sections, hinged to the bottom, and the wire in the upper edges of alternate sections sufficiently loose to turn therein, the ends of said wire in said alternate sections being provided with clasps or clamps for binding the adjacent sections together when they are turned up in contact preparatory to charging the pan with its contents for baking; the object of the invention being to permit the sections forming the circumference to be let down for the purpose of removing the baked contents of the pan without breaking the same, as will hereinafter more fully appear.

In the accompanying drawing, the bottom A of a square pan has its edges wired. The sections B B' and C C' have their upper and lower edges wired, and are hinged to the bottom A. The end edges of each of the sections B B' C C' are provided with flanges d, which, when the sections are turned up and brought in contact to form the circumference of the pan, unite and form tight unsoldered seams. The wires E E' in the upper edges of the sections B B' turn in their bearings, and are provided with the clasps or clamps $f f'$, one at each end, which, when turned inwardly, bind the several sections together, thus forming the pan.

Fig. 3 shows an application of my invention to an octagonal pan, in which the bottom G is wired, as is A. The upper and lower edges of the sections H H', I I', J J', and K K' are wired, and the said sections hinged to G. The end edges of said sections are provided with flanges l, which, when the sections are turned up to form the pan, unite and form tight unsoldered seams. The wires R in the upper edges of the alternate sections H I J K turn in their bearings, and are provided with clasps or clamps $m m'$, which, when turned inwardly, bind the adjacent sections firmly together, and thus form an octagonal pan.

The construction of the two pans is the same, the form only being different. The hinges at the bottom leave a small air-space, n, between the lower edges of the sections and the upper surface of the bottom. The air-space n is not large enough to permit the contents of the pan to escape, but is large enough to permit air to enter and prevent the contents from being burned.

The operation of the invention is very simple. The contents of the pan having been baked, it is only necessary to turn the clasp $f f'$ or $m m'$ outwardly and lower the sections, when the contents can be removed without breaking.

Having thus described my invention, what I claim as new and useful, and desire to secure by Letters Patent, is—

In a baking-pan in which the portion surrounding the bottom to form the sides and ends or circumference is constructed in sections, hinged to the bottom of the pan, the combination of flanges on the end edges of each section with clasps at the ends of the upper wired edges of alternate sections, operating substantially as and for the purposes set forth.

In testimony that I claim the foregoing improvement, as above described, I have hereunto set my hand and seal this 28th day of August, 1874.

    EMMA E. O. WARNER. [L. S.]

Witnesses:
 DANIEL SAYER,
 J. P. WARNER,
 D. C. LIONBERGER.

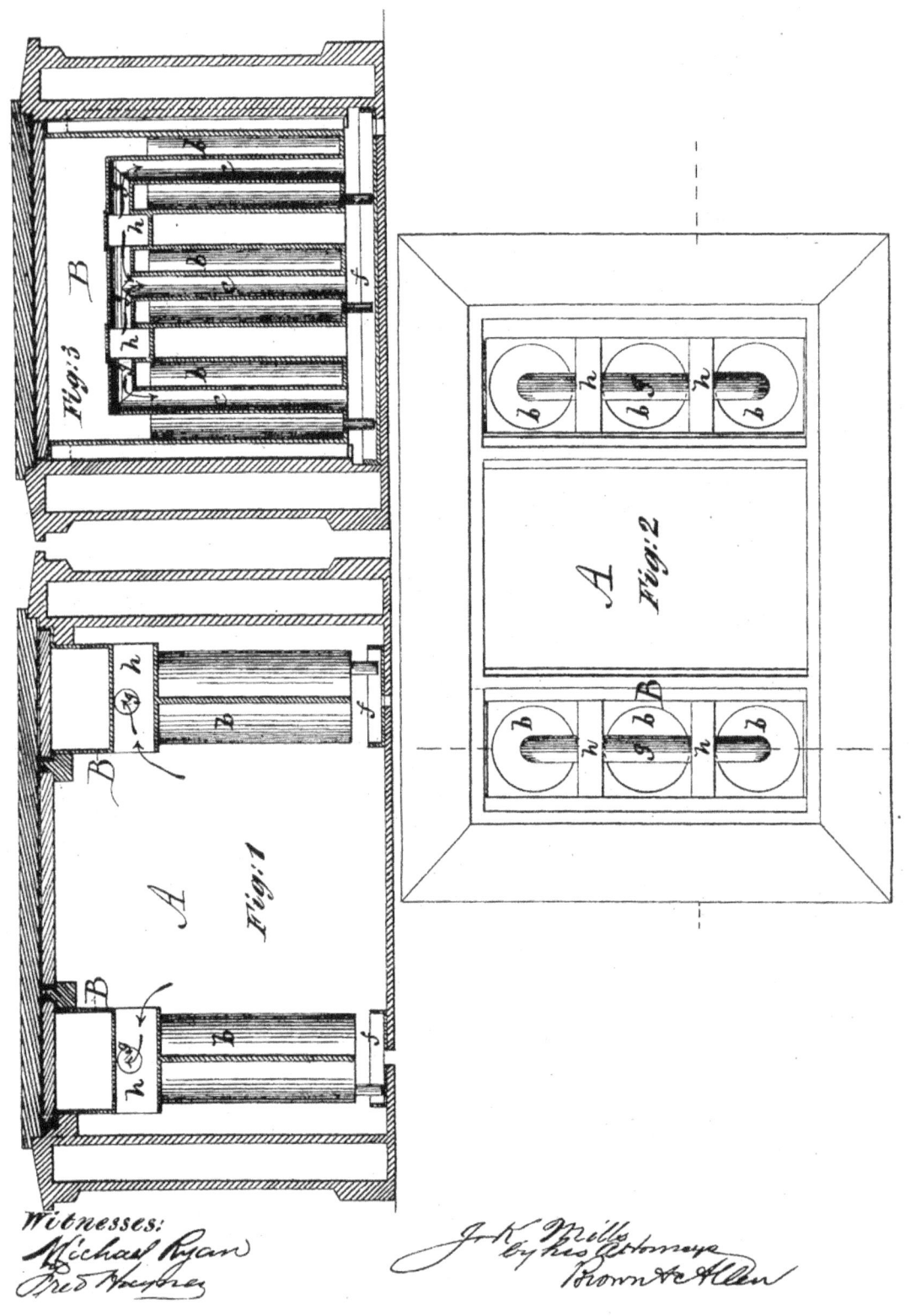

UNITED STATES PATENT OFFICE.

JOSEPH K. MILLS, OF DENVER, COLORADO TERRITORY.

IMPROVEMENT IN REFRIGERATORS.

Specification forming part of Letters Patent No. **157,019**, dated November 17, 1874; application filed March 26, 1874.

To all whom it may concern:

Be it known that I, J. K. MILLS, of Denver, in the county of Arapahoe and Territory of Colorado, have invented certain Improvements in Refrigerators, of which the following is a specification:

My invention consists in the combination, with a chest or refrigerator, of an ice-tank of peculiar construction, provided with air-tubes surrounded by receptacles for the ice, whereby a current of cold air is kept in circulation through the tank and the chest or apartment in which it is placed.

In the accompanying drawing, Figure 1 is a longitudinal vertical section of a refrigerator with one of my improved ice-tanks at each end. Fig. 2 is a top view of the same. Fig. 3 is a central vertical section through one of the tanks.

The chest or apartment A may be of any suitable form and dimensions, and may contain two tanks, one at each end. The tank B is divided into three or more chambers, b, in each of which is a pipe, c, connected at the upper end with a transverse pipe communicating with the chest or refrigerator outside of the tank. The chambers b may be of cylindrical or other suitable form, extending downward to within a short distance of the bottom of the chest A, and are provided with waste pipes for carrying off the drippings from the ice, which waste-pipes communicate with a pan, f. The lower ends of the pipes c pass through the bottoms of the chambers b, so as to communicate with the chest or refrigerator below said chambers, and their upper ends communicate with each other by means of a pipe, g, running longitudinally of the tank. Transverse pipes h pass from one side of the tank to the other, communicating with the chest A outside of the tank, and also with the longitudinal pipe g. The ice is placed in the upper part of the tank, resting upon the pipes $g\ h$. As the air circulates through said pipes it is cooled by the ice, and, as it has free communication with the chest outside of the tank, the tendency is to reduce the temperature of all the air in the chest. The drippings from the tank flow into the pan f, from whence they are carried off by a waste-pipe.

What I claim as new, and desire to secure by Letters Patent, is—

In a refrigerator having a tank divided into compartments, the combination of the pipe g communicating with the vertical pipes c, with the pipes h communicating with the chest A, and the pipes g, all arranged to operate substantially as described, for the object specified.

JOSEPH K. MILLS.

Witnesses:
T. A. GREATOREX,
WM. D. TODD.

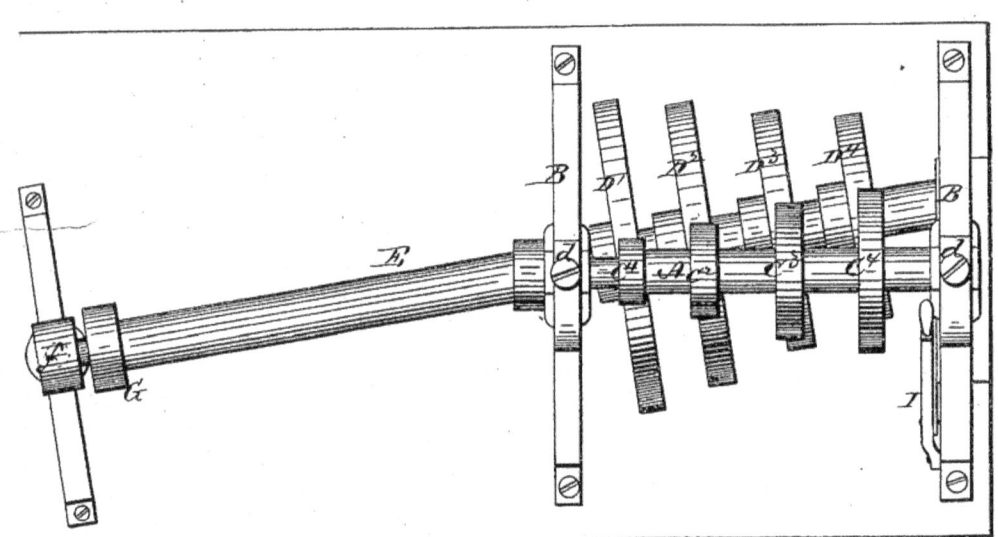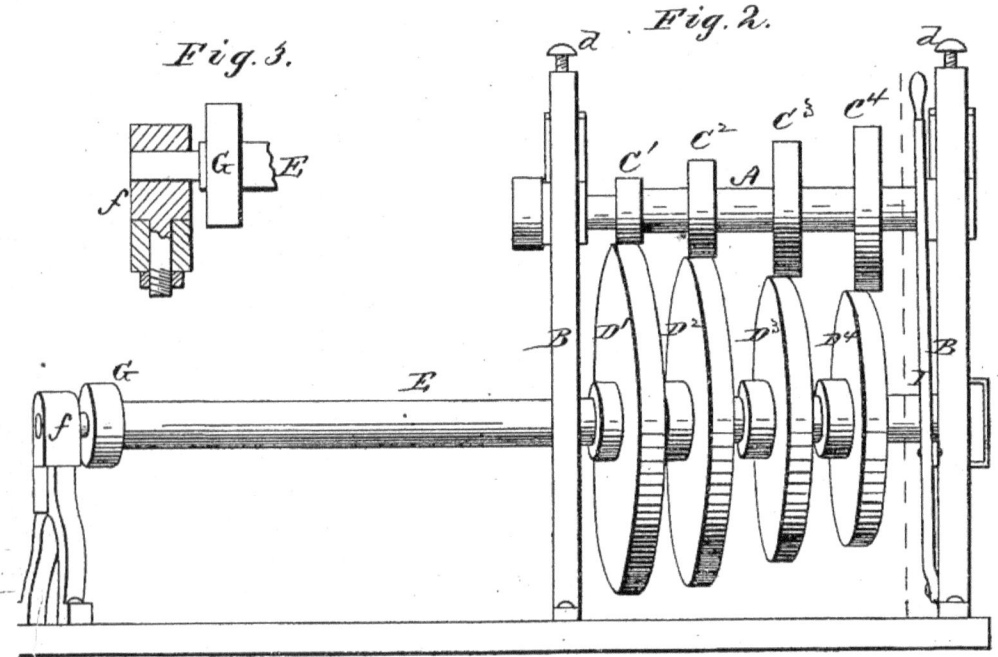

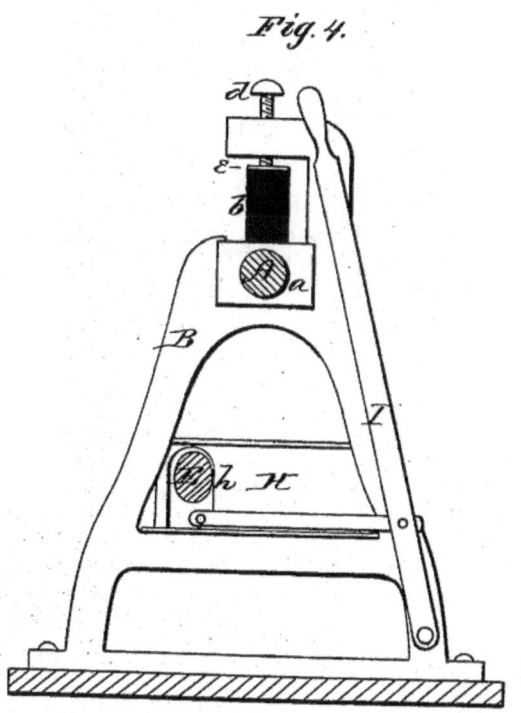

UNITED STATES PATENT OFFICE.

HERMAN D. HALL, OF DENVER, COLORADO TERRITORY.

IMPROVEMENT IN SAW-MILLS.

Specification forming part of Letters Patent No. **158,703**, dated January 12, 1875; application filed December 19, 1874.

To all whom it may concern:

Be it known that I, HERMAN D. HALL, of Denver, in the county of Arapahoe and in the Territory of Colorado, have invented certain new and useful Improvements in Saw-Mills; and do hereby declare that the following is a full, clear, and exact description thereof, reference being had to the accompanying drawings and to the letters of reference marked thereon, making a part of this specification.

The nature of my invention consists in the construction and arrangement of a mechanism for feeding the log-carriage of a saw-mill, whereby the log may be fed at any desired rate of speed, while the power or driving shaft is being run at the same rate of speed, as will be hereinafter more fully set forth.

In order to enable others skilled in the art to which my invention appertains to make and use the same, I will now proceed to describe its construction and operation, referring to the annexed drawing, in which—

Figure 1 is a plan view, and Fig. 2 is a front elevation, of my machine. Fig. 3 is a vertical section of a pivoted journal-box. Fig. 4 is a vertical section through the line x x, Fig. 2.

A represents the driving-shaft, connected, by a belt or otherwise, with any suitable power for running the same. This shaft has its bearings in boxes a, which are placed in slots in vertical frames B B, and are held down by means of rubber springs b, the tension of said springs being regulated by means of set-screws d bearing upon metal plates e, placed on top of the rubber springs. On the driving-shaft A, at suitable distances apart, are secured a series of wheels, C^1 C^2 C^3 C^4, increasing gradually in the length of their diameter from one end to the other. E represents the shaft, which communicates motion to the log-carriage by means of a cog-wheel, G, secured on the inner end of the shaft, and gearing with a rack-bar on the carriage. The inner end of the shaft E has its bearing in a journal-box, f, which is pivoted, as shown in Fig. 3, on top of a suitable standard or frame. The outer end of the shaft E has its bearing in a journal-box, h, which is placed in a horizontal way or guide, H, attached to the outer frame B, and the box h moved back and forth therein by a lever, I, or other suitable means. On the shaft E are secured a series of wheels, D^1 D^2 D^3 D^4, which correspond with the wheels upon the driving-shaft A, and increase gradually in the length of their diameter in the opposite direction from that of the wheels on the driving-shaft. The shafts A and E are arranged relatively to each other in such a manner that when they are parallel with each other they will be in different vertical planes, and none of the wheels on one shaft will be in contact with a wheel on the other. As the outer end of the shaft E is moved so as to bring it under the driving-shaft A, the wheel D^4 nearest the outer end will come in contact with the wheel C^4 on the driving-shaft, while none of the others are in contact. By moving the shaft still farther, the wheels D^4 C^4 will be thrown out of contact, and the wheels D^3 C^3 brought in contact with each other, and so on any one of the wheels on the shaft E may be thrown in contact with the corresponding wheel on the driving-shaft, and thus move the log-carriage at any desired speed, while the driving-shaft continues at the same rate of speed.

Having thus fully described my invention, what I claim as new, and desire to secure by Letters Patent, is—

1. In a mechanism for feeding the log-carriage for saw-mills, the combination of the driving-shaft A and the movable shaft E, arranged in different vertical planes, and each provided with a series of wheels of different diameters, substantially as and for the purposes herein set forth.

2. The combination of the driving-shaft A, with wheels C^1 C^2 C^3 C^4, rubber springs d, and the shaft E, with wheels D^1 D^2 D^3 D^4, pivoted box f, and sliding box h, all constructed and arranged to operate substantially as and for the purposes herein set forth.

In testimony that I claim the foregoing I have hereunto set my hand this 18th day of December, 1874.

HERMAN D. HALL.

Witnesses:
C. L. EVERT,
WM. L. BRAMHALL.

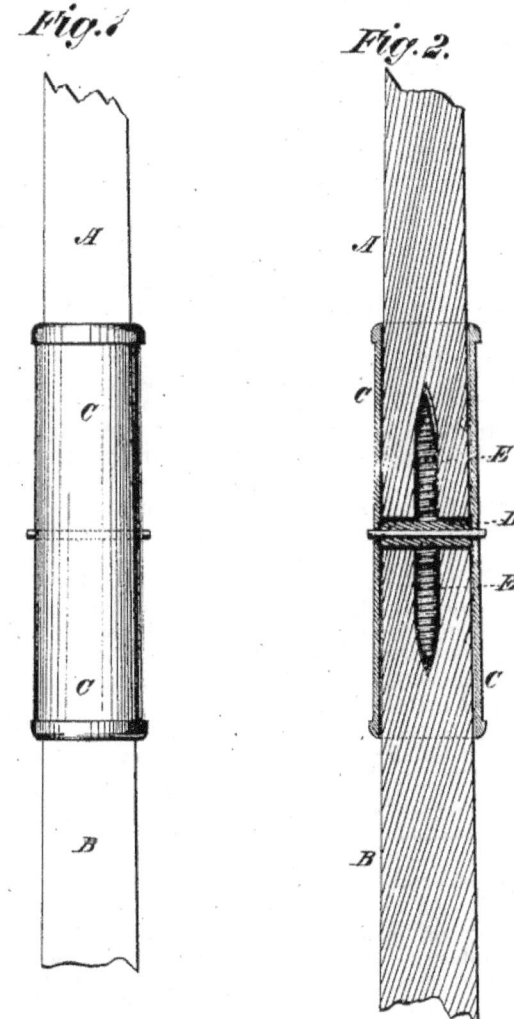

UNITED STATES PATENT OFFICE.

EDWARD B. LIGHT, OF DENVER, COLORADO TERRITORY.

IMPROVEMENT IN WHIP-TIP FERRULES.

Specification forming part of Letters Patent No. **159,105**, dated January 26, 1875; application filed October 17, 1874.

To all whom it may concern:

Be it known that I, EDWARD B. LIGHT, of Denver, Arapahoe county, Colorado Territory, have invented a new and Improved Whip-Tip Ferrule, of which the following is a specification:

Figure 1 is a side view of a portion of a whip-tip and stock to which my improvement has been applied, and Fig. 2 is a longitudinal section of the same.

Similar letters of reference indicate corresponding parts.

The invention will first be fully described, and then pointed out in the claim.

A represents a whip-tip, and B represents a whip-stock, about the construction of which there is nothing new. C is a ferrule, which is so formed as to fit upon the adjacent ends of the tip A and stock B. D is a short solid cylinder, which is fitted into the center of the ferrule C, and secured there by a pin, rivet, or screw. E is a rod, which passes longitudinally through the center of the cylinder D, and is rigidly secured to said cylinder. Upon each end of the rod E is cut a screw-thread, as shown in Fig. 2. I prefer to cut a right-hand screw-thread upon one end of rod E, and a left-hand screw-thread upon the other end of said rod; but this is not essential. If desired, one end of the rod E may be cut off or omitted, and that end of the ferrule C secured in place by teeth formed in the body of said ferrule C. In using the device the butt-end of the tip is screwed into the ferrule C until it strikes the end of the cylinder D. The small end of the whip-stock B is afterward screwed into the other end of the ferrule C until it strikes against the end of the cylinder D. A small quantity of a suitable glue or cement may be put into the ferrule C before screwing in the parts A B, to fill the interstices and make the joint firm and strong.

I am aware that ferrules have been used for covering the adjacent ends of a whip-tip and stock, and also that a screw has been used screwing partly into each of said adjacent ends. These parts I do not claim, broadly; but I am aware that whips have been made with a wire center in place of whalebone, and in two parts, the bottom part or butt having a wire center, and in some cases the wire extending beyond the rattan and provided with a screw on it. The butt is then screwed on the point, and the joint in the whip is covered with a ferrule. But this is a process of making a whip. The difference between mine and this class of whips is, that the screw and ferrule are one in mine, while in these the whip is secured to the handle. I use a ferrule having a screw in its center, made solid, which becomes a manufacture, which is sold independently of the whip, so that by different sizes of ferrules a whip, when broken, can be cut into at the break and conveniently and immediately repaired without the use of any tool whatever. This ferrule is also applicable to the repairing and making of fish-rods, fastening cane-heads on canes, &c.

Having thus described my invention, I claim as new and desire to secure by Letters Patent—

As a new article of manufacture, a tube, D, provided with opposite screws E E, as and for the purpose described.

EDW. B. LIGHT.

Witnesses:
  JNO. R. HANNA,
  C. G. GROSVENOR.

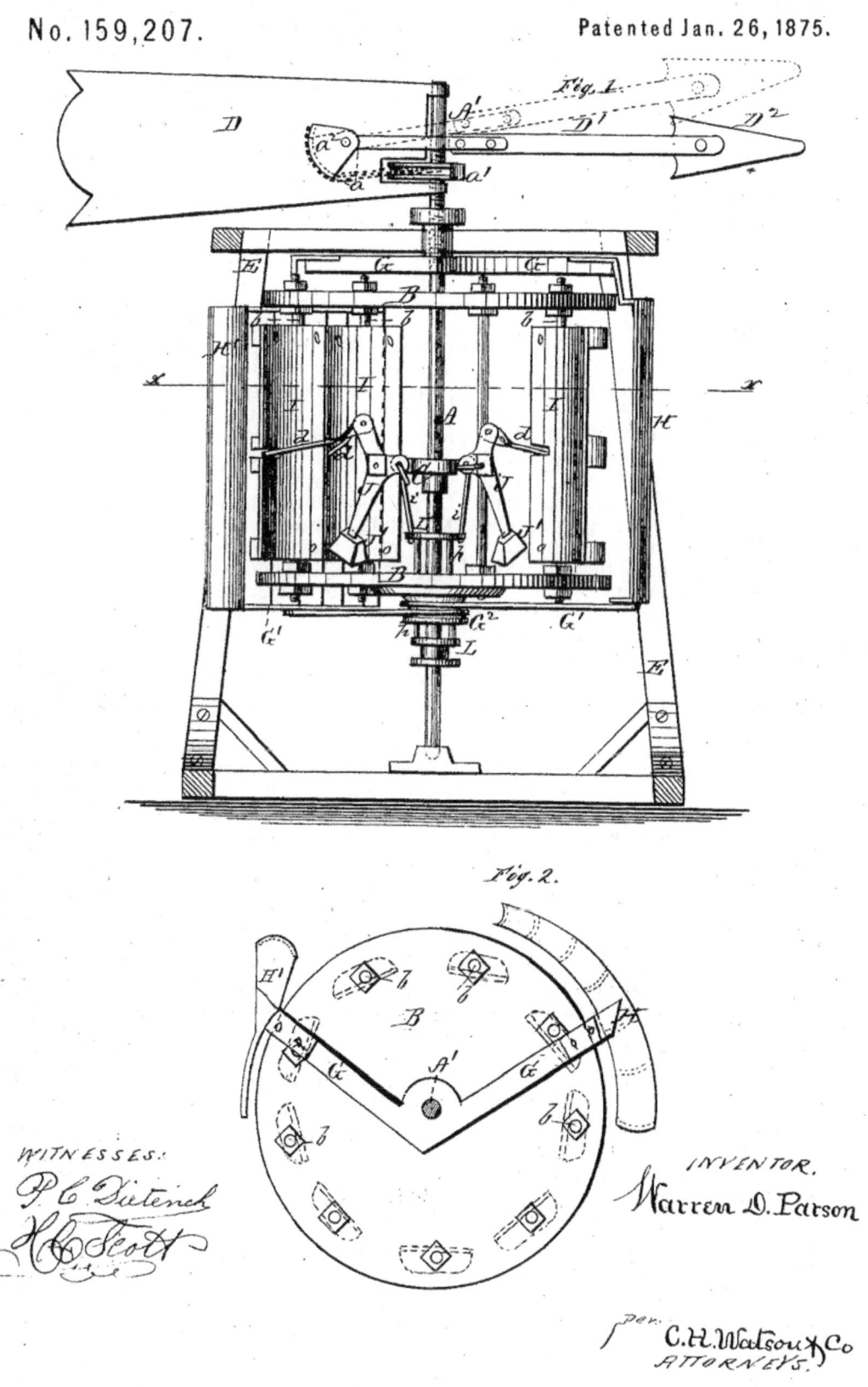

UNITED STATES PATENT OFFICE.

WARREN D. PARSON, OF DENVER, COLORADO TERRITORY.

IMPROVEMENT IN WINDMILLS.

Specification forming part of Letters Patent No. **159,207**, dated January 26, 1875; application filed August 10, 1874.

To all whom it may concern:

Be it known that I, WARREN D. PARSON, of Denver, in the county of Arapahoe and Territory of Colorado, have invented certain new and useful Improvements in Windmills; and I do hereby declare that the following is a full, clear, and exact description thereof, which will enable others skilled in the art to which it pertains to make and use the same, reference being had to the accompanying drawings, and to the letters of reference marked thereon, which form a part of this specification.

The nature of my invention consists in the construction and arrangement of a windmill, as will be hereinafter more fully set forth.

In the accompanying drawing, Figure 1 is a side elevation of my entire windmill, and Fig. 2 is a plan view of the wheel thereof.

A represents the main shaft, to which are keyed, or otherwise fastened, the heads B B of the wheel, and the spider C at a suitable point between the heads. To this shaft should also be attached a gear or other suitable device for transmitting power. A′ represents a shaft, made to turn in suitable boxes secured in the frame E of the windmill. The lower end of this shaft A′ enters a socket secured on the upper end of the shaft A, or at the top of the wind-wheel, so that the two shafts may revolve independent of each other, though being on one axial line. D is the weather-vane, hinged loosely on the shaft A′. a^1 is a segment of a grooved pulley, made fast to the shaft A′, and connected by a chain, a, with a similar grooved segment, a^2, which works loosely on a stud or pin projecting from the side of the vane D. To the segment a^2 is fastened a lever, D¹, provided at its outer end with a weight, D², said lever extending in the opposite direction from the vane. On the lower end of the shaft A′ is attached a spider for holding the arms G G, and to the outer ends of these arms are attached the fenders or guards H H. Below the wheel are other arms, G¹ G¹, to which the lower ends of the fenders are attached, the inner ends of said arms G¹, being formed or provided with a ring, which works on a collar, G², made fast to the bottom head of the wheel. I I represent the buckets or vanes of the wind-wheel, hinged at the center on rods $b\ b$, which are fastened to the heads B B by nuts or other suitable means. J J represent three-armed levers, hinged or pivoted to the spider C, and provided with weights J′ J′. The third arms of the levers are, by rods d, connected with the vanes I. Below the wheel on the shaft A is a slide, L, connected by rods $h\ h$ with a slide, L′, within the wheel below the spider C, and through this slide L′ are loosely passed rods $i\ i$, with nuts upon their lower ends, and these rods connect with the middle arms of the levers J J. The guards or fenders H H′ prevent the wind from striking the wheel in such a direction as to run it backward, and also convey into the wheel the portion of wind which would otherwise be thrown off and lost, thus causing the same to be converted into power. The two fenders are constructed as shown in Fig. 2— one, H, having a series of inclined vertical and curved slats, the tendency of which, under a pressure of wind, is to recede and go back of the wheel. The other, H′, is constructed so as to convey more wind into the wheel, and thus enlarge the working area. The hinged vane D and weighted lever D¹, with their connections $a\ a^1\ a^2$, allow or cause the fender to recede in heavy wind, and the weighted lever brings them back in place after the wind has subsided. As the former fender recedes the latter is brought in front of the wheel, thus shutting out the wind from the wheel, while the receding fender allows a contrary current of wind to strike the wheel. These parts being properly adjusted, an automatic governor is formed, which causes a large amount of wind to strike the wheel, if the breeze be light, and throwing it off if the wind be heavy, and guarding against any dangerous strain from wind-pressure. To make the wheel doubly safe in high winds, and to make it adaptable to all kinds of work, another governor is provided, consisting of the levers J. The weighted ends of these levers rise by centrifugal force, throwing their upper ends inward, drawing the buckets or vanes I with them, shutting out all wind not required to run the wheel at a certain speed. If the wind be variable the weights J′ will rise and exclude the wind if there be an excess, and drop of their own gravity, and open the buckets and receive more wind if the wind be light, or if more work be attached. By hanging the buckets in the center on the rods b the pressure of wind is equal on both sides, thus forming a balance, and requiring but little or no power to reef or furl the buckets, as the case may be.

The construction of the centrifugal governor admits of dispensing with any weights or springs to unfurl the sails after the governor had reefed them, the resistance of such weights or springs having necessarily to be overcome before the governor could act. My governor hangs perfectly free to act without this resistance to overcome, making it extremely sensitive to any variation of speed in the wind-wheel. This governor holds the buckets at the most desirable angle (forty-five degrees) to receive power from the wind when open.

The wind-wheel may be stopped from below, at pleasure, by a suitable connection, with the slide L to pull the same downward, when the levers J will close the buckets tightly all around the wheel.

Having thus fully described my invention, what I claim as new, and desire to secure by Letters Patent, is—

1. The fenders or guards H H', constructed as described, and operated by means of the lever D^1, substantially as and for the purposes herein set forth.

2. The combination of the vane D, grooved segments a^1 a^2, chain a, and lever D^1, all constructed substantially as and for the purposes herein set forth.

3. The shafts A A', independently connected to the frame, in combination with vane D, lever D^1, weight D^2, and fenders or guards, substantially as and for the purpose specified.

In testimony that I claim the foregoing as my own I affix my signature in presence of two witnesses.

WARREN D. PARSON.

Witnesses:
 FRANK CHURCH,
 EDWARD F. BISHOP.

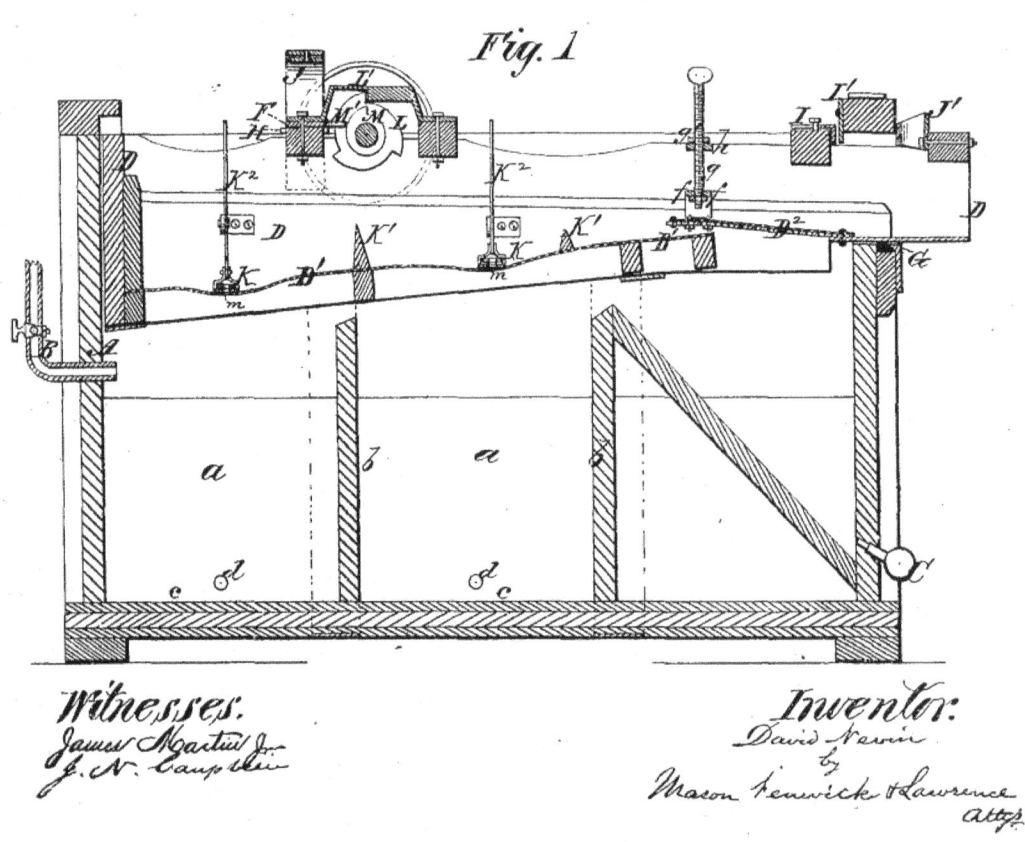

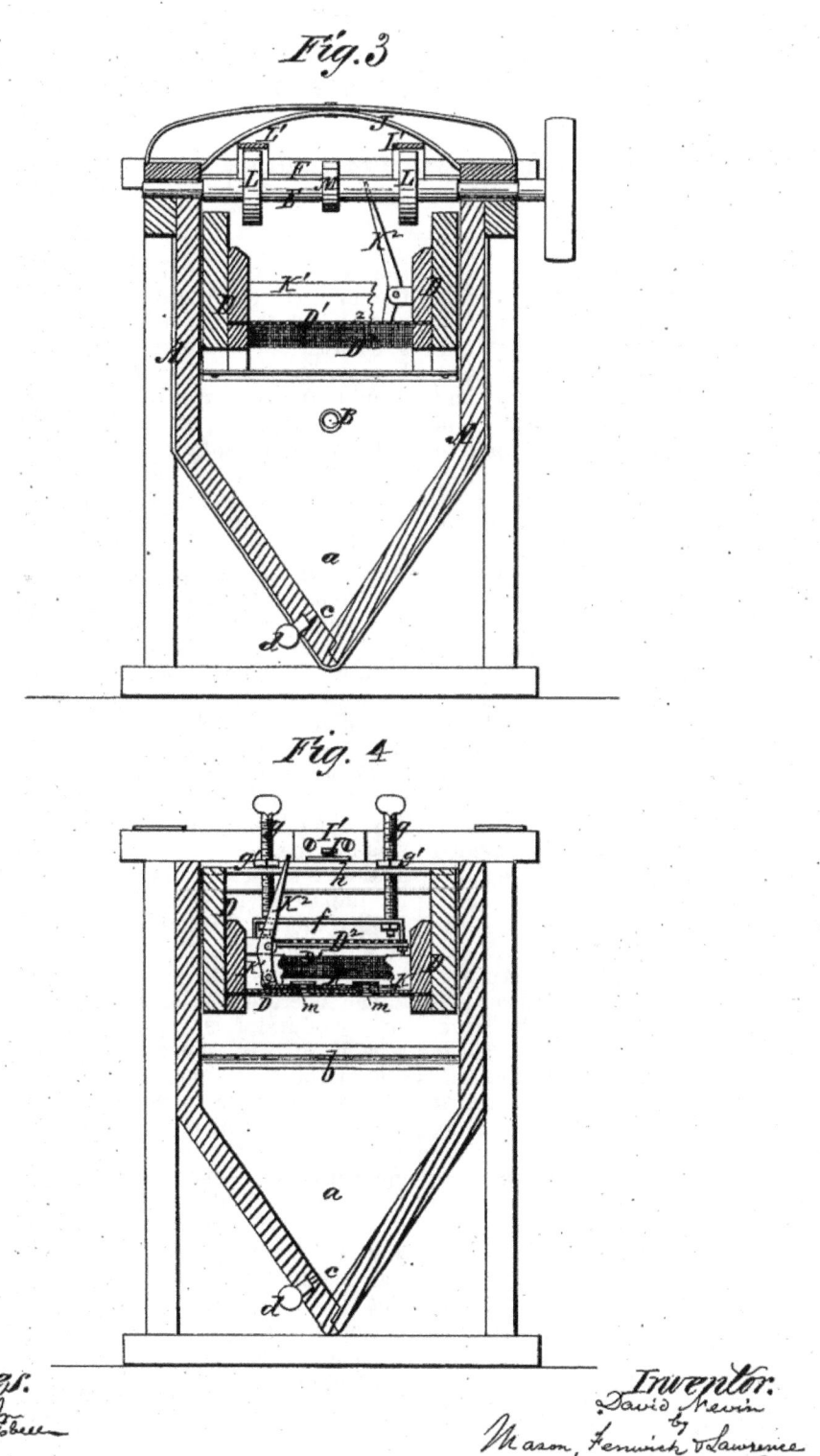

UNITED STATES PATENT OFFICE.

DAVID NEVIN, OF GEORGETOWN, COLORADO TERRITORY, ASSIGNOR TO HIMSELF, ROBERT NEVIN, AND J. OSCAR STEWART, OF SAME PLACE.

IMPROVEMENT IN ORE-SEPARATORS.

Specification forming part of Letters Patent No. **159,347**, dated February 2, 1875; application filed November 30, 1874.

To all whom it may concern:

Be it known that I, DAVID NEVIN, of Georgetown, county of Clear Creek and Territory of Colorado, have invented a new and useful Improvement in Ore-Separators; and I do hereby declare that the following is a full, clear, and exact description thereof, reference being had to the accompanying drawings making part of this specification, in which—

Figure 1 is a longitudinal section of my improved ore-separator. Fig. 2 is a top view of the same. Fig. 3 is a cross view of the same in the line $x\ x$ of Fig. 2. Fig. 4 is also a cross view in the line $y\ y$.

The nature of my invention consists in certain constructions and combinations of parts in an ore-separator which has a partitioned water-tank, a horizontally and vertically vibrating sorting-sieve, which is hung with one end extended through the frame, and kept water-tight at said end, while moving up and down and back and forth, by a suitable packing-bar or stuffing-box.

A is a water-tank, of oblong form, divided into several chambers, a, by transverse partitions b. Each of these chambers is formed with a funnel or hopper shaped bottom, c, at the angle of which a draw-off cock, d, is provided. B is a water-supplying pipe, and C a water-discharging pipe. These pipes are furnished with suitable cocks. $D\ D^1\ D^2$ is the sieve, consisting of an oblong frame, D, a wire-gauze or finely-reticulated metal bottom, $D^1\ D^2$. The adjustable portion D^2 serves for shearing or dividing the grades of ore, and for guiding them into an appropriate receptacle or receptacles after the ore has been treated upon the portion D^1. The portion D^2 of the sieve is suspended by an arched bar, f, and screws $g\ g$, upon a cross-bar, h, of the sieve-frame D. The screws work in taps in the bar h, and are fastened by nuts $g'\ g'$. This sieve is suspended between the upright sides of the tank A with a downward inclination toward the receiving end thereof, being held a little forward of its receiving end by means of a cam-shaft, E, and a sliding cross-bar, F, which have their support upon the upper edge of the tank, and is sustained at its discharging end by a packing or stuffing bar, G, of the frame, and, if desirable, by pivoted hangers pendent from the inner sides of the tank. H H are rubbers, upon which the ends of the bar F slide back and forth, and also bump. I is an adjustable bumper for controlling the extent of the longitudinal movement of the sieve. This bumper strikes a plate, I', of the frame of the tank. J J' are elliptic springs arranged near the respective ends of the sieve. The spring J receives the force of the sieve as it is moved upward, and the spring J' the force as it is moved forward. These springs serve to return the sieve to its normal position after being operated upon by the cams of the shaft E. K K are adjustable slide-valves, operated by levers K^2, attached to the side of the sieve-frame, over relief passages m, formed through the wire-gauze bottom of the sieve. K^1 are riffles, placed across the sieve bottom D^1 for retarding or arresting the heavy minerals. L L are cams on the shaft E, and working against tappets L' L', attached to the sieve for imparting a vertical motion to the sieve, and M is a smaller cam, also on the shaft E, and working against a tappet, M', also attached to the sieve for imparting a horizontal motion, or longitudinal motion, to the sieve. The counter or reciprocal movements of the sieve are produced by the springs J J', as above mentioned.

The operation is as follows: A continual supply of water is kept in the tank by the pipe B, so as to immerse the wire-gauze bottom of the sieve, and the ore or material to be separated is fed over the top of the frame into the receiving-end of the sieve, and the sieve is rapidly vibrated by suitable power applied to the cam-shaft E. The agitation of the sieve vertically in the water causes the lighter particles to separate from the heavier, and the lighter rise nearer to the surface, while the heavier settle at the bottom; and while this is being effected the horizontal or longitudinal motion of the sieve carries the lighter particles forward to the discharging end, where it is sorted, divided, or sheared by the portion D^2 of the sieve, and discharged into an appropriate receptacle or receptacles. The particles of ore which settle on the bottom of the sieve pass through the sieve and valve-passages into the hoppers below, and are drawn off by the cocks d. The water, which flows in by pipe B, is discharged by pipe C'.

What I claim as my invention is—

1. The combination of the springs J J', slide-bar F, cams L L and M, tappets L' L' and M', with the ore-separating sieve and tank, the whole operating to produce an up-and-down and back-and-forward vibration of the sieve within the tank, substantially as and for the purpose described.

2. The relief-passages m m in the wire sieve bottom D, in combination with the valves K and levers G² for opening and closing the valves, substantially in the manner shown and described.

3. The bar F, having the cams M' and L' L' applied to it, attached to the sieve-frame D, and hung loosely upon the tank, and combined with the tappets and tappet-shaft, substantially in the manner shown and described.

DAVID NEVIN.

Witnesses:
L. W. DOLLOFF,
THOS. J. CAMPBELL.

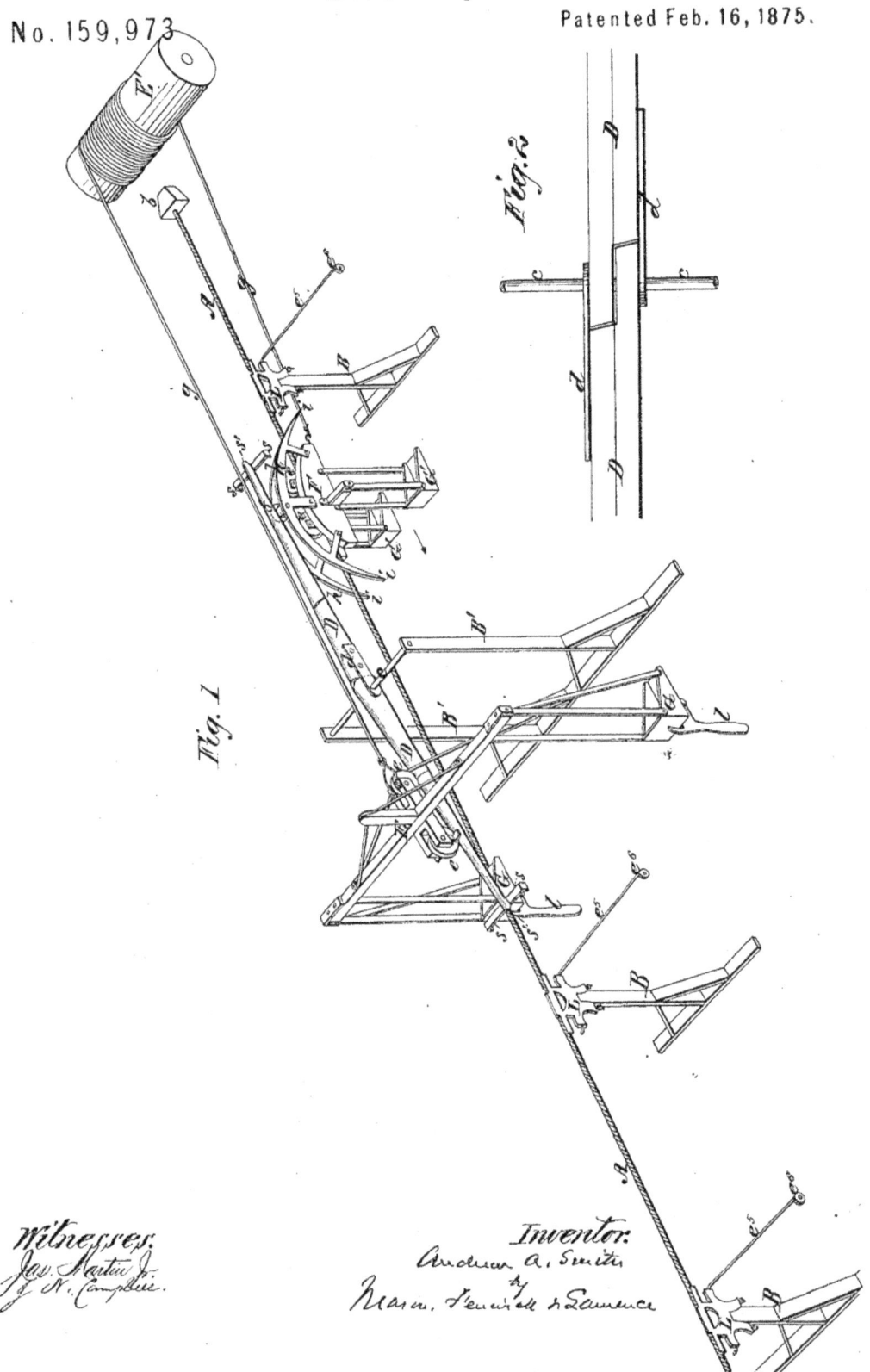

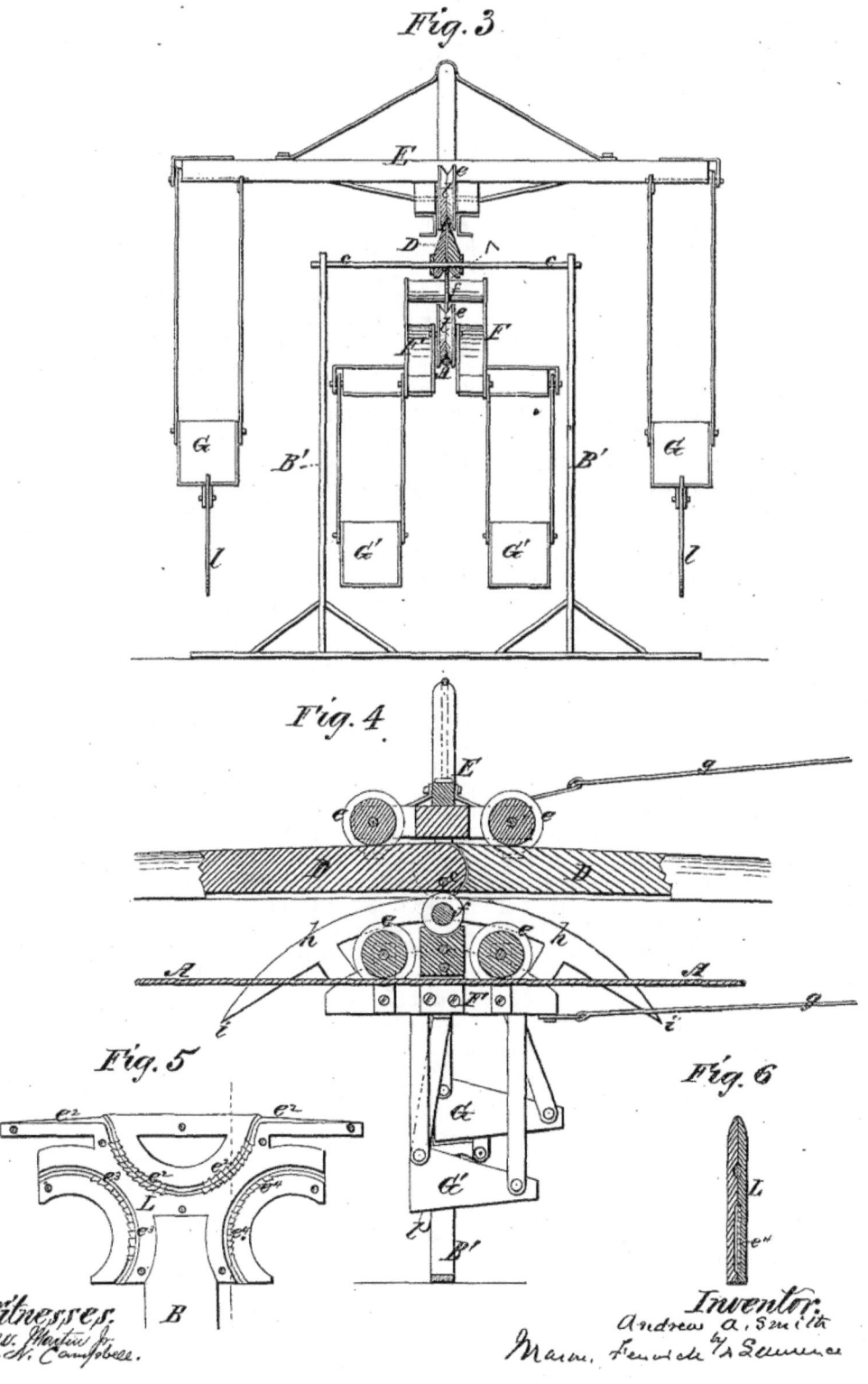

UNITED STATES PATENT OFFICE.

ANDREW A. SMITH, OF GEORGETOWN, COLORADO TERRITORY.

IMPROVEMENT IN WIREWAYS.

Specification forming part of Letters Patent No. **159,973**, dated February 16, 1875; application filed December 30, 1874.

To all whom it may concern:

Be it known that I, ANDREW A. SMITH, of Georgetown, county of Clear Creek, Territory of Colorado, have invented a new and Improved Cable-Way for Mining and other purposes; and I do hereby declare that the following is a full clear, and exact description thereof, reference being had to the accompanying drawings, making part of this specification, in which—

Figure 1 is a perspective view; Fig. 2, plan view of the jointed riding-track; Fig. 3, a view in cross-section of the riding-track, the two transporting-cars, and the cable-track. Fig. 4 is a longitudinal section of Fig. 3. Fig. 5 is a longitudinal section of the cable and guy-clamp; and Fig. 6 a cross-section of same.

The object of my invention is the construction of a "cable-way," particularly adapted for mining operations, which can be cheaply constructed, and only utilize a metallic cable for a single transporting-track in the place of two transporting-tracks, as heretofore used.

In Fig. 1 I have shown my invention in perspective view, with a cable, A, supposed to be anchored in the side of a mountain at b, with its opposite end anchored below, at the foot of the mountain. The cable is rigidly stretched over, and supported at proper intervals upon, posts B B B. About centrol of the length of the cable are posts B' B, one on each side of the cable, and tied together, near their upper ends, by a strong metal rod, c, which rod is to be made large enough to support the weight of the load which may be passed over a riding-track, D, through which said rod passes, and upon which the riding-track articulates. Fig. 2 shows the riding-track D jointed upon the rod c, the joint being strengthened by iron plates d, secured to the main parts of the riding-track, with the rod c passing through said plates. This riding-track D D is made, on its top, and along its whole length, in the form of the letter **V** inverted, while its under side is grooved in like form, such form being adapted on its top to receive the tread of the grooved wheels $e\ e$ of the car E on its passage over the riding-track D D, while the groove along on the under side of the riding-track is adapted to receive a guide-roll, f, of the car F (clearly shown in Fig. 4) during its passage beneath said riding-track and on the cable A.

In Figs. 3 and 4 I have shown the transporting-cars E and F in the act of passing each other over my cable-way. A rope, G, as shown in Fig. 1, is attached at one end to the car E, which, after winding around a drum, E', has its opposite end attached to the car F, so that by the rotation of the drum the car E may be drawn up the mountain on the cable-way, while the car F is allowed to pass down, or the reverse thereof, as circumstances may require. These cars, in their movement up and down the mountain, pass each at a central point of the line of cable-way. The supports B' B' indicate such point; and, by an inspection of Fig. 1, it will be seen that the car E is riding upon one section of the riding-track D D, while the other car F is passing beneath the other section of said riding-track and upon the cable A. Thus, that section of the riding-track which supports the car E, as shown in Fig. 1, has its lower end resting upon the cable A, while its upper jointed end is supported by the rod c of the supports B' B', and during this time the other section of the riding-track is elevated upon the guide-roll f of the car F while the car F is passing toward the bar c, at which point c the two cars pass each other, one upon the riding-track D D, and the other upon the cable A beneath the said track.

By reference to Fig. 3 it will be seen that the frame-work of the car F is of such width as to allow its passage between the supporting-posts B' B', while the frame-work of the car E is of such width as to freely pass on either side of such posts.

Figs. 1 and 4 show the frame of the car F made with curved guards h, the extreme ends i of which extend down below the cable on which the car is riding, so that when the car approaches the riding-track D D such end i will, at the proper time, pass under a cross-bar, s, attached to the extreme outer ends of each of the sections of the riding track D D, and thus elevate the same, according to the direction, either up or down the cable A in which the car F may be passing.

When the car F (supposing it to be moving in the direction of the arrow) is passing beneath one section of the riding-track, such section will gradually be lowered down, so that its extreme end s' will rest upon the cable A, and thus afford a passage-way for the car E to move down off from the riding-track upon the cable; and, while the car E is so moving down, the car F will be passing beneath the section of the riding-track which the car E has just passed over. In this manner the cars may pass each other in either direction, the one upon the riding-track, and the other beneath it on the cable A. I would state that when the cars pass each other at the bar c the sag of the cable A beneath such point will permit the under car to pass without bearing any of the weight of the car above it, the weight of the upper car being thrown upon the cross-bar c.

G G are buckets or vessels suspended from the car E, and G' G' are buckets or vessels suspended from the car F, into which the load to be transported over the cable-way is placed. These buckets are suspended by jointed rods, as shown in Fig. 3; which rods and buckets may so articulate as to keep the buckets in proper upright position while they are being transported up and down the mountain. To the buckets G tripping-levers l are applied, in order to facilitate the discharge of the load from the buckets, and like levers may be applied to buckets G', if desired.

In order to sustain and hold the cable-track A in a direct line, and prevent it from swaying from such line, I securely attach, in any proper manner, to the posts B B B, guy-clamps L. These clamps (see Figs. 5 and 6) may be of cast-metal plates bolted together, and having a groove, as at e^2, in which the cable A lies, and in which it is firmly clamped between the two plates which compose the guy-clamp. Serrations are formed in such groove in such manner as to hold the cable with a bite or grip, and thus prevent the slipping of the cable after adjustment therein. Like serrated grooves, as at e^3 and e^4, are formed in the inner faces of the guy-clamp L, in which guy-ropes e^5 are placed and held in a fixed position, as indicated in Fig. 1. One end of the guys e^5 is anchored in the rock or ground at e^6, immediately under cable A. The guys e^6 may be secured in position immediately under the cable at points in the ground above the connection of the guy with the cable at the posts, the guy running horizontal, or nearly so, from the ground to the clamp at the head of the post.

By my application of the guy-clamp L the cable A or transporting-track is divided into sections or divisions, although the strands of the cable are continuous, each section consisting of that portion of the cable A which lies between any two guys, or, at the extremities between the end and the nearest guy.

The strain from the weight of the car, as well as from the gravity of the cable or other cause, is thus brought upon a section of the cable A, instead of upon the cable throughout its whole stretch at one time; and, except upon the section where the cars pass, the weight of only one car can bear upon any one section at one time. The cable is thus held firm in place, and prevented from forward slip; and the lateral swing or other swaying of the cable is diminished in proportion as the length of the whole cable is to a single section.

What I claim as new is—

1. The cars E and F, in combination with the single cable A, substantially as and for the purpose described.

2. The riding-tracks D D, in combination with the cable-track A, substantially as and for the purpose described.

3. The support B' B' and bar c, in combination with the hinged riding-track D, substantially as described.

4. A transporting-car, E, constructed with curved guards h, or their equivalent, substantially as and for the purpose set forth.

5. Guy-clamps L, in combination with the cable A and guy-ropes e^5, substantially as and for the purpose set forth.

ANDREW A. SMITH.

Witnesses:
WM. STRUANCE,
WM. B. HOUGH.

J. BERNDT.
Sash-Balances.

No. 160,145

Patented Feb. 23, 1875.

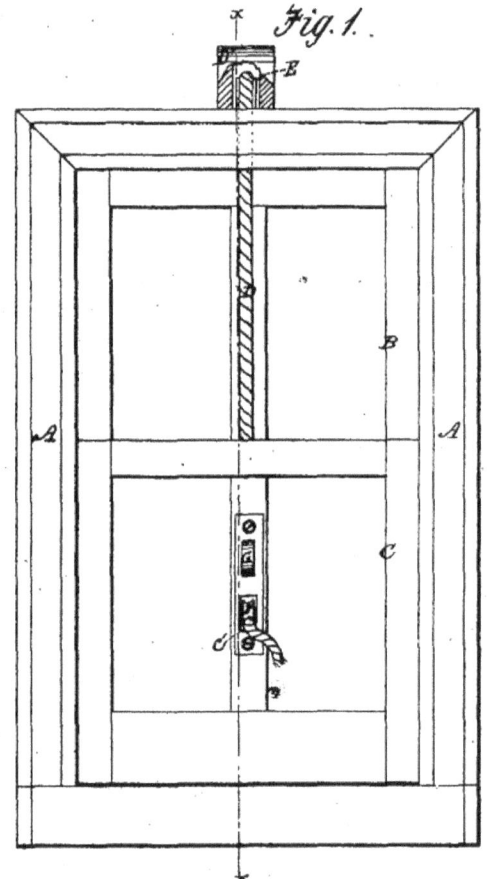
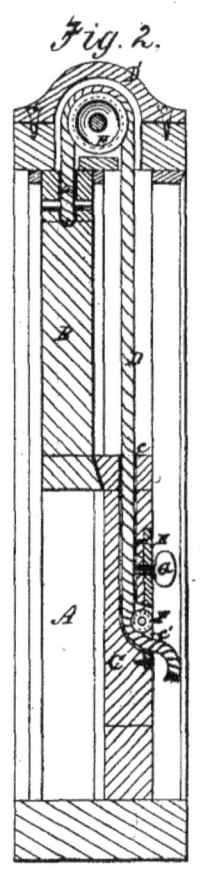

UNITED STATES PATENT OFFICE.

JOHN BERNDT, OF DENVER, COLORADO TERRITORY.

INPROVEMENT IN SASH-BALANCES.

Specification forming part of Letters Patent No. **160,145**, dated February 23, 1875; application filed December 28, 1874.

To all whom it may concern:

Be it known that I, JOHN BERNDT, of Denver, in the county of Arapahoe, Colorado Territory, have invented a new and Improved Sash Balance and Fastener; and I do hereby declare that the following is a full, clear, and exact description of the same, reference being had to the accompanying drawing, forming a part of this specification, in which—

Figure 1 is a front elevation partly in section; Fig. 2, a vertical section.

The invention consists in bringing down the cord that connects the two sashes through a vertical hole in the top of lower sash into and partly through the mullion, a cord-pulley being arranged within a slot, and a clamp being attached to the mullion surface, all as hereinafter more fully described.

A represents a window-frame, and B C the upper and lower sashes that slide up and down therein. I connect the sashes B C by a flexible connection wire or rope, D, having one end attached to the top sash, passing thence over a pulley, E, in the window-frame; thence down through a vertical hole, c, in the lower sash C, into and partly through the mullion, over a pulley, F, arranged within a slot, and out at a front hole, c', the free end projecting within convenient reach. G is a clamp-screw in the mullion of the lower sash that works across the hole c, and enables the connecting part of rope D between the two sashes to be shortened or lengthened. The pulley and rope E D may be covered by a plate, D', while a plate, E', may be used to support the clamp-screw and pulley F. By this means I can lower or raise the upper or lower sash without disturbing each other, or I can open them both relatively, as seems most desirable.

I am aware that two sashes have been heretofore conjoined by a cord so as to be held by a clamp at varying elevations; but

What I claim as new is—

The combination, with sashes B C, of the cord D, pulley F, and clamp G, the first being brought down through a vertical hole in the top of lower sash, and partly through the mullion thereof, the second arranged within a slot, and the third attached to the surface of said mullion, as and for the purpose specified.

JOHN BERNDT.

Witnesses:
 WILLIAM TENWINKLE,
 H. H. THOMAS.

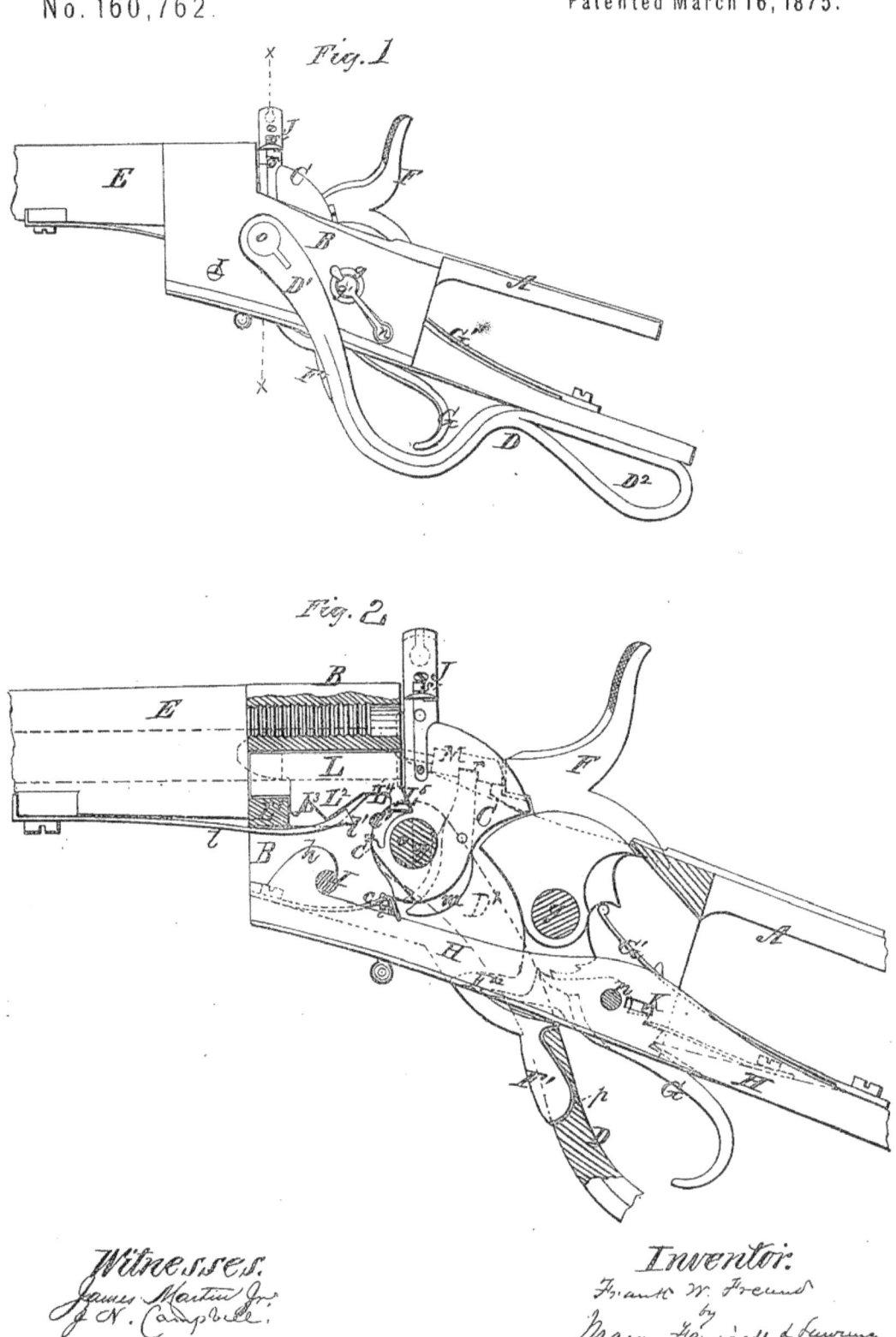

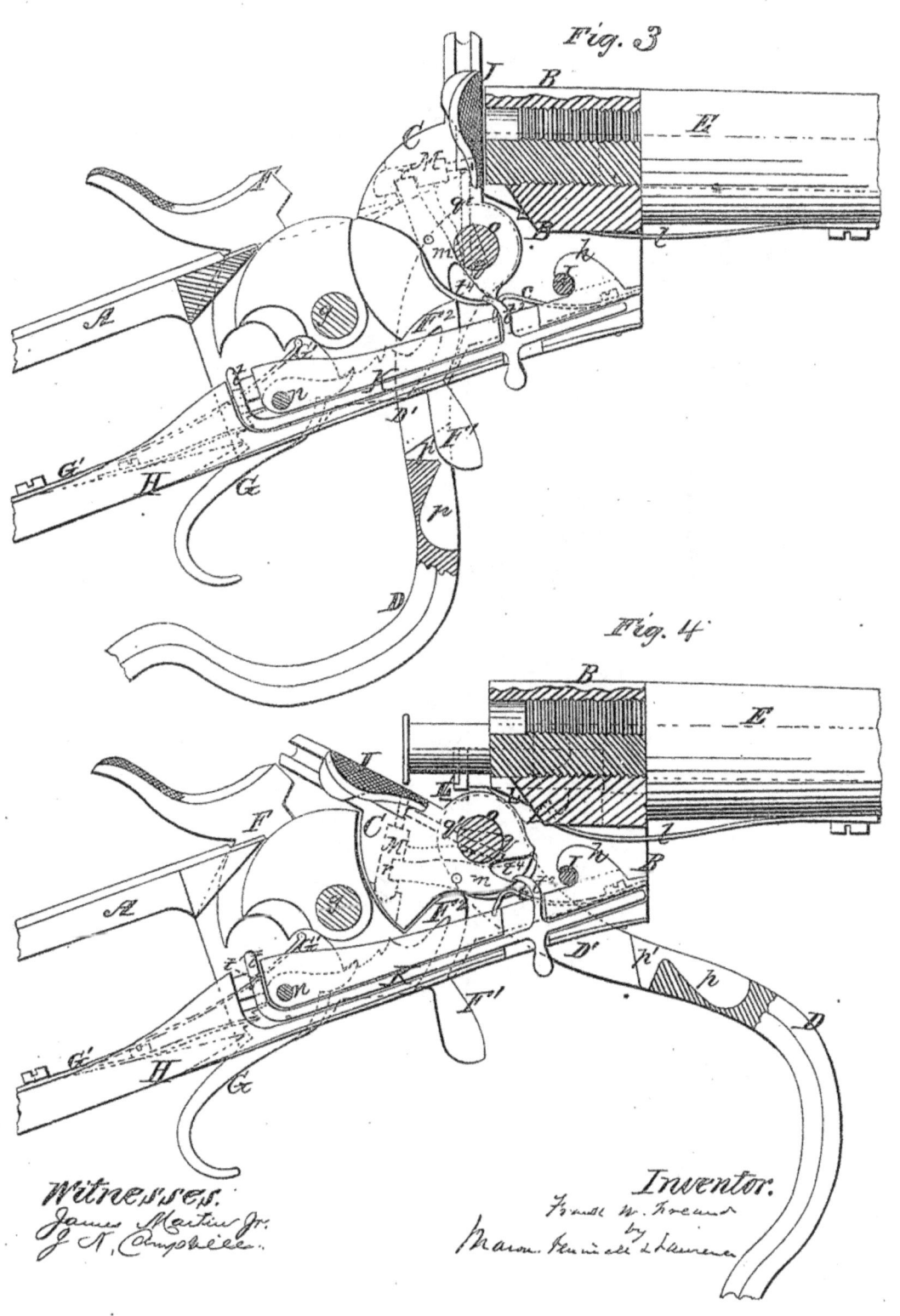

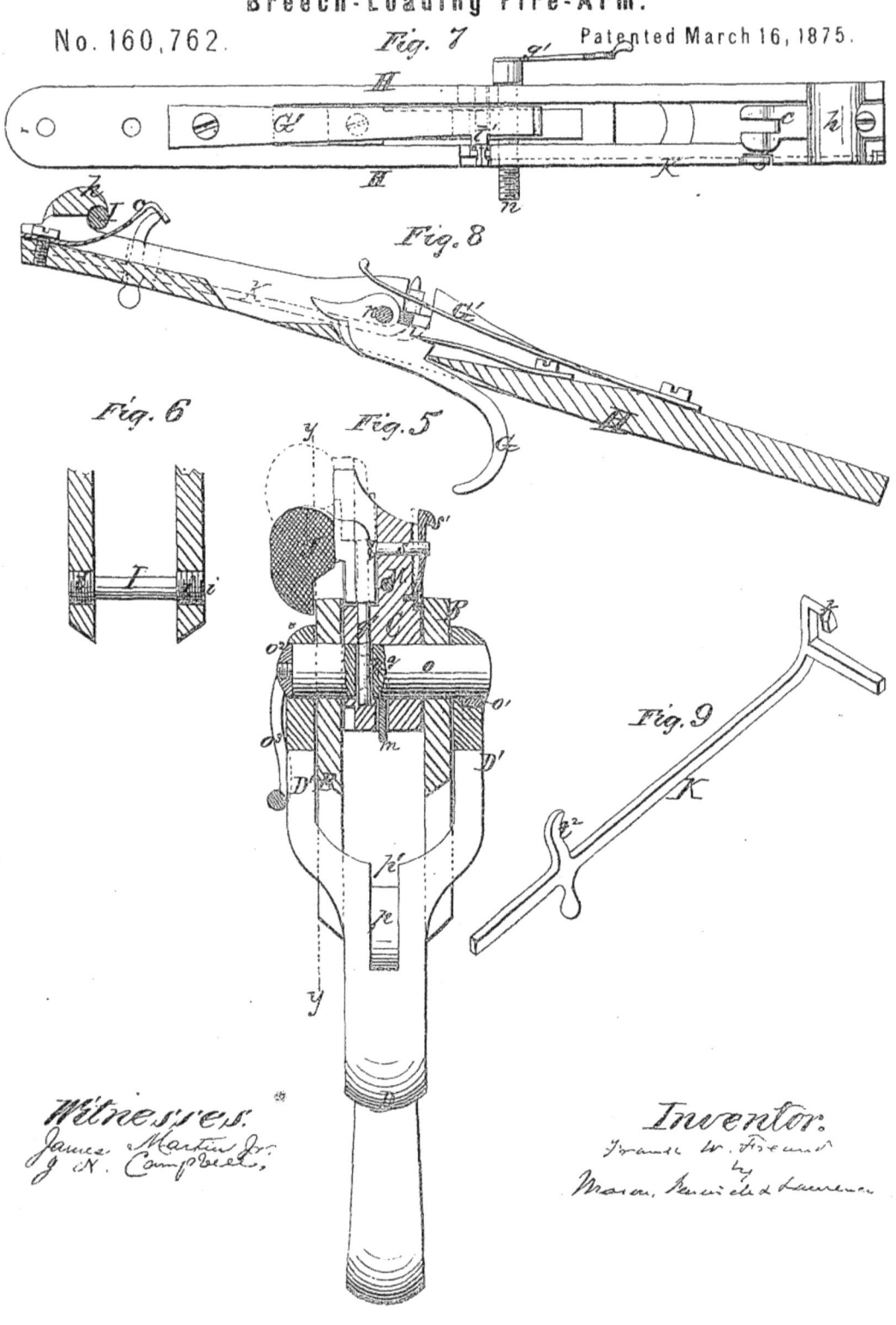

UNITED STATES PATENT OFFICE.

FRANK W. FREUND, OF DENVER, COLORADO TERRITORY.

IMPROVEMENT IN BREECH-LOADING FIRE-ARMS.

Specification forming part of Letters Patent No. **160,762**, dated March 16, 1875; application filed June 10, 1874.

To all whom it may concern:

Be it known that I, FRANK W. FREUND, of Denver, county of Arapahoe, Territory of Colorado, have invented a new and useful Improvement in Breech-Loading Fire-Arms; and I do hereby declare that the following is a full, clear, and exact description thereof, reference being had to the accompanying drawings, making part of this specification, in which—

Figure 1 is a side elevation of the arm as it appears after it has been fired. Fig. 2 is a longitudinal section of the arm, in the same position as in Fig. 1. Fig. 3 is a similar section in the line $y\,y$, Fig. 5, of the arm, cocked, and just previous to having the empty cartridge-shell extracted. Fig. 4 is a similar section of the arm in the line $y\,y$, Fig. 5, cocked, and with its breech-block thrown back to open the breech, and the empty shell partly withdrawn from the chamber of the barrel. Fig. 5 is a vertical transverse section in the line $x\,x$ of Fig. 1. Fig. 6 is a sectional view of the lugs of the breech, and pin which holds the front end of the trigger-plate. Fig. 7 is a plan of the trigger-plate and its attachments. Fig. 8 is a longitudinal section of the same. Fig. 9 is a perspective view of the slide which latches the hammer spring and hammer-trigger after the hammer is cocked.

The nature of my invention consists, first, in a tail on the lower part of the hammer, in combination with a notch of the guard-lever, the tail and the notch being peculiarly constructed, and enabling me to cock the arm before moving the breech-block by the movement of the lever to open the breech, and after the breech has been opened and the arm loaded, I am enabled to close the breech by the lever without striking the hammer with the lever, so as to interfere on its back movement.

It consists, second, in a nose or cam formed on the tail of the hammer, in combination with a lever and the firing-pin, whereby I am enabled to move the firing-pin back with a positive action, and hold it so after the arm is cocked and during the act of closing the block, and at a time when the block is nearly and quite closed, and then I am enabled to release the pin on the instant that the hammer is set free from its trigger-pawl. Thus, while the greatest safety is insured by a hold upon the firing-pin until the aim is taken and the hammer set free, a percussive blow with the hammer is produced, from the fact that the hold upon the pin is withdrawn the instant the hammer-trigger is drawn.

It consists, third, in a slide for latching the spring of the hammer and hammer-trigger during the act of loading the arm, in combination with the breech-block, whereby the slide is automatically made to latch and unlatch the said spring and hammer-trigger as the breech-block is opened and closed.

It consists, fourth, in a forked guard-lever, which receives the breech between its prongs and fastens rigidly upon a movable pin of the breech-block, in combination with a breech-block which is fitted loosely upon the said pin, and with a sliding thumb-piece having a coupling-pin attached to it, which pin is arranged to enter an oblong passage cut through the pin or pivot whenever it is desired to operate the breech-block by the guard-lever, and occupies a position outside of said passage when it is desired to operate the breech-block by the thumb-piece, whereby a fire-arm is provided in which the hammer can be cocked before the breech-block is opened. The breech-block can be opened and closed by the guard-lever, or by the thumb-piece, and thus, when the huntsman is in a position which necessitates the depression of his gun near the ground, and there is no room for the sweep of the lever, he can, by simply withdrawing the coupling-pin, release the breech-block from its rigid connection with the pin, and then, by taking hold of the thumb-piece, he can open and close the breech-block while the gun is depressed close to the ground. Further, this combination is such that the arm is rendered capable of being operated either by the thumb-piece or guard-lever interchangeably for rapid or slow firing, and in case the guard-lever is broken the arm is not disabled so as to be useless until repaired, as the thumb-piece is interchangeable with the guard-lever. This is a matter of some importance in localities where repair-shops and gunsmiths are not readily reached. This combination is also such that the hammer can be cocked by the guard-lever first, and then the breech-block opened by a continuation of the movement of the lever.

It consists, fifth, in a transverse spring-pin having a holding-catch, in combination with the thumb-piece and coupling-pin, whereby the thumb-piece, with attached coupling-pin, is held in an elevated position while the breech-block is to be operated by the thumb.

It consists, sixth, in a pin for receiving the hook of the trigger-plate, screw-threaded on both of its ends and screwed into the cheek-plates of the breech, whereby a firm brace between the cheeks and a support for the trigger-plate is provided by the use of a single pin.

It consists, seventh, in the forked guard-lever clasping the two sides of the breech-piece, in combination with the pivot of the breech, extended beyond the cheeks of the breech, and having the prongs of the guard-lever rigidly connected to the extended end, whereby the lever is applied without cutting into the breech or through the trigger-plate, and, while this is the case, can be operated in a more steady and perfect manner than heretofore.

It consists, eighth, in a peculiar construction of a cartridge-shell extractor, in combination with a peculiar spring combined therewith, and with a breech which admits of the arrangement of the extractor directly above the pivot of the breech-block, and in a recess formed on one side of the chamber of the arm. This feature of my invention is such that the extractor is applied and held in position without the aid of a pin or other fastening. Further, but three parts additional to the stock and barrel are necessary in its construction and application—viz., the breech-block, the spring, and the extractor itself. These parts are of such a construction that they are strong and not liable to get out of repair and become deranged; and the effect of the spring as applied is to hold the extractor firmly in place when the breech is closed, and at the proper moment, after the shell has been started out of the chamber by the breech-block, to suddenly act upon the extractor with a straight thrust, and thereby accelerate the discharge of the shell from the chamber of the arm.

To enable others skilled in the art to make and use my invention, I will proceed to describe it.

A represents the stock; B, the breech; C, the breech-block; c, its easing and steadying spring; o, its pivot or pin; D D^1 D^1 D^2, the guard-lever; E, the barrel, and q' the pin by which the guard-lever is coupled to the breech-block; F F^1 F^2, the hammer and its extensions; G, the hammer-trigger, and G' the hammer-spring; H, the trigger-plate; h, its hook; I, the hinge-pin of trigger-plate; $i\ i$, its screw-threaded ends. J is the thumb-piece for operating the breech-block when the lever is not used. K is the slide for latching the hammer-spring and hammer-trigger when the arm is being loaded. L is the cartridge-extractor, and l the spring for controlling and suddenly operating it. M is the firing-pin passed loosely through the breech-block, and m is the lever by which it is forced back after firing the arm. The hammer is hung and operated in the usual manner upon a pin, g, which is confined by means of a spring-catch, g', attached to a screw-pin, n, which holds the rear end of the trigger-plate between the cheek-pieces of the breech B. This catch springs into a notched socket in the end of the hammer-pivot, and prevents the said pivot from turning and moving endwise; but by moving the catch aside the pin can be withdrawn. The tail or extension F^1 of the hammer passes outside of the arm through a slot in the trigger-plate, while the extension F^2 projects obliquely toward the breech-block, and is long enough to impinge forcibly upon the lever m of the firing-pin when the hammer is cocked and the breech-block about half closed. The guard-lever is constructed with a finger-loop, D^2, at its rear, and forked at its front end, its prongs D^1 D^1 passing up on each side of the breech, and receiving through their perforated ends the projecting ends of the pin o of the breech-block C.

The connection between the pin and this lever is made rigid by means of a key, o^1, and a nut, o^2, which screws upon a threaded end of the pin, said nut having a spring-arm, o^3, formed on it to hold the nut from turning by falling into a groove in one of the prongs of the lever. At the junction of the prongs of the lever an oblique socket, p, is cut on the front of the lever, and just above this socket a notch, p', is cut in the lever from front to rear.

By this construction, and the extension F^1 of the hammer, the hammer can be cocked when the guard-lever is moved downward and forward for the purpose of opening the breech, and the lever can be drawn back without striking the tail or extension so as to interfere; but in order to cock the hammer before the breech is moved, an oblong slot, q, is cut through the pin o, on which the breech-block is hung, and the coupling-pin q' is made of smaller size than this slot, so that the pin o, with the lever, may be moved far enough to cock the hammer before the breech-block begins to move. The breech-block is formed with a slot in its rear, in which the lever m, for moving back the firing-pin M, is set, and confined by a pivot. This lever m, below its axial pin, projects out from the back and bottom edge of the breech-block, and has its projecting edge of a cam form, so as to ride up against and past the extension F^2 with a wedging action. The upper end of this lever is coupled to the firing-pin by entering a notch, r, in the bottom of said pin. The coupling-pin q' has a flat extension on its top, and this extension unites with the thumb-piece J. Said pin with flat extension is fitted in a transversely-grooved top piece or extension of the breech-block, and at right angles to this pin a latch-bolt, s, is passed through the extension, and fits under the shoulder formed by the junction of the coupling-pin and the flat extension thereof. This bolt has a shoulder or head, and in front thereof a spring-lever catch, s', is arranged, for the purpose of pulling the bolt from under the shoulder of the coupling-pin when it is desired to lower the coupling-pin into the oblong slot of the pin or pivot of the breech-block.

In Fig. 5 the dotted lines show the coupling-pin and thumb-piece raised, and the full black lines show it lowered. When the pin is raised the guard-lever is free from the breech-block, and the thumb-lever can move the block independently of the lever. When the pin is down the lever can move the breech-block as the pin q' couples the block to the lever. The slide K t t^1 t^2 t^3, for latching the hammer-spring and hammer-trigger, is constructed as represented in Fig. 9, and is fitted into grooves and slots cut in the trigger-plate, as shown in Figs. 2, 3, and 4. The part t of this slide which overhangs the lateral projection t^1 of the hammer-spring when the hammer is cocked ceases its connection with the spring, and does not press down upon the spring and interfere with its action upon the hammer, when the hammer is cocked and the breech-block is closed; but when the breech-block is being opened the said part t of the slide is moved in range with the projection t^1, and bears down upon the spring and relieves the hammer from the force thereof, and at the same instant the part t^3 of the slide which extends in laterally behind the shoulder of the hammer-trigger falls in behind the shoulder of the trigger, and latches the trigger in one of the notches of the hammer. Thus both hammer-spring and hammer-trigger are latched while the breech is being opened. This action of the slide is produced by the tooth t^2 gearing with a segment-notch, t^4, in the end of the breech-block, while the button t^5 protrudes through the breech and acts as a stop. The movement of the breech-block backward causes the shoulder of the segment-notch to strike the slide and force the rear end of the slide down upon the spring, thereby locking the hammer-spring and hammer-trigger, and the forward movement of the breech moves the slide out of range with the projection of the hammer-spring, and free from the hammer-trigger, and thereby sets the spring and trigger free.

It is plain that if the breech is being closed the lever m will be forcing the firing-pin back from the position the hammer left it when the arm was last fired, as it is impossible for the cam-surface of the lever m to pass by the extension T^2 until it (the lever) has been forced forward and its upper end forced backward against the firing-pin. It will also be equally plain that the extension moves out of the way on the instant that the hammer begins to fall, and thus the pin is free to act with a percussive force upon the fulminate of the cartridge. The cartridge-extractor L, in general form, is like other extractors so far as taking hold of the rim of the cartridge-shell is concerned, and it occupies a position on one side of the breech of the gun-barrel between the barrel and one of the cheek-pieces or locking plates of the stock—being set to slide in a guide, L^1, and held therein by the spring l. On the bottom edge of this extractor a projection, L^2, in form very nearly of the letter V, is provided. At the base of one of the inclined sides of the projection a shoulder, L^3, is formed, and at the base of the other inclined side an angular depression, L^4, is cut, thereby forming a lug, L^5, which is beveled on its rear end and slightly hooking on its front end. This lug fits down behind a shoulder, C^1, formed by cutting the open-sided recess C^2 on the breech-block C in the circumference thereof, as shown in Fig. 2. By means of the shoulder C^1 and the lug L^5 the extractor and breech-block are coupled together. The spring l is bowed slightly toward its rear end, and at the termination of this bowed portion it has its end l' thickened and shaped so as to stand parallel with the respective faces of the inclines of the projection L when in contact with the same. By this means the spring, when in rear of the projection, will hold the extractor from moving back; but the instant the spring escapes forward of the projection it will recoil and produce a sudden accelerated action upon the extractor and cause the shell to fly back out of the chamber, from which it has been started by the breech-hook C^2 taking hold of the lug L^5. The thrust and force of the spring being in nearly a straight line, and the fall of the spring forward of the lug being very quick, the effect upon the extractor is like that of the blow of a hammer, the concussion causing the cartridge to fly suddenly back out of the breech-chamber.

I am aware that cartridge-extractors composed of a greater number of parts have been devised, and that in some instances a spring is used to assist the movement; but I am not aware that any one has devised the plan I have shown, which is very simple, durable, and effective.

The construction of my fire-arm is such that by the removal of four pins—viz., the trigger-pin, the hammer-pin, the lever spring-pin, and the breech-pin—the trigger-plate, with all its attachments—viz., the guard-lever, breech-block, and the hammer—can be separated; and the same parts, together with the breech-piece, are held together and stayed by these three pins and the pin I. Further, the pins of the hammer-trigger, the hammer, and breech-block are held from turning by spring-stops, which enable me to separate the pieces without the aid of any instrument; and by my simple slide, which is held in position without a spring, screw, or pin extra of those used to unite the other parts, I am enabled in one movement to latch or unlatch both the hammer-spring and hammer-trigger, thus rendering the arm doubly safe against accidental discharge.

The provision which the slot q makes for an independent movement of the lever in order to cock the hammer before opening the breech-block may be made at the end of the breech-block pin or pivot, in connection with the prongs of the guard-lever, by means of a slide, or by shoulders projecting into the hole of the lever-prong; these shoulders fitting in the pin loosely, so as to permit the necessary play.

What I claim as new, and desire to secure by Letters Patent, is—

1. The tail or extension F^1 of the hammer, extended through the trigger-plate, in combination with the guard-lever D, substantially as and for the purpose described.

2. The nose or cam F^2, formed on the tail of the hammer, in combination with the lever m and the firing-pin M, whereby the firing-pin is moved out before the breech-block is moved, the said pin held out when the breech-block is fully closed, and the breech-block can be moved as much and as often as found necessary without releasing the firing-pin at a point where it will come in contact with the percussion, substantially in the manner and for the purpose described.

3. The slide K, having the stops t^3, for latching the hammer-spring and hammer-trigger, as shown and described, in combination with the breech-block C, notched at t^4, and the hammer-spring G' and hammer-trigger, substantially as and for the purpose set forth.

4. The forked guard-lever D D^1 D^1, fastened rigidly upon the extended ends of the pin o, on which the breech-block is hung, in combination with the breech-block C, which is fitted loosely upon the pin o, and with a sliding thumb-piece, J, having a coupling-pin, q', attached to it, which pin, at option, is passed into an oblong slot of the pin o, substantially in the manner and for the purpose herein set forth.

5. The combination of the guard-lever D, the hammer F, the breech-block C, the oblong slot q in pin o, and the coupling-pin q', whereby the hammer can be cocked before the breech is opened by the lever which is used to open the breech, and during the one movement of the lever, and the breech can be closed without uncocking the hammer by the back movement of the lever, substantially as described.

6. A guard-lever, forked and connected rigidly by its prongs D^1 D^1 to the outer ends of the pin o, substantially in the manner described, and for the purpose set forth.

7. The transverse spring-pin s, having a holding-catch, s', in combination with the thumb-piece J and its attached pin q', substantially as and for the purpose described.

8. The rectilinear moving cartridge-extractor L, fitted in the guide L^1, in combination with the spring l and the breech-block C, whereby the extractor is operated and held in position without any fastening-pin, as and for the purpose set forth.

9. The extractor having the hook L^5 and the projection L^2, in combination with the breech-block C, whereby the extractor is secured in place and operated by the breech-block, substantially as and for the purpose described.

10. The trigger-plate, constructed with a hook, h, on its forward end, in the manner specified, in combination with the permanent pin I, supported in the cheek-pieces of the breech, and, in turn, supporting said cheek-pieces against inward and outward pressure, whereby, while facilities for readily removing the trigger-plate and replacing it, by the removal of a single pin in rear of the pin I, are afforded, the cheek-plates are stayed firmly against any tendency to warp or spring, either outward or inward, during the hardening process and while in use, substantially as described.

11. The combination of the lever spring-stop g' with the socketed and notched pin g of the hammer, and with the trigger-pin n, substantially as and for the purpose described.

FRANK WM. FREUND.

Witnesses:
JOHN ELSNER,
GEORGE C. SCHLEIER.

F. W. FREUND.
Metallic-Cartridge.

No. 160,763

Patented March 16, 1875

Fig. 1

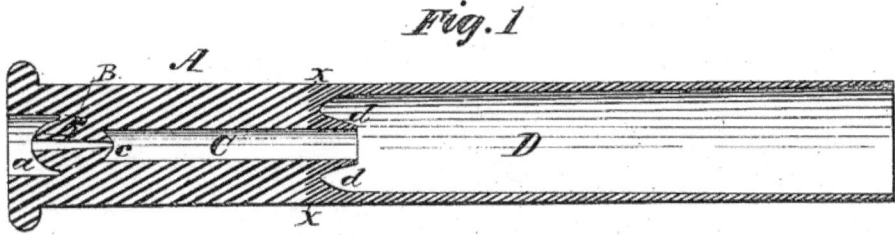

Fig. 2

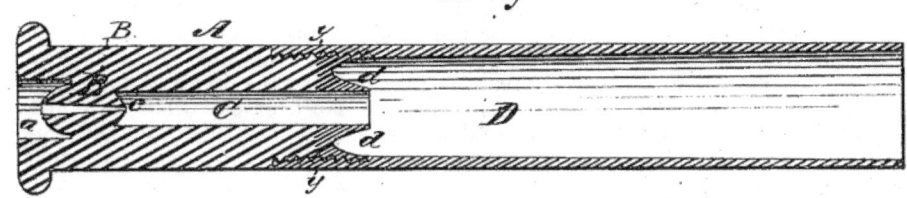

UNITED STATES PATENT OFFICE.

FRANK W. FREUND, OF DENVER, COLORADO TERRITORY.

IMPROVEMENT IN METALLIC CARTRIDGES.

Specification forming part of Letters Patent No. **160,763**, dated March 16, 1875; application filed February 4, 1874.

To all whom it may concern:

Be it known that I, FRANK W. FREUND, of Denver, county of Arapahoe, Territory of Colorado, have invented a new and Improved Reloading Rifle-Cartridge; and I do hereby declare that the following is a full, clear, and exact description thereof, reference being had to the accompanying drawings, making part of this specification, in which—

Figure 1 is a longitudinal central section, and Fig. 2 a like section, showing the thinned portion of the cartridge screwed upon the thick rear portion, as at $y\ y$.

One general fault with cartridges of heavy charge for breech-loading guns has been that the bulk of powder has occupied the rear end of the cartridge, and consequently in the extreme rear end of the barrel, where the barrel is subjected to the heaviest strain of the explosion, so that when the cartridge is exploded such explosion simultaneously expands both the cartridge and the barrel, which, contracting unequally, makes it difficult to withdraw the cartridge, and still more difficult to reinsert the cartridge after it has been reloaded. This difficulty I obviate in my improved cartridge by making it considerably longer than the cartridge in common use, and by constructing it with a solid or thickened head of such length as will cause the bulk of the powder to be located (when the cartridge is inserted in the barrel) at a point considerably in advance of the extreme rear end of the barrel. By my invention I overcome or avoid the objectionable expansion both of the barrel and the cartridge, which is incident to the use of the cartridges as now commonly constructed.

In the drawings, D, Fig. 1, indicates a portion of my cartridge, which is made thinned from about the point $x\ x$ to the mouth or muzzle, while in rear of the point $x\ x$ the cartridge is made solid or thickened, as indicated at A B. From the point $x\ x$ to the muzzle I harden the steel of which it is composed, making it of fine spring temper, and from said point $x\ x$ to the rear termination of the shell I leave the steel soft or unhardened. I construct the part of my shell shown at A B, in rear of the point $x\ x$, in a solid or thick condition, for the reason, first, that I thus prevent an expansion of the shell against the barrel; and, second, I make it of metal which is soft or unhardened, because, from actual trial, I have discovered that practically such metal will not granulate and become weakened by the shock of explosion, and so split and break. The part D is made of spring temper, so that it will, if expanded by explosion, immediately return to its normal condition.

In the drawings, a represents the anvil for the percussion-cap, with a fine perforation passing through the solid part B, and making connection with a reduced powder-chamber, C, which in turn makes connection with the main powder-chamber D.

The object of constructing the cartridge with a reduced powder-chamber, C, in connection with a main powder-chamber, D, is, first, to so divide the charge of powder that the least shock of explosion shall fall upon the rear end of the cartridge as well as the extreme rear end of the gun, while at the same time the heaviest shock will fall upon the gun-barrel at a point considerably forward of its extreme rear end; second, by thus dividing the charge of powder the shock of explosion is divided and distributed in the cartridge, and the main chamber D relieved of a portion of the shock and power of the explosion.

The main powder-chamber terminates in an annular recess or gas-cup, $d\ d$, and the reduced powder-chamber C also terminates in a like recess or gas-cup, c, as shown in Figs. 1 and 2.

The recoil of an explosion is received in and checked by recesses $c\ d$, and thus the shock of discharge is lessened in its effect both upon the cartridge and the gun-barrel itself. Besides this the gas is more or less prevented from being forced through the small aperture in the anvil a, leading into the reduced chamber C. It is believed, also, that if the bulk of the powder lies close to the rear end of the barrel the danger from accident is greater than when the charge is located farther forward, as when at the rear the explosion is near the joint or fastening of the breech, and being near the fire-tube connecting with the powder the fire-tube becomes worn more easily than when the bulk of the powder is removed to a point forward in the barrel.

The advantages of my improved shell, it will be seen, are, first, that its rear portion is made of solid metal of such thickness that no expansion of it can take place in the act of explosion; second, that such rear portion, which constitutes about one-third of the length of the shell, is made of soft metal, and thus resists a granulation and weakening of the shell, to which it would be subject under the successive jar and shock of constant refiring if it were made of hardened metal; third, that the bulk of powder occupies a position in the shell which, when the shell is inserted in the barrel, will be considerably forward of the extreme rear end of the gun-barrel; fourth, that an enlarged and a reduced powder-chamber are in conjunction utilized to divide the shock of an explosion, check recoil, and lessen liability to accident near the joint or fastening of the breech; fifth, that at a point in the main chamber D upon which the greatest force of the explosion falls the metal is made elastic or springy, so that if expanded by explosion it will at once return to its normal condition, and thus allow its easy retraction from the gun-barrel, as well as subsequent insertion thereof. These advantages, in a measure, relieve the breech end of the gun from undue strain when fired, and add to the safety as well as to the convenience and facility of manipulating the gun.

I will here state that the comparatively solid and thick portion of my shell A B, which is in rear of the line $x\,x$, may be made of brass, copper, or other suitable soft metal, instead of soft steel, and united to the forward portion D by screw-thread, as indicated at $y\,y$ in Fig. 2.

What I claim as my invention is—

1. A cartridge-shell made, substantially as described, of one piece of metal, with a small powder-tube, C, between a fire-tube and a main powder-chamber, D.

2. A cartridge-shell made, substantially as described, with a thin hard-metal portion, D, and a thick soft-metal portion, A B.

FRANK W. FREUND.

Witnesses:
L. K. JOHNSON,
L. C. CHARLES.

F. W. FREUND.
Sights for Fire-Arms.

No. 160,819
Patented March 16, 1875.

Fig. 1
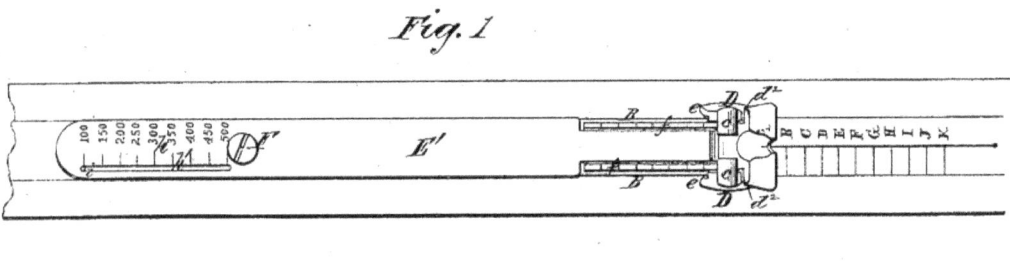

Fig. 2
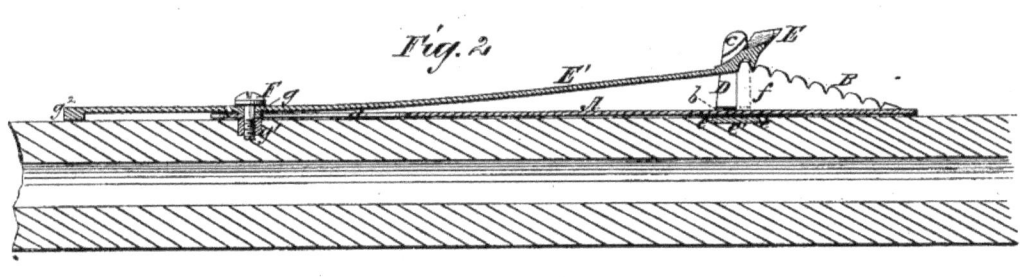

Fig. 3
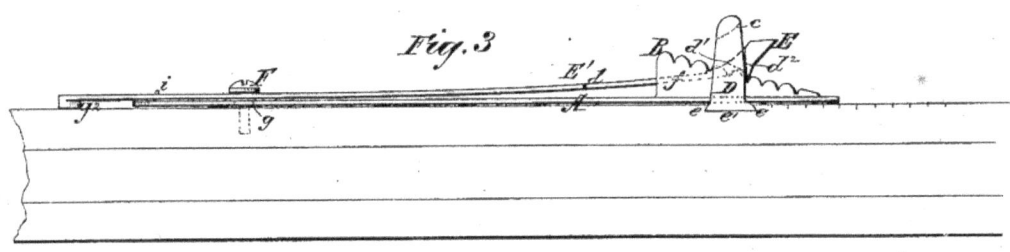

Fig. 4   Fig. 5   Fig. 6
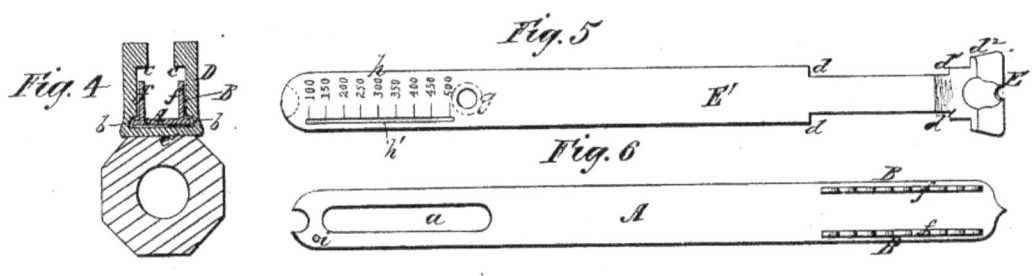

Witnesses.

Inventor:
Frank W. Freund.
by
Mason Fenwick & Lawrence
Attys.

THE GRAPHIC CO. PHOTO-LITH. 39 & 41 PARK PLACE, N.Y.

UNITED STATES PATENT OFFICE.

FRANK W. FREUND, OF DENVER, COLORADO TERRITORY.

IMPROVEMENT IN SIGHTS FOR FIRE-ARMS.

Specification forming part of Letters Patent No. **160,819**, dated March 16, 1875; application filed October 19, 1874.

To all whom it may concern:

Be it known that I, FRANK W. FREUND, of Denver, county of Arapahoe and Territory of Colorado, have invented a new and useful Improvement in Sights for Fire-Arms; and I do hereby declare that the following is a full, clear, and exact description thereof, reference being had to the accompanying drawing, making part of this specification, in which—

Figure 1 is a top view of my improved sight as applied to a rifle. Fig. 2 is a longitudinal section of the same. Fig. 3 is a side view. Fig. 4 is a cross-section in the line $x\ x$ of Fig. 3, the sight being removed. Figs. 5 and 6 are details of the sight.

My invention relates to certain improvements in adjustable sights; and the object of my improvements is to prevent casual change in the sight after it has been adjusted, hold the parts firmly together, and insure and facilitate accurate and nice adjustments.

A, in the accompanying drawings, is a broad tail attached to the stepped sight-support B. This tail is formed with a slot, a, between its rear end and the stepped support. The notches of the stepped support are very nearly of the shape of the letter V, and the partitions between the notches are rounded off at top. D is a guide, with grooves $b\ b$ on its inner edge just above the upper surface of its base, and with beveled shoulders $c\ c$ extending inward from its uprights a short distance. E is the sight, made with a long spring-tail, E', which is reduced in width between the sight and its rear end, so as to form shoulders $d\ d^1\ d^2$.

The parts described are united together and applied to the barrel as follows: The guide has the front and rear edges of its base portion beveled off, as at $e\ e$, so as to form a dovetail, and transversely through the upper part of the barrel an open dovetailed groove or channel, e, is cut, and into this dovetailed groove the guide is inserted, as shown.

The stepped sight-support, which is constructed with two inclined stepped side pieces, $f\ f$, into the upper edge of which the V-notches with rounded partitions are formed, is passed with its tail longitudinally through the guide D, so as to fit in the groove $b\ b$, and rest upon the top of the barrel. The tail of the sight is then passed through the guide, and between the stepped side pieces, over the tail of the support far enough to bring its shoulders d^2 up to the front of the uprights of the guide. The sight and sight-support being thus adjusted, a screw, F, (which may be a set or thumb screw,) is inserted through the thickened portion g of the tail of the sight, and passed down through the slot in the tail of the stepped support into a socket, g^1, in the barrel. With the parts thus connected the stepped support can be moved longitudinally through the guide, for the purpose of raising or lowering the sight from step to step, by simply lifting the spring-sight and pulling the stepped support in or outward, according to the adjustment required.

The tail of the sight is formed with the projecting offsets $g\ g^2$ on its under side, to prevent its bearing on the spring beneath it. The offset g passes through the slot and bears upon the nut-block g^1, and the offset g^2 bears upon the barrel. These offsets or projections are deep enough to hold the tail of the sight in relief from the tail of the stepped support.

The upper shoulders of the side grooves $b\ b$ prevent the sight-support from rising when the support is moved longitudinally through the guide D, and the guide and screw F prevent the support from moving laterally or shifting in any manner. The shoulders $c\ c$ prevent the sight from being raised too high and from being strained or injured, and the screw F, guide, and the side stepped supports keep it from casual displacement, after being set as desired.

In order to assist the user of the arm in adjusting the sight, a scale, h, may be marked on it, and a long slot, h', cut through it, for a small pointer, i, of the tail of the support to pass through, as shown in the drawings. Or, instead of this, the stepped support may have at its front end a central pointer, and a scale with alphabetical letters or characters, or marks expressive of certain adjustments, understood by the marksman, may be placed upon the barrel or on a plate attached thereto. Or both these plans may be provided and used in conjunction with one another, as judgment dictates or circumstances require. The scale may be placed on the edge of one of the tails, and the pointer on the other.

The great objection to the stepped spring-sights now in use lies in the liability of their being displaced or casually moved under a shock or jar, and, as a movement in even the slightest degree destroys the utility of the sight, all movement must be prevented.

Another objection is the falling off and losing of the sight-support, there being nothing to hold it in its position but the spring of the sight, and this is not sufficient for that purpose; and another objection is that the notches or steps are flat, and, being in the center, cannot be raised high enough for longer distances, or on an ascending and descending scale of incline planes the sight is easily displaced; the ordinary recoil from firing, or ordinary handling, or a fall or a jerk, displaces it. These objections I have overcome by shaping the notches of the step-support to hold in two directions, providing the stepped support with a long tail, and fitting its edges into the groove of the guide, and, in connection therewith, making the step with a long spring-tail, and fitting the sight under shoulders of the guide, and fastening the tails of the sight and support together and to the barrel in such a manner that the sight and support cannot casually move upon one another, and yet the support can be moved, when it is necessary to raise or lower the sight, to any extent desired.

The shoulders $c\ c$ may be formed by simply inserting pins through the uprights of the guide, and the stop-notches may have one straight and one beveled side, or they may be rectangular; or they might be formed by inserting pins at a proper distance apart into the upper edges of the inclined side supports.

The stepped support may be formed of one stepped piece passed through a slot in the spring-tail of the sight; but I prefer to have it made of two pieces, as by that construction the support is out of range of the sight, and thus can be raised to any desirable height, and when lowered for shorter range it is not in the way of a perfect range with the front sight, as would be the case on other sights now in use.

In operating the stepped support for adjusting the sight, the shoulders d^2 give a bearing to the sight upon the front of the uprights of the guide, while the projecting metal forward of the shoulders d^1 bear laterally against the inner sides of these uprights, and thus as it is being adjusted, and after it has been adjusted, is kept firm and true in position.

What I claim as my invention is—

1. The sight for a fire-arm, having a spring-tail, in combination with a stepped support having a tail, and with a guide, the sight and support being united together by a suitable fastening, F, and the supports being constructed and arranged to move in and out under the sight, and in its movement caused to adjust the sight to a higher or lower position with respect to the top of the barrel, substantially as and for the purpose described.

2. The guide D, constructed with stop-shoulders at b for the sliding stepped support, and with stop projections at c for the spring-sight, substantially in the manner and for the purpose described.

3. The spring-tail of the sight, constructed with the offsets $g\ g^2$, in combination with the slotted tail of the stepped supports, substantially in the manner described.

4. The tail E' of sight E, having an index thereon, and slotted at h', in combination with the indicator i on tail A of support B, substantially as and for the purpose described.

5. The gun-sight arranged to rise and fall in a guide which has stops $c\ c$, and constructed with a holding-tooth on its under side, in combination with a stepped support, the notches in which prevent the slide from moving back or forward unless the sight is raised high enough to clear the tooth from the highest parts of the partitions forming the notches, as and for the purpose herein described.

FRANK W. FREUND.

Witnesses:
F. M. DANIELSON,
GEO. M. HOWE.

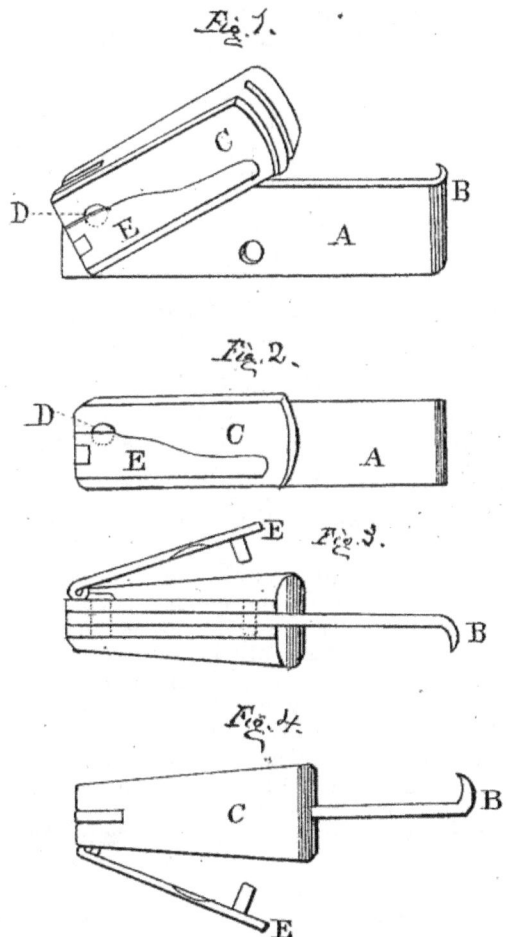

UNITED STATES PATENT OFFICE.

GEORGE BURT, OF DENVER, COLORADO TERRITORY.

IMPROVEMENT IN DOOR-CHECKS.

Specification forming part of Letters Patent No. **162,217**, dated April 20, 1875; application filed March 13, 1875.

To all whom it may concern:

Be it known that I, GEORGE BURT, of Denver, in the county of Arapahoe, in the Territory of Colorado, have invented certain Improvements in Door-Fasteners, of which the following is a specification:

The object of my invention is to securely fasten chamber or other doors upon the inside by attaching the pocket door-fastener herein described, and which is made of brass or other metal, to the jamb and edge of the door; and it consists in a novel construction and arrangement of parts, as will be hereinafter more fully described, and then pointed out in the claim.

Figure 1 is a plan view, showing the hook-end plate partly out of the jaws; and Figs. 2, 3, and 4 are detail views in various positions.

In the accompanying drawing, A represents a plate, terminating at one end in the curved hook B. This plate works upon the rivet D in the slitted jaw C. This jaw is made so as to present a surface or shoulder broad enough to catch and hold the door upon either side. Attached to it is a hinged bolt, E, opening outward, but which, when closed, goes through an orifice in the jaw and in the plate, so as to fasten the plate securely in its place, which, as will be seen, is especially necessary when placed upon a door opening from right to left, the jaw not then being retained in its place by its own weight, and makes it more firm and secure when placed upon a door opening from left to right.

I claim as my invention—

The hinged bolt E, in combination with and passing through the jaw C and the plate A, which plate works upon the rivet D, and terminates in a curved hook, B, all substantially as described and shown, for the purposes hereinbefore set forth.

GEORGE BURT.

Witnesses:
JAS. C. WHITALL,
SAM S. LANDON.

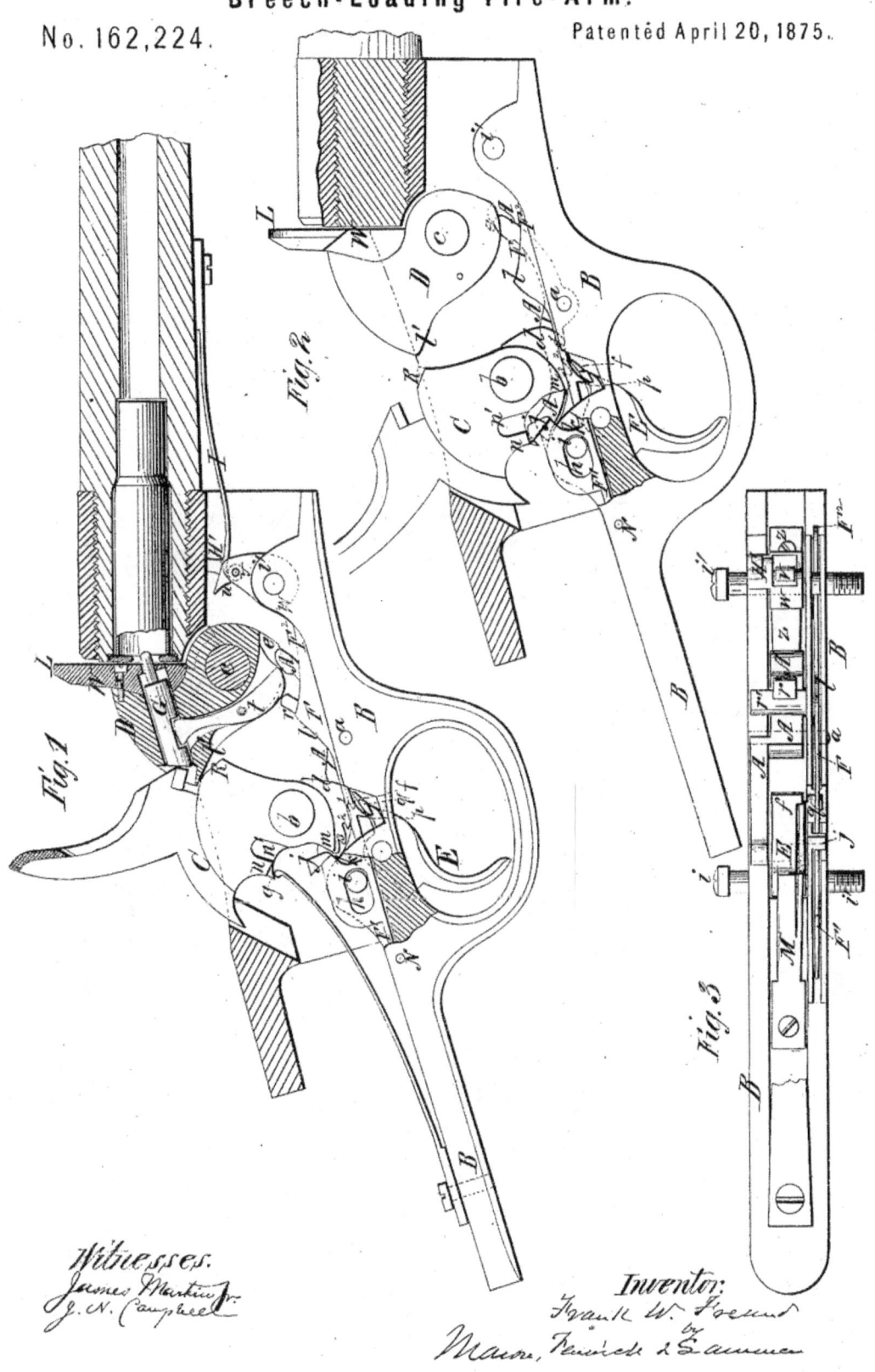

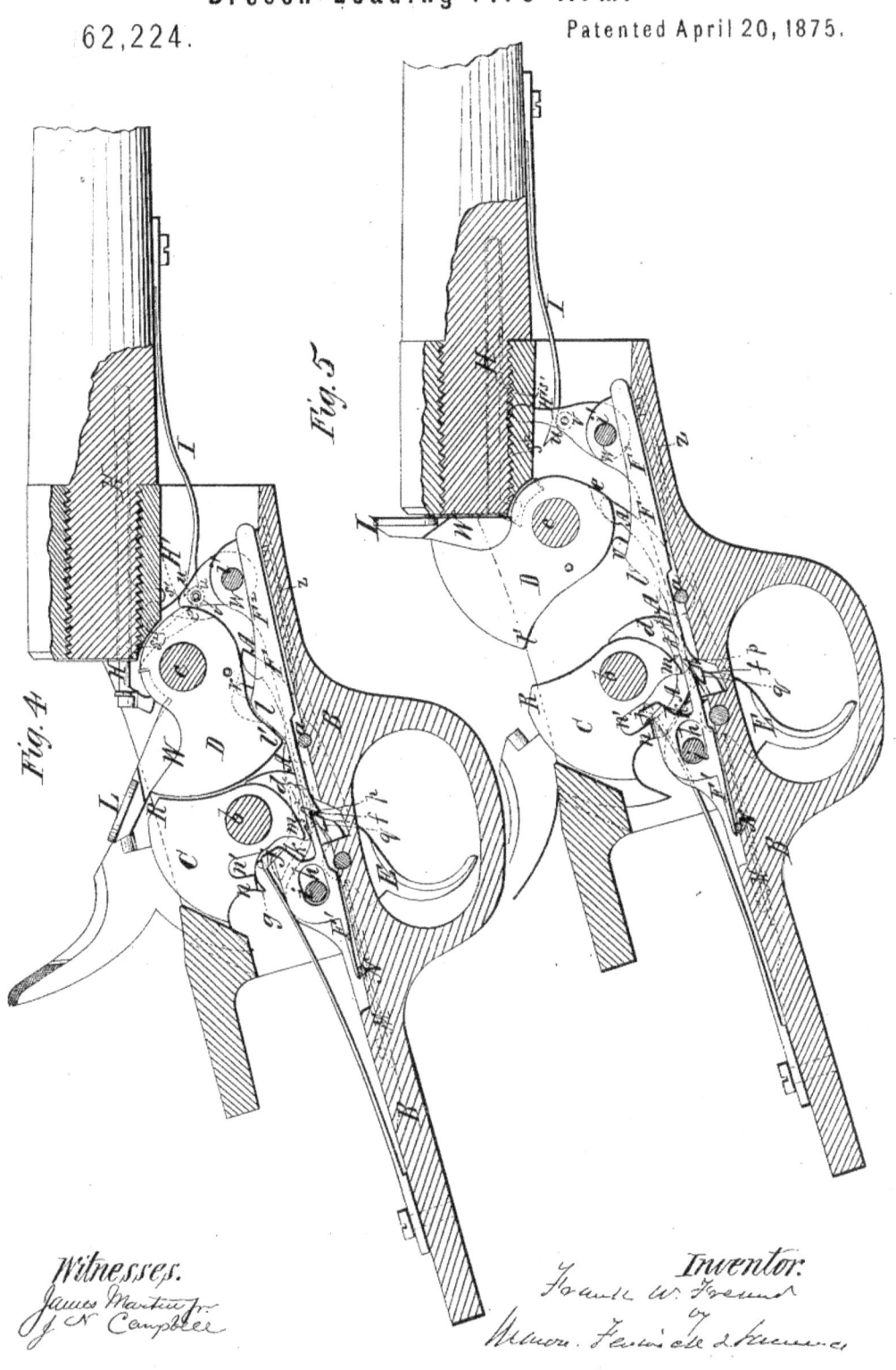

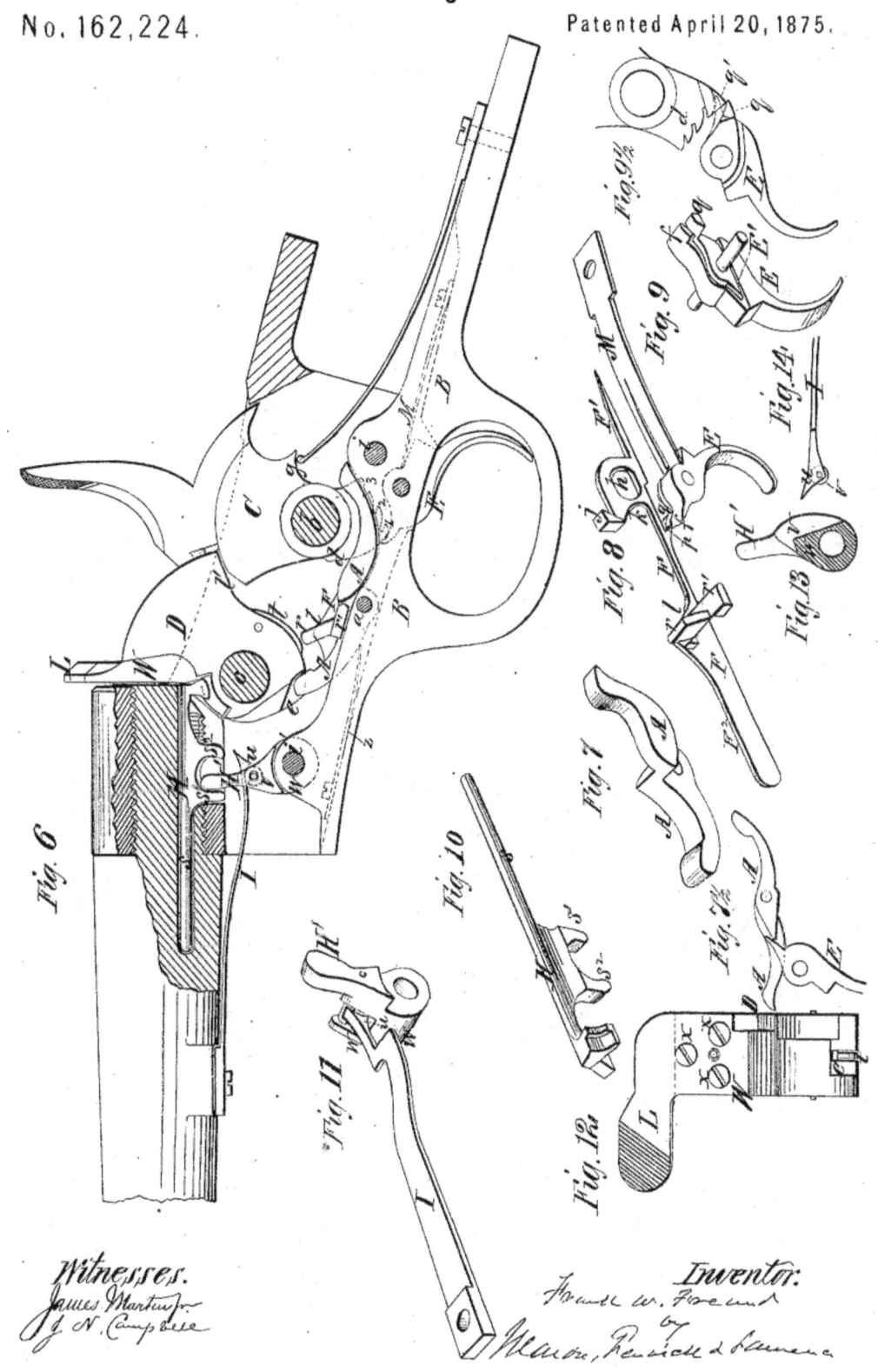

UNITED STATES PATENT OFFICE.

FRANK W. FREUND, OF DENVER, COLORADO TERRITORY.

IMPROVEMENT IN BREECH-LOADING FIRE-ARMS.

Specification forming part of Letters Patent No. **162,224**, dated April 20, 1875; application filed March 19, 1875.

CASE D.

To all whom it may concern:

Be it known that I, FRANK W. FREUND, of Denver, county of Arapahoe and Territory of Colorado, have invented an Improvement in Breech-Loading Fire-Arms; and I do hereby declare that the following is a full, clear, and exact description thereof, reference being had to the accompanying drawings making part of this specification, in which—

Figure 1 is a longitudinal view of the gun, partly in elevation and partly in section, as it appears just after being fired. Fig. 2 is a similar view of a portion of the gun as it appears when the hammer is cocked on the second notch, and before the breech has been opened and the empty shell extracted. Fig. 3 is a top view of the trigger-plate and its attachments. Fig. 4 is a longitudinal section of the gun as it appears when cocked on the second notch and when the breech-block has been opened and the empty cartridge-shell extracted. Fig. 5 is a similar section of the gun as it appears after it has been recharged, breech fully closed, and the hammer cocked on the third notch. Fig. 6 is a longitudinal view of the gun, partly in section and partly in elevation, the parts being in the same position as in Fig. 1, but viewed from the opposite side. Fig. 7 is a perspective view of the lever which fastens the breech block. Fig. 7½ shows a modification of the lever shown in Fig. 7, and which locks and controls the hammer. By this modification the trigger, as well as the breech-block and hammer, is controlled by said lever—that is, the trigger is locked against casual displacement. Fig. 8 is a perspective view of the slide carrying the hammer-check and firing-pin holder, and also of the slide-sear, trigger-sear, and forked sear-spring. Fig. 9 is a perspective view of the trigger and its sear, and of the slide-sear, showing clearly how the latter is hung independently on the trigger-pin and lies upon a shoulder of the trigger below said pin, and is operated by the trigger-sear as soon as it is released from the notches of the hammer-tumbler. Fig. 9½ shows a modification of the trigger, auxiliary sear, and tumbler of the hammer. By this modification the auxiliary sear q is unlocked by the projection q' of the tumbler d after the hammer has passed from the trigger beyond the first notch, No. 1, instead of by the trigger. Fig. 10 is a perspective view of the extractor. Fig. 11 is a perspective view of the lever, its hub, and the spring for operating the extractor. Fig. 12 is a front face view of the breech-block. Figs. 13 and 14 show a modification of the lever and its hub and spring for operating the extractor.

The object of my invention is: First, to provide for loading the gun while the hammer is held in a partly cocked and loading position without a possibility of its being fully cocked until the breech-block has been opened to admit the charge and again closed; second, to move and hold the firing-pin out of contact with the cartridge when the cartridge is in the chamber and the breech-block fully closed, and during the operation of closing the breech-block against the cartridge, and also during the operation of full-cocking the hammer and only to release the firing-pin when the trigger is pulled for firing the charge, and the hammer entirely free from the trigger; third, to permit the hammer to be lowered to the second or first notch without releasing the firing-pin, and also to permit the hammer to be full-cocked after it has been thus lowered, without releasing the firing-pin; fourth, another object is to modify and improve the mechanism employed for fastening the breech-block and preventing casual displacement thereof while the hammer is on the full-cock; fifth, to simplify the mechanism employed for holding the hammer when partly cocked; sixth, to make the rear end of the lever, which fastens the breech-block against casual displacement, act as a check against the full-cocking of the hammer in cases where the breech-block is left partly open; seventh, to effect a simultaneous movement of the slide which has the hammer-check connected to it, and of the shell-extractor, at the moment that the breech-block has been fully opened; eighth, to readjust the safety-checking mechanism at the last part of the movement of the hammer toward the firing-pin, or fulminate, and also by the same motion and at the same stage of the movement release the firing-pin; ninth, to improve cartridge-extractors so that they may be operated by percussive blows, both in their inward and outward movement; and, further, to lessen the expense of manufacturing and applying these extractors.

In the accompanying drawings, A represents a vertically-vibrating lever pivoted to the trigger-plate at a. One arm of this lever occupies a position within the channel of the trigger plate B and the other arm a position over one of the sides of said plate. This lever is curved, and its rear arm is on a higher plane than its front arm. The rear arm terminates in rear of the pin b of the hammer C, and the front arm a little in rear of the axis c of the breech-block D, and rests upon a flat spring, Z, attached to the trigger-plate. The rear arm is seated in a curved recess cut in one edge of the trigger-plate, and the front arm occupies a position in the channel of said trigger-plate. The pivot of the lever is supported by the side pieces of the trigger-plate. This construction of the lever affords room in rear of its pivot for the hammer-tumbler and other mechanism to be applied and operated in, and also prevents straining of the pivot of the lever when the hammer has been moved up as far as it is intended it shall be moved. d is a tumbler provided on the hammer, said tumbler having three cocking-notches, 1 2 3, two of which are safe. e is a socket formed on the under side of the breech-block. The hammer is chamfered off very slightly at the point R, so as to wedge very slightly upon the breech-block as it passes the hammer and breech-block. This is done in order to prevent hanging of the hammer upon the breech-block when the breech-block is slightly open, and to insure a perfect closing of the breech-block by the hammer as it is falling to fire the charge. The hammer is so shaped that the latter can be swung open past the former when the sear f of the trigger E is in notch 2 of the tumbler d. g is a shoulder formed on the hammer C for preventing the lever A from ceasing its hold upon the breech-block when the breech is closed and the hammer full-cocked, and the sear of the trigger is in notch No. 3. This shoulder comes against the rear end of the lever A when the hammer is full-cocked, and prevents a casual release of the breech-block. When the hammer is cocked on notch No. 1 or No. 2, or when it is bearing against the firing-pin, there is room for the rear end of the lever to move up and down in between the shoulder g and the trigger-plate B, as is plainly shown in Fig. 6. The curved rear side of the breech-block is so formed that the forward end of the lever A is depressed, and the rear end thrown up, by the act of opening the breech-block for charging the gun, and owing to this it is impossible to cock the hammer on notch No. 3 before the breech-block is again closed. F is a slide for preventing the hammer being fully cocked after the charge has been fired, and before a new charge has been put into the chamber, and thus avoiding accidental discharges during the charging operation. This slide is placed in a groove on the other side of the trigger-plate, and along the main portion of its length between its ends it is supported by the trigger plate or frame. A rear-spring extension, F^1, and a front tapering tail, F^2, are formed on it. It is held in place by a pin, i, passed through a slot, h, cut horizontally through it.

The rear end F^1 of the slide rests with a spring action upon a pin, N, and the forward end is passed under another pin, i'. The spring portion F^1 bearing down on pin N keeps the slide from moving casually after it is thrown back, and the tapering portion bearing against the pin i' effects the same result when the slide is thrown forward. Upon the slide near its rear end a check, j, and a hooking-offset, k, are constructed, and forward of these an inclined elevated projection, l, is formed on the upper edge of the slide. m is a hooking-tail on the hammer C, corresponding to the hooking-offset k. n' is a slot, and n a check, formed in and on the hammer. The check n corresponds with the check j in form, and the slot n' is of a form to admit the check j into it. The rear of the breech-block is curved or made with a slight concave, as at l', near its top. By providing the slide F, and constructing it and the parts just mentioned as described and shown, the hammer will, in falling to discharge the gun, quickly throw the slide backward by means of its tail m coming against the offset k, and thereby bring the check j in such a position with respect to the check n, as shown in Figs. 1 and 2, that it will prevent the hammer being full-cocked before the breech-block has been fully opened, and while the breech-block is being opened for recharging the gun the curved rear side l' of the breech-block takes hold of the projection l of the slide and forces the slide forward, and thereby brings the check j in such a position with respect to the slot n' that the said check will enter the slot n' when the hammer is moved for the purpose of full-cocking it, and thus all interference with full-cocking the hammer is withdrawn, when the arm is loaded and the breech-block closed; but not until this has been effected, and all is safe, does this occur. p is a stop-notch on the slide F, and q a slide-sear on the trigger E, for preventing the firing-pin G moving to a firing position while charging the gun, and while the breech-block is either partly or fully closed, and while carrying the gun loaded with the hammer either partly or full cocked.

It will be seen that the trigger is formed with a side projection or depressed shoulder, E', below its pivot, and that the slide-sear is hung over this shoulder, so that when the trigger is pulled and the hammer-sear freed the shoulder will lift the rear end of the slide, and thereby free its front end from the notch of the slide. The hammer-sear and slide-sear are both controlled by the one sear-spring M, which is forked, and its prongs made relatively weak and strong, the hammer-prong being strong and the slide-prong being weak, according to the work to be done by these respective prongs.

A projection, r, is provided on the slide for bearing against the lower end of the firing-pin lever t, and thereby preventing said lever from moving after it has withdrawn or forced back the firing-pin. This projection r can only move away from the lever t after the slide is forced back by the hook m of the hammer taking hold of the hooking-offset k, and this can only take place after the trigger has been pulled far enough to disengage the sear f from the notch 3 or the notches 1 and 2 of the hammer-tumbler, and the sear q from the notch p. The projection r' is sustained by resting on the sides of the trigger-plate.

It will be understood from Fig. 9 that the hammer-sear and the slide-sear are independent of each other when the hammer is being cocked, but combined in their movement when the trigger is pulled for firing the gun. The one spring, M, by being forked, acts against both sears, and yet permits either sear to operate independently, as occasion requires. The slide is readjusted in gear with the sear q, after the hammer is partly cocked, by the breech-block being opened and caused to strike the projection l, and thereby move the slide forward; such forward movement, as before stated, also moves the check j to the position shown in Figs. 4 and 5. Thus a two-fold object is obtained by this single slide and its connections.

The extractor H is very similar to the one heretofore patented by myself, so far as arrangement goes; but in this instance it is made with a round stem, s, which is fitted in a circular passage, formed either between the barrel and frame or in the frame itself.

This construction enables me to turn the stem in a lathe, and to channel or bore out the passage for its reception with boring and channeling tools of a lathe, and at very slight expense comparatively; and in order to use such stem, and not have it turn in its seat, flat-sided lugs s^1 s^2 are formed on the extractor in rear of the stem, which is dovetailed or made concave on its upper side, as shown, and the lugs are on a central offset, and the extractor is fixed in its position by inserting this offset in the barrel or frame in a corresponding dovetail. For moving the extractor a lever, H', and spring I are employed. The lever H' is pivoted to the trigger-plate B by the pin i', and the spring I is attached to the barrel of the gun. This lever extends up between the lugs s^1 s^2, and plays freely back and forth between these lugs. The spring has a beveled or V-shaped projection, u, on the under side of its free end, which moves upon a friction-roller, V, or upon a projection without a roller, set or formed in an eccentric hub, W, of the lever. Instead of the roller V being on the pin, it may be attached to the spring and roll over an incline of the hub, as shown in Figs. 13 and 14.

Under this construction, when the breech-block is opened the extractor will be drawn out a certain distance, and the V-shaped projection u of the spring will then suddenly fall behind the roller or projection of the hub of the lever, and give it a sudden blow, which will cause the lever to fly backward and give a percussive blow against the rear lug s^2, and thereby cause the extractor to completely expel the empty shell from the chamber with great power and rapidity. This construction of the extractor is very free from friction, cheap, durable, and convenient, and it avoids the use of extra pins and holes for fastening it in place, and it cannot fall out when the breech-block is opened, and this is the case even when the spring and lever are removed or broken. For avoiding difficulty and expense, experienced in attaching the thumb-piece L to the breech-block, a face-plate, W, corresponding to the front face of the ordinary extracting breech-block, is provided, and on this plate the thumb-piece L is forged, as shown in Fig. 12. This plate, with thumb-piece, is fastened to the breech-block by means of screws x x.

In practice, I make the plate of iron, and case-harden the same, and with a gradually-increased thickness from top to bottom, and curved at its back, so that the pressure of the exploded charge shall not be exerted against the screws alone, but against the breech-block in an oblique direction, and also that sharp angles or corners, which are liable to break out, being determined lines of fracture, shall be avoided.

The operation is as follows: Suppose the gun loaded and full-cocked, as in Fig. 5. Pull the trigger, so as to release the hammer-sear f and the slide-sear g, as in Fig. 1. The descent of the hammer forces and moves the check j directly in the path of the check n, and also releases the firing-pin. The raising of the hammer for reloading is arrested on the second notch by the check j, as shown in Fig. 2, and the opening of the breech fully starts the extractor, whereupon the empty cartridge-shell is expelled by a sudden percussive blow of the lever upon the lug s^1, caused by the V part of the spring I falling down forward of the eccentric hub and reacting against it, and at the same moment the projection l of the slide is struck by the part l' of the breech-block, and the check j is moved in the path of the slot n', and the sear of the slide interlocked with the notch p of said slide, and the projection r is brought in position for fastening the firing-pin out of position while the breech-block is closed, and when closed, and until the hammer is set free to fire the arm and passes beyond the first notch. The closing of the breech after a cartridge is introduced into the chamber causes the lever A to fall into the socket e.

The full-cocking of the hammer causes the shoulder-stop g of the hammer to fasten the lever A against the breech-block, so that the breech-block cannot be casually or otherwise opened or moved until the hammer is allowed to descend against the firing-pin, or to the second or first notch of the tumbler. The lowering of the hammer to the second notch or first notch does not change the position of the check j, but it releases the breech-block from the positive hold of the lever A. The firing of the gun on full-cock readjusts the check j, and releases the firing-pin from the projection r, said projection and its slide being forced back to the position shown in Fig. 1 by this movement, by the hammer-tail acting on the slide-offset k, in which position it is out of gear with the sear q. The recocking of the hammer on the second notch, and the opening and closing of the breech, readjust the parts to the position shown in Fig. 4, when the hammer can be full-cocked on the third notch, as shown in Fig. 5. The slide E is kept from any casual change in either of its extreme positions by pressing with its spring-extension F', on its rear end, against its pin or support N, and by wedging slightly with its tapering front end E^2 under the pin i', as illustrated in the drawings. The rear arm of the lever A is arrested and supported in its downward movement by the trigger-plate B, and thus the pin on which it turns cannot be strained to too great a degree.

By my invention a gun is made which can be safely carried while loaded, and such gun can be safely loaded without any possibility of its being brought to a full-cock while being loaded.

What I claim is—

1. The check j of the slide or part F, in combination with the hammer, for the purpose of preventing the full-cocking of the hammer, substantially as and for the purpose described.

2. The projection k of the slide or part F, in combination with the hammer, having a projection, m, for moving the slide back, substantially as and for the purpose described.

3. The projection l of the slide or part F, in combination with the breech-block, for the purpose of moving the slide forward to set the check, or to withdraw the firing-pin when the breech is open, substantially as and for the purpose described.

4. The sear-notch p of the slide or part F, in combination with the auxiliary sear q, and the hammer-trigger, substantially as described.

5. The combination of the projections l and k of the slide or part F, with the breech-block and hammer, for the purpose of moving the slide forward and backward, substantially as described.

6. The stop r of the slide or part F, suitably combined with the firing-pin, for preventing the firing-pin moving forward when the breech-block is fully closed, and while the part F is locked, substantially as described.

7. The lever A, in combination with the hammer, for fastening the breech-block when the hammer is full-cocked, substantially as described.

8. The combination of the lever A and the breech-block, for preventing the full-cocking of the hammer while the breech-block is open, or only partly closed, substantially as described.

9. The firing-pin, combined with and operated by the hammer and breech-block, and suitable means for withdrawing said pin, so that it is retracted when the breech-block is in any position in which the firing-pin might be brought in contact with the cartridge, and when the hammer is in any position except in contact with the firing-pin, substantially as described.

10. The combination of a hammer, a breech-block, a movable intermediate part, F, having suitable projections, and a lever, A, whereby the hammer is prevented from being cocked when the breech-block is open, and the breech-block prevented from being opened when the hammer is cocked, substantially as herein described.

11. A vibrating lever, H', combined with a cartridge-shell extractor, having separated lugs or shoulders s^1 s^2, for producing a sudden percussive blow upon the extractor, substantially as described.

Witnesses: FRANK. WM. FREUND.
J. N. CAMPBELL,
J. W. HAMILTON JOHNSON.

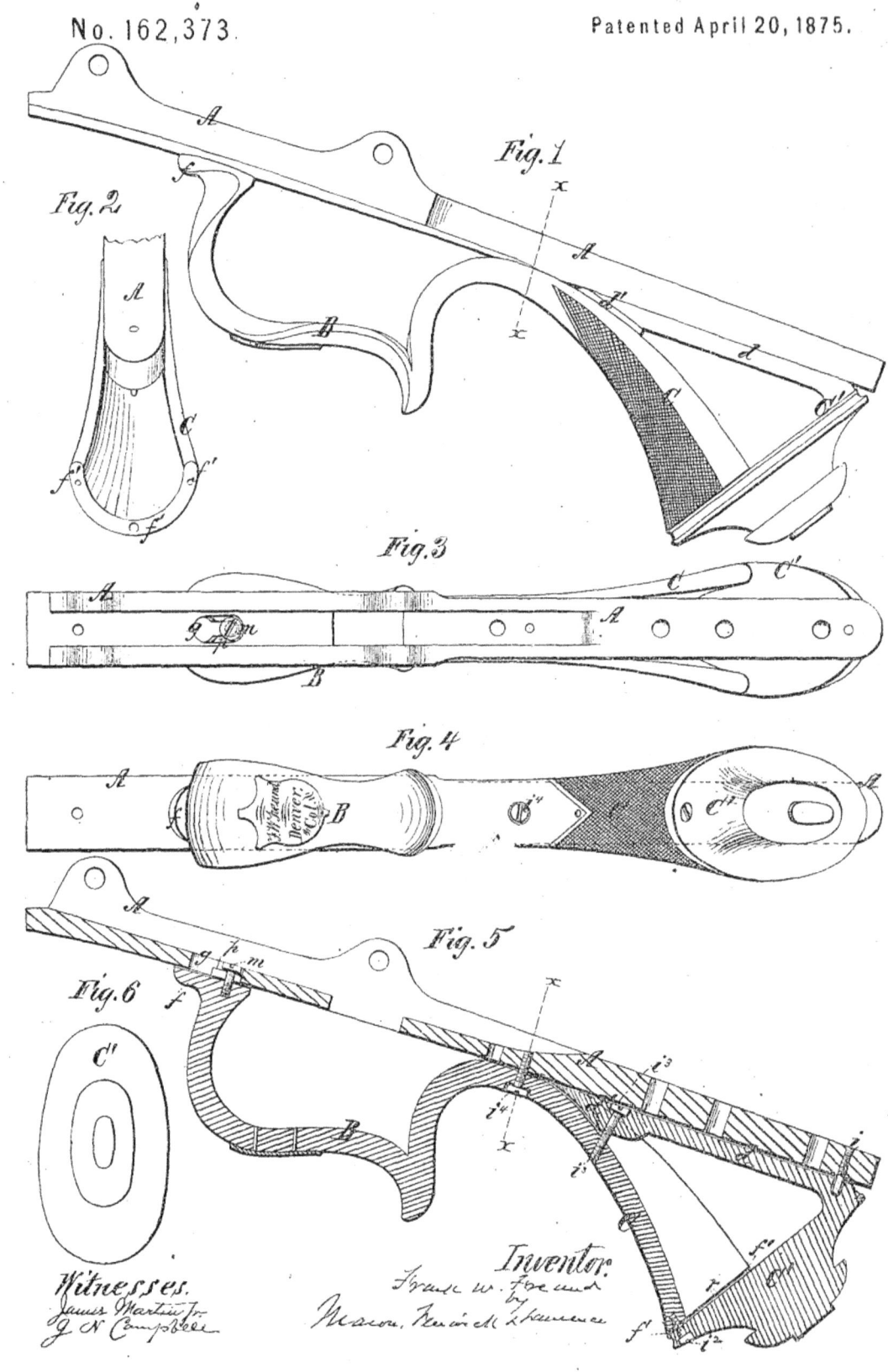

UNITED STATES PATENT OFFICE.

FRANK W. FREUND, OF DENVER, COLORADO TERRITORY.

IMPROVEMENT IN PISTOL-GRIP ATTACHMENTS FOR THE STOCKS OF FIRE-ARMS.

Specification forming part of Letters Patent No. 162,373, dated April 20, 1875; application filed March 19, 1875.

CASE B.

To all whom it may concern:

Be it known that I, FRANK W. FREUND, of Denver, county of Arapahoe and Territory of Colorado, have invented a new and useful Pistol-Grip and Trigger-Guard for Fire-Arms; and I do hereby declare that the following is a full, clear, and exact description thereof, reference being had to the accompanying drawings making part of this specification, in which—

Figure 1 is a side elevation of my combined pistol-gripe and trigger-guard; Fig. 2, a rear-end view of the lower and inner shell portion of the pistol-grip, and the rear end of the trigger-plate, with the butt of the pistol-grip removed; Fig. 3, a plan view, showing the perforations in the trigger-plate by means of which said plate can be attached to a gun, and also the button-slot through the plate, for affixing the forward end of the trigger-guard to said plate; Fig. 4, a plan view of the under side of the pistol-grip and trigger-guard; Fig. 5, a longitudinal central section; Fig. 6, a plan view of the rear end.

My invention has for its object the construction of a combined "pistol-grip" and trigger-guard, which, in connection with the trigger-plate of a fire-arm, can be readily applied to the ordinary guns now in use.

In the drawings, I have shown a trigger-plate as ordinarily applied to what is known as the "Remington," as well as other guns, which plate is provided with perforations for the reception of screws necessary to confine said plate to the gun-stock, as well as to confine in place those portions of the lock which are usually attached to or held in place by the trigger-plate. These perforations may be somewhat differently arranged in some trigger-plates to which my invention may be applied, according to the character or construction of the lock of the gun, and as other circumstances may require.

In the figures, and as clearly shown in Figs. 1 and 5, will be seen a trigger-guard, B, having its front extremity commencing at f, and terminating at a suitable point, as shown by dots at $x\ x$, from which point the material composing the trigger-guard is extended down with increasing diameter, and in oval form, until the extremity $f'\ f'$ is reached, as shown, thus composing from about the line $x\ x$ to the terminating points $f'\ f'$ the lower portion C of my pistol-grip. This shell or hollowed-out portion C, as plainly indicated in Fig. 2, may be composed of or struck up from any suitable metal. In Fig. 5 I have shown, in section, that part of my pistol-grip, which constitutes the butt C', which butt is formed with an extended piece, d, to fit against the under side of the trigger-plate, as shown in Fig. 5, and be held in place against said plate by a screw-fastening, as at i, while the lower portion of the butt is secured to the shell C by the screw-fastening i^2, the forward end of the extension d being also secured to the shell C by a like fastening, as at i^3. This latter fastening i^3 is made through a thickened part, d', of the butt extension d, for the additional security of such fastening, which part d' is so tapered and formed as to seat itself in the shell C adjacent to the dotted line $x\ x$, as indicated in Figs. 1 and 5.

In my application for a patent for a new and useful guard-lever and pistol-grip for breech-loading fire-arms, filed in the United States Patent Office on an even date herewith, I have shown a guard-lever, a pistol-grip, and a trigger-guard made of one piece of metal—that is to say, the whole of the grip in rear of the trigger-guard, including the butt of the grip, as therein shown, is made of one continuous piece of metal or other proper material. By my present invention I facilitate the manufacture of my pistol-grip by making it in two main portions, as shown in Figs. 1 and 5, since in such case the shell or concave portion C admits of the ready insertion of tools for finishing the same after it is formed, and since also the butt portion C', with its extension d, can be more readily made of metal than would be the case if the whole were made together. Besides this, it adds greatly to the general effect and beauty of the whole, when that portion of the grip and the trigger-guard, as shown at C in Fig. 5, is made in metal, while that portion shown at C', Fig. 5, is constructed either of horn or ivory, or suitable material other than metal, which advantage cannot be secured when the whole is made entirely of metal.

Heretofore the forward end f of trigger-guards have had a screw projecting from the inner face of such end, which screwed into a screw-hole in the plate, in order to secure the guard and plate together at that point, or else a screw has been passed entirely through such end and into the plate. By my construction I cut a button-slot, as at g, through the plate, one portion thereof being circular, while another portion is elongated and contracted in diameter, and leaving on either side thereof a shoulder, as at p, so that the head of a screw may pass freely through the circular opening, after which the body of the screw may be drawn back in the contracted portion of the button-slot, with the head upon the shoulder p, as shown, and thus hold the screw and the part into which the screw projects securely in place. As shown in Fig. 5, m is a screw partly screwed down into the inner face of the forward end of the trigger-guard, after which it may be made to seat itself, as shown in said figure.

Having finished the part in metal of a portion of my pistol-grip in the form as shown in Fig. 5, and inserted the screw m therein, as shown, and having finished in horn, ivory, gutta-percha, or metal, as the case may be, another portion, C', of my pistol-grip, the two parts are then placed in juxtaposition with each other, as indicated in Fig. 5, by means of the screw-fastenings i^2 and i^3. This being done, the screw m is inserted into the slotted opening g, and is then drawn back until the head of the screw seats itself on the shoulder p, after which act the screws i and i^4 are properly inserted, thus fastening the pistol-grip and trigger-guard securely to the trigger-plate. A pin, r, which projects from the butt C', serves also to retain said butt in proper position.

I would also state that when the main portions of my invention are made in detached parts, as shown, the ornamental figures which constitute a part of the butt C' can be wrought with much greater facility, and at much less cost, than can be done when the whole is constructed of a single piece of metal or other material.

What I claim is—

1. A pistol-grip consisting of a hand portion and a separate butt portion, substantially as described.

2. A pistol-grip having the metallic part, as at C, struck up from thin or sheet metal, substantially as described.

3. A trigger-guard provided with an adjustable head or screw, m, in combination with a trigger-plate having a slot, g, and shoulder p, substantially as and for the purpose described.

FRANK WM. FREUND.

Witnesses:
J. N. CAMPBELL,
J. W. HAMILTON JOHNSON.

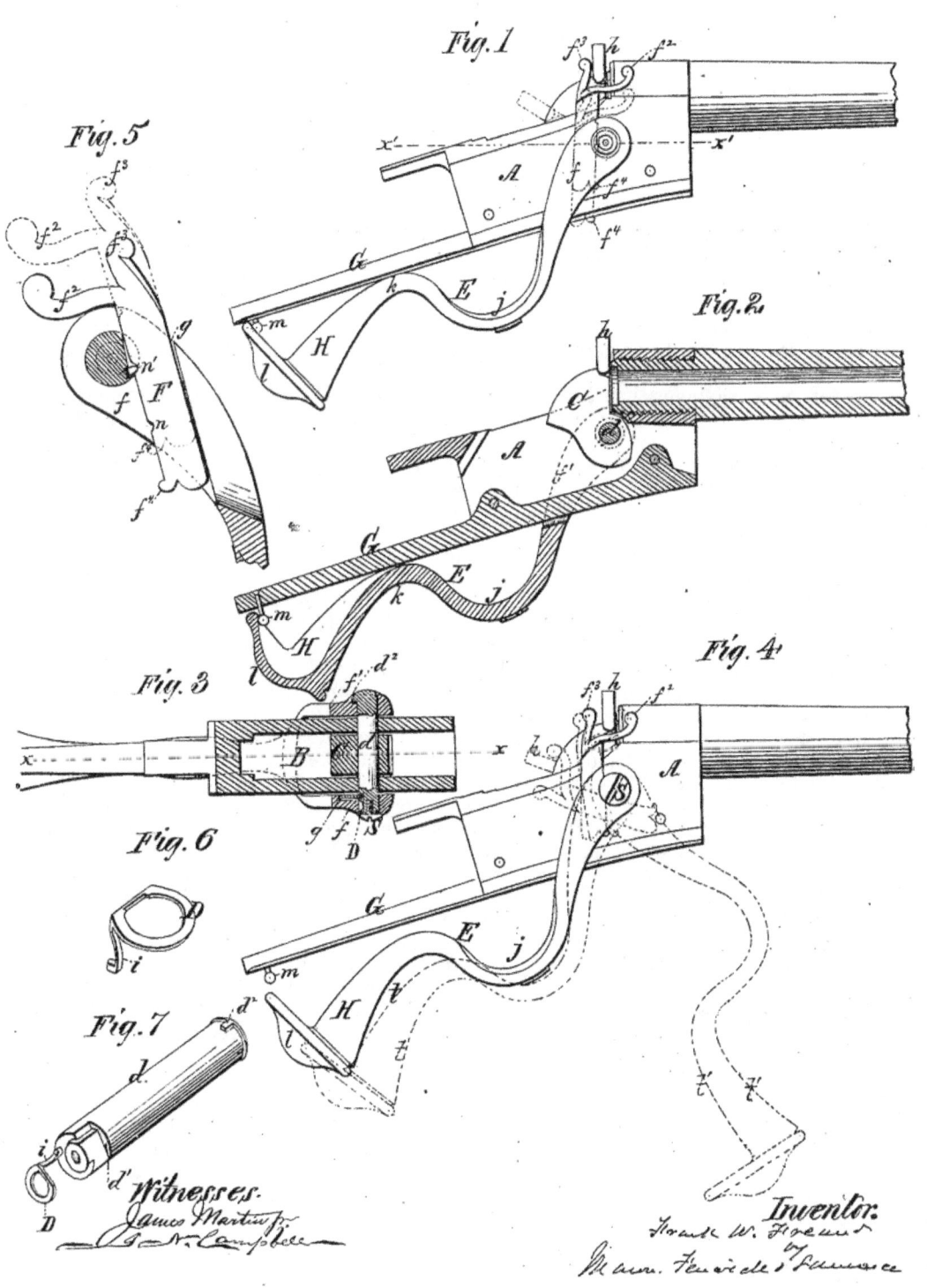

UNITED STATES PATENT OFFICE.

FRANK W. FREUND, OF DENVER, COLORADO TERRITORY.

IMPROVEMENT IN GUARD-LEVERS AND MEANS FOR OPERATING THE BREECH-BLOCK OF BREECH-LOADING FIRE-ARMS.

Specification forming part of Letters Patent No. **162,374**, dated April 20, 1875; application filed March 19, 1875.

CASE C.

To all whom it may concern:

Be it known that I, FRANK W. FREUND, of Denver, county of Arapahoe and Territory of Colorado, have invented a new and Improved Guard-Lever and Pistol-Grip, and a means for operating the breech-block of breech-loading fire-arms; and I do hereby declare that the following is a full, clear, and exact description thereof, reference being had to the accompanying drawings making a part of this specification, in which—

Figure 1 is a side elevation; Fig. 2, a longitudinal section in line $x\,x$ of Fig. 3; Fig. 3, a section on line $x'\,x'$ of Fig. 1; and Fig. 4, a side elevation, showing the movements of the guard-lever when used to open the breech of the gun. Figs. 5, 6, and 7 show parts of the gun in detail.

In this improvement, A is the frame which supports in position the several operating parts, and upon which they articulate. This frame is constructed with an opening or longitudinal slot, B, in which the breech-block C articulates upon a pin, d, which passes transversely through said frame and the breech-block C and prongs of the guard-lever E, as shown.

The main object of this invention is to afford the means whereby the breech-block may be operated, either separately or by the guard-lever, as may be desired. To effect this a slide, F, is attached between one of the forks of the forked guard-lever and the frame A, and in rear of the transverse pin d, on which pin the forward ends of the forks f and f^1 articulate during the movements of said guard-lever. This slide F is guided in its up-and-down movements by an open slot or groove, g, cut in the inner face of the prong f, into which slot the said slide is seated, as shown; and when properly seated in said slot the forward edge of the slide is made to travel against the pin d, which for such purpose is cut away, so as to form a shoulder, d^1, which shoulder, abutting against the inner face of the slide F, prevents the slide from frictional contact with the side of the frame A during the up-and-down movements of said slide.

By reference to Fig. 7 it will be seen that the pin d is provided near one end with a detent, d^2, projecting therefrom, as shown, which detent, when in place, seats itself into a corresponding slot cut in the prong f^1, so that when the pin is in working position the pin and guard-lever are made to articulate together simultaneously whenever the guard-lever is moved, and during which act the slide F is carried bodily forward or back in accord with the forward or back movement of the guard-lever.

The slide F is constructed of a single piece of metal, terminating at its upper end in projections somewhat in forked form, as at f^2 and f^3, one of which forked ends, f^2, occupies a position in front, and the other, f^3, in rear, of the thumb-piece h of the breech-block C, when it is desired to open or close the breech-block by the movement of the guard-lever. In other words, when the slide F is moved up, as in Fig. 1, so as to open the breech-block by the movement of the guard-lever, the projections f^2 and f^3 of the slide F will straddle the thumb-piece h, so that the movement of the guard-lever, carrying with it the slide, will cause the projections f^2 and f^3 to strike the thumb-piece h, and so open or close the breech-block, as the case may be.

It will be seen that when the breech-block is closed, and the guard-lever in position, as shown in Fig. 1, the projection f^3 impinges against the rear of the thumb-piece h, while the projection f^2 is some distance forward of, and out of contact with, the front face of the thumb-piece, which condition allows of the depression of the guard-lever for the purpose of half-cocking or full-cocking the gun (as may be desired, through proper mechanism connecting the lower guard with the gun-lock) before the projection f^2 shall strike the thumb-piece on the depression of the guard-lever.

In order to arrest an undue upward movement of the slide F, a slight projection, or other equivalent means, as at f^4, is made on the lower end of the slide, which projection strikes against a portion of the forked end f of the guard-lever, when the slide is elevated to a proper extent; and the downward movement of the slide is limited by a portion of the projection f^2, which overlaps and rests upon the forward part of the end f of the guard-lever when said slide is thrown down, as indicated in Fig. 1, so that its forked ends f^2 and f^3 do not straddle the thumb-piece h.

When the slide F is thrown down to its lowest extent and the guard-lever closed, the gun can then be cocked and the breech-block manipulated by the hand of the operator without any movement of the guard-lever and slide, during which act the lower edge of the thumb-piece h, in its movements, will be out of contact with every portion of the slide F. By reference to Figs. 6 and 7 it will be seen that the pin d has a metal spring-cap adapted to be seated upon its shouldered end. This spring-cap D is in D form, so that when the corresponding end of the pin is inserted into the cap, the latter will be prevented from turning on the pin, and both will then turn together to and fro by the movement of the guard lever. This cap has a small spring, i, projecting from its main portion, as shown in Figs. 6 and 7, so that when the slide F is placed in working position, the inner edge thereof will slightly press upon or force back the spring i. The slide, then, being elevated to a position to work the breech-block, this spring will seat itself into the notch n, thus retaining the slide in such elevated position; and when the slide is depressed to its lowest extent, the said spring will then seat itself in the notch n' of the slide, and thus in either case retain the slide in a desired position. The pin d having been inserted through the frame A, forks f and f^1, and breech-block C, all of these several parts, including the spring-cap on said pin, are secured in place by the screw S applied thereto, as shown.

In order to retain the slide F entirely out of contact with the frame A, this slide is dovetailed on its rear edge and made to travel in a corresponding groove (shown in Fig. 3) properly cut in the back of the open slot g.

The guard-lever E, it will be seen, is peculiarly constructed—first, in that it is made entirely of one piece; and, second, that it terminates, as at H, in the likeness of the "butt" of a pistol, in that portion which is grasped by one of the hands of the operator in the act of firing, thus affording a pistol-grip on this lever during such act.

It is made as clearly represented in Figs. 1, 2, and 3, having a bow form at j for the trigger-guard, and from the point k, at which the rear of the trigger-guard terminates, it is made of increased width and oval form in cross-section in the outline of a pistol-butt, as shown. Its extreme rear end l is formed like the rear end of pistols, which have such end in egg form in plan view. The guard-lever thus forms a pistol-gripe, H, in that portion which is in rear of the trigger-guard j, which rear portion may be hollowed out, so as, in fact, to form a partial shell rather than a solid portion of metal for such grip. The rear end of the trigger-blade G is provided with a pin-button, m, projecting therefrom, as shown, over which button the hollowed-out end l (see Fig. 2) of the pistol-grip may be sprung, so as to cause a portion of the button m to enter the cavity of the part l, and thus retain the parts in the position shown in said figure.

The operation is as follows: The gun having been fired off, the guard-lever, slide, and breech-block will then be in the position as shown in Fig. 1. To reload by the use of the guard-lever, such lever is then slightly depressed, as shown in full lines in Fig. 4, which act, through proper mechanical appliances in connection with such lever, will half-cock the gun. This act will cause the projection f^2 of the slide F to approach a certain distance toward the thumb-piece h. A still further depression of the guard-lever, as shown by dotted lines $t\,t$ in Fig. 4, is then made, thus causing the gun to be fully cocked and the projection f^2 to approach still nearer, but not touch, the thumb-piece h. A further and full depression of the guard-lever, as indicated by dotted lines $t'\,t'$ in said figure, will then cause the projection f^2 to throw open the breech-block to its full extent, and force out of the gun-barrel the cartridge which has been exploded, and allow a new cartridge to be inserted in its place. This being done the guard-lever is then brought back to its original position shown in Fig. 1, the projection f^3 during this movement coming in contact with the thumb-piece, and forcing the breech-block against the rear end of the gun-barrel, and thus completing the forcing home of the newly-inserted cartridge into the gun-barrel, after which the gun is fully ready to again be fired.

Under certain circumstances the operator may be in such a position that he cannot, or may not wish to, use the guard-lever and slide to prepare the gun for firing. In such case the slide F is shoved down out of contact with the thumb-piece h of the breech-block, and he can then cock the gun and manipulate the breech-block with his fingers alone without moving the guard-lever at all.

It is obvious that the distance between the projections f^2 and f^3 may be such as to operate the breech-block when the hammer is either half or full cocked, whether the guard-lever solely or the hand of the operator is used for opening the breech and cocking the hammer, as in my patent dated March 16, 1875; and, further, that the mechanical appliances for holding the hammer and breech-block in given positions, as shown in my application for a patent for improvement in breech-loading fire-arms filed in the Patent Office concurrent with this application may be applied in connection with this improvement when the arm is to be operated by either the hand or guard-lever; but under such construction, if the lever is connected with the thumb-piece, the hammer can only be moved to the half-cock by the lever, and must be fully cocked by hand.

It will be seen that by my construction and application of the slide F for effecting the movements of the breech-block, I leave such block, and also the breech-pin, solid, and thus utilize the full strength of these parts for resisting the explosion of a heavy charge of powder.

What I claim is—

1. The combination of a breech-block, an operating-lever, and an intermediate connecting device, the lever and connecting device being applied outside of the frame of the arm, substantially as described.

2. A guard-lever having its rear end constructed in the form of the lower part of a pistol-stock, substantially as described.

3. The slide F, constructed with the projections or arms $f^2 f^3$, with a play-space between, adapted to operate the breech-block, substantially as described.

4. The cap-spring D, in combination with the pin d and slide F, substantially as and for the purpose described.

FRANK WM. FREUND.

Witnesses:
J. N. CAMPBELL,
J. W. HAMILTON JOHNSON.

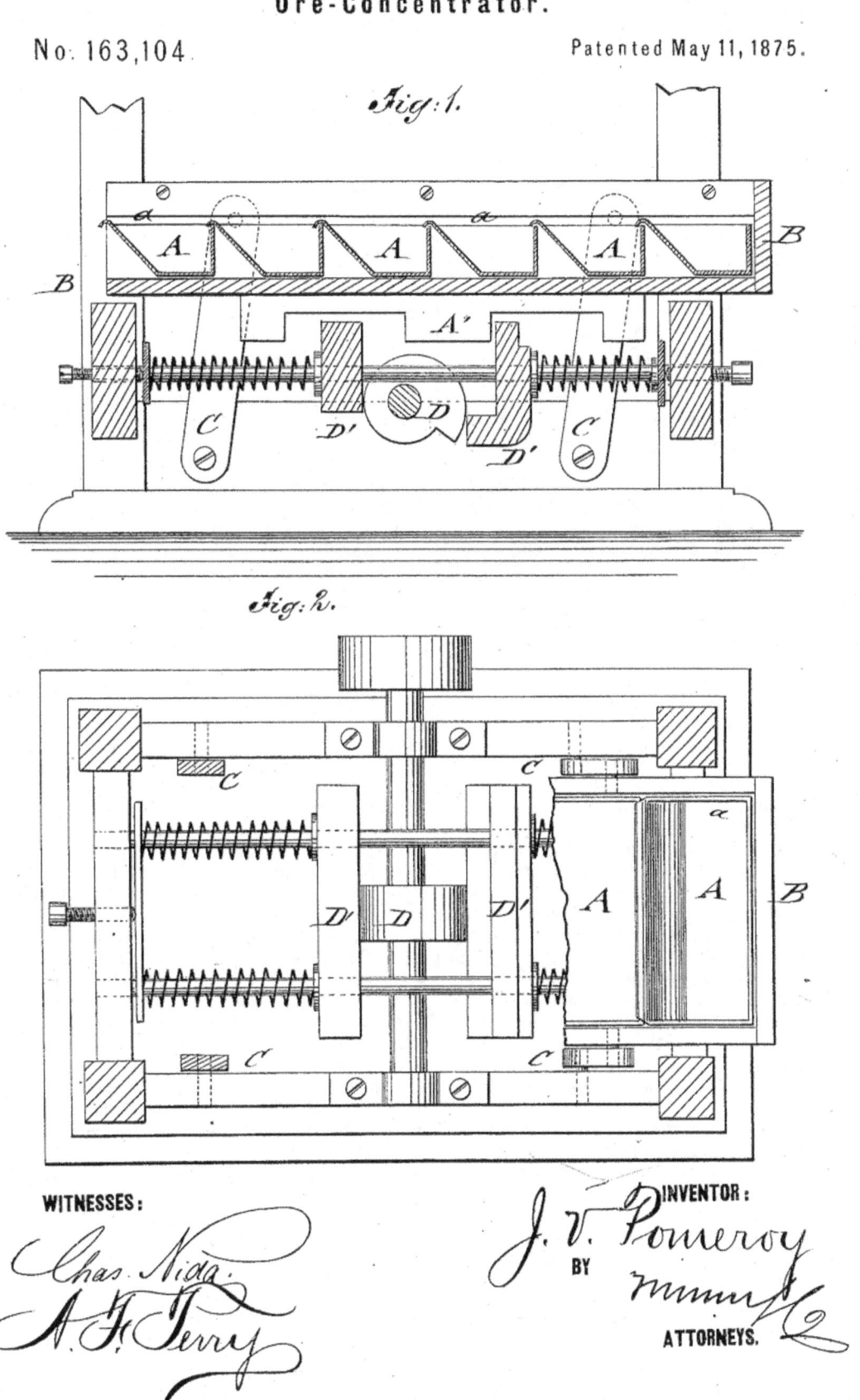

UNITED STATES PATENT OFFICE.

JAMES V. POMEROY, OF BOULDER, COLORADO TERRITORY.

IMPROVEMENT IN ORE-CONCENTRATORS.

Specification forming part of Letters Patent No. **163,104**, dated May 11, 1875; application filed March 1, 1875.

To all whom it may concern:

Be it known that I, JAMES V. POMEROY, of Boulder, in the county of Boulder and Territory of Colorado, have invented a new and Improved Ore-Concentrator, of which the following is a specification:

In the accompanying drawing, Figure 1 represents a vertical longitudinal section of my improved ore-concentrator, and Fig. 2 a top view of the same with parts broken away to show mechanism below.

Similar letters of reference indicate corresponding parts.

My invention relates to a simple and effective ore-concentrator, by which the heavier metallic parts of the pulp are rapidly separated from the lighter particles.

The invention consists of a series of ore pans or troughs, which are placed in detachable manner in a supporting-frame, to which reciprocating motion is imparted by concussions with suitable actuating mechanism. The pans are connected by one of the sides being of suitable inclination, and overlapping the edge of the adjoining pan, for facilitating the wave motion of the water, and the separation of light particles on the motion of the frame.

In the drawing, A are the concentrating-pans, which are made of suitable sheet metal, and placed into a supporting-frame, B, being held therein by detachable side strips a, which bind on the top part of the pans, so that they are firmly retained in position without being detached by the concussions to which frame B is exposed. One of the lateral sides of each pan is produced at a certain angle of inclination, with curved or bent upper edge that overlaps the vertical side of the adjoining pan, and enables thereby the water to pass readily by, the sudden motion of the frame into the adjoining pans carrying the lighter particles along. The supporting-frame is hung on oscillating standards or rods C, by which reciprocating motion is imparted to the same. To accelerate the separation of the lighter particles from the heavier metallic parts, sudden motion is given to the supporting-frame by concussions produced by a revolving eccentric cam, D, acting on spring-acted plates D', that strike lugs A' of the frame, so that by the sudden starting of the frame, and suitable intervals of rest between the strokes, sufficient time is given for the flowing over and receding of the wave of water.

Any other mode of hanging the frame from above or below or on friction-rollers may be employed, and also any mechanism for producing the sudden motion may be used, as I do not confine myself to the special construction shown in the drawing. The detachable pans may also be dispensed with, provided troughs or a continuous pan of the same shape is arranged in the reciprocating frame, the main advantage of the separating-pans consisting in the convenient discharge of the concentrated ore, and the placing of the last pans, containing a quantity of lighter particles intermixed with metallic parts, at the head of the pan, to work them over again for more complete separation.

The pulp is discharged through the screens from a stamp-mill or other crushing machinery onto a level apron extending at suitable length at the head or first pan, being fed in a steady regular flow or supply to the pans. The motion, together with the concussion, causes the mineral to settle, while the light particles form a covering to the heavier mineral on the surface. The lighter particles are propelled forward from the first pan by the concussion and wave action of the water, no mineral accumulating in the second pan until the first pan is filled with mineral and overflows to second pan, and so on through all the pans consecutively. The layer of lighter material on the top of the heavier particles forms a covering against the action of the water.

The old concussion-tables are mostly hung on a suitable inclination, and depend entirely on the flow of water for carrying off the refuse, by which a large amount of fine mineral or "slimes" and coarse ore is also carried along and lost. The concussion of the table, and the wave motion of the water following the same, produce on the level apron already a settling of the heavier minerals, while the coarse rock and lighter material remain on the top and go forward to the pans, which can then be subjected to any amount of wave motion without loss of fine mineral, as it accumulates on the level surface of the pan, forming an inclined plane toward the adjoining pan. The coarse and lighter material is carried over from pan to pan, while the heavier particles are settled on the apron, and consecutively in the level pans, producing in one machine with the concentrating also the sizing of the minerals.

When the pans are filled with concentrated mineral parts the fastenings are detached, and the pans removed for dumping, the last, with its mixed contents, being then placed at the head. The concussion-table, in connection with wave motion of the water, produces very effective and satisfactory results, and renders the concentrator more advantageous than the more complicated devices hitherto employed for the same purpose.

Having thus described my invention, I claim as new and desire to secure by Letters Patent—

The combination of level table B, having lugs A', the series of overlapping pans A, supported at both ends by oscillating standards C C, the revolving cam D, and the sliding spring-plates D' D', all arranged substantially as and for the purpose specified.

JAMES V. POMEROY.

Witnesses:
P. A. LEONARD,
GEO. C. CORNING.

G. W. DUNN.
Water-Wheel Gate.

No. 163,754. Patented May 25, 1875.

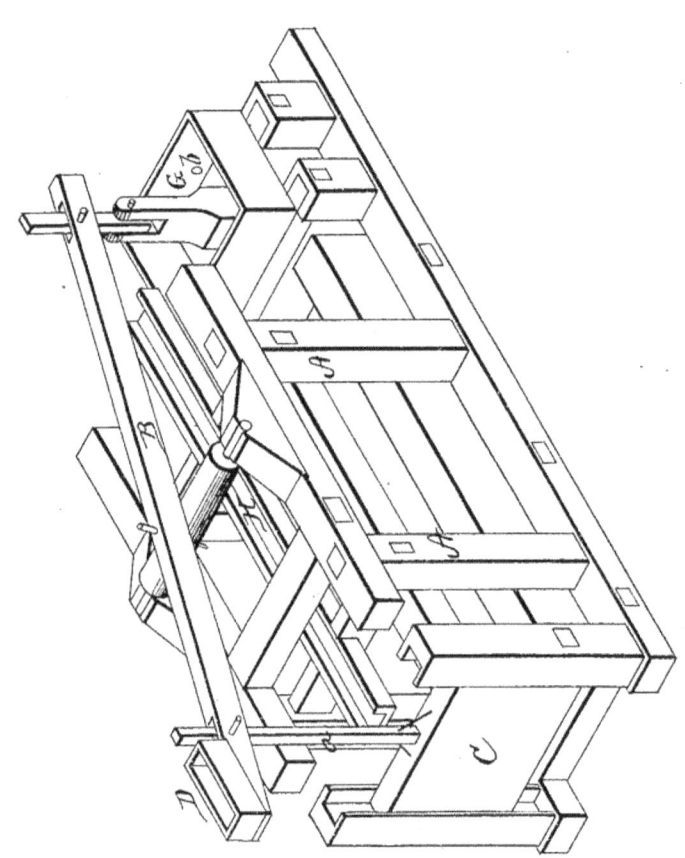

WITNESSES
Chas. H. Ourand
C. L. Everk.

INVENTOR
George W. Dunn
per Alexander Mason
ATTORNEY

UNITED STATES PATENT OFFICE.

GEORGE W. DUNN, OF TEXAS CREEK, COLORADO TERRITORY.

IMPROVEMENT IN WATER-WHEEL GATES.

Specification forming part of Letters Patent No. **163,754**, dated May 25, 1875; application filed March 6, 1875.

To all whom it may concern:

Be it known that I, GEORGE W. DUNN, of Texas Creek, in the county of Fremont and in the Territory of Colorado, have invented certain new and useful Improvements in Water-Gate; and do hereby declare that the following is a full, clear, and exact description thereof, reference being had to the accompanying drawings and to the letters of reference marked thereon, making a part of this specification.

The nature of my invention consists in the construction and arrangement of a self-acting water-gate for mining purposes, as will be hereinafter more fully set forth.

In order to enable others skilled in the art to which my invention appertains to make and use the same, I will now proceed to describe its construction and operation, referring to the annexed drawing, which represents a perspective view of my invention.

A represents a suitable frame-work erected below any water-reservoir, and having a walking-beam or lever, B, suitably journaled in its upper part. C represents the gate for the reservoir, connected by a rod or bar, a, with the inner end of the lever B, said end of the lever being provided with a box, D, for the reception of weights to bear down this end of the lever and gate. From the other end of the lever B is suspended a box, G, as shown. H represents a trough arranged in such a manner that when the water rises in the reservoir above the gate C it will pass through this trough and fill the box G so that the box will overbalance the weighted end of the lever and raise the gate, allowing a portion of the water to pass out through the same. As soon as the water in the reservoir falls low enough that no more will go through the trough H the water in the box G will pass out through an aperture, b, therein. The weighted end of the lever, then overbalancing the box, will close the gate C. In like manner, every time the water rises above the water-line the gate will open, and as soon as it falls below the gate will close.

Having thus fully described my invention, what I claim as new, and desire to secure by Letters Patent, is—

The combination of the gate C, connecting-rod a, lever or walking-beam B, with weight-box D, the box G, with outlet b, and the trough H, all constructed and arranged substantially as and for the purposes herein set forth.

In testimony that I claim the foregoing I have hereunto set my hand this 15th day of April, 1874.

GEORGE W. DUNN.

Witnesses:
L. D. HUBBELL,
JAS. M. RILAND.

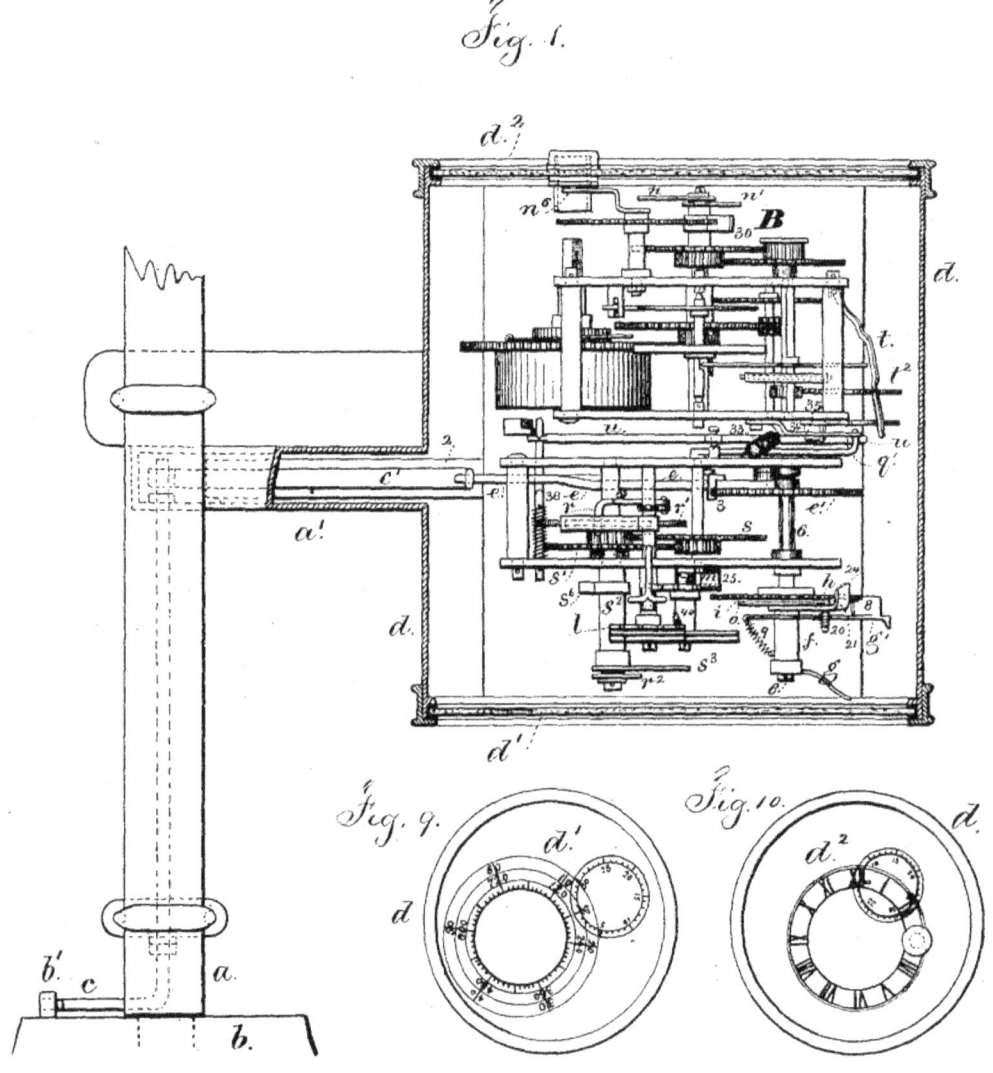

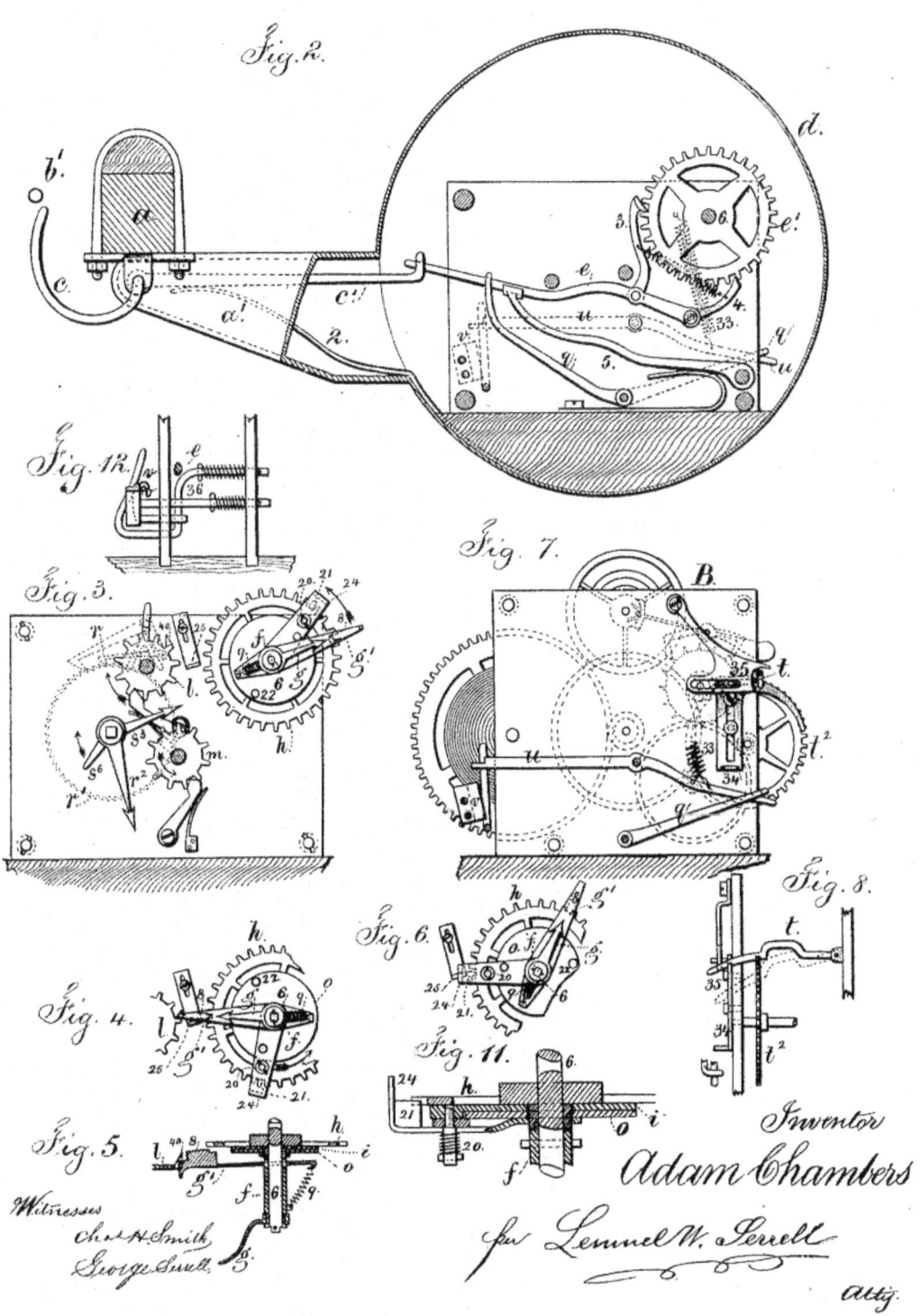

UNITED STATES PATENT OFFICE.

ADAM CHAMBERS, OF PUEBLO, COLORADO TERRITORY.

IMPROVEMENT IN ROTARY MEASURES.

Specification forming part of Letters Patent No. **164,424**, dated June 15, 1875; application filed April 7, 1875.

To all whom it may concern:

Be it known that I, ADAM CHAMBERS, of Pueblo, in the county of Pueblo and Territory of Colorado, have invented an Improvement in Odometers, of which the following is a specification:

Odometers have been attached both to the wheel and to the axle for registering the number of revolutions of a wheel, and the consequent distance traveled.

My invention is made for accomplishing this object by mechanism that can be easily adapted to the irregular counting motion consequent upon the circumference of the wheel not being contained an even number of times in a mile. Besides this, my improvement provides for combining, with the odometer, a time-register that is maintained in motion while the vehicle is moving, and is stopped when such vehicle stops; thereby a complete record is kept of the number of hours the vehicle is in motion, so as to indicate the average rate of speed and prevent questions arising between owners of vehicles and persons hiring the same as to the time occupied in journeying the distance traveled, or the time during which the vehicle was at rest. I accomplish these objects by a clock movement and stop that is kept out of action by the movement of the odometer; hence such stop becomes operative automatically when the vehicle ceases to move.

In the drawing, Figure 1 is a general plan view, with the case of the odometer in section. Fig. 2 is a sectional view of the counting appliances. Fig. 3 is an elevation of the computating mechanism. Figs. 4, 5, and 6 represent parts of the computating-wheels. Figs. 7 and 8 represent the stop motion for the clock, and Figs. 9 and 10 show face views of the dials.

Upon the axle a the hub b of the wheel revolves, and, by the pin b' acting upon the bent cam-shaped arm c, motion is given to the shaft that runs along below the axle, and passes into the case a', and connects with the lever c', that is moved by the spring 2, when c is liberated from the pin b'. It is preferable to have a rubber packing or washer to exclude dust where the shaft enters the case a'. The works of the odometer are in the case d—that is, at the end of the hollow arm or case a'—and at one end is a cap and dial, d^1, Fig. 9, and at the other end is the cap and dial d^2 (See Fig. 10.) These are preferably painted upon glass, so that the hands show behind the glass, and the works of the odometer are entirely excluded from dust by elastic packings or washers, and the dials are attached in place or secured by locks, so that the works cannot be injured or misplaced. The lever c' operates the lever e and pawl 3, that moves the first counting-wheel e', and 4 is the stop-pawl to such wheel, and 5 is a spring-lever to give the return movement to the lever e and pawl 3. The shaft 6 of the wheel e' has at its end a loose sleeve, f, to which a pointer, g, is connected, and also a lever, g', that swings on this sleeve, and has a tooth, 8, at the back of the lever that is pressed between the teeth upon the wheel h by the spring 9. This wheel h is fastened firmly to its shaft 6; hence every revolution of the wheels e' and h by the step-by-step movement the end of the lever g' comes in contact with one tooth of the second counting-wheel l, and turns the same one space.

It is seldom that the carriage-wheel is of such diameter that the circumference will be contained in a mile an even number of times, so that one mile will be traveled when the wheels h and e' have gone around a sufficient number of times to make one turn of the second counting-wheel l. Hence I employ a compensating device that turns the mile dial or counter l the last movement of the revolution, whereby I am enabled to drop from the computation as many revolutions of the carriage-wheel as may be required to make up the deficiency and reach the end of the miles as the mile-wheel is moved.

To accomplish this I employ two disks, i and o, upon the shaft 6. They are clamped together at any required point by the screw 20. One disk carries the spring-tooth 21, and the other the stop 22. These parts are shown in larger size in Fig. 11. One of the star-teeth, 40, of the dial l, is inclined, so that as the end of the lever g' comes against it the lever end is pushed back enough to throw the tooth 8 at the back of the lever g' out from between the teeth of the wheel h, as shown in Figs. 4 and 5, and hence said wheel h will continue to revolve without turning the lever or counting on the second dial l until the stop 22 of the disk o, coming around against the side of the lever g', completes the movement of the lever g', and turns the second counter l its last notch of the mile as the vehicle reaches the end of the mile. The movement of the wheels e' and h continuing, the inclined end 24 of the arm of the disk i stops against the stationary incline 25, as shown in Fig. 6, and thereby it is pressed back sufficiently to disconnect its stop 21 from the wheel h, and thus it remains until the lever g' coming around against the arm of such disk i, the end 24 is carried off the incline 25, its stop 21 takes the teeth of h, and the parts are replaced in the first position without the movement of the arm g' being again checked.

By this construction a final turn of the second dial l will be made to complete the mile record by a greater number of revolutions of the carriage-wheel than usual, and according to the position in which the two disks i and o are clamped together, so the lever g' will remain inoperative during a greater or less number of revolutions of the carriage-wheel in reaching the end of the mile.

A projection upon the shaft of the dial l acts upon a swinging pawl, r, that takes up one tooth at a time upon the counting-wheel r^1 of the hand r^2, and from this wheel r^1 motion is taken to the wheel s by a pinion, and thence back to the wheel s^1, sleeve s^2, and hand s^3, so as to keep accounts of miles and hundreds of miles, and a fourth counter, m, may be used—that is, turned one tooth each revolution of s by a tooth, s^6, upon the sleeve s^2, thereby computing to thousands of miles, if desired.

For determining the number of hours during which the vehicle is moving I employ an ordinary spring marine or balance clock movement, B, of any ordinary character, with hands n n^1 and and tooth 30, that turns the indicating-hand n^6 one space every twelve hours, so as to keep records of days. In order, however, to stop the clock-movement when the vehicle is standing still, I employ the fly-stop t, that is made of a light piece of metal jointed at one end to the clock-frame, so that it has a limited movement, and can be lifted out of the teeth of the wheel t^2 of the clock-movement, and thrown backward to fall at a distance down the wheel, and be brought up upon the wheel again. This is done each revolution of the carriage-wheel, so that when the carriage is moving the fly-stop is constantly moved back out of the way; but when the carriage stops the fly-stop arrests the movement of the clock. As the lever e is raised it moves the rocking lever q, and depresses the back end of the fly-lever u, straining the spring 33, and allowing the slide 34 to descend, and the hanging ejector 35 to drop; but when the lever e is depressed the spring 33 draws the lever u, so that the end rests upon the spring-latch block v, and the lever e, in its further movement, acts upon the spring-finger slide 36, (see Fig. 12,) to move the same by passing down between a portion of the slide and the frame, and in so doing the lever u is pressed off the latch-block v, and the other end flies up and strikes the slide 34, so that that and the ejector throw the stop t back farther down the wheel t^2, and prevent its arresting the clock-movement, as aforesaid.

I claim as my invention—

1. The two disks i and o, with their respective stops turning upon the shaft of the wheel h, in combination with the sleeve f, lever g', stationary incline 25, second counting-wheel l, and its incline 40, substantially as and for the purposes set forth.

2. The combination, with the odometer, of a clock-movement and a stop, operated by the odometer so as to compute the period of time in which the vehicle is in motion, as set forth.

3. The fly-stop t, slide 34, and ejector 35, operated by the spring-lever u, that receives motion from the lever e, in combination with the clock-movement and odometer-register, substantially as set forth.

Signed by me this 30th day of November, A. D. 1874.

ADAM CHAMBERS.

Witnesses:
H. J. SEWARD,
JOHN W. PYLE.

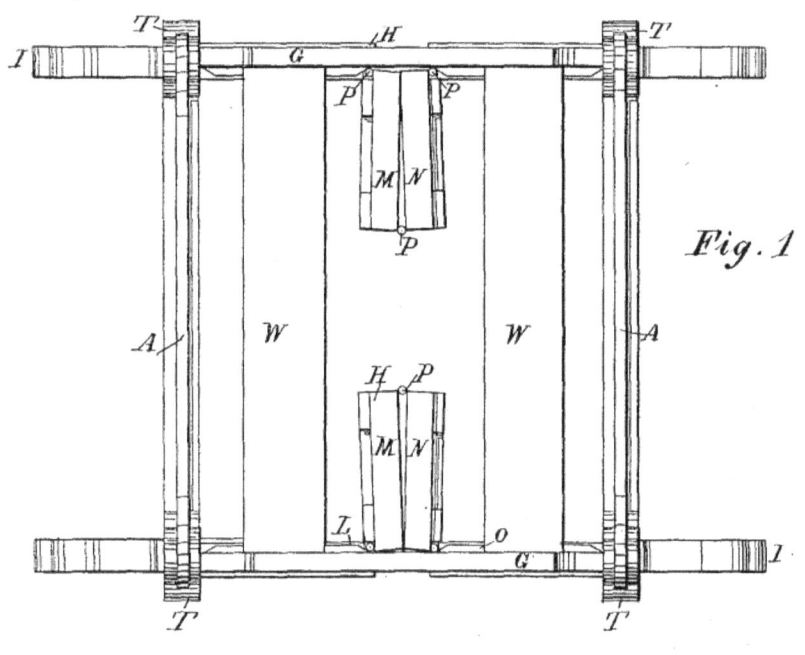
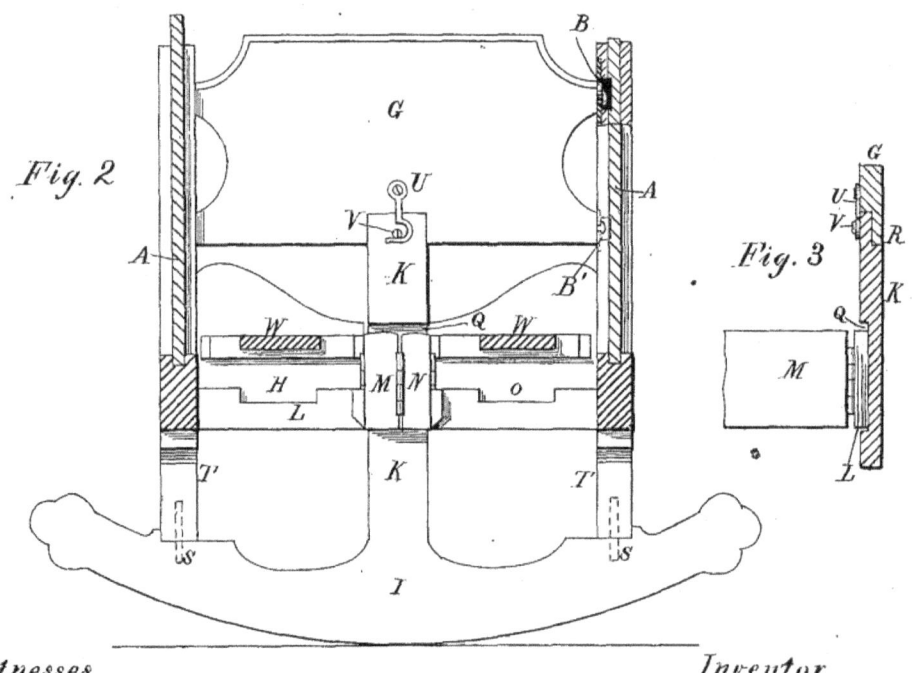

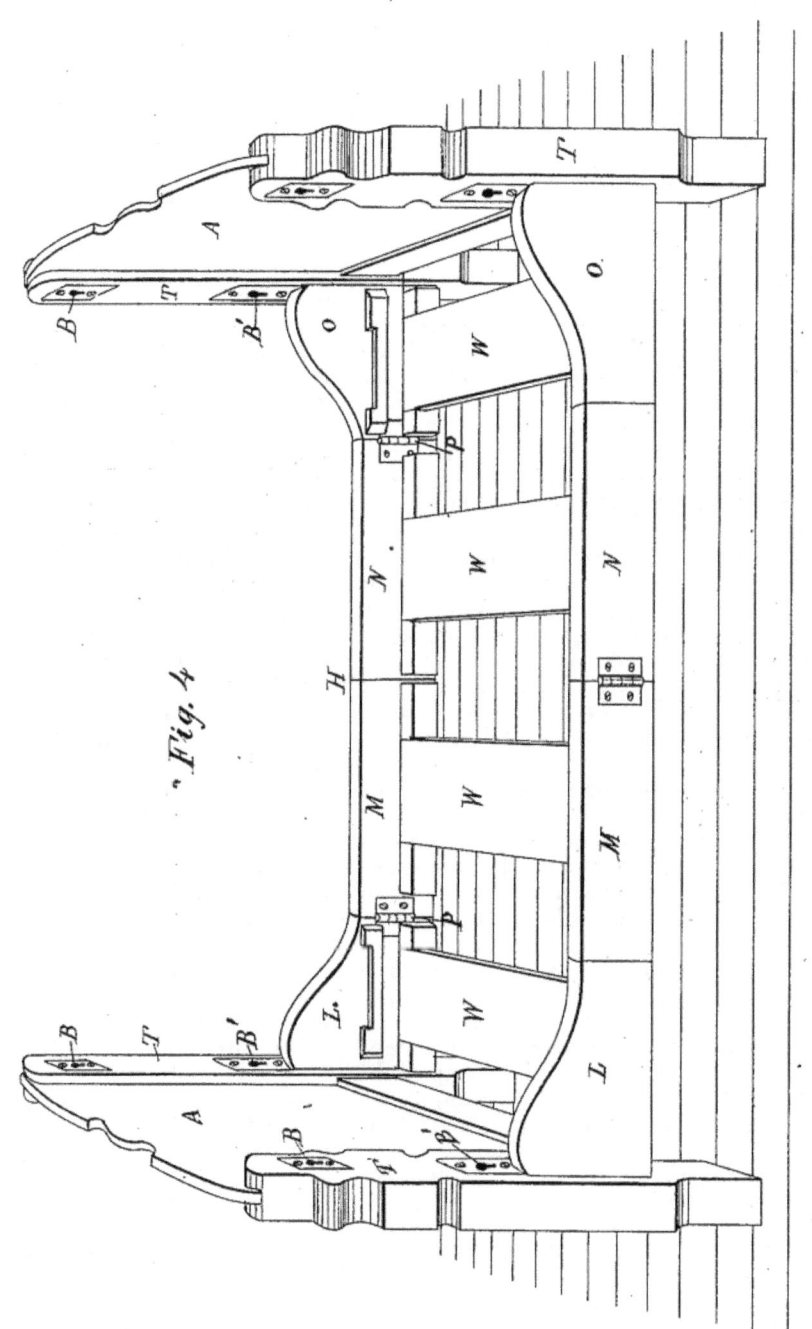

UNITED STATES PATENT OFFICE.

CARRIE W. CHAMBERLAIN, OF DENVER, COLORADO TERRITORY.

IMPROVEMENT IN COMBINED CRADLES AND BEDSTEADS.

Specification forming part of Letters Patent No. **164,639**, dated June 22, 1875; application filed May 14, 1875.

To all whom it may concern:

Be it known that I, CARRIE WELLS CHAMBERLAIN, of Denver, in the county of Arapahoe and Territory of Colorado, have invented a new and useful Improvement in a Combined Cradle and Bedstead; and I hereby declare the following to be a full, clear, and exact description of the same, reference being had to the accompanying drawing making a part of this specification, in which—

Figure 1 is a plan view of a combined cradle and bedstead embodying the improvements in this invention. Fig. 2 is a transverse vertical sectional view taken through the center of Fig. 1. Fig. 3 is a detached sectional view taken through the longitudinal vertical center of Fig. 2, and Fig. 4 is a perspective view of the invention extended and converted into a bedstead.

This invention relates to an improvement in a cradle and bedstead combined; and consists in the combination of the two side pieces provided with legs, two removable hinged end rails, two removable end pieces, and two removable anchor-shaped rockers; the object of the invention being to produce a combined cradle and bedstead, to be used as a cradle for an infant while it is quite small, and to be changed by the removal of the rockers and end pieces, and the extension of the hinged end rails, into a bedstead, to be occupied by the infant when it has grown too large for the cradle, all of which will hereinafter more fully appear.

In the accompanying drawing, the side pieces A A are provided with slotted plates B B' in the posts T, for receiving the studs on the ends of the removable end pieces G G and the hinged end rails H H. The anchor-shaped rockers I I are so called because the uprights K K and rockers resemble an anchor. The end-rails H H are constructed in four sections, L, M, N, and O, connected together by hinges P, and when in use in the cradle are folded to form a letter, T, with a recess at the top of the vertical portion of the letter T, which receives one of the uprights K. A recess, Q, in the latter receives the top ends of the vertical portion of the letter T. The tops of the uprights K are tenoned and enter recesses R R in the lower inside edges of the end pieces G G. The rockers I I have pins S S, which enter holes in the lower ends of the posts T of the side pieces A A. A hook, U, upon each end piece G engages with a stud, V, upon each upright K, and secures the anchor-shaped rockers I I to the cradle. Slats W W' traverse the cradle longitudinally.

The parts hereinbefore described, when put together, form an infant's cradle, which may be occupied by the infant until it has grown too large to occupy it longer. The rockers I I and end pieces G G may be then removed, and the hinged end rails H H extended to form the side rails of a bedstead, as shown in Fig. 4, and the slats W, all placed in the same plane, which change converts the cradle into a bedstead of greater dimensions than when the parts formed the cradle. It will be seen that the side pieces A A of the cradle become the head and foot of the bedstead. Casters may be inserted in the holes formerly occupied by the pins S S.

Having thus described my invention of improvements, what I claim as new and useful, and desire to secure by Letters Patent, is—

A combined cradle and bedstead, composed of the side pieces A A, end rails H H, end pieces G G, and anchor-shaped rockers I I, constructed to permit the removal of the end pieces G G and anchor-shaped rockers I I, and the extension of the hinged end rails H H, substantially as and for the purposes set forth.

In testimony that I claim the foregoing improvement as above described, I have hereunto set my hand and seal this 6th day of May, 1875.

CARRIE W. CHAMBERLAIN. [L. S.]

Witnesses:
FRANCIS GALLUP,
JOHN W. HORNER.

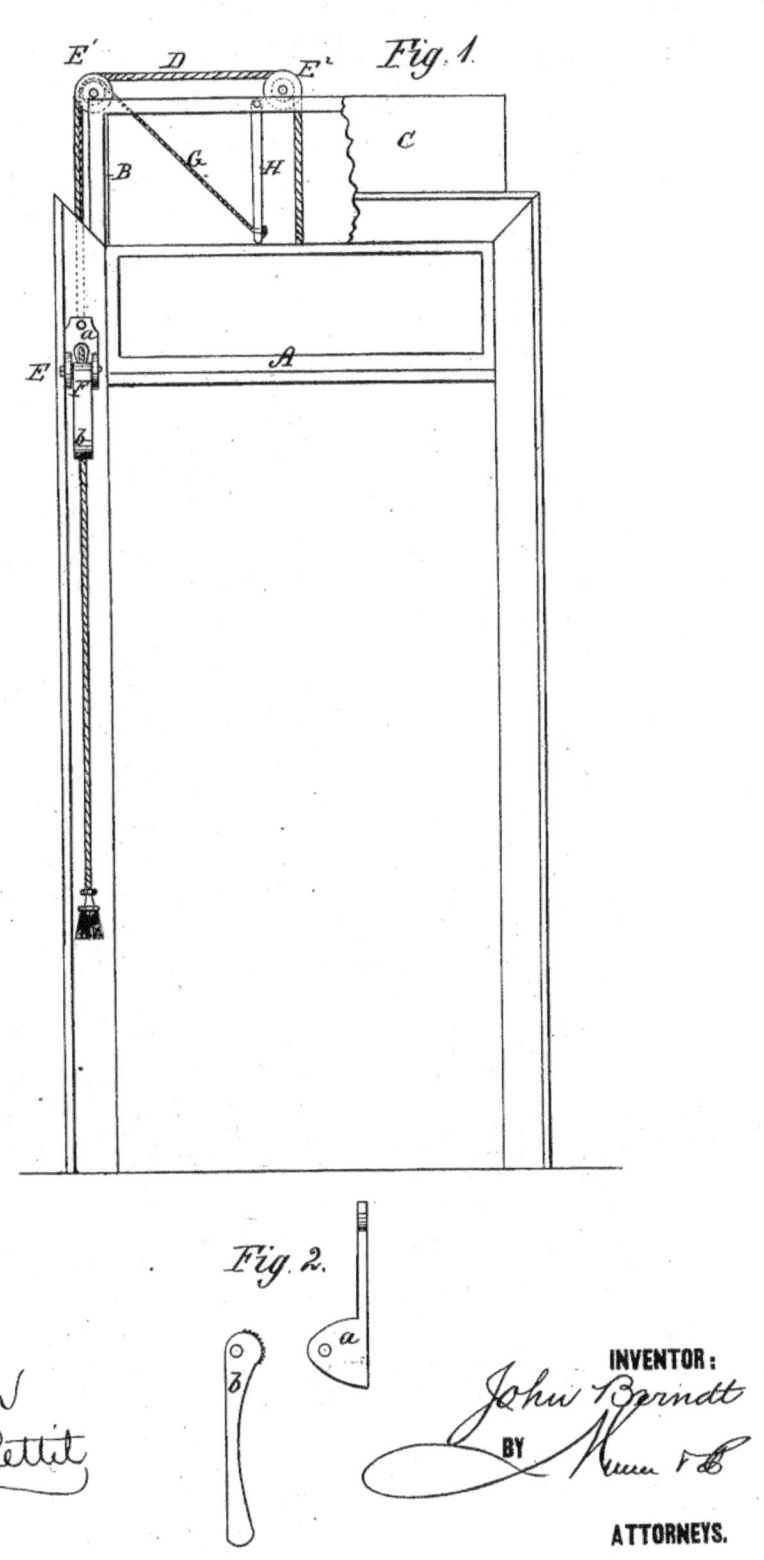

UNITED STATES PATENT OFFICE.

JOHN BERNDT, OF DENVER, COLORADO TERRITORY.

IMPROVEMENT IN TRANSOMS FOR DOORS.

Specification forming part of Letters Patent No. **164,794**, dated June 22, 1875; application filed May 18, 1875.

To all whom it may concern:

Be it known that I, JOHN BERNDT, of Denver, in the county of Arapahoe, and Territory of Colorado, have invented a new and Improved Transom for Doors; and I do hereby declare that the following is a full, clear, and exact description of the same, reference being had to the accompanying drawing, forming a part of this specification, in which—

Figure 1 is a vertical side elevation with parts broken away; Fig. 2, details of the fastening device.

This invention relates to cetain improvements in transoms for doors; and it consists in a transom-sash that is made to slide into a casing above, by means of a branched cord moving over pulleys, one of the branches of which cord is attached to the sash for the purpose of raising it, and the other attached to a suspended detent or locking-bar, which prevents the raising of the sash except by the cord upon the inside of the house, the cord being fastened below by a self-closing cam-lever, and so arranged at its branched ends, as to raise the sash and lift the locking-bar away at the same time.

In the drawing, A represents the sash of the transom, having grooves upon its edges which receive and slide over tongues attached to the frame B, to exclude dust, snow, and wind. C is a casing or chamber above the transom, into which the transom-sash slides when raised. D is a cord, which passes over pulleys E E^1 E^2 in the casing, and is attached to the top part of the transom-sash at one end, and is fastened at a convenient distance below by a self-acting device, F. Said device consists of a frame, *a*, and a lever, *b*, having a serrated or ridged cam edge, which presses against the cord from the weight of the lever, and holds the said cord at any adjustment. G is a branch cord attached to cord D at one end, and at the other end to a swing detent or locking-bar, H. This locking-bar serves to hold the sash down, and acts as a safety-catch to prevent entrance from the outside by burglars, the bar being so arranged as to be removed from its locking position only by a traction upon the cord upon the inside.

By means of this improved construction and arrangement of parts, the transom may be readily adjusted at any height for ventilation, the sash automatically locked, when closed or down, and all dust, snow, &c., excluded.

Having thus described my invention, what I claim as new is—

The transom-sash A, in combination with the casing C, the cord D, pulleys E E^1 E^2, fastening F, branch cord G, and the locking-bar H, substantially as and for the purpose described.

JOHN BERNDT.

Witnesses:
WM. PENWINKLE,
HENRY GOODRIDGE.

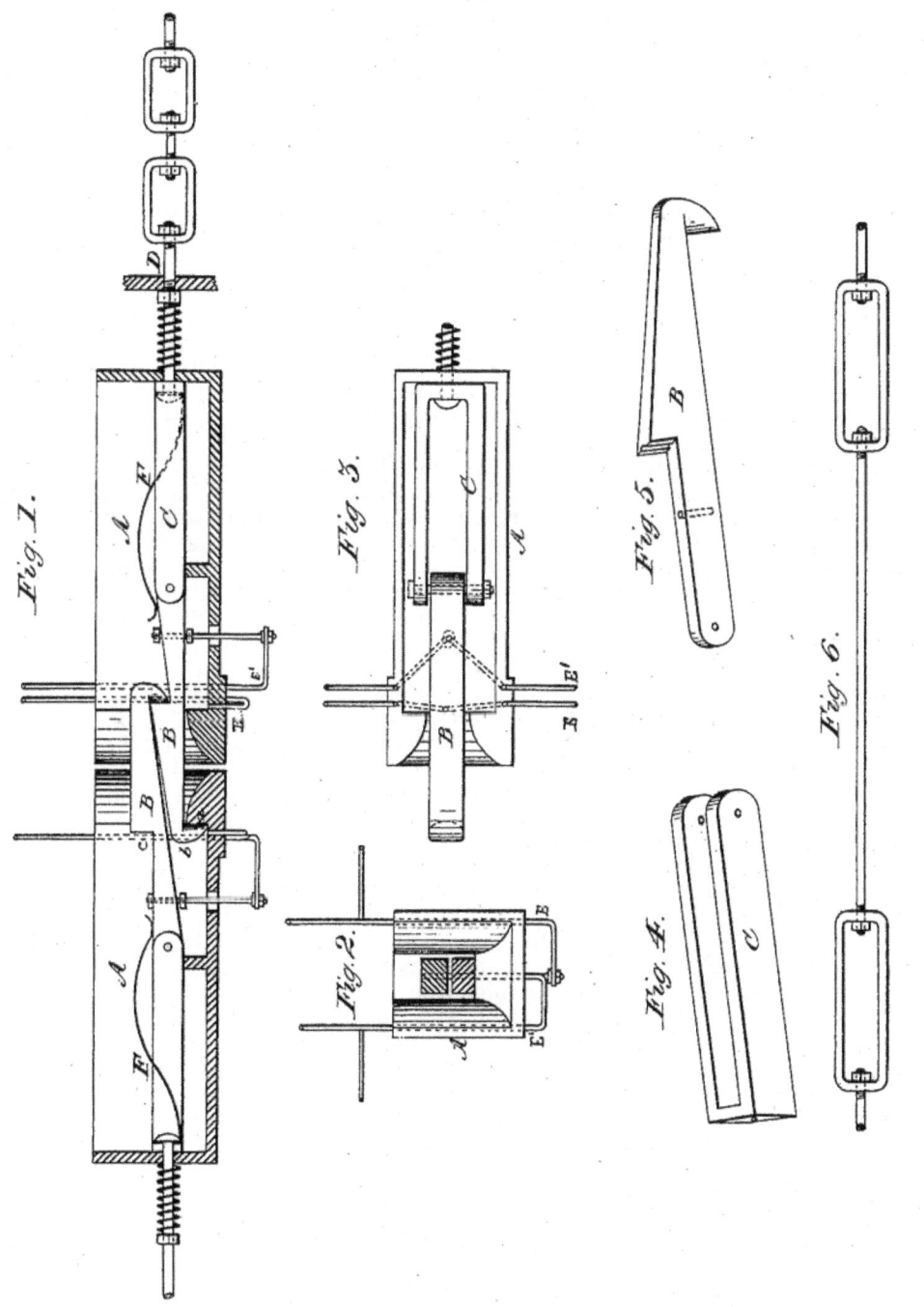

UNITED STATES PATENT OFFICE.

JOHN DINSMORE, OF DENVER, COLORADO TERRITORY.

IMPROVEMENT IN CAR-COUPLINGS.

Specification forming part of Letters Patent No. **165,484**, dated July 13, 1875; application filed March 2, 1875.

To all whom it may concern:

Be it known that I, JOHN DINSMORE, of Denver, county of Arapahoe, Colorado Territory, have invented an Improvement in Car-Couplings, of which the following is a specification:

The object of my invention is to furnish a safe and reliable automatic coupling device for railroad-cars, reference being had to the accompanying drawings forming a part of this specification, in which—

Figure 1 is a vertical longitudinal section of my improved coupling, and Figs. 2, 3, 4, 5, and 6 detached portions of the same.

A represent the draw-head; B, the double-catch latch; C, the clevis to which the latch is secured; D, the draw-bar; E, the rod for lifting the latch and uncoupling the car; E', the rod for setting and fastening the latch; F, a spring which holds the latch down on the lower side of the opening of the draw-bar and prevents the latches from displacement. The opening to the interior of the draw-bar is inclined, so that the lower catch will be raised and carried over the catch a, where it is held securely by the pressure of the spring F. The use of this spring F can be obviated by the use of the rod E'. The double-catched latches have a catch or shoulder, b, on the under side of one end, and another catch, c, about midway on the upper side. The one on the end engages with the catch a on the draw-head, or in the catch c on the upper side of the adjacent double latch. It will be seen that it does not matter which of the latches engages or enters the draw-head first, the other latch will ride over it and engage with the catch c, thus forming a sure and safe coupling. The double latches B are secured to a square link or clevis, C, which in turn is secured to the draw-bar D.

The rod E extends down from the top of the car or from the platform below the draw-head, the lower end of which is bent at a right angle, and to the end of which is secured a short rod which enters the draw-head below the double latches, and when the rod is pulled up the latch is raised and the cars disconnected. The rod E' is of a similar construction, except that the short rod passes through the latch, and is used for setting the latch, and the end of which is provided with a screw-thread, on which is placed nuts both above and below the latch. As the latch is raised it describes the arc of a circle. The lifting-rod, still remaining in a vertical position, infringes on the sides of the opening in the latch through which it passes, thus holding the latch in an elevated position until forced down by the operator.

Having thus described my invention, what I desire to secure by Letters Patent is—

1. The double-catch latches B, pivoted to the square link or clevis C, in combination with the catches a of the draw-head, substantially as and for the purpose specified.

2. In combination with the double-catch latches B, the rods E and E', substantially as and for the purpose specified.

3. In combination with the double-catch latches, the strap-spring F, substantially as and for the purpose specified.

4. In a car-coupling the double-catch latches B, draw-head A, draw-head catches a, link or clevis C, draw-bar D, spring F, rods E and E', all arranged to operate in the manner set forth, and for the purpose specified.

JOHN DINSMORE.

Witnesses:
THOMAS GEORGE,
HUNTER GUNNELL.

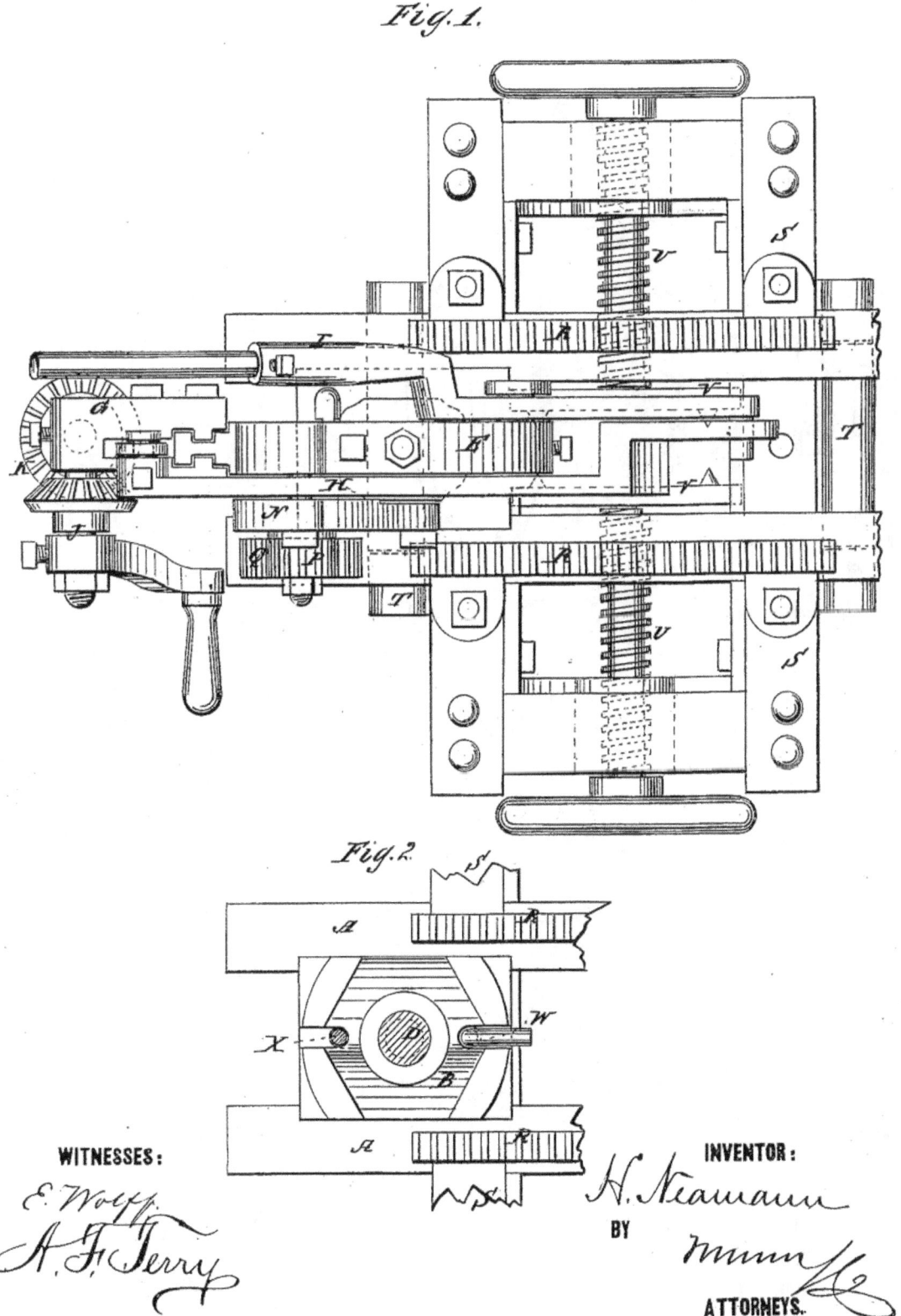

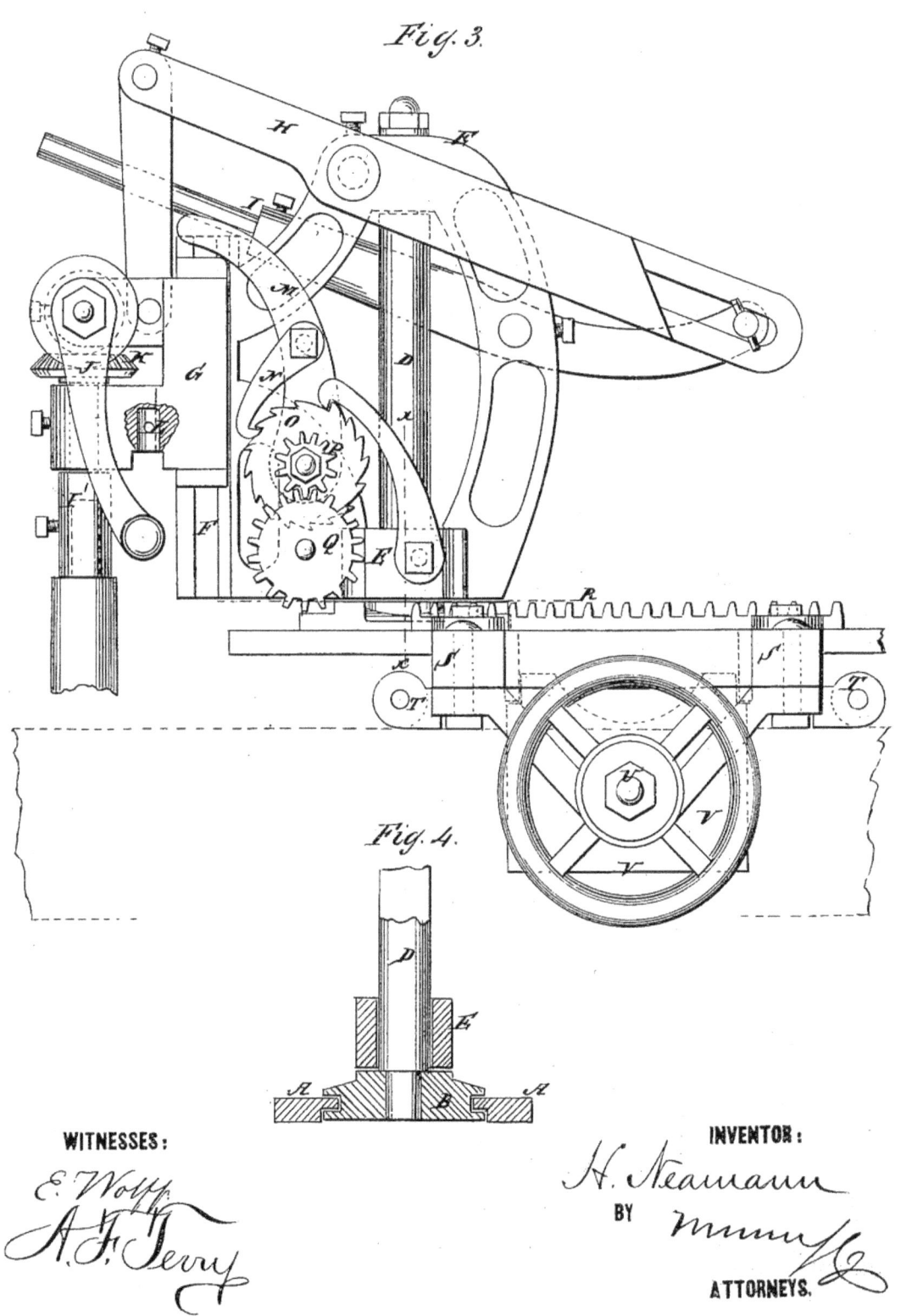

UNITED STATES PATENT OFFICE.

HENRY NEAMANN, OF CENTRAL CITY, COLORADO TERRITORY.

IMPROVEMENT IN BORING AND MORTISING MACHINES.

Specification forming part of Letters Patent No. **165,495**, dated July 13, 1875; application filed May 22, 1875.

To all whom it may concern:

Be it known that I, HENRY NEAMANN, of Central City, in the county of Gilpin and Territory of Colorado, have invented an Improvement in Boring and Mortising Machines, of which the following is a specification:

The invention consists of the sliding support for the tool-slide, contrived to be shifted around on its sliding base, in combination with feed-racks on both sides, whereby the mortising-tool may be fed up to both ends of the mortise.

The invention also consists in a portable boring and mortising machine, having rollers for shifting it along the timber easily, and provided with clamps and screws for attaching it to the latter.

Figure 1 is a plan view of my improved boring and mortising machine. Fig. 2 is a detail in horizontal section, showing some of the contrivance for shifting the mortising-tool about for feeding both ways. Fig. 3 is a side elevation; and Fig. 4 is a detail in sectional elevation taken on line $x\,x$ of Fig. 3.

Similar letters of reference indicate corresponding parts.

A represents a couple of parallel ways, on which a bed-piece, B, is fitted to slide forward and backward, in which is supported the vertical shaft D, on which is pivoted the frame E, carrying the vertical ways F on which the boring tool-head G is made to reciprocate by the levers H and I, so that said head may be shifted to the front either way on the ways A, and thus be worked up to both ends of the mortise. I is the boring-tool stock. J the crank, and K the wheels for turning it, all being contrived in the ordinary way. L is a socket for the head G for the mortising-chisel. M is the pawl-lever for feeding the machine along when using the chisel by means of the pawl N, ratchet O, pinion P, wheel Q, and toothed bar R, the lever being raised by the head G, when it is raised to work the chisel, and falling back by its own gravity. When using the boring-tool the pawl-lever does not work, and the machine does not feed, but it may be shifted along by hand to shift the auger for the different holes. W is a pin for fastening the sliding bed on the ways, so as not to slide when it is required to stand still for boring, and X a pin for fastening the revolving-frame E in working position. The ways A are mounted on a strong frame, S, having rollers T under them for shifting the machine along the timber easily, and also having clamp-screws U, and clamping-plates V, by which the ways are made fast to the timber.

Having thus described my invention, I claim as new and desire to secure by Letters Patent—

The sliding tool-carrying frame E, arranged to revolve horizontally, and the feed mechanism thereon, in combination with a feeding-rack, R, on both sides of the ways in which the frame slides, substantially as specified.

The clamp screws U, clamping-plates V, frame S, rollers T, and the ways A, combined and arranged substantially as specified.

HENRY NEAMANN.

Witnesses:
 HARLEY B. MORSE,
 I. N. WILCOXEN.

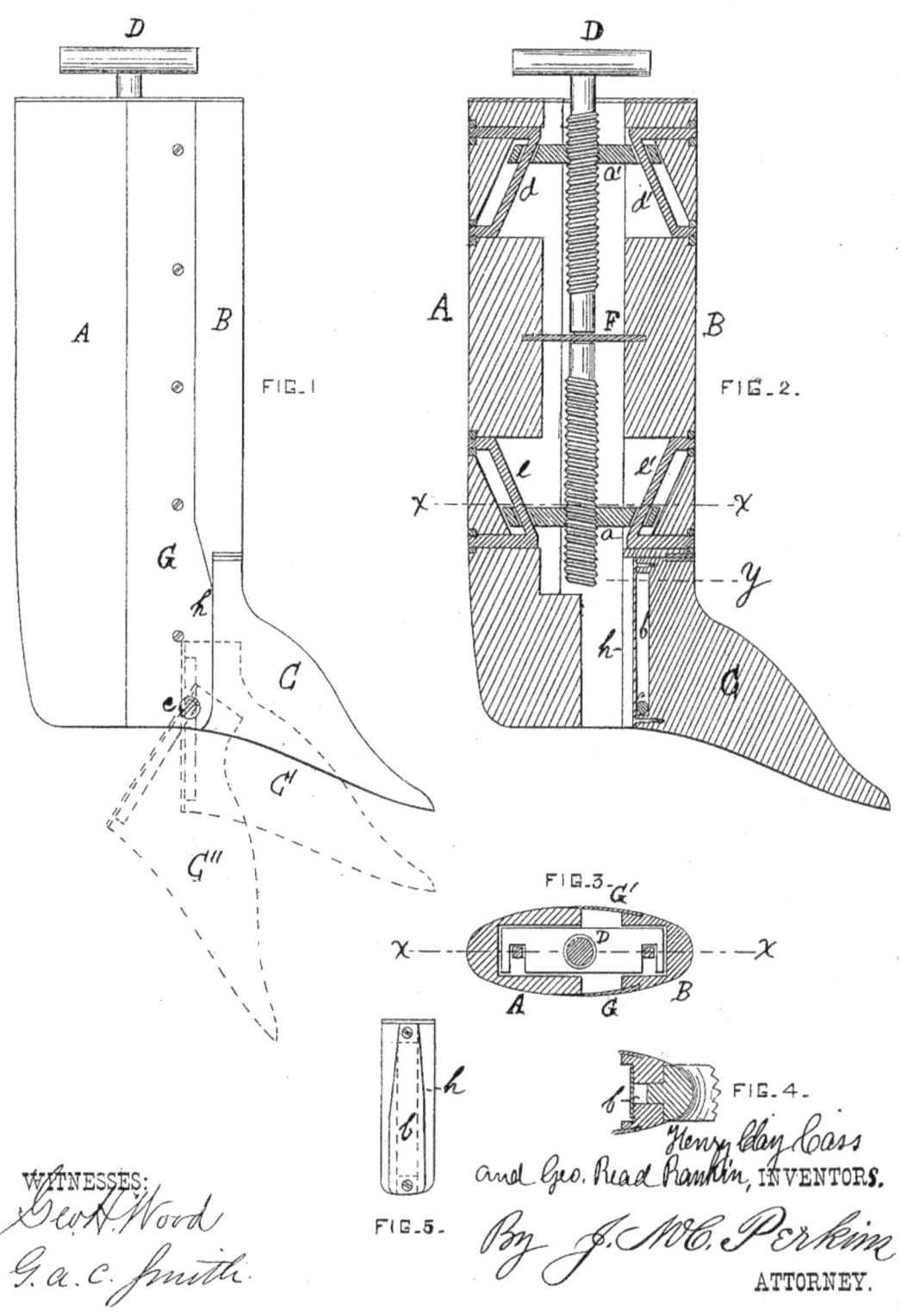

UNITED STATES PATENT OFFICE.

HENRY CLAY CASS AND GEORGE READ RANKIN, OF ALMA, COLORADO TERRITORY.

IMPROVEMENT IN BOOT-TREES.

Specification forming part of Letters Patent No. **166,499**, dated August 10, 1875; application filed May 25, 1875.

To all whom it may concern:

Be it known that we, HENRY CLAY CASS and GEORGE READ RANKIN, of Alma, in the county of Park and Territory of Colorado, have invented certain new and useful Improvements in Boot-Trees; and we do hereby declare that the following is a full, clear, and exact description thereof, that will enable others skilled in the art to which it appertains to make and use the same, reference being had to the accompanying drawings, and to the letters and figures of reference marked thereon, which form a part of this specification.

The same letters and figures of reference are used to indicate the corresponding parts.

After describing the invention, its nature and extent will be shown in the claims.

Figure 1 is a side view. Fig. 2 shows a vertical section, and Fig. 3 a horizontal section, of my boot-tree, taken through the line $x\ x$. Fig. 4 is a horizontal view of the foot, taken through the line y; and Fig. 5 is a rear view of the foot detached from the boot-tree.

A is the rear part of the leg, and B the front part. G G' are the flanges, which are screwed to the front B, and serve to entirely cover the spaces caused by the separation of A and B, as will hereafter be shown. C is the foot provided with an elongated slot, b, in its rear. In this slot the screw c plays. D is a rod which reaches from the top of the boot-tree to the point where the movable foot C is connected with it. It is provided with a right-and-left-hand screw at either end. F is a thin iron plate, the ends of which are supported in a slot in A and B, respectively. The rod D is kept in the same relative position by the plate F, as shown. The plate a' moves by the screw on D, and is provided at either end with inclined slots by which it moves on the keepers d and d'. The plate a' is made in a similar manner, and moves on the keepers e and e'. By turning the rod D to the right, the plates a and a' moved from the plate F, and so separate the parts A and B until the two plates, respectively, reach the points on the keepers $e\ e'$ and $d\ d''$, which approach nearest to each other. Then the boot-tree has reached its utmost capacity in stretching the boot-leg. By turning the rod D to the left, the action is reversed, and the parts A and B are brought together again. When the boot-tree is to be placed in the boot the foot C is knocked down, as shown by C''. When the foot reaches the bottom of the boot it assumes the position shown by C'. By pressing the tree downward the screw c falls to the bottom of the slot b, and the foot then is in the position shown by C. Then the boot may be stretched both in the leg and in the foot, as before described. The foot C may be removed at pleasure, and replaced by one of larger or smaller size, so that the foot may be enlarged more or less, as desired.

Having now fully described our invention, what we claim, and desire to secure by Letters Patent, is—

1. In a boot-tree, the rod D, provided with a right-and-left-hand screw, in combination with the movable plates $a\ a'$, and the fixed plate F, as shown and described.

2. The laterally-adjustable parts A and B, provided with the keepers $d\ d'$ and $e\ e'$, in combination with the movable foot C, substantially as before shown and described.

3. In a boot-tree, the movable foot C, provided with an elongated slot, b, in combination with the screw c, substantially as shown and described.

4. The keepers $e\ e'$ and $d\ d'$, in combination with the plates $a\ a'$ and F, rod D, and foot C, and parts A B.

In testimony that we claim the foregoing we have hereunto set our hands this 14th day of May, A. D. 1875.

HENRY CLAY CASS.
GEORGE READ RANKIN.

Witnesses:
C. E. EDGAR,
JAMES V. DEXTER.

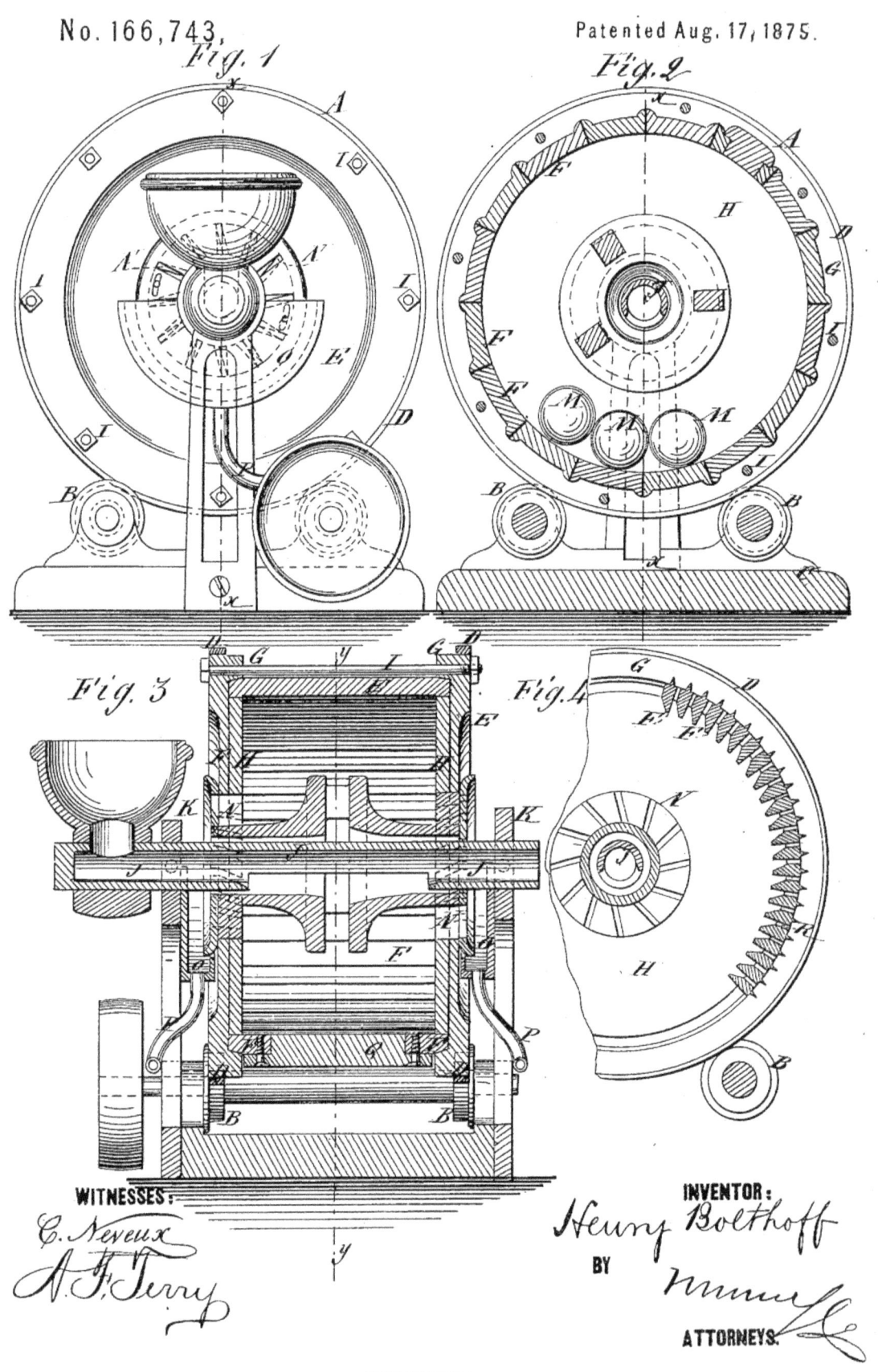

UNITED STATES PATENT OFFICE.

HENRY BOLTHOFF, OF CENTRAL CITY, COLORADO TERRITORY, ASSIGNOR TO HIMSELF AND CHARLES F. HENDRIE, OF SAME PLACE.

IMPROVEMENT IN WET AND DRY ORE CRUSHERS.

Specification forming part of Letters Patent No. **166,743**, dated August 17, 1875; application filed May 1, 1875.

To all whom it may concern:

Be it known that I, HENRY BOLTHOFF, of Central City, in the county of Gilpin and Territory of Colorado, have invented a new and Improved Ball-Pulverizer, of which the following is a specification:

The invention will first be described in connection with the drawing, and then pointed out in the claims.

Figure 1 is an end elevation of my improved machine. Fig. 2 is a transverse section taken on the line $y\ y$ of Fig. 3. Fig. 3 is a longitudinal sectional elevation on line $x\ x$ of Figs. 1 and 2, and Fig. 4 is a section showing the arrangement of staves for dry-pulverizing.

Similar letters of reference indicate corresponding parts.

A is a hollow cylinder of any required size, made of cast-iron or other suitable material, and caused to revolve upon four truck-wheels, B, placed in a frame, C. The motive power is applied to one of the truck-wheel shafts, driving the mill by friction of the truck-wheels on the periphery of the heads, which are banded with tires D, to prevent wear of machine.

The cylinder consists of two heads, E, connected together by staves F, made of cast-iron or other suitable material. The heads have a flange, G, on the outer rim, and are protected from wear on inner side by liners H.

The staves are fitted between the outside flange of heads and the outer rim of liners, and are tapered at the ends to fit taper on flanges, so that when the connecting-bolts I are drawn up the taper acts like a hoop on a barrel, to tighten the staves together.

For wet-crushing these staves are made water-tight by the insertion of proper packing between them and at the ends, each stave having projecting ribs to help hold the packing and stiffen the stave.

Through the center of the cylinder, which is open, is placed a hollow pipe, J, held in place by two stands, K. Through this pipe is fed the ore and water, the pipe having openings, L, for discharge of same into inside of cylinder. I propose to utilize this pipe for the shaft of the cylinder. Balls M, of cast-iron or other suitable material, are placed inside, and by the motion of cylinder the ore and balls are brought into contact, and the crushing is done by concussion and abrasion, and when the ore is sufficiently fine to float, it rises to the top of the water and passes out in form of pulp through registers N on either side near the center into hoppers O, fastened to the stands; thence it passes in pipes P to the amalgamating-coppers, as used with stamps. The registers N may be contrived to discharge the pulp higher or lower by means of regulators, to regulate the concentration by specific gravity. At intervals the feeding of the ore can be stopped, and some mercury put into the cylinder, which will take up all the loose, free gold there may be left in the cylinder, and then, after a thorough mixing of mercury with the pulp, the hand-hole plates Q can be removed from the stave, and a grate inserted in the place with holes small enough to prevent the balls escaping, but let all the pulp discharge into a dolly-tub or settler, in which the amalgam and concentrated tailings can be separated and obtained, the amalgam retorted, and the gold and tailings, or ore that will not amalgamate, will be sufficiently concentrated to heat by smelting.

The above is the arrangement as used for wet-crushing, and principally on gold ores.

For dry-crushing, of course the ore is fed in dry, and instead of discharging at the centers, it discharges around the periphery through interstices R between each stave, which are made much narrower than the wet-mill stave, to give more discharging capacity, and are so shaped on inside as to form corrugations, thus preventing packing of ore and balls, and thus aiding free discharge. These staves are slightly thicker at each end than the rest, to separate them for the interstices and spaces for the discharge of the ore.

In my dry-crusher, the pulverized ores are discharged at the periphery through interstices between staves, whose narrowness enables the discharge-space to be increased, and whose corrugated shape on the inside prevents the balls and unbroken ore from interfering with the discharge. The pulverizing capacity of a given machine is thus greatly augmented.

Having thus described my invention, I claim

as new and desire to secure by Letters Patent—

1. A wet-pulverizer for ores, discharging the pulp near its center through a series of registers, N, of varying altitude, thereby regulating the fineness of the crushed ore by its own gravity.

2. The combination of heads E E, having flanges G and lining H, with end-tapered staves F, having rib, the said staves and heads being bolted together in the manner described.

3. A dry-pulverizer for ores, having staves made narrow, intervaled and corrugated on the inside, as and for the purpose specified.

HENRY BOLTHOFF.

Witnesses:
  CHAS. WITHROW,
  JAMES BURRELL.

D. NEVIN.
Ore-Sizing Machine.

No. 167,191. Patented Aug. 31, 1875.

Fig. 1

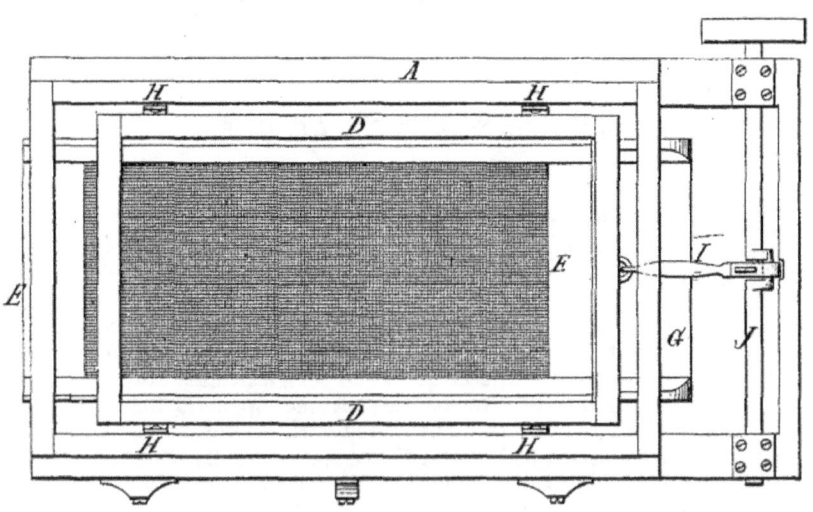

Fig. 2

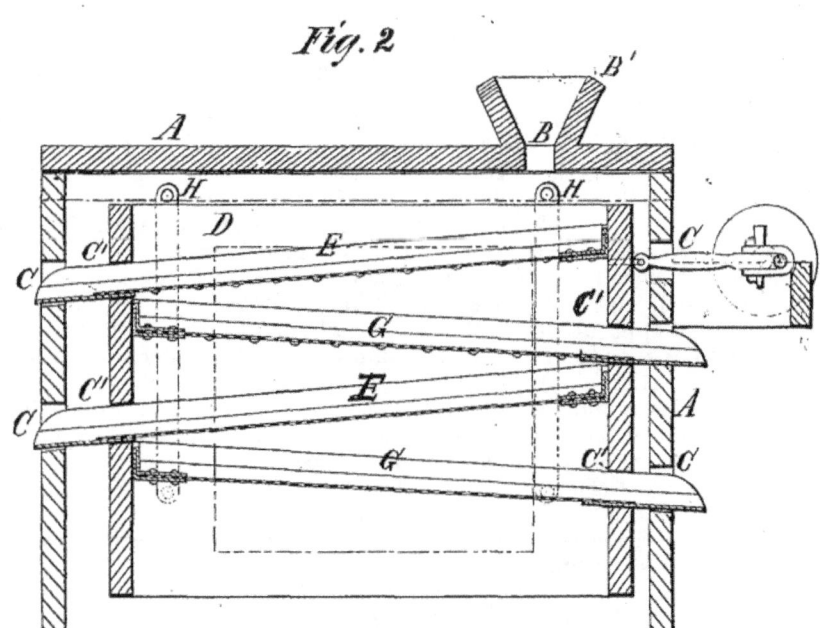

UNITED STATES PATENT OFFICE

DAVID NEVIN, OF GEORGETOWN, COLORADO TERRITORY, ASSIGNOR TO HIMSELF, ROBERT A. NEVIN, AND JAMES OSCAR STEWART, OF SAME PLACE.

IMPROVEMENT IN ORE-SIZING MACHINES.

Specification forming part of Letters Patent No. **167,191**, dated August 31, 1875; application filed August 2, 1875.

To all whom it may concern:

Be it known that I, DAVID NEVIN, of Georgetown, county of Clear Creek and Territory of Colorado, have invented a new and Improved Ore-Sizing Machine; and I do hereby declare that the following is a full, clear, and exact description thereof, reference being had to the accompanying drawings making part of this specification, in which—

Figure 1 is a top view, and Fig. 2 a vertical longitudinal section, of the machine.

The object of my invention is to provide a simple, cheap, and effective machine for use in connection with "concentrating-machines," whereby ore can be assorted or sized in a rapid and perfect manner. The sizing-machines in use have been constructed with revolving screens, and such screens have not been found to answer the purpose intended near as well as the plan which I have invented.

The nature of my invention consists in two or more sieves, with meshes or openings of appropriate sizes, arranged fixedly on a vibrating frame, so as to incline in opposite directions, and have their respective ends extend through the sieve-frame and through an outer supporting-frame. This construction is such that the ore not discharged over the end of the first sieve is discharged through meshes of this sieve upon a second sieve, and caused to move in a reverse direction to that in which it moved when on the first sieve. This construction is also such that the refuse or finer particles of matter are confined and prevented from flying about, and finally pass through the sieves upon the floor or into a receiver.

To enable others skilled in the art to make and use my invention, I will proceed to describe it.

A is an outer frame closed in at top and on all sides, and left open at its bottom, and provided with suitable inlet and outlet openings B and C. The opening B, which is in the top of the frame, is for the introduction of the ore to be sorted or sized, and it is surrounded by a feed-hopper, B', and the openings C, which are in the ends of the frame, are for the discharge of the sorted or sized ore. D is an interior sieve-frame, open at top and bottom, and provided with flow-passages C' in its ends. E and G are sieves rigidly fastened within the frame D. The discharge ends of these sieves extend through the flow-passages C' and discharge-passages C of the two frames A and D, as shown in the drawing. The top sieve E is inclined in one direction, and the sieve directly under it in an opposite direction. The meshes or openings of the respective sieves will be graduated in size to suit the requirements of the operator. The sieve-frame D, with its sieves, is suspended within the frame A by means of pendulous straps H. This frame is also connected to a pitman, I, of a revolving crank-shaft, J, which is mounted on the frame A, and by means of said shaft and pitman the frame D, with both sieves, is reciprocated within said frame A.

The ore is passed through the hopper upon the first sieve, and the finer portions pass through and fall upon the second sieve. The two sizes of ore pass off in different directions through flow-passages C' of frame D, and through discharge-openings C of frame A into proper receivers. The refuse falls upon the floor or into a receiver.

In the drawings two sets of sieves are shown, and the second set works precisely the same as the first. The number of sets may be increased, as described. Three sieves might be used instead of four, or any other unequal number above three.

What I claim is—

Two or more reversely-inclined ore-sizing sieves, partly inclosed in frames A and D, one of which frames is stationary, and the other reciprocating, substantially as and for the purpose set forth.

DAVID NEVIN.

Witnesses:
HENRY C. HARRINGTON,
EDWARD A. CLARK.

J. KNIGHT.
Key-Fastener.

No. 167,674. Patented Sept. 14, 1875.

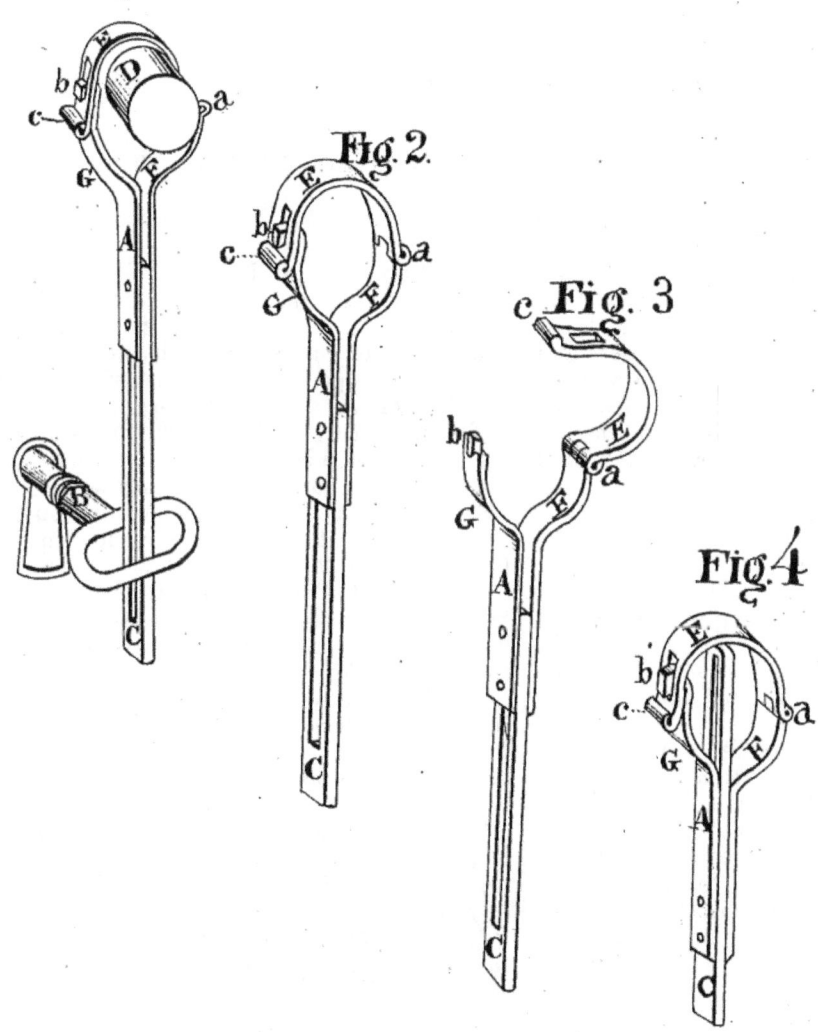

UNITED STATES PATENT OFFICE.

JAMES KNIGHT, OF DENVER, COLORADO TERRITORY.

IMPROVEMENT IN KEY-FASTENERS.

Specification forming part of Letters Patent No. **167,674**, dated September 14, 1875; application filed July 9, 1875.

To all whom it may concern:

Be it known that I, JAMES KNIGHT, of Denver, in the county of Arapahoe and Territory of Colorado, have invented a new and Improved Key-Fastener; and I do hereby declare the following to be a full and exact description of the same, reference being had to the accompanying drawings forming a part of this specification, in which—

Figure 1 is a perspective view of my key-fastener applied to a key that is in the lock of a door. Fig. 2 is a perspective view of the key-fastener, detached from the door. Fig. 3 is a view showing the clasp unfastened and top turned back on its hinges. Fig. 4 shows the key-fastener with the top closed and the slotted arm pressed up against the top in the most compact manner.

Similar letters of reference in the accompanying drawings denote the same parts.

This invention relates to key-fasteners, by the use of which the key in a door is prevented from being turned by any means from the opposite side, in which it is, and has for its object to provide for the public an inexpensive and efficient means of securing their doors against being opened by professional burglars or sneak-thieves.

To these ends the invention consists in the peculiar construction of the device, as hereinafter more fully described and definitely claimed.

In the drawings, A represents the key-fastener in position, to prevent the key from being turned. B is the key through which the slotted arm C passes. D is the shank of the knob, around which the hinged top E closes and holds itself in position. F is a bent arm, hinged at *a*, with top E. G is a bent arm, at the upper end of which is the catch *b*, for holding clasp *c* in position. The slotted arm C slides between the bent arms F and G, which are held in proper position by two rivets passing through the slot in the arm C.

To apply this device to the purpose for which it is intended, take it in its most compact form, as shown in Fig. 4, draw the slotted arm down as far as possible, unclasp the top from the catch *b*, and turn back on the hinge until the top is open, as shown in Fig. 3; then put the slotted arm C through the key B, clasp the top around the shank D, and make fast with catch *b* and clasp *a* altogether, as shown in Fig. 1.

It will now be seen that the key cannot be turned in the lock without detaching the key-fastener, which cannot be done by any means or appliances from the opposite side of the door.

The whole arrangement is simple, inexpensive, and effective.

I claim as my invention and desire to secure by Letters Patent—

1. In a key-fastener, the slotted arm C, sliding between the bent arms F and G, substantially as described and shown.

2. The bent arms F and G, hinged and clasped to the top E, substantially as set forth and shown.

3. The combination of the slotted arm C, with the bent arms F and G, and the hinged top E, substantially as shown and described.

JAMES KNIGHT.

Witnesses:
GEO. BURT,
JAY A. MERRILL.

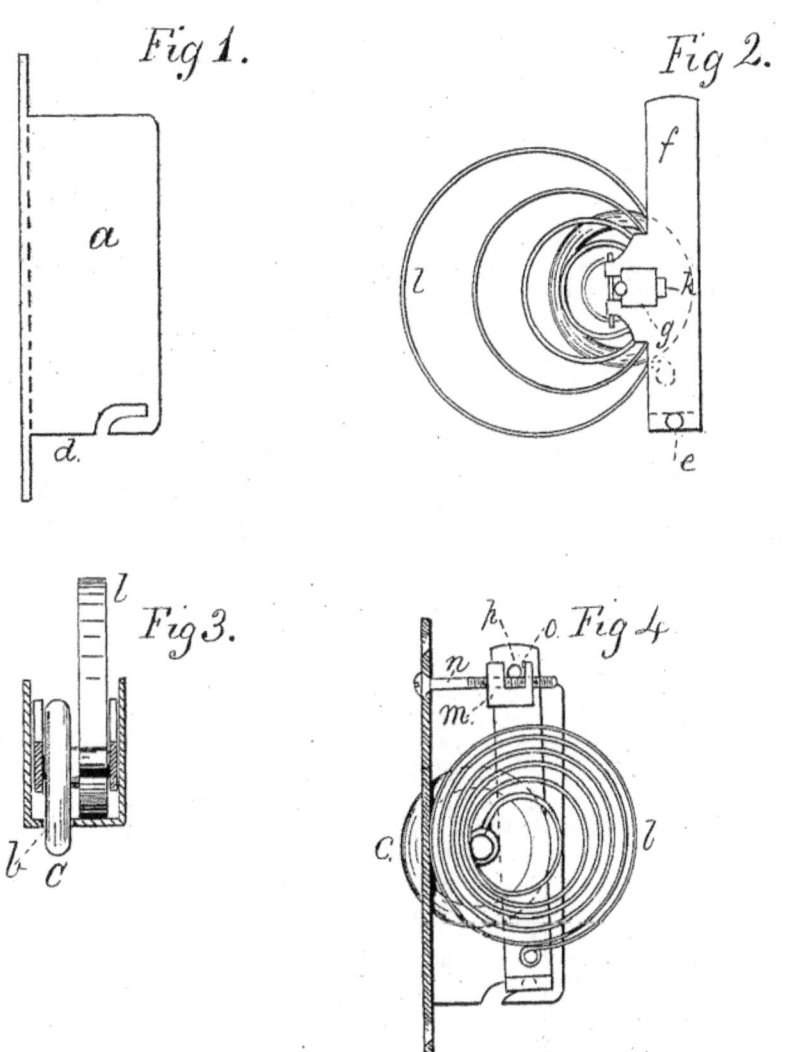

UNITED STATES PATENT OFFICE.

WILLIAM J. LEWIS, OF DENVER, COLORADO TERRITORY.

IMPROVEMENT IN SASH-BALANCES.

Specification forming part of Letters Patent No. **167,677**, dated September 14, 1875; application filed August 4, 1875.

To all whom it may concern:

Be it known that I, WILLIAM J. LEWIS, of Denver, county of Arapahoe and Territory of Colorado, have invented a Self-Adjusting Sash-Balance.

The following description, taken in connection with the accompanying plate of drawings hereinafter referred to, forms a full and exact specification, wherein are set forth the nature and principles of the invention, by which the same may be distinguished from others of a similar class, together with such parts thereof as are claimed as new and are desired to be secured by Letters Patent of the United States.

My invention relates to that class of appliances for windows commonly known as sash-balances; and the nature thereof consists in certain improvements in the construction of the same and novel combination of parts hereinafter described—that is to say, my invention relates to the employment of spring-cylinders or rollers upon one or both edges of the window-sash, the periphery of each roll being preferably covered with rubber, and each roller being hung upon an arbor actuated by a spring, and wound upon an arbor against the stress of a coiled spring, in such a manner that, when the sash is put in its casing, the tendency of the spring to rotate the roll creates a stress upon the sash tending to throw it upward. The novel combination of parts constituting the invention is designated in the claims.

In the accompanying plate of drawings, in which corresponding parts are designated by the same letters, Figure 1 represents the exterior of the casing. Fig. 2 is a detached view of mechanism by which the pulley is actuated. Fig. 3 is a vertical section. Fig. 4 illustrates the interior of the casing.

The casing a is fitted within a slot cut for its reception in that portion of the frame which is next to the sash, and is provided with an elongated aperture, b, for the reception of the projecting portion of the pulley c, and curvilinear openings d, for the reception of the lugs e, which project from and form a part of inner frame-work f. The axle of the said pulley c has its bearings in the journal-boxes g, which are arranged to slide in slots or openings cut in said frame-work f, and rest against rubber pieces k, arranged at the bases of the said slots or openings. l designates a spiral spring, one end of which is secured to a projecting lug attached to the said frame-work f, and the other end of which is secured to the axle of said pulley. When the said spring is wound or coiled upon said axle the force of elasticity developed will cause the said pulley to rotate and exert its force upon the sash of the window in such a manner as to prevent the said window from falling. m designates a nut arranged upon the screw n, in such a manner that it may be made to travel in or out with facility, by means of a screw-driver applied to the head of the screw, which occupies a position, when the window is raised, immediately beneath the lower sash. The said nut is provided with elongated slots o, for the reception of lugs p, rigidly attached to the inner sides of said frame-work f.

By this combination of parts, as will be obvious to those skilled in the art to which the invention relates, the pulley or roller which is provided with a periphery of rubber will be rotated by the falling sash in such a manner as to cause the spring to be wound up or coiled upon the axle thereof. It will also be obvious that the pressure of the said roller may be accurately adjusted by means of said screw n.

Having thus described my invention, I claim and desire to secure by Letters Patent of the United States—

1. In a sash-balance containing a spring, the stress of which tends to turn the roll and to raise or support the sash, the combination of the casing a, provided with curvilinear openings d, the frame f, the nut m, and the screw n, all constructed as described, and co-acting as described.

2. In a sash-balance containing a spring, the stress of which tends to turn a roll, and raise the sash, the pulley c, the periphery of which is covered with rubber, in combination with the journal-box g and elastic pad k, as and for the purposes described.

In testimony that I claim the foregoing I have hereunto set my hand this 6th day of July, 1875.

WILLIAM J. LEWIS.

Witnesses:
H. Y. ANDERSON,
JAY A. MERRILL.

I. A. LOVEJOY.
Stove-Leg.

No. 167,915. Patented Sept. 21, 1875.

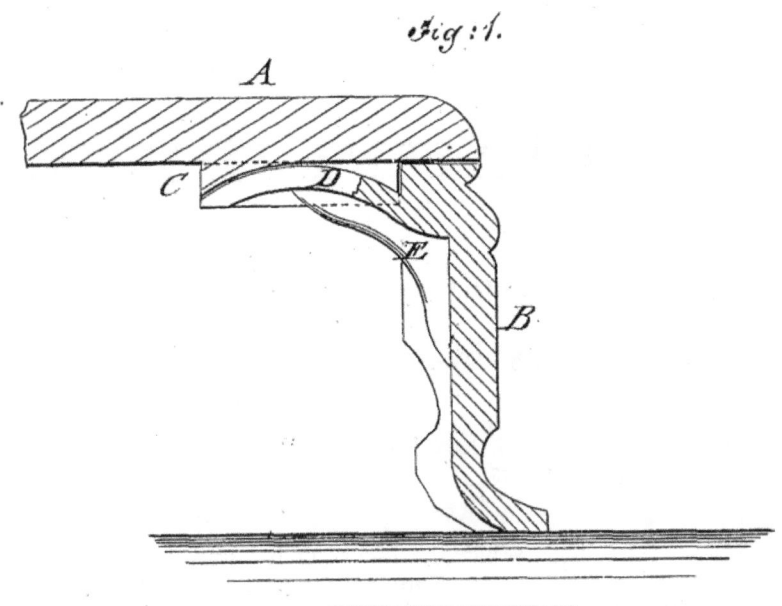

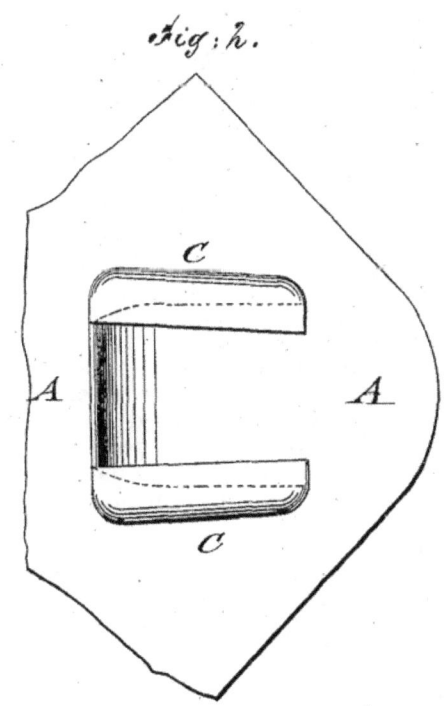

WITNESSES: INVENTOR:
  Ira A. Lovejoy
  BY
  ATTORNEYS.

UNITED STATES PATENT OFFICE.

IRA A. LOVEJOY, OF DENVER, COLORADO TERRITORY.

IMPROVEMENT IN STOVE-LEGS.

Specification forming part of Letters Patent No. **167,915**, dated September 21, 1875; application filed August 21, 1875.

To all whom it may concern:

Be it known that I, IRA A. LOVEJOY, of Denver, in the county of Arapahoe and Territory of Colorado, have invented a new and Improved Stove-Leg, of which the following is a specification:

In the accompanying drawing, Figure 1 represents a vertical central section of my improved stove-leg, and Fig. 2 a bottom view of the hearth or base plate of the stove.

Similar letters of reference indicate corresponding parts.

My invention relates to an improved stove-leg, which is firmly seated in the socket-groove of the hearth-plate of the stove, in such a manner that it does not get detached when the stove is raised for the purpose of changing the position.

The invention consists of a stove-leg with curved and braced tongue, fitting into a curved groove formed by recessed socket-projections at the under side of the bottom or hearth plate.

In the drawing, A represents the base or hearth plate of the stove, and B the stove-leg, which is applied to the base-plate by a curved tongue, D, that slides into a curved groove formed by recessed or dovetailed socket-projections C at the under side of the base-plate A.

When the stove-leg is completely set into the socket-projections, so that the main part comes in contact with the same, the leg is seated and retained therein without getting detached when raising the stove for removal.

The curved tongue B is strengthened by a brace or rib, E, in the bottom of leg, for preventing its breaking off.

The curved socket-pieces hold the leg firmly in position when the stove is standing, and, as the tongue is fully pressed into the groove, the curve prevents any slipping out on the raising of the stove, so that the annoyance of dropping the legs when moving the stove is fully avoided.

Having thus described my invention, what I claim as new, and desire to secure by Letters Patent, is—

The combination of a stove-leg, having curved and braced tongue, with a curved groove formed by recessed socket projecting at the under side of the stove-base plate, substantially in the manner and for the purpose specified.

IRA A. LOVEJOY.

Witnesses:
JAMES M. BLOOD,
ELIZA R. BLOOD.

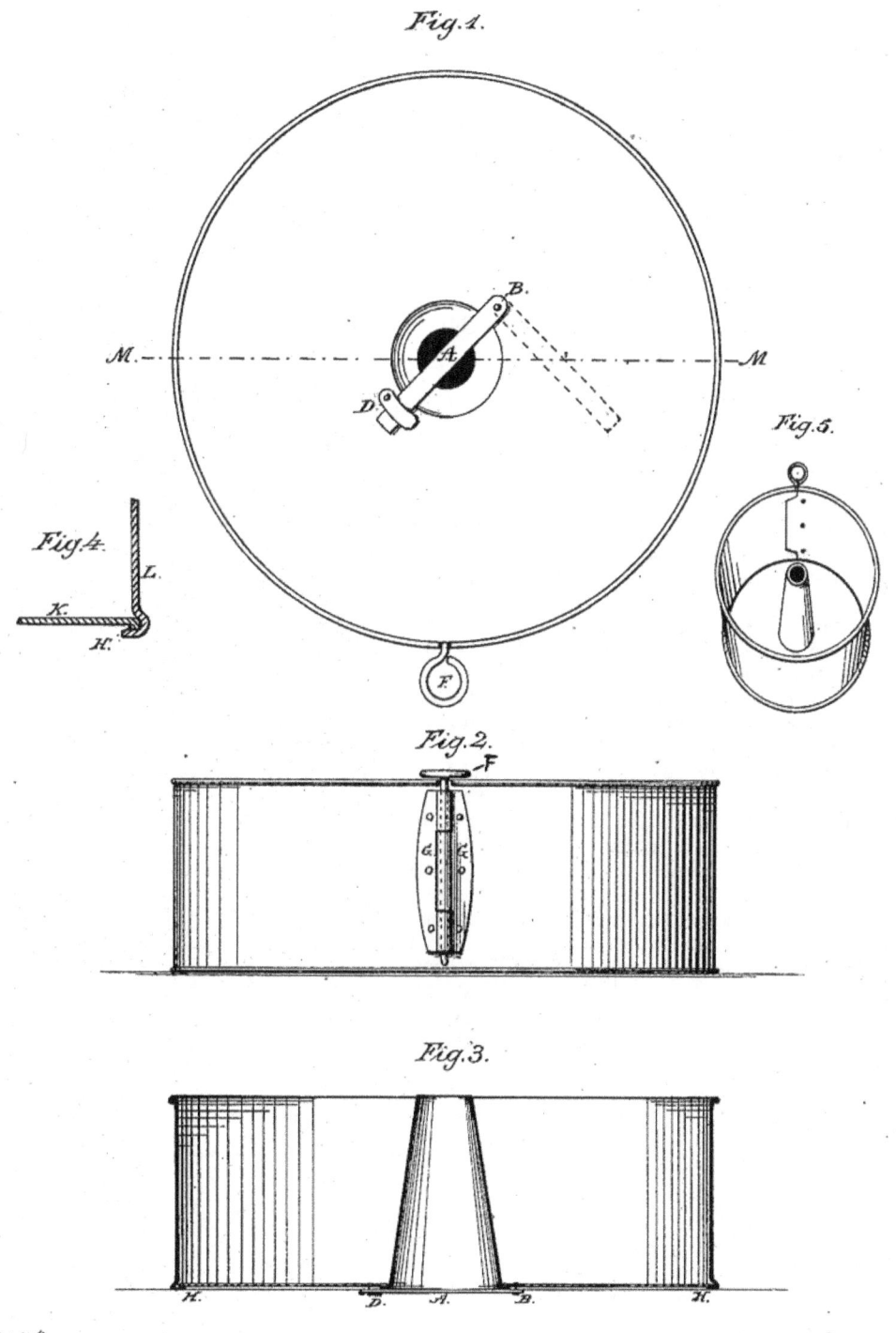

UNITED STATES PATENT OFFICE.

LYDIA A. FRISTOE, OF DENVER, COLORADO TERRITORY.

IMPROVEMENT IN BAKING-PANS.

Specification forming part of Letters Patent No. **168,089**, dated September 28, 1875; application filed June 5, 1875.

To all whom it may concern:

Be it known that I, LYDIA A. FRISTOE, of Denver, Colorado Territory, have invented an Improvement in Baking-Pans, of which the following is a specification:

The object of this improvement is, first, to provide a means of removing the baked contents of the dish or pan without injury or soiling; second, provide a raised groove on the bottom of the pan or dish, to allow air between the oven and pan-bottom, thus preventing the contents from being burned.

Figure 1 is a plan of the bottom of the pan, showing the means of removing the center funnel from the inside of the baked contents.

A is a metal bar, that turns freely on its joint B and slips under the clasp D. To remove the funnel, it is only necessary to move back the bar A to the position indicated by the dotted lines, and the center piece can be readily drawn out.

Fig. 2 is a plane elevation, showing the means of clasping and unclasping the outside or circumference from the bottom. To remove the bottom, together with the baked contents, withdraw the pin F from out the clasp G, thus releasing the sides or circumference, and the bottom drops out of the groove H.

Fig. 4 is a section of this groove H on an enlarged scale. K is the bottom; L, the sides.

Fig. 3 is a section of the dish on the lines M M. Fig. 5 is a perspective view of the dish put together, ready for charging with its contents.

What I claim as new and useful, and desire to secure by Letters Patent, is—

The combination of the hoop L, provided with the clasp, pin, and groove, as specified, and the bottom K, as shown and described.

In witness whereof I have hereunto set my hand and seal this 27th day of May, 1875.

LYDIA A. FRISTOE. [L. S.]

Witnesses:
W. H. J. NICHOLS,
W. S. NEWMAN,
C. H. FRISTOE.

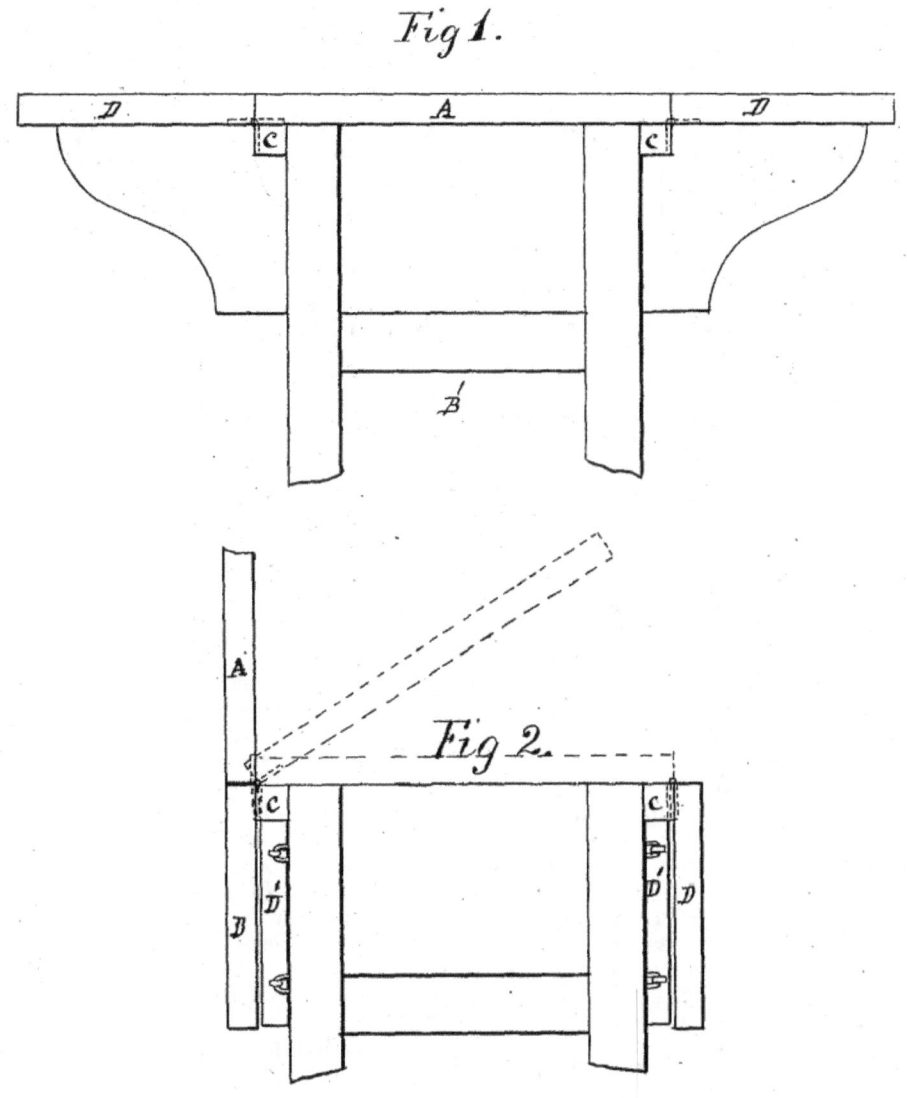

UNITED STATES PATENT OFFICE.

JOHN C. RICKETTS, OF DENVER, COLORADO TERRITORY.

IMPROVEMENT IN KITCHEN-TABLES.

Specification forming part of Letters Patent No. **168,288**, dated September 28, 1875; application filed July 9, 1875.

To all whom it may concern:

Be it known that I, JOHN C. RICKETTS, of Denver, in the county of Arapahoe and Territory of Colorado, have invented a new and Improved article of Kitchen Furniture; and I do hereby declare the following to be a full and exact description of the same, reference being had to the accompanying drawings, forming part of this specification.

My invention relates to that class of tables which are adapted to kitchen use; and the nature thereof consists in certain improvements in the construction of the same, and novel combinations of parts, hereinafter shown and described.

In the accompanying plate of drawings, in which corresponding parts are designated by the same letters, Figure 1 is an end elevation, showing the leaves raised. Fig. 2 is an end elevation, showing the leaves lowered.

In said drawings, A designates the top of the table, which is hinged to the block C, arranged longitudinally beneath said top, and rigidly attached to the sides of the table. The leaves D are also hinged to the said blocks C in such a manner that with facility they may be made to assume the horizontal position shown in Fig. 1, or the vertical position illustrated in Fig. 2. D' designates hinged brackets, which are swung outward in such a manner as to support the said leaves, as is shown in Fig. 1.

I claim—

The combination of the blocks C, arranged longitudinally beneath the top, and rigidly attached to the sides of the table, the leaves D, hinged to the blocks C, the hinged brackets D', and the cover A, hinged to the blocks C, as and for the purposes described.

JOHN C. RICKETTS.

Witnesses:
JAY A. MERRILL,
W. A. LEWIS.

G. BURT.
Door-Securer.

No. 168,556. Patented Oct. 11, 1875.

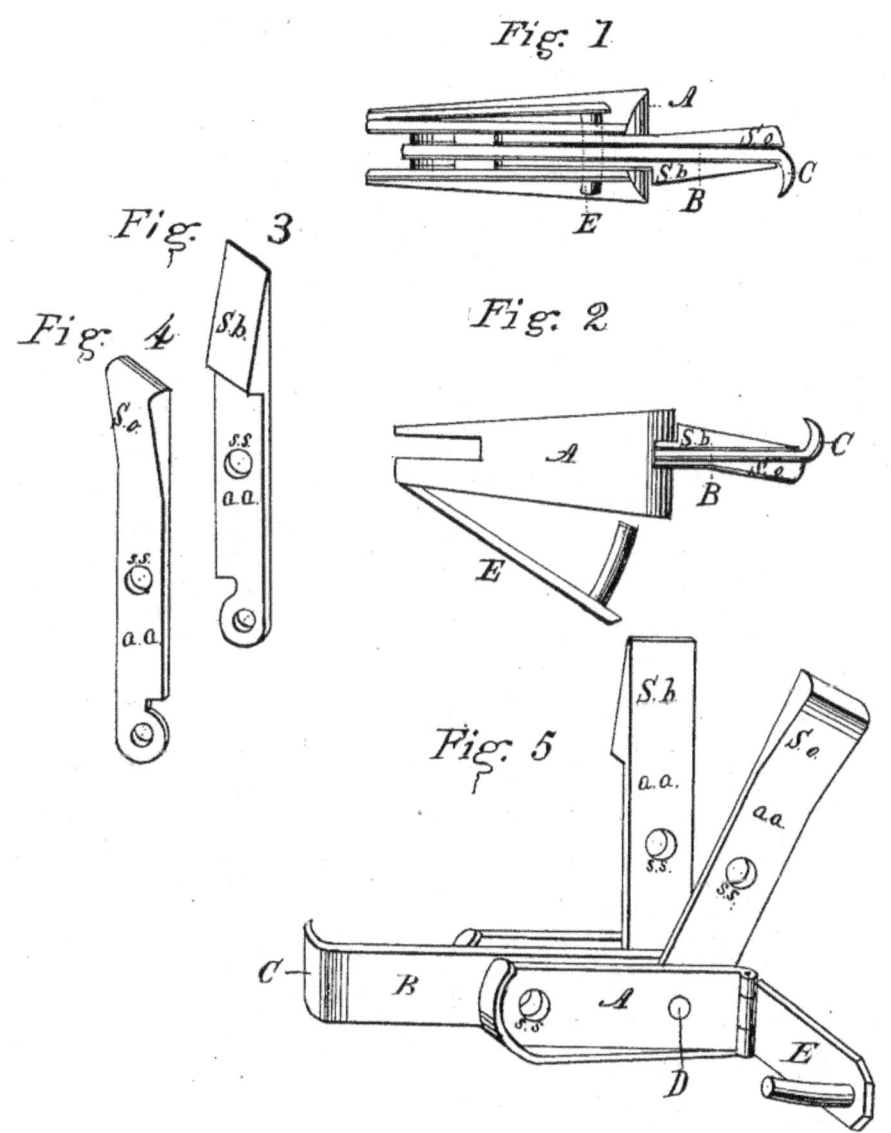

UNITED STATES PATENT OFFICE.

GEORGE BURT, OF DENVER, COLORADO TERRITORY.

IMPROVEMENT IN DOOR-SECURERS.

Specification forming part of Letters Patent No. **168,556**, dated October 11, 1875; application filed May 28, 1875.

CASE B.

To all whom it may concern:

Be it known that I, GEORGE BURT, of Denver, in the county of Arapahoe, in the Territory of Colorado, have invented certain Improvements in Door-Fasteners, of which the following is a specification:

The object of my invention is to furnish new appliances to fill up the space between the edge of the door and the jamb where the space is of more than ordinary thickness, and also to hold the fastener securely in position. It consists of a novel adaptation of reversed wedges, the application of my wedge-plates in this relation producing very desirable and useful results, as will be hereinafter more fully described, and then pointed out in the claim.

Figure 1 is a plan view, showing the reversed wedge-plates in position with the other parts of the fastener. Fig. 2 is a top view of the same. Figs. 3 and 4 are views of the wedge-plates detached from the device. Fig. 5 is a view, in detail, of the door-fastener, with the wedge-plates attached; also, a new arrangement or change of position of the slot in the jaw, the slot being placed nearer the hook or jamb side of the jaw, so that the fastener can be affixed to doors where there is a molding round the casing.

In the accompanying drawing, A represents a slotted jaw; B, a plate, terminating at one end with a curved hook, C. This plate works upon a rivet, D, in the slotted jaw A; S b and S o, the reversed wedges, affixed at the end of each plate $a\ a$, these plates also working on the rivet D, on either or each side of the curved hook-plate B. The wedge-plates $a\ a$ are provided with orifices $s\ s$, corresponding with the orifices in the jaw A and the curved hook-plate B, through which the hinged bolt E passes, and holds the wedge-plates $a\ a$ firmly in position and together with the curved hook-plate B.

The reversed wedges can be used singly or together, as the thickness or dimensions of the aperture between the edge of the door and the casing may require. When the reversed wedges are not required they can be dropped down out of the way, and do not interfere with the working of the fastener when the curved hook-plate is only used or needed.

I claim as my invention—

The two plates $a\ a$, working upon the rivet D, with the orifices $s\ s$, by means of which they may be locked in position, in combination with the reversed wedges S b and S o, attached thereto, respectively, in the position and substantially as described and shown, for the purposes hereinbefore set forth.

GEO. BURT.

Witnesses:
EDMUND A. WILLOUGHBY,
J. O. PATTERSON.

J. M. BLOOD.
DOOR-SPRING.

No. 169,405.   Patented Nov. 2, 1875.

Fig. 1.

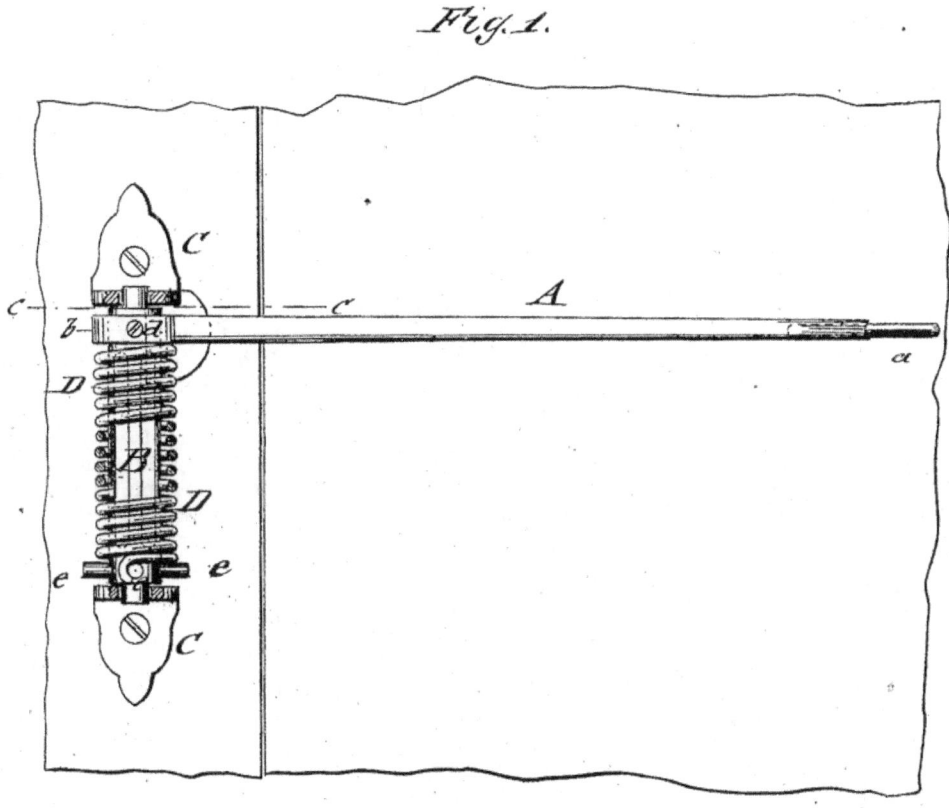

Fig. 2.

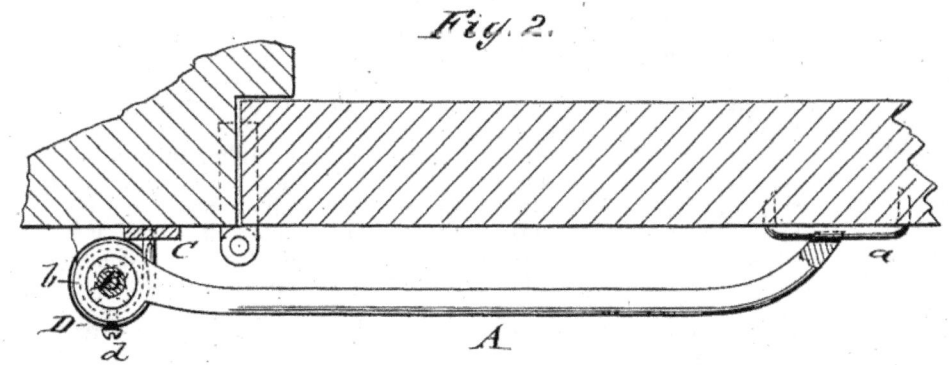

WITNESSES:
E. Wolff
A. F. Terry

INVENTOR:
J. M. Blood
BY
[signature]
ATTORNEYS.

UNITED STATES PATENT OFFICE.

JAMES M. BLOOD, OF DENVER, COLORADO TERRITORY.

IMPROVEMENT IN DOOR-SPRINGS.

Specification forming part of Letters Patent No. **169,405**, dated November 2, 1875; application filed September 17, 1875.

To all whom it may concern:

Be it known that I, JAMES M. BLOOD, of Denver, in the county of Arapahoe and Territory of Colorado, have invented a new and Improved Door-Spring, of which the following is a specification:

In the accompanying drawing, Figure 1 represents a front elevation of my improved door-spring; and Fig. 2, a top view of the same, partly in horizontal section on the line $c\ c$, Fig. 1.

Similar letters of reference indicate corresponding parts.

The invention is an improvement in the class of door-closing devices which consist of a journaled shaft or roller encircled by a spiral spring, and provided with a laterally-projecting arm, whose outer end bears upon the door with a pressure corresponding to the power and tension of the spring.

The invention consists in the novel construction and arrangement of parts, as hereinafter described and claimed, whereby the tension of the spring may be quickly and conveniently changed, and the action of the device thereby regulated.

In the drawing, A represents the curved lever, that presses and slides with its outer grooved end on a wire staple, or the aperture of a thumb-screw hook, a, of the door, during the opening and closing of the same. The lever A is attached to an annular collar, b, and clamp-screw d to a fluted barrel, B, that turns by top and bottom pivots or gudgeons in brackets C, screwed firmly to the door-frame. The spiral spring D is coiled around the fluted barrel, which reduces, by its small contact-surface, the friction of the spring during the winding and unwinding operations of the same. The spring D is applied by one end to the bracket-plate or door-frame; by the other end to one of the radially-extending spurs or pins e of the barrel. The spurs e serve for the purpose of regulating the tension of the spring according to the size and weight of the door to be closed, or for readjusting the same after having been in use for some time, by simply detaching the lever from the adjustable thumb-screw hook, turning the same a quarter round, so that the end of the lever is clear, swinging then the lever up, and placing a clog below one of the spurs, so that the lever is prevented from swinging back. The clamp-screw of the lever is then loosened, and the lever carried back to its position on the door, and fastened again by the clamp-screw. The clog is then taken off, and thus the tension of the spring adjusted in a very simple and convenient manner, without detaching the spring from the door-frame.

The barrel turns with the lever and tightens the spring attached thereto, which works very easily and satisfactorily, as the exact degree of tension can be readily imparted to the same.

Having thus described my invention, I claim as new and desire to secure by Letters Patent—

As the improvement hereinbefore described, the journaled roller or barrel B, having the series of fixed radially-projecting pins e, and the curved adjustable arm A, and clamp-screw d, and the spiral spring D, all combined and arranged as set forth and shown, for the purpose specified.

JAMES M. BLOOD.

Witnesses:
 IRA A. LOVEJOY,
 JNO. A. RYAN.

C. DUHEM.
GALVANIC-BATTERY.

No. 169,529.   Patented Nov. 2. 1875.

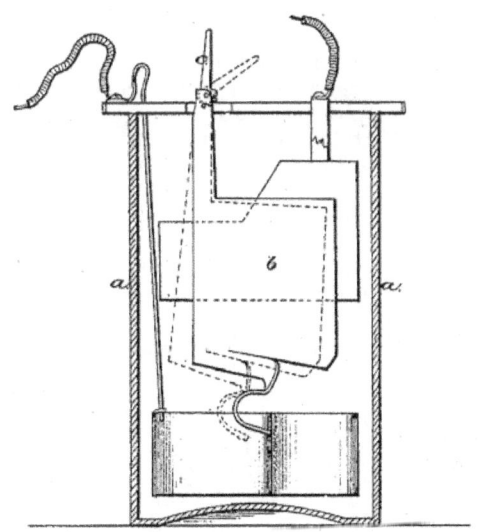

Attest:
M. Gardner.
Edw. W. Donn

C. Duhem   Inventor: by
CS Whitman.
attorney

UNITED STATES PATENT OFFICE.

CONSTANT DUHEM, OF DENVER, COLORADO TERRITORY.

IMPROVEMENT IN GALVANIC BATTERIES.

Specification forming part of Letters Patent No. **169,529**, dated November 2, 1875; application filed July 9, 1875.

To all whom it may concern:

Be it known that I, CONSTANT DUHEM, of Denver, in the county of Arapahoe and Territory of Colorado, have invented a new and improved mode of increasing the electrical force of galvanic batteries by a simple mechanical attachment, which I will call "Duhem's Positive Supplementary Electrode," which I will now proceed to describe, reference being had to the accompanying drawing forming part of this specification, in which—

Figure 1 is a perspective view of a galvanic battery or cup with my invention attached, showing the device connected; also a lever arrangement, by which it is held in or out of connection.

Similar letters of reference in the accompanying drawings denote the same parts.

This invention relates to galvanic batteries for telegraph or other purposes, in which, by the use of my invention, the current can be doubled in quantity instantly by moving the lever c to nearly a perpendicular position, as shown, and has for its object to provide for the public a means for a more economical use of electricity, which shall be simple in its construction, sure and efficient in its operation, and by its use the same amount of work can be done with at least one-half of the ordinary number of cups and one-third the expense.

To these ends the invention consists in providing any cup or battery for telegraph or other purposes with a plate or piece of any of the different positive metals, suspended by any proper means in the exciting liquid between the positive and negative elements, the size and shape of the plate or piece of metal varying according to the cup or battery in which it is to be used.

In the drawings, $a\,a$ represent a galvanic battery or cup, and b the plate or piece of metal called "Duhem's positive supplementary electrode." c is the lever by which Duhem's positive supplementary electrode is connected or disconnected with the positive electro-pole of a battery without perceptibly disturbing the liquid. When in connection with the positive electro-pole the current is double in quantity, and remains so as long as desired, and falls to its original strength by being disconnected, as shown by dotted lines, thereby causing no unnecessary waste or use of material when not in use.

Having thus fully described my invention, what I claim as new, and desire to secure by Letters Patent, is—

The application to any galvanic battery of a positive supplementary electrode, capable of being easily and quickly connected or disconnected with the positive plate of a battery within the liquid, as described.

CONSTANT DUHEM.

Witnesses:
JAY A. MERRILL,
BART C. HEFLEY.

J. W. NESMITH.
SPARK-ARRESTER.

No. 169,831. Patented Nov. 9. 1875.

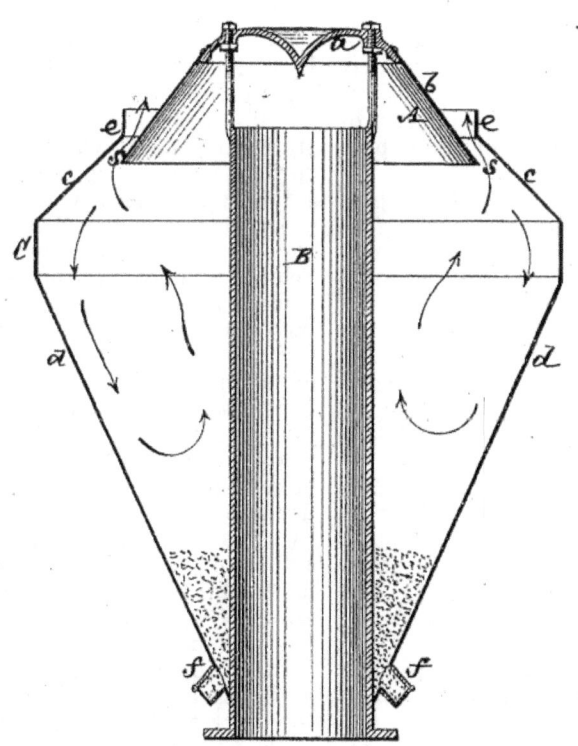

UNITED STATES PATENT OFFICE.

J. WELLINGTON NESMITH, OF GOLDEN, COLORADO.

IMPROVEMENT IN SPARK-ARRESTERS.

Specification forming part of Letters Patent No. **169,831**, dated November 9, 1875; application filed October 6, 1875.

To all whom it may concern:

Be it known that I, J. WELLINGTON NESMITH, of Golden, Jefferson county, and State of Colorado, have invented a new and useful Improvement in Smoke-Stacks for Locomotive-Engines; and I do hereby declare that the following is a full, clear, and exact description of the same, reference being had to the accompanying drawing, which forms part of this specification.

This invention has for its object the production of a smoke-stack for coal-burning locomotive-engines, which, while it possesses every efficiency in point of draft and economy as regards the consumption of fuel by the engine, serves most effectually to prevent the escape of sparks and cinders from the stack.

The invention consists in a peculiarly-constructed spark arrester and deflector, arranged within the upper portion of the stack-head, in combination with a smoke-flue, arranged to enter up within the mouth of the deflector, whereby reverse currents are produced within the stack-head during the escape and stoppage of the exhaust-steam from the engine, and an eddying action of the currents in said head is obtained, giving increased efficiency to the stack.

The drawing represents a sectional elevation of a locomotive-engine smoke-stack having my invention applied.

A is a hollow cone or inverted conical pot, the upper part a of which may be of cast-iron, and its lower and larger portion or sides b, which are free from excessive wear, be made of sheet-iron, and riveted to the upper part a. B is the smoke-flue, up through which the products of combustion from the furnace and exhaust-steam of the engine pass. Said flue has no flaring top, but may be straight throughout its length, and is extended to enter partly up within the hollow cone A, the interior of the top of which latter I prefer to make of a concave annular form, for the purpose of more effectually distributing and deflecting the incandescent particles or cinders. The lower end or mouth of the hollow cone A is considerably larger than the entering top of the smoke-flue, in order that said cone may present a full and sufficient opening for the arrested hot or burning particles to be deflected and discharged below, as hereinafter described. C is the stack-head, which consists of two frustums of cones, $c\,d$, connected at their bases, and a contracted upper portion, e. Said stack-head is made of more than ordinary large diameter at its bilge for an engine having a given diameter of cylinders; and to utilize all the room for a proper action of the stack the cone A, which may be secured by springs, or in any other suitable manner, is set as high as possible above the entering end of the flue B, and so that its lower open and widest end or mouth comes within or slightly below the contracted upper portion e of the stack-head, leaving a contracted opening, s, between the stack-head and mouth of the cone.

The operation is as follows: The products of combustion are carried forcibly up by the exhaust-steam from the engine, through the flue B, and strike the cone A. This arrests the whole current, and, by means of the cone or conical deflector A, causes it not only to be deflected downward, but outward, following the direction given by the sides b of said cone, and impinging against the upper part of the lower conical portion d of the stack-head, all around the latter, and from thence following the portion d of the stack-head downward. Now, the only point of egress from the inside of the stack-head C to the atmosphere is by the contracted opening s between the mouth of the deflecting-cone A and the upper part of the stack-head; but a current, to pass up through this space s, must also pass from the inside of the stack-head through the obliquely-downward and outer current from the flue B, which gets its direction from the sides b of the cone A, and the exhaust downward and outward from said sides b cuts off the upward current from the stack-head, and stops it for a time—that is, during each escape of exhaust-steam from the cylinder. In this manner the currents have an alternating and eddying action—that is to say, a downward current is produced at the instant of each exhaust from the engine through the flue B and cone A into the stack-head, and then an upward current—that is, between the periods of exhaust from the engine—out through the opening s. It consequently will be seen that the deflecting of the current of the products of combustion and steam downward and outward toward the portion *d* of the stack-head is absolutely essential to secure the action as described.

By the arrangement of the parts and enlarged size of the stack-head as described, there is provided all possible chance and the greatest amount of room for the currents to become more gentle and easier broken up and thrown into eddies by the action of the currents crossing each other, thereby affording a perfect opportunity for the sparks or hot solid particles and cinders to settle down within the bottom of the stack-head, from whence they may be withdrawn from time to time, as required, by one or more openings, *f*, which should be closed by lids or doors.

I claim—

The hollow cone A, arranged to project above the lower edge of the upper reduced portion *e* of the stack-head C, but with its mouth arranged to project within or below said upper reduced portion *e*, leaving a contracted opening, *s*, between it and said head, and with its sides *b* inclining in a reverse direction to the sides or portion *d* of the head, in combination with the flue B, arranged to enter up and open within the mouth of the cone A, substantially as shown and described.

J. WELLINGTON NESMITH.

Witnesses:
 E. W. ROLLINS,
 W. C. ARMOR.

J. ERNST.
BOTTLE.

No. 170,073. Patented Nov. 16, 1875.

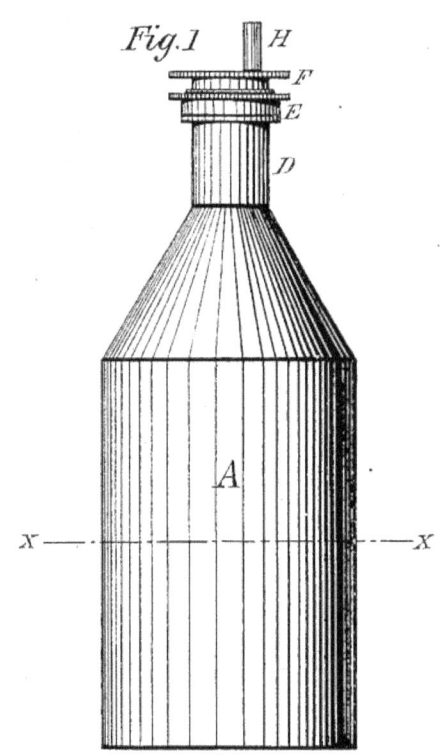

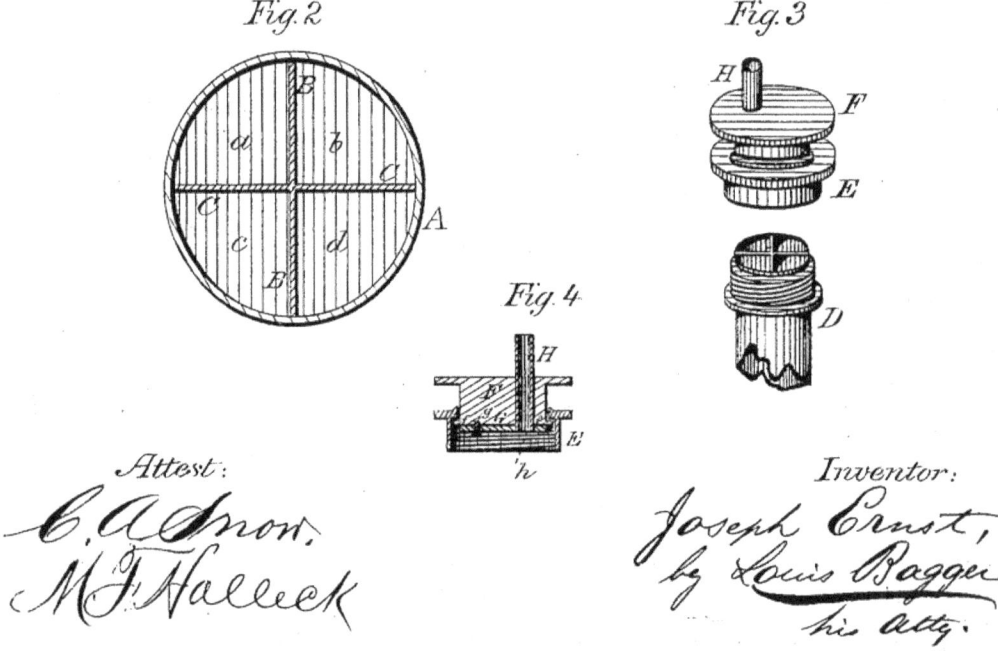

UNITED STATES PATENT OFFICE.

JOSEPH ERNST, OF CENTRAL CITY, COLORADO TERRITORY, ASSIGNOR OF ONE-HALF HIS RIGHT TO JOSEPH KEMPF, OF SAME PLACE.

IMPROVEMENT IN BOTTLES.

Specification forming part of Letters Patent No. **170,073**, dated November 16, 1875; application filed September 14, 1875.

To all whom it may concern:

Be it known that I, JOSEPH ERNST, of Central City, in the county of Gilpin and Territory of Colorado, have invented certain new and useful Improvements in Bottles; and I do hereby declare that the following is a full, clear, and exact description thereof, which will enable others skilled in the art to which it appertains to make and use the same, reference being had to the accompanying drawings and to the letters of reference marked thereon, which form a part of this specification.

Figure 1 is a side view of a bottle with the cap attached. Fig. 2 is a horizontal section after the line indicated by $x\ x$ in Fig. 1. Fig. 3 is a perspective view of the neck of the bottle and cap, detached; and Fig. 4 is a vertical section of the cap.

Similar letters of reference indicate corresponding parts in all the figures.

This invention consists in the combination of a compartment-bottle with a revolving screw-cap of peculiar construction, so that the tube in said cap may readily be placed over either of the compartments.

The bottle A has two or more compartments, denoted by $a\ b\ c\ d$, formed by the interior dividing-walls B C. The neck of the bottle is provided with a screw-thread, D, as shown. The cap consists of the sleeve E, which has an inside screw-thread corresponding to D, and the revolving top piece F, which is secured upon the sleeve E by the annular flange f, as shown in Fig. 4. The rim of the top piece F is ribbed or serrated, so the fingers may readily seize it when it is desired to turn it. G is a washer made of rubber or other suitable material and secured onto the under side of the top piece F by rivets g. This washer is perforated at h, care being taken when the washer is riveted to the top piece that the said perforation comes directly under the tube H, which is affixed to and rotates with the top piece F.

From the foregoing description the manner of operating the cap will be readily understood.

The various compartments in the bottle having been filled with the various kinds of liquor they are desired to contain, the screw-cap is adjusted by turning the rotating top piece F, so that the tube H is placed over the compartment from which it is desired to pour the liquor. A band or label may be placed around the neck of the bottle below the screw-cap, having upon it the names of the liquors or fluids contained in the bottle, and so arranged that each name shall come just opposite to the compartment to which it refers. By this arrangement the tube may be readily placed in its proper position, even if the bottle is made of opaque glass.

It is obvious that this invention may be applied to a variety of purposes, such as barkeeper's bottles, barber's bottles, medicine-bottles, or casters for table use, the compartments being varied in number and configuration to suit the various circumstances of the case, and the shape and dimensions of the tube H being also modified according to circumstances.

Having thus described my invention, I claim as new and desire to secure by Letters Patent of the United States—

The combination of a bottle or other vessel having two or more compartments formed by vertical walls or divisions B C with a screw-cap having a rotating top piece, F, and tube H, that may be adjusted over either compartment, substantially for the purpose and in the manner hereinbefore described.

In testimony that I claim the foregoing as my own I have hereunto affixed my signature in presence of two witnesses.

JOSEPH ERNST.

Witnesses:
HARLEY B. MORSE,
HENRY GOETZE.

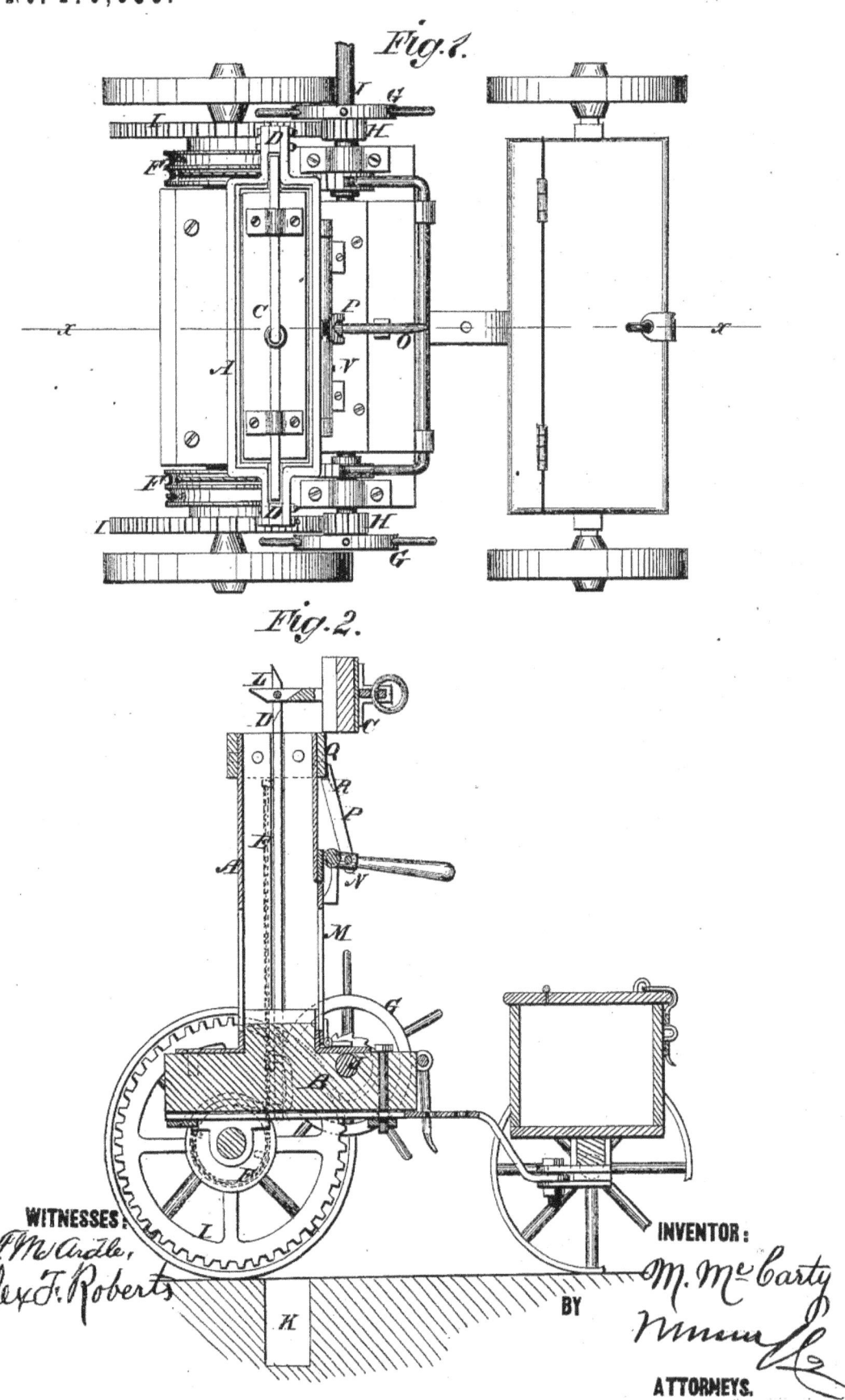

UNITED STATES PATENT OFFICE.

MICHAEL McCARTY, OF PUEBLO, COLORADO TERRITORY.

IMPROVEMENT IN PORTABLE HAY-PRESSES.

Specification forming part of Letters Patent No. **170,636**, dated November 30, 1875; application filed October 23, 1875.

To all whom it may concern:

Be it known that I, MICHAEL McCARTY, of Pueblo, in the county of Pueblo and Territory of Colorado, have invented a new and Improved Portable Press, of which the following is a specification:

The invention is an improvement in that class of presses whose follower is operated vertically by means of rods worked by chains and windlass or equivalent means.

The improvement consists, first, in jointing the rods to enable the follower to be tilted to one side of the top of the press-case, to allow the hay or other material to be inserted; and, second, the invention relates to means for fastening the door of the case out of which the bales are discharged.

Figure 1 is a top view of my improved press, and Fig. 2 is a sectional elevation taken on the line $x\ x$ of Fig. 1.

Similar letters of reference indicate corresponding parts.

A represents the vertical press-case, which is erected on a strong base, B, that is mounted on the hind portion of a truck for moving the press about from place to place. C is the follower; D, rods for working the follower; E, chains for working said rods; F, drums for working the chains; G, hand-wheels; H, pinions, and I wheels for working the drums. The hand-wheels and pinions are on a shaft, J, arranged in suitable bearings in the bed-piece B, and extending across the truck from side to side, so that power can be applied at both sides, and at one end the shaft projects, so that a pulley and a rope may be applied for the use of horse-power to work the press.

The wheels I are fitted on the axle of the truck so as to turn loosely, to work the press when the truck is at rest.

Instead of the drums and chains for working the bars D, the latter may be toothed, and gear with pinions connected with the wheels I.

K represents holes to be made in the ground, to allow the bars room for sliding down to work the follower. The bars are jointed at L, to allow the follower to swing over to one side of the press-case to open it for stuffing. The fastening for the door consists of the shaft N, with lugs M and handle O, and the fastening-dog P.

By the lever the lugs are pressed hard against the door to hold it, and let the dog P drop under the cross-bar Q at R, to hold the lugs.

The press is designed more particularly for pressing hay from stacks, by the side of which the case is to be adjusted, so as to pitch down into it; but the hay may also be pitched up into it from the ground.

Having thus described my invention, I claim as new and desire to secure by Letters Patent—

1. The combination, with the follower and vertical press-case, of the bars D, jointed at L, as shown and described, to enable said follower to tilt, in the manner specified.

2. The shaft N, lugs M, lever O, and locking-dog P, combined and arranged with the door, substantially as specified.

MICHAEL McCARTY.

Witnesses:
 M. G. BRADFORD,
 THOMAS W. SAYLES.

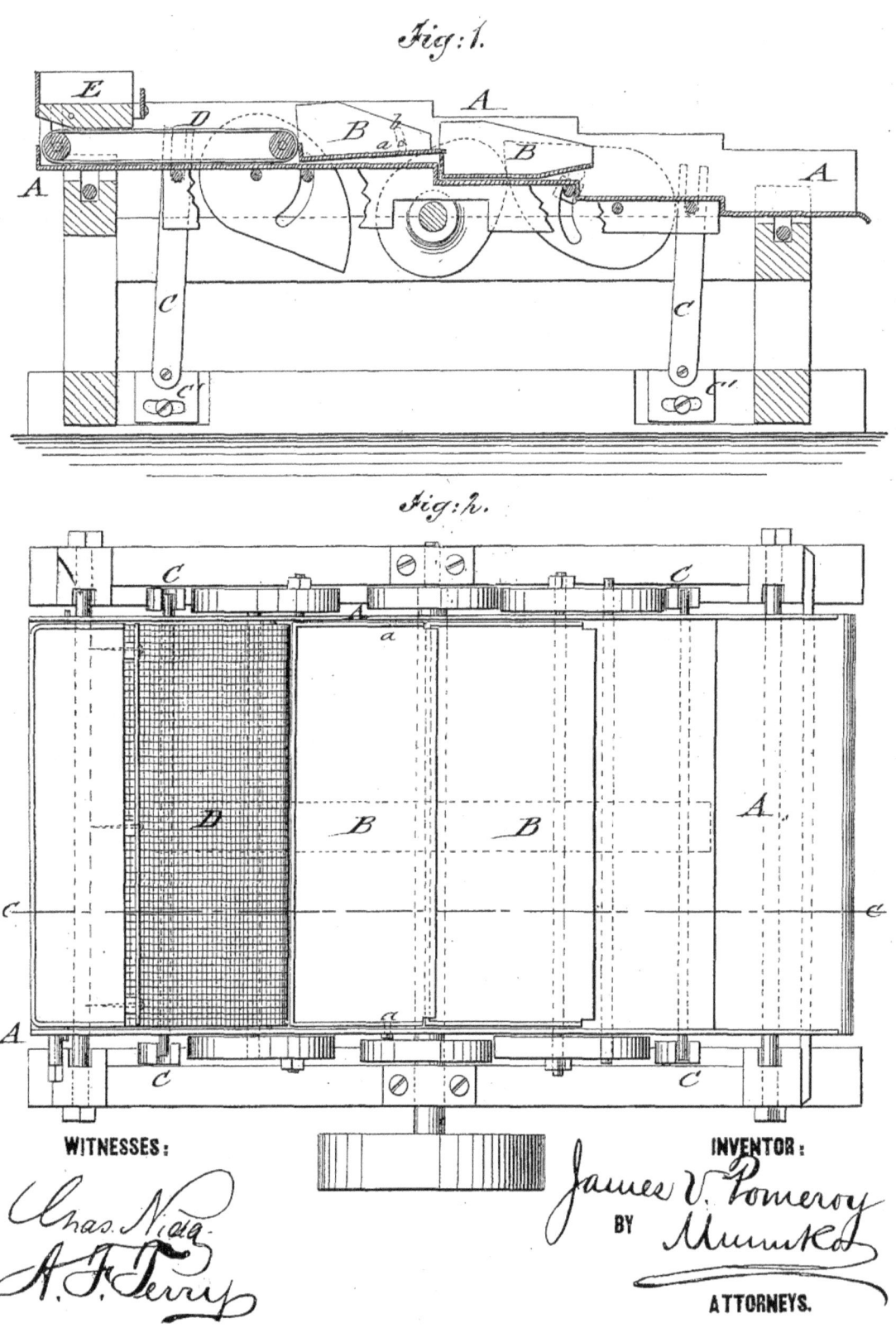

UNITED STATES PATENT OFFICE.

JAMES V. POMEROY, OF BOULDER, COLORADO TERRITORY.

IMPROVEMENT IN ORE-CONCENTRATORS.

Specification forming part of Letters Patent No. **170,642**, dated November 30, 1875; application filed August 21, 1875.

To all whom it may concern:

Be it known that I, JAMES V. POMEROY, of Boulder, in the county of Boulder and Territory of Colorado, have invented a new and Improved Ore-Concentrator, of which the following is a specification:

In the accompanying drawing, Figure 1 represents a vertical longitudinal section of my improved ore-concentrator on the line c c, Fig. 2; and Fig. 2, a top view of the same.

Similar letters of reference indicate corresponding parts.

My invention relates to improvements in the ore-concentrator which has been patented to me under date of May 11, 1875, and numbered 163,104, so that the operation of the same is more effective, and the same can be worked with or without the concentrating-pans.

The invention will first be described in connection with drawing, and then pointed out in claims.

A in the drawing represents the supporting-table, which is constructed with a step-shaped bottom, that forms a series of levels for the concentrating-pans B, the steps and head-walls producing a wave action of the water in each level or pan. The table A is supported on oscillating standards C, which are pivoted to adjustable slide-boxes C' at the lower part of the table-supporting frame, so that the center of gravity of the table may be changed, and a heavier or lighter shock be imparted to the same, according to the quality of the material.

Reciprocating motion is imparted to the table by means of a revolving eccentric and adjustable cam-pieces of the table, which mechanism is so arranged that the motion and shock imparted to the table is quick and sudden when moving toward the feed end, and slower and less violent at the discharge end.

This variable motion and shock of the table produces vibrations and waves, which convey and discharge the light material, and precipitate the heavy parts.

The table A may be used with or without the pans, the steps serving as pans, and creating the waves at each stroke of the reciprocating mechanism.

The pans B are placed on the levels of the table, with the bottom of one lapping or extending over the head or wall of the one next below. They may be arranged level with the table or adjusted by side bolts and nuts a in slots b of the side walls of the table to any suitable inclination.

A level of greater length is arranged at the head of the table, and on the same placed an endless belt or canvas, D, onto which the pulp is fed through gate of hopper E, that is hinged at the head of the table, and seated water-tight on the belt D by suitable spring-clamps, so that it forms in this position a wall for producing a wave over the belt.

When the belt is charged with mineral, the hopper is raised for an instant, and the canvas moved forward to discharge its load, forming a new surface for the mineral to settle thereon.

I do not confine myself to any special construction of cams and levers by which the reciprocating motion is imparted; but I deem it a point of main importance for producing satisfactory results of concentration that the shocks at each end should be variable, and regulated at the head or feed end of the machine exactly in accordance with the gravity of the ore, and at the discharge end with the gravity of the rock, so as to hold the one and discharge the other. The mineral is thereby regulated and controlled on the levels and in the pans, and separated in a very satisfactory and rapid manner from the lighter materials.

As the table A is vibrated or reciprocated to and fro, the ore is caused to drop between the hopper and gate, that are separated by suitable spacing-blocks, while the hopper, being pivoted, rises and falls, so as to allow the ore to escape readily.

Having thus described my invention, I claim as new and desire to secure by Letters Patent—

1. In reciprocating ore-concentrators, a step-shaped table, having a series of levels at different elevations, as and for the purpose described.

2. The combination in an ore-concentrator, with a series of levels at different elevations, of a head-level, made longer than the others, and provided with an endless belt, as and for the purpose set forth.

3. The combination of the pans, side bolts,

and nuts with the slotted side walls of the table, to adjust the pans to any inclination, substantially as set forth.

4. The standards pivoted to slide-boxes, as and for the purpose specified.

5. The combination, with concentrating-table and endless belt, of the hopper, pivoted and having gate, as and for the purpose specified.

JAMES V. POMEROY.

Witnesses:
T. J. GRAHAM,
E. L. HUBBARD.

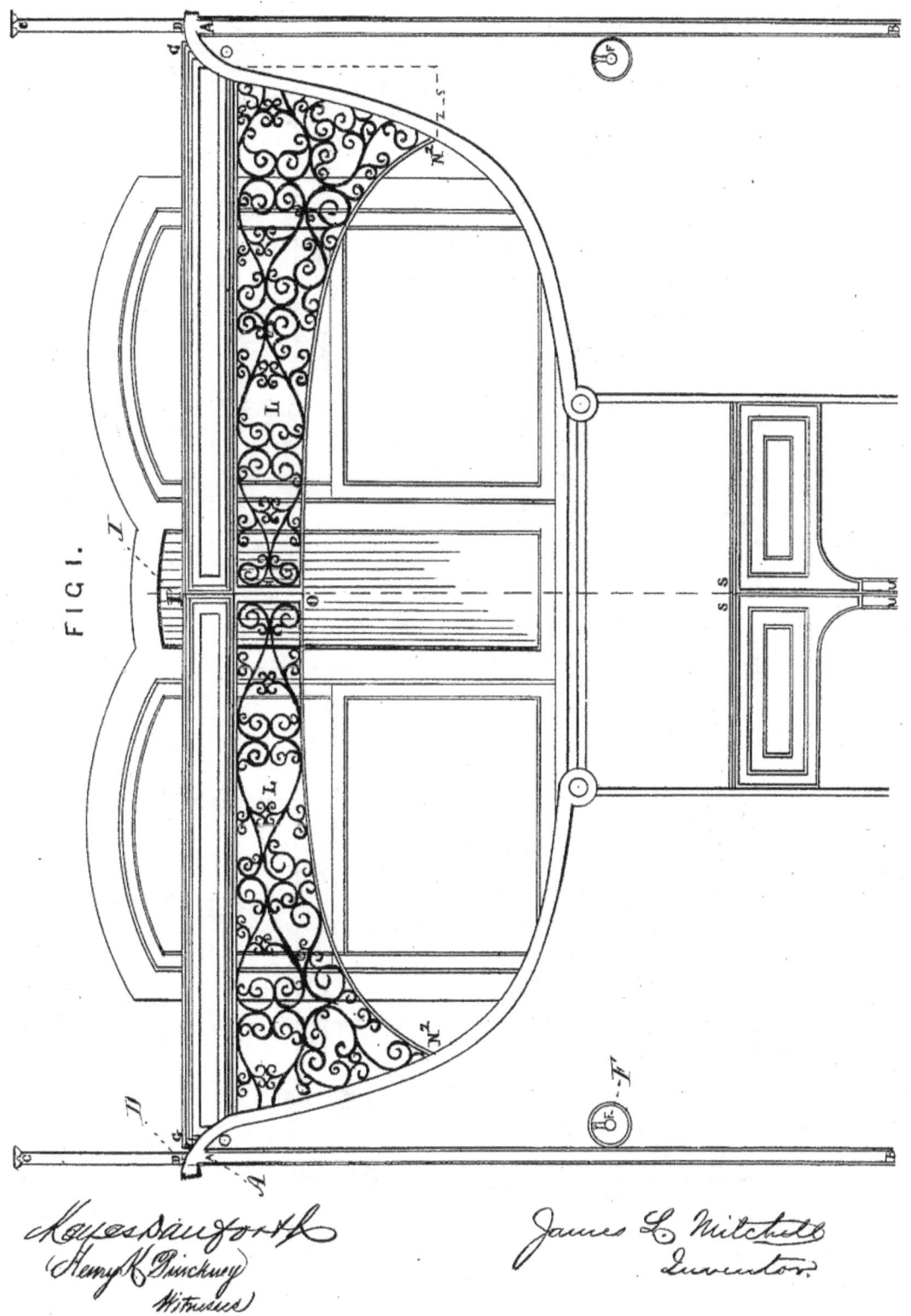

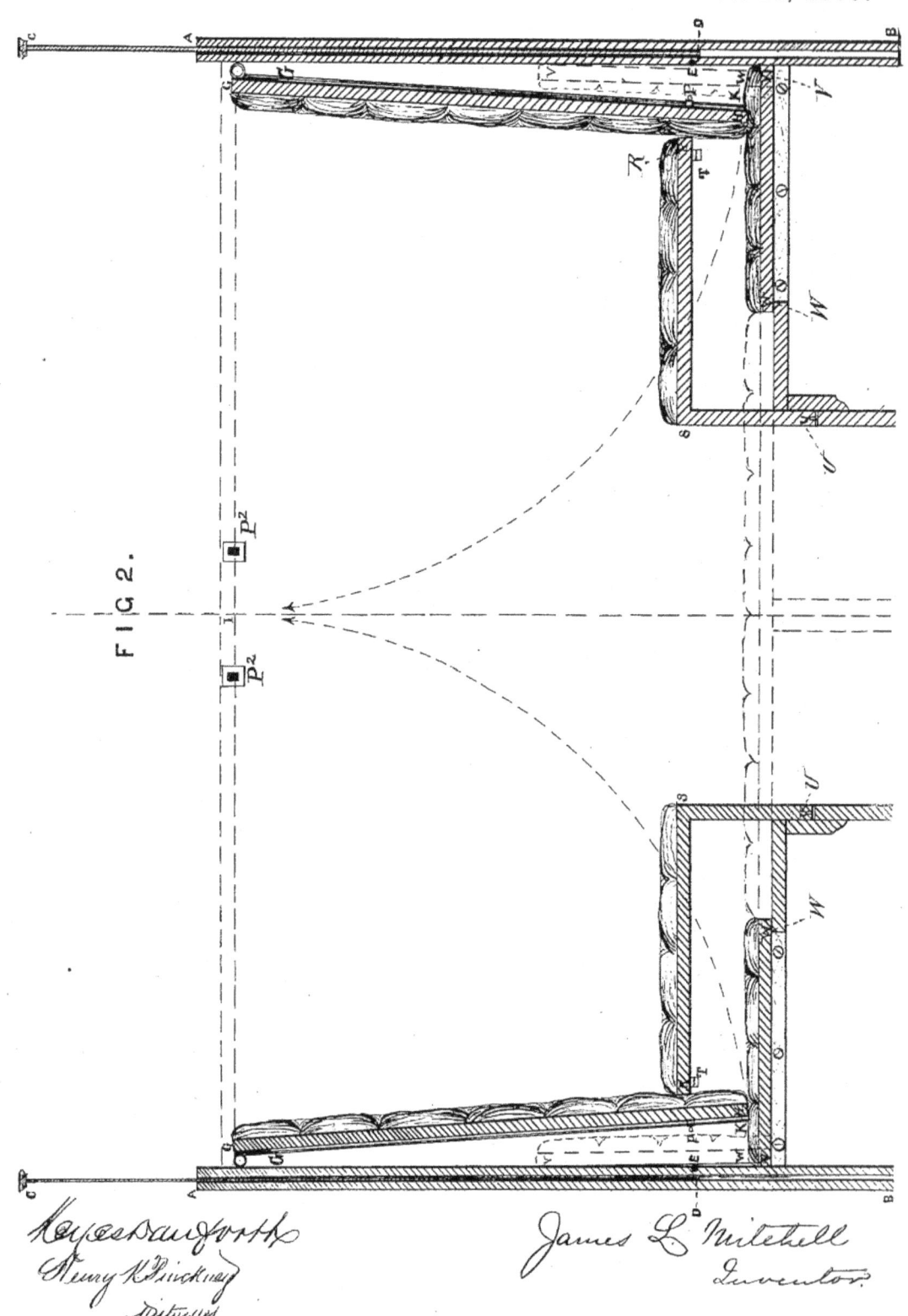

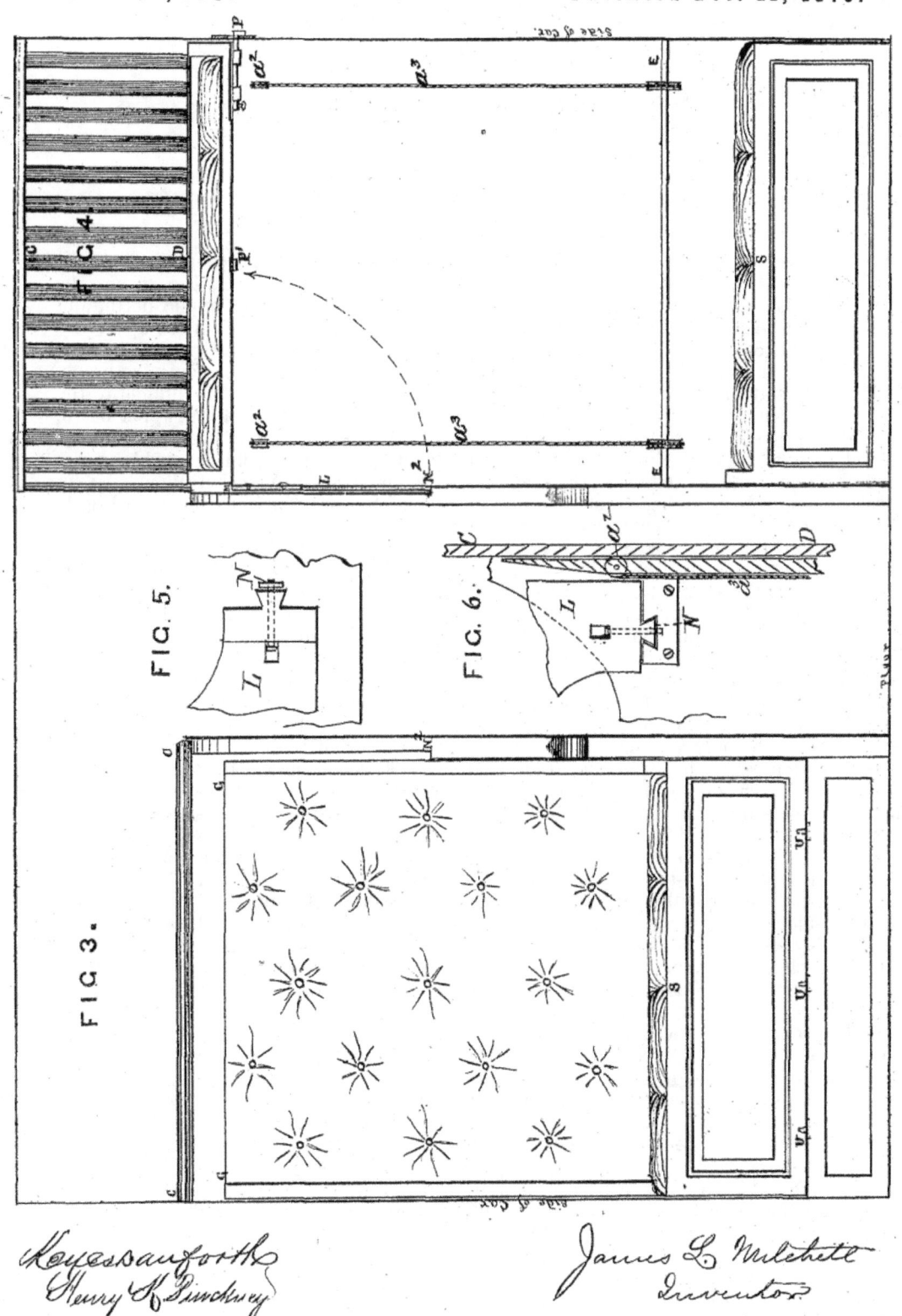

UNITED STATES PATENT OFFICE.

JAMES L. MITCHELL, OF PUEBLO, COLORADO TERRITORY.

IMPROVEMENT IN SLEEPING-CARS.

Specification forming part of Letters Patent No. **171,238**, dated December 21, 1875; application filed June 21, 1875.

To all whom it may concern:

Be it known that I, JAMES L. MITCHELL, of Pueblo, Pueblo county, Colorado Territory, have invented certain Improvements in the Seats or Couches of Sleeping-Cars, of which the following is a specification:

My invention relates to railway-cars adapted for both day and night travel; and a special feature of improvement consists of brackets hinged to the seat-backs in a novel manner, and combined with fastenings in the seat ends, car-wall, and seat-backs, in such manner that the bracket of each seat-back can be dropped down in front of the couch to form a continuous arch-support for the aisle side of the upper couch, and fastened at two points—the heel and the middle—and turned under and fastened to the seat-back out of the way when the seat-backs are lowered. The feature of the continuous arch-support at the front of the couch is entirely new, so far as I know, and the manner of securing these brackets when so arched is not only advantageous, but new in connection with such front spanning arches. These arch-supports fold under against the inner side of the seat-backs, when the latter are adjusted for day travel, and the same bolts which serve to secure them as arched supports serve also to fasten them to the seat-backs. The vertically-sliding panels are raised and lowered by crank-shafts having cord and pulley connections with said panels. This renders the adjustment of the panels very convenient from the floor of the car.

Figure 1 is an elevation of one section of a sleeping-car prepared for the night embodying my invention. Fig. 2 is a longitudinal section of the same in form of seats. Fig. 3 is an end elevation of one-half of a section in the form of a seat. Fig. 4 is an end elevation of one-half of a section made up into berths or couches.

A B, Figs. 1 and 2, are the divisions between the sections or compartments of the car, and are made hollow to admit the sliding panels C D. E E, Fig. 2, are shafts fitted with either pinions working into racks on the side of panels C D, or with spools and cords a^2 a^3, Fig. 4, attached to panels for raising and lowering the same. The shafts E E are turned by means of the cranks F, Fig. 1, which cranks will be arranged with a clamp-screw to hold at any point. G H, Fig. 2, are the seat-backs which form the upper berth, and are hinged at G, so as to be turned up readily into the horizontal position G I, Fig. 1. The double line G K, Fig. 2, represents the brackets L, Figs. 1 and 4, which are hinged to the outer edge M of its half of the upper berth, Fig. 4, and when in form of seats folds under and behind the backs, and are held by the bolts N shooting into socket P' on the inner side of the seat-back, as shown in Fig. 5, which is a view of the heel of the bracket L as it appears when folded and fastened to the seat-back by the bolt N. When, however, the brackets are dropped down into vertical positions, as shown in Figs. 1 and 4, the same bolts N serve as the means for securing the brackets in their arched positions, as shown in Fig. 6, which is a section looking at the inner side of the heel of the bracket when its bolt N and dovetail are fastened into the socket on the inner side of the seat end. In Fig. 1 these brackets are shown as forming a front arched support to the upper couch. In Fig. 4 one of them is shown as fastened down at N^2, and in Fig. 2 a double line at the inner side of the seat-back shows the bracket folded the full length of the seat-back. The brackets L are supplied at the points N^2 O, Fig. 1, with couplings, consisting of a dovetail with a spring-bolt, Figs. 5 and 6; or, in lieu of this, thumb-screws may be used to lock them securely in the arch form N^2 O N, Fig. 1. P P, Figs. 2 and 4, are hook-bolts, which support the upper berth, and secure it to the side of the car. R S, Fig. 2, are the shifting-seat bottoms which form the lower berth, and which are secured in their position as seats by the pins U and bearing T. Pass from the arrangement of seats to that of sleeping-berths, the upper seat body R S U is slightly raised and carried forward to the position indicated by the dotted lines, Fig. 2. The seat-backs G H, Fig. 2, are then swung to the horizontal position G I G, and the bolts P shot into the sockets P^2 in the side of car. The bracket-bolts N are then withdrawn from the socket P^1, Fig. 4, allowing bracket to swing down and again lock at N^2, Figs. 1 and 4. The thumb-screw at O is then screwed up, securing the brackets in the arch form. The cushion V W, which may stand in rear of seat-back, in position indicated by dotted lines, is then placed in the position shown in Fig. 2. Sliding panels C D are then run up by turning the cranks F, Fig. 1, thus closing the space between the compartments of the car between the upper berth and roof of car. Reverse this operation to return to seats.

Supporting the upper couch by brackets hinged to the chair-frames has been done before in different ways, and I do not claim a bracket-support, as such, for the upper berth, but only the novel manner of hinging the brackets along the front edge of the seat-backs, so that they meet in the middle of the berth, and are there fastened to each other, while by means of a heel-extension it is fastened to the seat end, and in which the joining and heel fastenings of these brackets are readily unfastened to allow them to be turned under the seat-backs and there fastened.

I claim as my invention—

1. The brackets L, hinged to the seat-backs, as described, and combined therewith, and with the seat ends to form, when dropped down, a continuous front arch-support fastened together for the aisle side of the upper couch, and turned out of the way when the seat-backs are lowered, as herein set forth.

2. The brackets L, hinged to the seat-backs, as described, in combination with the fastening device N P^1, by which said brackets are held in place when folded.

3. The brackets L, hinged to the seat-backs, as described, in combination with the seat-end-fastening device, as shown and described.

4. The brackets L, hinged to the seat-backs, as described, each having a heel-extension provided with a bolt, N, which serves as the means by which the brackets are both secured in their arched and folded positions, as described.

5. The combination with the vertical sliding panels C D of the crank-shaft E F, and the cords and pulleys a^2 a^3 connecting said panels with the winding and unwinding shafts, whereby the panels are raised and lowered from the floor of the car.

JAMES L. MITCHELL.

Witnesses:
KEYES DANFORTH,
HENRY K. PINCKNEY.

J. L. MITCHELL.

SLEEPING-CAR.

No. 171,239. Patented Dec. 21, 1875.

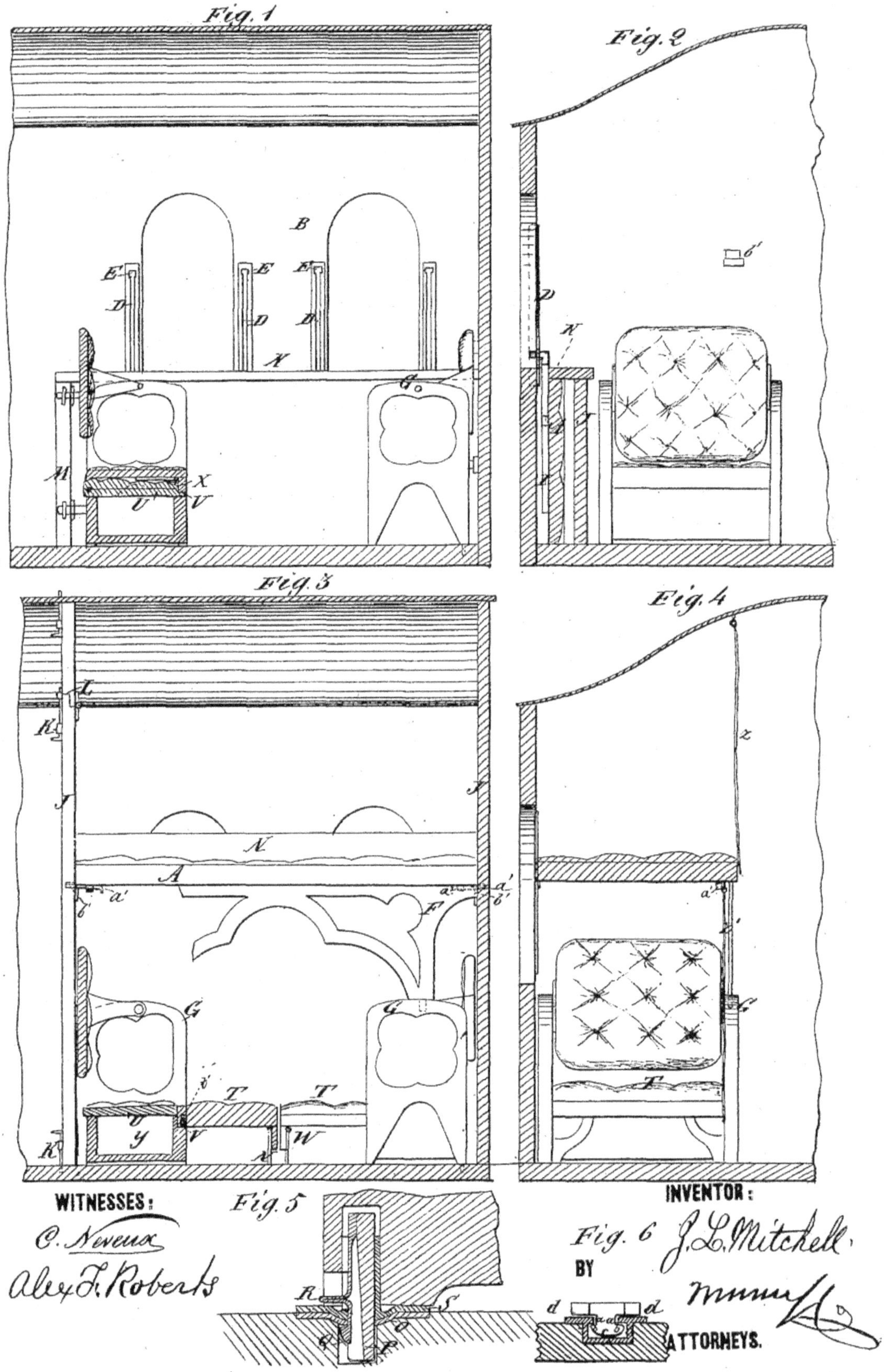

UNITED STATES PATENT OFFICE.

JAMES L. MITCHELL, OF PUEBLO, COLORADO TERRITORY.

IMPROVEMENT IN SLEEPING-CARS.

Specification forming part of Letters Patent No. **171,239**, dated December 21, 1875; application filed November 27, 1875.

To all whom it may concern:

Be it known that I, JAMES L. MITCHELL, of Pueblo, in the county of Pueblo and Territory of Colorado, have invented a new and Improved Sleeping-Car, of which the following is a specification:

The invention relates to connecting the upper berth to the side or wall of the car by a sliding hinge, for allowing it to shift from one position to another, as required or not required for use, without becoming detached from the wall. It also relates to the construction of the hinge thereof, and a partition-section, adapted to be secured vertically, to aid in supporting the upper berth, or horizontally alongside the same. It also relates to the construction whereby a detachable middle section of the lower seat-section is adapted to be applied as a cover or top of said seats, sections, or an extension thereof. It also relates to other features, as hereinafter specified.

Figure 1 is a longitudinal section of a car with my improved sleeping-berth contrivance, the same being adjusted for day use. Fig. 2 is a transverse section of Fig. 1. Fig. 3 is a longitudinal section, showing the contrivance for night use. Fig. 4 is a transverse section of Fig. 3. Fig. 5 is a detail section of the contrivance for holding the seats, so that they may be shifted as required, and at the same time preventing them from moving out of place by the shaking of the car. Fig. 6 is a detail of the hook employed to connect the upper berth to the side of the car-body. Said figure also shows the arrangement of the hook, or its mode of connection with the slotted plate attached to the side of the car.

Similar letters of reference indicate corresponding parts.

A is the frame of the upper berth, which is connected to the side B of the car-body by hooks C and slotted plates D, so that it can be dropped down and folded against the side of the car-body under the window, as shown in Fig. 1, and also be supported at the upper end of the slotted plates for a bed, as shown in Figs. 3 and 4. The slots are wider at the top E than below, and the hooks have a narrow part, a, and a wide part, b, so contrived that when the berth swings down parallel to the side of the car-body, the part a allows the berth to slide up or down freely; but when, after raising the hooks to the top of the slots, the berth is swung up level, the wide parts b of the hooks swing through the parts E of the slots and drop behind the shoulders, so that the berth is supported on said shoulders, and at the same time held securely against disconnecting from the wall. The hooks have shoulders d inside of the part a, which prevent the disconnection of the berth while sliding up and down, but they disconnect readily at the top of the slots whenever it may be required to do so for cleaning and for other purposes. The upper berth is supported at the front by the legs F resting on the seat-arms G, the legs being hinged to the bottom of the berth, so as to fold up against the bottom, as shown at I. The section-partition J, except a small portion, M, is made entirely independent of the car-seats, and fastened up detachably by bolts K, or other suitable means, and has a folding joint at L, so that it can be taken down and placed in front of the bed, and be fastened in that position by its bolts, which catch in small sections M of said partitions, which is permanently set up and made separate from the main portions, which section incloses at the end the space containing the bed. The back side rail N of the upper berth A forms the shelf or ledge under the window, corresponding to the ordinary projecting ledge of the car-body, but being a little wider than common. To allow of folding the top berth down this way the seats are contrived to move out from the wall; and to hold them so as to allow of such movements, and at the same time secure them against shaking out of place by the jarring of the cars, the legs will drop into little cavities o in the floor, and one leg will have a slide-bolt, P, passing through the plate O, forming the cavity, and fastening below by a spring-catch, Q, having a thumb-bit, R, by which to disengage it. On the bottom the legs will be shod with a convex plate, S, corresponding to the cavity-plate O, and being suitable for the seats to slide back and forth on when shifting from one position to the other. The middle sections T of the lower berth are constructed to rest on the end sections V, and form part of the seat in the day-time, and they are supported, when adjusted for the bed, in the rabbets V of the

437

end sections, and by hinged legs W, which fold under them when on the seat. The rabbets V are filled by the ribs X when the seats are made up, the said ribs hiding the cushions of the sections V, and making a suitable finish. Studs t' are set vertically in the rabbeted portion V, and coincident holes are formed in the under side of the rib X of sections V. The latter are secured to the seat U in either position by means of said studs.

By having the section-partitions independent of the seat-backs, the latter are forced to turn over for fronting either way, and by having the seats movable they can be shifted about to front the windows or the opposite seats, or in any desired direction. The seats are boxed below at Y, for stowing the bedding.

The curtains will be made separate for each berth, the upper one, Z, being suspended from the roof of the car, and the lower one, Z', from the upper berth.

When the berths are made up the seats will be shifted back toward the side of the car the width of the space made vacant by the removal of the upper berth and the partition, thus affording a little more middle space in the car at night. Two sets of cavities, o, will be provided for this purpose.

The upper berth has a hook-ended slide-bolt, a', at each end, which slides out a certain distance, and hooks into a catch, b', on the section-partition, to hold the berth temporarily when let down, till the supports F are adjusted. These bolts connect all the berths and section-partitions of one side of a car, and thus make all more substantial than they otherwise would be.

Having thus described my invention, I claim as new and desire to secure by Letters Patent—

1. The upper berth N, having a sliding hinge-connection with the side of the car, substantially as shown and described, whereby it is adapted to be raised and assume a horizontal position, or to be lowered and maintain a vertical position against or parallel to the wall, as shown and described.

2. The detachable partition-sections J, having the hinged and folding parts, and provided with fastenings, as described, whereby it is adapted to be secured in a vertical position as a partition, or horizontally alongside the upper berth, to form a panel-protector for the same, as shown and described.

3. The combination, with a lower seat-section having a rabbet along the front edge, and studs t', set vertically therein, of a detachable part, T, having folding legs, and provided with holes in its ribs X, to receive said studs when in either of its allotted positions, as shown and described.

4. The combination, with the upper berth, arranged to fold down against the side of the car, of the side rail N, forming the ledge below the window, and the section J, forming the side panel of the car-body, substantially as specified.

5. The combination of the hooks C, having the parts $b\ a\ d$, and the slotted plates D, having upper wide notch E, with the upper berth and the car-body, substantially as specified.

6. The combination of convex plates on the seat-legs with cavity-plates O in the car-floor, substantially as specified.

7. The combination, with movable seats having a slide-bolt and spring-catch in the leg, of a catch-plate in the floor, substantially as specified.

JAMES L. MITCHELL.

Witnesses:
A. P. THAYER,
ALEX. F. ROBERTS.

J. S. CALVERT.
GOLD-WASHER.

No. 171,597. Patented Dec. 28, 1875.

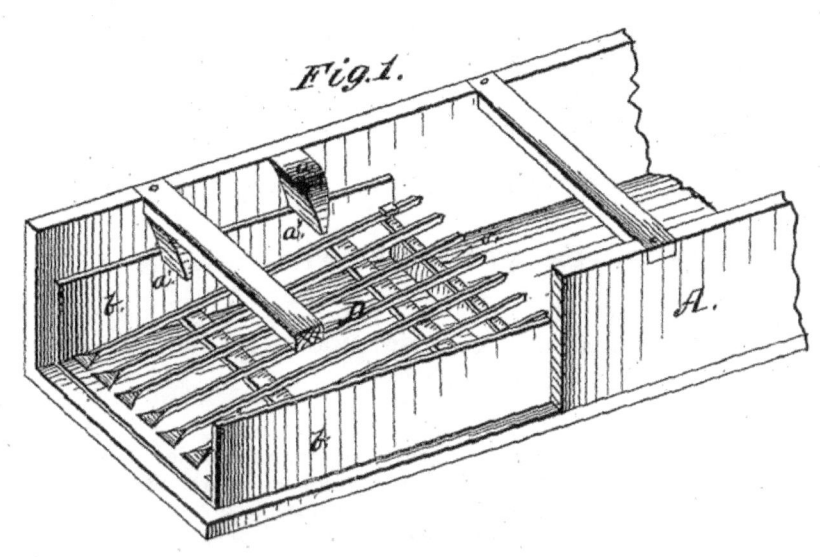

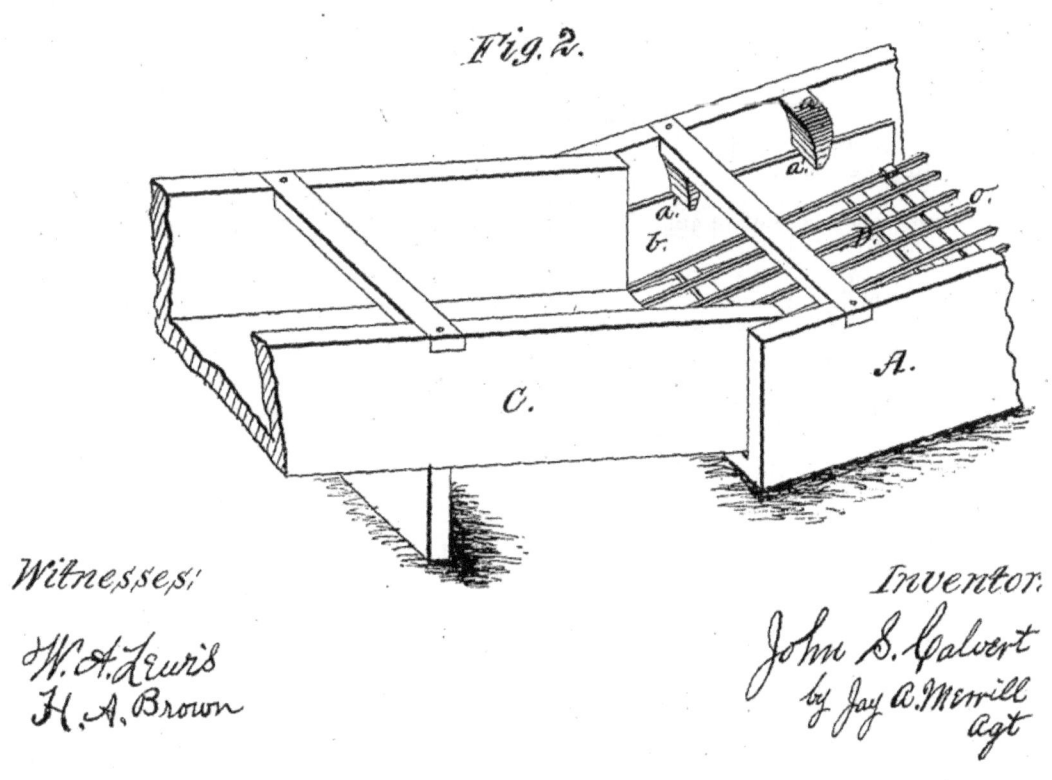

UNITED STATES PATENT OFFICE.

JOHN S. CALVERT, OF DENVER, COLORADO TERRITORY.

IMPROVEMENT IN GOLD-WASHERS.

Specification forming part of Letters Patent No. **171,597**, dated December 28, 1875; application filed July 9, 1875.

To all whom it may concern:

Be it known that I, JOHN S. CALVERT, of Denver, in the county of Arapahoe and Territory of Colorado, have invented a new and Improved Gold-Washer; and I do hereby declare the following to be a full and exact description of the same:

My invention relates to that class of devices made use of for washing gold commonly known as the "sluice;" and the nature thereof consists in certain improvements in the details of the construction of the same, and novel combinations of parts hereinafter shown and described.

In the accompanying plate of drawings, in which corresponding parts are designated by similar letters, Figure 1 is a perspective view of a sluice-box, having a part thereof removed in order to more clearly illustrate my improvements. Fig. 2 represents two of the sluice-boxes joined together in the ordinary manner.

The sluice commonly made use of in gold-mining is a long wooden trough, having a considerable inclination, into which "pay dirt" is shoveled, and through which a rapid stream of water is continually flowing. The bottom of this trough is provided with a series of riffles, generally containing mercury, by which the gold is retained, while the clay, sand, and gravel are carried off by the force of the current. The ordinary sluice is composed of a series of rough wooden boxes, the ends of which are fitted into each other.

In the drawings, A represents a sluice-box having my improvements applied thereto. C designates another sluice-box, through which the water and gravel pass before reaching said box A. B is the quicksilver-box, having vertical sides b, and an end piece, o, upon which rests the inclined grate D. Attached to each side of the box A are flanges or projections a, having inclined and curvilinear sides a, which deflect the water and dirt, held in suspension, downward through the grate.

The advantages of the improvement will be obvious to those skilled in the art to which the invention relates without further description.

Having thus described my invention, I claim and desire to secure by Letters Patent of the United States—

The combination of the sluice-boxes A and C; the quicksilver-box B, having vertical sides b and an end piece, o; the inclined grate D resting upon the end piece o, and the flanges or projections a attached to the sides of the box A, and arranged above the quicksilver-box, as and for the purpose described.

JOHN S. CALVERT.

Witnesses:
 JAY A. MERRILL,
 W. A. LEWIS.

F. M. F. CAZIN.
NUT-LOCK.

No. 172,387. Patented Jan. 18, 1876.

Fig. 1.

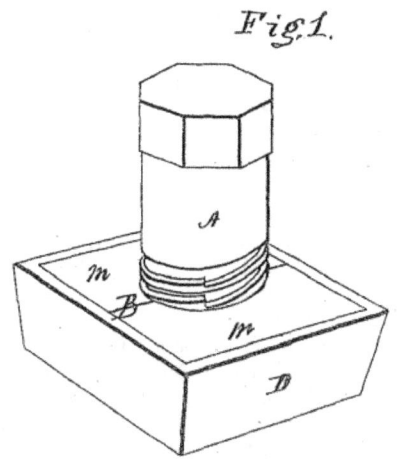

Fig. 2.

Fig. 3.

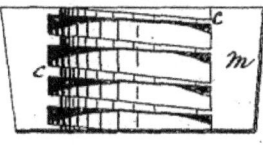 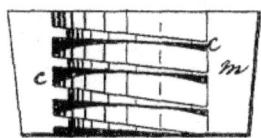

Witnesses:
F. B. Townsend
R. K. Evans

Inventor:
Francis M. F. Cazin
by A. H. Evans & Co
his attys.

UNITED STATES PATENT OFFICE.

FRANCIS M. F. CAZIN, OF DENVER, COLORADO TERRITORY.

IMPROVEMENT IN NUT-LOCKS.

Specification forming part of Letters Patent No. **172,387**, dated January 18, 1876; application filed September 1, 1875.

To all whom it may concern:

Be it known that I, FRANCIS M. F. CAZIN, of Denver, Colorado, have invented certain new and useful Improvements in Lock Nuts and Bolts, of which the following is a full, clear, and exact description, reference being had to the accompanying drawings, making a part of this specification, in which—

Figure 1 is a perspective view of my invention. Fig. 2 is a side view of the bolt's thread. Fig. 3 is an inside view of the nut.

My invention will be first fully described, and subsequently pointed out in the claim.

To enable others skilled in the art to make and use my invention, I will proceed to described the exact manner in which I have carried it out.

In the said drawings, A represents a bolt having a square thread, a, and distinguished from ordinary square threads by the lower or inside plane of the thread (the plane facing toward the head of the bolt) forming a continuous zigzag line, dividing the circumferential screw-line in as many offsets as are necessary for the special purpose of the lock-bolt. The offsets on each single thread form, with the offsets on the other single threads, a line parallel to the axis of the bolt, thereby forming as many parallel lines to the axis of the bolt as there are offsets on one turn of the thread. The shoulders or offsets b on the threads of the bolt face toward the head of the bolt. B is the nut, made in two sections, $m\ m$, whose sides are slightly beveled. This nut is so constructed that when the two sections are placed together the threads have shoulders or offsets c on the upper plane of their surfaces, corresponding with those on the bolt-thread. When the nut is screwed on the bolt sufficiently tight to cause a pressure in an opposite direction, the shoulders or offsets on the bolt-thread are caused to come in contact with those on the thread of the nut, thereby securely holding or locking the nut to the bolt. When the outward pressure is removed the nut can be screwed off the bolt, as there is sufficient space between the bolt-threads to allow the shoulders of the nut-thread to pass. D is a frame or band, constructed with beveled sides to receive and hold the sections $m\ m$ of the nut B.

Although I have shown the bolt A and nut B provided with a single thread, the same may be constructed with two or more parallel threads, as will be readily understood by those skilled in the art.

It is also evident, from the foregoing description, that the beveled frame D and the two halves of the outside beveled nut fit together, whereby the pressure exercised on the bolt-head and nut in screwing up forces the two halves of the nut together, especially so if the frame projects, on the narrow or in side, over the half-nut. Thus the nut answers its full purpose, without being welded or otherwise joined permanently, by the pressure caused in screwing it up.

Having thus described my invention, what I claim as new, and desire to secure by Letters Patent, is—

The combination, with a bolt, A, constructed with a zigzag or ratchet-faced thread or threads, of a nut, B, formed in sections $m\ m$, provided with a correspondingly-formed zigzag thread or threads, and held together by a band, D, substantially as shown and described.

FRANCIS MICHAEL FREDERICK CAZIN.

Witnesses:
C. F. ADOLPH FISCHER,
OWEN E. LE FEVRE.

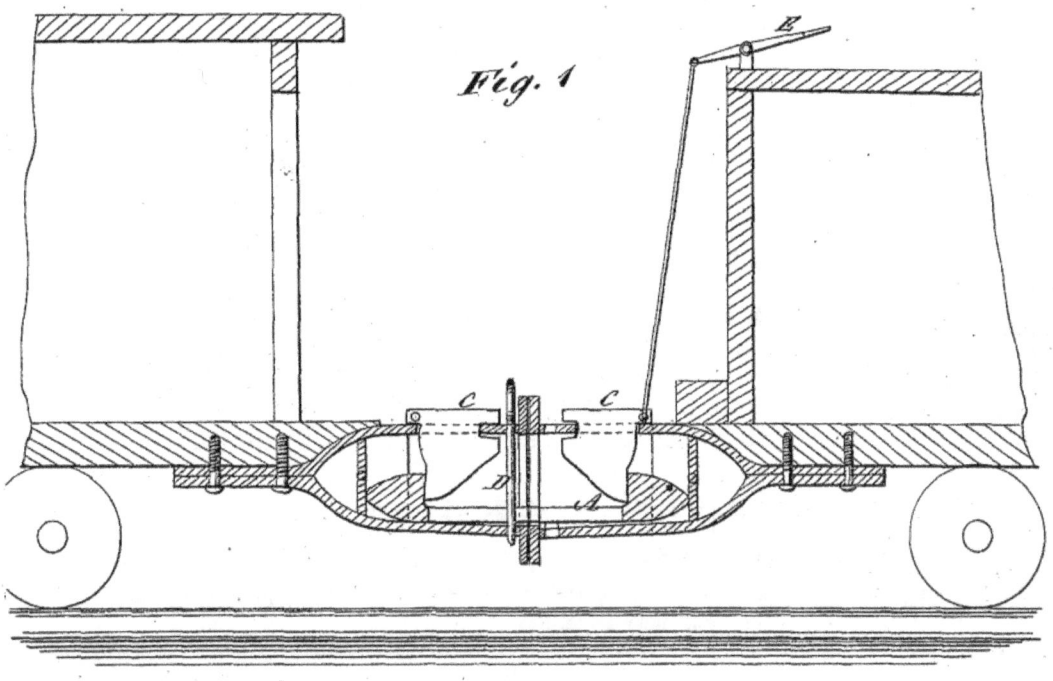
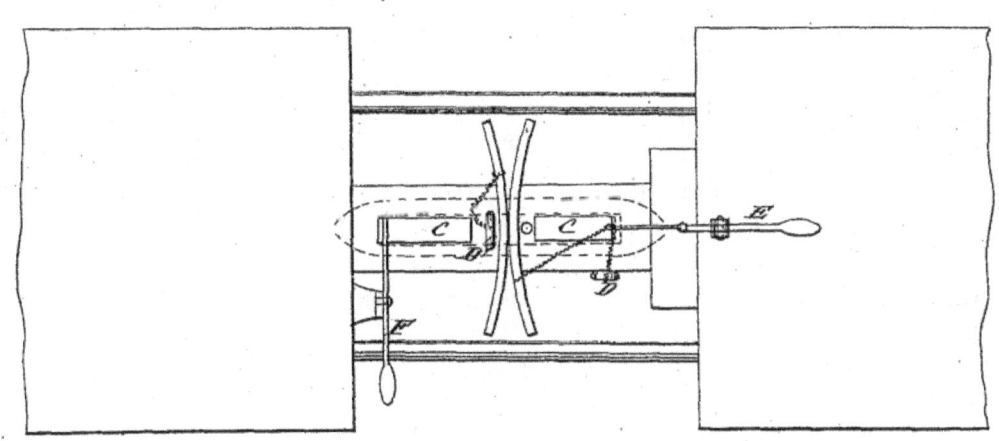

UNITED STATES PATENT OFFICE.

CHARLES H. BRIGGS, OF BLACK HAWK, COLORADO TERRITORY.

IMPROVEMENT IN CAR-COUPLINGS.

Specification forming part of Letters Patent No. **174,187**, dated February 29, 1876; application filed January 15, 1876.

To all whom it may concern:

Be it known that I, CHARLES H. BRIGGS, of Black Hawk, Gilpin county, Territory of Colorado, have invented a new and Improved Car-Coupling, of which the following is a specification:

My invention consists of a combined link and hook-headed coupler, in combination with a catch in the draw-bar behind the hole for a coupling-pin, which may be used with cars only adapted for the ordinary link-and-pin connection. The catch is contrived to work vertically in opening and closing, so that it will fall and couple self-actingly, and can be uncoupled from the top of the car or from the side.

Figure 1 is a longitudinal sectional elevation of my improved coupling, and Fig. 2 is a top view.

Similar letters of reference indicate corresponding parts.

A is the link, which I construct with a hook-head, B, on the upper side of each end, and for which I contrive the gravity-catch C in the draw-head behind the hole for the coupling-pin D, thus converting the ordinary link-and-pin coupling into a self-coupler, and at the same time having it so that it can be used in either way. The hook may be connected to a lever, E, on the top of the car for uncoupling therefrom, and it may also be connected with a lever, F, for working it from the side.

I am aware that a gravity-catch has been heretofore used in connection with a hook-coupler; but

What I claim is—

A gravity-catch, C, hinged on the end of slot in draw-bar and behind the ordinary hole for the coupling-pin, as and for the purpose specified.

CHARLES H. BRIGGS.

Witnesses:
ADRIAN MOUSTER,
E. C. BEACH.

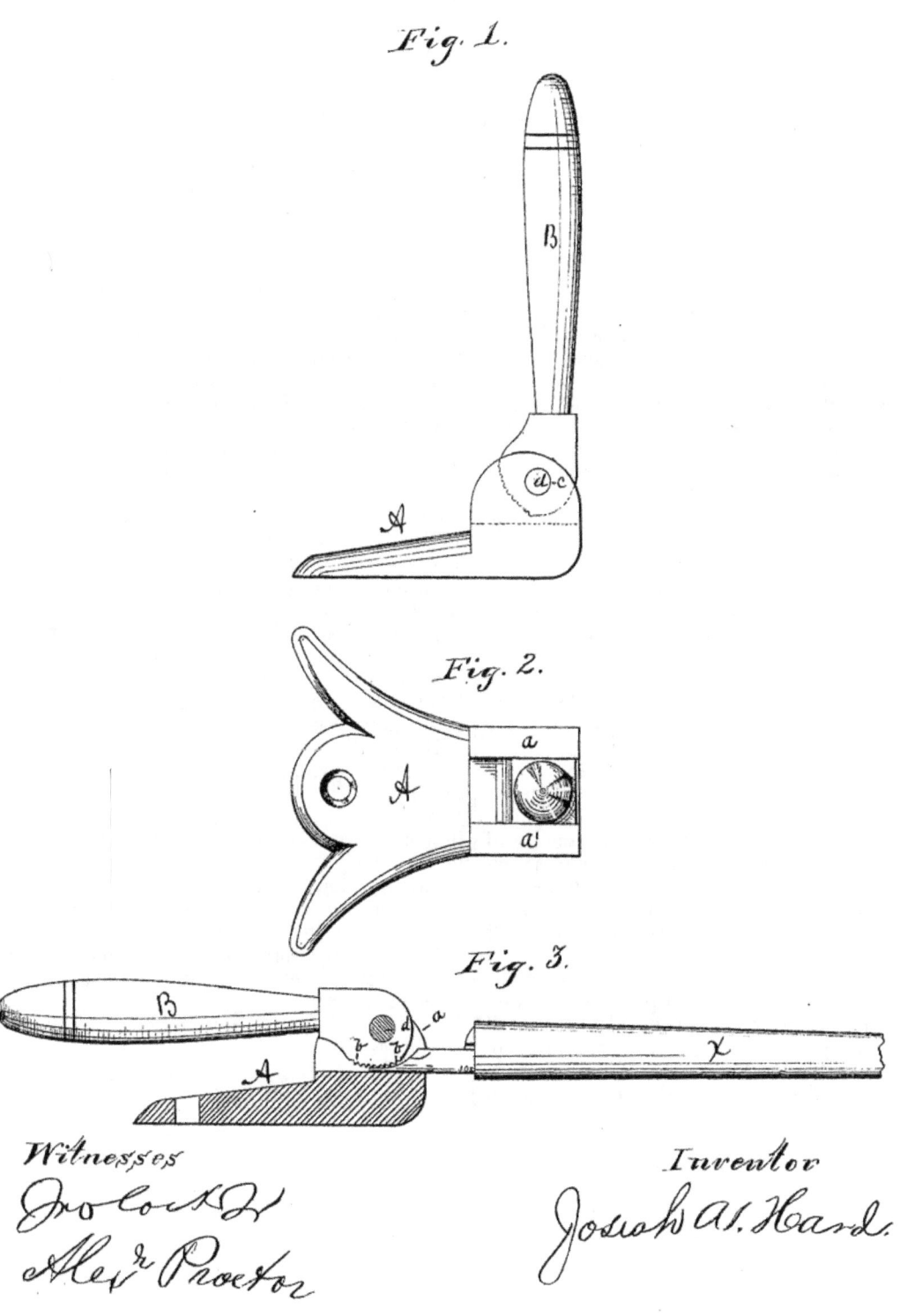

UNITED STATES PATENT OFFICE.

JOSIAH A. HARD, DENVER, COLORADO TERRITORY.

IMPROVEMENT IN PEN-EXTRACTORS.

Specification forming part of Letters Patent No. **175,082**, dated March 21, 1876; application filed January 14, 1876.

To all whom it may concern:

Be it known that I, JOSIAH A. HARD, of Denver, in the county of Arapahoe and Territory of Colorado, have invented an Improved Device for Extracting Pens from their Holders; and I do hereby declare the following to be a full, clear, and exact description thereof, sufficient to enable others to make and use the same, reference being had to the accompanying drawings, and to the letters of reference marked thereon, which form a part of this specification.

My invention relates to an improved device for extracting pens from their holders; and it consists of a metallic base, having two uprights at one end, between which is pivoted a lever, having its lower end provided with a series of corrugations, the parts being arranged and adapted to operate as will be hereinafter more fully described, and pointed out in the claim.

Referring to the drawings, Figure 1 is a side elevation of my invention, with the lever raised for the introduction of the pen-point. Fig. 2 is a top plan view of the same, and Fig. 3 is a side view in partial section, showing the lever depressed upon the pen-point.

Similar letters of reference occurring on the several figures indicate corresponding parts.

A represents a metallic base, which may be of any suitable ornamental pattern or configuration, and which is provided at one end with two parallel, upright bearings, $a\ a'$, in which are formed holes $c\ c'$. B represents a lever, provided with a fluted or corrugated cam projection, b, on its inside lower end, said lever being pivoted or supported between the bearings $a\ a'$ by a rivet, d, which passes through the side bearings and the lower part of the lever, as fully shown in the drawings.

In the practical operation of my invention the point or nib of the pen is pushed in between the upright bearings below the foot of the lever, and is caught and retained in that position by depressing the lever, as fully illustrated in Fig. 3 of the drawings. The holder is then drawn away, leaving the pen in the embrace of the vice formed by the depression of said lever upon the base A. The advantage of my invention will be readily apparent, inasmuch as it entirely obviates the difficulties hitherto experienced in extracting pens from their holders, and without necessitating the soiling of the fingers from the ink which may have accumulated upon the pen.

Having thus described my invention, what I claim as new, and desire to secure by Letters Patent, is—

As a new article of manufacture, the hereinbefore-described pen-extractor, consisting of the base A, having upright bearings $a\ a'$, between which is pivoted the lever B, having the fluted cam b upon its lower end, substantially as described and shown.

In testimony that I claim the foregoing I have hereunto set my hand this 24th day of December, 1875.

JOSIAH A. HARD.

Witnesses:
JNO. COOK, Jr.,
ALEXR. PROCTOR.

E. F. WILLIAMS.
FRICTION-CLUTCH.

No. 175,401. Patented March 28, 1876.

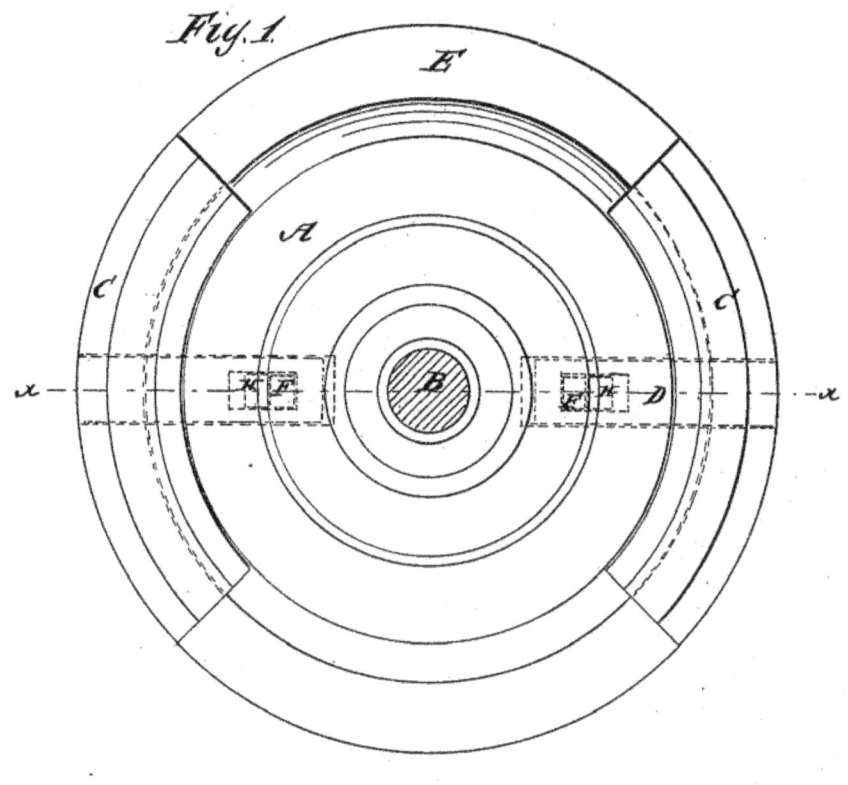

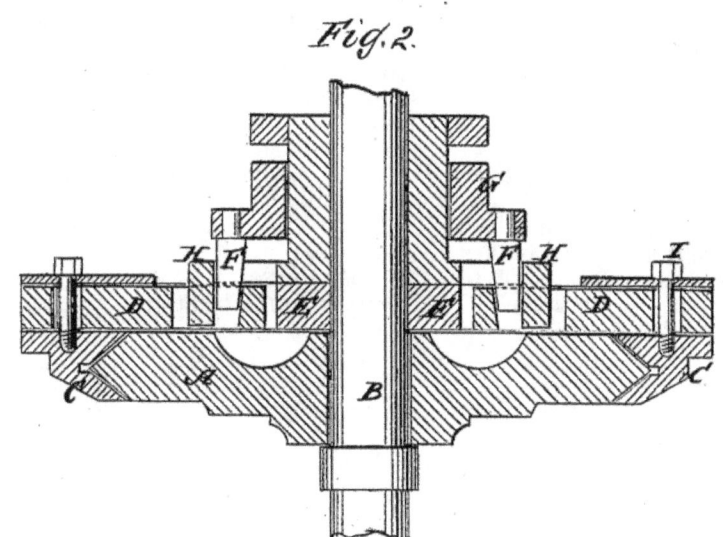

UNITED STATES PATENT OFFICE.

EDWIN F. WILLIAMS, OF BALD MOUNTAIN, COLORADO TERRITORY.

IMPROVEMENT IN FRICTION-CLUTCHES.

Specification forming part of Letters Patent No. **175,401**, dated March 28, 1876; application filed March 13, 1876.

To all whom it may concern:

Be it known that I, EDWIN F. WILLIAMS, of Bald Mountain, Gilpin county, Colorado Ter., have invented a new and Improved Friction Clutch, of which the following is a specification:

The invention consists of brakes which are drawn against the face of a disk-wheel by wedges moved by the sliding head on the shaft moved by the levers, the disk and the wedges being of V-shape, or any other approved form best calculated to cause friction.

Figure 1 is a side elevation of my improved clutch. Fig. 2 is a section taken on line $x\,x$.

Similar letters of reference indicate corresponding parts.

A is the disk, which is keyed on the shaft B, for stopping it. C represents the brakes for pressing against the face of the disk to stop it. They are connected to the slides D, working in radial grooves in the disk E, and being forced in by the wedges F on the sliding hub G, and working in slots in the slides and against the supports H of the disk E.

The brakes are adjustably connected to the slides by bolts I, so as to be shifted along to take up the wear.

The construction is simple and cheap, and the arrangement is calculated to be very efficient.

Having thus described my invention, I claim as new and desire to secure by Letters Patent—

The combination of disk A, brakes C, slides D, disk E, wedges F, and the sliding head G, substantially as specified.

EDWIN F. WILLIAMS.

Witnesses:
DEFOREST H. ANDREWS,
SAMUEL MCCLURE.

L. B. WELCH.
WAGON-BRAKE.

No. 175,799. Patented April 4, 1876.

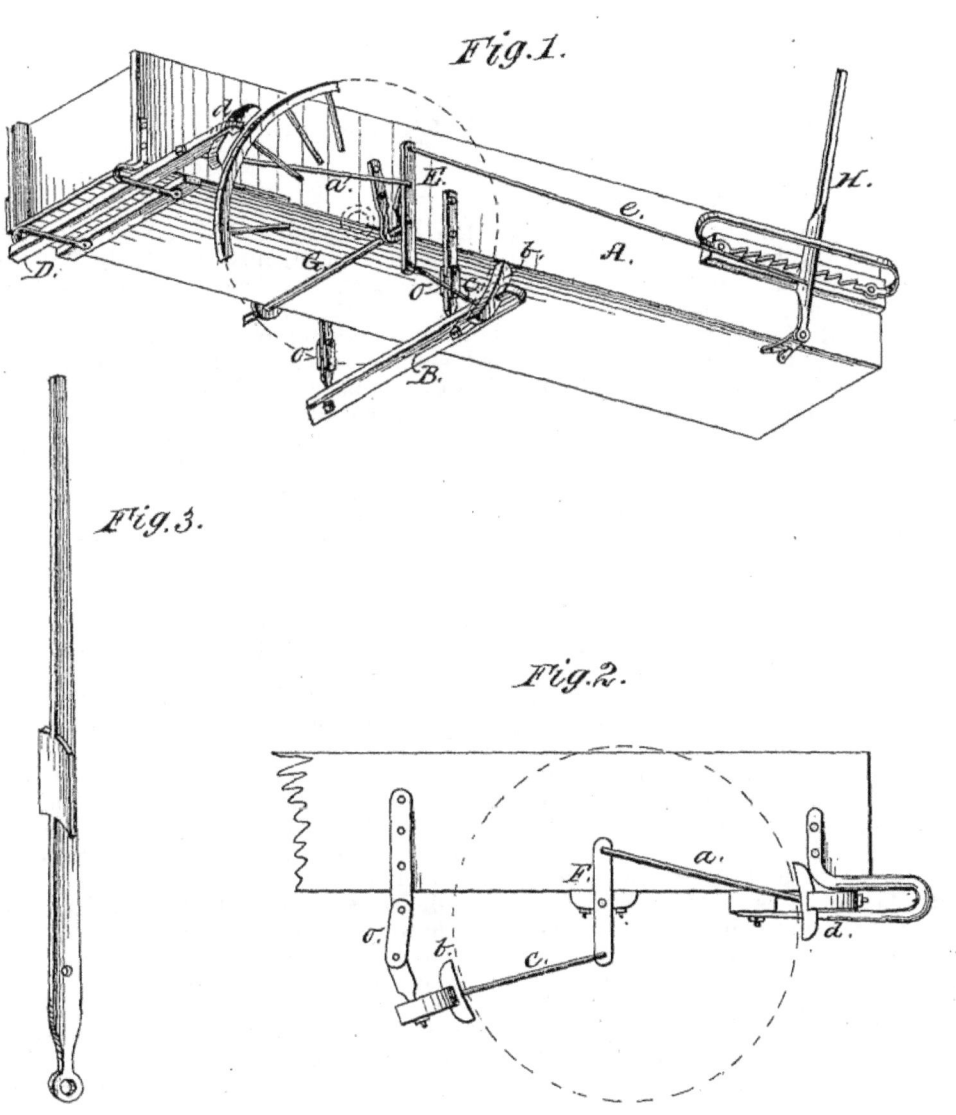

Witnesses:
Geo Burt
W. A. Lewis

Inventor,
Lester B Welch
by Jay A Merrill
agt

UNITED STATES PATENT OFFICE.

LESTER B. WELCH, OF MOUNT VERNON, COLORADO TERRITORY.

IMPROVEMENT IN WAGON-BRAKES.

Specification forming part of Letters Patent No. **175,799**, dated April 4, 1876; application filed July 9, 1875.

To all whom it may concern:

Be it known that I, LESTER B. WELCH, of Mount Vernon, in the county of Jefferson and Territory of Colorado, have invented a new and Improved Wagon-Brake; and I do hereby declare the following to be a full and exact description of the same, reference being had to the accompanying drawings, forming part of this specification, in which—

Figure 1 is a side view of a wagon-box supplied with my invention. Fig. 2 is also a side view, showing the other side of the wagon-box. Fig. 3 is the hand-lever for applying the brake to the rear wheels of a wagon, showing that the whole device can be reversed and adjusted to either side of the wagon.

Similar letters of reference in the accompanying drawings denote the same parts.

This invention relates to a wagon-brake employing two cross-bars or double-acting levers whereby a brake-shoe is pressed against the front and rear of each wheel on the same axle in place of the single cross-bar and brake-shoes that press only on the front of the wheels; and has for its object to provide a more effectual wagon-brake than has before been used, which shall be simple in construction, sure and efficient in operation, and that will stop instantly both wheels from turning when the wagon is going down the steepest hill.

To these ends the invention consists in the peculiar construction of the device as I will now proceed to describe.

In the drawings, A represents a wagon-box and B the front cross-bar lowered from the wagon-box so that the brake-shoes $b\ b$ will press the wheels below the center, thereby having the greater pressure on the wheels. The double joint $o\ o$ allows the forward and backward movement of the front bar B, at the same time holding it firmly in its proper place below the wagon-box. D is the rear cross-bar in position against the bottom of the wagon-box, so that the brake-shoes $d\ d$ will press the wheels above the center, thereby having the greater power on the wheels. E is the double-acting lever, as shown in Fig. 1. F is the double-acting lever, as shown in Fig. 2. G is the connecting rod under the wagon, at each end of which is fastened the double-acting levers E and F. H is the hand-lever by which the power is applied. The cross-bars B and D are connected with the double-acting levers E and F by rods $a\ a$ and $c\ c$. The hand-lever is connected by rod e, as shown in Fig. 1. The cross bars B and D and the connecting-rod G can be held in proper position by any convenient device, as shown in Figs. 1 and 2.

To apply the brake the hand-lever H must be pressed forward, which will draw the rear cross-bar D forward and the front cross-bar B backward. The brake-shoes $b\ b$ will then press the wheels in front and below the center, while the brake-shoes $d\ d$ will press the wheels at the rear and above the center. By this arrangement a very small power at the hand-lever will stop both wheels from turning, however heavy the load or steep the hill may be. The whole arrangement of parts is simple and the operation is certain and effective.

I claim as my invention and desire to secure by Letters Patent—

The connecting-rod G, double-acting levers E and F, and connecting-rods $a\ a$ and $c\ c$, in combination with the cross-bars B and D, substantially as described.

LESTER B. WELCH.

Witnesses:
CONSTANT DUHEM,
JAY A. MERRILL.

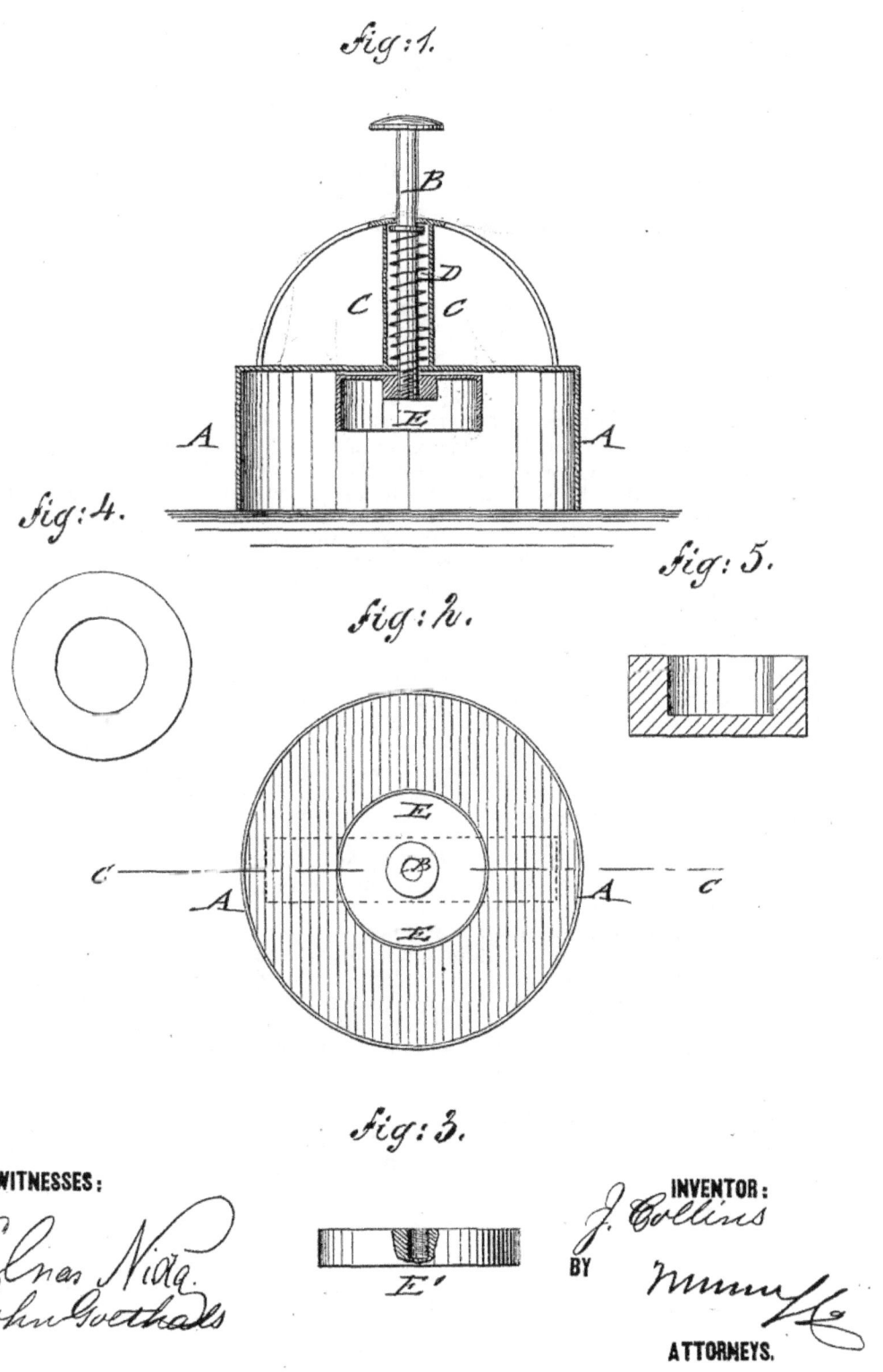

UNITED STATES PATENT OFFICE.

JAMES COLLINS, OF CENTRAL CITY, COLORADO TERRITORY.

IMPROVEMENT IN CAKE-CUTTERS.

Specification forming part of Letters Patent No. **176,217**, dated April 18, 1876; application filed February 28, 1876.

To all whom it may concern:

Be it known that I, JAMES COLLINS, of Central City, in the county of Gilpin and Territory of Colorado, have invented a new and Improved Dough-Cutter, of which the following is a specification:

In the accompanying drawing, Figure 1 represents a vertical central section on the line $c\ c$, Fig. 2, of my improved dough-cutter. Fig. 2 is a bottom view of the same. Fig. 3 is a side view of the central detachable former of the same. Figs. 4 and 5 are different shapes, which may be made by the cutter.

Similar letters of reference indicate corresponding parts.

The object of my invention is to provide an improved dough-cutter, which may be employed for making tarts, doughnuts, biscuits, &c., with greater convenience and with a saving of labor and time.

The invention consists of a cutter with a central sliding and spring acting part for forming and cutting, simultaneously with the outer part, the tart or other article to be produced.

In the drawing, A represents a dough-cutter of any suitable size, material, or shape, which is provided with a central sliding bolt, B, that is guided in a suitable casing, C, at the top of the cutter A. The bolt B is acted upon by a spiral spring, D, so as to be carried in an upward direction after each depression of said spring D. The upper end of the bolt is provided with a knob, while the lower threaded end projects to the interior of the cutter and allows either the screwing on or attachment of a smaller interior cutter, E, that corresponds in shape to the outer cutter, as shown in Fig. 1, or the attaching of a solid disk or former, E', as shown in Fig. 3.

By using the outer cutter without the interior cutter, biscuits and cakes may be cut from the dough in the common manner, while doughnuts and similar articles in which the central part is to be removed, may be produced in one cutting by the simultaneous depression of the inner cutter.

When the solid former E is used in combination with the outer cutter, tarts and rimmed bakings may be formed from the dough, as the former merely presses on the central part, providing thus a simple yet very effective and convenient implement for domestic and general purposes.

Having thus described my invention, I claim as new and desire to secure by Letters Patent—

A dough-cutter for making tarts, doughnuts, biscuits, &c., composed of an outer cutter, and an interior sliding spring acted shaping device, that may be worked simultaneously with the outer cutter or not, as desired, substantially as set forth.

JAMES COLLINS.

Witnesses:
J. S. D. MANVILLE,
BEN. E. SEYMOUR.

J. COLLINS.
DOOR-CHECK.

No. 176,598. Patented April 25, 1876.

UNITED STATES PATENT OFFICE.

JAMES COLLINS, OF CENTRAL CITY, COLORADO TERRITORY.

IMPROVEMENT IN DOOR-CHECKS.

Specification forming part of Letters Patent No. **176,598**, dated April 25, 1876; application filed February 28, 1876.

To all whom it may concern:

Be it known that I, JAMES COLLINS, of Central City, in the county of Gilpin and Territory of Colorado, have invented a new and Improved Door-Stop, of which the following is a specification:

In the accompanying drawing, Figure 1 represents a sectional front view, and Fig. 2 a vertical transverse section, of my improved door-stop taken on the line *c c*, Fig. 1.

Similar letters of reference indicate corresponding parts.

My invention relates to a device for holding the door without the use of wooden blocks, chains, &c., and without injury to the carpet or floor.

The invention consists of a spring-acted and rubber-headed bolt that slides in a casing or groove of the door, and is operated by connecting-lever rod and crank, as hereinafter more fully described and definitely claimed.

In the drawing, A represents a sliding bolt that is guided either in a casing, B, screwed to the lower part of the door, or in a socket-groove of the same, as desired. The lower part of the bolt is lined or cushioned with rubber, or other elastic material, to bear on the carpet or floor without scratching or otherwise injuring the same. The bolt A is acted upon by a spiral spring, C, that is placed between the top part of the casing and the enlarged bottom part of the bolt, being forced in a downward direction to bear with considerable pressure on the floor. The upper end of the bolt projects to the outside of casing B, and is pivoted to a lever-rod, D, that is again pivoted at its upper end to a crank, E, at a short distance from the pivot-pin or turning-point of the same.

When the crank is carried below its pivot the pressure of the spring is sufficient to throw the bolt downward, so as to hold the door in firm position.

When the door is desired to be moved in either direction the crank is raised above the pivot, and carried by the force of the spring against a stop-pin, *a*, holding thereby the pressure-bolt in a stationary raised position without a chance of forming contact with the floor.

The spring may be readily replaced when weakened by use by lowering the bolt sufficiently to insert a new one. The whole stop is readily applied, and of great convenience and durability.

Having thus described my invention, what I claim as new, and desire to secure by Letters Patent, is—

The combination, with pivoted spring-bolt A working in a guide, of the lever-rod D and the crank E, the former pivoted to the latter at a short distance from its turning-point, and between the pivot and the handle, substantially as and for the purpose specified.

JAMES COLLINS.

Witnesses:
  J. S. D. MANVILLE,
  BEN E. SEYMOUR.

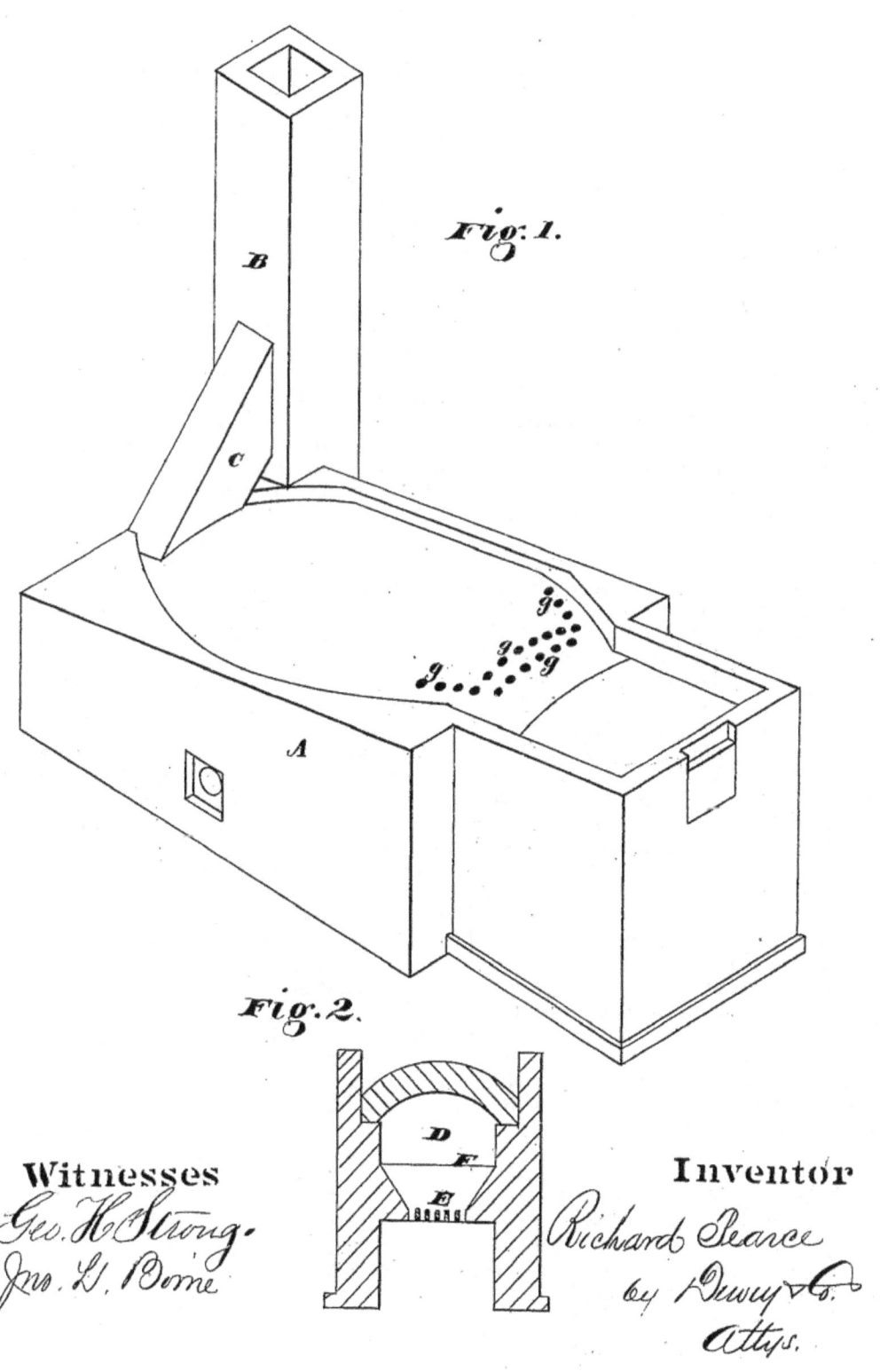

UNITED STATES PATENT OFFICE.

RICHARD PEARCE, OF BLACK HAWK, COLORADO TERRITORY.

IMPROVEMENT IN REVERBERATORY FURNACES.

Specification forming part of Letters Patent No. **176,994**, dated May 2, 1876; application filed April 15, 1875.

To all whom it may concern:

Be it known that I, RICHARD PEARCE, of Black Hawk, Gilpin county, Colorado Territory, have invented an Improvement in Reverberatory Furnaces; and I do hereby declare the following description and accompanying drawings are sufficient to enable any person skilled in the art or science to which it most nearly appertains to make and use my said invention or improvement without further invention or experiment.

The object of my invention is to provide certain improvements in reverberatory furnaces, and it is more especially adapted for use in such furnaces as burn wood as a fuel, and as a large grate-surface has been used heretofore, much of the products of the combustion would find its way to the stack or chimney unconsumed, and therefore wasted.

My improvement contemplates a more perfect combustion of the fuel, and a consequent economy of heat; and it consists in a novel construction of the fire-place, together with the employment of openings at certain points, whereby air is admitted, so that sufficient oxygen will be supplied to insure a complete combustion.

Referring to the accompanying drawings for a more complete explanation of my invention, Figure 1 is a perspective view of my furnace. Fig. 2 is a transverse section taken through the fire-place.

A is the body of a reverberatory furnace. B is the stack or chimney, and C is the flue leading to the stack. D is the fire-place, and E is the grate upon which the wood is placed. In order to reduce the grate-surface without making the body of the fire-place too small, I make the walls of the fire-place inclining from a point a short distance above the grate down to its surface, where, it will be seen, the distance becomes very much narrowed. The fuel is, consequently, not spread over so large a surface as in other fire-places.

The gases of combustion pass over the bridge-wall F, and are deflected upon the hearth of the furnace and its contents in the usual manner, but an insufficiency of oxygen causes a considerable loss of heat from the incomplete combustion.

In order to supply the necessary amount of oxygen to make the combustion perfect, I perforate the top or roof of the furnace with a series of openings, $g g$, just above and behind the bridge-wall, and also extending a short distance along the sides, as shown. Through these openings the air passes, and, meeting the flame as it passes over the bridge-wall, a sufficient quantity of oxygen will be supplied to completely consume all the gases and make a most intense heat.

I am aware that atmospheric passage-ways have been constructed through the arch over the fire-room and bridge-wall, for the purpose of passing broad thin currents of air heated in passing through the wall, and discharge at a line over, or nearly over, the rear side of the bridge-wall, downwardly and diagonally across the current of the gaseous products of combustion; but this is not my invention.

Having thus described my invention, what I claim, and desire to secure by Letters Patent, is—

The furnace A, having the roof perforated with openings $g g$ over and behind the bridge-wall, and arranged along the sides, substantially as and for the purpose described.

In witness whereof I hereunto set my hand and seal.

RICHARD PEARCE. [L. S.]

Witnesses:
HENRY P. COWENHOVEN,
HENRY WILLIAMS.

J. C. STANTON.
SHEET-METAL PIPE-JOINT.

No. 177,361. Patented May 16, 1876.

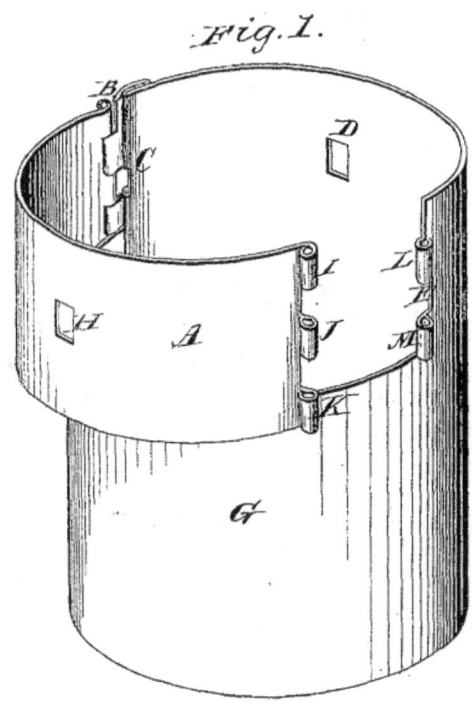

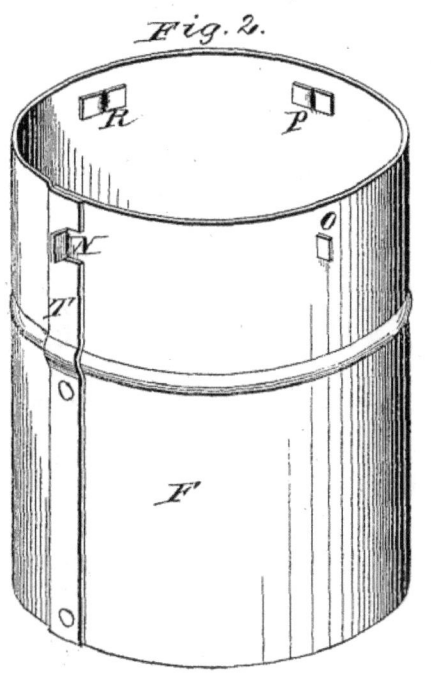

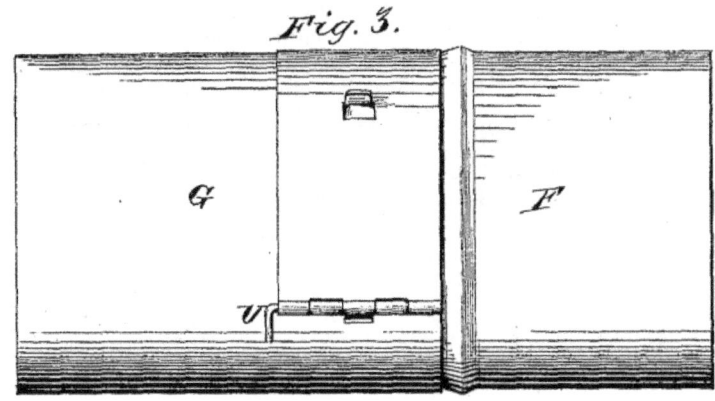

Witnesses
J. W. Grow
J. J. Smith

Inventor
J. Clark Stanton

UNITED STATES PATENT OFFICE.

J. CLARK STANTON, OF HUTCHINSON, ASSIGNOR OF ONE-HALF HIS RIGHT TO CASSIUS G. HALL, OF HALL VALLEY, COLORADO TERRITORY.

IMPROVEMENT IN SHEET-METAL-PIPE JOINTS.

Specification forming part of Letters Patent No. **177,361**, dated May 16, 1876; application filed February 14, 1876.

To all whom it may concern:

Be it known that I, J. CLARK STANTON, of Hutchinson, in the county of Jefferson, Territory of Colorado, have invented a new and useful Improvement in Jointing and Fastening Sheet-Metal Piping, which improvement is fully set forth in the following specification, reference being had to the accompanying drawings.

By means of the hinged flap A, Figure 1, working upon a hinge, B, whereby the same is closed around the joint F, Fig. 2, after insertion of three of the four studs N O P R into the three openings C D E, Fig. 1, the opening H closes over the remaining stud, after which the whole is securely fastened together by a metal pin, U, Fig. 4, passing through the eyes I J K L M, the whole presenting the appearance shown in Fig. 3.

The studs N O P R, Fig. 2, are made in the following manner: N, by turning up a portion of the seam T; O P R, by strips of metal doubled, and the ends turned outward at right angles, Fig. 5, and firmly fastened in, Fig. 2, by swaging into openings made for the purpose at O, P, and R. P and R show the back side of the studs.

I claim—

The combination, in a sheet-metal pipe, of the hinged flap, studs, openings, eyes, and metallic pin for connecting the sections together, substantially as described.

J. CLARK STANTON.

Witnesses:
J. W. GROW,
J. J. SMITH.

J. METZ & E. HINMAN.
TAG-HOLDER- FOR MAIL-POUCHES.

No. 179,040. Patented June 20, 1876.

Fig.1.

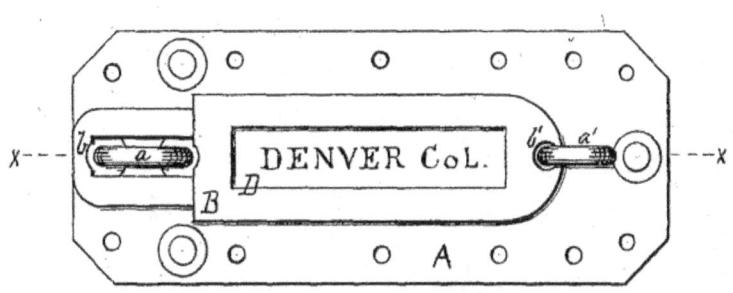

Fig.2.

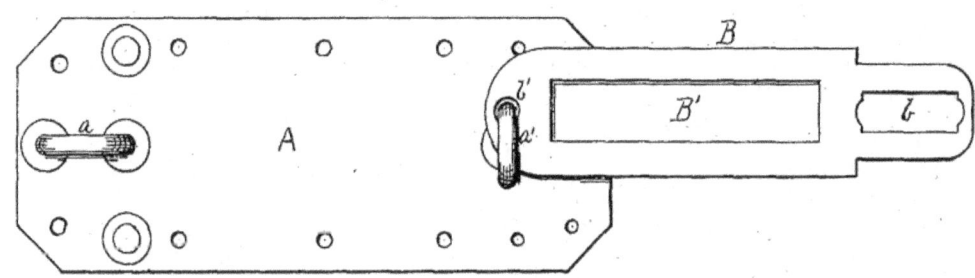

Fig.3.

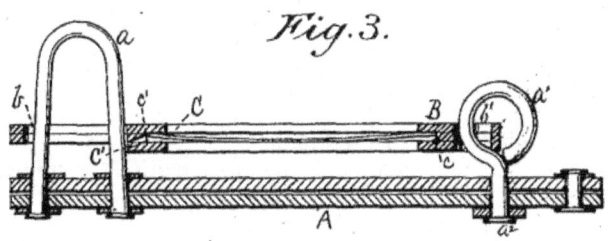

Witnesses;
F. W. Howard.
Edwin James.

Inventors.
Julius Metz.
Egbert Hinman.
per J. E. F. Holmead,
Attorney.

UNITED STATES PATENT OFFICE.

JULIUS METZ AND EGBERT HINMAN, OF DENVER, COLORADO TERRITORY.

IMPROVEMENT IN TAG-HOLDERS FOR MAIL-POUCHES.

Specification forming part of Letters Patent No. **179,040**, dated June 20, 1876; application filed May 19, 1876.

To all whom it may concern:

Be it known that we, JULIUS METZ and EGBERT HINMAN, both of Denver, in the county of Arapahoe and Territory of Colorado, have invented an Improved Tag-Holder for Mail-Pouches, of which the following is a full, clear, and exact description, reference being had to the accompanying drawing, and to the letters of reference marked thereon, making part of this specification, in which—

Figure 1 is a top-plan view, the tag-holder being in position. Fig. 2 is a top-plan view, the tag-holder being reversed. Fig. 3 is a longitudinal sectional view on the line $x\ x$, Fig. 1.

The object of our invention is to so construct the tag-holder that there will be no necessity of pulling out the labeled tag from the holder and reversing the same in order to read the address on the opposite side, as is now the case with mail-pouches.

The nature of our invention consists in constructing the holder in the form of a rectangular plate having a hollow center with an open slot at one end, and a hole or orifice at the other. The hollow center is so constructed as to provide bearings at each of its shorter sides for springs, which extend a little more than the entire distance of the length of the hollow center, and has a slot entering into it for the ready insertion of the tag, all arranged as will be more fully hereinafter described.

The construction and operation of our invention are as follows: A is the leather base, to which the tag-holder is attached, it being a portion of the mail-pouch. B is the tag-holder, and is so constructed as to leave a hollow space, B', at its center, as clearly shown in Fig. 2. Preferably this holder is constructed of three sheets of metal, as shown in Fig. 3, the same being riveted or otherwise securely fastened together. One end of the holder B is provided with a slot, b, which is designed to fit over the staple a, attached to the base A, and through which passes the lock. The other end of the holder B is provided with a hole or orifice, b', by means of which it is attached to the swivel a^1. This swivel passes through a hole in the base A, so as to be readily turned, having a nut, a^2, at the end of its shank to prevent it from being drawn out. The middle section of the hollow center B' of the holder B is a little longer than the top and bottom sections, so as to provide bearings $c\ c'$ for the springs C, as clearly shown in Fig. 3. C' is an inclined slot, which terminates on its lower side in a shoulder, c', against which rests one end of the springs C, and through which is inserted the labeled tag D.

The operation is as follows: The tag D is passed down through the slot C', and secured between the top plate and springs C, its index-face being exposed through the hollow center B', the springs C retaining it in position. Both sides of the tag being labeled, when it is desired to change the direction the holder is lifted up and reversed, as shown in Fig. 2, when, by turning the same on the swivel a^1, it is again brought to the position shown in Fig. 1, except that the opposite side of the tag is exposed.

What we claim as new, and desire to secure by Letters Patent of the United States, is—

The tag-holder B, provided with a hollow center or card-receptacle, B', which extends longitudinally nearly the length of the plate, and vertically through the same, bearings c c', slot b, hole b', springs C, and mouth C', in combination with swivel a^1 and staple a, substantially as and for the purpose described.

In testimony whereof we have signed our names to this specification in the presence of two subscribing witnesses.

JULIUS METZ.
EGBERT HINMAN.

Witnesses:
W. D. ANTHONY,
S. W. FRENCH.

A. B. SMITH.
GEARING.

No. 179,737. Patented July 11, 1876.

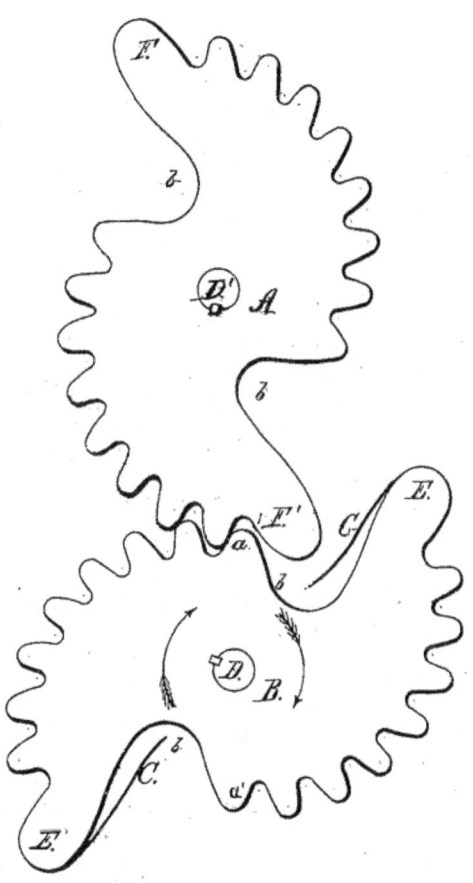

UNITED STATES PATENT OFFICE.

ANSELMO B. SMITH, OF DENVER, COLORADO TERRITORY.

IMPROVEMENT IN GEARING.

Specification forming part of Letters Patent No. **179,737**, dated July 11, 1876; application filed June 24, 1876.

To all whom it may concern:

Be it known that I, ANSELMO B. SMITH, of Denver, Colorado Territory, have invented a new and useful Improvement in Irregular or Cammed Geared Wheels, which improvement is fully set forth in the following specification, reference being had to the accompanying drawings:

The object of my invention is to convert a regular rotary motion into an irregular rotary motion by the means of what may be termed double-cammed gears A and B, secured on shafts D' D, B being the driving-shaft and regular motion, and A being the driven shaft and irregular motion, which is produced by the increasing diameter of the driver B, and the decreasing diameter of the driven, A, making an increased motion of A from slow to fast, while the driver B turns half-way over, and then at once drops from fast motion to a momentary pause, and then repeats the same motion again from slow to fast, and so keeps repeating. When the cog a comes in contact with the long cammed-shaped cog F', the motion of A is very slow, and, as B revolves, increasing the motion of A until the long cammed-shaped cog E' reaches the deep depression b', when there is an extra increase in the motion of A, consequent by the nearer approach of E' to the center of A, until E' shall have arrived to about in a line with shafts D D', at which time the momentary pause occurs, and then the same motion commences again. The extra increased motion referred to is doubly necessary—first, to get the long cammed cog F sufficiently advanced to drop into the depression b' before the cog a intervenes; second, to increase the motion of A to a greater extent, which will more fully appear when the present use is set forth.

The springs C' C may be made as shown in the drawings, or of rubber inserted in a cavity in the edge of the wheel, and are used to prevent any backlash in the cogs while changing from a fast to a slow motion, and making a enter its proper place, instead of, perhaps, striking against the cog beyond. The same result of motion may be obtained by using a pair of single-cammed cog-wheels having the cammed-shaped cog and depression, thereby causing the driving-shaft to make a complete revolution before the motion commences to repeat again from slow to fast.

The ratio of increased motion or (by a slight change in the construction of the long-cammed cog and the depression) decreased motion, by reversing the motion of the driver, may be more or less, to suit the purpose to which it is applied, by varying the center of the irregular wheels—in other words, by decreasing or increasing the distance from a to D, and increasing or decreasing the distance from E' to D, thereby increasing or decreasing the ratio, as desired.

The object to which I apply the motion at present is to reciprocate the tables used in stamp-mills for reducing and concentrating ores, which tables of themselves are quite heavy, and, when loaded with pulverized quartz, are still more so, and have to be run at a given speed to produce the desired effect on the pulverized quartz, as the tables strike a solid resistance at each end of the stroke, and hence, when started in an opposite direction, it must be done by commencing to move slowly, so as to not create any undue strain or jar on the machinery, and more especially so as not to slide the pulverized quartz on the table, and at the completion of the stroke it must be quick to give the shock. I get the above-required motion by having a crank attached to the shaft D', and, by a pitman, transmit the motion to the table. Right here comes in the point referred to heretofore about extra-increased motion. As the crank nears its so-called dead-centers, there is little or no lateral motion—hence the second reason heretofore named.

I am aware that there are many irregular motions by cammed gears and eccentric gears, which run from slow to fast, and then back again in a reverse motion, but know of no one that runs from slow to fast, and almost instantly drops to slow motion, and then repeats again in a rotary motion.

I claim as my invention—

The two peculiarly double or single cams, cogged, depressed, and otherwise formed as shown and described, the depressions being furnished with springs to prevent backlash, the whole as substantially described.

ANSELMO B. SMITH.

Witnesses:
A. M. SMITH,
JOSEPH E. WALKER.

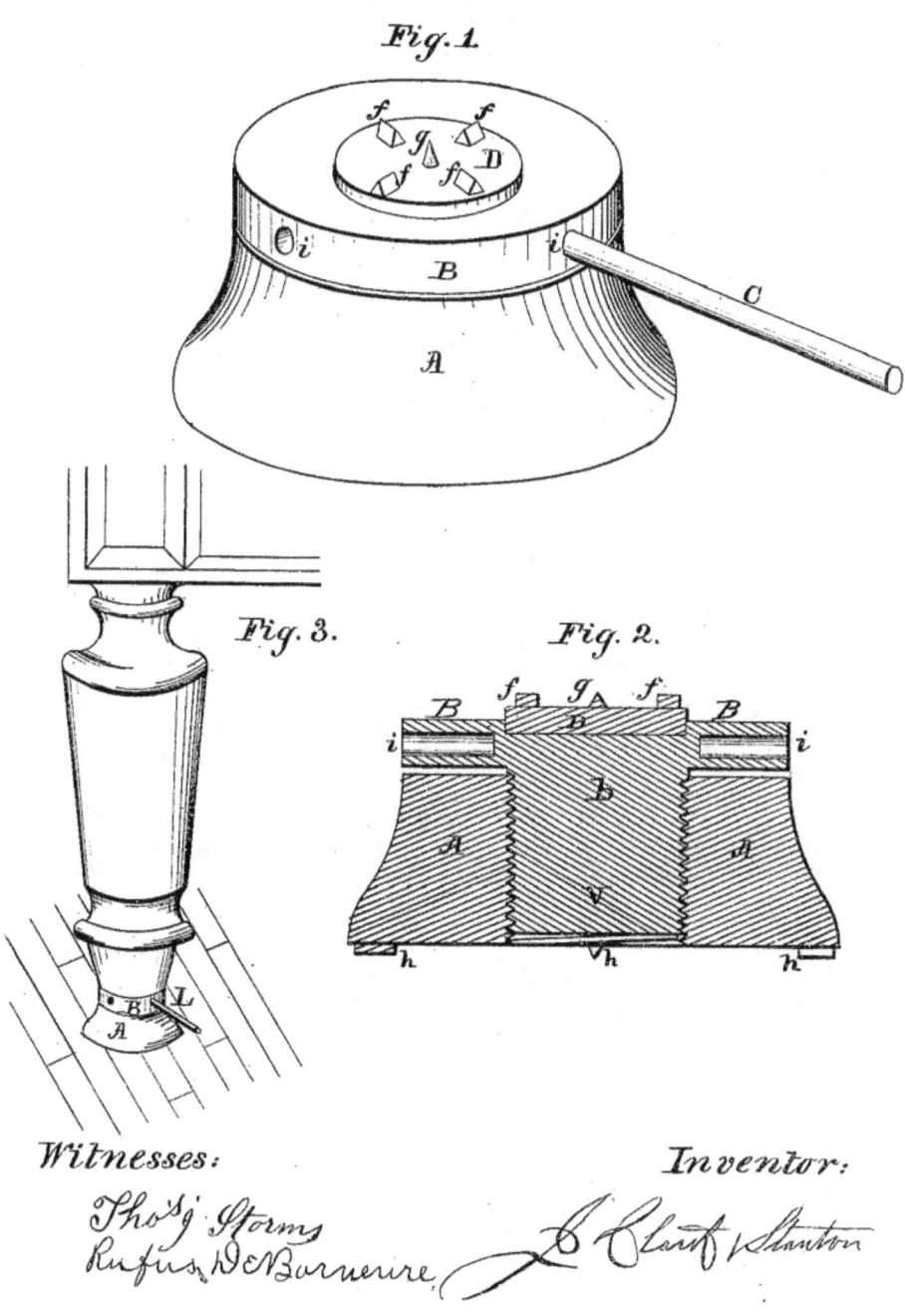

UNITED STATES PATENT OFFICE.

J. CLARK STANTON, OF HUTCHINSON, ASSIGNOR OF ONE-HALF HIS RIGHT TO FRANSANA HALL, OF HALL VALLEY, COLORADO TERRITORY.

IMPROVEMENT IN BILLIARD-TABLE LEVELERS.

Specification forming part of Letters Patent No. **179,740**, dated July 11, 1876; application filed April 26, 1876.

To all whom it may concern:

Be it known that I, J. CLARK STANTON, of Hutchinson, in the county of Jefferson, Territory of Colorado, have invented a new and useful invention for Leveling Billiard-Tables, Pool-Tables, Pigeon-Hole Tables, and Bagatelle-Tables, which improvement is fully set forth in the following specification, reference being had to the accompanying drawings.

The object of my invention is to level the tables by applying to each leg a screw as a permanent fixture.

The machine is shown in perspective in Figure 1, also in vertical section, Fig. 2; and it consists, essentially, of a screw, b, Fig. 2, working in base A, Figs. 1 and 2, and worked by means of the capstan head or block B, Figs. 1 and 2, which is revolved by a lever, C, Fig. 1, that is inserted into any of the four holes contained in the capstan-head B, two of which holes are shown at $i\ i$ in Figs. 1 and 2, and illustrate an application of the screw.

The circular piece D, containing sharp spuds at $f\ f\ f\ f$ and g, (shown in perspective, Fig. 1, and vertical section in Fig. 2,) is let into the capstan-head one-half its thickness, thereby giving the piece sufficient elevation to insure freedom of motion to the capstan-head when the machine is applied to the table.

The spuds at $f\ f\ f\ f$ and g, Fig. 1, are for the purpose of being pressed into the leg of the table, to prevent the slipping of the piece D when the capstan-head is revolved.

The sharp spuds at $h\ h\ h$, Fig. 2, are to prevent the slipping of the base A upon the floor. This manner of applying the screw is shown at L, Fig. 3.

I claim—

The combination, in a billiard-table leveler, of the base A, provided with spuds $h\ h$, the capstan-block B, with screw V and recessed upper face, and the circular piece D, fitting said recessed face, and having spuds $f\ f\ f\ f$, all combined and arranged to operate as described.

J. CLARK STANTON.

Witnesses:
W. F. KENDRICK,
CASSIUS G. HALL.

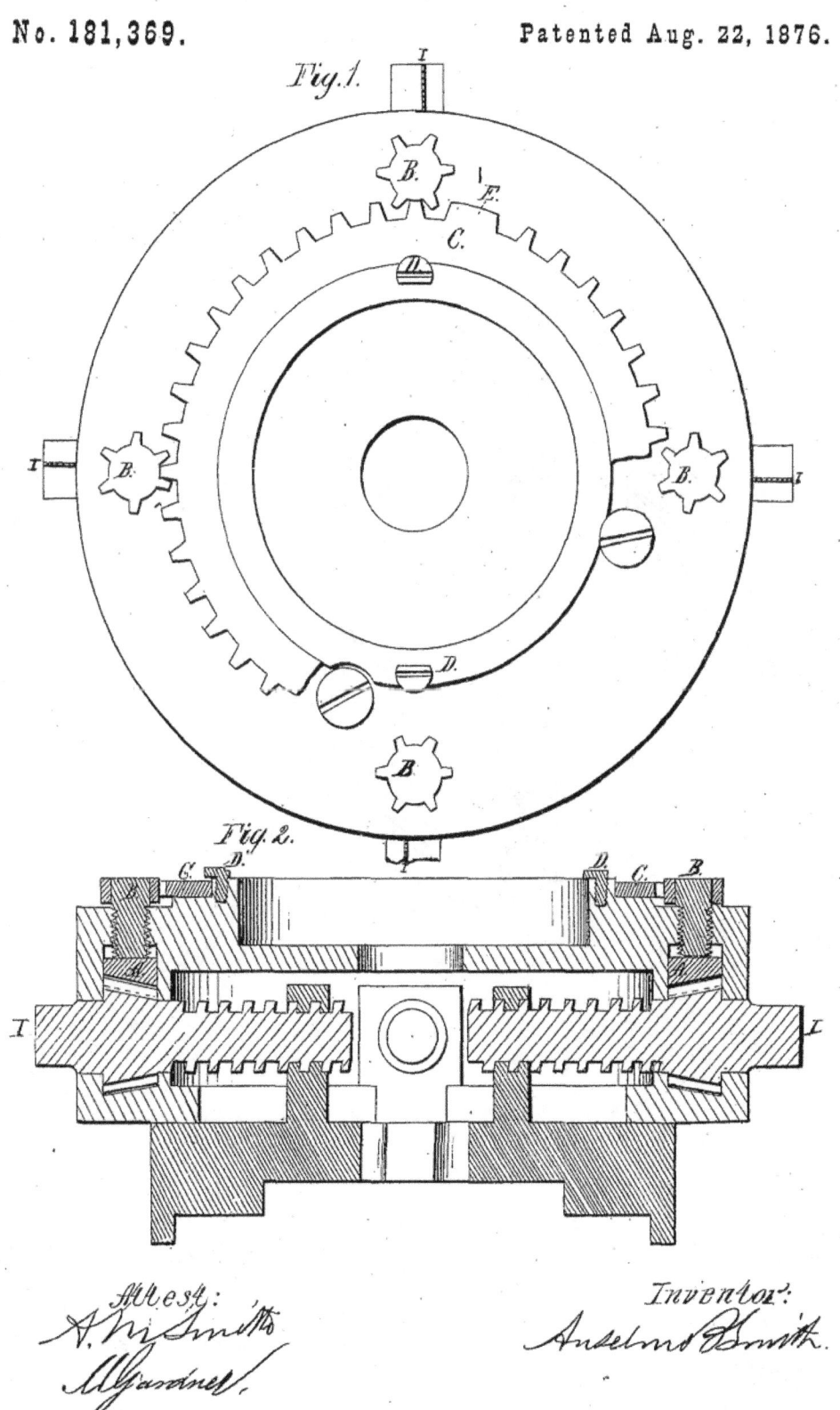

A. B. SMITH.
CHUCKS FOR METAL LATHES.

No. 181,369.

2 Sheets—Sheet 2.

Patented Aug. 22, 1876.

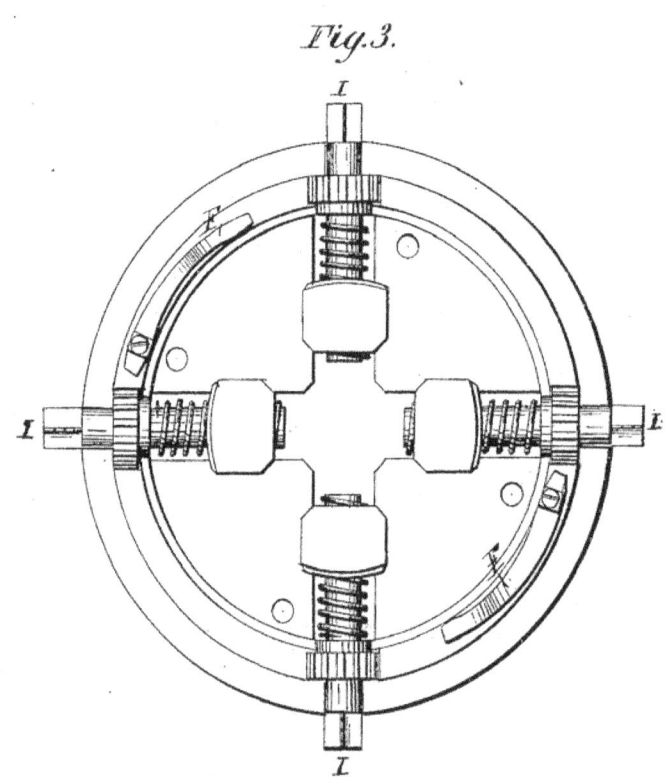

Fig. 3.

Attest:
A. M. Smith
M. Gardner

Inventor:
Anselmo Smith

UNITED STATES PATENT OFFICE.

ANSELMO B. SMITH, OF DENVER, COLORADO TERRITORY.

IMPROVEMENT IN CHUCKS FOR METAL-LATHES.

Specification forming part of Letters Patent No. **181,369**, dated August 22, 1876; application filed June 24, 1876.

To all whom it may concern:

Be it known that I, ANSELMO B. SMITH, of Denver, Colorado, have invented a new and useful Improvement in Chucks for Metal-Lathes, of which the following is a specification:

The object of my invention is to provide a chuck that can be used as a universal, independent, concentric or eccentric chuck, and that can readily be changed from one of these to the other.

My invention consists of the combination and arrangement of the several parts, as hereinafter described, and specifically pointed out in the claims.

Referring to the accompanying drawings, Figure 1 is a plan view of the rear side of the chuck, showing the toothed ring for operating the pinion-headed screws B. Fig. 2 is a cross-section of my improved chuck; and Fig. 3, a plan view of the under side of the jaw-carrying part of the same, showing the springs for throwing the ring for operating the pinions on the jaw-screws out of gear.

My invention is an improvement upon the chuck patented to Eli Horton, November 13, 1855, No. 13,787, and a detailed description of the several parts common to both chucks is, therefore, unnecessary.

B represents the gear-headed screws, which throw the toothed ring A into gear with the pinions of the jaw-screw. C is a toothed ring, which is used for turning all of the gear-headed screws B at once, and it is held in place by means of the screws D, each of which has one side of its head cut away, so that, by turning it half-way around, the toothed ring C can be readily removed, to enable the gear-headed screws B to be properly adjusted. The ring C in the drawing, Fig. 1, is cut away to show the location of the bolts for holding the two halves of the chuck together. I represents an index formed on one of the corners of the square end of each jaw-screw. A corresponding index is formed on the edge of the face-plate over each squared end, in virtue of which all of the jaws can be properly positioned, each at an equal distance from the center, by turning, by means of a wrench applied to the squared ends, each jaw-screw until its index-corner is directly under the index upon the edge of the face-plate. The face-plate is also divided by circles, which are of the same distance apart as are the threads of the jaw-screws; and these circles are also of service in approximating the position of the jaws. A jaw might be set nearly accurate by these circles, but by the aid of the index I there can be no mistake when the chuck has once been properly indexed. The blank space just above the toothed ring A (being about one-tenth ($\frac{1}{10}$) of an inch) shows the whole extent that I increase the bulk of the chuck. Attached to the frame of the jaw-holding half of the chuck between the jaw-screws are the springs F, (see Fig. 3,) which bear directly upon the face of the cogs of ring A, and not only serve to throw the said ring out of gear with the pinions of the jaw-screws when the gear-headed screws B are turned back, but also prevent it from rattling when the device is employed as an independent chuck.

When used as a universal chuck the toothed ring A moves with much less friction on the ends of the gear-headed screws B than when it wears all the way around the chuck, as in all other chucks of this class.

The geared ring C has a blank-cog, E, which prevents the gear-headed screws B from being turned too far in or out.

I claim and desire to secure by Letters Patent—

1. The combination of the pinions of the jaw-screws, provided with square indexed ends I, toothed ring A, springs F, and screws B, substantially as described.

2. The combination of the gear-headed screws B and the rings A C, substantially as described.

ANSELMO B. SMITH.

Witnesses:
A. M. SMITH,
D. P. COWL.

T. J. McMAHON.
SPARK-ARRESTER.

No. 182,214. Patented Sept. 12, 1876.

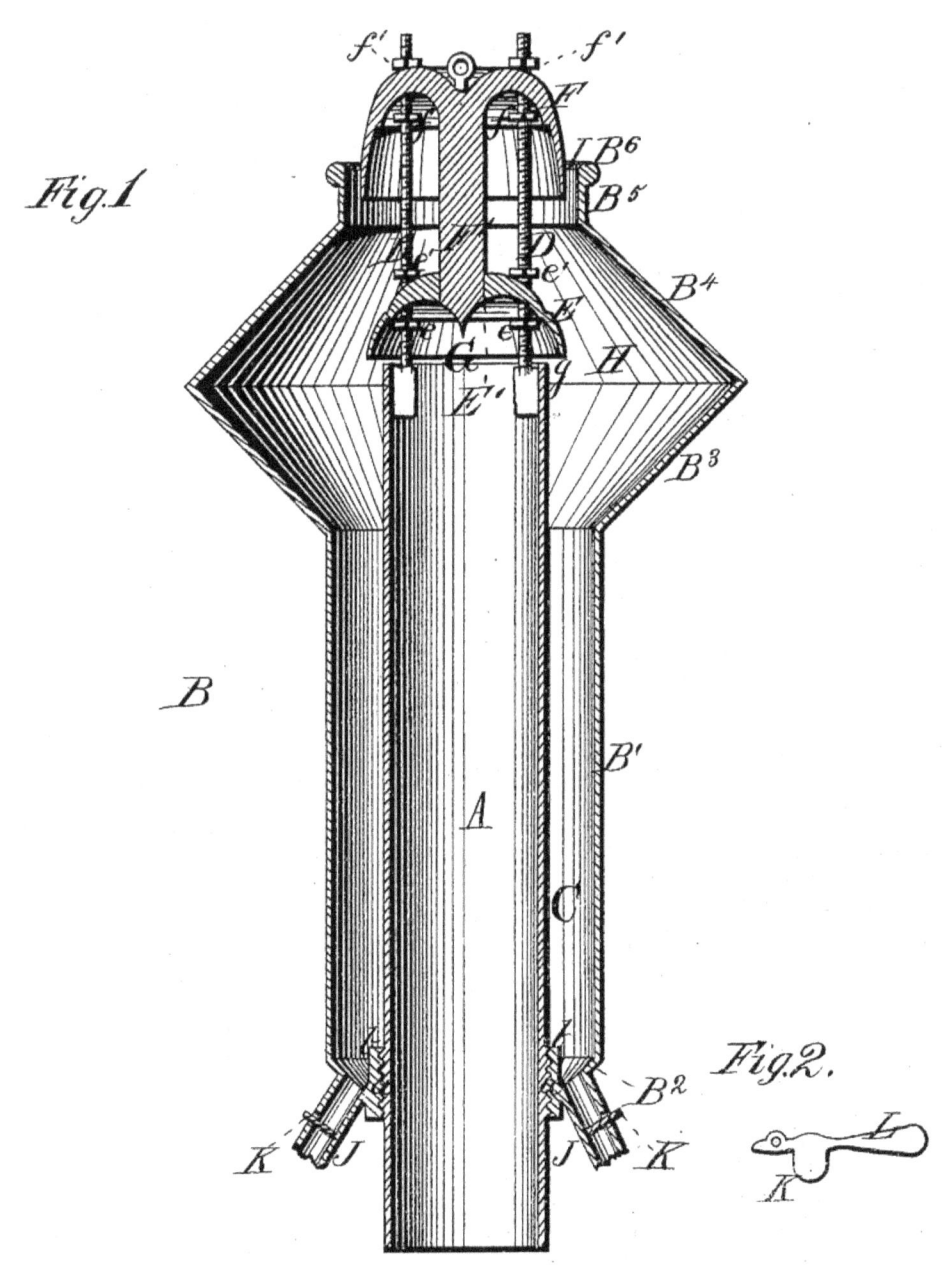

UNITED STATES PATENT OFFICE.

TERRENCE J. McMAHON, OF GOLDEN CITY, COLORADO.

IMPROVEMENT IN SPARK-ARRESTERS.

Specification forming part of Letters Patent No. **182,214**, dated September 12, 1876; application filed July 29, 1876.

To all whom it may concern:

Be it known that I, TERRENCE J. McMAHON, of Golden City, in the county of Jefferson and State of Colorado, have invented a new and valuable Improvement in Spark-Arresters; and I do hereby declare that the following is a full, clear, and exact description of the construction and operation of the same, reference being had to the annexed drawings, making a part of this specification, and to the letters and figures of reference marked thereon.

Figure 1 of the drawings is a representation of a longitudinal vertical section of my spark-arrester, and Fig. 2 is a detail view of the same.

The object of this invention is to provide a spark-arrester for the smoke-stacks of steam-engines which will effectually arrest and extinguish the sparks flying upward among the products of combustion without interfering with the draft, and which will also promote economy in the consumption of fuel.

The nature of said invention consists in certain improvements in spark-arresters, hereinafter particularly described.

In the accompanying drawings, A designates the main pipe or smoke-flue, through which the products of combustion are carried upward by the exhaust steam. Said smoke-flue A is screw-threaded on its outer surface at a, to receive an internally screw-threaded ring, b, which forms the bottom of stack-head B. Said stack-head consists of a cylindrical portion, B^1, which surrounds a part of smoke-flue A like a sleeve, leaving a spark-receiving chamber, C, of cylindrical form, between said portion B^1 of the stack-head and said smoke-flue A; also, of an inclined bottom portion, B^2, which connects the lower end of said cylindrical portion B^1 with bottom ring B, and forms an inclined floor for cinder-receiving chamber C; also, of two conoidal hollow portions, B^3 B^4, the lower one, B^3, of which rests on the top of cylindrical portion B^1, and flares upward, while the upper conoid B^4 flares downward with its outer rim resting on the upper edge of B^3; and, finally, of an annular upper flange, B^5, surmounted by a turned rim, B^6. The parts b B^1, B^2, B^3, B^4, B^5, and B^6 are all made in one piece, and of iron, copper, brass, or other suitable material, according to the uses for which the engine is designed.

The above-described construction produces a stack-head of very neat and attractive external appearance, and one which is susceptible of considerable ornament. This would be desirable in case of engines used on passenger railway-trains.

D D D designate screw-threaded rods, which are permanently attached to the upper end of smoke-flue A, on the inside thereof. Their function is to support inverted cones or cups E F by means of nuts e e e, which set under lower cup or cone E, and nuts f f f, which set under upper cone F. Said rods pass through perforations in said cups or cones, the sides of which perforations so bind against said rods as to materially assist in the support of said cups or cones. Lower cup or cone E is provided with a central perforation, E', and upper cup or cone F is provided with a downwardly-extending weighted pointed bar, F', which sets into perforation E', and the point of which passes a little below the same, so as to complete the inner deflecting-curve of said lower cup or cone. Said bar operates, also, by its weight to prevent the displacement of said cups or cones by wind or other accidental cause. Lower cup or cone E sets down nearly to the top of smoke-flue A, leaving a space, G, between the two, and also an annular side exit, g. Said cup E also sets into a space, H, which is bounded exteriorly by flaring portions B^3 B^4 of stack-head B, and which communicates with cylindrical space C. The lower part of upper inverted cup or cone F sets within annular flange B^5, leaving an annular exit, I, between the outside of said cone and the inside of upper rim B^6 of stack-head B. The upper part of said upper inverted cup F extends entirely above said stack-head, and adds to the ornamental appearance thereof. Additional nuts e' e' e' are screwed home above cup E, to hold it in place, and additional nuts f' f' f' are screwed home above upper cup or cone F, to hold it in place.

In the inclined part B^2 of stack-head B are discharge-pipes J J, each of which is slotted at right angles to its length, to allow the play of a slide, K, which is rigidly attached to a lever, L, pivoted to the side of discharge-pipe

469

J. By operating said lever from the cab of the engine, said discharge-pipe can be closed or opened at will.

All the above-described parts of my apparatus are preferably made of metal, though in the case of lever L, and, perhaps, some others, a different material might be substituted.

The operation of my device is as follows: The exhaust steam carries the products of combustion up smoke-flue A, causing an upward current of air, smoke, steam, cinders, and sparks. Said current then comes in contact with the curved face formed by the pointed end of bar F' and the under side of lower cup E, which face, by reason of its peculiar shape, will cause eddies and counter-currents in space G, as that part of the current which is deflected outward from the point of bar F will come into collision with the part of said current which is deflected inward from the inside of cup E. Said current then escapes from space G through narrow annular exit g into space H. It is next deflected from the inside of conoidal portion B⁴ of stack-head B into the hollow of upper cone or cup F. There it is again deflected inward by said cup, and outward by central bar F, which action produces more eddies and counter-currents in and below said cup. At last said current escapes through narrow annular exit I; but the sparks are previously nearly all extinguished by successively impinging against so many surfaces, and in the end most of them fall into space C, at the bottom of which they lie until the discharge-pipes J J are opened, when they fall to the ground. Even if some sparks of fire still remain in them, they will no longer prove an annoyance, as the elevation of said discharge-pipes above the ground is not sufficient to allow said sparks to get afloat in the air again. The lower deflecting cup or cone E may be perforated, if preferred; but in this case the course of the ascending air, steam, and smoke current will be somewhat changed, and the action of the cups and stack-head on the sparks will be correspondingly modified.

What I claim as new, and desire to secure by Letters Patent, is—

1. The combination of lower inverted cup or cone E, perforated at E', with its supporting-rods, the smoke-flue A, and upper inverted cup or cone F, having central weighted pointed bar F', substantially as and for the purpose set forth.

2. The combination of stack-head B, having cylindrical portion B¹, flaring portions B³ B⁴, lower inclined portion B², and upper annular flange B⁵, with smoke-flue A, inverted deflecting cones or cups E and F, and screw-threaded rods D, substantially as and for the purpose set forth.

In testimony that I claim the above I have hereunto subscribed my name in the presence of two witnesses.

TERRENCE J. McMAHON.

Witnesses:
J. M. JOHNSON, Jr.,
A. H. DE FRANCE.

C. J. EVERETT.
PROCESS OF PRESERVING ANIMAL AND VEGETABLE SUBSTANCES DURING TRANSPORTATION.

No. 182,426.   Patented Sept. 19, 1876.

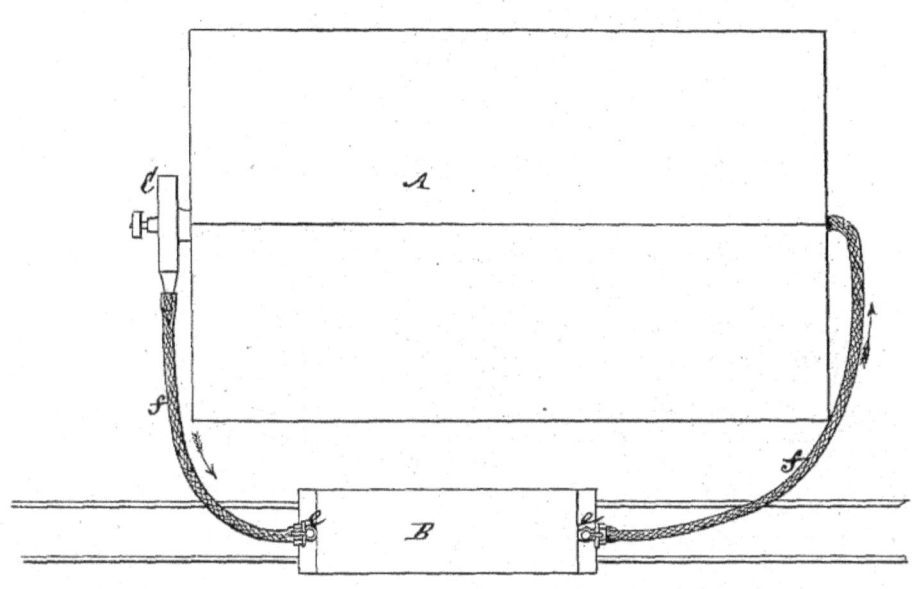

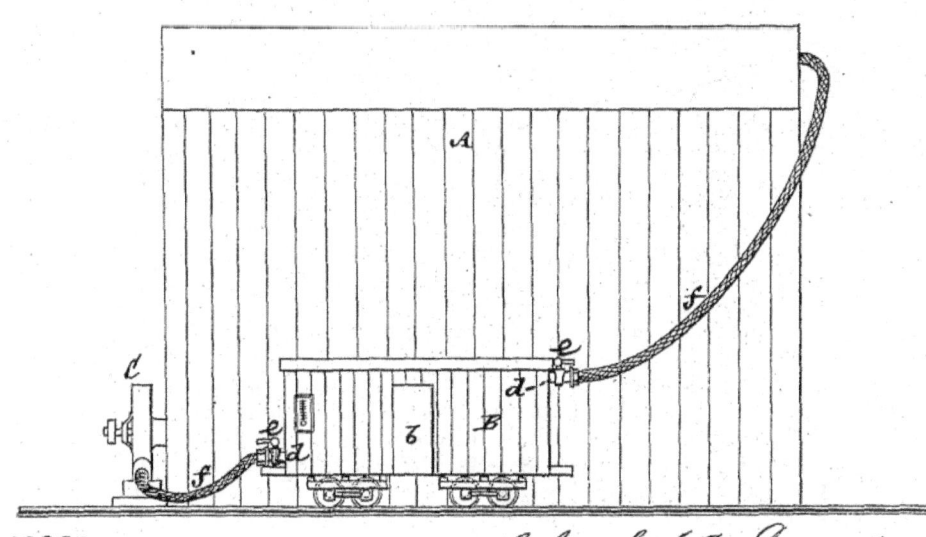

UNITED STATES PATENT OFFICE.

CHARLES J. EVERETT, OF TENAFLY, NEW JERSEY, ASSIGNOR TO HIMSELF AND RADCLIFFE B. LOCKWOOD, OF BOULDER, COLORADO.

IMPROVEMENT IN PROCESSES OF PRESERVING ANIMAL AND VEGETABLE SUBSTANCES DURING TRANSPORTATION.

Specification forming part of Letters Patent No. **182,426,** dated September 19, 1876; application filed August 2, 1876.

To all whom it may concern:

Be it known that I, CHARLES J. EVERETT, of Tenafly, in the county of Bergen and State of New Jersey, have invented a new and useful Improvement in the Preservation of Animal and Vegetable Substances; and I do hereby declare that the following is a full, clear, and exact description of the same, reference being had to the accompanying drawing, which forms part of this specification.

This invention relates more particularly to the preservation of animal and vegetable substances during transportation from one place to another, without the use of ice or other refrigerating material during such transportation.

The following preliminary remarks will serve to explain more fully the objects and value of my invention.

Animal and vegetable substances of a perishable character are often produced in large quantities in localities distant one or more days' travel by railroad, or other system of conveyance, from extensive markets, or other places of consumption. Heretofore it has been usual, during warm weather, to transport such perishable substances in railway-cars, vessels, or wagons by inclosing them in a non-conducting chamber, and surrounding them by atmospheric air, kept constantly cool or at a low temperature by means of ice, or other refrigerating material, or by chemical compounds or processes. But all these previous methods involve the continuous use, proximity to the substance being preserved, and waste of large quantities of ice or cooling chemical substances, or the active continuance of the cooling processes heretofore practiced during such transportation. Furthermore, most, if not all, of such previous methods require frequent if not continuous currents of such artificially-cooled air to pass over and around the perishable substances intended to be preserved. If these air-currents are induced for the purpose of ventilation, and to remove strong odors or foul gases, it is customary to keep up a continuous circulation by fresh quantities of atmospheric air passed into and through the chamber where the perishable substances are confined. This is not only wasteful of the ice or other refrigerating material, but is otherwise objectionable. On the other hand, when the same confined air is constantly circulated through the chamber containing the substances to be preserved, it is found, in practice, that by frequent deposition of the natural moisture of the air on the colder surfaces of the ice, or of the ice-box, or of other refrigerating medium, that that abnormally dry air extracts from the animal or vegetable substances their moisture, and with it much of the characteristic flavor of said substances. Furthermore, it is obvious that when the low temperature of a refrigerating-car or other vehicle or vessel is maintained by any of the customary or hereinbefore-described processes, a large portion of the carrying capacity of the car or vehicle is occupied by the refrigerating material, or apparatus used to carry on the refrigerating process, thus adding so much dead weight to the vehicle, and reducing the space available to the meat, fruit, or other substance to be preserved.

If the animal or vegetable substances to be transported during warm weather should simply first be cooled down in an ice-house to the lowest temperature which they will safely bear, and be then quickly placed in a car constructed with non-conducting walls, but the inside temperature of which is much higher than that of the ice-house, it is evident that the heat of the contained air and of the interior sides of the car would soon raise the temperature of the cooled contents to an unsafe or prejudicial degree, so that some method of renewed or additional refrigeration must be adopted after the car is filled and closed.

My invention obviates these difficulties, and its object is to simplify and economize the preservation of animal and vegetable substances of a perishable character, during comparatively short periods of time. It is alike applicable, by merely substituting a furnace or heater for an ice-house, to preserving said substances from freezing during winter as from decay during warm weather.

My invention consists in confining the substances to be preserved in an air-tight car, or other vehicle or chamber, having non-conducting walls, and then making a temporary communication between such vehicle or chamber and an ice-house or a heater, accordingly as it is required to cool or heat the vehicle or chamber, till the latter and its contents reach or approximate the same temperature as the ice-house or heater, by means of either a natural or artificial or induced circulation kept up between the car or preserving-chamber and ice-house or heater during their connection, after which said connection is severed, and external air excluded from entering the car or preserving-chamber, which maintains its modified temperature by reason of the non-conducting character of its construction. Chemical absorbents or disinfectants may also be used to advantage within the car in combination with this process.

In the drawing, Figure 1 represents a plan of certain means used to illustrate my improved process, as applied to the preservation of perishable animal or vegetable substances during their transportation by railroad, and the same will here, mainly, be described as adapted to warm weather. Fig. 2 is a side elevation of the same.

At the place of production or collection of large quantities of perishable animal or vegetable substances I propose to construct one or more houses or other receptacles, A, for the storage of moderate quantities of ice. If on the line of a railroad, close air-tight cars will be prepared as follows:

The sides, ends, tops, and floors of the car B are double, with intervening spaces, which are filled with any good non-conducting material. Said car has but one door, b, for ingress and egress, which door is constructed so that when closed all circulation of air to or from the interior of the car entirely ceases. At either end of the car, say, at the upper part of one end and at the lower part of the other end, are air-pipes d, of three or four inches diameter, more or less, opening into the outer air, and communicating with the interior of the car. These pipes are provided with air-tight valves $e\ e$ to exclude the outer air, and with screw-threads or other suitable means for connecting thereto flexible pipes or hose $f\!f$, which may be of the same diameter as the pipes, and which are made to communicate with the ice-depot or storehouse A before mentioned. The hose is connected with a fan-blower, air-pump, or other device C for forcing or drawing the cold air from the ice-house into the car at one end, while the warmer air previously contained in the car flows from the other end back into the ice-house, to be there cooled and again forced into and through the car.

The same effect—that is, the cooling to the required temperature of the contained air of the car—may be effected automatically by using larger pipes, and so connecting them with the ice-house that the colder and heavier air of the ice-house will flow continually, though more slowly, into the lower part of the car, and force the warm and lighter air of the car upward. A thermometer is placed in the car, visible through a glass window, to enable the operator to see when the required temperature is attained.

The car and the requisite connections with the ice-house, hereinbefore described, having been prepared, and a quantity of meat, fish, fruit, or other animal or vegetable substances having been accumulated at, in, or near the ice-house, the same is placed in the car, the door of the latter tightly closed, the temporary communication with the ice-house effected, and the cold air forced or drawn through the car until the thermometer shows that the requisite temperature has been attained by the contained air and contents of the car. The valves of the air-pipes are then closed, and the hose-pipes disconnected. The car is then ready to proceed on its journey, and need not have its interior again exposed to the outside atmosphere until the car has arrived at its destination for distribution of its contents, or certain of them.

When economy is not so much of an object as expedition, and the perishable substances to be preserved and to be transported are stored in the ice-house, temporary connection may be made between the car door and the door of the ice-house, the air-pipe connection made, and, as soon as the loading of the car is commenced, the circulation of the cooled air is also begun, so that by the time the car is filled the interior of the car and its contents will have been cooled down to the requisite temperature. This mode of carrying out the process, although more wasteful, allows the displaced warm air of the car to escape into the outer air, and to be replaced by the cooled air from the ice-house.

When it is required to transport the contents of the car an unusually prolonged distance for such a system of preservation, and to maintain the low temperature for a proportionately-extended period of time, it will be necessary to repeat the process hereinbefore described of cooling the car as often as the thermometer in the car indicates the approach of too high a temperature within the car. If it is desired to transport the substances to be preserved several days' journey, ice-depots should be constructed at distances apart equal to one or two days' travel, with sidings or switches alongside the main track, upon which the cars may be run and the operation herein described repeated.

To adapt the process to the preservation of animal or vegetable substances from freezing or being injured by cold in the winter season, it is only necessary to substitute a furnace or heater for the ice-house to elevate the temperature of the contained air of the car to a degree which will have the desired effect upon the contents of the car, at least for a short period of time or during transportation, the same means and mode of operation being resorted to as in cooling the car for transportation during warm weather.

When the substances to be preserved are such as emit strong odors or offensive gases during their confinement in the air-tight car or chamber, I introduce dry vegetable carbon or any other inodorous absorbent or suitable disinfectant for the purpose of absorbing or neutralizing such odors or gases as fast as they are generated.

I do not limit the application of my process to any specific form or kind of car, chamber, or package for the purpose of receiving and transporting the substances to be preserved, so long as such car, chamber, or package is air-tight when closed, and has walls of a non-conducting character; nor do I confine myself to any specific means of cooling or heating the air to be supplied to the car or chamber, as there are many well-known modes of accomplishing either result.

I claim—

The process herein described of preserving animal or vegetable substances during transportation by confining them in an air-tight car or other vehicle or chamber, having its walls built to obstruct the passage of heat, and then making temporary communication between such vehicle or chamber and an ice-house or heater, and establishing circulation between either of the latter and the vehicle or preserving-chamber, and subsequently severing such communication, and excluding the external air from the interior of the car or chamber, substantially as specified.

CHAS. J. EVERETT.

Witnesses:
HENRY T. BROWN,
FRED. HAYNES.

R. McDONALD.
COMBINED STEP AND HUB-BAND.

No. 182,839. Patented Oct. 3, 1876.

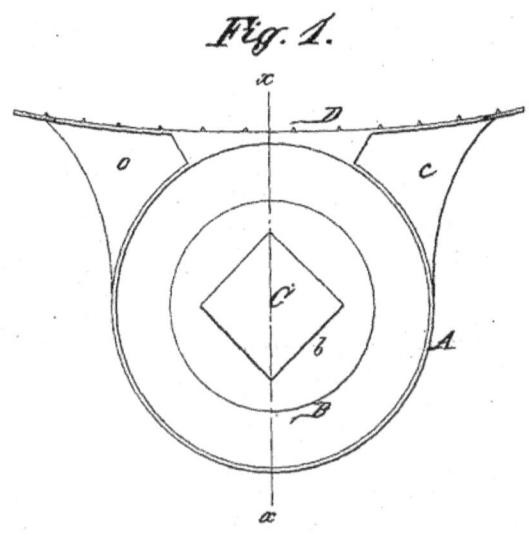

UNITED STATES PATENT OFFICE.

ROBERT McDONALD, OF GEORGETOWN, COLORADO.

IMPROVEMENT IN COMBINED STEP AND HUB-BAND.

Specification forming part of Letters Patent No. **182,839**, dated October 3, 1876; application filed August 28, 1876.

To all whom it may concern:

Be it known that I, ROBERT MCDONALD, of Georgetown, in the county of Clear Creek and State of Colorado, have invented a new and Improved Safety-Step, Hub-Band, Nut, and Dust-Box for Carriages, of which the following is a specification:

Figure 1 is a front elevation. Fig. 2 is a vertical section on line $x\,x$ in Fig. 1.

Similar letters of reference indicate corresponding parts.

This invention consists in the combination of a step, hub-band, nut, and dust-box for carriages, comprised in a single casting.

A is a band, which is of sufficient size to inclose the end of the carriage-hub, and is divided in the center by a web, B. A nut, C, is formed at the center of the web, and is provided with the usual recess for the washer a, and with the square portion b. D is a step, cast upon one side of the band A, and strengthened by ribs or brackets c. The upper surface of the step is roughened or serrated to insure a firm foot-hold. An aperture, d, is cut in the lower side of the band to permit the escape of dust.

This invention is applicable to carriages and wagons of every description. It provides a step at the most desirable point and answers the purpose of a nut and hub-band.

If desirable the device may be made in two or more parts, fixed together by rivets, screws, or otherwise, and finished by plating or gilding.

Having thus described my invention, I claim as new and desire to secure by Letters Patent—

A step, hub-band, nut, and dust-box combined in a single casting or piece of metal, or made in several parts, permanently fixed together, substantially as shown and described.

ROBT. McDONALD.

Witnesses:
H. B. BEIGHLEY,
THOS. S. CAUTTON.

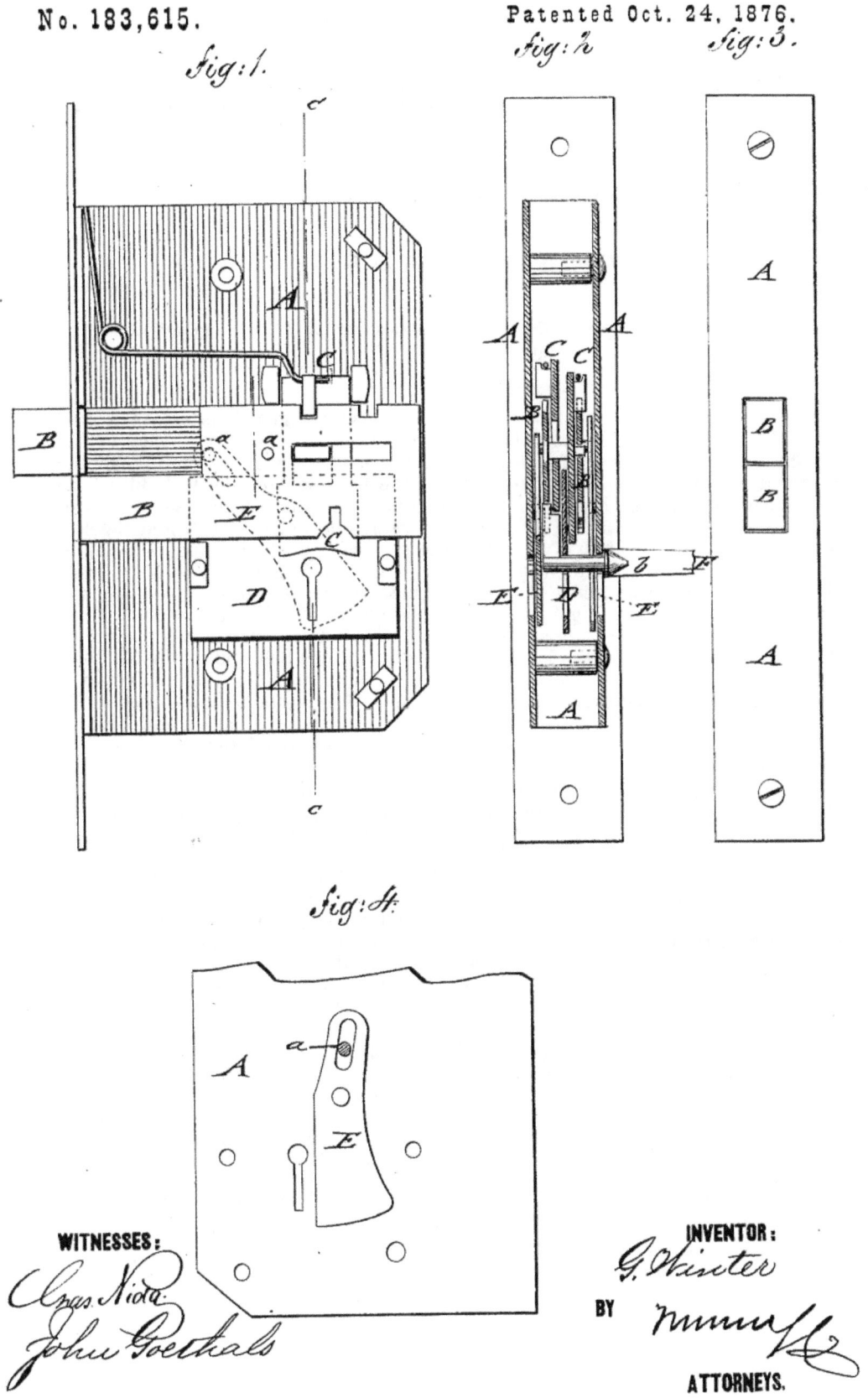

UNITED STATES PATENT OFFICE.

GUSTAV WINTER, OF DENVER, COLORADO TERRITORY.

IMPROVEMENT IN DOOR-LOCKS.

Specification forming part of Letters Patent No. **183,615,** dated October 24, 1876; application filed July 1, 1876.

To all whom it may concern:

Be it known that I, GUSTAV WINTER, of Denver, Arapahoe county, Territory of Colorado, have invented a new and Improved Door-Lock, of which the following is a specifiation:

Figure 1 represents a side elevation of my improved door-lock, with inclosing side plate detached. Fig. 2 is a vertical transverse section of the same on line *c c*, Fig. 1; Fig. 3, an end view of the lock, showing face-plate and bolts; and Fig. 4 is a detail view of the keyhole guard-plate.

Similar letters of reference indicate corresponding parts.

My invention relates to an improved safety-lock for hotels, private houses, and other purposes, which prevents, by a cheap and simple construction, the opening of the lock from the outside and the forcing of anesthetics through the key-hole.

The invention consists of a door-lock with two or more bolts and tumblers, which are so arranged in connection with the key-hole guard-plates, pivoted to the casing of the lock and operated by the bolts and key, that the key-hole is closed at the side opposite to that from which the key is introduced.

In the drawing, A represents the casing of my improved door-lock, which is arranged with two or more bolts, B, and tumblers C, that are separated by a division-plate, D, so as to be operated independently of each other by the key F. The bolts, B, are connected by pins *a* with the slotted ends of key-hole guard-plates E, that are pivoted to the casing A, and operated by the sliding bolts in such a manner that when the bolts are thrown forward the guard-plates of the same are swung over to close the key-hole, and when the bolts are thrown back the guard-plates are moved away from the key-hole. The heads of the bolts B run parallel, and are one above the other in the face-plate of the lock, filling up the recess of the same. The key-hole guard-plate E swings between the bolt and the casing, the key being made without an end pin, but with a guard, *b*, that permits it to enter the required distance without touching the guard-plate and hindering its motion.

The bit of the key is only equal in width to the thickness of one bolt and its tumbler, and when introduced operates the tumbler and bolt at the side opposite to that from which the key is inserted, the tumbler and bolt on the side of the key remaining in its position.

By locking, therefore, the door from the outside, the inner lock and guard-plate are closed, while by locking the door from the inside the outer lock and guard-plate are closed.

The tampering with the lock from either side, and the introduction of chloroform or other stupifying anesthetics, are thus prevented, and a safety lock of simple and reliable construction, especialty for hotel purposes, furnished.

Having thus described my invention, I claim as new and desire to secure by Letters Patent—

The combination in case A of bolts B and tumblers C, separated by plate D, the bolts being connected by pins *a* with pivoted key-hole guards E, and provided with parallel heads, one above another, in the face-plate, as shown and described.

GUSTAV WINTER.

Witnesses:
CHAS. MERSEBURG,
HERRMAN HOLST.

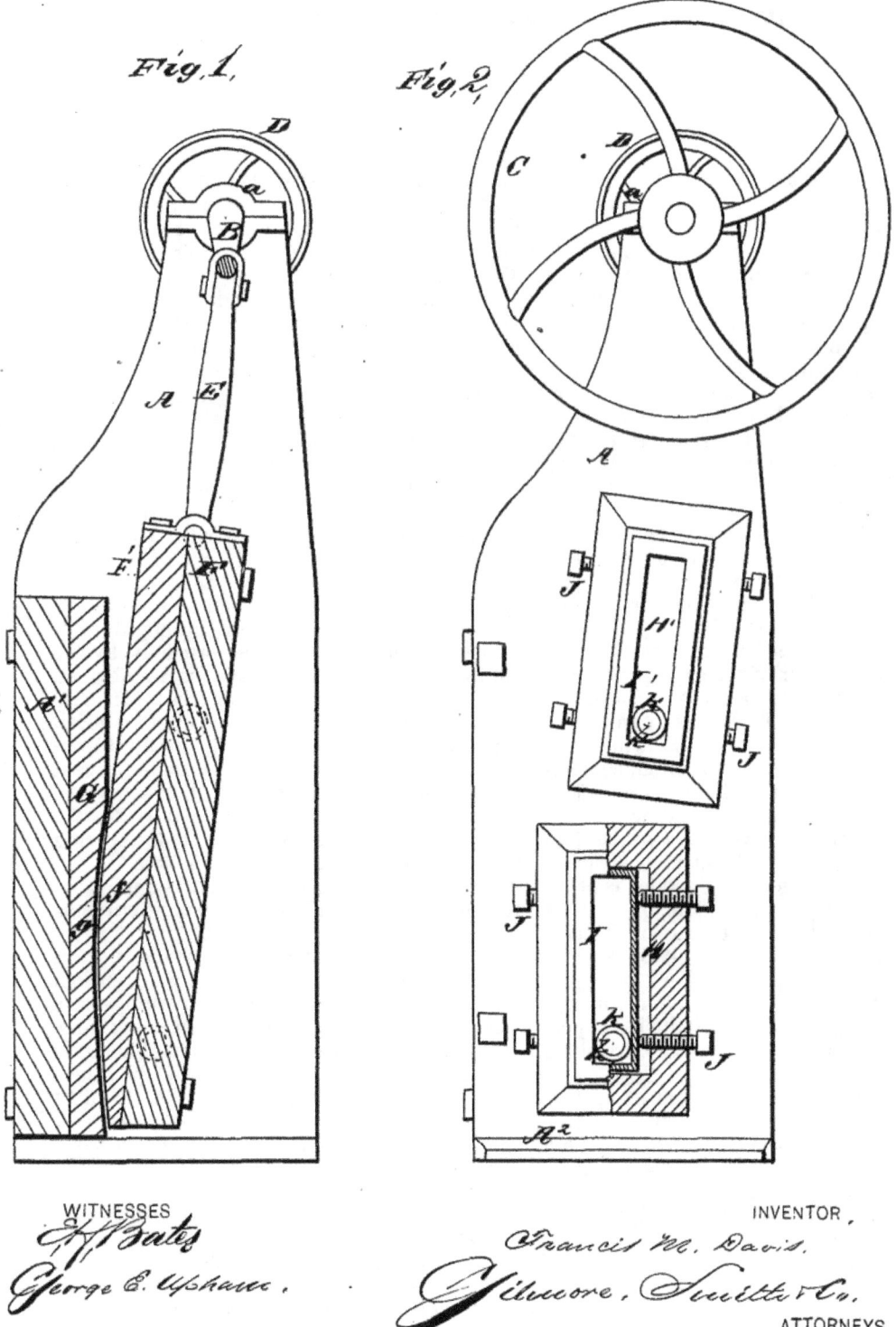

UNITED STATES PATENT OFFICE.

FRANCIS M. DAVIS, OF DENVER, COLORADO.

IMPROVEMENT IN QUARTZ-CRUSHERS.

Specification forming part of Letters Patent No. **183,648**, dated October 24, 1876; application filed July 29, 1876.

To all whom it may concern:

Be it known that I, FRANCIS M. DAVIS, of Denver, in the county of Arapahoe and State of Colorado, have invented a new and valuable Improvement in Quartz-Crushers; and I do hereby declare that the following is a full, clear, and exact description of the construction and operation of the same, reference being had to the annexed drawings, making a part of this specification, and to the letters and figures of reference marked thereon.

Figure 1 of the drawings is a representation of a longitudinal vertical section of my quartz-crusher; and Fig. 2 is a side elevation, part sectional, thereof.

This invention relates to quartz-crushers; and it consists in certain improvements therein, as will be hereinafter more fully set forth.

In the annexed drawings, A designates one of the two standards which constitute, together with front piece or block A^1, the supporting-frame and box of the casing. On the tops of standards A, in boxes a, is journaled a rotating double-crank shaft, B, carrying a fly-wheel, C, and a belt-wheel, D, where the power is applied. Said double crank communicates vertically reciprocating and oscillating motion to a strong metal rod or pitman, E, the lower end of which is pivotally connected to a crushing-block, F. Said block is constructed with a face, F′, of chilled metal, which is plane from the top nearly to the middle, but convex at f from the middle to the bottom. G is a stationary crushing block or plate, also of chilled metal, and secured to front piece A^1. The face of crushing-block G is plane for part of the way down, and concave in its lower portion g. Concavity g and convexity f are made to fit one another.

Standards A A are each slotted at H and H′, the former slot being vertical, the latter inclined upward and backward. In said slots are set metal boxes I I′, somewhat narrower than said slots, so as to be capable of lateral adjustment therein, said adjustment being effected by means of adjusting-screws J J. The function of said boxes is to guide rigid gudgeons or trunnions K K, which slide therein. Said gudgeons are connected to and form a part of crushing-block F, and are provided with loose anti-friction sleeves kk, of Babbitt's metal or any other suitable material. By adjusting boxes I I′ backward or forward the distance between the tops of the crushing-faces may be increased or diminished at will. The crushing-plates F′ and G are made of chilled metal, and detachable from block F and front piece A^1, which should be of cast-iron or similar heavy and strong material.

In practice, the quartz is fed into the space between the tops of the crushing-plates as block F rises. When said block descends, the crushing-plate F′ grinds and crushes said quartz against plate G with a compound vertical and forward and back motion, due to pitman E, to inclined slot H′ and vertical slot H, and to the boxes I I′, secured in said slots. By adjusting the crushing-plates close together, their action is made more powerful, and the peculiar conformation of their lower portions makes it possible to thoroughly pulverize the quartz, as well as crush it, by the continuous operation of the same devices. The standards A A and the front piece A^1 must be made of thick and strong material, especially the latter, which is preferably of iron; and the joints are made close to prevent the escape of quartz, except at the bottom. Foot-pieces A^2 are attached rigidly to the standards A A, for the purpose of securing said standards in an upright position.

The above-described apparatus is applicable to crushing any kind of ores, coal, or stone as well as quartz.

Various modifications may be made without departing from the spirit of my invention. For instance, the reciprocating crushing-plate may be made concave, and the stationary one convex. Also, the means of adjustable boxes I I′ may be any known mechanical equivalent for screws J J. The crushing-plates may also be made in one piece with the blocks to which they are secured; and the double-crank shaft B may be operated by any suitable known mechanism.

What I claim as new, and desire to secure by Letters Patent, is—

1. The combination of standards A, having inclined slots H′ and vertical slots H, with crushing-block F and trunnions or gudgeons K K, substantially as and for the purpose set forth.

2. The combination of standards A, having inclined slots H' and vertical slots H, provided with adjustable boxes I I, with crushing-block F and trunnions K K, substantially as and for the purpose set forth.

3. Trunnions K, provided with loose metal sleeves L, in combination with boxes I I' and adjusting-screws J J, substantially as and for the purpose set forth.

In testimony that I claim the above I have hereunto subscribed my name in the presence of two witnesses.

FRANCIS MARION DAVIS.

Witnesses:
H. C. ENSMINGER,
H. M. BEMIS.

W. WEST.
PULVERIZED FUEL-FEEDER FOR SMELTING FURNACES.

No. 184,122. Patented Nov. 7, 1876.

Fig. 1.

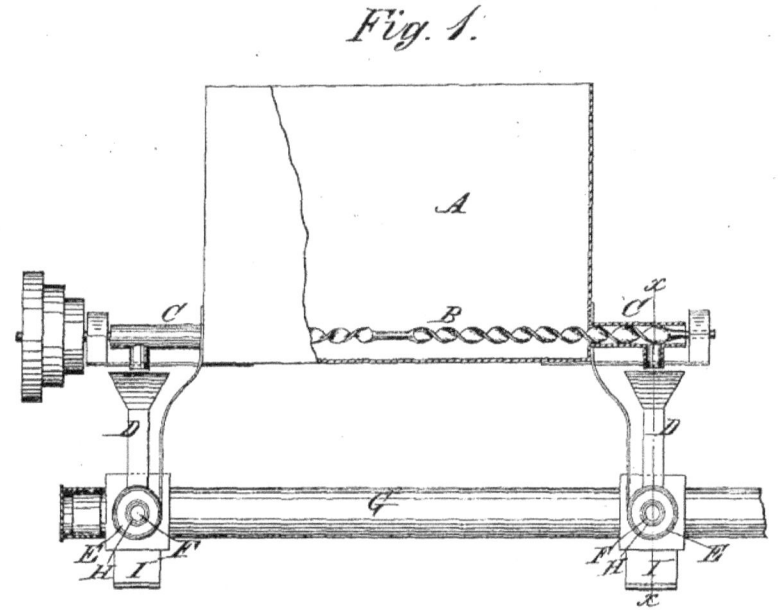

Fig. 2.

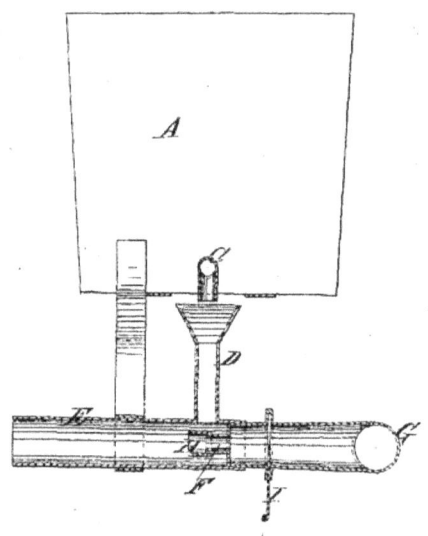

United States Patent Office.

WILLIAM WEST, OF GOLDEN CITY, ASSIGNOR OF ONE-HALF HIS RIGHT TO IRA S. ELKINS, OF DENVER, COLORADO TERRITORY.

IMPROVEMENT IN PULVERIZED FUEL FEEDER FOR SMELTING-FURNACES.

Specification forming part of Letters Patent No. **184,122**, dated November 7, 1876; application filed July 1, 1876.

To all whom it may concern:

Be it known that I, WILLIAM WEST, of Golden City, in the county of Jefferson and Territory of Colorado, have invented a new and Improved Pulverized Fuel Feeder for Smelting-Furnaces, of which the following is a specification:

My invention consists of a contrivance for feeding smelting-furnaces with coal-dust by means of the air-blast.

Figure 1 is partly a side elevation and partly a sectional elevation of my improved coal-dust feeder, and Fig. 2 is a section on the line $x\,x$ of Fig. 1.

Similar letters of reference indicate corresponding parts.

A is a hopper, in which the dust is placed, for being fed into the furnace. B is a screw-conveyer for feeding out the dust into one or more tubes, C, from which it drops through the funnel-mouthed pipes D into the large blast-pipes E upon the nozzles F, through which the blasts enter E from the main pipe G, to be carried along by the air into the furnace. H represents a movable piece of pipe to regulate the mixing of the air and coal, and I is a damper or valve to regulate the air.

The screw will have a cone-pulley for the driving-belt, or other means for varying the speed at the will of the operator. Other means of giving a regular supply of coal-dust to the pipe D may be employed.

Having thus described my invention, I claim as new and desire to secure by Letters Patent—

The combination of hopper-box A, right-and-left screw-conveyer B inclosed in tube C, funnel-mouthed tube D, pipe E, and blast-pipe G, the latter having the adjustable nozzle H, substantially as described.

WILLIAM WEST.

Witnesses:
SILAS BERTENSHAM,
H. H. STEBBIN.

J. COLLINS.
ENVELOPE.

No. 185,727.   Patented Dec. 26, 1876.

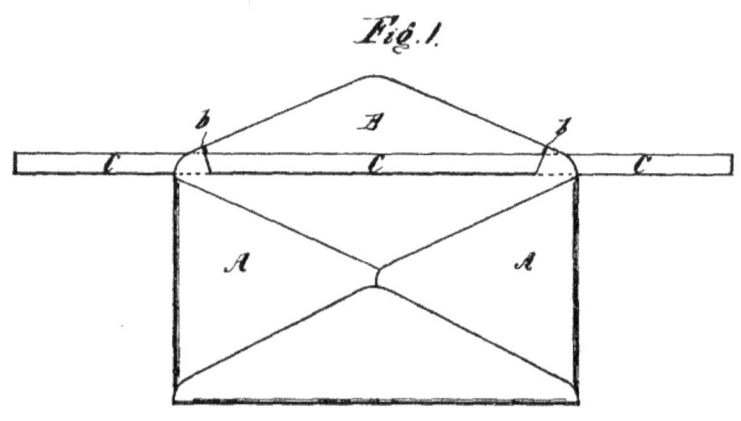

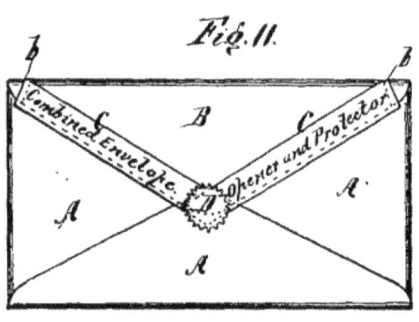

UNITED STATES PATENT OFFICE.

JAMES COLLINS, OF CENTRAL CITY, COLO., ASSIGNOR OF TWO-THIRDS HIS RIGHT TO NATHAN A. SEARS AND WM. C. HENDRICKS, OF SAME PLACE.

IMPROVEMENT IN ENVELOPES.

Specification forming part of Letters Patent No. **185,727**, dated December 26, 1876; application filed October 20, 1876.

To all whom it may concern:

Be it known that I, JAMES COLLINS, of Central City, Gilpin county, State of Colorado, have invented a new and useful Improvement in Combined Envelope Opener and Protector; and I do declare that the following is a clear and exact description, which will enable others to make and use my improved combined envelope opener and protector.

My invention consists in bending a narrow strip of parchment, placed under the flap of the envelope, down over said flap to near the middle of the envelope, where they are crossed and secured together or sealed.

I prefer to make two incisions, one in each side of the lap, near to the corners; but these incisions are not absolutely required. If desired, they can be dispensed with.

After the envelope has been sealed, and the ends of the strip are projecting from each corner of the envelope under the closed lap, I bend these ends over the lap edge of the envelope, the strips at the bends being inserted in the aforementioned incisions in the flap, and let them cross each other over the central point. On this point the ends are fastened by aid of mucilage or any other convenient adhesive material, which may be applied to the ends of the strip before it is used. After the ends are fastened down, a seal made of sealing-wax or stamped wafer, or made in any other suitable manner, is placed over the ends, which prevents the letter being opened without injuring the seal. The strip covering the edge of the flap or lap, where it is fastened down to the back of the envelope, prevents the edge of the lap from being moistened, and access gained into the interior of the envelope. On the outside of that part of the strip covering the edge of the lap is printed "Combined Envelope Opener and Protector," indicating its purpose to the public.

The envelope is opened by destroying the seal and loosening one of the ends of the strip, or one end of the strip may be cut by a pair of scissors. By taking hold of the loosened end of the strip and ripping up the top edge of the envelope, access is gained to the interior of the same.

In order to more fully describe my invention, I refer to the accompanying drawings, forming a part of this specification.

Figure I is a back view of an envelope with the lap opened, showing the position of my improved combined envelope opener and protector before the letter is placed into the envelope. Fig. II is a back view of an envelope with the lap fastened down, showing the position of my combined envelope opener and protector.

A is the envelope; B, the lap, with the incisions $b\ b$; C, the envelope opener and protector; D, the seal.

Having thus described my invention, I desire to claim—

The combined envelope opener and protector, consisting of the strip C and seal D, in combination with the envelope A B, substantially as described.

JAMES COLLINS.

Witnesses:
ROBERT CAMERON,
JAMES NICHOLSON.

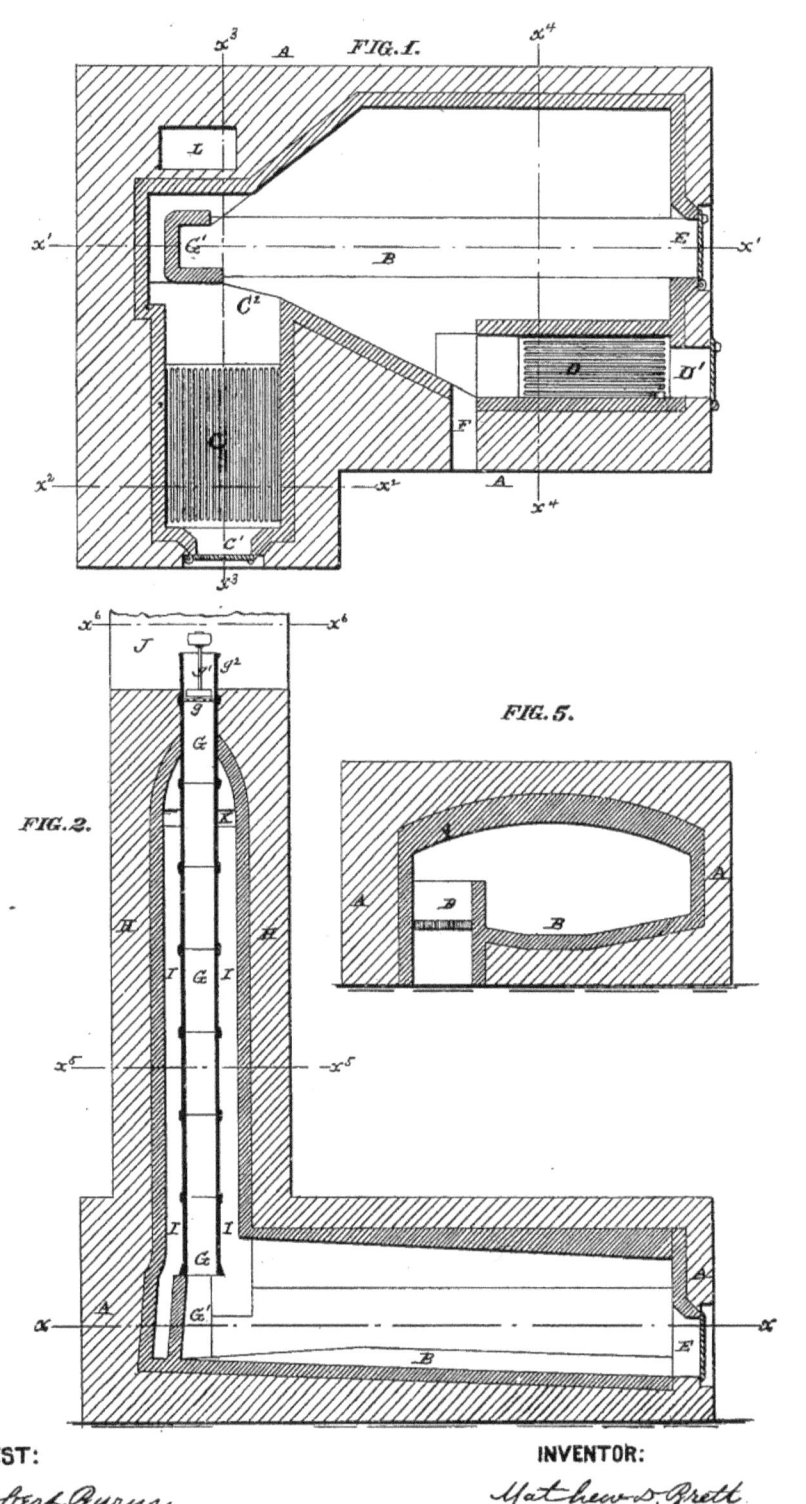

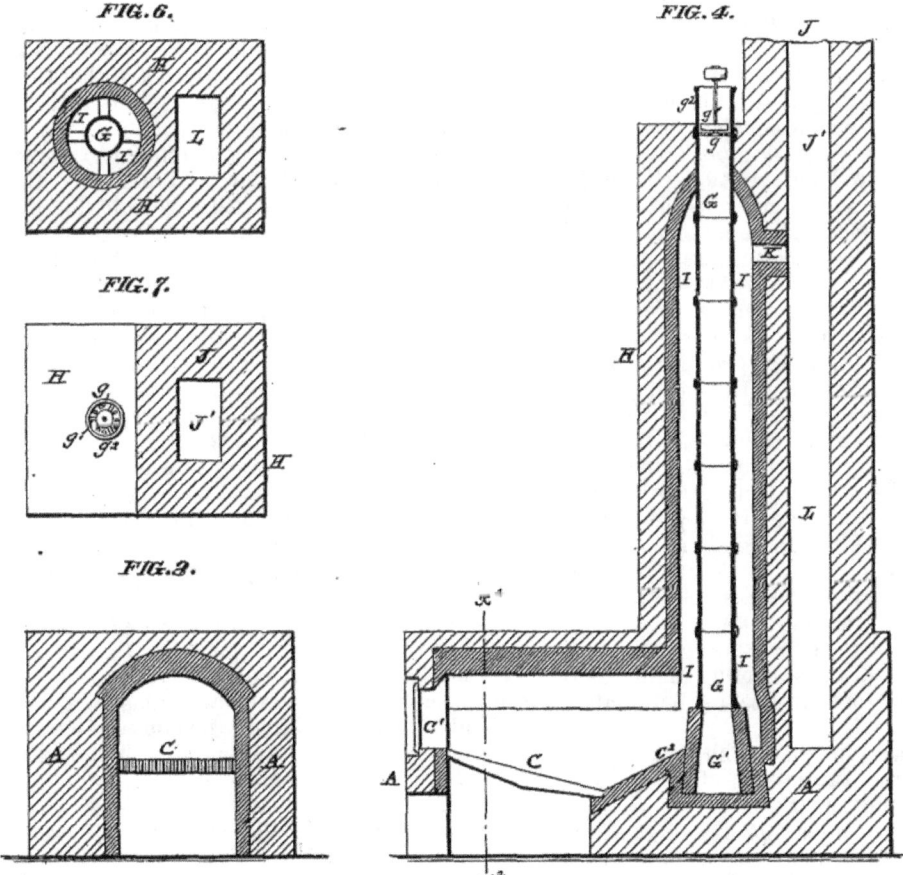

UNITED STATES PATENT OFFICE.

MATHEW D. BRETT, OF BOULDER, COLORADO.

IMPROVEMENT IN SHAFT-FURNACES FOR TREATING ORES.

Specification forming part of Letters Patent No. **188,098**, dated March 6, 1877; application filed September 8, 1876.

To all whom it may concern:

Be it known that I, MATHEW D. BRETT, of Boulder, in the county of Boulder and State of Colorado, have invented certain new and useful Improvements in Shaft-Furnaces for Treating Ores, of which the following is a specification:

My invention relates to that class of furnaces used for oxidizing and reducing metallic ores.

My improvement consists, first, in the combination of a vertical pipe, down which the ore is showered onto the hearth, and a base having an open front, the pipe being surrounded by an annular flue, through which the products of combustion pass upwardly.

My improvement consists, secondly, in combining with the pipe and base two furnaces arranged in a peculiar manner—one furnace so located as to direct the product of combustion in front of and around the base, and the other furnace in such a position as to maintain a flame at the exit of the pipe.

My improvement consists, thirdly, in combining a hearth and furnace with an annular flue, for the passage of the products of combustion, a side flue communicating with a smoke-stack, and a dust-chamber formed by the continuation of the stack, opening downwardly past the side flue.

My improvement consists, fourthly, in a combination of devices forming an improved construction of ore-furnace, as hereinafter more fully explained.

A process in which this apparatus is employed forms the subject of a separate application for Letters Patent.

In the accompanying drawings, Figure 1 is a horizontal section on the line $x\ x$, Fig. 2. Fig. 2 is a vertical longitudinal section on the line $x^1\ x^1$, Fig. 1. Fig. 3 is a vertical longitudinal section on the line $x^2\ x^2$, Figs. 1 and 4. Fig. 4 is a vertical transverse section on the line $x^3\ x^3$, Fig. 1. Fig. 5 is a vertical transverse section on the line $x^4\ x^4$, Fig. 1. Fig. 6 is a horizontal section on the line $x^5\ x^5$, Fig. 2. Fig. 7 is a horizontal section on the line $x^6\ x^6$, Fig. 2.

A is the main furnace-wall, inclosing a hearth, B, main furnace-grate C, and auxiliary furnace-grate D, as shown in Fig. 1. E is a door, through which the reduced ore is raked from the hearth B. F is an opening in the wall A, through which air is admitted into the furnace to assist in the oxidation of the ore, &c. Air is also admitted through furnace openings or doors D', C¹, and E for the same purpose. G is a pipe, arranged in a tower, H. This pipe, at top, has a perforated plate or partition, g, through which the ore is showered into the pipe by a stirrer, g^1, turning in the hopper g^2.

The ore-pipe G is surrounded by an annular flue, I, up which the products of combustion pass to the stack J, through side flue K. L is a dust chamber, formed by the continuation of the stack-opening J' down past the flue K, as shown in Fig. 4.

It will be seen that by my construction the ore is dropped down through the pipe G without being subjected to contact with the products of combustion while within the pipe. The pipe G is supported on a base, G', having an opening onto the hearth B.

The operation of my improved furnace is as follows: On the grate C is the main fire, and on the grate D a moderate fire, so that the fire at C will supply a large per cent. of carbureted hydrogen, which passes over the bridge-wall C², (with or without a supply of air from opening C¹,) to the open side of the base G¹, where it meets with a supply of heated air admitted into the furnace through openings D' E F, and an intense heat is generated at that point, the products of combustion ascending the annular flue I, then through flue K into the stack J.

It is evident that the intensity of the heat at the mouth of the base G' can be regulated and controlled by the amount of fuel used, and the quantity of air supplied through openings C¹ D' E F. The heat in the annular flue I keeps the ore-pipe G very hot, especially at the bottom, and the pulverized ore being fed in at the top of said pipe G is subjected to a gradually-increasing heat as it is showered down through said pipe, its velocity being in proportion to the amount of gases evolved from the ore, combined with the amount of draft, which is downward in this pipe. The ore, when it reaches the opening in the base G, has acquired sufficient momentum to carry it through the flame at that point onto the hearth B, from which it is removed through door E.

Having thus described my invention, the following is what I claim as new, and desire to secure by Letters Patent:

1. The combination of the vertical pipe G, surrounded by an annular flue, I, and a base, G^1, having an open front, as and for the purpose set forth.

2. The combination, with the pipe G, having open base G^1, of the furnaces C and D, the furnace C arranged to direct the products of combustion in front of the opening in said base and around the same, and the furnace D arranged to maintain a flame at the exit of said pipe, as and for the purpose set forth.

3. The hearth B and furnace C, in combination with the flues I and K, stack J, and dust-chamber L, as and for the purpose set forth.

4. The hearth B, furnaces C and D, pipe G, open base G', annular flue I, perforated partition g, stirrer g^1, and hopper g^2, in combination with the flue K, stack J, and dust-chamber L, as and for the purpose set forth.

MATHEW D. BRETT.

Witnesses:
ROBERT BURNS,
C. W. H. BROWN.

H. G. WEIBLING.
Axle.

No. 1,768.

Reissued Sept 13, 1864.

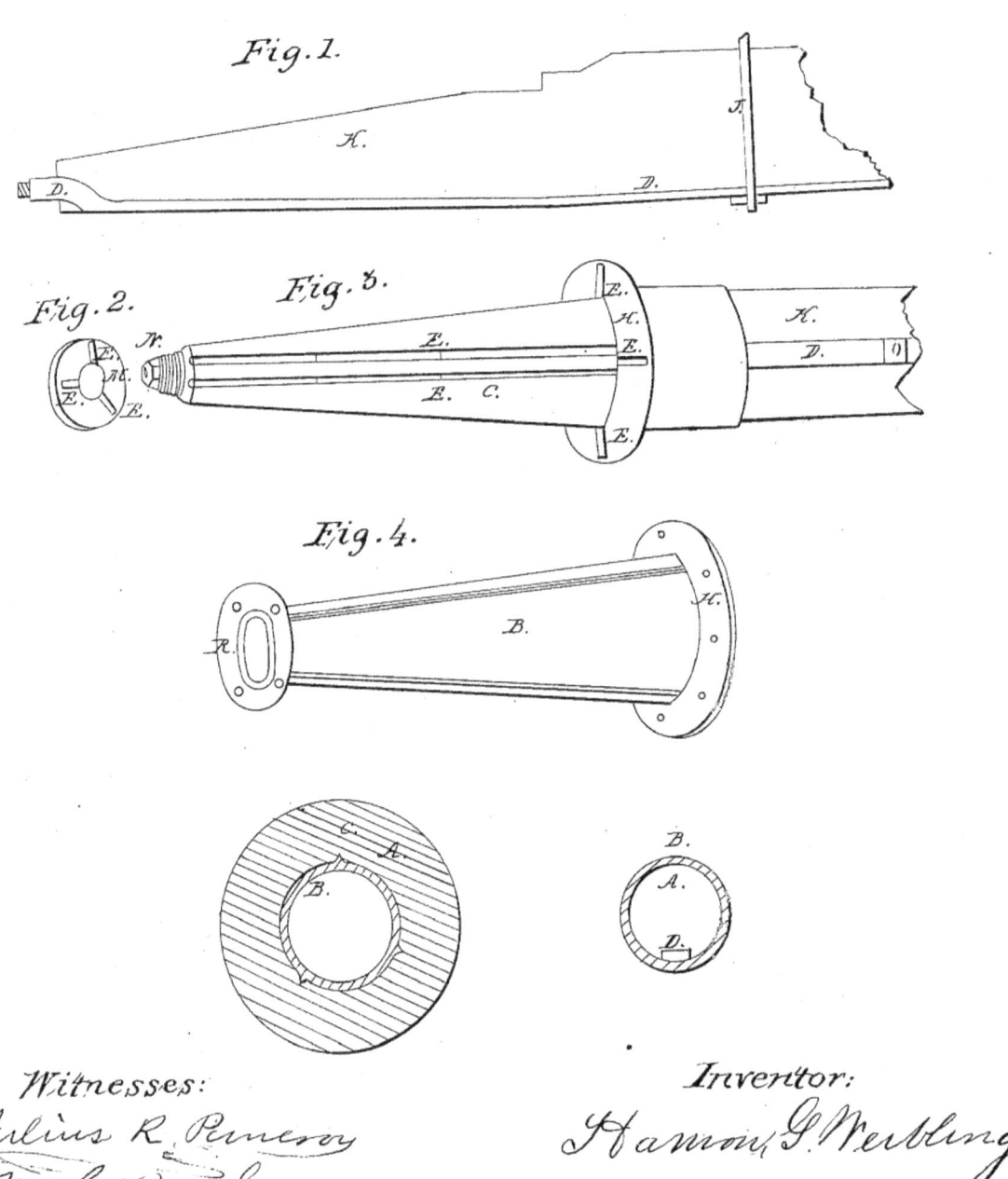

UNITED STATES PATENT OFFICE.

HARMON G. WEIBLING, OF DENVER, COLORADO.

IMPROVEMENT IN CARRIAGE-WHEELS.

Specification forming part of Letters Patent No. 37,480, dated January 20, 1863; Reissue No. **1,768**, dated September 13, 1864.

To all whom it may concern:

Be it known that I, HARMON G. WEIBLING, of Denver city, in the Territory of Colorado, have invented a new and Improved Axle, by means of which the friction of the wheel turning thereon is greatly lessened; and I do hereby declare that the following is a full and exact description thereof, reference being had to the accompanying drawings, and to the letters of reference marked thereon.

The nature of my invention consists in applying friction-rollers longitudinally to the under side of the spindle forming the outside of the axle upon which the wheel rests, the rollers being embedded to a little more than half their diameter in a groove or grooves cut in the under side of such spindle. Thus the axle, preserving its relative position, will rest within the hub of the wheel upon these longitudinal rollers, and as the wheel turns the rollers embedded partially within the axle will turn also, thereby greatly lessening the friction, care being also taken to keep them properly lubricated.

My invention also consists in applying friction-rollers to the shoulder of the axle against which the hub of the wheel rests when pressed onto the axle, and also to the inside surface of the nut which keeps the wheel from coming off when it has been placed upon the axle. These rollers are also partially embedded in the shoulder and in the nut in grooves, permitting the rollers to turn when pressed against by the wheel, but holding them in their relative places. By these means I oppose to the turning wheel within its hub, and at each end thereof, friction-rollers, turning themselves whenever the wheel is in motion, and thereby decreasing the amount of friction which would otherwise exist.

In the drawings, Figure 1 represents a longitudinal section of the axle before the skein or spindle is placed upon it, along the under side of which is an iron strap, (shown at D,) bent at the end of the axle and projecting slightly from it, having a thread cut upon its end to receive a nut.

Fig. 3 represents the spindle C as placed upon the axle K, showing at E E the friction-rollers running longitudinally along the under side of the spindle as attached to the axle. The shoulder against which the hub or the flange of the box receiving the axle rests when the wheel is on appears at H, and the short rollers embedded in this shoulder are seen at E E E. The strap D may be seen in this figure projecting from the spindle at N, when the nut M is to be applied.

In Fig. 2 the rollers to be opposed to the outside flange of the box within which the spindle rests when the wheel is on the axle are shown at E E E on the inner surface of the nut M.

Fig. 4 represents the box which forms the inside surface of the hub of the wheel, and in which the spindle C, as shown in Fig. 3, rests when the wheel is on its axle. The flanges of this box are shown at R and H, against which come the rollers in the shoulder and nut, heretofore named.

The friction-rollers above named should be made of steel or chilled iron, and the grooves in which they are contained, and in which they roll, should be concave, approaching a cylinder in form, so as to hold the rollers in place and yet leave them projecting along their entire length from the surface of the spindle in which the grooves are cut. The grooves in the material of which the spindle is made may be lined with Babbitt metal or other material. I have generally used two of these longitudinal grooves in the under side of each spindle; but more may be used, if deemed best. The rollers should be made in short pieces whenever the spindle is cone-like in shape, as shown in the figures. I generally use three to fill one groove in length for a wagon-wheel of ordinary size. Each roller should act independently of any other in its own position in the groove in which it is placed. The rollers in the shoulder H and in the nut M should be placed in a position perpendicular to the axis of the axle, the grooves being cut to correspond thereto, so that the rollers may impinge regularly against the hub of the wheel. They may be made of two or more pieces to turn separately.

The spindle C may be fastened to the axle K with gutta-percha packing, the gutta-percha to be dissolved to the consistency of thick tar and then spread on the surface of the axle K and the inner surface of the spindle C, which is then forced upon the axle to its proper place and secured by means of the iron strap or bar D, inserted in a groove in the lower side of the axle, and extending from one end to the other of the axle, or to the bolt J, as shown in Fig. 1. Any kind of cement may be used instead of gutta-percha packing.

I am aware that friction-rollers have been hitherto used in the boxes of wheels and attached to them, on which the axle has rested, and I do not claim to have invented the use of friction-rollers; but

What I claim as my invention, and desire to secure by Letters Patent, is—

1. The application of friction-rollers partially embedded in a groove in the under side of the axle or spindle upon which the wheel is placed, substantially as and for the purposes above described.

2. The application of friction-rollers E E E, embedded partially in the surface of the shoulder H and the nut M, as and for the purposes above described.

HARMON G. WEIBLING.

Witnesses:
JULIUS R. POMEROY,
W. H. BOUGHTON.

THOMAS BATES.
Improvement in Grinding and Amalgamating Ores.

No. 4,380. Reissued May 16, 1871.

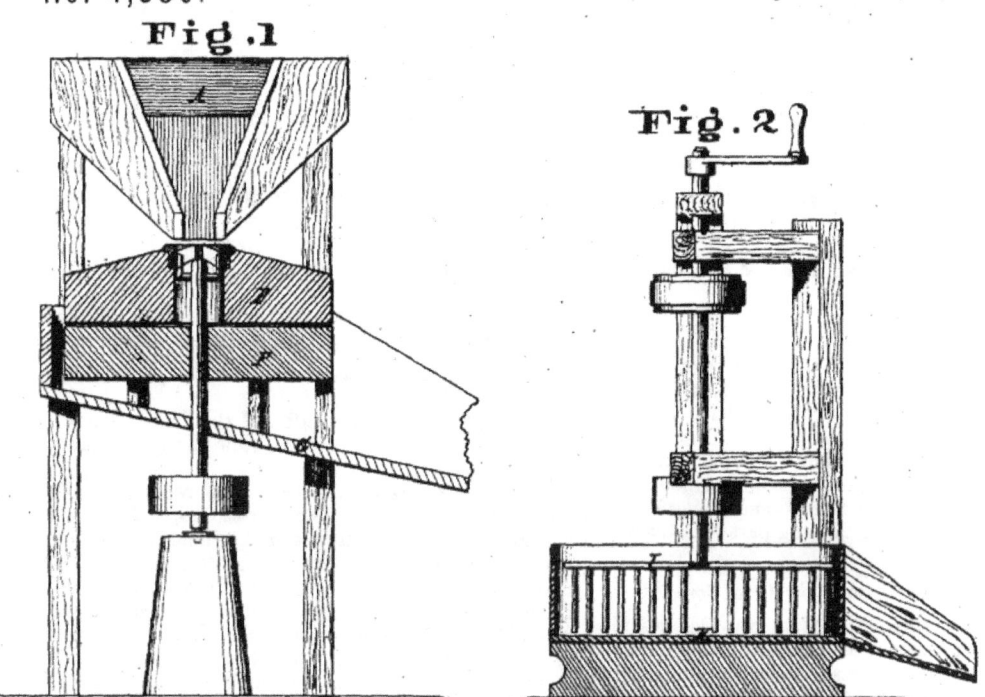

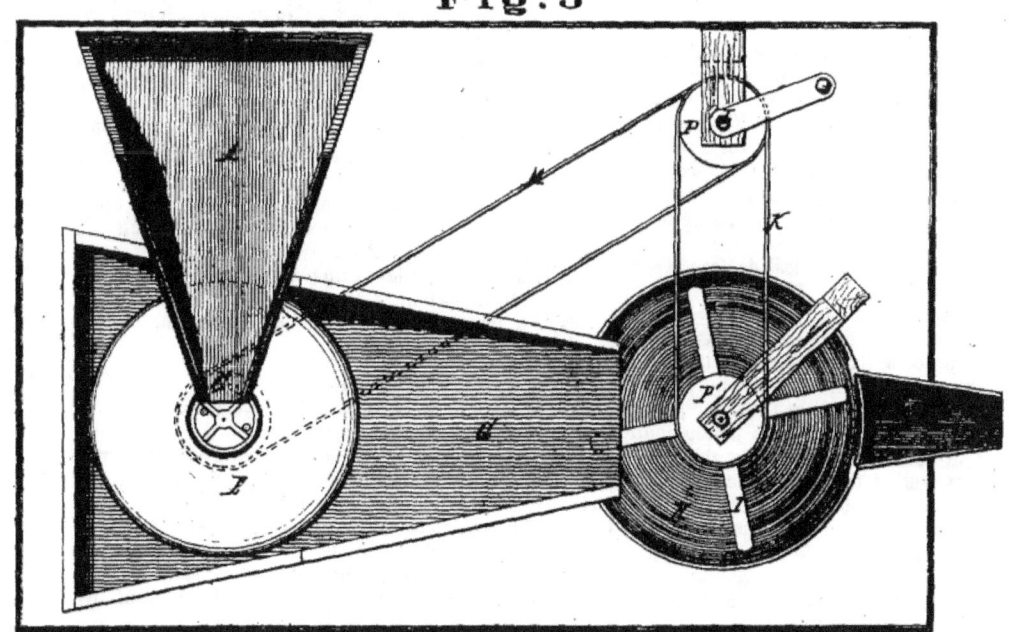

United States Patent Office.

THOMAS BATES, OF CENTRAL CITY, COLORADO TERRITORY.

Letters Patent No. 102,476, dated May 3, 1870; reissue No. 4,380, dated May 16, 1871.

IMPROVEMENT IN GRINDING AND AMALGAMATING ORES.

The Schedule referred to in these Letters Patent and making part of the same.

To all whom it may concern:

Be it known that I, THOMAS BATES, of Central City, Colorado Territory, formerly of Pinos Altos, in the county of Grant and Territory of New Mexico, have invented a new and improved Ore-Separator; and I do hereby declare that the following is a full, clear, and exact description thereof, which will enable others skilled in the art to make and use the same, reference being had to the accompanying drawing forming part of this specification.

Nature and Objects of the Invention.

The object of my invention is to provide a simple and efficient arrangement of means for receiving the tailings of gold and other ores from the battery, or ore crushed by any suitable means, and to pulverize, scour, and burnish the same, ready for separating; and

Secondly, to provide a simple means for amalgamating or separating the gold from the pulverized mass by the use of quicksilver.

The invention comprises—

First, a process for pulverizing, scouring, and burnishing the gold contained in crude ores after it has been crushed in a battery, or by other suitable means.

Second, a process of amalgamating the gold in a suitable amalgamator, disconnected from the pulverizing apparatus after it has been pulverized, scoured, and burnished, enabling me to separate the gold from the pulverized ore, independent of the pulverizing process.

Third, providing suitable mechanical devices to carry these methods into effect.

In methods heretofore used no plan of pulverizing, scouring, and burnishing the material, independent of the amalgamating process, has been successfully employed. The Mexican "arastrar" crushes, pulverizes, and burnishes the gold, but does it in the same pan or pit in which the quicksilver is used to amalgamate the gold, and the two processes are inseparable.

Stamping-mills pulverize the gold, independent of the separating method, but do not scour, polish, or burnish it—that is, do not free the gold from the quartz, sulphurets, or other minerals with which it is frequently allied.

My method accomplishes the pulverizing, scouring, and burnishing gold more rapidly than the arastrar, and, like the stamping-mills, pulverizes independent of the separating process, while, in addition, it scours and burnishes the gold and saves a larger percentage thereof than any other method, and at a less expense.

Description of the Accompanying Drawing.

Figure 1 is a vertical section of the pulverizing-mill.

Figure 2 is a vertical section of the amalgamator.

Figure 3 represents a plan view of figs. 1 and 2 when connected.

To pulverize the ore and scour or burnish the small particles of gold, I take two bur-stones, E F, with a suitable dress and set, and arrange them in a similar manner to those of an ordinary grain-grinding mill, except that I do not use any casing immediately around them, leaving their entire peripheries free for the discharge of the pulverized material. This burnishing-mill E F I use in direct connection with a suitable stamping-mill or crusher, to which it is attached by the spout A, which acts as a hopper, and also conveys the tailings from the stamping-mill and the water necessary to be used. The mill E F may be operated by any known motor.

Underneath the mill is a table or spout, lined with quicksilver, placed at an angle, as seen in fig. 1, to save the gold as the ore passes from the mill, and this table may be used to conduct the material to the amalgamator.

My amalgamator is a circular vessel, H, the interior of which is made of amalgamating-plates, prepared in the usual way.

I is a horizontal rake or stirrer, which works upon a vertical axis, and is made to revolve by a belt, K, running upon pulleys P P'.

P is a driving-pulley, which is here shown connected to a driving-shaft, L.

N is a spout for carrying off the residuum.

Claims.

I claim as my invention—

1. The continuous process of pulverizing, scouring, and amalgamating the tailings of an ordinary battery by means of the grinding-mill E F and amalgamator H, connected by suitable spouts to each other and to the battery, substantially as herein set forth.

2. The combination of the table or spout A, grinding-mill E F, table G, amalgamator H, stirrer I, when constructed, arranged, operated, and adapted for application to and use with a battery, all substantially as specified.

THOMAS BATES. [L. S.]

Witnesses:
CHASE WITHROW,
M. McLAUGHLIN.

J. E. AMBROSE.
Lamps.

No. 5,412. Reissued May 20, 1873.

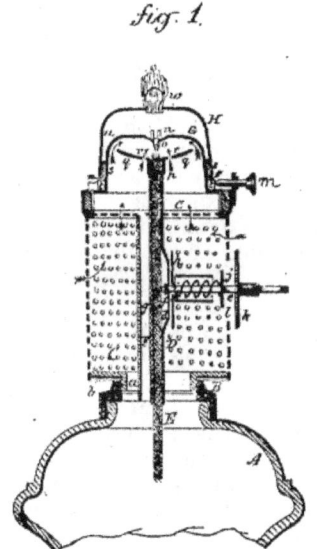

UNITED STATES PATENT OFFICE.

JOSHUA E. AMBROSE, OF COLORADO SPRINGS, COLORADO TERRITORY, ASSIGNOR, BY MESNE ASSIGNMENTS, TO SARAH T. AMBROSE, OF SAME PLACE, AND EDWARD MILLER, OF MERIDEN, CONNECTICUT.

IMPROVEMENT IN LAMPS.

Specification forming part of Letters Patent No. 30,381, dated October 16, 1860; reissue No. **5,412**, dated May 20, 1873; application filed February 12, 1873.

To all whom it may concern:

Be it known that I, JOSHUA E. AMBROSE, of Colorado Springs, in the Territory of Colorado, have invented a new and Improved Lamp; and I do hereby declare the following, when taken in connection with the accompanying drawing and the letters of reference marked thereon, to be a full, clear, and exact description of the same, and which said drawing constitutes part of this specification, and represents, in—

Figure 1, a vertical central section; Fig. 2, a top view; Fig. 3, a top view with the heater detached; and in Fig. 4, a detached plan or top view of the wick-adjuster.

This invention relates to an improvement in that class of burners designed for burning hydrocarbons. In this class of burners the wick-adjuster must necessarily penetrate the wick tube in order to come in contact with the wick. In the use of these burners it is found that the gas which is unavoidably generated within the lamp will escape through the tube around the wick-adjuster and pass off to mingle with the surrounding atmosphere to the discomfort of persons near, if not detrimental to their health, and as this gas is highly inflammable it frequently ignites from the flame of the lamp and often causes explosion. The object of this invention is to combine with the wick tube and adjuster such a means of escape for the gas that it may pass so freely directly to the flame as to be there consumed, and thus prevent its escape around the adjuster; also, the construction of a burner which may be used without a chimney.

The invention consists, first, in combining with the wick tube and adjuster, an auxiliary passage leading directly from the lamp up to within such proximity to the flame that the gas from the lamp, flowing freely through this auxiliary passage, will pass to and be consumed by the flame; second, in the employment of a perforated cap, wick-tube, heaters, and deflecting-plate, combined and arranged as hereinafter described; third, in a wick-adjusting mechanism, arranged so as to admit of the wick being elevated with certainty, and when not in use allow the wick to be loose and free within the tube—that is, without any pressure from the adjuster—to allow the free flow of the oil.

A represents the upper or neck portion of the body of a lamp, provided at its upper end with the usual socket B to receive the cap C, the lower end of the cap being provided with a threaded flange, a, to fit the corresponding thread in the socket. The cap c is, by preference, of cylindrical form, and constructed from perforated sheet metal, the lower end having a plate, b, fitted into it, the said plate being a part of or attached to the flange a. The upper end of the cap is covered by a perforated plate, c. D, the wick tube, extends vertically from the socket upward, opening both into the lamp and at or near the deflector, in substantially the usual manner. Within the tube the wick E is arranged, and the tube is fitted with an adjuster, here represented as an improved adjuster, to be hereinafter described. An auxiliary tube or passage, F, is formed, the lower end of which communicates with the interior of the body of the lamp, and the upper end opening near the upper end of the wick-tube, so that the gas which is generated within the lamp, instead of passing out through the opening in the tube for the wick-adjuster, as it otherwise would, will pass up through this tube or passage in such proximity to the flame that it is consumed. The termination of this tube is here represented as at the perforated plate c, the perforations of the plate being sufficient for the free passage of gas to the flame. On the upper end of the cap c there is placed a copper dome-shaped heater, G, which is secured in proper position by a thumb-screw, m. This heater is slotted at its upper end, as shown at n, and at the center of the slot there is fitted a longitudinal bar, O, the latter dividing the slot n into two equal longitudinal parts. The wick tube F extends some distance above the perforated plate c, and on its upper end a collar, p, is fitted, the said collar having plates q projecting from it slightly inclined from a horizontal plane. Between the outer edges of the plates q and the collar p there are openings r. On the outer side of the heater G there are vertical ribs s, at the lower ends of which there are projections t. These projections t serve as bearings for a heater, H, which is similar to G in form. The ribs and projections t admit of a space, u, being between the two heaters, and the upper end of the heater H is slotted, as shown at v, Fig. 2, and has plates w extending upward from each end of it and inclined toward each other at an angle of about forty-five degrees. The plates q of the collar p and the openings r cause a draft to ascend directly upward to the flame, and air is also deflected directly against the inner sides of the heater G, and becomes intensely heated, so as to supply the flame with warm oxygen. The bar o in the slot n of the heater G serves to divide the flame, and prevents it from ascending up through the slot n before the carbon is consumed. Between the two heaters G H oxygen passes and becomes highly rarefied, and unites with the carbon in the flame, insuring perfect combustion.

The plates w at the ends of the slot v of the heater H serve to spread the flame and diminish its height, thereby keeping the flame at the point where the heat is most intense. The flame at the slot n in the heater G is merely a gas-generating flame, the illuminating flame having its base at the slot v of the heater H.

The wick-tube D at one side—the side opposite that to which the tube F is attached—has an enlarged space or a chamber, d, in which the inner end of a horizontal shaft, e, passes. This shaft e has a horizontal rod, f, fitted on it, containing spurs G, the rod and spurs being within the chamber d. On the shaft e there is placed loosely a metal plate, h, the said plate being at the outer side of the chamber d, the latter having its side slotted to admit the shaft e and rod f. On the shaft e there is placed a spiral spring, i, the inner end of which bears against the plate h, the outer end bearing against a plate or step, j, which is attached permanently to the shaft e. The spring i, it will be seen, has a tendency to keep the shaft e shoved outward to the extent of this movement, and keep the rod f and spurs g within the chamber d and free from the wick E. On the shaft e, and at the outer side of the cap C, there is secured a plate, k. The shaft e passes through a slot, l, in the cap C.

In order to raise or lower the wick E the shaft e is pressed inward, and the spurs g will penetrate the wick, and by raising or lowering the shaft e the wick will be raised or lowered accordingly. The plate h covers the slot in the side of the chamber d, and prevents the escape of gas or vapor from the wick-tube and chamber d; the plate k retains the rod e in a horizontal position as it is raised and lowered.

I claim as my invention—

1. In combination with the wick-tube and a mechanism for adjusting the wick, an auxiliary tube or passage leading from the lamp upward to conduct the gas from within the lamp to the flame, substantially as set forth.

2. The arrangement of the heaters G H, with a space between them communicating directly with the external air, in connection with the collar p and plates q q, fitted on the top of the wick tube E, and the perforated cap C, substantially as and for the purpose set forth.

3. The shaft e provided with the rod f and spurs g, which are within the chamber d of the wick-tube, in connection with the plates h j k and spring i on the said shaft, all being arranged to operate as and for the purpose set forth.

JOSHUA E. AMBROSE.

Witnesses:
A. J. TIBBITS,
JOHN E. EARLE.

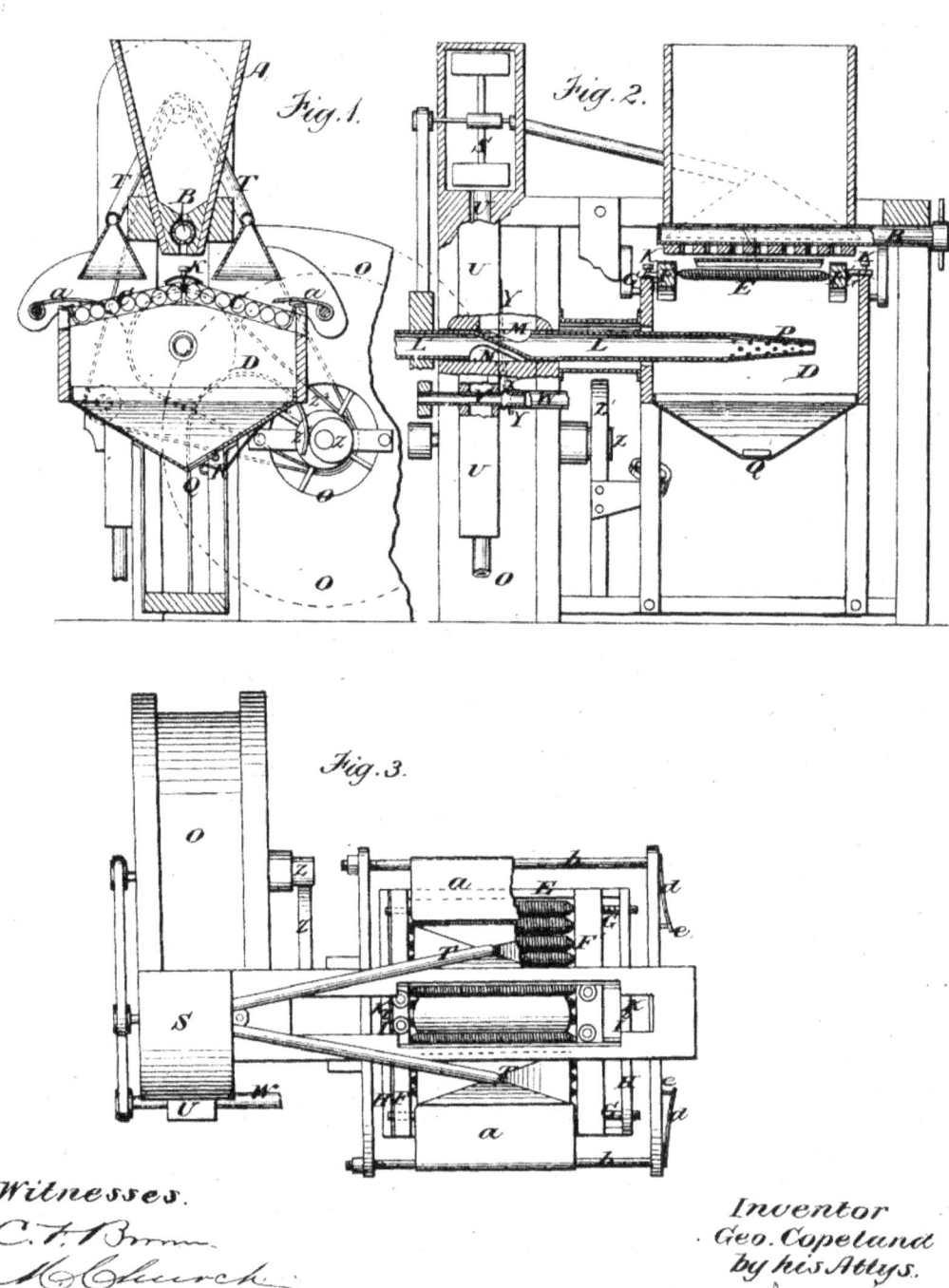

UNITED STATES PATENT OFFICE.

GEORGE COPELAND, OF DENVER, COLORADO TERRITORY, ASSIGNOR TO CHARLES E. WHITMORE.

IMPROVEMENT IN ORE-SEPARATORS.

Specification forming part of Letters Patent No. 103,574, dated May 31, 1870; reissue No. **5,944**, dated June 30, 1874; application filed June 25, 1874.

To all whom it may concern:

Be it known that I, GEORGE COPELAND, of Denver, in the county of Arapahoe and Territory of Colorado, have invented certain new and useful Improvements in Separators; and I do hereby declare the following to be a full, clear, and exact description of the same, reference being had to the accompanying drawings forming part of this specification, in which—

Figure 1 is a transverse sectional elevation of my improved separator. Fig. 2 is a sectional elevation, taken at right angles to the plane of Fig. 1; and Fig. 3 is a top-plan view, partly in section.

Similar letters of reference indicate the same parts in the several figures of the drawings.

This invention relates to that class of separators employed for separating dry pulverized or granular substances, according to the relative weight and size of their particles, by the action of a sieve or screen, combined with a current or currents of air, and has for its object to effect the more perfect separation of such substances.

The invention consists, first, in the improved process of separating the different particles according to their size and weight; secondly, in the following improvements in mechanism adapted for the purpose of such separation, viz: First, combining a sieve or screen with an air-blast beneath and an air suction or exhaust above it; second, combining an inclined sieve or screen with an air-blast beneath and an air suction or exhaust above it; third, combining a movable sieve or screen with an air-blast beneath and an air suction or exhaust above it; fourth, combining a longitudinally reciprocating or vibrating sieve or screen with an air-blast beneath and an air suction or exhaust above it; fifth, combining a vertically-adjustable sieve or screen with an air-blast beneath it and an air suction or exhaust above it, or with either of them; sixth, combining a sieve or screen, having its inclination adjustable, with an air-blast beneath it and an air-suction or exhaust above it, or with either of them; seventh, arranging a sieve or screen, an air exhaust or suction above it, and an air-blast beneath it, in such manner that the suction shall assist the blast in creating an upward current through or from the sieve; eighth, combining, in a separator, a sieve or screen, through which a blast passes in one direction, while the finer and heavier substances to be separated pass in the other, with an auxiliary pipe, with jets from an independent fan-blower; ninth, combining a movable sieve or screen with an air suction or exhaust above it, and mechanism for clearing the under side of the screen; tenth, combining with a sieve or screen an air-pipe beneath it, to deliver the air in thin currents or jets against the under side of the screen for the purpose of clearing the meshes thereof, and lifting into the air the light particles thereon; eleventh, combining with a sieve or screen a rotary air-blast pipe beneath it, the fine air currents or jets from which impinge against the under side of the sieve; twelfth, combining with a sieve or screen a traveling air-blast beneath it, and impinging against its under side; thirteenth, dividing the air-blast so as to cause a portion of it to act upon one part of the vibrating screen, while another portion is operating upon a different part of the same screen; fourteenth, combining an intermittent air-blast under a sieve or screen with an air-suction or exhaust above it; fifteenth, dividing the sieve or screen into sections, and causing the several sections to be cleaned by blasts from the same fan; sixteenth, the combination of one or more covering-chambers, a suction-fan, and one or more conducting-pipes, with a vibrating or reciprocating sieve or screen; seventeenth, the combination of one or more covering-chambers, a suction-fan, and one or more conducting-pipes with a movable screen having an air-blast beneath it; eighteen, the combination of a receiving-hopper having a sieve or screen at the top, with an air-blast pipe underneath the sieve, and a blower to deliver the air in thin currents or jets; nineteenth, an adjustable feed extending substantially the whole width of the sieve or -screen, or at right angles to the line of its movement; twentieth, regulating the movement and discharge of the material upon the sieve or screen by varying the inclination of the latter; twenty-first, a sieve or screen capable of being rendered coarser or finer by the adjustment of its reticulations; twenty-second, arranging the air-blast of several separating-machines to be operated by a single fan.

In the accompanying drawings, which show one form of machine for carrying out my invention, A is a hopper, into which the substance or material to be separated or treated is conveyed by any suitable means. It is provided with numerous holes along the bottom for the delivery of the material, and a rotary perforated valve, B, for regulating or stopping the discharge. C is a sieve placed under the hopper A and over another hopper, D, and in this instance is arranged to shed each way from the line of the delivery-orifices of the hopper above. The material is fed from this hopper in a thin sheet or series of small streams across the width of the sieve, and in a line at right angles or nearly so to the line of its reciprocations or vibrations. The material is, therefore, spread evenly over and across the receiving portion of the sieve, and its flow is regulated or stopped by the adjustable valve B.

The sieve shown in this example of my invention is formed of spiral-wire coils or springs E, stretched from the end blocks F F¹, parallel with each other, forming meshes or reticulations, which may be varied for finer or coarser material by adjusting the end blocks to or from each other through the medium of the screw rods G G¹, by which they are connected, and by which they are supported on the bars H of the frame. The end blocks are jointed at the center, and the screw-rods G¹ thereat rest at the ends on plates I on the top of the bars H, having adjusting-screws K, by which they may be raised or lowered to vary the angle of the shed or inclination, for the purpose of regulating the movement and discharge of the material upon such sieve. Other sieves, however, may be used instead of such as I have described.

The sieve has a reciprocating or shaking motion imparted to it by an eccentric-wheel, Z, on the shaft of a fan, O, acting on a spring, Z¹, connected to the sieve supports, which are arranged in any suitable way for vibration. L is a two-way-revolving blast-pipe, receiving air alternately through the orifices M N from a fan, O, and projecting into the hopper D, where it has a perforated nozzle, P, through which the air is delivered in gusts and jets among the particles of heavier matter, and acting on the lighter and coarser matters on the sieve to toss them up and separate them from the heavier. S is a suction or exhaust fan attached to the top of the machine, and having two covering-chambers or funnel-mouthed pipes arranged above the sieves to take up the fine light dust or particles and convey them away through the pipe U to a receptacle.

As the sieve vibrates or reciprocates the heavy and valuable substances fall through it into the hopper D. The coarser and lighter particles are held in suspension over the sieve by means of the ascending air-currents, and float down over the sieve to the tail thereof, where they are discharged. The light fine dust and impurities, rising above the light coarse particles, are drawn off by the suction-fan and conveyed away to a receptacle. By this means the pure and valuable materials fall through the sieve, the coarse light particles are discharged at the end, and the light fine particles are drawn up and carried off by the suction or exhaust fan.

An upward current of air has a tendency to cause particles of matter to adhere to the under side of the sieve, and to counteract this the under side of the sieve should be swept by some force moving laterally, to clear it from such particles. The perforated nozzle of the blast-pipe projects the air in thin currents or jets against the under side of the sieve at almost every angle, and the rotation or oscillation of the pipe causes these fine currents or jets to travel along the under side of the sieve and brush off any particles that may have attached themselves thereto. This action of the air currents or jets is facilitated or increased by the constant changing of the angle at which they strike the sieve, by the traveling movement of the sieve itself, and by the vibrations or percussion of the sieve, due to the action of the driving cam and the spring. The air-blast has the further function of removing any particles that may become lodged in the meshes of the sieve. The suction assists the blast in creating an upward current through or from the sieve.

The sieve shown in the drawings is divided into sections, which are cleaned by the fan-blast, and while one portion of the blast is acting upon one part of the sieve another portion of it acts upon a different part of the sieve. The vertical adjustment of the sieve adapts it to operate nearer to, or farther from, the suction and blast, or at any desired point between the two.

The hopper D is closed, except at the top, and is provided with an escape-valve, Q, at the bottom, held closed by a spring, R, which will resist the force of the blast, but will yield under the weight of an accumulation of the treated substance sufficiently to let it escape from time to time and prevent the hopper from filling. The part L¹ of the air-pipe is intended to conduct the air admitted through the passage N to another similar hopper at the other side of the blast fan, to which like attachments are connected, constituting a double-acting machine, whereby the continuous blast from the fan O is delivered to each set in alternate gusts. The pipe U may receive jets of water from a revolving perforated pipe, V, to which a hose-pipe, W, is jointed at X, and held in contact by a spring, Y, or other suitable means. These water-jets may be mixed with the dust drawn up by the suction-fan, to prevent it from being carried away in the air. The air-blast tube L L¹ is operated by a belt, Z², from the fan-shaft, working over a pulley thereon; and the suction and water-jet tube may also be operated by belts from the same shaft, or they may be operated in any approved way

a are skimmers, arranged at the lower edges of the sieves and lapping over the upper surfaces a short distance. They are arranged on oscillating shafts *b*, having spring-arms *d* and holding-pins *e*, by which they may be raised or lowered and held in any desired position when it is necessary to skim off the coarse and light particles of matter which are floated down over the sieve and above the heavier particles by the action of the air and the sieves.

The feed-hopper and valve B may be dispensed with and the substance fed directly to the sieves by hand or other means, as preferred.

Having thus described my invention, what I claim is—

1. The process of separating pulverized or granular substances by spreading them onto a suitable bed, blowing air up through the bed to lift and lighten up the substance thereon, and employing a suction or exhaust above the bed to carry off the fine light particles or impurities, substantially as described.

2. In a separating-machine, a sieve or screen in combination with an air-blast beneath and an air suction or exhaust above it.

3. In a separating-machine, an inclined sieve or screen combined with an air-blast beneath and an air suction or exhaust above it.

4. In a separating-machine, a movable sieve or screen combined with an air-blast beneath and an air suction or exhaust above it.

5. In a separating-machine, a longitudinally-reciprocating or vibrating sieve or screen combined with an air-blast beneath and an air suction or exhaust above it.

6. In a separating-machine, a vertically-adjustable sieve or screen combined with an air-blast beneath and an air suction or exhaust above it.

7. In a separating-machine, a sieve or screen, having its inclination adjustable, combined with an air-blast beneath it.

8. In a separating-machine, a sieve or screen, having its inclination adjustable, combined with an air suction or exhaust above it.

9. In a separating-machine, a sieve or screen, having its inclination adjustable, combined with an air-blast beneath and an air suction or exhaust above it.

10. In a separating-machine, a sieve or screen, an air exhaust or suction above it, and an air-blast beneath it, arranged and operated in such manner that the suction shall assist the blast in creating an upward current through or from the sieve.

11. In a separating-machine, a sieve or screen through which a blast passes in one direction while the finer and heavier substances to be separated pass in the other, combined with an auxiliary pipe with jets from an independent fan-blower.

12. In a separating-machine, a movable sieve or screen with an air suction or exhaust above it and mechanism for cleaning the under side of the screen.

13. In a separating-machine, a sieve or screen combined with an air-pipe beneath it, to deliver the air in thin currents or jets against the under side of the screen, for the purpose of clearing the meshes thereof and lifting into the air the light particles thereon.

14. In a separating-machine, a sieve or screen combined with a rotary air-blast pipe beneath it, the fine air currents or jets from which impinge against the under side of the sieve.

15. In a separating-machine, a sieve or screen combined with an air-blast beneath it, the air current or currents from which impinge against and travel along the under surface of the sieve.

16. In a separating-machine, having a vibrating sieve or screen, a number of air currents or jets divided so that a portion of them acts upon one part of the screen while another portion acts upon a different part of the same screen.

17. In a separating-machine having a sieve or screen, an intermittent air-blast under the sieve combined with an air suction or exhaust above it.

18. In a separating-machine, a sieve or screen divided into sections cleaned by blasts of air from the same fan.

19. In a separating-machine, a vibrating or reciprocating sieve or screen combined with one or more covering-chambers, a suction or exhaust fan, and one or more conducting-pipes, arranged to receive the light fine particles directly over the sieve.

20. In a separating-machine, the combination of one or more covering-chambers with a suction-fan, one or more conducting-pipes, and a movable screen having an air-blast beneath it.

21. In a separating-machine, the combination of a receiving-hopper having a sieve or screen at the top, with an air-blast pipe underneath the sieve constructed to deliver the air in thin currents or jets.

22. In a separating-machine, an adjustable feed to deliver the material substantially the whole width of the reciprocating or vibrating sieve.

23. In a separating-machine, a sieve or screen capable of being rendered coarser or finer by the adjustment of its reticulations.

24. The combination of a single fan with the blast-pipe, of several separating-machines, substantially as described.

GEO. COPELAND.

Witnesses:
H. R. WHITMORE,
JNO. B. CHURCH.

J. E. AMBROSE.
LAMP.

No. 6,844.   Reissued Jan. 11, 1876.

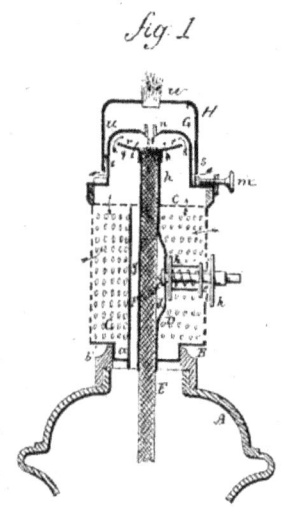

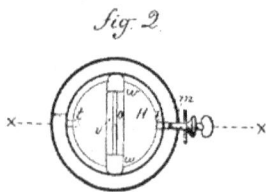
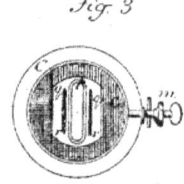

Witnesses:
J. H. Shumway
Clara Broughton

Joshua E. Ambrose
Inventor
By Atty.
John F. Earle

UNITED STATES PATENT OFFICE.

JOSHUA E. AMBROSE, OF PLATTSVILLE, COLORADO TER., ASSIGNOR, BY MESNE ASSIGNMENTS, TO EDWARD MILLER & CO., OF MERIDEN, CONN.

IMPROVEMENT IN LAMPS.

Specification forming part of Letters Patent No. 30,381, dated October 16, 1860; reissue No. 5,412, dated May 20, 1873; reissue No. **6,844**, dated January 11, 1876; application filed December 9, 1875.

To all whom it may concern:

Be it known that I, JOSHUA E. AMBROSE, of Plattsville, in the county of Weld and Territory of Colorado, have invented a new Improvement in Lamps; and I do hereby declare the following, when taken in connection with the accompanying drawings and the letters of reference marked thereon, to be a full, clear, and exact description of the same, and which said drawings constitute part of this specification, and represent, in—

Figure 1, vertical central section; Fig. 2, top view; Fig. 3, a top view with the heater detached; Fig. 4, detached plan or top view of the wick-adjuster.

This invention relates to an improvement in that class of burners designed for burning hydrocarbons. In this class of burners the wick-adjuster must necessarily penetrate the wick-tube in order to come in contact with the wick. In the use of these burners it is found that the gas which is unavoidably generated within the lamp will escape through the tube around the wick-adjuster and pass off to mingle with the surrounding atmosphere to the discomfort of persons near, if not detrimental to their health, and as this gas is highly inflammable it frequently ignites from the flame of the lamp, and often causes explosion.

The object of this invention is to combine with the wick tube and adjuster such a means of escape for the gas that it may pass so freely directly to the flame as to be there consumed, and thus prevent its escape around the adjuster; also, the construction of a burner which may be used without a chimney.

The invention consists, first, in combining with the wick tube and adjuster an auxiliary passage leading directly from the lamp up to within such proximity to the flame that the gas from the lamp, flowing freely through this auxiliary passage, will pass to and be consumed by the flame; second, in combining in a lamp-burner a deflector, a perforated air-distributer, with the deflector forming the combustion-chamber, a wick-tube extending from the fount to the combustion-chamber, an adjusting device to regulate the elevation of the wick, and a tube to conduct the gas from the fount to the chamber above the air-distributer; third, in the employment of a perforated cap, wick-tube, heaters, and deflecting plate, combined and arranged as hereinafter described; fourth, in a wick-adjusting mechanism, arranged so as to admit of the wick being elevated with certainty, and when not in use allow the wick to be loose and free within the tube—that is, without any pressure from the adjuster—to allow the free flow of the oil.

A represents the upper or neck portion of the body of a lamp, provided at its upper end with the usual socket B, to receive the cap C, the lower end of the cap being provided with a threaded flange, *a*, to fit the corresponding thread in the socket. The cap C is, by preference, of cylindrical form, and constructed from perforated sheet metal, the lower end having a plate, *b*, fitted into it, the said plate being a part of, or attached to, the flange *a*. *c* is a perforated air-distributer, which, with the deflector, forms the combustion-chamber, into which the wick-tube D extends. Within the tube the wick E is arranged, and the tube is fitted with an adjuster, (here represented as an improved adjuster,) to be hereinafter described. An auxiliary tube or passage, F, is formed, the lower end of which communicates with the interior of the body of the lamp, and the upper end opening near the upper end of the wick-tube, so that the gas which is generated within the lamp, instead of passing out through the opening in the tube for the wick-adjuster, as it otherwise would, will pass up through this tube or passage in such proximity to the flame that it is consumed. The termination of this tube is here represented as at the perforated plate *c*, the perforations of the plate being sufficient for the free passage of gas to the flame. On the upper end of the cap C there is placed a copper dome-shaped heater, G, which is secured in proper position by a thumb-screw, *m*. This heater is slotted at its upper end, as shown at *n*, and at the center of the slot there is fitted a longitudinal bar, *o*, the latter dividing the slot *n* into two equal longitudinal parts. The wick-tube D extends some distance above the perforated plate *c*, and on its upper end a collar, p, is fitted, the said collar having plates q projecting from it, slightly inclined from a horizontal plane. Between the outer edges of the plates q and the collar p there are openings r. On the outer side of the heater G there are vertical ribs s, at the lower ends of which there are projections t. These projections t serve as bearings for a heater, H, which is similar to G in form. The ribs and projections t admit of a space, u, being between the two heaters, and the upper end of the heater H is slotted, as shown at v, Fig. 2, and has plates w, extending upward from each end of it, and inclined toward each other at an angle of about forty-five degrees. The plates q of the collar p and the openings r, cause a draft to ascend directly upward to the flame, and air is also deflected directly against the inner sides of the heater G, and becomes intensely heated, so as to supply the flame with warm oxygen. The bar o in the slot n of the heater G serves to divide the flame, and prevents it from ascending up through the slot n before the carbon is consumed. Between the two heaters G H oxygen passes, and becomes highly rarefied, and unites with the carbon in the flame, insuring perfect combustion.

The plates w, at the ends of the slot v of the heater H, serve to spread the flame and diminish its height, thereby keeping the flame at the point where the heat is most intense. The flame at the slot n in the heater G is merely a gas-generating flame, the illuminating flame having its base at the slot v of the heater H. The wick-tube D at one side (the side opposite that to which the tube F is attached) has an enlarged space or a chamber, d, in which the inner end of a horizontal shaft, e, passes. This shaft e has a horizontal rod, f, fitted on it, containing spurs g, the rod and spurs being within the chamber d. On the shaft e there is placed loosely a metal plate, h, the said plate being at the outer side of the chamber d, the latter having its side slotted to admit the shaft e and rod f. On the shaft e there is placed a spiral spring, i, the inner end of which bears against the plate h, the outer end bearing against a plate or step, j, which is attached permanently to the shaft e. The spring i, it will be seen, has a tendency to keep the shaft e shoved outward to the extent of this movement, and keep the rod f and spurs g within the chamber d, and free from the wick E. On the shaft e, and at the outer side of the cap C, there is secured a plate, k. The shaft e passes through a slot, l, in the cap C.

In order to raise or lower the wick E the shaft e is pressed inward, and the spurs g will penetrate the wick, and by raising or lowering the shaft e the wick will be raised or lowered accordingly. The plate h covers the slot in the side of the chamber d, and prevents the escape of gas or vapor from the wick-tube and chamber d. The plate k retains the rod e in a horizontal position as it is raised and lowered.

I claim as my invention—

1. In combination with the wick-tube and a mechanism for adjusting the wick, an auxiliary tube or passage leading from the lamp upward, to conduct the gas from within the lamp to the flame without the mixture of air with the gas below the upper orifice of the tube, substantially as set forth.

2. The combination, in a lamp-burner, of the following elements: first, a deflector; second, a perforated air-distributer, which, with the deflector, forms the combustion-chamber; third, a wick-tube extending from the fount to the combustion-chamber; fourth, a tube or passage to conduct the gas from the fount to said combustion-chamber, substantially as described.

3. The combination, in a lamp-burner, of the following elements; first, a deflector; second, a perforated air-distributer, which, with the deflector, forms the combustion-chamber; third, a wick-tube extending from the fount to the combustion-chamber; fourth, a tube or passage to conduct the gas from the fount to said combustion-chamber; fifth, an adjusting device to regulate the elevation of the wick, substantially as described.

4. The combination of the heaters G H, with a space between them, communicating directly with the external air, in connection with the collar p and plates q q, fitted on the top of the wick-tube E, and the perforated cap C, substantially as and for the purpose set forth.

5. The shaft e, provided with the rod f and spurs g, which are within the chamber d of the wick-tube, in connection with the plates h j k and spring i on the said shaft, all being arranged to operate as and for the purpose set forth.

JOSHUA E. AMBROSE.

Witnesses:
 N. B. DEARBORN,
 W. H. AMBROSE.

Index

A

A H Evans & Co 441
Adams, Charles B 211
Adams, Orwin 255
Adervice, J 77
Alden, Frank S 87
Alexander & Mason 226, 332, 382
Alexander, Calvin C 9
Allen (Brown & Allen) 259, 330, 421, 471
Allen (Wales, Brown & Allen) 250
Allen, Walter 261
Almquist, A W 178, 195, 269
Alphonse, George E 468
Ambrose, Joshua E 495, 502
Ambrose, Sarah T 495
Ambrose, W H 502
Anderson, H Y 407
Andrews, DeForest H 447
Anthony, W D 459
Arey, John P 134, 192, 201
Armor, W C 314, 421
Armor, William 42, 102, 118, 119
Armor, Wm 107
Arnett, William D 182, 199, 209, 234
Arnold, A 282
Ashkettle, W C 79
Atkins, Alex W 73
Atkins, Horace H 75
August, Anthony J 277

B

Backus, G B 108
Baggen, Louis 424
Baldauff, Ph P 9
Ball, David J 77
Barnay, Henry 143
Barrett, Franklin 484
Bartels, Louis T 20
Barth, Mortz 244
Barth, William 244
Bates, A C 248
Bates, E H 479
Bates, Thomas 493
Beach, E C 443
Becker, John 146, 188, 224, 259, 471
Behr & Ward 32
Behr, Adolph 32
Beighley, H B 475
Bemis, H M 479
Bendy, A 238
Bennerkendorf, A 236, 240, 252, 284, 314
Benton, Edward V 288
Berkley, G 103
Berndt, John 348, 391
Bertensham, Silas 482
Berthoud, Edward L 234
Bilhuber, E 232
Bilhuber, Ernst 229, 242
Bishop, Edward F 337
Blatchley, A 123
Blood, Eliza R 409
Blood, James M 409, 417
Bode, J 493
Bolthoff, Henry 174, 207, 215, 326, 400
Bome, Jno L 455
Bonnell, C E 273
Boone, John L 273
Boughton, W H 490
Boyd & Co 73
Boyd (Wood & Boyd) 493
Boyd, H L 112
Boyd, Sam'l E 73
Bradford, M G 426
Bramhall, Wm L 332
Breed, Abel D 318
Brennendorf, A 116
Brett, Mathew D 486
Briggs, C H 443
Brooks, John F 90, 103, 110, 114, 123, 166
Broughton, Clara 502
Brown & Allen 259, 330, 421, 471
Brown (Wales, Brown & Allen) 250
Brown, C F 263, 498
Brown, C W H 486
Brown, Edm F 59
Brown, F H 35
Brown, Geo E 238
Brown, George 171
Brown, H A 405, 439
Brown, Henry T 471
Bruckner, William 70, 99
Brush, Fred M 246
Buckland, Wm J 316
Burdett, LeBlond 486
Burns, Robert 261, 486
Burrell, Harvey M 90
Burrell, James 1, 400
Burridge, J H 87
Burt, George 363, 405, 415, 449

C

C H Watson & Co 337
Cairns, Thomas A 236
Calvert, John S 439
Cameron, Robert 484
Cammack, Wm 92
Campbell, J N 134, 182, 192, 199, 201, 209, 234, 282, 312, 340, 344, 350, 357, 360, 365, 372, 375
Campbell, R T 134, 182, 192, 199, 201, 209, 234
Campbell, Thos J 340
Cass, Henry Clay 398
Cass, J B 190
Cautton, Thos S 475
Cazin, Francis M F 441
Chaffee, Wm E 294
Chamberlain, Carrie Wells 388
Chambers, Adam 384
Charles, L C 312, 357
Chase, I Q 38
Chase, L W 116
Chenowith, Joel T 244
Chiniquy, Charles L 45
Church, Frank 337
Church, Jno B 498
Church, M 498
Church, Melville 263
Churchill, Caleb W 302
Clark, Edward A 403
Clark, F A 222
Clark, James 326
Clark, W T 121
Clark, Wm T 110, 114
Clarke, R W 134
Clausen, C F 140
Clovis, Henry 22
Coe, Edward D 252
Collier, Cushman & Farrell 79
Collier, David C 79
Collins, James 451, 453, 484
Collins, S G 250
Collom, John 166, 266, 269, 271
Cook, Jno Jr 445
Coombs, J J 56
Coombs, J W 1, 11, 13
Coombs, Jos L 59
Coon, John 56
Copeland, George 132, 137, 229, 498
Corning, Geo C 379
Cotton, G C 84
Courvoisier, Auguste 121

Cowenhoven, Henry P 455
Cowl, D P 465
Cramer, Frederick 188
Critchel, Wesley 174
Crosby & Thompson 24
Crosby, Augustine B 24
Crosby, W B 39
Cross, J M 112
Cumings, J W 105
Cumings, James W 226
Cushman (Collier, Cushman & Farrell) 79
Cushman, Samuel 79
Cutshaw, L 411

D

D E Jones & Co 100
D P Holloway & Co 140
Danforth, Keyes 431
Danielson, F M 360
Davids, Wm B 110
Davidson, Alexander 73
Davis, Francis Marion 479
Dean, Thos J 266, 269, 271
Dearborn, N B 502
DeBorneirre, Rufus 463
DeFrance, A H 468
Delany, W R 20
Dennis, J Jr 99
Dennis, Wm 99
Dewey & Co 273, 455
Dexter, James V 398
Dibble, Almon 4, 6
Dick, Ewell 294
Dickson, Joseph 73
Dieterich, Gustave 171, 176
Dieterich, P C 337
Dinsmore, John 393
Dodge, M B 15, 22
Dodge, W C 30
Dolloff, L W 340
Douglas, James Jr 304
Drips, James W 195
Drury, E N 30
DuBois, F N 42
Duhem, Constant 419, 449
Dunn, Edw W 419
Dunn, George W 382
Dyer, Geo W 413
Dyer, John P 308

Index

E

Earle, John E 495, 502
Edgar, C E 398
Edson, O E 13
Eils, P Edw J 100
Elkins, Ira S 482
Elliott, Henry R 294
Ellsworth (Hill & Ellsworth) 204, 211, 263, 498
Ellsworth, H K 204
Ellsworth, N K 211
Ellsworth, Nathan K 263
Elsner, John 350
Ensminger, H C 479
Ernst, Joseph 424
Evans (A H Evans & Co) 441
Evans, Elihu 112
Evans, John 224
Evans, R K 441
Everett, Charles J 471
Everett, Robert 468
Evert, C L 226, 332, 382
Eyster, Christian S 140

F

Farrell (Collier, Cushman & Farrell) 79
Farrell, Newell E 79
Fay, William J 236
Feeser, Louis 9
Fenwick (Mason, Fenwick & Lawrence) 134, 182, 192, 199, 201, 209, 234, 277, 282, 312, 340, 344, 350, 357, 360, 365, 372, 375, 403
Fischer, C F Adolph 441
Folelis, L C 174
Ford, B L 68
Foster, C E 20
Foster, J R 176
Fraser, John 68
French, S W 459
French, S Willis 415
Freund, Frank W 312, 350, 357, 360, 365, 372, 375
Fristoe, C H 411
Fristoe, Lydia A 411
Froggatt (Johnson & Froggatt) 84
Froggatt, Edwin 84, 90
Fusch, Fred 250
Fusche, Theo 75, 77, 79

G

Gallemore, J M 63
Gallemore, Jas R 45
Gallup, Francis 388
Gardner, A 419, 461, 465
George, Robert 92, 148, 155, 160
George, Thomas 393
Gerner, Henry 484
Gerner, Richard 484
Gill, Andrew J 190, 222
Gilmore, Smith & Co 468, 479
Given, John W 174
Gleason, W B 39
Godwin, Thomas J 388
Goethals, John 443, 447, 451, 453, 475, 477, 482
Goetze, Henry 424
Goodridge, Henry 391
Gould, F 39
Graham, T J 428
Graham, W A 236, 240
Grannis, Henry 70
Greatorex, T A 330
Green, Samuel 38
Gribble, Edwin 226
Grinnell, James S 140
Griswold, Lyman 188
Gross, Edgar J 306, 309, 318
Grosvenor, C G 335
Grow, J W 457
Gunn, James 146
Gunnell, Hunter 393
Gunnison, W C 171

H

Hagar, E L 77
Hagmann, Victor 128, 130
Hale, H M 312
Hale, J P 22
Hall, Amos W 105
Hall, Assyria 176
Hall, Cassius G 457, 463
Hall, Frank 79
Hall, Fransana 463
Hall, Herman D 332
Hall, John N 288
Hall, W F 45, 52, 63
Halleck, M F 424
Hanna, Jno R 335
Hard, Josiah A 445

Harkness, C A 204
Harlan, Jesse H 73
Harlan, William H 73
Harold, Thos Geo 17
Harrington, Henry C 240, 403
Harris, Arthur C 98, 107
Harris, Richard H 102, 118, 119
Hart, A W 123, 238
Hartley, Jesse 178
Haskins, K 134
Hastings, John I 188
Hatch, Saml F 204
Hatch, Samuel F 211
Hauff (Van Santvoord & Hauff) 217, 229, 232, 242
Havemeyer, H C 32
Haymanie, W 123
Haynes, Fred 250, 259, 330, 421, 471
Hedrick, B S 24, 277
Hefley, Bart C 419
Henchman, O 103, 166
Hendricks, Wm C 484
Hendrie, Charles F 400
Herron, Charles 100
Hicks, Charles D 13
Hill & Ellsworth 204, 211, 263, 498
Hill, Geo D 65
Hine, Henry B 238
Hinman, Egbert 459
Hitchings, John A 45, 63
Hobbs, B 63
Hoffman, Benjamin W 421
Hollingsworth, W W 348
Holloky 294
Holloway (D P Holloway & Co) 140
Holmead, J E F 459
Holst, Herrman 477
Hook, Charles H 273
Horner, John W 388
Horr, M L 182
Hough, Wm B 344
Howard, F W 459
Howard, Geo H 413
Howe, Geo M 360
Howery, Henry 20
Hubbard, E L 428
Hubbell, L D 382
Hunt, Thomas Sterry 304
Hunter, H M 318
Hunter, John 244
Hunter, R M 306, 309

Hurlbut, F B 42
Hurlbut, H E 42
Hussey, Hyatt 121
Husted, Calvin R 324
Hutchinson, Wm N 240

I

Irwin, Wm 75

J

Jackson, F A 222
Jackson, T A 190
Jacobs, C W J 393
James, Edwin 459
Jensen, F 217, 232, 242, 259
Johnson & Froggoatt 84
Johnson, H C 148, 155, 160
Johnson, J M Jr 468
Johnson, J W Hamilton 365, 372, 375
Johnson, L K 357
Johnson, Mary 116
Johnson, P C 84, 100, 105, 116
Jones (D E Jones & Co) 100

K

Kastenhuber, E G 232
Keith, N Shepard 32
Kemon, Solon C 128, 130
Kempf, Joseph 424
Kempton, David W 263
Kendall, S P 84, 116
Kendrick, W F 463
Kennedy, Joseph W 174
Kennedy, William R 114, 123
Kennon, Solom C 391
Kenyon, Joseph 17
Kernon, John C 348
Kirby, J P 143
Kirby, John F 238
Klaucke, Alexander A C 50, 52
Knight & Bros 261, 486
Knight, Edward H 45
Knight, James 405
Knight, Saml 261
Kurtz, Julius 70

L

Lake, D D   215
Landon, Sam S   363
Lang, J F Theodore   403
Larsen, Neils   302
Lathrop, H S   4
Lathrop, Henry S   6
Lathrop, Sperry L   4
Lawrence (Mason, Fenwick & Lawrence)   182, 192, 199, 201, 209, 234, 277, 282, 312, 340, 344, 350, 357, 360, 365, 372, 375, 403
Lawton, Herm   238
Leas, George W   199
LeFevre, Owen E   441
Leland, Charles M   100
Leonard, P A   379
Levy, M W   236
Lewis, W A   405, 413, 439, 449
Lewis, William J   407
Light, Edward B   335
Light, William   166
Lionberger, D C   328
Livingston, M M   15, 22
Lockwood, Radcliffe B   471
Long, William H   35
Loos, Fredrich   20
Lovejoy, Ira A   409
Lovejoy, Ira A   417
Ludlow, W J   217
Lynch, Chas H   308
Lynch, J A   9
Lynd, William J   107
Lynd, William John   98, 102, 118, 119, 294

M

Mabee, Geo W   108, 123, 224
Mabee, L S   180, 132, 137, 146, 176, 178, 188
Mahany, Jerry G   277
Mahany, Jerry G   304
Mallinckrodt, John F   273
Manahan, Jas M   314
Manville, J S D   451, 453
Markham, Vincent D   209
Martin, Charles A   70
Martin, James Jr   277, 282, 312, 340, 344, 350, 357, 360, 365, 372, 375, 403
Martin, Wm   92, 148, 155, 160
Mason (Alexander & Mason)   226, 332, 382
Mason, Fenwick & Lawrence   134, 182, 192, 199, 201, 209, 234, 277, 282, 312, 340, 344, 350, 357, 360, 365, 372, 375, 403
Mathys, G   288
Matthews, E G   222
Maus, W E   35
McArdle, Francis   335, 426
McCabe, Wm H   98
McCarty, Michael   316, 426
McClure, Samuel   447
McCormic, T B   236
McDonald, Robert   475
McFarland, James Maxey   252
McIntyre & Reeves   28
McIntyre, Douglass   28
McLaughlin, M   493
McMahon, Terrence J   468
McNeil, J L   250
McPherson, Charles Henry   324
Menger, B O   20
Merns, Henry   13
Merrell, Herman   493
Merrill, Jay A   263, 405, 407, 413, 419, 439, 449
Merseburg, Chas   477
Metz, Julius   459
Meyer, Herman H   217, 232, 242, 250, 259
Miller, Edward   495, 502
Miller, Henry N   226, 332
Miller, John D   316
Mills, Joseph K   330
Millward, Frank   306, 309, 318
Mitchell, D H   304
Mitchell, George R   75
Mitchell, James L   431, 436
Modill, H J   143
Morgan, C H   146
Morgan, Wm A   84, 105
Morris, Henry   15, 28
Morse, Frederick C   176
Morse, Harley B   395, 424
Mosher, T B   224, 284
Mouster, Adrian   443
Mowbray, Roscoe C   282
Mungen, Theo   328, 388
Munn & Co   1, 22, 28, 45, 52, 63, 68, 75, 77, 79, 84, 90, 103, 105, 108, 110, 112, 114, 116, 121, 123, 128, 130, 132, 137, 146, 166, 171, 176, 178, 180, 188, 195, 207, 215, 224, 236, 240, 252, 255, 266, 269, 271, 275, 284, 288, 302, 314, 316, 326, 335, 348, 379, 391, 395, 400, 409, 417, 426, 428, 436, 443, 447, 451, 453, 475, 477, 482

Munn (John Munn & Co) 13
Munson, Geo C 77
Munson, George C 185
Musgrove, William E 261

N

Nathan, S 38
Neamann, Henry 395
Nesmith, J W 42
Nesmith, J Wellington 108, 314, 421
Neveux, C 400, 436, 443
Nevin, David 103, 146, 180, 240, 340, 403
Nevin, Robert 340
Nevin, Robert A 403
Newell, C 318
Newman, W S 411
Nichols, J N 255
Nichols, W H J 411
Nicholson, James 484
Nida, Chas 105, 137, 266, 326, 379, 428, 451, 453, 477

O

Olds, Amandrin M 246, 248
Ostrander, Othello R 302
Ourand, Chas H 382
Overhood, H M 108

P

Parmelee, Ed C 70
Parris, Albion K 407
Parson, Warren D 337
Patterson, J O 415
Pearce, Richard 455
Pearce, W H 261
Peck, C C 30
Peck, C E 39
Penrose, William H 204, 211
Penwinkle, Wm 391
Perkins, J M C 398
Perley, F L 328, 388
Perrenoud, J G 121
Pettit, C A 112
Pettit, Charles A 50, 128
Pettit, Chas A 130, 391
Peyton, W J 217
Pinckney, Henry K 431
Platt, H H 324

Pole, B C 407
Pollard, Chas W 180
Pomeroy, James V 379, 428
Pomeroy, Julius R 490
Pomeroy, Thos 73
Pool, S M 140
Post, Wm H 246, 248
Potter, W T 1
Proctor, Alexander 445
Pyle, John W 384

R

Raettig, C 90, 207, 215
Randall, John G 11
Rankin, George Read 398
Rawlings, A C 211
Raymond, Wm 182
Reeves (McIntyre & Reeves) 28
Reeves, George C 28, 87
Reichard, Adolph L 242
Resor, Edward A 222
Revnon, T C 112
Rice & Van Deren 114
Rice, C A H 114
Richardson, Alfred H 68
Richardson, C M 273
Ricketts, John C 413
Riland, Jas M 382
Roberts, Alex F 116, 121, 224, 426, 436
Roby, John D 110
Rogers, Andrews N 284
Rollins, E W 421
Rood, M L 110
Ross, W A 266, 269, 271
Rowland, John Henry 275
Ruch, G W 11
Rudd, Anson 11
Ruppert, A 140, 328
Ryan, Jno A 417
Ryan, Michael 330
Rydquist, H 475, 482

S

Sarner, Phil F 190
Sarner, Phil P 222
Sarrell, Wm M B 234
Sayer, Daniel 328
Sayles, Thomas W 426
Sayr, Hal 255

Schleier, George C 350
Schoenfeld, F 90
Schulze, Louis 148, 155, 160
Schuyler, Fred 324
Scott, H C 337
Sears, Nathan A 484
Sears, W F 84
Sedgwick, C 252, 255, 266, 269, 271, 275, 284, 302, 314, 324
Seller, Willard 114
Sellers, Henry M 326
Seward, H J 384
Seymour, Ben E 451, 453
Shumway, J H 495, 502
Sieterich, P C 180
Simington, M W 1
Smith (Gilmore, Smith & Co) 468, 479
Smith, A M 461, 465
Smith, Andrew A 344
Smith, Anselmo B 461
Smith, Anselmo B 465
Smith, Austin 178
Smith, C D 52
Smith, Chas H 17, 384
Smith, G A C 398
Smith, J J 457
Smith, L J 252
Smith, Percy B 229
Smith, T C 294
Smith, Wm H C 195, 207, 215
Snow, C A 424
Sorah, S I 4
Spicer, Wells 143
Spruance, Wm 195
Stanley, Gilbert 229, 275
Stanton, J Clark 457, 463
Stanton, J O, MD 65
Stanton, J W 22
Staples, James 275
Stebbin, H H 482
Stebbins, G I 282
Stewart, J Oscar 340
Stewart, James O 277
Stewart, James Oscar 304, 403
Stillings, Edw'd B 75
Stokes, T T 215
Storms, Thos G 463
Strong, Geo H 455
Struance, Wm 344
Surrell, George 384

T

Tappan, Henry S 123
Taylor, James G 132
Taylor, James G 137
Teats, Robert 306, 309, 318
Tenwinkle, Wm 348
Terrell, Lemuel W 384
Terry, A F 316, 326, 335, 379, 395, 400, 417, 428
Thayer, A P 284, 436
Thomas, H H 348
Thomas, Jerome 178
Thompson (Crosby & Thompson) 24
Thompson, Robt L 24
Thompson, S V 24
Thornton, John S 185
Tibbits, A J 495
Todd, Wm D 330
Topleff, C L 22
Topliff, C L 28
Townsend, Alfred H 195
Townsend, F B 441
Treadway, James Wilson 171
Treurn, Wm 68

U

Updegraff, Joseph S 207
Upshaw, George E 479

V

Van Deren (Rice & Van Deren) 114
Van Deren, A J 1, 114
Van Santvoord & Hauff 217, 229, 232, 242
Van Slarter (Wm Van Slarter & Co) 143
Veasey, John M 128, 130, 132, 137, 238
Ventz, Wm 185
Vorlander, M 108, 171
Wagoner, H O 68
Wahlers, C 229, 242
Waite, E E 87
Wales, Brown & Allen 250
Walker, Joseph E 461
Ward (Behr & Ward) 32
Ward, R H 308
Ward, William James 32
Warner, Emma E O 328
Warner, J P 328
Wartmann, J L 309
Watson (C H Watson & Co) 337
Watson, C H 143

Watson, James F 363
Weber, E P 148, 155, 160
Webster, John W 199, 209, 217, 232, 259
Weibling, Harmon B 490
Weibling, Harmon G 4, 6
Welch, C C 326
Welch, Lester B 449
West, William 482
Whitall, Jas C 363
Whitman, Charles S 407, 413, 419
Whitmore, Charles E 498
Whitmore, H R 498
Whittemore, Oliver A 171
Wiedersheim, John 63
Wilcox, Lewis V 207
Wilcoxen, I N 395
Wilcoxen, J N 100
Wilder, Eugene 79
Williams, C D 226
Williams, Edwin F 447
Williams, George 50, 52
Williams, Henry 455
Willoughby, Edmund A 363, 415

Wilson, D P 11
Winter, Gustav 477
Withrow, Chase 400, 493
Witter, H 13
Wm Van Slarter & Co 143
Wolff, E 255, 271, 275, 302, 316, 395, 417, 447
Wood & Boyd 493
Wood, Geo H 398
Wood, Wm C 190, 222
Woodhull, Alfred A 204
Woodworth, J B 190
Worrall, Thomas D 56, 59, 65
Wright, Alpheus 103

Y

Yates, Lemuel F 180
Yenley, J H 166
Young, John 28
Young, Nathaniel 28

Z

Zurns, Robert 486

Additional Colorado Research Titles

If you borrowed this copy from a library and would like to order a copy, please send a check or money order to: Iron Gate Publishing, P.O. Box 999, Niwot, CO 80544. Our books are available online to institutions through Lightning Source, to individuals at Amazon.com and on our website:

www.irongate.com

Boulder County, Colorado District Court Civil Appearance Docket, 1878-1882: An Annotated Index
ISBN 978-1-68224-019-9 $19.95 + $5.00 S&H

Boulder County, Colorado County Court Will Record, Volume A, 1875-1889: An Annotated Index
ISBN 978-1-68224-018-2 $11.95 + $4.00 S&H

Boulder County, Colorado, County Court Probate Record, Vol 1, 1875-1884: An Annotated Index
ISBN 978-1-68224-017-5 $11.95 + $4.00 S&H

Early Land Owners Along the St. Vrain Creek, Colorado Territory, 1860-1861: An Annotated Index
ISBN 978-1-68224-006-9 $11.95 + $4.00 S&H

Boulder County, Colorado District Court Widow's Relinquishment, Volumes 1 & 2, 1889–1937: An Annotated Index
ISBN 978-1-68224-009-0 $11.95 + $4.00 S&H

Boulder County, Colorado, District Court Guardians Bonds, Vol. A, 1876-1902: An Annotated Index
ISBN 978-1-879579-78-1 $11.95 + $4.00 S&H

Boulder County, Colorado Probate Court Fee Book, 1874-1890: An Annotated Index
ISBN 978-1-879579-88-0 $11.95 + $4.00 S&H

Boulder City Town Company Lot Sales 1859-1864: An Annotated Map Guide
ISBN 978-1-879579-87-3 $15.95 + $5.00 S&H

Brainard's Hotel Register, Boulder, Colorado, 1880: An Annotated Index
ISBN 978-1-879579-86-6 $15.95 $5.00 S&H

Boulder County Commissioner's Journal, 1861-1871: An Annotated Transcription
ISBN 978-1-879579-77-4 $45.99 + $5.00 S&H

Boulder County Commissioners Journal, 1871-1874: An Annotated Transcription
ISBN 978-1-879579-91-0 $39.95 + $5.00 S&H

Colorado's Territorial Masons: An Annotated Index of the Proceedings of the Grand Lodge of Colorado, 1861–1876

ISBN 978-1-879579-85-9 $29.95 + $5.00 S&H

Boulder, Colorado Teachers, 1878-1900: An Annotated Index

ISBN 978-1-879579-93-4 $11.95 + $4.00 S&H

Boulder County, Colorado District Court Execution Docket, 1875-1885: An Annotated Index

ISBN 978-1-879579-94-1 $11.95 + $4.00 S&H

Denver, Colorado Police Force Record, 1879-1903: An Annotated Index

ISBN 978-1-879579-81-1 $11.95 + $4.00 S&H

Boulder, Colorado Births 1892–1906: An Annotated Index

ISBN 978-1-879579-79-8 $11.95 + $4.00 S&H

Arapahoe County, Colorado Territory Criminal Court Index, 1862-1879: An Annotated Index

ISBN 978-1-879579-70-5 $11.95 + $4.00 S&H

Boulder County Probate Court Appraisement Record A, 1875-1888: An Annotated Index

ISBN 978-1-879579-72-9 $11.95 + $4.00 S&H

Boulder County Assessor's Tax List, 1875: An Annotated Index

ISBN 978-1-879579-55-2 $11.95 + $4.00 S&H

Boulder County Assessor's Tax List, 1876: An Annotated Index

ISBN 978-1-879579-56-9 $11.95 + $4.00 S&H

Boulder Valley Presbyterian Church Records, 1863-1900: An Annotated Index

ISBN 978-1-879579-58-3 $11.95 + $4.00 S&H

Boulder's Masonic Pioneers, 1867-1886: Members of Columbia Lodge No. 14, Boulder County, Colorado Territory

ISBN 978-1-879579-57-6 $15.95 + $4.00 S&H

Map: Boulder City Town Company 1859 Original Survey Map

ISBN 978-1-68224-000-7 $24.95 (PAPER) + $7.00 S&H

ISBN 978-1-68224-001-4 $74.95 (MYLAR) + $7.00 S&H

Map: Boulder City Town Company, 11 Aug 1859 Land Lottery Map Showing Lot Purchases

ISBN 978-1-68224-002-1 $24.95 (PAPER) + $7.00 S&H

ISBN 978-1-68224-003-8 $74.95 (MYLAR) + $7.00 S&H

Map: Boulder City Town Company 20 Sept 1859 Map Showing Stock Certificates Issued by Lot
ISBN 978-1-68224-004-5 $24.95 (PAPER) + $7.00 S&H
ISBN 978-1-68224-005-2 $74.95 (MYLAR) + $7.00 S&H

Publishing Titles

If you would like to order one of these books, please send a check or money order to: Iron Gate Publishing, P.O. Box 999, Niwot, CO 80544. Our books are available online to institutions through Ingram, to individuals at Amazon.com and on our website:

www.irongate.com

Set Yourself Up to Self-Publish: A Genealogist's Guide
    ISBN 978-1-879579-99-6 $19.95 + $5.00 S&H

Publish Your Genealogy: A Step-by-Step Guide for Preserving Your Research for the Next Generation
    ISBN 978-1-879579-62-0 $24.95 + $5.00 S&H

Publish Your Family History: A Step-by-Step Guide to Writing the Stories of Your Ancestors
    ISBN 978-1-879579-63-7 $24.95 + $5.00 S&H

Publish a Local History: A Step-by-Step Guide from Finding the Right Project to Finished Book
    ISBN 978-1-879579-64-4 $24.95 + $5.00 S&H

Publish a Memoir: A Step-by-Step Guide to Saving Your Memories for Future Generations
    ISBN 978-1-879579-65-1 $24.95 + $5.00 S&H

Publish a Biography: A Step-by-Step Guide to Capturing the Life and Times of an Ancestor or a Generation
    ISBN 978-1-879579-66-8 $24.95 + $5.00 S&H

Publish a Photo Book: A Step-by-Step Guide for Transforming Your Genealogical Research into a Stunning Family Heirloom
    ISBN 978-1-879579-67-5 $24.95 + $5.00 S&H

Publish a Source Index: A Step-by-Step Guide to Creating a Genealogically Useful Index, Abstract or Transcription
    ISBN 978-1-879579-68-2 $24.95 + $5.00 S&H

Publish Your Specialty: A Step-by-Step Guide for Imparting Your Research Expertise to Others
    ISBN 978-1-879579-76-7 $24.95 + $5.00 S&H

www.ingramcontent.com/pod-product-compliance
Lightning Source LLC
Chambersburg PA
CBHW080530300426
44111CB00017B/2664